W9-AWA-624

Functions and Relations

11

**Addison-Wesley
Secondary
Mathematics
Authors**

Elizabeth Ainslie
Paul Atkinson
Maurice Barry
Cam Bennet
Barbara J. Canton
Ron Coleborn
Fred Crouse
Garry Davis
Jane Forbes
George Gadanidis
Liliane Gauthier
Florence Glanfield
Katie Pallos-Haden
Carol Besteck Hope
Terry Kaminski
Brendan Kelly
Stephen Khan
Ron Lancaster
Duncan LeBlanc
Rob McLeish
Jim Nakamoto
Nick Nielsen
Paul Pogue
Brent Richards
David Sufrin
Paul Williams
Elizabeth Wood
Rick Wunderlich
Paul Zolis
Leanne Zorn

Robert Alexander
Mathematics Teacher and
Consultant
Richmond Hill

Peter Taylor
Professor
Department of Mathematics
and Statistics
Queen's University
Kingston

Peter J. Harrison
Mathematics Teacher
Riverdale Collegiate Institute
Toronto

Kevin Maguire
Instructional Leader, Mathematics
Toronto District School Board
Toronto

Linda Rajotte
Mathematics Teacher
G.P. Vanier Secondary School
Courtenay

Margaret Sinclair
Vice Principal
Dante Alighieri Academy
Toronto

Kevin Spry
Head of Mathematics
Centre Dufferin District High School
Shelburne

Toronto

Senior Consulting Mathematics Editor
Lesley Haynes

Coordinating Editor
Mei Lin Cheung

Production Coordinator
Stephanie Cox

Developmental Editor
Nirmala Nutakki

Editorial Contributors

Marg Bukta   David Gargaro
Rosina Daillie   Susan Hall
William Dodd   Gay McKellar

Managing Editor
Enid Haley

Marketing Manager
Dawna Day Harris

Product Manager
Reid McAlpine

Publisher
Claire Burnett

Design/Production
Pronk&Associates

Art Direction
Pronk&Associates

Electronic Assembly/Technical Art
Pronk&Associates

Copyright © 2002 Pearson Education Canada Inc., Toronto, Ontario

All Rights Reserved. This publication is protected by copyright, and permission should be obtained from the publisher prior to any prohibited reproduction, storage in a retrieval system, or transmission in any form or by any means, electronic, mechanical, photocopying, recording, or likewise. For information regarding permission, write to the Permissions Department.

The publisher has taken every care to meet or exceed industry specifications for the manufacturing of textbooks. The spine and the endpapers of this sewn book have been reinforced with special fabric for extra binding strength. The cover is a premium, polymer-reinforced material designed to provide long life and withstand rugged use. Mylar gloss lamination has been applied for further durability.

ISBN: 0-201-72657-2

This book contains recycled product and is acid free.

Printed and bound in Canada

1 2 3 4 5 GG 05 04 03 02 01

Program Consultants

Ron Bender

Faculty of Engineering
University of Ottawa

Bill Chambers

Former Head of Mathematics
John Fraser Secondary School
Mississauga

John Kitney

Head of Mathematics
Bayridge Secondary School
Kingston

Jamie Pyper

Head of Mathematics
H.B. Beal Secondary School
London

Assessment Consultant

Lynda E.C. Colgan

Professor
Department of Education
Queen's University
Kingston

Reviewers

Ron Bender
Faculty of Engineering
University of Ottawa

Heather Boychuk
Confederation Secondary School
Sudbury

Katie Branovacki
Former Mathematics Consultant
Greater Essex County District School Board

Karen Bryan
Head of Mathematics
North Dundas District High School
Chesterville

Anita Casella
Sir Allan MacNab Secondary School
Hamilton

Bill Chambers
Former Head of Mathematics
John Fraser Secondary School
Mississauga

Tom Chapman
Curriculum Coordinator
Hastings and Prince Edward District School Board
Belleville

Lynda E.C. Colgan
Professor
Queen's University
Kingston

Jacqueline Hill
Port Perry High School
Port Perry

Stan Hugel
Head of Mathematics
Philip Pocock Catholic Secondary School
Mississauga

John Kitney
Head of Mathematics
Bayridge Secondary School
Kingston

Victoria Kudrenski
Head of Mathematics
Sir Allan MacNab Secondary School
Hamilton

John McGrath
Head of Mathematics
Adam Scott CVI
Peterborough

Betty Morrison
Head of Mathematics
Delhi District Secondary School
Delhi

Jamie Pyper
Head of Mathematics
H.B. Beal Secondary School
London

John Santarelli
Head of Mathematics
Cathedral High School
Hamilton

Wendy Solheim
Head of Mathematics
Thornhill Secondary School
Thornhill

Geoff Taylor
Head of Mathematics
Cawthra Park Secondary School
Mississauga

Wally Webster
Assessment and Evaluation Coordinator
Avon Maitland District School Board
Seaforth

Contents

Contents

5 Trigonometric Functions

6 Graphing Trigonometric Functions

Contents

To the Teacher

About *Addison-Wesley Functions and Relations 11: Ontario*

Addison-Wesley Functions and Relations 11: Ontario is organized according to our authors' best interpretation of the Ontario curriculum. Several sequences of topics would have been possible — and teachers might decide to modify the sequences — but the authors had several goals in mind when they established the final chapter sequence:

- *We wanted to make the Functions course a clean subset of the Functions and Relations text.*
  Chapters 8 and 9 are for Functions and Relations students only. This means that the Functions course is contained in all but the last two chapters of the book.

- *Students should have a fresh start after grade 10, by opening with new, but accessible, material.*
  This is why Chapter 1 is on Sequences and Series, which are number patterns with some algebraic analysis. Although this content was in a higher grade level in a previous curriculum, the numerical approach we emphasize makes it accessible for younger students. Some teachers may decide to teach this chapter later in the course.

- *Students should have the algebraic tools they need, when they need them.*
  This is why Chapter 2, Rational Expressions, appears between Chapter 1 and Chapter 3, Financial Mathematics. While Chapters 1 and 3 have many conceptual connections, students benefit from seeing some algebraic principles first.

- *Many students will thrive on the finance work.*
  Chapter 3, Financial Mathematics, appears early in the book since students should be ready for it. Teachers may delay this unit without affecting the logical flow of the course.

- *It's important to allow students to examine specific cases, and work with familiar material, before generalizing results.*
  This is the thinking behind the sequencing of Chapters 4, 5, 6, and 7. Chapter 4 builds on grade 10 work with the parabola; trigonometric functions involve similar ideas but the quadratic work is more familiar. Chapter 5, Trigonometric Functions, also extends grade 10 work, and sets up concepts for working with graphs of trigonometric functions in Chapter 6.

Curriculum Quote

Process and content, together, are important aspects of learning mathematics. An emphasis on one over the other tends to reduce the usefulness and the effectiveness of the learning. It is the integration of various aspects of mathematical knowledge that provides a powerful tool for reasoning and problem solving. This curriculum reflects a meaningful blend of both process and content.

The Ontario Curriculum Grades 11 and 12

Chapter 7 serves as a strong culminating unit for the Functions course, while it also wraps up important concepts for the Functions and Relations students before they proceed to the last two chapters.

- ***For the conic sections, students need time for visual work before they proceed to the algebra.***
  This explains why two chapters cover the single strand on conics. Chapter 8 highlights a geometric approach, introducing the concept of a locus. Students trace a locus and build equations from geometric definitions. In Chapter 9, students use algebraic approaches to examine properties of conics, while examining practical applications in which conic sections arise.

- ***The title of the book is Functions and Relations; the idea of connecting algebraic and geometry or graphing approaches should underlie the thinking of the content development.***
  Even though some curriculum expectations do not explicitly mention functions or relations, there are possible links in all the content. In topics such as Sequences and Series, or Financial Mathematics, the authors have used graphical representations whenever relevant to help support understanding. With some of the algebraic work, the functions connection will come into play when students proceed to the Advanced Functions and Introductory Calculus course in grade 12.

- ***The overriding purpose of the course is to engage students with meaningful mathematical activities and problems that challenge, stretch, and reward them.***
  For grade 11 students, the authors wanted to take the inquiry process to a new level, in which the organizing problem for each chapter opens up more room for thoughtful investigation of concepts, not just context. This vision contributed to the overall structure of each chapter in the student book.

  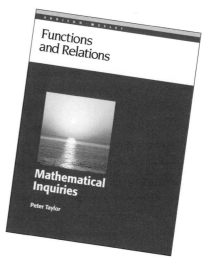

  The idea of problems that take the inquiry process to a new level is also the driving force behind ***Addison-Wesley Functions and Relations 11 Ontario, Mathematical Inquiries.*** This short collection of problems offers springboards for meaningful mathematical investigations into a variety of contextual applications.

To the Student

About *Addison-Wesley Functions and Relations 11 ...*

If you're an Ontario student using this book, you're probably registered in **Functions 11** or **Functions and Relations 11**. Both courses are outlined in the Ontario Ministry of Education curriculum document for Grades 11 and 12, released in 2000. This curriculum grew out of a discussion that included mathematics teachers, university professors, business representatives, and secondary school students. Many of the people behind this curriculum had a vision of mathematics as an engaging, vibrant discipline that is best learned through investigative problem solving and a process of mathematical inquiry.

Still, the curriculum also had to address the content requirements related to your future destination. What academic opportunities might you pursue? What field will you follow? What mathematical knowledge would you need to bring to it? These questions take on a new, serious tone in grade 11.

The result of the vision (the big picture) and the need to prepare for future destinations (the content detail) are represented in the two courses

- **Functions** (University and College bound), and
- **Functions and Relations** (University bound)

Both courses qualify you to study grade 12 courses in

- **Advanced Functions and Introductory Calculus,**
- **The Mathematics of Data Management,** or
- **Mathematics for College Technology**

The Functions and Relations course also leads to Geometry and Discrete Mathematics in grade 12. The path from Functions and Relations to Geometry and Discrete Mathematics was designed for students who intend to pursue university studies in engineering, mathematics, or the physical sciences.

The Inquiry Process: An Organizing Influence for Each Chapter

The destinations described above highlight the importance of the inquiry process: mathematical inquiry extends in scope at this level. In previous grades, you may have completed activities that were designed to bring you to a particular mathematical concept. In this book, **Insights into a Rich Problem** in each chapter presents an open-ended problem that intrigues mathematicians, and can lead to many different directions.

The authors share their insights, and solutions, to that problem. Then, they pose new and related problems for you to solve. We think you'll find many of these problems, and the thinking you bring to them, exciting and rewarding.

Other Chapter Elements

Each **Insights into a Rich Problem** ties closely to the curriculum content the chapter covers. Other chapter elements build from there.

Necessary Skills

In mathematics, new concepts build on what has gone before. **Necessary Skills** gives a quick refresher in the prerequisite skills you need for the chapter. Your teacher may use these as a diagnostic tool before starting a chapter, or leave them to you for independent study.

Occasionally, a "New" skill comes up in Necessary Skills. You didn't learn this skill in previous grades, usually because it wasn't included in the curriculum. We teach it in **Necessary Skills** because it's relatively straightforward, and you have all the related concepts you need to develop an understanding quickly.

Numbered Sections

These develop the new content of the course. Investigative activities are included whenever the curriculum requires them.

Exercises are organized into A, B, and C categories according to their level of difficulty. Each exercise set contains many exercises; don't feel you must complete every one. Their quantity provides choice.

 You'll see that some exercises have a check mark beside them; try these exercises to be sure you have covered all core curriculum requirements.

Each exercise set identifies one exercise for each of the four categories of the provincial **Achievement Chart**. These show you what to expect when you are assessed on any of the four categories. We have highlighted exactly four exercises as examples only. Each exercise set has several exercises that relate to one, or more, of the categories of achievement. Exercises that are labelled are not limited to one category only, but the focus helps to simplify assessment.

To the Student

Review

Self-Checks are one-page reviews that occur mid-chapter. They let you check your knowledge and understanding of the previous sections.

The **Mathematics Toolkit** in each chapter review summarizes important chapter results. Use the toolkit and the **Review Exercises** to study each chapter.

Self-Test at the end of each chapter helps you prepare for a class test. Each Self-Test includes several **Assessment Tasks:** these exercises consolidate chapter concepts, and allow for a full range of responses, up to a level 4 performance.

Cumulative Review after Chapter 7 provides additional support when you're preparing for examinations at the end of the course.

Communication

Communication is a key part of all learning. *Discuss* questions in this book prompt you to reflect on solutions or the implications of new concepts. Exercises ask you to explain your reasoning, or describe your findings. Each numbered section contains an exercise highlighted with a "Communication" emphasis.

Technology

When technology arises in this book, the authors have assumed that you have some familiarity with graphing calculator technology and *The Geometer's Sketchpad*, based on your work in grades 9 and 10. When new uses of the technology arise, we provide explicit instructions in the book.

Assessment

Several features of this book relate to a balanced assessment approach.

- **Achievement Chart Categories** highlighted in each exercise set
- **Communication** opportunities in Examples and exercises
- **Self-Checks** to support your knowledge and understanding
- **Insights into a Rich Problem** with intriguing problems for you to solve
- **Self-Tests**, including **Assessment Tasks** with opportunities for a level-4 performance

INSIGHTS INSI
INTO A INTO
RICH RICH R
PROBLEM
INSIGHT

You may have noticed that when you drop a ball onto a hard surface, the ball bounces to a lower height. If the ball continues to bounce, the height to which it bounces decreases with each subsequent bounce.

At the end of this chapter, you will investigate the relationship between the distance travelled by a bouncing ball and time. You will use sequences and series.

Curriculum Expectations

By the end of this chapter, you will:

- Write terms of a sequence, given the formula for the nth term (or given a recursion formula).

- Determine a formula for the nth term of a given sequence.

- Identify sequences as arithmetic or geometric, or neither.

- Determine the value of any term in an arithmetic or a geometric sequence, using the formula for the nth term of the sequence.

- Determine the sum of the terms of an arithmetic or a geometric series, using appropriate formulas and techniques.

- Demonstrate an understanding of the relationship between ..., arithmetic sequences, and linear growth.

- Demonstrate an understanding of the relationship between ..., geometric sequences, and exponential growth.

- Simplify and evaluate expressions containing integer and rational exponents, using the laws of exponents.

- Solve exponential equations.

Necessary Skills

1. Review: Percent

Calculations that involve percent are used in many applications.

Example 1

Express each percent as a decimal.

a) 68%   **b)** 6.8%

Solution

a) $68\% = \dfrac{68}{100}$

$\qquad = 0.68$

b) $6.8\% = \dfrac{6.8}{100}$

$\qquad = 0.068$

Example 2

Express each decimal as a percent.

a) 0.37   **b)** 1.27

Solution

a) $0.37 = \dfrac{37}{100}$

$\qquad = 37\%$

b) $1.27 = \dfrac{127}{100}$

$\qquad = 127\%$

Example 3

Determine 35% of $245.

Solution

Change the percent to a decimal, then multiply.

$35\% \text{ of } \$245 = 0.35 \times \$245$

$\qquad\qquad\quad\;\; = \$85.75$

Example 4

Express 38 as a percent of 70.

Solution

$\dfrac{38}{70} \doteq 0.542\ 857\ 1$

$\qquad \doteq 54\%$

Exercises

1. Express each percent as a decimal.

　a) 20%　　　**b)** 4%　　　**c)** 15%　　　**d)** 75%　　　**e)** 110%

　f) 8.75%　　**g)** $1\frac{1}{2}$%　　**h)** $3\frac{1}{4}$%　　**i)** 0.5%　　**j)** 0.1%

2. Express each decimal as a percent.

　a) 0.25　　**b)** 0.472　　**c)** 0.08　　**d)** 0.003　　**e)** 1.37

3. Calculate:

　a) 73% of $129.66　　　　　　　**b)** 8.2% of $120 000

　c) 173% of $129.66　　　　　　**d)** 0.82% of $120 000

4. Express:

　a) 44 as a percent of 79　　　　　**b)** 5.43 as a percent of 11.82

　c) 79 as a percent of 44　　　　　**d)** 11.82 as a percent of 5.43

5. A mountain bike has a "For Sale" sign, and a price of $399. The dealer wants a quick sale, so she adds a "15% off this price" sticker to the sign.

　a) What is the new price for the mountain bike?

　b) The purchaser will have to pay the PST of 8% and the GST of 7%. What is the total price of the mountain bike?

6. Economists predict that heating fuel costs will increase by 22% over the next year. This year, a family spent $1175 on heating fuel. How much might that family expect to pay next year?

2. New: Exponent Laws for Integer Exponents

Recall the definition of a power: $a^n = a \times a \times a \times ... \times a$, n factors

This definition yields a set of rules for working with exponents.

Take Note

Law of Multiplication	$x^m \times x^n = x^{m+n}$
Law of Division	$\frac{x^m}{x^n} = x^{m-n}$ $(x \neq 0)$
Power of a Power	$(x^m)^n = x^{mn}$
Zero Exponent	$x^0 = 1$ $(x \neq 0)$
Negative Exponent	$x^{-n} = \frac{1}{x^n}, x^n = \frac{1}{x^{-n}}$ $(x \neq 0)$

The base x represents any real numbers for which the expressions are defined. The exponents m and n are any integers.

Two more rules can be added to those studied in earlier grades.

Power of a Product Law

Since $(xy)^4$ means $(xy) \times (xy) \times (xy) \times (xy)$,

then
$$
\begin{aligned}
(xy)^4 &= (xy) \times (xy) \times (xy) \times (xy) \\
&= x \times x \times y \times x \times x \times y \times x \times x \times y \times x \times x \times y \\
&= x \times x \times x \times x \times x \times x \times y \times y \times y \times y \\
&= x^4 y^4
\end{aligned}
$$

Each factor is raised to the power 4.

We would get similar results for other numbers inside the brackets or a different exponent.

So, $(xy)^n = x^n \times y^n$

Power of a Quotient Law

Since $\left(\frac{x}{y}\right)^4$ means $\left(\frac{x}{y}\right) \times \left(\frac{x}{y}\right) \times \left(\frac{x}{y}\right) \times \left(\frac{x}{y}\right)$,

then
$$
\begin{aligned}
\left(\frac{x}{y}\right)^4 &= \left(\frac{x}{y}\right) \times \left(\frac{x}{y}\right) \times \left(\frac{x}{y}\right) \times \left(\frac{x}{y}\right) \\
&= \frac{x \times x \times x \times x}{y \times y \times y \times y} \\
&= \frac{x^4}{y^4}
\end{aligned}
$$

The numerator and denominator are raised to the power 4.

We would get similar results for other numbers inside the brackets or a different exponent.

So, $\left(\frac{x}{y}\right)^n = \frac{x^n}{y^n}$

Take Note

Power of a Product	$(xy)^n = x^n y^n$
Power of a Quotient	$\left(\frac{x}{y}\right)^n = \frac{x^n}{y^n} \ (y \neq 0)$

Example 1

Evaluate each expression.

a) $\left(\frac{3}{5}\right)^2$ b) $\left(\frac{3}{5}\right)^{-2}$ c) $\left(\frac{3}{5}\right)^0$ d) $(3 \times 2)^3$

Solution

a) Use the power of a quotient law.
$$
\begin{aligned}
\left(\frac{3}{5}\right)^2 &= \frac{3^2}{5^2} \\
&= \frac{9}{25}
\end{aligned}
$$

b) Use the negative exponent law.
$$
\begin{aligned}
\left(\frac{3}{5}\right)^{-2} &= \left(\frac{5}{3}\right)^2 \\
&= \frac{25}{9}
\end{aligned}
$$

c) Use the zero exponent law.
$$
\left(\frac{3}{5}\right)^0 = 1
$$

d) Use the power of a product law.
$$
\begin{aligned}
(3 \times 2)^3 &= 3^3 \times 2^3 \\
&= 27 \times 8 \\
&= 216
\end{aligned}
$$

Example 2

Evaluate each expression.

a) $(-3)^2$ **b)** -3^2 **c)** $(-3)^{-2}$ **d)** -3^{-2}

Solution

a) $(-3)^2 = (-3)(-3)$
$$= 9$$

b) $-3^2 = -(3)(3)$
$$= -9$$

c) $(-3)^{-2} = \dfrac{1}{(-3)^2}$
$$= \dfrac{1}{9}$$

d) $-3^{-2} = -\dfrac{1}{3^2}$
$$= -\dfrac{1}{9}$$

Discuss

How do the brackets in each expression affect the answers?

Exercises

1. Evaluate.

a) 2^3 **b)** 3^{-1} **c)** 5^{-2} **d)** $\left(\dfrac{1}{4}\right)^{-1}$ **e)** $\left(\dfrac{2}{3}\right)^4$

f) 0.5^{-1} **g)** 10^0 **h)** 1^{-2} **i)** 0.1^{-2} **j)** $\dfrac{1}{2^{-3}}$

2. Evaluate.

a) 2^4 **b)** 2^{-4} **c)** $(-2)^4$ **d)** -2^4 **e)** $(-2)^{-4}$

f) -2^{-4} **g)** $\left(\dfrac{1}{2}\right)^4$ **h)** $\left(\dfrac{1}{2}\right)^{-4}$ **i)** $\left(-\dfrac{1}{2}\right)^4$ **j)** $-\left(\dfrac{1}{2}\right)^4$

3. Evaluate.

a) $(2^{-2})(2^5)$ **b)** $(2^{-2})(2^{-5})$ **c)** $(2^2)(2^{-5})$ **d)** $(2^2)(2^5)$

e) $\dfrac{2^{-2}}{2^5}$ **f)** $\dfrac{2^{-2}}{5^{-5}}$ **g)** $\dfrac{2^2}{5^{-5}}$ **h)** $\dfrac{2^2}{2^5}$

i) $(2^{-2})^5$ **j)** $(2^{-2})^{-5}$ **k)** $(2^2)^{-5}$ **l)** $(2^2)^5$

4. Write each expression as a single power.

a) $\dfrac{10^5 \times 10^{11}}{10^{-3} \times 10^0}$ **b)** $\dfrac{(6^4)^5}{6^8 \times 6^{-3}}$ **c)** $\dfrac{3^{-5} \times 3^{-9}}{3^{-10}}$

5. Simplify, then evaluate.

a) $\dfrac{2^2 \times 2^7 \div 2^{-5}}{(2^3 \times 2^{-4})^6}$ **b)** $\left(\dfrac{7.2^{-1}}{3.6^{-1}}\right)^3$ **c)** $\left(\dfrac{2^3 \times 3^2}{2^4 \times 3^{-2}}\right)^4$

6. When you *multiply* $2^4 \times 2^3$ to obtain 2^7, you *add* the exponents. There are other examples like this in the exponent laws where you carry out a certain operation on powers by performing a different operation on the exponents. Create numerical examples to illustrate each of these laws.

Necessary Skills

3. New: Numerical Roots

Since $\sqrt{9} = \sqrt{3^2} = 3$, the positive *square* root of 9 is 3.

Since $\sqrt[3]{8} = \sqrt[3]{2^3} = 2$, the *cube* root of 8 is 2.

Since $\sqrt[4]{16} = \sqrt[4]{2^4} = 2$, the positive *fourth* root of 16 is 2.

Since $\sqrt[5]{-32} = \sqrt[5]{(-2)^5} = -2$, the *fifth* root of –32 is –2.

Higher roots are defined in the same way.

For even roots, the radical sign, $\sqrt{\ }$, denotes only the *positive* root. So, the square roots of 9 are 3 and –3, but $\sqrt{9} = 3$.

To determine the root of a number, we use mental math if we can write the number as a power. Otherwise, we use a calculator.

Example 1

Determine each value without using a calculator.

a) $\sqrt{36}$ b) $\sqrt[3]{-27}$ c) $\sqrt[4]{81}$ d) $\sqrt{-82}$

Solution

a) Since $36 = 6^2$, $\sqrt{36} = \sqrt{6^2} = 6$

b) Since $-27 = (-3)^3$, $\sqrt[3]{-27} = \sqrt[3]{(-3)^3} = -3$

c) Since $81 = 3^4$, $\sqrt[4]{81} = \sqrt[4]{3^4} = 3$

d) Since we cannot determine the square root of a negative number, $\sqrt{-82}$ is not defined for real numbers.

Example 2

Use a calculator to determine each value to 2 decimal places.

a) $\sqrt{283.4}$ b) $\sqrt[3]{30}$ c) $\sqrt[5]{-356}$

Solution

The key sequences are for a Texas Instruments TI-30X IIS scientific calculator. If you have a different calculator, check the manual.

a) For $\sqrt{283.4}$, key in: [2nd] [x²] 283.4 [ENTER =] to display 16.83448841
$\sqrt{283.4} \doteq 16.83$

b) For $\sqrt[3]{30}$, key in: 3 [2nd] [^] 30 [ENTER =] to display 3.107232506
$\sqrt[3]{30} \doteq 3.11$

c) For $\sqrt[5]{-356}$, key in: 5 [2nd] [^] [(-)] 356 [ENTER] to display -3.238098083

$$\sqrt[5]{-356} \doteq -3.24$$

Exercises

1. Determine each value without using a calculator.

a) $\sqrt{49}$ b) $\sqrt[3]{27}$ c) $\sqrt[4]{81}$ d) $\sqrt[7]{-128}$

e) $\sqrt[6]{1\,000\,000}$ f) $\sqrt[3]{-64}$ g) $\sqrt{81}$ h) $\sqrt[4]{10\,000}$

2. Use a calculator to determine each value to 2 decimal places.

a) $\sqrt{6.2}$ b) $\sqrt[3]{17.8}$ c) $\sqrt[4]{60}$ d) $\sqrt[5]{-83.4}$ e) $\sqrt[10]{2.85}$

3. A 1-L can of paint covers an area of 12 m².

a) Suppose one can of paint is used to cover a square panel with one coat. What are the dimensions of the panel?

b) Suppose one can is used to cover a different square panel with two coats. Assume each coat uses the same amount. How long is one side of the panel?

4. a) The ancient Egyptians could pound gold into very thin sheets. A volume of 1 cm³ of gold could produce a square sheet 0.0005 cm thick with an area of 2000 cm². How long is one side of this square sheet?

b) Modern methods produce much thinner sheets. A volume of 1 cm³ of gold can produce a square sheet with an area 100 times as great as the sheet in part a. How long is one side of this square?

5. The Ladner Creek Gold Mine in British Columbia estimates that its gold reserves are 395 700 cm³. Suppose all this gold is cast into a cube. What would be the dimensions of the cube?

4. New: Patterns and Sequences

IQ tests sometimes contain problems in which a sequence of letters, numbers, or geometric figures is given. The problem is to discover a pattern that relates the items, and to predict the next item.

1. What is the next number? Describe the pattern you used.

a) 5, 10, 15, ▧ b) 5, 10, 20, 40, ▧

c) 18, 27, 36, ▧ d) 100, 10, 1, ▧

e) 400, 100, 25, ▧ f) 1, 3, 6, 10, 15, ▧

2. Each sequence begins with 1, 2, 3. What is the next number? Describe each pattern.

a) 1, 2, 3, 4, 5, 6, ■

b) 1, 2, 3, 1, 2, 3, ■

c) 1, 2, 3, 2, 5, 2, ■

d) 1, 2, 3, 5, 8, 13, ■

e) 1, 2, 3, 6, 12, 24, ■

3. Each sequence begins with 2, 3, 5. What is the next number? Describe each pattern.

a) 2, 3, 5, 8, 12, 17, ■

b) 2, 3, 5, 8, 13, 21, ■

c) 2, 3, 5, 10, 20, 40, ■

d) 2, 3, 5, 6, 8, 9, ■

e) 2, 3, 5, 3, 8, 3, ■

f) 2, 3, 5, 9, 17, 33, ■

4. Describe each pattern, then predict the next two numbers.

a) 1, 3, 5, 7, ■, ■

b) 10, 20, 40, 80, ■, ■

c) 15, 30, 45, ■, ■

d) 100, 90, 80, 70, ■, ■

e) 1, 3, 9, 27, ■, ■

f) 2, –2, 2, –2, ■, ■

g) 1, –10, 100, –1000, ■, ■

h) 8, 3, –2, –7, ■, ■

i) $\frac{1}{2}, \frac{3}{4}, \frac{5}{6}$, ■, ■

j) 9, 3, 1, $\frac{1}{3}$, ■, ■

k) 1, 5, 9, 13, ■, ■

l) 1, 4, 9, 16, ■, ■

The numbers in a sequence are called *terms*.

In some sequences, each term is obtained from the one before it by adding the same number. These kinds of sequences are called *arithmetic sequences*. For example, 3, 7, 11, 15, … is an arithmetic sequence because each term is calculated by adding 4 to the preceding term.

In other sequences, each term is obtained from the one before it by multiplying by the same number. These kinds of sequences are called *geometric sequences*. For example, 3, 6, 12, 24, … is a geometric sequence because each term is calculated by multiplying the preceding term by 2.

5. In exercise 4

a) Which sequences are arithmetic?

b) Which sequences are geometric?

c) Which sequences are neither arithmetic nor geometric?

6. Create at least two different patterns that start with 2, 4, 8, … . Describe each pattern.

Suppose you have a part-time job. You earn $30 per day. You start with $100 in your savings. Each evening you add the $30 you earned that day to your savings. So, after the first day you have $130 saved, and after the second day you have $160, and so on.

How much will you have saved after 12 days?

To answer this question, we tabulate the amount at the end of each of the first few days. In the last column, we "analyse" the amount, to try to obtain a simple mathematical expression.

Day	Amount ($)	Analysis ($)	
0	100	100	$= 100$
1	130	$100 + 30$	$= 100 + 1 \times 30$
2	160	$100 + 30 + 30$	$= 100 + 2 \times 30$
3	190	$100 + 30 + 30 + 30$	$= 100 + 3 \times 30$
4	220	$100 + 30 + 30 + 30 + 30$	$= 100 + 4 \times 30$
5	250	$100 + 30 + 30 + 30 + 30 + 30$	$= 100 + 5 \times 30$

There is a pattern in the growth of the amount. At the end of the 5th day, $30 have been added 5 times. So, at the end of the 12th day, $30 have been added 12 times. The amount after 12 days is:

$$100 + 12 \times 30 = 100 + 360$$
$$= 460$$

At the end of the 12th day, you will have $460 saved.

This kind of growth is called *additive growth* because we add the same amount each day. The graph shows how the amount changes at the end of each day. The points lie on a straight line with slope 30, because the amount grows by $30 each day. For this reason, additive growth is often called *linear growth*.

The Amount at the End of Each Day

$$\text{slope} = \frac{\text{rise}}{\text{run}}$$

$$= \frac{\$30}{1 \text{ day}}, \text{ or } \$30/\text{day}$$

Example 1

A local music store has a guitar on sale for $900. The dealer will reduce the price by $25 at the end of each week until it is sold. Thus, for the first week, the price is $900, for the second week it is $875, and so on. Assume the guitar has not been sold.

a) What is the price of the guitar during the 10th week?

b) Draw a graph to illustrate the price of the guitar at the beginning of each week, for 6 weeks.

Solution

a) During the 10th week, the price of the guitar has been reduced nine times by $25. Therefore, the price that week is:

$$\$900 - 9 \times \$25 = \$900 - \$225$$
$$= \$675$$

b) Make a table of values, then use the data to draw a graph.

Week	1	2	3	4	5	6
Price ($)	900	875	850	825	800	775

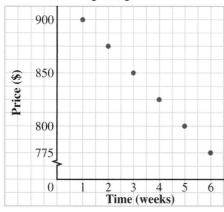

Price of the Guitar at the Beginning of a Week

Discuss

Why do the points lie on a straight line?

Should the points be joined? Explain.

What is the slope of the line?

Suppose the initial price was different. How would the graph change?

Suppose the weekly reduction was different. How would the graph change?

Look at the successive numbers in the two sequences above:

100, 130, 160, 190, 220, 250, ...
900, 875, 850, 825, 800, 775, ...

These are examples of arithmetic sequences. In an arithmetic sequence, each term after the first is found by adding the same number to the preceding term. In the first sequence, that number is 30 and the terms increase. In the second sequence, −25 is added, and the terms decrease.

Arithmetic Sequence

In an *arithmetic sequence*, the number obtained by subtracting any term from the next term is a constant. This constant is the *common difference*.

These are arithmetic sequences.

4, 9, 14, 19, ...   common difference: $9 - 4 = 5$

17, 17.5, 18, 18.5, ...   common difference: $17.5 - 17 = 0.5$

10, 9.5, 9, 8.5, ...   common difference: $9.5 - 10 = -0.5$

12, 2, –8, –18, ...   common difference: $2 - 12 = -10$

Discuss

In an arithmetic sequence, you always add the same number to a term to get the next term. Why is the number you add called a *difference*?

Example 2

The arithmetic sequence 2, 9, 16, ... is given.

a) Determine the 20th term.

b) Suppose you know the term number. How can you calculate the term?

Solution

2, 9, 16, ...
Each term is 7 more than the preceding term, so the common difference is 7. The first term is 2. We get the second term by adding 7 once, the third term by adding 7 twice, and so on. So, we get the 20th term by adding 7 nineteen times to the first term.

a) The common difference is $9 - 2 = 7$.

The 20th term is $2 + 19 \times 7 = 2 + 133$
$$= 135$$

b) Analyse the method in part a. To get the 20th term: subtract 1 from 20, multiply by 7, then add 2. In general, subtract 1 from the term number, multiply by the common difference, then add the first term.

Example 3

Insert two numbers between 17 and 59, so the four numbers form an arithmetic sequence.

Solution

Let d represent the common difference. Visualize the numbers in the sequence:

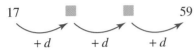

17   ■   ■   59

$+d$ $+d$ $+d$

To go from the 1st term to the 4th term, add d three times. Write an equation to represent this.

$$17 + 3d = 59$$
$$3d = 42$$
$$d = 14$$

The arithmetic sequence is 17, 17 + 1(14), 17 + 2(14), 59; or 17, 31, 45, 59.

1.1 Exercises

A

1. Which sequences are arithmetic? If a sequence is arithmetic, state its common difference.

   a) 6, 10, 14, 18, …

   b) 9, 7, 5, 3, …

   c) 5, 10, 20, 40, …

   d) $1, \frac{1}{2}, \frac{1}{3}, \frac{1}{4}, \dots$

   e) –11, –4, 3, 10, …

   f) 4, –6, 8, –10, …

   g) 2, –3, 4, –5, …

   h) –3, –5, –7, –9, …

   i) –8, –7, –6, –5, …

   j) 1, 1, 2, 3, 5, …

 2. State the common difference, then list the next three terms of each arithmetic sequence.

   a) 12, 15, 18, …

   b) 25, 21, 17, …

   c) 27, 37, 47, …

   d) 31, 21, 11, …

   e) –8, –5, –2, …

   f) 1.8, 2.3, 2.8, …

   g) –3, –8, –13, …

   h) 200, 250, 300, …

   i) 66, 55, 44, …

   j) 1.23, 1.87, 2.51, …

3. Eight dollars were put in an empty piggy bank on January 1. Three dollars are put in the piggy bank on the 1st day of each month after that. How much will be in the piggy bank on July 2?

4. From a computer manufacturer's web site, customers can order their own computer. Customers must choose the processor speed, the amount of memory, and the hard drive capacity. Each choice involves a sequence. Determine if the sequence is an arithmetic sequence. Explain.

a) processor speeds in megahertz: 733, 800, 866, 933, 1000, 1133

b) random access memory in megabytes: 128, 256, 384, 512

c) hard drive capacity in gigabytes: 10, 20, 30, 45, 75

✓ **5. Knowledge/Understanding**

a) Determine the indicated term of each arithmetic sequence.

i) 6, 11, 16, …	7th term	**ii)** 18, 15, 12, …	8th term
iii) 23, 34, 45, …	10th term	**iv)** 45, 37, 29, …	9th term
v) 5, 10, 15, …	12th term	**vi)** −10, −4, 2, …	10th term

b) Choose one sequence from part a. Explain how you could calculate any term in the sequence if you know the term number.

✓ **6. Thinking/Inquiry/Problem Solving** Here is a pattern of natural numbers in three rows. Assume the pattern continues.

Row 1	1	4	7	10	13	…
Row 2	2	5	8	11	14	…
Row 3	3	6	9	12	15	…

a) What are the next five numbers in row 2?

b) In which row will the number 100 appear? Explain.

c) Describe a procedure you could use to determine in which row any given natural number appears. Test your procedure with some examples.

7. A month from a calendar is shown.

a) Explain why the numbers in each row form an arithmetic sequence.

b) Explain why the numbers in each column form an arithmetic sequence.

c) Find some numbers that form a diagonal line. Do these numbers form an arithmetic sequence? Explain.

Sunday	Monday	Tuesday	Wednesday	Thursday	Friday	Saturday
1	2	3	4	5	6	7
8	9	10	11	12	13	14
15	16	17	18	19	20	21
22	23	24	25	26	27	28
29	30	31				

8. The Chinese calendar associates years with animals. There are 12 animals. They are always used in the order shown below. After 2011, the pattern repeats with 2012 as the year of the dragon.

dragon	snake	horse	ram	monkey	rooster
2000	2001	2002	2003	2004	2005
dog	pig	rat	ox	tiger	rabbit
2006	2007	2008	2009	2010	2011

a) The year 2000 was the year of the dragon. List the next three years that will be the year of the dragon.

b) On July 1, 2067, Canada will be 200 years old. Which animal will be associated with 2067?

c) After 2011, list the next three years each animal will appear.

  i) the tiger   **ii)** the rooster   **iii)** the rat

9. The disappearance of the dinosaurs about 65 million years ago is one of the great mysteries of science. Scientists have recently found that mass extinctions of Earth's creatures are separated by periods of roughly 26 million years.

a) About when did other mass extinctions occur?

b) Suppose the scientific theory is correct. Estimate when the next mass extinction might occur.

10. Suppose the first term and the common difference of an arithmetic sequence are equal. How are all the terms related to the first term? Explain.

11. After the start-up year, the annual production of a northern gold mine has remained constant at 22 000 ounces per year. At the end of last year, the total output of the mine, since it was opened, was 90 000 ounces of gold.

a) What will the total output be at the end of this year? At the end of next year?

b) Draw a graph to show the total output of the mine for the next five years.

c) Suppose the annual output is more than 22 000 ounces per year. How would the graph change?

12. **Application** The Olympic Winter Games are held every four years. The first Winter Olympics were held in 1924.

   a) Begin with 1924. List the years that should have been the first six Winter Olympics.

   b) In two of those years, the Winter Olympics were cancelled. What years do you think they were? Explain your answer.

   c) The Winter Olympics followed the pattern of being held every four years until 1992. Beginning in 1994, another pattern of holding the Winter Olympics every four years was begun. How many Winter Olympics followed the first pattern?

   d) Why do you think the first pattern was broken in 1994?

13. **Communication** Give examples to illustrate your answers to these questions.

   a) Is it possible to have an arithmetic sequence in which all terms are the same?

   b) Is it possible to have an arithmetic sequence in which some, but not all, terms are the same?

14. a) Copy, then complete each arithmetic sequence.
      i) ■, 7, 12, ■, ■   ii) ■, ■, 29, 25, ■
      iii) 5, ■, 21, ■, ■   iv) 50, ■, ■, 35, ■
      v) ■, –8, ■, ■, ■, 32   vi) 43, ■, ■, ■, 77

   b) Choose one sequence from part a. Explain how you determined the missing terms.

15. Insert two numbers between 8 and 30, so the four numbers form an arithmetic sequence.

16. Insert three numbers between 10 and 55, so the five numbers form an arithmetic sequence.

17. Determine the first five terms of each arithmetic sequence.

   a) The 2nd term is 14 and the 5th term is 23.

   b) The 3rd term is 35 and the 7th term is 55.

   c) The 5th term is 4 and the 8th term is –2.

C

18. Here is a game for two people, *A* and *B*. *A* begins by mentioning a single-digit number. *B* may add any single-digit number to the number mentioned by *A*. *A* may add any single-digit number to the result. Players alternate in this manner, always adding any single-digit number to the previous result. The winner is the first person to reach 50. Play this game with a friend, and determine a winning strategy.

An antique apple peeler is now worth $100. Its value increases by 9% every year. How much will the antique apple peeler be worth after 8 years?

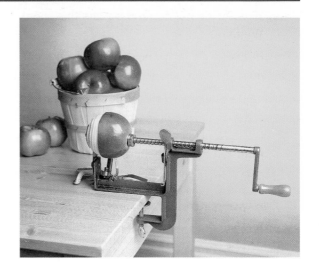

We will solve this problem in two different ways.

Method 1: Calculating the annual increases in value

Start with $100 the first year.
After one year, the antique apple peeler's value will be 9% greater.
9% of $100 is 0.09 × $100 = $9.
After one year, its value is $100 + $9 = $109.

After two years, its value will be 9% greater than its value after the first year.
9% of $109 is 0.09 × $109 = $9.81.
After two years, its value is $109.00 + $9.81 = $118.81.

This pattern continues. Look at the calculation of the value after two years. The increase after the second year was 81¢ more than the increase after the first year. The extra 81¢ is 9% of the $9 increase from the first year. The process by which we get this extra increase is called *compounding*. In situations that involve percent growth, these extra increases are always accumulating. The table shows the results for the first 8 years.

Year	Method	Value ($)
0	100.00 = 100.00	100.00
1	100.00 + 0.09 × 100.00 = 109.00	109.00
2	109.00 + 0.09 × 109.00 = 118.81	118.81
3	118.81 + 0.09 × 118.81 = 129.50	129.50
4	129.50 + 0.09 × 129.50 = 141.16	141.16
5	141.16 + 0.09 × 141.16 = 153.86	153.86
6	153.86 + 0.09 × 153.86 = 167.71	167.71
7	167.71 + 0.09 × 167.71 = 182.80	182.80
8	182.80 + 0.09 × 182.80 = 199.26	199.26

Discuss

How can you use your calculator efficiently to determine successive values?

After 8 years, the antique apple peeler is worth $199.26.

Method 2: Using a multiplier

Look at the method in the second row of the table on page 16. There is a common factor of 100 in the expression $100 + 0.09 \times 100$. We can use this common factor to calculate the value after the second year in a different way:

$$100 + 0.09 \times 100 = 100(1 + 0.09)$$
$$= 100(1.09)$$
$$= 109$$

Instead of calculating 9% of 100, then adding the result to 100, we multiply 100 by 1.09. We could multiply by 1.09 in each of the other rows as well.

Take Note

Multiplier Principle for Growth

Increasing a quantity by 9% is the same as multiplying by $(1 + 0.09)$, or 1.09.

We could use the multiplier principle to complete the calculations.

Year	Method		Value ($)
0	100	$= 100$	100.00
1	100×1.09	$= 100 \times 1.09^1$	109.00
2	$100 \times 1.09 \times 1.09$	$= 100 \times 1.09^2$	118.81
3	$100 \times 1.09 \times 1.09 \times 1.09$	$= 100 \times 1.09^3$	129.50
4	$100 \times 1.09 \times 1.09 \times 1.09 \times 1.09$	$= 100 \times 1.09^4$	141.16
5	$100 \times 1.09 \times 1.09 \times 1.09 \times 1.09 \times 1.09$	$= 100 \times 1.09^5$	153.86

There is a pattern in the calculations. After 5 years, we have multiplied by 1.09 five times. So, after 8 years, we will have multiplied by 1.09 eight times.

The value of the apple peeler can be determined:

$$100(1.09)^8 \doteq 100 \times 1.992\,562\,6$$
$$\doteq 199.26$$

After 8 years, the antique apple peeler is worth $199.26.

This kind of growth is called *multiplicative growth* because we multiply by the same factor each year. The graph on page 18 shows how the value of the apple peeler changes over time.

Discuss

Describe why we cannot solve the problem this way: The value of the antique apple peeler increases by 9% each year; so, after 8 years, it will have increased by 9% eight times, for an overall increase of 72%. After 8 years, the apple peeler will be worth $172.

Since repeated multiplication is represented by a power, multiplicative growth is called *exponential growth*. The points lie on a curve.

Value of an Antique Apple Peeler against Time

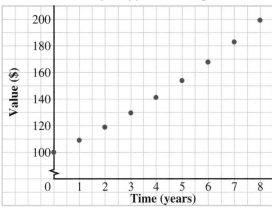

Example 1

A mountain bike is worth $1000. Each year it loses 8% of its value.

a) What will the bike be worth after 6 years?

b) Draw a graph to show how the value of the bike changes during the 6 years.

Solution

a) Solution 1

Calculate the annual decreases in value.

Start with $1000 the first year.

After one year, the mountain bike's value will be 8% less.

8% of $1000 is $0.08 \times \$1000 = \$80$.

After one year, its value is $\$1000 - \$80 = \$920$.

These calculations are continued in the table.

Year	Method	Value ($)
0	1000 = 1000	1000.00
1	$1000 - 0.08 \times 1000 = 920.00$	920.00
2	$920.00 - 0.08 \times 920.00 = 846.40$	846.40
3	$846.40 - 0.08 \times 846.40 = 778.69$	778.69
4	$778.69 - 0.08 \times 778.69 = 716.39$	716.39
5	$716.39 - 0.08 \times 716.39 = 659.08$	659.08
6	$659.08 - 0.08 \times 659.08 = 606.35$	606.35

The mountain bike is worth $606.35 after 6 years.

Solution 2
Use a multiplier.

Each year, the mountain bike loses 8% of its value.
Therefore, at the end of each year, the bike is worth $100\% - 8\% = 92\%$ of its value for the preceding year.
So, each year, multiply the previous year's value by 0.92.

Year	Method		Value ($)
0	1000	$= 1000$	1000.00
1	1000×0.92	$= 1000 \times 0.92^1$	920.00
2	920.00×0.92	$= 1000 \times 0.92^2$	846.40
3	846.40×0.92	$= 1000 \times 0.92^3$	778.69
4	778.69×0.92	$= 1000 \times 0.92^4$	716.39
5	716.39×0.92	$= 1000 \times 0.92^5$	659.08
6	659.08×0.92	$= 1000 \times 0.92^6$	606.35

From the table, the value after 6 years is $606.35.

b) Draw a graph using either table of values from part a.

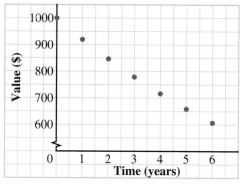

Value of a Mountain Bike against Time

Discuss

What are the advantages and disadvantages of the two solutions in part a?

How can you tell from the graph that the decreases in value are not constant?

In Solution 2 of *Example 1*, we used the following principle:

Take Note

Multiplier Principle for Decay

Decreasing a quantity by 8% is the same as multiplying by $(1 - 0.08)$, or 0.92.

We can use the pattern in the table in Solution 2 to write an expression for the value of the mountain bike after any number of years. For example:

After 10 years, the mountain bike would be worth $1000(0.92)^{10}$.
After 12 years, the mountain bike would be worth $1000(0.92)^{12}$.

Look at the successive values of the antique apple peeler and the mountain bike.

100.00, 109.00, 118.81, 129.50, 141.16, 153.86, 167.71, ...
1000.00, 920.00, 846.40, 778.69, 716.39, 659.08, 606.35, ...

These are examples of geometric sequences. In a geometric sequence, each term after the first is found by multiplying the preceding term by the same number. In the first sequence, that number is 1.09 and the numbers increase. In the second sequence, each term is multiplied by 0.92 and the numbers decrease.

Take Note

Geometric Sequence

In a *geometric sequence*, the number obtained by dividing any term by the preceding term is a constant. This constant is the *multiplier* or the *common ratio*.

These are geometric sequences:

1, 3, 9, 27, 81, ...   common ratio: $\frac{3}{1} = \frac{9}{3} = \frac{27}{9} = 3$

2, 10, 50, 250, ...   common ratio: $\frac{10}{2} = 5$

12, 6, 3, 1.5, 0.75, ...   common ratio: $\frac{6}{12} = 0.5$

3, –12, 48, –192, ...   common ratio: $\frac{-12}{3} = -4$

Discuss

In a geometric sequence, you always multiply a term by the same number to get the next term. Why is the number you multiply by called a ratio?

Example 2

The geometric sequence 2, 6, 18, ... is given.

a) Determine the 10th term.

b) Suppose you know the term number. How can you calculate the term?

Solution

2, 6, 18, …

Each term is 3 times the preceding term, so the common ratio is 3. The first term is 2. We get the second term by multiplying by 3 once, the third term by multiplying by 3 twice, and so on. So, we get the 10th term by multiplying the first term, 2, by 3 nine times.

a) The common ratio is $\frac{6}{2} = 3$.

The 10th term is $2 \times 3^9 = 2 \times 19\ 683$
$$= 39\ 366$$

b) Analyse the method in part a. To get the 10th term, subtract 1 from 10 to determine the exponent, calculate 3^9, then multiply by 2. In general: subtract 1 from the term number to determine the exponent, calculate the common ratio raised to that exponent, then multiply by the first term.

Example 3

Insert two numbers between 5 and 320, so the four numbers form a geometric sequence.

Solution

Let r represent the common ratio. Visualize the numbers in the sequence:

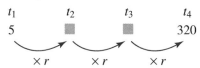

t_1 t_2 t_3 t_4
5   ▪   ▪   320

$\times r$ $\times r$ $\times r$

To go from the 1st term to the 4th term, multiply by r three times. Write an equation to represent this.

$$5 \times r^3 = 320$$
$$r^3 = 64$$

Since $4 \times 4 \times 4 = 64$,
$$r = 4$$

The geometric sequence is 5, 5(4), $5(4)^2$, 320;
or 5, 20, 80, 320.

Discuss

Suppose only one number is inserted between 5 and 320 so the three numbers are in a geometric sequence. What numbers are possible? Explain.

How can you test a sequence to determine whether it is geometric, arithmetic, or neither?

A

1. Which sequences are geometric? If a sequence is geometric, state its common ratio.

a) 1, 2, 4, 8, 16, …

b) 2, 4, 6, 10, 16, …

c) $4, -2, 1, -\frac{1}{2}, \frac{1}{4}, \ldots$

d) $1, -\frac{1}{3}, \frac{1}{9}, -\frac{1}{27}, \ldots$

e) −3, 2, 7, 12, 17, …

f) 6, 0.6, 0.06, 0.006, …

g) 3, 7, 15, 31, …

h) 10, 100, 1000, 10 000, …

i) $2 \times 10^{-3}, 2 \times 10^{-5}, 2 \times 10^{-7}, \ldots$

j) $1.08^2, 1.08^3, 1.08^4, \ldots$

2. State the common ratio, then list the next three terms of each geometric sequence.

a) 2, 20, 200, …

b) 48, 24, 12, …

c) 5, −10, 20, …

d) 3, 9, 27, …

e) 4, −2, 1, …

f) 1, −1, 1, …

g) 2, 4, 8, …

h) −1, −3, −9, …

i) $\frac{1}{2}, \frac{1}{6}, \frac{1}{18}, \ldots$

j) $\frac{64}{81}, \frac{32}{27}, \frac{16}{9}, \ldots$

3. Determine whether each sequence is arithmetic, geometric, or neither. Explain your choice.

a) 1, 100, 10 000, …

b) 1, 3, 6, 10, 15, …

c) 1, 5, 9, 13, …

d) 1, 4, 9, 16, 25, …

e) 22, 15, 8, 1, …

f) 2, 0.2, 0.02, 0.002, …

g) 1, −1, 1, −1, …

h) 2, 2, 2, 2, …

i) $1, \frac{1}{4}, \frac{1}{64}, \frac{1}{256}, \ldots$

j) $\frac{1}{2}, \frac{3}{4}, \frac{5}{6}, \ldots$

B

4. A colony of 100 insects doubles every week. How many insects are there after each time?

a) 2 weeks

b) 4 weeks

c) 6 weeks

5. Sequences of numbers are involved in photography. Determine if each sequence is geometric. Explain.

a) shutter speeds in seconds: $1, \frac{1}{2}, \frac{1}{4}, \frac{1}{8}, \frac{1}{15}, \frac{1}{30}, \frac{1}{60}$

b) film speeds: 100, 200, 400, 800

c) lens aperture markings: 1.4, 2, 2.8, 4, 5.6, 8, 11, 16, 22

6. I have a metre stick. I break off $\frac{1}{10}$ of it and throw the piece away. I then break off $\frac{1}{10}$ of what remains and throw that piece away. I repeat this process many times, each time breaking off $\frac{1}{10}$ of what remains and throwing the piece away.

   a) What is the length of the piece I have after the first break? The second break? The third break?

   b) Explain why the sequence of lengths of the pieces I have is geometric.

   c) How long is the piece I have after the 10th break?

✓ **7. Knowledge/Understanding**

   a) Determine the indicated term of each geometric sequence.
   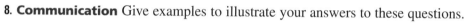
   i) 3, 6, 12, ...   6th term   **ii)** 3, –6, 12, ...   6th term
   iii) 200, 20, 2, ...   5th term   **iv)** 5, 20, 80, ...   7th term
   v) 100, 20, 4, ...   5th term   **vi)** 6, –2, $\frac{2}{3}$, ...   6th term

   b) Choose one sequence from part a. Explain how you could calculate any term in the sequence if you know the term number.

✓ **8. Communication** Give examples to illustrate your answers to these questions.

   a) Is it possible to have a geometric sequence in which all terms are the same?

   b) Is it possible to have a geometric sequence in which some, but not all, terms are the same?

   c) Is it possible for a sequence to be both arithmetic and geometric? Explain.

✓ **9.** An oil painting is worth $400. Its value increases by 7% each year.
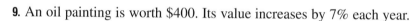

   a) What is the value of the painting after 6 years?

   b) Draw a graph to show how the value changes during the 6 years.

   c) How would the graph change if the initial value of the oil painting was more than $400? Less than $400?

   d) How would the graph change if the value increased each year by more than 7%? Less than 7%?

✓ **10.** A hockey card is worth $250. Its value increases by 9% each year. What is the card worth after 10 years?

11. A $1000 investment increases in value by 6% each year, for 8 years. What is the investment worth after 8 years?

✓ **12.** A new vehicle is worth $30 000. It decreases in value by 20% each year.

   a) What will the vehicle be worth after 5 years?

   b) Draw a graph to show how the value changes during the 5 years.

   c) How would the graph change if the initial value of the vehicle was more than $30 000? Less than $30 000?

d) How would the graph change if the value decreased each year by more than 20%? Less than 20%?

13. A store has a sale in which 10% is taken off the cost of an item at the end of each day. Suppose an item originally cost $250. Determine its cost for each of the next five days.

✓ **14.** A sailboat was bought for $2000. Its value decreases by 9% each year. What will the sailboat be worth in 5 years?

15. Application A rectangular piece of paper measures 30 cm by 20 cm. It is cut into four smaller congruent rectangular pieces. These pieces are arranged one on top of another to form a pile of 4 sheets that measures 15 cm by 10 cm.

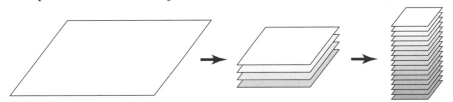

This pile of 4 sheets is cut into smaller congruent pieces. These smaller pieces are arranged to form a pile of 16 sheets that measures 7.5 cm by 5.0 cm.

Suppose the above steps are repeated many times.

a) Copy and complete this table to the 4th step.

Step	Number of pieces	Length of one piece (cm)	Width of one piece (cm)	Area of one piece (cm²)
Start	1	30	20	
1				
2				
3				
4				

b) Explain why the numbers in each column (except the first) form a geometric sequence.

16. Suppose the first term and the common ratio of a geometric sequence are equal. How are all the terms related to the first term?

17. Strep throat is an infection caused by the bacteria streptococci. After you have been infected, these bacteria could double in number every 20 min.

a) Suppose a single bacterium began reproducing at noon. About how many bacteria would be present at each time?
12:20 P.M.; 12:40 P.M.; 1 P.M.; 1:20 P.M.; 1:40 P.M.; 2 P.M.; 2:20 P.M.; 2:40 P.M.

b) Show the results of part a on a graph. Should the points on the graph be joined? Explain.

18. In exercise 17, the way you calculated the number of bacteria every 20 min and the graph of the results are called *models* of the growth of the bacteria.

  a) Give some reasons why the actual number of bacteria present every 20 min might be different from the numbers predicted by the model.

  b) Do you think the growth could continue indefinitely? Explain.

19. Thinking/Inquiry/Problem Solving Suppose you know the first term and the common ratio of a geometric sequence. How can you tell from these numbers whether the terms of the sequence become greater or smaller as you extend the sequence? What other possibilities are there for what happens to the terms as you extend the sequence? How can you tell when these will happen? Support your explanations with examples.

20. Copy and complete each geometric sequence.

  a) ■, 8, 16, ■, ■

  b) ■, ■, 12, 4, ■

  c) 1, ■, ■, −27, ■

  d) 1, ■, 16, ■, ■

  e) ■, 160, ■, ■, ■, 10

  f) 10, ■, ■, ■, 6250

21. Insert two numbers between 2 and 54, so the four numbers form a geometric sequence.

22. Insert three numbers between 4 and 2500, so the five numbers form a geometric sequence.

23. Choose either exercise 21 or exercise 22. Explain how you determined the numbers.

C

24. a) Use the y^x or $\wedge$ key on a calculator to express the first five terms of this sequence in decimal form.

  $2^{2.0}, 2^{2.1}, 2^{2.2}, 2^{2.3}, 2^{2.4}, \ldots$

  b) Determine whether this is a geometric sequence. Explain.

25. Determine whether it is possible for 3 numbers to form both an arithmetic sequence and a geometric sequence.

26. Determine the geometric sequence with each property.

  a) The sum of the 3rd and 4th terms is 36. The sum of the 4th and 5th terms is 108.

  b) The sum of the first 2 terms is 3. The sum of the next 2 terms is $\frac{4}{3}$.

1.3 The General Term of a Sequence

General Term of an Arithmetic Sequence

Consider the arithmetic sequence 4, 7, 10, ...
Each term is 3 more than the preceding term.
We can write the terms as follows.

$$t_1 = 4$$
$$t_2 = 4 + 1(3) = 7$$
$$t_3 = 4 + 2(3) = 10$$
$$t_4 = 4 + 3(3) = 13$$
$$\vdots \qquad \vdots$$

To determine any term, we add a certain number of 3s to the first term.
The number of 3s to add is 1 less than the term number.
For example, $t_{20} = 4 + 19(3)$
$$= 61$$

Similarly, $t_n = 4 + (n - 1)(3)$
$$= 4 + 3n - 3$$
$$= 3n + 1$$

The term, $t_n = 3n + 1$, is the *general term* of the sequence. The general term is a formula that can be used to calculate any term in this sequence.

For example, to determine the 80th term, t_{80}, substitute $n = 80$ in $t_n = 3n + 1$.
$$t_{80} = 3(80) + 1$$
$$= 241$$
The 80th term of the sequence above is 241.

The general arithmetic sequence has first term a and common difference d.

$$a, a + d, a + 2d, a + 3d, \ldots$$

To determine t_n, add $(n - 1)$ common differences to the first term.

$$t_n = a + (n - 1)d$$

Take Note

General Term of the General Arithmetic Sequence

The general term of the arithmetic sequence
$a, a + d, a + 2d, a + 3d, \ldots$ is
$$t_n = a + (n - 1)d$$

Example 1

Determine the 35th term of the arithmetic sequence 4, 7, 10, … .

Solution

Use the formula for the general term, $t_n = a + (n - 1)d$.
The first term is 4. The common difference is $7 - 4 = 3$.
Substitute $n = 35$, $a = 4$, and $d = 3$ in $t_n = a + (n - 1)d$.

$$t_{35} = 4 + 34(3)$$
$$= 4 + 102$$
$$= 106$$

The 35th term of the sequence is 106.

Discuss

The common difference is 3. Describe how the terms grow.

Example 2

The formula for the *n*th term of a sequence is $t_n = 12 - 5n$.

a) Write the first four terms of the sequence.

b) Use the results of part a to explain how the formula for t_n was derived.

Solution

a) Use the formula $t_n = 12 - 5n$. Substitute $n = 1, 2, 3$, then 4.
$$t_1 = 12 - 5(1) = 7$$
$$t_2 = 12 - 5(2) = 2$$
$$t_3 = 12 - 5(3) = -3$$
$$t_4 = 12 - 5(4) = -8$$

The first four terms of the sequence are 7, 2, –3, –8.

b) The sequence 7, 2, –3, –8, … is an arithmetic sequence with 1st term 7
and common difference –5.

Use the general term of an arithmetic sequence, $t_n = a + (n - 1)d$.
Substitute $a = 7$ and $d = -5$.
$$t_n = 7 + (n - 1)(-5)$$
$$= 7 - 5n + 5$$
$$= 12 - 5n$$

General Term of a Geometric Sequence

The development of the general term of a geometric sequence is similar to that
of an arithmetic sequence.

Consider the geometric sequence 2, 6, 18, ...
Each term is 3 times the preceding term. We can write the terms as follows.

$t_1 = 2$
$t_2 = 2(3) = 6$
$t_3 = 2(3)^2 = 18$
$t_4 = 2(3)^3 = 54$
$\vdots \quad \vdots$

To determine any term, we multiply the first term by a certain number of 3s.
The number of 3s to multiply by is 1 less than the term number.

For example, $t_{10} = 2(3)^9 = 39\ 366$
Similarly, $t_n = 2(3)^{n-1}$
The term, $t_n = 2(3)^{n-1}$, is the general term of the sequence.

We can use this general term to calculate any term in this sequence.
For example, to determine the 8th term, t_8, substitute $n = 8$ in $t_n = 2(3)^{n-1}$.

$t_8 = 2(3)^{8-1} = 2(3)^7 = 4374$

The 8th term of the sequence above is 4374.
The general geometric sequence has first term a and common ratio r.

$a, ar, ar^2, ar^3, ...$

To determine t_n, multiply a by $(n - 1)$ common ratios.

$t_n = ar^{n-1}$

Take Note

General Term of the General Geometric Sequence
The general term of the geometric sequence $a, ar, ar^2, ar^3, ...$ is
$$t_n = ar^{n-1}$$

Example 3

Determine the 11th term of the geometric sequence 3, 6, 12, 24, ...

Solution

Use the formula for the general term, $t_n = ar^{n-1}$.
The first term is 3 and the common ratio is 2.
Substitute $n = 11$, $a = 3$, and $r = 2$ in $t_n = ar^{n-1}$.

$t_{11} = 3(2)^{10}$
$= 3(1024)$
$= 3072$

The 11th term of the sequence is 3072.

Discuss

The common ratio
is 2. Describe how the
terms grow.

Some sequences are neither arithmetic nor geometric.

Example 4

Determine a formula for the nth term of the sequence $\frac{1}{2}, \frac{3}{4}, \frac{5}{8}, \frac{7}{16}, \dots$.

Solution

The numerators form an arithmetic sequence 1, 3, 5, 7, … .

Use the expression for the general term of an arithmetic sequence: $a + (n - 1)d$

Substitute $a = 1$ and $d = 2$.

The nth term of the sequence of numerators is

$$1 + (n - 1) \times 2 = 1 + 2n - 2$$
$$= 2n - 1$$

The denominators form a geometric sequence 2, 4, 8, 16, … .

Use the expression for the general term of a geometric sequence: ar^{n-1}

Substitute $a = 2$ and $r = 2$.

The nth term of the sequence of denominators is

$$2 \times 2^{n-1} = 2^1 \times 2^{n-1}$$
$$= 2^n$$

The formula for the nth term of the sequence

is $t_n = \frac{2n - 1}{2^n}$.

Discuss

What other way is there to determine the nth term of the sequence of denominators?

Is the sequence $\frac{1}{2}, \frac{3}{4}, \frac{5}{8}, \frac{7}{16}, \dots$ arithmetic, geometric, or neither? Explain.

1.3 Exercises

A

1. The formula for the nth term of a sequence is given. Write the first four terms of each sequence.

   a) $t_n = 2 + 5n$
   b) $t_n = 18 - 2n$
   c) $t_n = 2^n$
   d) $t_n = 2 \times 3^n$
   e) $t_n = n^2 + 1$
   f) $t_n = n(n + 1)$

2. Identify each sequence in exercise 1 as arithmetic, geometric, or neither.

3. The formula for the nth term of a sequence is given. Determine the 10th term.

   a) $t_n = 7 + 2n$
   b) $t_n = -20 + 3n$
   c) $t_n = 6 - n$
   d) $t_n = n^2 - 1$
   e) $t_n = \frac{1}{n}$
   f) $t_n = n(n - 1)$

4. For the arithmetic sequence 4, 10, 16, 20, …, determine each term.

    a) t_n **b)** t_{10} **c)** t_{20}

5. For the arithmetic sequence 11, 8, 5, 2, …, determine each term.

    a) t_n **b)** t_8 **c)** t_{25}

6. For the geometric sequence 3, 6, 12, …, determine each term.

    a) t_n **b)** t_7 **c)** t_{12}

7. For the geometric sequence 3, –6, 12, …, determine each term.

    a) t_n **b)** t_7 **c)** t_{12}

8. Compare the results in exercises 6 and 7. In what ways are they similar? In what ways are they different?

B

9. Write the general term for each arithmetic sequence.

    a) 5, 8, 11, 14, …   **b)** 5, 3, 1, –1, …

    c) –4, –2, 0, 2, …   **d)** 3, 9, 15, 21, …

10. Each sequence is an arithmetic sequence. Write a formula for t_n, then use it to determine the indicated term.

    a) 2, 5, 8, … t_{20} **b)** 10, 12, 14, … t_{50}

    c) 20, 17, 14, … t_{80} **d)** 45, 43, 41, … t_{100}

11. Write the general term for each geometric sequence.

    a) 1, 2, 4, 8, …   **b)** 1, –2, 4, –8, …

    c) 8, 4, 2, 1, …   **d)** 8, –4, 2, –1, …

12. Each sequence is geometric. Write a formula for t_n, then use it to determine the indicated term.

    a) 2, 6, 18, … t_6 **b)** 3, 15, 75, … t_9

    c) 10, 5, 2.5, … t_8 **d)** 4, –12, 36, … t_{10}

13. Knowledge/Understanding Four sequences have the general terms listed below.

    Sequence 1: $t_n = n + 1$
    Sequence 2: $t_n = 2n + 1$
    Sequence 3: $t_n = 3n + 1$
    Sequence 4: $t_n = 4n + 1$

    a) List the first four terms of each sequence.

    b) How are the 1st terms of these sequences related? Explain.

    c) How are the 2nd terms of these sequences related? Explain.

d) How are the 3rd terms of these sequences related? Explain.

e) How are the 4th terms of these sequences related? Explain.

14. A pile of bricks is arranged in rows. The number of bricks in each row forms the arithmetic sequence 65, 59, 53, … .

a) One row contains 17 bricks. Which row is this?

b) How many rows of bricks are there? Explain your assumptions and answer.

15. An arithmetic sequence is 8, 14, 20, 26, … . Which term is 92?

16. For each arithmetic sequence, a later term in the sequence is given. Which term is it?

a) 1, 4, 7, 10, …   94   **b)** 3, 5, 7, 9, …   119

c) 2, 7, 12, 17, …   187   **d)** −7, −5, −3, −1, …   57

e) 30, 26, 22, 18, …   −50   **f)** 2, 3.5, 5, 6.5, …   152

17. Thinking/Inquiry/Problem Solving In an arithmetic sequence, the 3rd term is 25 and the 9th term is 43. How many terms of the sequence are less than 100?

18. Application You have 2 parents 1 generation ago, 4 grandparents 2 generations ago, 8 great-grandparents 3 generations ago, and so on. Determine how many ancestors you had each number of generations ago.

a) 5   **b)** 10   **c)** 20   **d)** 40

19. Assume one generation lasts about 25 years. Then 40 generations ago was about 1000 years ago. Historians estimate the world population was about 300 000 000 at that time. Your answer to exercise 18d is approximately 1 000 000 000 000. Explain why the calculated number of ancestors 40 generations ago is much greater than the entire world population.

20. Each year, the value of a car depreciates to 70% of its value the previous year. A car was bought new for $25 000.

a) Determine its approximate value at the end of every year, for 5 years.

b) Draw a graph to show how its value drops during the 5 years.

c) Write an expression to represent its value after n years.

21. Communication Suppose you know the first term and the common difference of an arithmetic sequence. How can you tell from these numbers whether the terms of the sequence become greater or smaller as you extend the sequence? What other possibilities are there for what happens to the terms as you extend the sequence? How can you tell when these will happen? Support your explanations with examples.

22. Determine a formula for the nth term of each sequence.

a) $\dfrac{1}{2}, \dfrac{2}{3}, \dfrac{3}{4}, \dfrac{4}{5}, \dots$

b) $\dfrac{1}{1}, \dfrac{3}{2}, \dfrac{5}{3}, \dfrac{7}{4}, \dots$

c) $\dfrac{2}{1}, \dfrac{6}{3}, \dfrac{10}{5}, \dfrac{14}{7}, \dots$

23. Determine a formula for the nth term of each sequence.

a) $1 \times 2, 2 \times 3, 3 \times 4, 4 \times 5, \dots$

b) $1 \times 2, 3 \times 5, 5 \times 8, 7 \times 11, \dots$

c) $1 \times 2, 2 \times 4, 3 \times 8, 4 \times 16, \dots$

d) $2 \times 3, 6 \times 5, 10 \times 7, 14 \times 9, \dots$

24. This advertisement appeared in a local newspaper.

BOAT WORLD

BIG TEN

SALE

10% will be taken off each boat's price each week for the next four weeks. 60-day warranty on all items. First come, first served.

Boat	Retail price ($)	Week 1 price ($)	Week 2 price ($)	Week 3 price ($)	Week 4 price ($)
15' Chrysler Tri Hull	2000	1800	1620	1458	1312
14' Starcraft, 20 Yamaha	7000	6300	5670	5103	4593
16' Wilker, 100 Javelin	9000				
19' Steury, 105 Chrysler	5699				

a) In the first two rows, check that the prices for each week are correct.

b) Calculate the prices in the other two rows.

c) Let x dollars represent the retail price of a boat. Write an expression to represent the price of the boat in each of the next four weeks.

25. Suppose a cottage is bought for $120 000. Assume its value increases by about 8% each year. What is its approximate value after each time?

a) 5 years

b) 10 years

c) n years

C

26. The general term of a certain sequence is given by this formula.

$$t_n = 2n + 0.1(n - 1)(n - 2)(n - 3)(n - 4)(n - 5)$$

a) Determine the first 6 terms of the sequence.

b) Describe the pattern in the first 5 terms. Explain why the pattern does not apply to the terms after the 5th term.

27. The arithmetic sequence 200, 185, 170, … is given. What is the first negative term of this sequence? Explain.

1. A $1000 investment certificate increases in value by 5% each year. How much will it be worth after 2 years?

2. Determine the 10th term of the sequence with each general term.

   a) $t_n = 12 - 2n$

   b) $t_n = 5(2)^{n-1}$

3. Write the first 3 terms of the sequence with each general term.

   a) $t_n = n^2 - 1$

   b) $t_n = 10(1.5)^n$

4. State which sequences in exercises 2 and 3 are:

   a) arithmetic

   b) geometric

   c) neither arithmetic nor geometric

5. Write the general term for each arithmetic sequence.

   a) 5, 8, 11, 14, …

   b) 5, 3, 1, –1, …

6. Write the general term for each geometric sequence.

   a) 1, 2, 4, 8, …

   b) 8, –4, 2, –1, …

7. Write a formula for the nth term of each sequence.

   a) 2, 10, 50, 250, …

   b) $\dfrac{1}{2}, \dfrac{3}{5}, \dfrac{5}{8}, \dfrac{7}{11}, \ldots$

8. Determine a formula for the nth term of each sequence.

   a) $1 \times 1, 3 \times 4, 5 \times 7, 7 \times 10, \ldots$

   b) $\dfrac{1 \times 3}{2 \times 4}, \dfrac{3 \times 5}{4 \times 6}, \dfrac{5 \times 7}{6 \times 8}, \dfrac{7 \times 9}{8 \times 10}, \ldots$

1.4 Recursion Formulas (Functions and Relations)

In Section 1.3, we developed formulas for the general term of an arithmetic or geometric sequence. For some sequences, the general term can be expressed in a different way. For example, consider the following arithmetic sequence.

$$2, 12, 22, 32, \dots$$

The first term is 2, and each term is 10 more than the preceding term. Hence, the nth term is 10 more than the $(n - 1)$th term. We write:

$$t_1 = 2, t_n = t_{n-1} + 10, n > 1$$

This is a *recursion formula*. A recursion formula is a "recipe" for generating the terms, starting with the first term. A recursion formula has two parts. The first part begins the sequence. The second part is used to write the terms, one after the other.

Example 1

Write the first 5 terms of the sequence defined by each recursion formula.

a) $t_1 = -7, t_n = t_{n-1} + 4, n > 1$ **b)** $t_1 = 2, t_n = 3t_{n-1}, n > 1$

Solution

The first part of the formula is the first term. Substitute $n = 2, 3, 4, \dots$ in turn in the second part of the formula to determine the other terms.

a) $t_1 = -7$

$t_2 = t_1 + 4$	$t_3 = t_2 + 4$	$t_4 = t_3 + 4$	$t_5 = t_4 + 4$
$= -7 + 4$	$= -3 + 4$	$= 1 + 4$	$= 5 + 4$
$= -3$	$= 1$	$= 5$	$= 9$

The first 5 terms of the sequence are $-7, -3, 1, 5, 9$.

b) $t_1 = 2$

$t_2 = 3t_1$	$t_3 = 3t_2$	$t_4 = 3t_3$	$t_5 = 3t_4$
$= 3(2)$	$= 3(6)$	$= 3(18)$	$= 3(54)$
$= 6$	$= 18$	$= 54$	$= 162$

The first 5 terms of the sequence are $2, 6, 18, 54, 162$.

Example 2

The recursion formula $t_1 = 1; t_2 = 1; t_n = t_{n-1} + t_{n-2}, n > 2$ defines the Fibonacci sequence.

Write the first 6 terms of the Fibonacci sequence. Is this sequence arithmetic, geometric, or neither?

Solution

$$t_1 = 1$$
$$t_2 = 1$$
$$t_3 = t_2 + t_1 = 1 + 1 = 2$$
$$t_4 = t_3 + t_2 = 2 + 1 = 3$$
$$t_5 = t_4 + t_3 = 3 + 2 = 5$$
$$t_6 = t_5 + t_4 = 5 + 3 = 8$$

The Fibonacci sequence is neither arithmetic nor geometric.

Discuss

Why does the recursion formula include the condition that $n > 2$?

The sequence in *Example 2* is named for Leonardo Fibonacci, an Italian mathematician. His publication, *Liber abaci* in 1202, introduced the Arabic number system to Europe.

1.4 Exercises

A

1. Write the first 5 terms of the sequence defined by each recursion formula.

   a) $t_1 = 1$, $t_n = t_{n-1} + 2$, $n > 1$
   b) $t_1 = 2$, $t_n = t_{n-1} + 3$, $n > 1$
   c) $t_1 = 5$, $t_n = t_{n-1} + 5$, $n > 1$
   d) $t_1 = -4$, $t_n = t_{n-1} + 2$, $n > 1$
   e) $t_1 = 8$, $t_n = t_{n-1} - 5$, $n > 1$
   f) $t_1 = 10$, $t_n = t_{n-1} + 100$, $n > 1$

2. Write the first 5 terms of the sequence defined by each recursion formula.

   a) $t_1 = 1$, $t_n = 2t_{n-1}$, $n > 1$
   b) $t_1 = 2$, $t_n = 2t_{n-1}$, $n > 1$
   c) $t_1 = 3$, $t_n = 2t_{n-1}$, $n > 1$
   d) $t_1 = 3$, $t_n = -2t_{n-1}$, $n > 1$
   e) $t_1 = 1$, $t_n = 10t_{n-1}$, $n > 1$
   f) $t_1 = 16$, $t_n = 0.5t_{n-1}$, $n > 1$

3. **Communication**

   a) Suppose you know the first part of a recursion formula but not the second. Explain why you would not be able to write the terms of the sequence.

   b) Suppose you know the second part of a recursion formula but not the first. Explain why you would not be able to write the terms of the sequence.

4. **a)** Write the first 5 terms of each sequence.

   i) $t_1 = 1$, $t_n = t_{n-1} + 1$, $n > 1$
   $t_1 = 1$, $t_n = t_{n-1} + 2$, $n > 1$
   $t_1 = 1$, $t_n = t_{n-1} + 3$, $n > 1$
   $t_1 = 1$, $t_n = t_{n-1} + 4$, $n > 1$

   ii) $t_1 = 1$, $t_n = t_{n-1} + 1$, $n > 1$
   $t_1 = 2$, $t_n = t_{n-1} + 2$, $n > 1$
   $t_1 = 3$, $t_n = t_{n-1} + 3$, $n > 1$
   $t_1 = 4$, $t_n = t_{n-1} + 4$, $n > 1$

   b) Describe any patterns you found in part a.

   c) Explain why these patterns occur.

5. a) Write the first 5 terms of each sequence.

i) $t_1 = 1, t_n = t_{n-1}, n > 1$
$t_1 = 1, t_n = 2t_{n-1}, n > 1$
$t_1 = 1, t_n = 3t_{n-1}, n > 1$
$t_1 = 1, t_n = 4t_{n-1}, n > 1$

ii) $t_1 = 1, t_n = -t_{n-1}, n > 1$
$t_1 = 1, t_n = -2t_{n-1}, n > 1$
$t_1 = 1, t_n = -3t_{n-1}, n > 1$
$t_1 = 1, t_n = -4t_{n-1}, n > 1$

b) Describe any patterns you found in part a.

c) Explain why these patterns occur.

B

6. Write the first 5 terms of the sequence defined by each recursion formula.

a) $t_1 = 100, t_n = t_{n-1} + 7, n > 1$ **b)** $t_1 = -9, t_n = t_{n-1} + 10, n > 1$

c) $t_1 = 1, t_n = 0.5t_{n-1}, n > 1$ **d)** $t_1 = 1, t_n = -0.5t_{n-1}, n > 1$

e) $t_1 = 2, t_n = 2 - t_{n-1}, n > 1$ **f)** $t_1 = 6, t_n = (1 + n)t_{n-1}, n > 1$

✓ **7. Knowledge/Understanding** For each recursion formula, determine whether the sequence is arithmetic, geometric, or neither. Explain your choice.

a) $t_1 = 5, t_n = -t_{n-1}, n > 1$ **b)** $t_1 = 3, t_n = 1 - t_{n-1}, n > 1$

c) $t_1 = 2, t_n = \dfrac{1}{t_{n-1}}, n > 1$ **d)** $t_1 = 2, t_n = (t_{n-1})^2, n > 1$

8. Thinking/Inquiry/Problem Solving A sequence is defined by the recursion formula $t_1 = 3, t_n = t_{n-1} + 10, n > 1$.

a) Determine the 100th term of this sequence.

b) Explain how you determined the 100th term.

9. The recursion formula $t_1 = 2, t_n = 5t_{n-1}, n > 1$ defines a sequence.

a) Determine the 10th term of this sequence.

b) Write to explain how you determined the 10th term.

✓ **10.** Write the first 5 terms of the sequence defined by each recursion formula.

a) $t_1 = 1, t_n = t_{n-1} + n, n > 1$ **b)** $t_1 = 1, t_n = t_{n-1} + 2n, n > 1$

c) $t_1 = 1, t_n = 2t_{n-1} + 1, n > 1$ **d)** $t_1 = 1, t_n = 2(t_{n-1} + 1), n > 1$

✓ **11.** For some recursion formulas, the nth term depends on the two preceding terms. Write the first 5 terms of the sequence defined by each recursion formula.

a) $t_1 = 1, t_2 = 2, t_n = t_{n-1} + t_{n-2}, n > 2$

b) $t_1 = 1, t_2 = 3, t_n = t_{n-1} + t_{n-2}, n > 2$

c) $t_1 = 1, t_2 = 2, t_n = t_{n-1} + 2t_{n-2}, n > 2$

d) $t_1 = 1, t_2 = 2, t_n = t_{n-1} + 3t_{n-2}, n > 2$

✓ **12. a)** Write a recursion formula for each sequence.

i) $4, 11, 18, 25, \ldots$ ii) $32, 26, 20, 14, \ldots$
iii) $1, -10, 100, -1000, \ldots$ iv) $32, 16, 8, 4, \ldots$

b) Choose one sequence from part a. Explain how you determined the recursion formula.

✓ **13.** Write a recursion formula for each sequence.

    a) the general arithmetic sequence $a, a + d, a + 2d, a + 3d, \ldots$

    b) the general geometric sequence $a, ar, ar^2, ar^3, \ldots$

✓ **14.** A sequence is defined by the recursion formula $t_1 = a$, $t_n = mt_{n-1} + b$, $n > 1$. For what values of m and b is the sequence:

    a) arithmetic?   **b)** geometric?   **c)** neither arithmetic nor geometric?

✓ **15. Application** Visualize drawing a sequence of rectangles by following these steps.

    i) Draw a square with sides 1 unit long.

    ii) Draw a square beside it.

    iii) Draw a square below them.

    iv) Draw a square at the side.

    v) Draw a square below.

    vi) Draw a square at the side.

Visualize continuing this process indefinitely.

    a) Write the sequence formed by the side lengths of the squares that are drawn at each step.

    b) Write a recursion formula for this sequence.

C

16. The areas of the squares in exercise 15 form a sequence.

    a) Write the first 4 terms of this sequence.

    b) Write a recursion formula for the sequence.

17. Is it possible for a sequence to have two different recursion formulas? If your answer is no, give a convincing explanation. If your answer is yes, give an example.

1. A \$5000 investment certificate increases in value by 4% each year. How much will it be worth after 3 years?

2. Determine the 8th term of the sequence with each general term.

   a) $t_n = 32 - 3n$

   b) $t_n = 4(2)^{n-1}$

3. Write the first 3 terms of the sequence with each general term.

   a) $t_n = n^2 + 1$

   b) $t_n = 8(1.4)^n$

4. State which sequences in exercises 2 and 3 are:

   a) arithmetic

   b) geometric

   c) neither arithmetic nor geometric

5. Write the general term for each arithmetic sequence.

   a) 7, 11, 15, 19, …

   b) 7, 4, 1, –2, …

6. Write the general term for each geometric sequence.

   a) 2, 8, 32, 128, …

   b) $99, -33, 11, -\dfrac{11}{3}, \ldots$

7. Write a formula for the nth term of each sequence.

   a) 3, 12, 48, 192, …

   b) $\dfrac{1}{2}, \dfrac{5}{4}, \dfrac{9}{6}, \dfrac{13}{8}, \ldots$

8. Determine a formula for the nth term of each sequence.

   a) $2 \times 3, 4 \times 6, 6 \times 9, 8 \times 12, \ldots$

   b) $\dfrac{1 \times 4}{2 \times 3}, \dfrac{4 \times 7}{3 \times 4}, \dfrac{7 \times 10}{4 \times 5}, \dfrac{10 \times 13}{5 \times 6}, \ldots$

9. Write the first 5 terms of the sequence defined by each recursion formula.

   a) $t_1 = 7, t_n = 2t_{n-1} - 3n, n > 1$

   b) $t_1 = 2.5, t_n = t_1(t_{n-1})^{n-1}, n > 1$

10. Write a recursion formula for each sequence.

    a) 32, 26, 20, 14, …

    b) $p, pq^2, pq^4, pq^6, \ldots$

1.5 Defining Rational Exponents

A power with a positive integral exponent is defined using repeated multiplication. Powers with rational exponents, such as $3^{\frac{1}{2}}$ and $3^{-\frac{1}{2}}$, must be defined in another way. Mathematicians have defined powers with rational exponents so the exponent laws, as summarized on pages 3 and 4, still apply.

Apply the law of multiplication, $x^m \times x^n = x^{m+n}$, when m and n are rational numbers. Then we can write:

$$3^{\frac{1}{2}} \times 3^{\frac{1}{2}} = 3^{\frac{1}{2}+\frac{1}{2}}$$
$$= 3^1$$
$$= 3$$

We also know $\sqrt{3} \times \sqrt{3} = 3$

Therefore, $\quad 3^{\frac{1}{2}} \times 3^{\frac{1}{2}} = \sqrt{3} \times \sqrt{3}$

and thus $\quad\quad 3^{\frac{1}{2}} = \sqrt{3}$

$$5^{\frac{1}{3}} \times 5^{\frac{1}{3}} \times 5^{\frac{1}{3}} = 5^{\frac{1}{3}+\frac{1}{3}+\frac{1}{3}}$$
$$= 5^1$$
$$= 5$$

We also know $\sqrt[3]{5} \times \sqrt[3]{5} \times \sqrt[3]{5} = 5$

Therefore, $\quad 5^{\frac{1}{3}} \times 5^{\frac{1}{3}} \times 5^{\frac{1}{3}} = \sqrt[3]{5} \times \sqrt[3]{5} \times \sqrt[3]{5}$

and thus $\quad\quad 5^{\frac{1}{3}} = \sqrt[3]{5}$

These examples suggest that an exponent of $\frac{1}{2}$ means the positive square root of the number, and an exponent of $\frac{1}{3}$ means the cube root of the number.

Apply the power of a power law, $x^{mn} = (x^m)^n = (x^n)^m$, when m and n are rational numbers. Then we can write:

$$6^{\frac{3}{4}} = \left(6^{\frac{1}{4}}\right)^3 \quad\quad \text{or} \quad\quad 6^{\frac{3}{4}} = \left(6^3\right)^{\frac{1}{4}}$$
$$= \left(\sqrt[4]{6}\right)^3 \quad\quad\quad\quad\quad = \sqrt[4]{6^3}$$

$$7^{\frac{2}{3}} = \left(7^{\frac{1}{3}}\right)^2 \quad\quad \text{or} \quad\quad 7^{\frac{2}{3}} = \left(7^2\right)^{\frac{1}{3}}$$
$$= \left(\sqrt[3]{7}\right)^2 \quad\quad\quad\quad\quad = \sqrt[3]{7^2}$$

These examples suggest that rational exponents and radical signs are just different mathematical notation that can be used to express the same number.

$$7^{\frac{1}{2}} = \sqrt{7} \quad\quad\quad\quad 4^{\frac{2}{3}} = \left(\sqrt[3]{4}\right)^2 \quad\quad\quad\quad 9^{\frac{5}{4}} = \left(\sqrt[4]{9}\right)^5$$

Take Note

Defining Powers with Rational Exponents

$$x^{\frac{1}{n}} = \sqrt[n]{x} \quad\quad\quad\quad x^{\frac{m}{n}} = \left(\sqrt[n]{x}\right)^m = \sqrt[n]{x^m}$$

n is a natural number, $x \geq 0$ when n is even.

Since even roots of negative numbers are not defined for real numbers, when $x < 0$, n must be an odd number.

Radical signs are often used in mathematical expressions to indicate square roots and cube roots. Rational exponents are normally used to indicate roots for which $n > 3$.

Apply the law for negative exponents, $x^{-n} = \frac{1}{x^n}$, when m and n are rational numbers. Then we can write:

$$3^{-\frac{1}{2}} = \left(3^{\frac{1}{2}}\right)^{-1} \qquad 5^{-\frac{1}{3}} = \left(5^{\frac{1}{3}}\right)^{-1}$$
$$= \frac{1}{3^{\frac{1}{2}}} \qquad\qquad = \frac{1}{5^{\frac{1}{3}}}$$

Take Note

Defining Powers with Negative Rational Exponents

$$x^{-\frac{1}{n}} = \frac{1}{\sqrt[n]{x}} = \frac{1}{x^{\frac{1}{n}}} \qquad x^{-\frac{m}{n}} = \frac{1}{\left(\sqrt[n]{x}\right)^m} = \frac{1}{x^{\frac{m}{n}}}$$

n is a natural number, $x \neq 0$; $x > 0$ when n is even.

With the definition above, and on page 39, all the exponent laws apply to rational exponents.

Example 1

Determine each value.

a) $27^{\frac{1}{3}}$

b) $-16^{-\frac{1}{4}}$

c) $15^{-\frac{1}{4}}$

Solution

Write each base as a power, where possible.

a) $27^{\frac{1}{3}} = \left(3^3\right)^{\frac{1}{3}}$

$= 3^{3 \times \frac{1}{3}}$

$= 3$

b) $-16^{-\frac{1}{4}} = -\left(2^4\right)^{-\frac{1}{4}}$

$= -2^{4 \times \left(-\frac{1}{4}\right)}$

$= -2^{-1}$

$= -\frac{1}{2}$

c) We cannot calculate $15^{-\frac{1}{4}}$ mentally. Use a calculator.

Key in: 15 ⌃ ((-) 1 ÷ 4) ENTER to display 0.508132748

$15^{-\frac{1}{4}} \doteq 0.508$

Example 2

Determine each value.

a) $27^{\frac{2}{3}}$ **b)** $16^{-\frac{3}{4}}$ **c)** $48^{\frac{7}{11}}$

Solution

a) $27^{\frac{2}{3}} = \left(3^3\right)^{\frac{2}{3}}$
$= 3^{3 \times \frac{2}{3}}$
$= 3^2$
$= 9$

b) $16^{-\frac{3}{4}} = \left(2^4\right)^{-\frac{3}{4}}$
$= 2^{4 \times \left(-\frac{3}{4}\right)}$
$= 2^{-3}$
$= \dfrac{1}{2^3}$
$= \dfrac{1}{8}$

c) For $48^{\frac{7}{11}}$, we cannot calculate $\sqrt[11]{48}$ mentally. Use a calculator.
Key in: 48 ⌃ (7 ÷ 11) ENTER = to display 11.74575093
$48^{\frac{7}{11}} \doteq 11.746$

Example 3

Determine each value.

a) $(-32)^{\frac{1}{5}}$ **b)** $(-32)^{\frac{2}{5}}$ **c)** $(-40)^{\frac{3}{5}}$

Solution

a) $(-32)^{\frac{1}{5}} = [(-2)^5]^{\frac{1}{5}}$
$= (-2)^{5 \times \frac{1}{5}}$
$= (-2)^1$
$= -2$

b) $(-32)^{\frac{2}{5}} = [(-2)^5]^{\frac{2}{5}}$
$= (-2)^{5 \times \frac{2}{5}}$
$= (-2)^2$
$= 4$

c) $(-40)^{\frac{3}{5}}$

When a power has a negative base, we may not be able to use
a calculator directly.
When we key in: ((-) 40) ⌃ (3 ÷ 5),
we get an error message.
So, calculate $(-40)^{\frac{1}{5}}$ first, then cube the result.
Key in: ((-) 40) ⌃ (1 ÷ 5) ENTER = to display –2.091279105
Do not clear the display. Key in: ⌃ 3 ENTER = to display –9.146101039
$(-40)^{\frac{3}{5}} \doteq -9.146$

Example 3c illustrates that, to raise a negative base to a rational exponent, use
the power of a power rule. Take the root of the base first, then raise the result
to a power.

Example 4

In studies of mammals, scientists have discovered an approximate formula that relates the brain mass to the body mass. The formula is $b = 0.01m^{0.7}$, where b is the brain mass in kilograms and m is the body mass in kilograms. Calculate the brain mass of each animal.

a) a 900-kg steer

b) a 120-g hamster

Solution

a) Use the formula $b = 0.01m^{0.7}$.
Substitute $m = 900$.
$b = 0.01(900)^{0.7}$
Use a calculator.
$b \doteq 0.01(116.941\ 795\ 2)$
$\doteq 1.17$
The mass of the steer's brain is about 1.17 kg.

b) 120 g = 0.12 kg
Use the formula $b = 0.01m^{0.7}$.
Substitute $m = 0.12$.
$b = 0.01(0.12)^{0.7}$
Use a calculator.
$b \doteq 0.01(0.226\ 687\ 1)$
$\doteq 0.0023$
The mass of the hamster's brain is about 0.0023 kg, or 2.3 g.

Discuss

Which animal's brain represents the greater part of its body? Explain.

1.5 Exercises

1. Determine each value without using a calculator.

  a) $1^{\frac{1}{2}}$ **b)** $4^{\frac{1}{2}}$ **c)** $9^{\frac{1}{2}}$ **d)** $16^{\frac{1}{2}}$ **e)** $25^{\frac{1}{2}}$

  f) $1^{\frac{3}{2}}$ **g)** $4^{\frac{3}{2}}$ **h)** $9^{\frac{3}{2}}$ **i)** $16^{\frac{3}{2}}$ **j)** $25^{\frac{3}{2}}$

2. Determine each value without using a calculator.

a) $1^{\frac{1}{3}}$ **b)** $8^{\frac{1}{3}}$ **c)** $27^{\frac{1}{3}}$ **d)** $64^{\frac{1}{3}}$ **e)** $125^{\frac{1}{3}}$

f) $1^{\frac{2}{3}}$ **g)** $8^{\frac{2}{3}}$ **h)** $27^{\frac{2}{3}}$ **i)** $64^{\frac{2}{3}}$ **j)** $125^{\frac{2}{3}}$

3. Determine each value without using a calculator.

a) $(-1)^{\frac{1}{3}}$ **b)** $(-8)^{\frac{1}{3}}$ **c)** $(-27)^{\frac{1}{3}}$ **d)** $(-64)^{\frac{1}{3}}$ **e)** $(-125)^{\frac{1}{3}}$

f) $(-1)^{\frac{2}{3}}$ **g)** $(-8)^{\frac{2}{3}}$ **h)** $(-27)^{\frac{2}{3}}$ **i)** $(-64)^{\frac{2}{3}}$ **j)** $(-125)^{\frac{2}{3}}$

B

4. Knowledge/Understanding

a) Determine each value without using a calculator.

i) $8^{\frac{1}{3}}$ **ii)** $8^{\frac{2}{3}}$ **iii)** $-8^{\frac{1}{3}}$ **iv)** $-8^{\frac{2}{3}}$

v) $(-8)^{\frac{1}{3}}$ **vi)** $(-8)^{\frac{2}{3}}$ **vii)** $-(-8)^{\frac{1}{3}}$ **viii)** $-(-8)^{\frac{2}{3}}$

b) Use the results of part a. Explain the difference between $(-8)^{\frac{2}{3}}$ and $-8^{\frac{2}{3}}$.

5. Determine each value without using a calculator.

a) $4^{\frac{1}{2}}$ **b)** $4^{\frac{2}{2}}$ **c)** $4^{\frac{3}{2}}$ **d)** $4^{\frac{4}{2}}$ **e)** $4^{\frac{5}{2}}$

f) 4^{0} **g)** $4^{-\frac{1}{2}}$ **h)** $4^{-\frac{2}{2}}$ **i)** $4^{-\frac{3}{2}}$ **j)** $4^{-\frac{4}{2}}$

6. Determine each value without using a calculator.

a) $27^{\frac{1}{3}}$ **b)** $27^{\frac{2}{3}}$ **c)** $27^{\frac{3}{3}}$ **d)** $27^{\frac{4}{3}}$ **e)** $27^{\frac{5}{3}}$

f) 27^{0} **g)** $27^{-\frac{1}{3}}$ **h)** $27^{-\frac{2}{3}}$ **i)** $27^{-\frac{3}{3}}$ **j)** $27^{-\frac{4}{3}}$

7. Use a calculator to determine each value to 3 decimal places.

a) $7^{0.4}$ **b)** $12^{1.35}$ **c)** $5^{2.75}$ **d)** $8^{1.93}$ **e)** $2^{4.32}$

f) $7^{-0.4}$ **g)** $12^{-1.35}$ **h)** $5^{-2.75}$ **i)** $8^{-1.93}$ **j)** $2^{-4.32}$

8. Use the formula in *Example 4*. Calculate the brain mass of each animal.

a) a 360-kg moose   **b)** a 30-g mouse

9. The formula in *Example 4* does not apply to humans. For humans, the formula relating brain mass to body mass is $b = 0.085m^{0.66}$.

a) Calculate the brain mass of a person with a mass of 45 kg.

b) Calculate the mass of your brain.

10. An approximate formula for the surface area of the body in square metres is $A = 0.096m^{0.7}$, where m is the person's mass in kilograms.

a) Calculate the surface area of a newborn baby with mass 3.8 kg.

b) Calculate the surface area of a person with mass 140 kg.

c) Calculate your surface area.

11. A student thought that $40^{\frac{3}{4}} = \frac{3}{4}$ of 40, or 30.

    a) Explain why this is not correct.

    b) Use a calculator to determine the value of $40^{\frac{3}{4}}$ to 2 decimal places.

12. a) Determine each value without using a calculator.

    i) $16^{\frac{3}{4}}$ **ii)** $32^{\frac{2}{5}}$ **iii)** $49^{\frac{3}{2}}$ **iv)** $4^{\frac{7}{2}}$ **v)** $100^{\frac{5}{2}}$

    vi) $25^{-\frac{1}{2}}$ **vii)** $9^{-\frac{3}{2}}$ **viii)** $27^{-\frac{4}{3}}$ **ix)** $81^{-\frac{1}{4}}$ **x)** $1000^{-\frac{2}{3}}$

    b) Choose one power from part a. Explain how you determined the value.

13. Use a calculator. Determine each value to 3 decimal places.

    a) $15^{\frac{3}{4}}$ **b)** $33^{\frac{2}{5}}$ **c)** $48^{\frac{3}{2}}$ **d)** $5^{\frac{7}{2}}$ **e)** $99^{\frac{5}{2}}$

    f) $24^{-\frac{1}{2}}$ **g)** $10^{-\frac{3}{2}}$ **h)** $28^{-\frac{4}{3}}$ **i)** $80^{-\frac{1}{4}}$ **j)** $1001^{-\frac{2}{3}}$

14. Communication Compare the expressions in exercise 13 with those in exercise 12. The only difference is that the bases in exercise 13 differ by 1 compared with the corresponding bases in exercise 12.

    a) Explain why the results in exercise 12 were exact, but the results in exercise 13 were not exact.

    b) Compare the answers to the corresponding exercises. Explain any patterns you find.

15. Application

    a) The area of each face of a cube is 25 cm². Determine the length of each edge and the volume of the cube.

    b) Repeat part a for a cube with face area A square centimetres.

    c) Write the expressions from part b for the edge length, face area, and volume as a sequence. Is the sequence arithmetic, geometric, or neither? Explain.

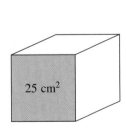

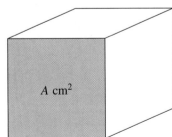

16. a) The volume of a cube is 800 cm^3. Determine the length of each edge and the area of each face.

b) Repeat part a for a cube with volume V cubic centimetres.

c) Write the expressions from part b for the edge length, face area, and volume as a sequence. Is the sequence arithmetic, geometric, or neither? Explain.

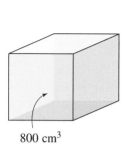

800 cm^3

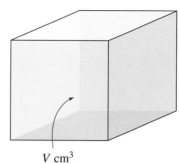

V cm^3

17. Determine each value without using a calculator.

a) $(-8)^{\frac{1}{3}}$ **b)** $-36^{\frac{3}{2}}$ **c)** $(-64)^{\frac{2}{3}}$ **d)** $400^{\frac{3}{2}}$ **e)** $(-8000)^{\frac{2}{3}}$

f) $\left(\frac{9}{16}\right)^{\frac{-1}{2}}$ **g)** $\left(\frac{25}{49}\right)^{\frac{3}{2}}$ **h)** $\left(\frac{-1}{32}\right)^{\frac{2}{5}}$ **i)** $-\left(\frac{8}{27}\right)^{-\frac{2}{3}}$ **j)** $\left(\frac{81}{16}\right)^{-\frac{3}{4}}$

 18. Some scientists believe that the exponent in the formula in *Example 4* should be $\frac{2}{3}$ instead of 0.7.

a) Use the formula $b = 0.01m^{\frac{2}{3}}$ for brain mass. Calculate the brain mass of each animal in this list.

Elephant	6400 kg
Cat	6.4 kg
Shrew	0.0064 kg

b) How are the masses of the three animals in part a related? How are the masses of their brains related?

19. Thinking/Inquiry/Problem Solving The formulas in *Example 4* and exercises 9 and 10 are based on actual measurements. The exact values of the coefficient and the exponent in the formula depend on the data that are used. The formulas give average brain masses, and the actual brain mass of any particular mammal may differ from the calculated result.

a) Do you think a mammal with a larger brain might be more intelligent than a mammal with a smaller brain? Give a reason to support your answer.

b) Do you think the saying "an elephant never forgets" might have some justification? Explain.

20. Scientists have determined the following approximate formulas for resting animals with mass m kilograms.

Heartbeat frequency, h beats per minute: $h = 241m^{-0.25}$
Respiratory frequency, b breaths per minute: $b = 53.5m^{-0.25}$

a) Calculate the heartbeat frequency and the respiratory frequency for each animal in exercise 18.

b) What happens to each frequency as the mass of the animal decreases?

C

21. In the solution of *Example 4a*, we determined the value of $900^{0.7}$.

a) Write to explain what $900^{0.7}$ means.

b) Use your answer to part a to determine the value of $900^{0.7}$ a different way.

22. On average, animals tend to live for approximately 1.5 billion heartbeats.

a) Use the first formula in exercise 20. Determine a formula for the average lifetime in years of an animal with mass m kilograms.

b) Estimate the average lifetime of each animal in exercise 18.

23. Check that $17^{\frac{3}{4}} \doteq 8.372\ 144\ 029$. The result is close to 8.5, which is one-half of 17. This suggests the following problems.

a) Find a number that, when raised to the exponent $\frac{3}{4}$, becomes one-half the number.

b) Find the value of x so that $17^x = 8.5$.

24. Three students discussed the meaning of the statement: $2.3^{3.7} \doteq 21.7968$. Their discussion went as follows:

Sean: "It means 2.3 multiplied by itself 3.7 times equals about 21.7968."

Vince: "That's not right. In $2^3 = 2 \times 2 \times 2$, the 2 is multiplied by itself 2 times, not 3 times. So, it means 2.3 multiplied by itself 2.7 times equals about 21.7968."

Emily: "Neither of you is right. You can't multiply a number by itself a fractional number of times."

Emily is correct. Explain the meaning of the statement $2.3^{3.7} \doteq 21.7968$.

1.6 Applying the Exponent Laws

We can use the exponent laws to simplify expressions that involve powers with rational exponents. Recall the exponent laws from pages 3 and 4.

Example 1

Simplify each expression.

a) $(x^{\frac{2}{3}})(x^{\frac{1}{2}})$ **b)** $\dfrac{x^{\frac{2}{3}}}{x^{\frac{1}{2}}}$ **c)** $(x^{\frac{2}{3}})^{\frac{1}{2}}$

Solution

a) $(x^{\frac{2}{3}})(x^{\frac{1}{2}}) = x^{\frac{2}{3}+\frac{1}{2}}$
$= x^{\frac{4}{6}+\frac{3}{6}}$
$= x^{\frac{7}{6}}$

b) $\dfrac{x^{\frac{2}{3}}}{x^{\frac{1}{2}}} = x^{\frac{2}{3}-\frac{1}{2}}$
$= x^{\frac{4}{6}-\frac{3}{6}}$
$= x^{\frac{1}{6}}$

c) $(x^{\frac{2}{3}})^{\frac{1}{2}} = x^{\frac{2}{3}\times\frac{1}{2}}$
$= x^{\frac{1}{3}}$

Example 2

Write each expression as a single power. Then evaluate the power.

a) $(9^{-2})(9^{\frac{1}{2}})$ **b)** $\dfrac{8^2}{8^{\frac{2}{3}}}$ **c)** $(27^{\frac{2}{3}})^{\frac{1}{2}}$

Solution

a) $(9^{-2})(9^{\frac{1}{2}}) = 9^{-2+\frac{1}{2}}$
$= 9^{-\frac{3}{2}}$
$= (3^2)^{-\frac{3}{2}}$
$= 3^{-3}$
$= \dfrac{1}{3^3}$
$= \dfrac{1}{27}$

b) $\dfrac{8^2}{8^{\frac{2}{3}}} = 8^{2-\frac{2}{3}}$
$= 8^{\frac{6}{3}-\frac{2}{3}}$
$= 8^{\frac{4}{3}}$
$= (2^3)^{\frac{4}{3}}$
$= 2^4$
$= 16$

c) $(27^{\frac{2}{3}})^{\frac{1}{2}} = 27^{\frac{2}{3}\times\frac{1}{2}}$
$= 27^{\frac{1}{3}}$
$= (3^3)^{\frac{1}{3}}$
$= 3$

Discuss

What other ways are there to complete Example 2?

Example 3

Solve the equation $4^x = 8^{x+3}$.

Solution

$4^x = 8^{x+3}$

Each side of the equation is expressed as a power. Both 4 and 8 are powers of 2. Write each base as a power of 2.

$$4^x = 8^{x+3}$$
$$(2^2)^x = (2^3)^{x+3}$$

Use the exponent law for the power of a power.

$$2^{2x} = 2^{3(x+3)}$$

Since the bases of this equation are equal, the exponents must also be equal.

$$2x = 3(x + 3)$$
$$2x = 3x + 9$$
$$-x = 9$$
$$x = -9$$

Discuss

How could you check the solution of the equation?

Some exponential equations can be solved by factoring.

Example 4

Solve the equation $2^{2x} - 7(2^x) - 8 = 0$.

Solution

$2^{2x} - 7(2^x) - 8 = 0$ can be written as $(2^x)^2 - 7(2^x) - 8 = 0$.

This is a quadratic equation in 2^x.

Solve by factoring.
$(2^x + 1)(2^x - 8) = 0$

Either $2^x + 1 = 0$ or $2^x - 8 = 0$

$2^x = -1$ $2^x = 8$

This is not possible. $x = 3$

The solution is $x = 3$.

Discuss

Why is $2^x = -1$ not possible?

48   CHAPTER 1 SEQUENCES AND SERIES

We often encounter rational exponents when we work with sequences.

Example 5

The growing number of Canada geese in southern Ontario is causing concern in some locations. A 1976 survey showed there were about 19 300 Canada geese in southern Ontario. A 1998 survey indicated that the number had grown to about 350 000. As the population grows, there are more adult geese laying eggs each year.

Assume the growth of the goose population is exponential.

a) Estimate the population of Canada geese in southern Ontario in 1990.

b) Predict the population of Canada geese in southern Ontario in 2010.

Solution

Since the growth of the goose population is exponential, use a geometric sequence. Calculate the common ratio.

Assume that the population each year is a term of a geometric sequence with common ratio r and first term a.
Since the population in 1976 is 19 300, the first term is $a = 19\ 300$.
Since $1998 - 1976 = 22$, the year 1998 is the term ar^{22}.
The 23rd term is $ar^{22} = 19\ 300r^{22}$.

Write an equation.
$$19\ 300r^{22} = 350\ 000$$
Divide each side by 19 300.
$$r^{22} = \frac{350\ 000}{19\ 300}$$
$$\doteq 18.134\ 715\ 03$$
Take the 22nd root of each side.
$$r \doteq 18.134\ 715\ 03^{\frac{1}{22}}$$
$$\doteq 1.140\ 788$$
The geometric sequence that represents the populations has a common ratio of approximately 1.140 788.

Discuss

Why is 1998 t_{23} and not t_{22}?

a) For the population in 1990:
1990 − 1976 = 14, so the year 1990 is the term ar^{14}.
$$t_{15} = ar^{14}$$
$$ar^{14} \doteq 19\ 300(1.140\ 788)^{14}$$
$$\doteq 122\ 019$$
The estimate for 1990 is about 122 000 Canada geese.

b) For the population in 2010:

$2010 - 1976 = 34$, so the year 2010 is the term ar^{34}.

$t_{35} = ar^{34}$

$ar^{34} \doteq 19\ 300(1.140\ 788)^{34}$

$\doteq 1\ 700\ 299$

The prediction for 2010 is about 1 700 000 Canada geese.

Discuss

What major assumption are we making in this example? Do you think this assumption is reasonable?

What would be the effect on the predictions if the growth was assumed to be arithmetic? Is this reasonable?

What is the percent increase in Canada geese each year?

1.6 Exercises

1. Write each expression as a single power.

a) $(x^{\frac{1}{2}})(x^{\frac{1}{4}})$ **b)** $(x^{\frac{2}{3}})(x^{\frac{1}{2}})$ **c)** $(x^{\frac{1}{2}})^{\frac{1}{4}}$ **d)** $(x^{\frac{2}{3}})^{\frac{1}{4}}$

e) $\dfrac{x^{\frac{3}{4}}}{x^{\frac{1}{2}}}$ **f)** $\dfrac{x^{\frac{2}{3}}}{x^{\frac{1}{4}}}$ **g)** $\dfrac{x^{\frac{1}{2}}}{x^{\frac{3}{4}}}$ **h)** $\dfrac{x^{\frac{1}{4}}}{x^{\frac{2}{3}}}$

 2. Write each expression as a single power. Then evaluate the power.

a) $(36^{-2})(36^{\frac{1}{2}})$ **b)** $(25^{-1})(25^{\frac{3}{2}})$ **c)** $(64^{\frac{1}{2}})(64^{-1})$ **d)** $(16^{\frac{1}{4}})(16^{\frac{1}{2}})$

e) $\dfrac{9^2}{9^{\frac{1}{2}}}$ **f)** $\dfrac{-8}{-8^{\frac{1}{3}}}$ **g)** $\dfrac{9^2}{9^{-\frac{1}{2}}}$ **h)** $\dfrac{-8}{(-8)^{-\frac{1}{3}}}$

3. Simplify.

a) $(8^2)(8^{\frac{1}{3}})$ **b)** $(8^2)(8^{\frac{2}{3}})$ **c)** $(8^2)(8^{-\frac{1}{3}})$ **d)** $(8^2)(8^{-\frac{2}{3}})$

e) $(8^{-2})(8^{\frac{1}{3}})$ **f)** $(8^{-2})(8^{\frac{2}{3}})$ **g)** $(8^{-2})(8^{-\frac{1}{3}})$ **h)** $(8^{-2})(8^{-\frac{2}{3}})$

4. Simplify.

a) $(4^2)(4^{\frac{1}{2}})$ **b)** $(4^2)(4^{-\frac{1}{2}})$ **c)** $(4^2)^{\frac{1}{2}}$ **d)** $(4^2)^{-\frac{1}{2}}$

e) $\dfrac{4^2}{4^{\frac{1}{2}}}$ **f)** $\dfrac{4^2}{4^{-\frac{1}{2}}}$ **g)** $\dfrac{4^{\frac{1}{2}}}{4^2}$ **h)** $\dfrac{4^{-\frac{1}{2}}}{4^2}$

5. Simplify.

a) $(a)(a^{\frac{1}{2}})$ **b)** $(b^{\frac{1}{3}})(b)$ **c)** $(s^{\frac{1}{4}})(s^{\frac{1}{2}})$ **d)** $(k^{\frac{3}{2}})(k^{\frac{1}{2}})$

e) $y \div y^{\frac{1}{3}}$ **f)** $c \div c^{\frac{2}{5}}$ **g)** $p^{\frac{3}{4}} \div p^{\frac{1}{2}}$ **h)** $n^{\frac{2}{3}} \div n^{\frac{1}{2}}$

6. Write each expression as a single power.

   a) $(3^2)(3^{\frac{1}{2}})$
   b) $(3^2)(3^{\frac{3}{2}})$
   c) $(3^2)(3^{\frac{5}{2}})$
   d) $(3^2)(3^{\frac{7}{2}})$

7. Write each expression as a single power.

   a) $\dfrac{7}{7^{\frac{1}{4}}}$
   b) $\dfrac{7}{7^{\frac{3}{4}}}$
   c) $\dfrac{7}{7^{\frac{5}{4}}}$
   d) $\dfrac{7}{7^{\frac{7}{4}}}$

8. Knowledge/Understanding Write each expression as a single power. Then evaluate the power.

   a) $(5^{0.2})(5^{1.2})$
   b) $(3^{2.75})(3^{1.15})$
   c) $\dfrac{2^{8.66}}{2^{3.12}}$
   d) $(7^{1.5})^{0.4}$

B

9. Solve each equation.

   a) $2^{x+1} = 4$
   b) $2^{x-1} = 8$
   c) $3^{x-5} = 9$
   d) $5^{x+3} = 25$
   e) $4^{x+2} = 16$
   f) $2^{2x+1} = 8$
   g) $3^{2x-1} = 9$
   h) $9^{1-2x} = 81$

10. a) Solve each equation.

   i) $4^x = 8^{x+3}$
   ii) $4^x = 8^{x+2}$
   iii) $4^x = 8^{x+1}$
   iv) $4^x = 8^x$
   v) $4^x = 8^{x-1}$
   vi) $4^x = 8^{x-2}$
   vii) $4^x = 8^{x-3}$
   viii) $4^x = 8^{x-4}$

   b) Choose one equation from part a. Explain how you solved the equation.

11. Thinking/Inquiry/Problem Solving Consider the equation $8^{x-2} = 64^{x+1}$. Solve the equation in two different ways.

12. Solve each equation.

   a) $2^{2x} - 9(2^x) + 8 = 0$
   b) $3^{2x} - 12(3^x) + 27 = 0$
   c) $2^{2x} - 2(2^x) - 8 = 0$
   d) $4^{2x} - 15(4^x) - 16 = 0$
   e) $2^{2x} - 18(2^x) + 32 = 0$
   f) $3^{2x} + 3^x - 2 = 0$
   g) $3^{2x} - 6(3^x) + 9 = 0$
   h) $4^{2x} - 17(4^x) + 16 = 0$
   i) $4^{2x} - 16 = 0$

13. Application Scientists have measured many bird eggs. From these data, they have established approximate formulas to represent various measurements. In the two formulas below, m represents the mass of the bird in grams. The formulas give average results. The properties of a particular egg from a particular bird may differ from the calculated result.

Mass of the egg, e grams: $e = 0.277m^{0.770}$
Mass of the eggshell, s grams: $s = 0.0482e^{1.132}$

   a) Use the first formula. Write an expression for the mass of the egg as a fraction of the mass of the bird.

   b) Use the second formula. Write an expression for the mass of the eggshell as a fraction of the mass of the egg.

14. Refer to the formulas in exercise 13. Determine an expression for the mass of the eggshell as a percent of the mass of the body.

15. A herd of caribou, known as the Qamanirjuag, ranges in the Northwest Territories west of Hudson Bay. After decades of decline, a census in 1980 indicated a population of 39 000. During the next 5 years, the population increased dramatically, growing to 200 000 animals in 1985. By 1994, there were 500 000 animals. Copy the table. Calculate to complete the table, showing the populations to the nearest thousand. Assume the growth is exponential.

Qamanirjuag Caribou Herd

Year	1985	1986	1987	1988	1989	1990	1991	1992	1993	1994
Population (thousands)	200									500

16. Communication Przewalski's Wild Horse is the only known species of wild horse left in the world. In 1956, there were only 36 of them. They were taken into protective captivity and there was an international effort toward registered breeding. By 1977, there were 300 wild horses and, in 1998, there were 1510. Copy the table. Calculate to complete the table, showing the populations to the nearest whole number. Assume the growth is exponential. Explain how you completed the table.

Przewalski's Wild Horse

Year	1977	1980	1983	1986	1989	1992	1995	1998	2001
Population	300							1510	

C

17. a) Solve each equation. Write the value of x to 3 decimal places.

    i) $2^x = 7$ **ii)** $7^x = 2$

  b) Determine whether the two values in part a are related. If they are, explain.

18. Use a calculator to confirm that $10^{0.3} \doteq 1.995$. Then, without using a calculator, determine each value.

  a) $10^{1.3}$ **b)** $10^{2.3}$ **c)** $10^{3.3}$ **d)** $10^{4.3}$

  e) $10^{-0.7}$ **f)** $10^{-1.7}$ **g)** $10^{-2.7}$ **h)** $10^{-3.7}$

1. Determine each value without using a calculator.

a) $1^{\frac{7}{5}}$

b) $64^{\frac{2}{3}}$

c) $8^{\frac{5}{3}}$

d) $-125^{\frac{4}{3}}$

e) 7^0

f) $4^{-\frac{1}{2}}$

g) $(-27)^{-\frac{2}{3}}$

h) $-25^{-\frac{3}{2}}$

2. Use a calculator to determine each value.

a) $11^{0.4}$

b) $12^{1.1}$

c) $13^{2.62}$

d) $14^{-2.19}$

e) $15^{\frac{3}{4}}$

f) $-17^{-0.213}$

3. Write each expression as a single power.

a) $(x^{\frac{3}{4}})(x^{\frac{4}{5}})$

b) $(x^{\frac{1}{2}})^{\frac{7}{3}}$

c) $\dfrac{x^{\frac{2}{5}}}{x^{\frac{3}{5}}}$

d) $\dfrac{x^{\frac{1}{3}}}{x^{\frac{1}{4}}}$

4. Simplify.

a) $(8^2)(8^{\frac{2}{3}})$

b) $(4^{\frac{3}{2}})(16^{\frac{3}{4}})$

5. Write each expression as a single power. Then evaluate that power.

a) $(5^{0.29})(5^{1.81})$

b) $\dfrac{7.2^{1.93}}{7.2^{-0.66}}$

6. Solve each equation.

a) $8^x = 4^{x+3}$

b) $2^{2x+3} = 8$

1.7   The Sum of an Arithmetic Series

Each of two summer jobs is for 3 months, or 12 weeks.

Job A pays $500 per month.
Job B pays $100 per week with a $5 raise each week, if the person performs well.

Which is the better-paying job?

Job A

Job A pays a total of $3 \times \$500 = \$1500$.

Job B

The weekly payments are the first 12 terms of an arithmetic sequence:
100, 105, 110, …

The pay in the last week is the 12th term of this sequence.

$$t_{12} = 100 + 11(5)$$
$$= 155$$

The total pay, in dollars, is $100 + 105 + 110 + \cdots + 155$.

This expression indicates that the terms of an arithmetic sequence are to be added. It is an example of an *arithmetic series*. An arithmetic series is the indicated sum of the terms of an arithmetic sequence. The sum of the series can be found by adding all 12 terms. Instead of adding 12 terms, here is a more efficient method.

Let S represent the sum of the series: $S = 100 + 105 + 110 + \cdots + 155$

Write the sum in reverse order: $S = 155 + 150 + 145 + \cdots + 100$

Add the left sides and the right sides: $2S = 255 + 255 + 255 + \cdots + 255$

$$2S = 12 \times 255 \quad \text{(since there are 12 terms)}$$
$$2S = 3060$$
$$S = 1530$$

The sum of the series is 1530.
Job B pays a total of $1530. It is the better-paying job.

We can use the above method to determine a formula for the sum of the first n terms of the general arithmetic series $a + (a + d) + (a + 2d) + \cdots$.

Let S_n represent the sum of the first n terms of the series.

The last term is: $\qquad\qquad t_n$

Term before the last term: $\quad t_{n-1} = t_n - d$

Term before that one: $\qquad t_{n-2} = t_n - 2d$

Hence: $\qquad S_n = a + (a + d) + (a + 2d) + \cdots + (t_n - 2d) + (t_n - d) + t_n$

Reversing: $\qquad \underline{S_n = t_n + (t_n - d) + (t_n - 2d) + \cdots + (a + 2d) + (a + d) + a}$

Adding: $\qquad 2S_n = (a + t_n) + (a + t_n) + (a + t_n) + \cdots + (a + t_n) + (a + t_n) + (a + t_n)$

$\qquad\qquad 2S_n = (a + t_n) \times n$ (since there are n terms)

$$S_n = \frac{(a + t_n) \times n}{2}$$

$$S_n = \left(\frac{a + t_n}{2}\right) \times n$$

Take Note

Sum of an Arithmetic Series

For the general arithmetic series $a + (a + d) + (a + 2d) + \cdots + t_n$, the sum of the first n terms is:

$$S_n = \left(\frac{\text{first term + last term}}{2}\right) \times (\text{number of terms}); \text{ that is,}$$

$$S_n = \left(\frac{a + t_n}{2}\right) \times n$$

or $\quad S_n = (\text{mean of first and last terms}) \times (\text{number of terms})$

or $\quad S_n = \frac{n}{2}[2a + (n - 1)d]$

Example 1

Determine the sum of the first 30 terms of the arithmetic series $5 + 5.3 + 5.6 + \cdots$.

Solution

$5 + 5.3 + 5.6 + \cdots$

For the series, $a = 5$, $d = 0.3$, $n = 30$

Substitute these values in the formula $S_n = \frac{n}{2}[2a + (n - 1)d]$.

$$S_{30} = \frac{30}{2}[2(5) + (30 - 1)0.3]$$

$$= 15[10 + 8.7]$$

$$= 280.5$$

The sum of the first 30 terms of the series is 280.5.

Example 2

Determine the sum of the arithmetic series $-4 - 10 - 16 - \cdots - 94$.

Solution

$-4 - 10 - 16 - \cdots - 94$

To use a formula for S_n, we need to know the number of terms, n. Since we know that $t_n = -94$, we can use the formula for t_n to determine n.

Use $t_n = a + (n - 1)d$.
Substitute $t_n = -94$, $a = -4$, $d = -6$.

$$-94 = -4 + (n - 1)(-6)$$
$$-94 = -4 - 6n + 6$$
$$-94 = 2 - 6n$$
$$6n = 96$$
$$n = 16$$

There are 16 terms in the series and $t_{16} = -94$.

Use the formula $S_n = \left(\frac{\text{first term} + \text{last term}}{2} \right) \times (\text{number of terms})$.

Substitute first term $= -4$, last term $= -94$, number of terms, $n = 16$.

$$S_{16} = \left(\frac{-4 - 94}{2} \right) \times 16$$
$$= (-49)(16)$$
$$= -784$$

The sum of the series is -784.

Discuss

How did we know which formula to use to find the sums in *Examples 1* and *2*? In each case, could we have used the alternative formula? Explain.

1.7 Exercises

A

1. Determine the sum of each arithmetic series.

 a) $2 + 4 + 6 + 8 + 10$

 b) $12 + 10 + 8 + 6 + 4$

 c) $-2 - 4 - 6 - 8 - 10$

 d) $-12 - 10 - 8 - 6 - 4$

2. Determine the sum of each arithmetic series.

 a) $3 + 12 + 21 + 30 + 39 + 48$

 b) $19 + 31 + 43 + 55 + 67 + 79 + 91$

 c) $6 + 13 + 20 + 27 + 34 + 41 + 48 + 55$

 d) $25 + 31 + 37 + 43 + 49 + 55 + 61 + 67 + 73$

3. Determine the sum of each arithmetic series.

a) $75 + 70 + 65 + 60 + 55 + 50$ b) $-20 - 18 - 16 - 14 - 12 - 10 - 8$

c) $9000 + 8000 + 7000 + 6000 + 5000$

d) $-47 - 52 - 57 - 62 - 67 - 72$

4. Determine the sum of the first 8 terms of each arithmetic series.

a) $1.24 + 1.28 + 1.32 + \cdots$ b) $7.33 + 7.22 + 7.11 + \cdots$

c) $4.2 - 0.9 - 6.0 - \cdots$ d) $-7 - 11 - 15 - \cdots$

5. Determine the sum of the first 20 terms of each arithmetic series.

a) $1 + 3 + 5 + 7 + \cdots$ b) $1 + 4 + 7 + 10 + \cdots$

c) $1 + 6 + 11 + 16 + \cdots$ d) $1 + 1.5 + 2 + 2.5 + \cdots$

B

6. Determine the sum of the first 10 terms of each arithmetic series.

a) $3 + 7 + 11 + 15 + \cdots$ b) $5 + 11 + 17 + 23 + \cdots$

c) $-2 - 8 - 14 - 20 - \cdots$ d) $45 + 39 + 33 + 27 + \cdots$

e) $6 + 16.2 + 26.4 + 36.6 + \cdots$ f) $-21 - 15.5 - 10 - 4.5 - \cdots$

7. Determine the sum of each arithmetic series.

a) $1 + 2 + 3 + \cdots + 10$ b) $1 + 2 + 3 + \cdots + 100$

c) $1 + 2 + 3 + \cdots + 1000$ d) $1 + 2 + 3 + \cdots + 10\,000$

8. a) Determine the sum of each arithmetic series.

i) $2 + 7 + 12 + \cdots + 62$ ii) $-4 - 11 - 18 - \cdots - 88$

iii) $3 + 5.5 + 8 + \cdots + 133$ iv) $20 + 14 + 8 + \cdots - 40$

b) Choose one series from part a. Explain how you determined the sum.

9. Determine the sum of each arithmetic series.

a) $31 + 35 + 39 + \cdots + 107$ b) $13 + 10 + 7 + \cdots - 62$

c) $11.5 + 14 + 16.5 + \cdots + 56.5$ d) $-10 - 9.5 - 9 - 8.5 - \cdots + 18.5$

e) $4 + 2.5 + 1 + \cdots - 33.5$ f) $1 + 0.9 + 0.8 + \cdots - 5.3$

10. For three summer months (12 weeks), Job A pays $325 per month with a monthly raise of $100. Job B pays $50 per week with a weekly raise of $10. Which is the better-paying job? What assumptions do you make?

11. Communication For three summer months (12 weeks), Job A pays $400 per month with a monthly raise of $20. Job B pays $100 per week with a weekly raise of $5. Do the jobs pay the same total amount over the summer, or does one job pay more than the other? Explain your answer.

12. Determine a formula for the sum of the first n natural numbers:
$1 + 2 + 3 + \cdots + n$.

13. Knowledge/Understanding For the arithmetic series $6 + 9 + 12 + 15 + \cdots$

  a) Determine the 20th term.

  b) Determine the sum of the first 20 terms.

14. In a supermarket, cans are stacked in a display arranged in layers. The numbers of cans in the layers form an arithmetic sequence. There are 48 cans in the bottom layer and 20 cans in the top layer. There are 8 layers. How many cans are in the display?

 15. A pile of bricks is arranged in rows. The numbers of bricks in the rows form an arithmetic sequence. There are 35 bricks in the 4th row and 20 bricks in the 9th row.

  a) How many bricks are in the 1st row?

  b) How many rows of bricks are there?

  c) How many bricks are in the pile?

  Explain any assumptions you made.

16. In *Take Note*, page 55, the formula for the sum of the first n terms of the arithmetic series $a + (a + d) + (a + 2d) + \cdots$ is written as
$$S_n = \left(\frac{a + t_n}{2} \right) \times n.$$
Substitute the general expression for t_n into this formula. Simplify the result to obtain the other formula in *Take Note*, $S_n = \frac{n}{2}[2a + (n - 1)d]$.

 **17. Application** In the popular TV quiz show *Jeopardy*, a contestant gives each response as a question to a clue hidden behind a panel that shows amounts of money. When the contestant's response is correct, the contestant wins the money.

  a) In *Jeopardy* (below left), what is the total amount of money shown?

JEOPARDY

WORLD ORIGINS	OCEANS	SCIENCE	MOVIES	MODERN POETRY	THIS & THAT
$100	$100	$100	$100	$100	$100
$200	$200	$200	$200	$200	$200
$300	$300	$300	$300	$300	$300
$400	$400	$400	$400	$400	$400
$500	$500	$500	$500	$500	$500

DOUBLE JEOPARDY

FOOD	TV QUIZ SHOWS	SPORTS	MATH	DRAMA	ODDS & ENDS
$200	$200	$200	$200	$200	$200
$400	$400	$400	$400	$400	$400
$600	$600	$600	$600	$600	$600
$800	$800	$800	$800	$800	$800
$1000	$1000	$1000	$1000	$1000	$1000

  b) In *Double Jeopardy* (above right), what is the total amount shown?

18. A person's annual salary ranges from \$25 325 in the 1st year to \$34 445 in the 7th year. The salaries in this range form an arithmetic sequence.

   a) Determine the raise the person can expect each year.

   b) What is the salary in the 4th year?

   c) In which year does the salary exceed \$30 000 for the first time?

   d) What is the total amount the person will earn in the 7 years?

19. The sum of the first 4 terms of an arithmetic series is −8 and the sum of the first 5 terms is 85. Determine the first term and the common difference.

20. The sum of the first 6 terms of an arithmetic series is 297 and the sum of the first 8 terms is 500. Determine the sum of the first 3 terms.

21. **Thinking/Inquiry/Problem Solving** A formula for the sum of the first n terms of an arithmetic series is $S_n = n^2 + 4n$. Determine the first 4 terms of the series.

22. This sentence is called a "snowball sentence."
I do not know where family doctors acquired illegibly perplexing handwriting; nevertheless, extraordinary pharmaceutical intellectuality, counterbalancing indecipherability, transcendentalizes intercommunications' incomprehensibleness.

   a) What does this sentence mean?

   b) Why is the name "snowball sentence" appropriate?

   c) How many letters are in this snowball sentence?

23. Write to explain how arithmetic sequences and arithmetic series are related. Use examples to illustrate your explanation.

C

24. The arithmetic series $3 + 7 + 11 + 15 + \cdots$ is given.

   a) How many terms are less than 500?

   b) How many terms have a sum less than 500?

25. Ten equally spaced positive integers have a sum of 250. What are the possibilities for the integers?

26. A series of consecutive positive integers has a sum of 150. What are the possibilities for the integers?

1.8 The Sum of a Geometric Series

Some families succeed in tracing their roots back 10 generations or more. When you go back 10 generations, how many ancestors would there be in your family tree?

Every person has 2 parents, 4 grandparents, 8 great-grandparents, and so on. The number of ancestors through 10 generations is:

$$2 + 4 + 8 + 16 + 32 + 64 + 128 + 256 + 512 + 1024$$

This expression indicates that the terms of a geometric sequence are to be added. It is an example of a *geometric series*. A geometric series is the indicated sum of the terms of a geometric sequence. To determine the sum of the series, add all 10 terms. Instead of adding 10 terms, here is a more efficient method.

Let S represent the sum of the series: $S = 2 + 4 + 8 + \cdots + 512 + 1024$ ①

Multiply by the common ratio, 2: $2S = 4 + 8 + \cdots + 512 + 1024 + 2048$ ②

Subtract ① from ②: $S = -2 + 2048$

$$S = 2046$$

The sum of the series is 2046.
Going back 10 generations, each person has 2046 ancestors.

We can use the above method to determine a formula for the sum of the first n terms of the general geometric series $a + ar + ar^2 + \cdots + ar^{n-1}$.

Let S_n represent the sum of the first n terms of the series.

$$S_n = a + ar + ar^2 + \cdots + ar^{n-1} \qquad ①$$

Multiply by r: $rS_n = ar + ar^2 + \cdots + ar^{n-1} + ar^n \qquad ②$

Subtract ① from ②: $rS_n - S_n = -a + ar^n$

Factor: $S_n(r - 1) = a(-1 + r^n)$

Divide by $r - 1$: $S_n = \dfrac{a(r^n - 1)}{r - 1}, \ r \neq 1$

Discuss
Why is the restriction $r \neq 1$ necessary?

Take Note

Sum of a Geometric Series

For the general geometric series $a + ar + ar^2 + \cdots$, the sum of the first n terms is

$$S_n = \frac{a(r^n - 1)}{r - 1}, \quad r \neq 1$$

Example 1

Determine the sum of the first 8 terms of the geometric series
$6 + 24 + 96 + 384 + \cdots$.

Solution

$6 + 24 + 96 + 384 + \cdots$

Use the formula $S_n = \dfrac{a(r^n - 1)}{r - 1}$.

Substitute $a = 6$, $r = 4$, $n = 8$.

$$S_8 = \frac{6(4^8 - 1)}{4 - 1}$$

$$= 2(4^8 - 1)$$

$$= 131\ 070$$

Discuss

How would the
solution change for
this series?
$6 - 24 + 96 - 384 + \cdots$

Example 2

Determine the sum of the first 10 terms of the geometric series
$24 - 12 + 6 - 3 + \cdots$.

Solution

$24 - 12 + 6 - 3 + \cdots$

Use the formula $S_n = \dfrac{a(r^n - 1)}{r - 1}$.

Substitute $a = 24$, $r = -0.5$, $n = 10$.

$$S_{10} = \frac{24[(-0.5)^{10} - 1]}{-0.5 - 1}$$

$$= -16[(-0.5)^{10} - 1]$$

$$= 15.984\ 375$$

Discuss

How would the
solution change for
this series?
$24 + 12 + 6 + 3 + \cdots$

1.8 Exercises

A

1. Determine the sum of each geometric series.

a) $2 + 4 + 8 + 16 + 32$

b) $2 - 4 + 8 - 16 + 32$

c) $-2 + 4 - 8 + 16 - 32$

d) $3 + 9 + 27 + 81 + 243$

e) $3 - 9 + 27 - 81 + 243$

f) $-3 + 9 - 27 + 81 - 243$

2. Determine the sum of each geometric series.

   a) $1 + 2 + 4 + 8 + 16 + 32$ **b)** $3 + 9 + 27 + 81 + 243 + 729$

   c) $2 + 8 + 32 + 128 + 512$ **d)** $40 + 20 + 10 + 5 + 2.5$

   e) $1 - 2 + 4 - 8 + 16 - 32$ **f)** $40 - 20 + 10 - 5 + 2.5$

3. Determine the sum of the first 5 terms of each geometric series.

   a) $2 + 10 + 50 + \cdots$ **b)** $4 + 12 + 36 + \cdots$

   c) $3 + 6 + 12 + \cdots$ **d)** $24 + 12 + 6 + \cdots$

   e) $5 + 15 + 45 + \cdots$ **f)** $80 - 40 + 20 - \cdots$

4. Determine the sum of each geometric series.

   a) $0.1 + 0.01 + 0.001 + 0.0001$

   b) $2.1 + 6.3 + 18.9 + 56.7 + 170.1$

   c) $-3 - 9 - 27 - 81 - 243$

   d) $100 + 25 + 6.25 + 1.5625 + 0.390\,625$

   e) $0.5 + 0.25 + 0.125 + 0.0625$

   f) $8 - 7.2 + 6.48 - 5.832 + 5.2488$

5. Knowledge/Understanding Consider the geometric series
$4 + 12 + 36 + 108 + \cdots$.

   a) Determine the 10th term.

   b) Determine the sum of the first 10 terms.

6. Determine the sum of the first 12 terms of each geometric series.

   a) $1 - 2 + 4 - 8 + \cdots$

   b) $6 + 12 + 24 + 48 + \cdots$

   c) $3 + 12 + 48 + 192 + \cdots$

   d) $6561 - 2187 + 729 - 243 + \cdots$

   e) $96 + 48 + 24 + 12 + \cdots$

   f) $96 - 48 + 24 - 12 + \cdots$

7. Determine the sum of the first 10 terms of each geometric series.

   a) $5 + 10 + 20 + 40 + \cdots$ **b)** $5 - 10 + 20 - 40 + \cdots$

   c) $1 + \frac{1}{3} + \frac{1}{9} + \frac{1}{27} + \cdots$ **d)** $1 - \frac{1}{3} + \frac{1}{9} - \frac{1}{27} + \cdots$

   e) $5 + \frac{5}{2} + \frac{5}{4} + \frac{5}{8} + \cdots$ **f)** $5 - \frac{5}{2} + \frac{5}{4} - \frac{5}{8} + \cdots$

8. **Application** A contest winner is given a choice of two prizes:

Prize 1 You will receive $1 today, $2 a year from now, $4 two years from now, and so on, for 20 years. Each year you will receive twice as much as the year before.

Prize 2 You will receive $100 000 today.

a) Predict which prize would provide the most earnings.

b) Calculate the total amount of money a winner who chooses Prize 1 will receive.

c) Which prize would you choose? Explain.

9. Consider this geometric series:

$3 + 6 + 12 + \cdots + 3072$

a) Use the formula for t_n to determine the number of terms in the series.

b) Calculate the sum of the series.

10. Use the method of exercise 9. Calculate the sum of each series.

a) $2 + 4 + 8 + \cdots + 128$

b) $\frac{1}{25} + \frac{1}{5} + 1 + 5 + \cdots + 3125$

c) $4 + 12 + 36 + \cdots + 2916$

d) $\frac{1}{4} + \frac{1}{2} + 1 + 2 + \cdots + 1024$

11. In exercise 18, page 31, you calculated the numbers of ancestors for different numbers of generations. What is the total number of ancestors you have going back each number of generations?

a) 5   b) 10   c) 20   d) 40

12. Here are 3 levels in a school trip telephoning tree. The tree continues for many levels until all students have been contacted.

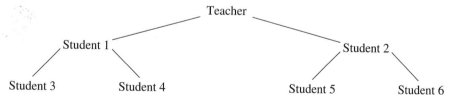

a) At what level are 64 students contacted?

b) How many students are contacted at the 8th level?

c) By the 8th level, how many students in total have been contacted?

d) By the nth level, how many students in total have been contacted?

e) Suppose there are 300 students in total. By what level will all the students have been contacted?

13. **Communication** Explain how geometric sequences and geometric series are related. Use examples to illustrate your explanation.

14. Thinking/Inquiry/Problem Solving Sixteen players enter a tennis tournament. When a player loses a match, the player drops out; the winners go on to the next round. The "draw" is a large board on which the players' names are entered, such as the one below. At the start of the tournament, the 16 names appear in the left column. Adjacent players play their matches, and the winners' names are written in the second column. The winners of these matches are written in the third column. The process repeats, and the tournament winner's name is written in the final column.

Anne
James } Anne
Kwan
Cheung } Cheung } Cheung
Fatima
Ali } Fatima } Fatima
Sarah
Thomas } Thomas } Fatima
Nicole
Max } Nicole } Tatiana
Heidi
Ernst } Ernst } Ernst
Colleen
Owen } Owen } Tatiana
Tatiana
Ivan } Tatiana } Tatiana

a) Suppose there are 16 players in the tournament. How many matches are needed?

b) A larger tournament can accommodate 32 players. How many matches are needed?

c) How many matches are needed when there are 64 players? Support your answer with a convincing explanation.

d) How many players can participate in a tournament if no player has a bye? Describe how to determine the number of games that must be played.

15. Determine the sum of the series $64 + 32 + 16 + \cdots + \dfrac{1}{1024}$.

16. Let $S_n = 1 + \dfrac{1}{2} + \dfrac{1}{4} + \dfrac{1}{8} + \cdots + \dfrac{1}{2^{n-1}}$.

a) Show algebraically that $S_n < 2$ for all values of n.

b) Explain why S_n becomes closer and closer to 2 as n becomes larger.

c) Draw a diagram to illustrate why $S_n < 2$.

17. Determine the sum of the factors of 3^8.

1. Determine the sum of each series. Identify the type of series.

   a) $4 + 9 + 14 + 19 + 24 + 29 + 34$

   b) $200 + 190 + 180 + 170 + 160 + 150$

   c) $1024 + 512 + 256 + 128 + 64 + 32 + 16$

   d) $0.3 + 0.42 + 0.588 + 0.8232 + 1.152\,48$

2. Determine the sum of the first 10 terms of each series.

   a) $10 + 11.5 + 13 + 14.5 + \cdots$

   b) $10 + 8.5 + 7 + 5.5 + \cdots$

   c) $1 + 3 + 9 + 27 + \cdots$

   d) $1 - 3 + 9 - 27 + \cdots$

   e) $1 + \dfrac{1}{2} + \dfrac{1}{4} + \dfrac{1}{8} + \cdots$

   f) $1 - \dfrac{1}{2} + \dfrac{1}{4} - \dfrac{1}{8} + \cdots$

3. Given the series $2 + 4.5 + 7 + 9.5 + \cdots$, determine t_{20} and S_{20}.

4. Given the series $\dfrac{1}{2} + 2 + 8 + 32 + \cdots$, determine t_{10} and S_{10}.

5. a) Determine the sum of $1 + 2 + 3 + 4 + \cdots + 526$.

   b) Determine the sum of $2 + 4 + 6 + 8 + \cdots + 526$.

6. Seven equally spaced positive integers have a sum of 203. Determine the integers.

7. Determine the sum of the series $3 + 6 + 12 + 24 + \cdots + 3072$.

8. Suppose you decide to save \$1 on a given day, \$2 one week later, \$4 a week later, and so on. How much will you have saved after 6 months?

The Bouncing Ball

Suppose we drop a superball from a height of 1 m. It hits the floor and bounces, returning to a height of 0.8 m. This height is 80% of its starting height. The ball bounces again and returns to a height of 0.64 m, which is 80% of its preceding height. The ball continues in this way, each time returning to 80% of its preceding height.

This graph shows the height of the ball as a function of time.

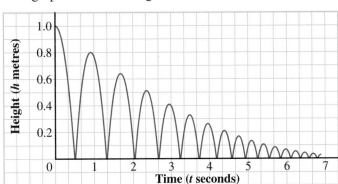

A ball that bounces on a hard surface always returns to the same fraction of its previous height. For a lively ball, such as a superball, that fraction can be close to 1.

This graph is not the path of the ball. The ball is moving straight up and down.

Look at the "hoops" on the graph. What kind of curve do they look like?

The tops of the hoops appear to lie on a curve. What kind of curve do you think it might be? Give two possibilities.

Formulating Questions

Here are the problems we want to investigate.

Suppose we let the ball bounce 16 times. That is, the ball moves down, then up 16 times.

Problem 1   How far does the ball travel?

Problem 2   How long does it take to bounce 16 times?

Representing the Distance in Mathematical Form

On the 1st bounce, the ball travels 1 m down and 0.8 m up.
On the 2nd bounce, it travels 0.8 m down and 0.8^2 m up.
On the 3rd bounce, it travels 0.8^2 m down and 0.8^3 m up.

⋮   ⋮   ⋮

On the 16th bounce, it travels 0.8^{15} m down and 0.8^{16} m up.

The total distance going down is $1 + 0.8 + 0.8^2 + \cdots + 0.8^{15}$.
This is a geometric series, and its sum is:

$$\frac{1(1 - 0.8^{16})}{1 - 0.8} = 5(1 - 0.8^{16}) \qquad ①$$

Distances covered, in metres

Bounce	Down	Up
1	1	0.8
2	0.8	0.8^2
3	0.8^2	0.8^3
4	0.8^3	0.8^4
⋮	⋮	⋮
16	0.8^{15}	0.8^{16}

The total distance going up is $0.8 + 0.8^2 + 0.8^3 + \cdots + 0.8^{16}$.
The sum of this geometric series is:

$$\frac{0.8(1 - 0.8^{16})}{1 - 0.8} = 4(1 - 0.8^{16}) \qquad ②$$

What is another way to find the sum of this series?

Add ① and ②:

$$5(1 - 0.8^{16}) + 4(1 - 0.8^{16}) = 9(1 - 0.8^{16})$$
$$\doteq 8.747$$

The ball travels about 8.747 m in 16 bounces.

In general, let D_n represent the total distance the ball travels when it bounces n times. By repeating the above steps using n instead of 16, we obtain this formula:

$$D_n = 9(1 - 0.8^n)$$

The graph of this function is shown at the right.

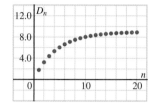

Interpreting Information and Forming Conclusions
What happens to the distance as *n* gets larger? Explain, using both the graph of D_n and the formula.

Representing the Time in Mathematical Form

We will add the down and up times just as we added the distances, but we need to determine these times. From physics, the formula that relates the distance, *d* metres, an object falls to the time *t* seconds is:

$$d = 4.9t^2$$

To determine the time to fall *d* metres, solve for *t*.

$$t^2 = \frac{d}{4.9}$$

Take the square root of each side, then use the exponent laws. The result is:

$$t \doteq 0.452d^{\frac{1}{2}}$$

Now we can determine the time for the ball to fall a given distance. Use the distances from the *Down* column of the table on page 66 and substitute into this formula. The results are shown in the table at the right. The total time travelling down is:

$$0.452\left[1 + 0.8^{\frac{1}{2}} + 0.8^{\frac{2}{2}} + 0.8^{\frac{3}{2}} + \cdots + 0.8^{\frac{15}{2}}\right]$$

The sum of this geometric series is:

$$\frac{0.452(1)\left[1 - \left(0.8^{\frac{1}{2}}\right)^{16}\right]}{1 - 0.8^{\frac{1}{2}}} \doteq 3.5631 \qquad ③$$

Elapsed times, in seconds

Bounce	Down	Up
1	0.452	$0.452(0.8)^{\frac{1}{2}}$
2	$0.452(0.8)^{\frac{1}{2}}$	$0.452(0.8)^{\frac{2}{2}}$
3	$0.452(0.8)^{\frac{2}{2}}$	$0.452(0.8)^{\frac{3}{2}}$
4	$0.452(0.8)^{\frac{3}{2}}$	$0.452(0.8)^{\frac{4}{2}}$
⋮	⋮	⋮
16	$0.452(0.8)^{\frac{15}{2}}$	$0.452(0.8)^{\frac{16}{2}}$

Use the information in the table on page 66 and the formula $t \doteq 0.452d^{\frac{1}{2}}$ to check that these times are correct.

Since each bounce is symmetrical, the ball takes the same time to rise to its maximum height as it takes to fall from that height. Use the distances from the *Up* column of the table on page 66 and substitute in the formula. The results are shown in the table on page 67. The total time travelling up is:

$$0.452\left[0.8^{\frac{1}{2}} + 0.8^{\frac{2}{2}} + 0.8^{\frac{3}{2}} + 0.8^{\frac{4}{2}} \cdots + 0.8^{\frac{16}{2}}\right]$$

The sum of this geometric series is:

$$\frac{0.452\left(0.8^{\frac{1}{2}}\right)\left[1 - \left(0.8^{\frac{1}{2}}\right)^{16}\right]}{1 - 0.8^{\frac{1}{2}}} \doteq 3.1869 \qquad ④$$

Add ③ and ④. The time for 16 bounces is about 6.75 s.

In general, let T_n represent the time for n bounces. By repeating the above steps using n instead of 16, we obtain this formula:

$$T_n \doteq 8.111\left(1 - 0.8^{\frac{n}{2}}\right)$$

The graph of this function is shown at the right.

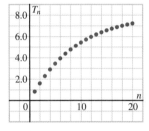

Interpreting Information and Forming Conclusions

What happens to the time as n gets larger? Explain, using both the graph of T_n and the formula.

Problems

1. Substitute $n = 16$ in the formulas for D_n and T_n to verify the answers to Problem 1 and Problem 2.

2. Are the sequences represented by D_n and T_n geometric sequences? Explain.

3. Look at the formula and graph for T_n. Some people may say that since the ball always bounces after hitting the ground, it can never stop bouncing and it bounces forever. So, it bounces for an infinite time. What do you think of this argument?

4. Let h_n represent the height of the ball after the nth bounce.

   a) Determine a formula for h_n.

   b) Graph h_n against n.

   c) What happens to the height as n gets larger?

   d) Compare your graph with the graph on page 66. Describe their similarities and differences.

Selecting Strategies, Resources, Technology, and Tools

We can create the graphs of D_n and T_n in different ways. We can use:
- a calculator and grid paper
- a spreadsheet
- a graphing calculator
- graphing software

Regardless of the method, the graph should consist of discrete points. Why is this?

Exercises 5 to 10 refer to the graph on page 66. You will also need the table on page 67. The word "hoop" refers to the curves as they appear on the graph. The first hoop is only a half hoop. It corresponds to the ball falling to the floor for the first time.

5. Look at the tops of the hoops.

   a) What do the horizontal coordinates of these points represent? Do they form a geometric sequence? Explain.

   b) What do the vertical coordinates represent? Do they form a geometric sequence? Explain.

6. Visualize little right triangles whose hypotenuses join the points at the tops of adjacent hoops.

   a) What do the horizontal legs of these triangles represent? Do their lengths form a geometric sequence? Explain.

   b) What do the vertical legs represent? Do their lengths form a geometric sequence? Explain.

7. The horizontal intercepts of the graph represent the times when the ball hits the floor. Do these times form a geometric sequence? Explain.

8. Explain your answer to each question.

   a) Are the hoops congruent?   b) Are the hoops similar?

Challenge Problems

9. Compare the graph on page 66 with the equation $d = 4.9t^2$ on page 67.

   a) What do the values of d in this equation represent? How are these related to the vertical coordinates of points on the first hoop?

   b) Use your answer to part a to determine the equation of the first hoop, and explain why it is a parabola.

   c) Determine the equation of the second hoop.

   d) The equations in parts a and b form a non-linear system of equations. Solve the system. What does the solution represent?

10. Suppose you have drawn one hoop. What is the simplest way to draw the next hoop?

11. On the outside of a tall building, there is a glass elevator that moves up at a constant speed of 5 m/s. Inside the elevator, the ball on page 66 is dropped from a height of 1 m above the floor. Draw a graph to show the height of the ball above the *ground* as a function of time. Assume the ball is dropped at the instant the elevator starts rising.

Reflecting on the Reasonableness of Results

The methods used to solve these problems are called *mathematical models*. The accuracy of the results obtained from a mathematical model depends on how closely it represents the situation.

For example, the graph on page 66 has a sharp corner at each bounce point. It assumes that the ball is a point and the bounce is instantaneous. In reality, the ball has a diameter and stays in contact with the floor for a short time. During this time the ball deforms, then springs back to its spherical shape.

Algebra Tools

Arithmetic Sequences and Series

- Arithmetic sequences and series describe linear or additive growth when the common difference is positive.

- General arithmetic sequence with n terms:
  $a, a + d, a + 2d, \ldots, a + (n - 1)d$

- General arithmetic series with n terms:
  $a + (a + d) + (a + 2d) + \cdots + [a + (n - 1)d]$

  The nth term $\qquad\qquad t_n = a + (n - 1)d$

  The common difference $\qquad d = t_n - t_{n-1}$

  Sum of the first n terms $\quad S_n = \left(\dfrac{a + t_n}{2}\right) \times n \quad$ or $\quad S_n = \dfrac{n}{2}[2a + (n - 1)d]$

Geometric Sequences and Series

- Geometric sequences and series describe exponential growth when the common ratio is greater than 1.

- General geometric sequence with n terms: $a, ar, ar^2, \ldots, ar^{n-1}$

- General geometric series with n terms: $a + ar + ar^2 + \cdots + ar^{n-1}$

  The nth term $\qquad\qquad t_n = ar^{n-1}$

  The common ratio $\qquad\quad r = \dfrac{t_n}{t_{n-1}}$

  Sum of the first n terms $\qquad S_n = \dfrac{a(r^n - 1)}{r - 1}, \ r \neq 1$

Recursion Formulas (Functions and Relations)

- $t_1 = a$, $t_n =$ (a function of earlier terms)

- Sequences and series produced using recursion formulas may be arithmetic, geometric, or neither.

Rational Exponents

- Rational exponents are defined by $\sqrt[n]{x} = x^{\frac{1}{n}}$ and $(\sqrt[n]{x})^m = \sqrt[n]{x^m} = x^{\frac{m}{n}}$.

- The exponent laws apply to rational exponents.
  Example: $81^{\frac{1}{4}} = (3^4)^{\frac{1}{4}} = 3$
  Example: $81^{\frac{3}{4}} = (3^4)^{\frac{3}{4}} = 3^3 = 27$

1. a) Determine the indicated term of each arithmetic sequence.

    i) 6, 10, 14, …   8th term   **ii)** 18, 13, 8, …   18th term
    iii) 13, 24, 35, …   11th term   **iv)** 55, 47, 39, ...   14th term

b) Choose one sequence from part a. Explain how you could calculate any term in the sequence if you know the term number.

2. Copy, then complete each arithmetic sequence.

  a) ■, 7, 15, ■, ■   **b)** ■, ■, 36, 25, ■

  c) 5, ■, 23, ■, ■   **d)** 50, ■, ■, 29, ■

  e) ■, –8, ■, ■, ■, 28   **f)** 41, ■, ■, ■, 97

3. For the arithmetic sequence 7, 15, 23, 31, …, determine each term.

  a) t_n **b)** t_{10} **c)** t_{20}

4. Determine the first 8 terms of each arithmetic sequence.

  a) The 2nd term is 42 and the 5th term is 99.

  b) The 3rd term is –1.64 and the 7th term is 10.2.

5. Determine whether each sequence is arithmetic, geometric, or neither. Explain your choice.

  a) 1, 10, 1000, …

  b) 1, 2, 4, 7, 11, …

  c) 2, 5, 8, 11, …

  d) 4, 9, 16, 25, …

  e) 1, 8, 27, 125, …

  f) 2.3, 0.23, 0.023, 0.0023, …

  g) 7, 7, 7, 7, …

  h) 3, –3, 3, –3, …

  i) $2 \times 3, 3 \times 6, 4 \times 12, 5 \times 24, …$

  j) $\frac{1}{2}, \frac{3}{4}, \frac{5}{8}, …$

6. a) Determine the indicated term of each geometric sequence.

    i) 2, 4, 8, …   8th term
    ii) 32, 16, 8, …   9th term
    iii) 1, 3, 9, …   10th term
    iv) 2, –6, 18, …   7th term

b) Choose one sequence from part a. Explain how you could calculate any term in the sequence if you know the term number.

Review Exercises

7. Copy, then complete each geometric sequence.

a) ■, 8, 24, ■, ■   **b)** ■, ■, 12, 3, ■

c) 1, ■, ■, –64, ■   **d)** 1, ■, 25, ■, ■

e) ■, 24 010, ■, ■, ■, 10   **f)** 6, ■, ■, ■, 7776

8. For the geometric sequence 3, 6, 12, …, determine each term.

a) t_n **b)** t_5 **c)** t_{11}

9. Determine the first 5 terms of each geometric sequence.

a) The 3rd term is –50 and the 4th term is 125.

b) The 2nd term is 8.37 and the 3rd term is 25.947.

1.3   **10.** The formula for the nth term of a sequence is given. Write the first 4 terms of each sequence. Identify the type of sequence.

a) $t_n = 2 - 5n$ **b)** $t_n = 13 + 3n$

c) $t_n = n + 2^n$ **d)** $t_n = 5 \times 3^n$

e) $t_n = 2n^2 + 3$ **f)** $t_n = n(n + 2)$

11. Each sequence is arithmetic. Write a formula for t_n, then use it to determine the indicated term.

a) 2, 6, 10, … t_{20} **b)** 100, 120, 140, … t_{50}

c) 33, 30, 27, … t_{80} **d)** 45, 44.5, 44, … t_{100}

12. Each sequence is geometric. Write a formula for t_n, then use it to determine the indicated term.

a) 2, 6, 18, … t_7 **b)** 3, 1.5, 0.75, … t_6

c) 10, –5, 2.5, … t_8 **d)** –4, –12, –36, … t_{10}

13. Determine a formula for the nth term of each sequence.

a) $\frac{1}{3}, \frac{2}{4}, \frac{4}{5}, \dots$ **b)** $\frac{1}{2}, \frac{3}{4}, \frac{5}{6}, \dots$

c) $1 \times 32, 2 \times 16, 3 \times 8, 4 \times 4, \dots$ **d)** $2 \times 3, 6 \times 4, 10 \times 5, 14 \times 6, \dots$

1.5   **14.** Determine each value without using a calculator.

a) $1^{\frac{1}{2}}$ **b)** $-4^{\frac{1}{2}}$ **c)** $9^{\frac{1}{2}}$ **d)** $-16^{\frac{1}{2}}$ **e)** $25^{\frac{1}{2}}$

f) $1^{\frac{2}{3}}$ **g)** $8^{\frac{2}{3}}$ **h)** $(-27)^{\frac{2}{3}}$ **i)** $64^{\frac{2}{3}}$ **j)** $(-125)^{\frac{2}{3}}$

k) $9^{\frac{1}{2}}$ **l)** $9^{\frac{3}{2}}$ **m)** $9^{-\frac{3}{2}}$ **n)** $9^{\frac{4}{2}}$ **o)** $-9^{\frac{5}{2}}$

p) $64^{\frac{1}{3}}$ **q)** $64^{\frac{2}{3}}$ **r)** $(-64)^{\frac{4}{3}}$ **s)** $64^{\frac{5}{3}}$ **t)** $64^{-\frac{4}{3}}$

15. Use a calculator. Determine each value to 3 decimal places.

a) $18^{\frac{3}{4}}$ **b)** $23^{\frac{2}{5}}$ **c)** $56^{\frac{3}{2}}$ **d)** $19^{\frac{7}{2}}$ **e)** $999^{\frac{5}{2}}$

f) $23^{-\frac{1}{2}}$ **g)** $110^{-\frac{3}{2}}$ **h)** $8^{-\frac{4}{3}}$ **i)** $180^{-\frac{1}{4}}$ **j)** $101^{-\frac{2}{3}}$

k) $17^{0.4}$ **l)** $12^{-1.16}$ **m)** $4.5^{-2.75}$ **n)** $8.32^{1.3}$ **o)** $1234^{4.321}$

16. Determine each value without using a calculator.

a) $(-125)^{\frac{1}{3}}$ **b)** $36^{\frac{3}{2}}$ **c)** $(-216)^{\frac{2}{3}}$ **d)** $400^{\frac{3}{2}}$

e) $(-27\,000)^{\frac{2}{3}}$ **f)** $\left(\frac{9}{16}\right)^{-\frac{1}{2}}$ **g)** $\left(\frac{25}{49}\right)^{\frac{1}{2}}$ **h)** $\left(\frac{-1}{32}\right)^{\frac{2}{5}}$

i) $\left(\frac{-8}{27}\right)^{-\frac{2}{3}}$ **j)** $\left(\frac{81}{16}\right)^{-\frac{3}{4}}$

1.6   **17.** Simplify without using a calculator.

a) $(8^2)(-27)^{\frac{1}{3}}$ **b)** $(3^2)(8^{\frac{2}{3}})$ **c)** $(4^2)(8^{-\frac{1}{3}})$ **d)** $(5^2)(8^{-\frac{2}{3}})$

e) $(2^{-2})(8^{\frac{1}{3}})$ **f)** $(2^{-2})(64^{\frac{2}{3}})$ **g)** $(8^{-2})(-27)^{-\frac{1}{3}}$ **h)** $(2^{-2})(8^{-\frac{2}{3}})$

i) $\dfrac{9^2}{9^{\frac{1}{2}}}$ **j)** $\dfrac{16^2}{4^{-\frac{3}{2}}}$ **k)** $\dfrac{64^{\frac{1}{3}}}{4^2}$ **l)** $\dfrac{4^{-\frac{1}{2}}}{4^2}$

18. A pond contains 100 insect larvae. Suppose the population triples every 2 days. How many insect larvae are there after each time?

a) 10 days   **b)** 24 days   **c)** 6 weeks

19. Write each expression as a single power. Then evaluate the power.

a) $(6^{0.2})(6^{1.2})$ **b)** $(8^{2.75})(8^{1.15})$ **c)** $\dfrac{5^{4.26}}{5^{-3.78}}$ **d)** $(7^{1.5})^{4.6}$

20. Solve each equation.

a) $2^{3x+1} = 4^2$ **b)** $2^{x-1} = 8^3$ **c)** $3^{x-5} = 9^{x+1}$ **d)** $5^{x+3} = 25^{2x}$

1.7   **21.** Determine the sum of the first 20 terms of each arithmetic series.

a) $2 + 5 + 8 + \cdots$ **b)** $1 - 1 - 3 - \cdots$

c) $11 + 16 + 21 + \cdots$ **d)** $1 + 1.7 + 2.4 + \cdots$

22. A formula for the sum of the first n terms of an arithmetic series is $S_n = n^2 - 2n$. Determine the first 4 terms of the series.

1.8   **23.** Determine the sum of the first 10 terms of each geometric series.

a) $5 + 15 + 45 + \cdots$ **b)** $-5 + 10 - 20 + \cdots$

c) $7 + \frac{7}{2} + \frac{7}{4} + \cdots$ **d)** $5 - 2.5 + 1.25 - \cdots$

24. A $1000 investment earns 9% interest each year.

   a) Suppose the investment earns simple interest. What will the investment be worth after 8 years?

   b) Suppose the investment earns compound interest. What will the investment be worth after 8 years?

25. Determine the sum of each series.

   a) $2 + 7 + 12 + \cdots + 72$ **b)** $4 + 11 + 18 + \cdots + 102$

   c) $3 + 12 + 48 + \cdots + 12\ 288$ **d)** $179.2 + 89.6 + 44.8 + \cdots + 1.4$

26. In a company telephone tree, each employee is to call 3 other employees. The tree begins with the company president.

   a) At what level are 243 employees contacted?

   b) How many employees are contacted at the 8th level?

   c) By the 8th level, how many employees in total have been contacted?

   d) Suppose there are 3500 employees in the company. By what level will all the employees have been contacted?

27. Insert three numbers between 5 and 1280, so the five numbers form a geometric sequence.

Functions and Relations

28. Write the first 5 terms of the sequence defined by each recursion formula.

   a) $t_1 = 1, t_n = t_{n-1} + 3, n > 1$ **b)** $t_1 = 2, t_n = t_{n-1} - 3, n > 1$

   c) $t_1 = 5, t_n = 2t_{n-1} + 1, n > 1$ **d)** $t_1 = -4, t_n = 3t_{n-1} + 0.2, n > 1$

29. Write the first 5 terms of the sequence defined by each recursion formula.

   a) $t_1 = 100, t_n = t_{n-1} + 7, n > 1$ **b)** $t_1 = -4, t_n = t_{n-1} - 5, n > 1$

   c) $t_1 = 1, t_n = 0.5t_{n-1}, n > 1$ **d)** $t_1 = 1, t_2 = 3, t_n = 0.7t_{n-2} - 0.5t_{n-1}, n > 2$

30. For each recursion formula, determine whether the sequence is arithmetic, geometric, or neither. Explain your choice.

   a) $t_1 = 3, t_n = t_{n-1} + 7, n > 1$ **b)** $t_1 = 7, t_n = 1 - 2t_{n-1}, n > 1$

   c) $t_1 = 4, t_n = \dfrac{1}{t_{n-1}}, n > 1$ **d)** $t_1 = 5, t_n = (t_{n-1})^2, n > 1$

Self-Test

1. **Knowledge/Understanding** Determine whether each sequence is arithmetic, geometric, or neither.

   a) 3, 7, 11, 15, …

   b) 2, 4, 8, 16, …

   c) 2×3, 3×4, 4×5, 5×6, …

   d) $\frac{1}{2}, \frac{2}{4}, \frac{3}{8}$, …

2. Determine the indicated term of each arithmetic sequence.

   a) 6, 17, 28, … 8th term

   b) 13, 10, 7, … 11th term

3. Determine the indicated term of each geometric sequence.

   a) 2, 10, 50, … 8th term

   b) 1, 4, 16, … 10th term

4. For the arithmetic sequence 7, 13.5, 20, 26.5 …, determine t_{18}.

5. For the geometric sequence 7, 21, 63, 189, …, determine t_{10}.

6. Simplify without using a calculator.

   a) $(3^2)(-27)^{\frac{1}{3}}$

   b) $(3^2)(64^{\frac{2}{3}})$

   c) $(3^2)(8^{-\frac{1}{3}})$

   d) $(2^3)(8^{-\frac{2}{3}})$

   e) $\dfrac{9^2}{9^{\frac{3}{2}}}$

   f) $\dfrac{8^2}{4^{-\frac{3}{2}}}$

   g) $\dfrac{64^{\frac{2}{3}}}{4^3}$

   h) $\dfrac{9^{-\frac{1}{2}}}{81^{-\frac{3}{4}}}$

7. Determine the sum of the first 20 terms of each arithmetic series.

   a) $11 + 19 + 27 + \cdots$

   b) $1.5 + 4.3 + 7.1 + \cdots$

8. Determine the sum of the first 10 terms of each geometric series.

   a) $1 + 5 + 15 + \cdots$

   b) $-10 + 5 - 2.5 + \cdots$

9. Use a calculator. Determine each value to 3 decimal places.

   a) $28^{\frac{3}{4}}$

   b) $283^{-\frac{1}{4}}$

   c) $1441^{-\frac{2}{3}}$

   d) $4.5^{-2.07}$

   e) $7.77^{1.77}$

   f) $43^{4.32}$

10. **Communication** Determine the first 8 terms of the arithmetic sequence, when the 2nd term is 42 and the 6th term is 72. Explain how you determined the terms.

    $$t_6 \quad t_2$$
    $$4d = 72 - 42$$

11. Determine the first 5 terms of the geometric sequence, when the 3rd term is −200 and the 4th term is 400.

12. **Application** The population of a city increases by 2% each year. On January 1, 2000, a city had a population of 530 000. What will the city's population be on January 1, 2020?

13. For the arithmetic series, $48 + 60 + 72 + \cdots$, determine t_{33} and S_{33}.

14. For the geometric series, $48 + 24 + 12 + \cdots$, determine t_9 and S_9.

15. Solve each equation.

a) $2^{4x-3} = 4^{-2}$

b) $5^{x-5} = 25^{x+1}$

16. Thinking/Inquiry/Problem Solving In an arithmetic sequence, the 2nd term is 25 and the 11th term is 79. How many terms of the sequence are less than 200?

Functions and Relations

17. Write the first 6 terms of the sequence defined by each recursion formula.

a) $t_1 = 1$, $t_n = t_{n-1} + 2$, $n > 1$

b) $t_1 = 2.4$, $t_n = 1.8t_{n-1}$, $n > 1$

Assessment Tasks

1. Consider this sequence:
$$101^{\frac{1}{2}}, \; 101^{\frac{3}{2}}, \; 101^{\frac{5}{2}}, \; \ldots$$

a) Use a calculator to investigate whether the sequence is arithmetic, geometric, or neither. Present your findings clearly.

b) Without using a calculator, establish the results you obtained in part a, so they are clear and easily verifiable by a person who does not have a calculator.

2. An antique roadster is increasing in value at the rate of 5% per year, while a new car is decreasing in value at the rate of 5% per year. After a number of years, the roadster will have doubled in value, while the new car will have halved in value.

a) Determine whether these events occur at the same time.

b) Investigate other situations of equal percent increase and decrease. Report your findings clearly.

3. This series is an *arithmetico-geometric* series.
$$1 \times 2^{10} + 2 \times 2^9 + 3 \times 2^8 + \cdots + 10 \times 2^1$$

a) Why do you think this series is called arithmetico-geometric? Give examples of other arithmetico-geometric series.

b) One strategy to calculate the sum without evaluating each term is to write each term vertically in a triangular array. The problem is now to add the row sums; explain why.
$$2^{10} + 2^9 + 2^8 + \cdots + 2^1$$
$$2^9 + 2^8 + \cdots + 2^1$$
$$2^8 + \cdots + 2^1$$
$$\vdots \quad \vdots \quad \vdots$$

Complete the calculation to determine the sum of the series.

⌐tigate other strategies for determining the sum of the series. Present ⌐gies clearly.

INSIGHTS
INTO A
RICH
PROBLEM

Some people always seem to be in a hurry when they drive a car. If they drive faster than the speed limit, they will arrive at their destination sooner than they would by obeying the speed limit. But, how much sooner will they arrive?

At the end of this chapter, you will investigate how the amount of time saved to travel a given distance is related to the amount by which a driver exceeds the speed limit. You will use rational expressions.

Curriculum Expectations

By the end of this chapter, you will:

- Add, subtract, and multiply polynomials.
- Add, subtract, multiply, and divide rational expressions, and state the restrictions on the variable values.
- Determine the real … roots of quadratic equations … by factoring.

- Communicate solutions to problems … clearly and concisely, orally and in writing, using an effective integration of essay and mathematical forms.
- Demonstrate the correct use of mathematical language, symbols, visuals, and conventions.

Necessary Skills

1. Review: Operations with Fractions

Skills with fractions are similar to the skills you will need to work with rational expressions.

Example

Simplify.

a) $\dfrac{8}{9} \times \dfrac{3}{2}$
b) $\dfrac{-2}{3} \div \dfrac{5}{7}$
c) $\dfrac{1}{4} + \dfrac{2}{5}$
d) $\dfrac{1}{4} - \dfrac{5}{6}$

Solution

a) $\dfrac{8}{9} \times \dfrac{3}{2} = \dfrac{\overset{4}{8} \times \overset{1}{3}}{\underset{3}{9} \times \underset{1}{2}}$

$= \dfrac{4}{3}$

Divide numerator and denominator by common factors.

b) $\dfrac{-2}{3} \div \dfrac{5}{7} = \dfrac{-2}{3} \times \dfrac{7}{5}$

$= \dfrac{(-2) \times 7}{3 \times 5}$

$= \dfrac{-14}{15}$, or $-\dfrac{14}{15}$

Multiply by the reciprocal of the divisor.

c) $\dfrac{1}{4} + \dfrac{2}{5} = \dfrac{1}{4} \times \dfrac{5}{5} + \dfrac{2}{5} \times \dfrac{4}{4}$

$= \dfrac{5}{20} + \dfrac{8}{20}$

$= \dfrac{5 + 8}{20}$

$= \dfrac{13}{20}$

Determine the lowest common denominator, 20.
The denominators are the same.

Add the numerators only. Keep the denominators the same.

d) $\dfrac{1}{4} - \dfrac{5}{6} = \dfrac{1}{4} \times \dfrac{3}{3} - \dfrac{5}{6} \times \dfrac{2}{2}$

$= \dfrac{3}{12} - \dfrac{10}{12}$

$= \dfrac{3 - 10}{12}$

$= \dfrac{-7}{12}$

Determine the lowest common denominator, 12.

Subtract the numerators.

Exercises

1. Reduce each fraction to simplest form.

a) $\dfrac{36}{15}$
b) $\dfrac{75}{10}$
c) $\dfrac{9}{12}$

2. Simplify each product.

a) $\frac{2}{15} \times \frac{5}{8}$ b) $\frac{16}{25} \times \frac{10}{-4}$ c) $\frac{-6}{49} \times \frac{14}{9}$

d) $\frac{16}{25} \times \frac{-10}{24}$ e) $\frac{-2}{3} \times \frac{15}{-18}$ f) $\frac{4}{7} \times \frac{77}{16}$

3. Simplify each quotient.

a) $\frac{6}{25} \div \frac{12}{5}$ b) $\frac{26}{3} \div \frac{39}{9}$ c) $\frac{-16}{35} \div \frac{-4}{14}$

d) $\frac{3}{-7} \div \frac{9}{-28}$ e) $\frac{8}{15} \div \frac{-24}{45}$ f) $\frac{63}{-72} \div \frac{9}{-8}$

4. Simplify each sum and difference.

a) $\frac{2}{5} + \frac{1}{5}$ b) $\frac{2}{3} - \frac{1}{2}$ c) $\frac{5}{12} + \frac{7}{8}$

d) $\frac{7}{12} + \frac{3}{5}$ e) $\frac{9}{11} - \frac{3}{22}$ f) $\frac{1}{4} - \frac{1}{5} + \frac{1}{6}$

2. Review: Operations with Monomials

Remember that a monomial is a constant or the product of a constant and one or more variables. We can add and subtract like monomials. We can multiply and divide monomials.

Example

Simplify.

a) $3x^2 + 7x - 5 + 4x^2 - 9x + 2$ b) $(4a^2b^3)(-5ab)^2$ c) $\frac{-12m^2n}{6mn^5}$

Solution

a) $3x^2 + 7x - 5 + 4x^2 - 9x + 2 = 3x^2 + 4x^2 + 7x - 9x - 5 + 2$ Group like terms.

                       $= 7x^2 - 2x - 3$ Combine like terms.

b) To multiply monomials, use the exponent laws.

     $(4a^2b^3)(-5ab)^2 = (4a^2b^3)(25a^2b^2)$ Apply the power of a power law to $(-5ab)^2$.

                  $= 100a^4b^5$ Apply the multiplication law.

c) To divide monomials, use the exponent laws.

     $\frac{-12m^2n}{6mn^5} = -2m^1n^{-4}$ Apply the division law.

          $= \frac{-2m}{n^4}$ Write all monomials with positive exponents.

Exercises

1. Simplify.

a) $3x + 5 + 6x - 1$

b) $-5a + 2 + a - 3$

c) $6x^2 + 5xy + 2y^2 - 4x^2 - 11xy + 6y^2$

d) $7a^2 - 2a - 2a + 5a^2 + 6a - 9a^2 - 4a$

2. Simplify.

a) $(3a)(2a)$ **b)** $(-3a^2)(2a)$ **c)** $(3a^2)(2a^3)$

3. Simplify.

a) $(6x)(3y)$ **b)** $(8p^2)(4q)$ **c)** $(-9r)(5rs^3)$

4. Simplify.

a) $\dfrac{12x^5}{3x^2}$ **b)** $\dfrac{54m^8}{-6m^2}$ **c)** $\dfrac{-24cd^3}{-6cd}$

5. Write each monomial as a product of two monomials, in three different ways. Which monomial(s) can be written as a product of two equal factors?

a) $36a^4b^2$ **b)** $-15xyz$ **c)** $-4m^4$

6. Write each monomial in exercise 5 as a quotient of two monomials, in three different ways.

7. Simplify.

a) $(2x^5)(3x^2)^3$ **b)** $(-3a^2b)(2a^4)^2$ **c)** $(5s^2t^5)(3s^4)^2$

8. Simplify.

a) $\dfrac{36r^6s^4}{8r^2s^2}$ **b)** $\dfrac{(2xy^2)(3x^5y^4)}{4x^2y^5}$ **c)** $\dfrac{(-7a^2b^4)(4a^3b^5)}{(-2ab^2)^3}$

3. Review: Factoring Polynomials

Remember that a monomial, and expressions formed by adding or subtracting monomials, are called *polynomials*. A polynomial with 2 terms is a binomial. A polynomial with 3 terms is a trinomial.

These expressions are polynomials:

$$18.3, \qquad 2x - 5, \qquad 6x^2 - 7x + 3, \qquad y^2$$

These expressions are not polynomials:

$$3\sqrt{x}, \qquad \sqrt{x^2 + 2x - 7}, \qquad y^3 + 3^y, \qquad \frac{3}{x}$$

Discuss

Why is each expression a polynomial?

Why is each expression not a polynomial?

When factoring a polynomial, first check whether there are any common factors.

Example 1

Factor.

a) $4x^2 - 6x$　　　　b) $x^2 - 7x + 12$　　　　c) $9m^2 - 16n^2$

Solution

a) $4x^2 - 6x$

The common factor of 4 and 6 is 2.
The common factor of x^2 and x is x.
So, the greatest common factor of $4x^2$ and $6x$ is $2x$.
$4x^2 - 6x = 2x(2x - 3)$

b) $x^2 - 7x + 12$

There are no common factors.
Find two numbers whose sum is -7 and whose product is 12.
The numbers are -3 and -4.
$x^2 - 7x + 12 = (x - 3)(x - 4)$

c) $9m^2 - 16n^2$

There are no common factors.
This is a difference of squares.
$$9m^2 - 16n^2 = (3m)^2 - (4n)^2$$
$$= (3m + 4n)(3m - 4n)$$

Example 2

Factor.

a) $2x^2 + 17x + 35$　　　　　　b) $12x^2 + 26x - 10$

Solution

a) $2x^2 + 17x + 35$

List the possibilities for the first and last terms, then look for a combination that gives a middle term of $17x$.

$2x$	x		5	7		$2x$	7	One factor
x	$2x$		7	5		x	5	Other factor

$$10x + 7x = 17x$$

$2x^2 + 17x + 35 = (2x + 7)(x + 5)$

b) $12x^2 + 26x - 10$

Remove the common factor of 2.

$12x^2 + 26x - 10 = 2(6x^2 + 13x - 5)$

List the possibilities for the first and last terms, then look for a combination that gives a middle term of $13x$.

$6x$	x	$2x$	$3x$	5	-5	$2x$ ⤬ 5		One factor
x	$6x$	$3x$	$2x$	-1	1	$3x$ ⤬ -1		Other factor

$$-2x + 15x = 13x$$

$12x^2 + 26x - 10 = 2(2x + 5)(3x - 1)$

We sometimes factor a polynomial to solve a quadratic equation.

Example 3

Solve by factoring.

a) $x^2 - x - 12 = 0$ **b)** $4y^2 - 9 = 0$

Solution

a) $x^2 - x - 12 = 0$

Factor the trinomial.

$(x - 4)(x + 3) = 0$

Either $x - 4 = 0$ or $x + 3 = 0$

         $x = 4$ $x = -3$

The roots are $x = 4$ and $x = -3$.

b) $4y^2 - 9 = 0$

Factor as a difference of squares.

$(2y + 3)(2y - 3) = 0$

Either $2y + 3 = 0$ or $2y - 3 = 0$

         $y = \frac{-3}{2}$ $y = \frac{3}{2}$

The roots are $y = \frac{-3}{2}$ and $y = \frac{3}{2}$.

Exercises

1. Factor.

a) $x^2 + 2x$

b) $3x^2 - 12$

c) $x^2 - 9$

d) $4m^2 - 25$

e) $2k^2 - 72$

f) $5x^2 - 20$

g) $36x^2 - 81$

h) $50x^2 - 2y^2$

i) $a^4 - b^4$

2. Factor.

a) $x^2 + 7x + 12$

b) $x^2 + x - 12$

c) $x^2 - x - 12$

d) $x^2 - 7x + 12$

e) $m^2 - 11m + 30$

f) $a^2 + 3a - 18$

g) $a^2 + 4a + 3$

h) $y^2 - 6y - 7$

i) $3a^2 + 3a - 6$

j) $2m^2 - 22m - 60$

k) $2x^2 + 2x - 144$

l) $13x^2 - 26x + 13$

m) $2x^2 - 14x + 20$

n) $3m^3 - 3m^2 - 18m$

3. Factor each polynomial, if possible. Examine the relationship between each polynomial and its factors. Write three different polynomials with a similar pattern. Factor these new polynomials, if possible.

a) $9x^2 - 30x + 25$

b) $9x^2 - 25$

c) $9x^2 + 25$

4. Factor.

a) $4x^2 - 12x + 9$

b) $2m^2 + 13m + 15$

c) $3a^2 - 13ab - 10b^2$

d) $2p^2 - 5p - 3$

e) $4m^2 + 12m + 9$

f) $25x^2 - 10x + 1$

5. Factor.

a) $7x^2 - 28y^2$

b) $5n^2 - 40n - 45$

c) $4a^2 + 7ab + 3b^2$

d) $2x^2 - 3x + 1$

e) $-8x^2 + 24x - 18$

f) $3x^2y - 9y^3$

6. Explain why $a - b$ is equal to $-(b - a)$.

7. Solve by factoring.

a) $m^2 - 2m + 1 = 0$

b) $x^2 - 3x - 40 = 0$

c) $9y^2 - 16 = 0$

d) $2x^2 + 5x + 2 = 0$

e) $4y^2 - 12y + 9 = 0$

f) $3x^2 - 7x - 6 = 0$

2.1 Operations with Polynomials

To add or subtract polynomials, remove any brackets then combine like terms.
Like terms have the same variables raised to the same exponents.

Example 1

Simplify.

a) $(2x^3 - 4xy^2 + 5x^2y^2) + (3x^3 + 2x^2y - 6x^2y^2)$

b) $(6y^2 - 5y + 3) - (2y^2 + 4y - 5)$

Solution

a) $(2x^3 - 4xy^2 + 5x^2y^2) + (3x^3 + 2x^2y - 6x^2y^2)$

    $= 2x^3 - 4xy^2 + 5x^2y^2 + 3x^3 + 2x^2y - 6x^2y^2$ Remove the brackets.

    $= 2x^3 + 3x^3 - 4xy^2 + 5x^2y^2 - 6x^2y^2 + 2x^2y$ Group like terms.

    $= 5x^3 - 4xy^2 - x^2y^2 + 2x^2y$ Combine like terms.

b) Remember that to subtract a polynomial, add its opposite.

    $(6y^2 - 5y + 3) - (2y^2 + 4y - 5)$

    $= 6y^2 - 5y + 3 + (-2y^2 - 4y + 5)$ Add the opposite.

    $= 6y^2 - 5y + 3 - 2y^2 - 4y + 5$

    $= 6y^2 - 2y^2 - 5y - 4y + 3 + 5$ Group like terms.

    $= 4y^2 - 9y + 8$ Combine like terms.

Discuss

In *Example 1b*, why could we not simply remove the brackets in one step, as we did in *Example 1a*?

To multiply a polynomial by a monomial, use the distributive law.

    $3x(2x - 7) = 3x(2x) + 3x(-7)$ Each term of the binomial is

                $= 6x^2 - 21x$ multiplied by $3x$.

Remember that multiplication using the distributive law is called *expanding*.

Take Note

The Distributive Law

    $a(x + y + z) = ax + ay + az$

Example 2

Expand.

a) $3(x + 5)$ b) $-7a(2a - 3b^2 + 4ab)$

Solution

a) $3(x + 5) = 3(x) + 3(5)$

           $= 3x + 15$

b) $-7a(2a - 3b^2 + 4ab) = -7a(2a) - 7a(-3b^2) - 7a(4ab)$
$$= -14a^2 + 21ab^2 - 28a^2b$$

Example 3

Expand, then simplify.

a) $3(2a - 7b) + 2(a + 5b)$ **b)** $9m(3m^2 - 4mn) - 5n(m^2 - 6n^2)$

Solution

a) $3(2a - 7b) + 2(a + 5b)$
$= 3(2a) + 3(-7b) + 2(a) + 2(5b)$ Apply the distributive law.
$= 6a - 21b + 2a + 10b$
$= 8a - 11b$ Combine like terms.

b) $9m(3m^2 - 4mn) - 5n(m^2 - 6n^2)$
$= 9m(3m^2) + 9m(-4mn) - 5n(m^2) - 5n(-6n^2)$
$= 27m^3 - 36m^2n - 5m^2n + 30n^3$
$= 27m^3 - 41m^2n + 30n^3$

The distributive law can also be used to multiply polynomials.
$$(a + b)(x + y) = a(x + y) + b(x + y)$$
$$= ax + ay + bx + by$$

Think: $(a + b)(x + y) = ax + ay + bx + by$

Similarly, $(a + b)(x + y + z) = a(x + y + z) + b(x + y + z)$
$$= ax + ay + az + bx + by + bz$$

Think: $(a + b)(x + y + z) = ax + ay + az + bx + by + bz$

Example 4

Expand, then simplify.

a) $(2x + 3)(x - 4)$ **b)** $(x - 5)^2$ **c)** $(a + 2b)^3$

Solution

a) $(2x + 3)(x - 4) = (2x + 3)(x - 4)$
$$= 2x^2 - 8x + 3x - 12$$
$$= 2x^2 - 5x - 12$$

b) $(x - 5)^2 = (x - 5)(x - 5)$

$\qquad = x^2 - 5x - 5x + 25$

$\qquad = x^2 - 10x + 25$

c) $(a + 2b)^3 = (a + 2b)(a + 2b)(a + 2b)$

$\qquad = (a + 2b)[a^2 + 2ab + 2ab + 4b^2]$

$\qquad = (a + 2b)(a^2 + 4ab + 4b^2)$

$\qquad = a^3 + 4a^2b + 4ab^2 + 2a^2b + 8ab^2 + 8b^3$

$\qquad = a^3 + 6a^2b + 12ab^2 + 8b^3$

Discuss

In *Example 4b*, the expression $(x - 5)^2$ is called a *binomial square*. Why do you think it has this name?

Example 5

Expand, then simplify. $\qquad (x - 2)(4x + 3) - (3x - 2)^2$

Solution

Use brackets to emphasize the order of operations; that is, multiply before subtracting.

$\quad (x - 2)(4x + 3) - (3x - 2)^2$

$= 4x^2 + 3x - 8x - 6 - (9x^2 - 6x - 6x + 4)$

$= 4x^2 - 5x - 6 - 9x^2 + 12x - 4$

$= -5x^2 + 7x - 10$

Discuss

In the third line of the solution, why do the signs of the terms change when the brackets are removed?

2.1 Exercises

A

1. Simplify.

a) $(3x + 4) + (2x - 5)$

b) $(7a - 2) + (5a - 3)$

c) $(4b - 6) + (-2b + 5)$

d) $(-y + 2) + (3 - 4y)$

e) $(-10b - 4a) + (8b + 7a)$

f) $(m + 2n) + (3m - 5n)$

2. Simplify.

a) $(3x + 4) - (2x - 5)$

b) $(7a - 2) - (5a - 3)$

c) $(4b - 6) - (-2b + 5)$

d) $(-y + 2) - (3 - 4y)$

e) $(-10b - 4a) - (8b + 7a)$

f) $(m + 2n) - (3m - 5n)$

3. Simplify.

a) $(4m^2 - 6m + 8) + (9m^2 + 3m - 8)$ **b)** $(8a^3 - 3a^2 + 6a) + (-4a^3 + 7a^2 - 3a)$

c) $(2x^2 - 6x + 7y) + (5x^2 + 16x - 12y)$ **d)** $(3x^2 + 4xy + 5y^2) + (2x^2 - 5xy - 4y^2)$

e) $(4m^2 - 6m + 8) - (9m^2 + 3m - 8)$ **f)** $(8a^3 - 3a^2 + 6a) - (-4a^3 + 7a^2 - 3a)$

g) $(2x^2 - 6x + 7y) - (5x^2 + 16x - 12y)$ **h)** $(3x^2 + 4xy + 5y^2) - (2x^2 - 5xy - 4y^2)$

 4. Expand.

a) $4(5m - 2)$ **b)** $6(2p - 3q)$ **c)** $-3(4mn + 2n - 1)$

d) $5(2x + 3y + 4)$ **e)** $7(-p + 8pq^2)$ **f)** $3(mn^2 - 11mn + n^3 - 4)$

5. Expand, then simplify.

a) $7(5m - 3n) - 11m$ **b)** $(3x + 2)(x - 5)$ **c)** $(2x + 11y)^2$

d) $(4m - 8n)(-11m + n)$ **e)** $(6x - 5)(2x + 1)$ **f)** $(3x - 7y)^2$

6. Expand.

a) $2(5x^2 - 10)$ **b)** $4(3a - 5)$ **c)** $-3(7k^2 - 8k)$

d) $2(2b^2 - 5b + 9)$ **e)** $-9(-8m^2 + 7m - 5)$ **f)** $11(4p^2 - 5p + 6)$

g) $12x(7x - 3)$ **h)** $4a(-5a + 8)$ **i)** $7p(2p - 3q)$

j) $-10n^2(4 - 9n)$ **k)** $6m^3(4mn - 5)$ **l)** $-7x^2(2x + 3y)$

 7. Expand and simplify.

a) $(x + 4)(x + 3)$ **b)** $(2a - 4)(a + 2)$ **c)** $(3 - 3b)(2 + b)$

d) $(t - 1)(t - 9)$ **e)** $(x + 3)(2x - 5)$ **f)** $(4 + k)(6 - k)$

g) $(y + 7)(4y - 5)$ **h)** $(k - 8)(k - 3)$ **i)** $(m + 6)(m - 5)$

8. Knowledge/Understanding

a) Expand each binomial square, then simplify.

   i) $(k + 2)^2$ **ii)** $(3m + 3)^2$ **iii)** $(a - 6)^2$

   iv) $(2b + 7)^2$ **v)** $(y - 1)^2$ **vi)** $(z + 6)^2$

   vii) $(8 - 4x)^2$ **viii)** $(a - 3b)^2$ **ix)** $(-4m - 3n)^2$

b) Look for a pattern in part a that you can use to write the square of a binomial in one line. Explain the pattern.

9. The sum of two polynomials is $15a + 4$. One polynomial is $3a - 6$. What is the other polynomial? Write to explain how you found it.

10. Write each polynomial as the sum of two polynomials.

a) $8a + 10$ **b)** $-6b + 15$ **c)** $-4m - 11n$ **d)** $16 - 17x$

11. Write each polynomial in exercise 10 as the difference of two polynomials.

12. The sum of two polynomials is $4x^2 - 7x + 3$. One polynomial is $-5x^2 - 8x + 5$. What is the other polynomial? Write to explain how you found it.

13. Here is a multiplication in arithmetic and the corresponding multiplication in algebra:

$$\begin{array}{r} 47 \\ \times\ 19 \\ \hline \end{array} \qquad\qquad \begin{array}{r} 4x + 7 \\ \times\ x + 9 \\ \hline \end{array}$$

a) Compare the two multiplications. In what ways are they similar? In what ways are they different?

b) Complete the two multiplications. In what ways are the steps the same? In what ways are the steps different?

c) How many individual multiplications do you do when you multiply two 2-digit numbers? How many do you do when you multiply two binomials?

✓ **14.** Expand the products in each list. Write to describe any patterns you see.

a) $(x + 2)(x + 3)$ **b)** $(x + 1)(x + 4)$ **c)** $(x + 6)(x + 3)$
$(x + 2)(x - 3)$ $(x + 1)(x - 4)$ $(x + 6)(x - 3)$
$(x - 2)(x + 3)$ $(x - 1)(x + 4)$ $(x - 6)(x + 3)$
$(x - 2)(x - 3)$ $(x - 1)(x - 4)$ $(x - 6)(x - 3)$

✓ **15.** Simplify.

a) $(5x^2 - 4y^2) + (y^2 - 4x^2) - (6x^2 + 3)$

b) $(2m^2 - 4n^2) - (2n^2 - 5m^2) + (3n^2 + 6m^2)$

c) $(3 + 9a^2 - 2a^3) + (3a^3 - 4a^2 - 9) - (13 - 8a^3 + 3a^2)$

d) $(5x^2 - 8x + 4) - (3x^2 - x + 10) - (9x^2 + 5x - 12)$

e) $(4x^2 - 2x^2y + y^2x - 2y) + (3xy^2 - y - 6x^2 + 4yx^2)$

f) $(5p^3q^2 + 8q^2p^2 - 4p) + (3q - 7p^2q^2 - 7q^2p^3)$

g) $(2xy + 4yx + 6x^2y - 8xy^2) - (xy + 5yx^2)$

h) $(-a^2b^2 - b^2) - (b^2a + a^2b) - (b^2 - 2b^2a^2 - b^2a)$

16. The sum of three polynomials is $-5x^2 - 8x + 5$. One polynomial is $4x^2 - 7x + 3$. What could the other two polynomials be? Write to explain how you found them.

✓ **17. Communication** A person thinks that $2x + 3y = 5xy$. Write to explain why this is not correct.

18. Expand, then simplify.

a) $2(x + 5) + 8$ **b)** $-64(2a + 7) + 21a$

c) $5(3y - 7) - 9y$ **d)** $3(7m - 5) - 13$

e) $-7(2p^2 + 9p) + 4p^2$ **f)** $2(5x - 8y) - 33x$

g) $2(x + 3) + 3(x - 7)$

h) $5(x - 9) - 2(x + 6)$

i) $8(3a + 10b - 5c) - 4(2a - 2b + 11c)$

j) $2(4m - 6n + 9) - 3(-4m + 5n - 6)$

19. Determine each product.

a) $(x + 2y)(4x + 9y)$

b) $(3a - 5b)^2$

c) $(6x - y)(5x + 4y)$

d) $(7x + 3y)(2x - 9y)$

e) $(4m - 3n)(6m - n)$

f) $(9x - 4y)(8x - 5y)$

✓ **20.** Expand, then simplify.

a) $4x^2(2x + y) + 3x^2(3x - 8y)$

b) $4a^3(3a - 2b) - 5a^3(7a + 9b)$

c) $p^2(3p - 2q) - 7p^2(p - 6q)$

d) $5a^3(-2a + 6b - 3) - 7a^3(a - 2b + 6)$

e) $-4m^2n(8mn + 2mn^2 - 3n^2)$

f) $6x(2x - 3y) - 5y(5x + y - 6) + 4y^2$

g) $3b^2(2b^2 - 5bc) - 7c(2b - c) + 4bc^2$

h) $2x(3x^2 - 6y^2) - 5xy - 7y(9x^2 + 2y^2)$

21. Expand each product of polynomials.

a) $(2x - 7)(3x^2 + 4x - 5)$

b) $(2n^2 - 5)(3n^2 - 9n + 14)$

c) $(a - 4)(3a^2 - 8a + 7)$

d) $(2p + 3)(13p^2 - 5p + 1)$

e) $(2m + 9)(3m^2 - 5m + 7)$

f) $(10y - z)(20y^2 - y - 13)$

22. Expand.

a) $(x + 1)^3$

b) $(x + y)^3$

c) $(2x + y)^3$

d) $(2x + 3)^3$

e) $(3x - 2y)^3$

23. Expand, then simplify.

a) $(x - 1)(x + 2) - (x - 3)^2$

b) $(2x - 1)^2 - (3x + 1)(2x + 5)$

c) $5(a - 2)(a + 3) + (a - 1)^2$

d) $(2a + 3)^2 + 3(a - 1)(3a + 2)$

✓ **24.** Expand, then simplify.

a) $(3x + 4)(x - 5)(2x + 8)$

b) $(b - 7)(b + 8)(3b - 4)$

c) $(2x - 5)(3x + 4)^2$

d) $(5a - 3)^2(2a - 7)$

e) $(5m - 2)^2(3m + 2)$

f) $(2k - 3)(2k + 3)^2$

✓ **25. Thinking/Inquiry/Problem Solving**

a) Expand the products in each list.

i) $(x + 3)(x + 1)$
$(x + 3)(x + 2)$
$(x + 3)(x + 3)$

ii) $(x + 1)(x - 1)$
$(x + 2)(x - 1)$
$(x + 3)(x - 1)$

iii) $(x + 5)(x - 5)$
$(x + 5)(x - 4)$
$(x + 5)(x - 3)$

b) Write to describe any patterns you found in part a.

c) Predict the next three products for each list in part a.

d) Suppose you extended the lists in part a upward. Predict the preceding three products in each list.

Application Use the following information to complete exercises 26 to 29.

A packaging company makes boxes with no tops. One style of box is made from cardboard 20 cm long and 10 cm wide. Equal squares are cut from the corners and the sides are folded up.

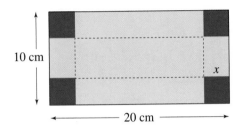

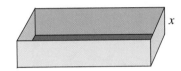

26. Let x centimetres represent the side length of each square cut out. Write a polynomial to represent the surface area of the box.

27. **a)** What values of x are possible in the polynomial in exercise 26? Describe how the size and the shape of the box change as x varies.

    b) Do you think all the boxes would have the same surface area? Describe how the surface area changes as x varies.

28. Complete a table like this for at least three different values of x.

Side length of square cut out (cm)	Total surface area (cm²)

29. Compare your results from exercise 28 with those of other students.

    a) Are any of the areas close to 150 cm²? Explain.

    b) What value of x is needed to make a box with a surface area of 150 cm²?

30. Determine each product. Investigate patterns in these products. Write to describe each pattern. Predict the next three lines in each list.

    a) $(x + 1)(x + 1)$
    $(x + 1)(x^2 + x + 1)$
    $(x + 1)(x^3 + x^2 + x + 1)$

    b) $(x + 1)(x - 1)$
    $(x + 1)(x^2 - x + 1)$
    $(x + 1)(x^3 - x^2 + x - 1)$

C

31. Determine each product. Investigate patterns in these products. Write to describe each pattern. Predict the next three lines in each list.

    a) $(x + 1)^2$
    $(x + 1)^3$
    $(x + 1)^4$

    b) $(x - 1)^2$
    $(x - 1)^3$
    $(x - 1)^4$

    c) $(x + 1)(x - 1)$
    $(x + 1)^2(x - 1)^2$
    $(x + 1)^3(x - 1)^3$

2.2 Evaluating Rational Expressions

Remember that a rational number can be written as a fraction in which the numerator and denominator are integers, and the denominator is not 0.

Take Note

Rational Number

A rational number can be written in the form $\frac{m}{n}$, where m and n are integers, and $n \neq 0$.

The numbers $\frac{2}{5}$, $7\frac{1}{3}$, 6, 2.83, and -3.45 are examples of rational numbers.

Discuss
How can each rational number be written in the form $\frac{m}{n}$?

A rational expression is a fraction in which the numerator and denominator are polynomials.

Discuss
Why is $a^3 - 8$ a rational expression?

These are rational expressions.

$$\frac{3x + 5}{2x + 7} \qquad \frac{m^2 - 4m + 3}{3mn} \qquad a^3 - 8$$

Take Note

Rational Expression

A rational expression can be written in the form $\frac{p}{q}$, where p and q are polynomials, and $q \neq 0$.

A rational expression indicates division. Thus, a rational expression is not defined when its denominator is 0.

To evaluate a rational expression, substitute the given number for each variable. A value of a variable that makes the denominator 0 is called a *non-permissible* value.

Example 1

Evaluate each rational expression, if possible, for $x = 2$ and $y = -1$.

a) $\frac{2x - 3y}{x}$
b) $\frac{x - 2}{y - 5}$
c) $\frac{5x}{y + 1}$

Solution

Substitute $x = 2$ and $y = -1$ in each rational expression.

a) $\dfrac{2x - 3y}{x} = \dfrac{2(2) - 3(-1)}{2}$

$\phantom{\dfrac{2x - 3y}{x}} = \dfrac{4 + 3}{2}$

$\phantom{\dfrac{2x - 3y}{x}} = \dfrac{7}{2}$

b) $\dfrac{x - 2}{y - 5} = \dfrac{(2) - 2}{(-1) - 5}$

$\phantom{\dfrac{x - 2}{y - 5}} = \dfrac{0}{-6}$

$\phantom{\dfrac{x - 2}{y - 5}} = 0$

c) $\dfrac{5x}{y + 1} = \dfrac{5(2)}{(-1) + 1}$

$\phantom{\dfrac{5x}{y + 1}} = \dfrac{10}{0}$

$\dfrac{10}{0}$ is not defined.

The expression $\dfrac{5x}{y + 1}$ cannot be evaluated when $y = -1$.

A rational expression is not defined when its denominator is 0.

In *Example 1c*, the expression $\dfrac{5x}{y + 1}$ is not defined when $y = -1$, since -1 is a value of y for which the denominator is 0. Thus, $y = -1$ is a non-permissible value.

Similarly, the expression in *Example 1a*, $\dfrac{2x - 3y}{x}$, is not defined when $x = 0$, since 0 is the value of x for which the denominator is 0. Thus, $x = 0$ is a non-permissible value.

Also, the expression in *Example 1b*, $\dfrac{x - 2}{y - 5}$, is not defined for $y = 5$, since 5 is the value of y for which the denominator is 0. Thus, $y = 5$ is a non-permissible value.

Example 2

State the non-permissible value(s) for each rational expression.

a) $\dfrac{6x}{5y}$
b) $\dfrac{b^2 - 3b}{b + 2}$
c) $\dfrac{a^3}{a^2 + 1}$
d) $\dfrac{3x}{x^2 + 9x + 18}$

Solution

A non-permissible value is the value of the variable that makes the denominator 0. So, equate each denominator to 0, then solve for the variable.

a) $\dfrac{6x}{5y}$

$5y = 0$

$y = \dfrac{0}{5}$

$\quad = 0$

$y = 0$ is a non-permissible value.

b) $\dfrac{b^2 - 3b}{b + 2}$

$b + 2 = 0$

$\quad b = -2$

$b = -2$ is a non-permissible value.

c) $\dfrac{a^3}{a^2 + 1}$

$a^2 + 1 = 0$

$\quad a^2 = -1$

The square of any real number is never negative. Therefore, $a^2 + 1$ is never equal to 0. The expression $\dfrac{a^3}{a^2 + 1}$ is defined for all real values of a.

d) $\dfrac{3x}{x^2 + 9x + 18}$

$x^2 + 9x + 18 = 0$

Solve by factoring.

$(x + 6)(x + 3) = 0$

Either $\quad x + 6 = 0 \qquad$ or $\qquad x + 3 = 0$

$\qquad\qquad x = -6 \qquad\qquad\qquad x = -3$

Thus, both $x = -6$ and $x = -3$ are non-permissible values.

2.2 Exercises

1. Knowledge/Understanding Evaluate each rational expression for $a = 1$.

a) $\dfrac{7}{-4}$

b) $\dfrac{a}{3}$

c) $\dfrac{2a}{3}$

d) $\dfrac{a + 4}{2a}$

e) $\dfrac{3a - 1}{a^2 + 9}$

f) $\dfrac{a + 1}{3a}$

g) $a^2 - a - 6$

h) $\dfrac{2a - 1}{a^2 - 1}$

i) $\dfrac{1}{a^2 - 9}$

2. Evaluate each rational expression for $x = 4$.

a) $\frac{x}{2}$

b) $\frac{-3}{x}$

c) $\frac{x-4}{3x}$

d) $x^2 + 5x + 1$

e) $\frac{x^3 + 1}{5}$

f) $\frac{-3x - 2}{x + 1}$

g) $\frac{-6}{x^2 - 2}$

h) $\frac{1}{x^2 - 4x}$

i) $\frac{-3x - 2}{3}$

3. Evaluate each rational expression in exercise 2 for $x = -1$.

B

4. In each of exercises 2 and 3, one rational expression is not defined for the given value of x. Explain why each expression is undefined.

5. Explain the difference between a rational number and a rational expression.

6. Evaluate each rational expression for $x = 2$ and $y = -3$.

a) $\frac{x + 2y}{2}$

b) $\frac{3x - 4y}{6}$

c) $\frac{x - y}{x}$

d) $\frac{3x - 2y}{xy}$

e) $\frac{3x + 2y}{x^2}$

f) $\frac{x - 2}{3y + 1}$

g) $\frac{x^3 + 1}{y - 3}$

h) $\frac{x^2 - 9}{x^2 - x - 6}$

i) $\frac{x^2 - 2x + 1}{x^2 - 1}$

7. Communication Suppose you were to evaluate each rational expression in exercise 6 for $x = -2$ and $y = 3$. Which expressions could not be evaluated? Explain.

8. Consider the rational expression $\frac{x + 4}{x - 5}$.

a) Evaluate this expression for $x = -4$.

b) Evaluate this expression for $x = 5$.

c) Explain why $x = -4$ is a permissible value, but $x = 5$ is a non-permissible value.

9. For which value(s) of x is each rational expression not defined?

a) $\frac{3}{x}$

b) $\frac{-2}{x + 1}$

c) $\frac{x + 2}{2x}$

d) $\frac{2x + 1}{5}$

e) $\frac{x^2}{2x - 7}$

f) $\frac{x^2 - 1}{x^3 - 1}$

g) $\frac{3x - 4}{x^2 - 9}$

h) $\frac{x^2 - 9}{x^2 + 1}$

i) $\frac{x^2 + 16}{x^2 + 3}$

10. a) Choose one part of exercise 9. Write to explain how you determined the value(s) of x for which the expression is not defined.

b) Three expressions in exercise 9 did not have any restrictions on the variable. Which rational expressions are they? Explain why all values are permissible.

11. a) Evaluate each rational expression for $x = 0.5$ and $y = -1.7$, to 2 decimal places.

i) $\dfrac{2x - y}{x - 3y}$

ii) $\dfrac{3x + 5y}{2x + y}$

iii) $\dfrac{4x - y}{2x - 7y}$

iv) $\dfrac{x + 7y}{x - 7y}$

v) $\dfrac{-3x + 4y}{6x - 8y}$

vi) $\dfrac{x^2 + 3y}{y^2 - 3x}$

b) Determine the non-permissible values of x and y for each expression in part a.

 12. Thinking/Inquiry/Problem Solving Consider the rational expression $\dfrac{5x + y}{x - 2y}$.

a) Suppose $x = 2$. What value of y would make the expression undefined?

b) Suppose $y = 3$. What value of x would make the expression undefined?

c) Copy and complete the table of values. List five ordered pairs that would make the expression undefined.

d) Plot these ordered pairs on a graph. Write an equation to describe your graph.

e) How is this equation related to the denominator of the rational expression?

x	y
2	
	3

13. Application The focal length of a lens is the distance from the centre of the lens to the point where incoming parallel light rays converge on the other side of the lens.

When an object is placed on one side of the lens, its image appears on the other side. The focal length, f, object distance, p, and image distance, q, are related by the *lens formula*:

$$f = \frac{pq}{p + q}$$

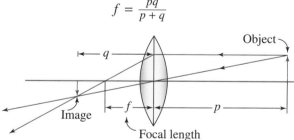

a) An object is placed 120 mm in front of a lens. The image appears 60 mm from the other side of the lens. Calculate the focal length of the lens.

b) An object is placed 60 mm in front of the lens in part a. Calculate the image distance.

c) A camera lens has a focal length of 55 mm. The camera takes a picture of a flower that is 60 cm in front of the lens. Calculate the distance between the lens and the film.

2.3 Simplifying Rational Expressions

To simplify a rational number, factor the numerator and the denominator.
Then, divide the numerator and the denominator by their greatest common factor.

For example, $\dfrac{24}{30} = \dfrac{\overset{1}{\cancel{6}}(4)}{\underset{1}{\cancel{6}}(5)}$

$= \dfrac{4}{5}$

Simplifying a rational expression is similar to simplifying a rational number.
For a rational expression, the non-permissible values of a variable are described
as *restrictions* on the variable.

Note that a simplified rational expression is defined only for the values of the
variables for which the original expression was defined.

Example 1

Simplify each rational expression. State any restrictions on the variables.

a) $\dfrac{12x^2}{15x}$ 　　　　　　**b)** $\dfrac{-6m^2n^3}{24mn^5}$ 　　　　　　**c)** $\dfrac{3x}{2x^2 - 10x}$

Solution

For each expression, first consider the denominator to determine restrictions
on the variables. Then factor the numerator and denominator and divide by
their greatest common factor.

a) $\dfrac{12x^2}{15x}$

Determine the restrictions on x.

Let $15x = 0$

　　$x = 0$

The expression $\dfrac{12x^2}{15x}$ is not defined when $x = 0$.

So, providing $x \neq 0$,

$\dfrac{12x^2}{15x} = \dfrac{\overset{1}{\cancel{(3x)}}(4x)}{\underset{1}{\cancel{(3x)}}(5)}$ 　　　　　Divide by the greatest common factor $3x$.

$= \dfrac{4x}{5}$

Therefore, $\dfrac{12x^2}{15x} = \dfrac{4x}{5}$ when $x \neq 0$

b) $\dfrac{-6m^2n^3}{24mn^5}$

Determine the restrictions on m and n.

Let $24mn^5 = 0$

　　　　$m = 0$ or $n = 0$

The expression $\dfrac{-6m^2n^3}{24mn^5}$ is not defined when $m = 0$ or $n = 0$.

So, providing $m \neq 0$ or $n \neq 0$,

$$\frac{-6m^2n^3}{24mn^5} = \frac{\overset{1}{6mn^3}(-m)}{\underset{1}{6mn^3}(4n^2)}$$ Divide by the greatest common factor $6mn^3$.

$$= \frac{-m}{4n^2}$$

Therefore, $\dfrac{-6m^2n^3}{24mn^5} = \dfrac{-m}{4n^2}$ when $m \neq 0$, $n \neq 0$

c) $\dfrac{3x}{2x^2 - 10x}$

Determine the restrictions on x.

Let $2x^2 - 10x = 0$

$\qquad 2x(x - 5) = 0$

Either $\qquad 2x = 0 \qquad$ or $\qquad x - 5 = 0$

$\qquad\qquad\quad x = 0 \qquad\qquad\qquad x = 5$

The expression $\dfrac{3x}{2x^2 - 10x}$ is not defined when $x = 0$ or $x = 5$.

So, providing $x \neq 0$, $x \neq 5$,

$$\frac{3x}{2x^2 - 10x} = \frac{3\overset{1}{(x)}}{2\underset{1}{(x)}(x - 5)}$$

$$= \frac{3}{2(x - 5)}$$

Therefore, $\dfrac{3x}{2x^2 - 10x} = \dfrac{3}{2(x - 5)}$, when $x \neq 0$, $x \neq 5$

For some rational expressions, the numerator and denominator may factor as the product of two binomials.

Example 2

Simplify each rational expression. State any restrictions on the variables.

a) $\dfrac{x^2 - 5x - 6}{x^2 - 36}$ b) $\dfrac{a^2 - 2a}{a^2 - a - 2}$ c) $\dfrac{2m^2 - 18}{m^2 - 6m + 9}$ d) $\dfrac{x - 7}{14 - 2x}$

Solution

For each expression, consider the denominator to determine the restrictions on the variables. Then factor the numerator and denominator. Divide by their greatest common factor.

a) $\dfrac{x^2 - 5x - 6}{x^2 - 36}$

Determine the restrictions on x.

Let $\qquad x^2 - 36 = 0$

$\qquad (x - 6)(x + 6) = 0$

$\qquad\qquad\qquad x = 6$ or $x = -6$

The expression $\dfrac{x^2 - 5x - 6}{x^2 - 36}$ is not defined when $x = 6$ or $x = -6$.

So, providing $x \neq 6$, $x \neq -6$,

$$\frac{x^2 - 5x - 6}{x^2 - 36} = \frac{\overset{1}{\cancel{(x - 6)}}(x + 1)}{\underset{1}{\cancel{(x - 6)}}(x + 6)} \qquad \text{Divide by the common factor } (x - 6).$$

$$= \frac{x + 1}{x + 6}$$

Therefore, $\dfrac{x^2 - 5x - 6}{x^2 - 36} = \dfrac{x + 1}{x + 6}$ when $x \neq 6$, $x \neq -6$

b) $\dfrac{a^2 - 2a}{a^2 - a - 2}$

Determine the restrictions on a.

Let $\quad a^2 - a - 2 = 0$

$\qquad (a - 2)(a + 1) = 0$

$\qquad\qquad a = 2$ or $a = -1$

The expression $\dfrac{a^2 - 2a}{a^2 - a - 2}$ is not defined when $a = 2$ or $a = -1$.

So, providing $a \neq 2$, $a \neq -1$,

$$\frac{a^2 - 2a}{a^2 - a - 2} = \frac{a\overset{1}{\cancel{(a - 2)}}}{\underset{1}{\cancel{(a - 2)}}(a + 1)}$$

$$= \frac{a}{a + 1}$$

Therefore, $\dfrac{a^2 - 2a}{a^2 - a - 2} = \dfrac{a}{a + 1}$ when $a \neq 2$, $a \neq -1$

c) $\dfrac{2m^2 - 18}{m^2 - 6m + 9}$

Determine the restrictions on m.

Let $\quad m^2 - 6m + 9 = 0$

$\qquad (m - 3)(m - 3) = 0$

$\qquad\qquad m = 3$

The expression $\dfrac{2m^2 - 18}{m^2 - 6m + 9}$ is not defined when $m = 3$.

So, providing $m \neq 3$,

$$\frac{2m^2 - 18}{m^2 - 6m + 9} = \frac{2(m^2 - 9)}{(m - 3)(m - 3)}$$

$$= \frac{2(m + 3)\overset{1}{\cancel{(m - 3)}}}{(m - 3)\underset{1}{\cancel{(m - 3)}}}$$

$$\frac{2m^2 - 18}{m^2 - 6m + 9} = \frac{2(m + 3)}{m - 3}, \text{ or } \frac{2m + 6}{m - 3}$$

Therefore, $\dfrac{2m^2 - 18}{m^2 - 6m + 9} = \dfrac{2(m + 3)}{m - 3}$ when $m \neq 3$

d) $\dfrac{x - 7}{14 - 2x}$

Determine the restrictions on x.

Let $14 - 2x = 0$

$\qquad\quad x = 7$

The expression $\dfrac{x - 7}{14 - 2x}$ is not defined when $x = 7$.

So, providing $x \neq 7$,

$$\frac{x-7}{14-2x} = \frac{x-7}{2(7-x)}$$
$$= \frac{-(7-x)^{1}}{2(7-x)_{1}}$$

$$\frac{x-7}{14-2x} = \frac{-1}{2}$$

Therefore, $\frac{x-7}{14-2x} = -\frac{1}{2}$ when $x \neq 7$

Discuss

Explain why $x - 7$ can be replaced by $-(7 - x)$.

In general, it is assumed that a rational expression is defined for all permissible values of the variables.

2.3 Exercises

A

1. Simplify.

a) $\frac{15x}{3}$

b) $\frac{44x}{-11y}$

c) $\frac{8a^3}{144a^2}$

d) $\frac{6ab}{12ac}$

e) $\frac{50m^2n}{75mn^3}$

f) $\frac{-9x^3y^2}{-y^5}$

g) $\frac{-5x^2yz}{10xyz^2}$

h) $\frac{-12ab^3}{6ab^2}$

2. Simplify.

a) $\frac{2x+2}{2x}$

b) $\frac{6a}{3a-3}$

c) $\frac{2x+6x^2}{4x}$

d) $\frac{4}{-2m-4}$

e) $\frac{4b^2-8b}{8b^2}$

f) $\frac{-9n^2}{-3n-3n^2}$

g) $\frac{-x+2x^2}{3x}$

h) $\frac{-10m^2}{6m+8m^2}$

B

 3. Knowledge/Understanding Simplify each rational expression. State any restrictions on the variables.

a) $\frac{3x+6}{5x+10}$

b) $\frac{x-5}{3x-15}$

c) $\frac{4x^2+6x}{2x}$

d) $\frac{2x^2-10x}{6x-30}$

e) $\frac{4x^2-12x}{x-3}$

f) $\frac{4a+10}{-6a-15}$

g) $\frac{-3m^2+2m}{-2m^2-2m}$

h) $\frac{-12+9n}{4n-3n^2}$

4. Simplify each rational expression where possible. Explain why some expressions are already in simplified form.

a) $\frac{x+1}{x+1}$

b) $\frac{x-1}{x-1}$

c) $\frac{x+1}{1+x}$

d) $\frac{x-1}{1-x}$

e) $\frac{x+1}{x-1}$

f) $\frac{x+1}{1-x}$

5. Simplify.

a) $\dfrac{2a + 2}{a^2 + 3a + 2}$

b) $\dfrac{x^2 - 4x + 3}{x^2 - x}$

c) $\dfrac{3m - 6}{m^2 - 5m + 6}$

d) $\dfrac{-n^2 - 2n}{n^2 - 4}$

e) $\dfrac{2 - 2b}{b^2 + b - 2}$

f) $\dfrac{x^2 - 4}{2 - x}$

g) $\dfrac{15 - 5x}{x^2 - 9}$

h) $\dfrac{x^2 - 6x + 9}{x - 3}$

i) $\dfrac{x + 3}{x^2 + 7x + 12}$

6. Consider the rational expression $\dfrac{2x^2 + 6x}{x^2 + 2x - 3}$.

a) Evaluate this expression for $x = 2$.

b) Determine any restrictions on x. Simplify the expression.

c) Evaluate the new expression in part b for $x = 2$.

d) Compare your answers to parts a and c.

e) How can you check whether you simplified an expression correctly?

7. Thinking/Inquiry/Problem Solving

a) Simplify $\dfrac{x^2 - 1}{x - 1}$.

b) A graphing calculator was used to display the graphs of the functions
$y = \dfrac{x^2 - 1}{x - 1}$ and $y = x + 1$. The screens are shown below. Look at the
screens carefully.

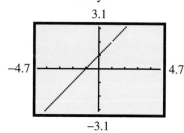
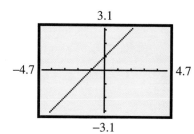

c) What is the same about each screen? What is different?

d) Which screen represents each function? Explain.

e) A student said that $\dfrac{x^2 - 1}{x - 1} = x + 1$ is true for all values of x. Is the student
correct? Explain.

8. Simplify.

a) $\dfrac{5n - 5m}{3m - 3n}$

b) $\dfrac{c - d}{d - c}$

c) $\dfrac{2a - 2b}{3b - 3a}$

d) $\dfrac{3xy - 18y^2}{12y^2 - 2xy}$

e) $\dfrac{10xy - 15x^2y}{6x^2 - 4x}$

f) $\dfrac{60a^2b^2 - 24ab}{16ab - 40a^2b^2}$

9. Simplify each rational expression, if possible.

a) $\dfrac{a^2 + 5a - 14}{a^2 - 6a + 8}$

b) $\dfrac{x - 3}{x^2 + 3x - 18}$

c) $\dfrac{m^2 - 7m + 10}{m - 2}$

d) $\dfrac{r^2 - 9}{r^2 + 6r + 9}$

e) $\dfrac{x + 4}{x^2 - 16}$

f) $\dfrac{x - 3}{x^2 + 9}$

10. **Application** A graphing calculator was used to display the tables of values for two rational expressions in exercise 9. Identify the expression from exercise 9 that was used for each table. Y1 represents the given expression and Y2 represents its simplified form.

a)

X	Y₁	Y₂
0	-5	-5
1	-4	-4
2	ERROR	-3
3	-2	-2
4	-1	-1
5	0	0
6	1	1

X=0

b)

X	Y₁	Y₂
0	-1.75	-1.75
1	-2.667	-2.667
2	ERROR	-4.5
3	-10	-10
4	ERROR	ERROR
5	12	12
6	6.5	6.5

X=0

11. Simplify.

a) $\dfrac{2xy - 12y^2}{18y^2 - 3xy}$

b) $\dfrac{3 - x}{x^2 - 9}$

c) $\dfrac{3x - 3y}{2y - 2x}$

d) $\dfrac{5x^2 - 15x}{5x^2 - 20x + 15}$

e) $\dfrac{3x^2 - 12}{x^2 + 14x + 24}$

f) $\dfrac{x^3 - 7x^2 + 12x}{x^3 - 16x}$

g) $\dfrac{48 - 3a^2}{4a^2 - 44a + 112}$

h) $\dfrac{4x^2 - 100}{6x^2 + 30x}$

i) $\dfrac{2a^2 + 4a - 48}{3a^2 + 3a - 60}$

12. Simplify.

a) $\dfrac{2x^2 - 3x - 2}{2x^2 + 3x + 1}$

b) $\dfrac{3a^2 + 5a - 2}{3a^2 + 2a - 1}$

c) $\dfrac{2m^2 - 5m + 2}{2m^2 + 3m - 2}$

d) $\dfrac{2d^2 - d - 3}{2d^2 - 5d + 3}$

e) $\dfrac{3n^2 - 2n - 1}{2n^2 - 3n + 1}$

f) $\dfrac{3x^2 + 4x - 4}{x^2 + x - 2}$

g) $\dfrac{4b^2 + 13b + 3}{4b^2 + 5b + 1}$

h) $\dfrac{4a^2 + 4a + 1}{4a^2 - 1}$

i) $\dfrac{4y^2 + 2y - 2}{4y^2 + 8y + 6}$

13. Simplify.

a) $\dfrac{7x^2 - 21x}{7x^2 - 28x + 21}$

b) $\dfrac{5x^2 - 20}{x^2 + 14x + 24}$

c) $\dfrac{32 - 2a^2}{4a^2 - 44a + 112}$

d) $\dfrac{3x^2 - 75}{6x^2 + 30x}$

e) $\dfrac{2x^3 - 28x^2 - 102x}{18x - 2x^3}$

f) $\dfrac{3b^2 + 3b - 60}{2b^2 + 4b - 48}$

g) $\dfrac{5g^2 - 5g - 10}{5g^2 - 9g - 2}$

h) $\dfrac{4h^2 - 12h + 8}{4h^2 - 4}$

i) $\dfrac{6x^2 - 8x + 2}{6x^2 - 2x - 4}$

14. **Communication** Three students were discussing how to simplify the rational expression $\dfrac{2x + 4}{x + 2}$.

Liz said: 2x divided by x is 2. Four divided by 2 is 2. Then, 2 + 2 equals 4.

Chantelle said: No, you must factor the numerator as $2(x + 2)$. Since the factor $x + 2$ is in the numerator and denominator, divide by this factor. They both become 1 and we get $\dfrac{2}{1}$, which is 2.

Lindsay said: No, divide 2 into the 2 in the denominator and the 2 in the numerator to get $\dfrac{x + 4}{x + 1}$.

Which student is correct? Explain how you know.

1. Simplify.

   a) $(3x^2 + 5x - 7) + (-2x^2 - 4x + 3)$

   b) $(4m^2 - m + 1) + (2m^2 + 3m - 4)$

   c) $(-10n^2 - 3n + 4) - (5n^2 + 5n + 7)$

   d) $(8b^2 + 4b + 10) - (10b^2 - 10b - 9)$

2. Expand, then simplify.

   a) $5x(2x - 7) + 4x(x + 9)$ **b)** $(3y + 4)(6y - 5)$

3. Expand, then simplify.

   a) $(5x + 2)^2$ **b)** $(6m - 7n)^2$

4. Expand, then simplify.

   a) $(x + 1)(x - 5) - (2x + 3)^2$ **b)** $(5y - 2)^3$

5. For what values of the variable(s) is each rational expression not defined?

   a) $\dfrac{7x}{2xy}$ **b)** $\dfrac{4}{x^2 + 4}$ **c)** $\dfrac{4}{x^2 - 4}$

6. Evaluate each rational expression for $x = 2$ and $y = -4$.

   a) $\dfrac{x + 2y}{3 - x}$ **b)** $\dfrac{x}{y + 5}$ **c)** $\dfrac{2x}{y - 4}$

7. Simplify.

   a) $\dfrac{5x^2y}{20xy^4}$ **b)** $\dfrac{4a^2 - 36}{5a - 15}$ **c)** $\dfrac{3a^3 - 4a^2b^2}{2a^3b^2 + a^2b^3}$

8. State any restrictions on the variable, then simplify.

   a) $\dfrac{x^2 - x - 6}{x^2 + 3x + 2}$ **b)** $\dfrac{x^2 - 16}{x^2 + 2x - 24}$ **c)** $\dfrac{x^2 - 4}{x^2 - 5x + 4}$

9. Simplify.

   a) $\dfrac{8a^2 + 2a - 15}{4a^2 - 4a - 15}$ **b)** $\dfrac{2x^2 + 3x + 1}{3x^2 + 2x - 1}$ **c)** $\dfrac{9a^3 - 16a^5}{6ab^3 - 8a^2b^3}$

10. State any restrictions on the variables, then simplify.

   a) $\dfrac{2a^2 + 4a + 2}{2a^2 - 2}$ **b)** $\dfrac{3b^2 - 3}{3b^2 + 6b + 3}$ **c)** $\dfrac{6c^2 - 12c + 6}{6c^2 - 6}$

Remember that to multiply rational numbers you multiply the numerators, multiply the denominators, and simplify. If possible, simplify before multiplying.

For example, $\dfrac{10}{21} \times \dfrac{7}{2} = \dfrac{\overset{5}{\cancel{10}}}{\underset{3}{\cancel{21}}} \times \dfrac{\overset{1}{\cancel{7}}}{\underset{1}{\cancel{2}}}$

$$= \dfrac{5}{3}$$

Rational expressions are multiplied the same way as rational numbers are multiplied. If possible, simplify by dividing numerator and denominator by common factors. Then multiply the numerators and multiply the denominators.

Example 1

Simplify.

a) $\dfrac{x^3}{6} \times \dfrac{3y}{2x}$ **b)** $6 \times \dfrac{5a}{2b^2}$ **c)** $\dfrac{3a^2(b+2)}{5(a-3)} \times \dfrac{10(a-3)}{ab}$

Solution

a) $\dfrac{x^3}{6} \times \dfrac{3y}{2x} = \dfrac{x^3}{\underset{2}{\cancel{6}}} \times \dfrac{\overset{1}{\cancel{3y}}}{2x}$ Divide numerator and denominator by 2.

$\qquad = \dfrac{x^3y}{4x}$ Divide numerator and denominator by x.

$\qquad = \dfrac{x^2y}{4}$

b) $6 \times \dfrac{5a}{2b^2} = \dfrac{\overset{3}{\cancel{6}}}{1} \times \dfrac{5a}{\underset{1}{\cancel{2b^2}}}$ Rewrite 6 as $\dfrac{6}{1}$. Divide numerator and denominator by 2.

$\qquad = \dfrac{15a}{b^2}$

c) $\dfrac{3a^2(b+2)}{5(a-3)} \times \dfrac{10(a-3)}{ab} = \dfrac{3a^2(b+2)}{\underset{1}{\cancel{5(a-3)}}} \times \dfrac{\overset{2}{\cancel{10(a-3)}}^{1}}{ab}$ Divide numerator and denominator by $5a(a-3)$.

$\qquad = \dfrac{6a(b+2)}{b}$

Remember that to divide two rational numbers, you multiply the dividend by the reciprocal of the divisor.

For example, $\dfrac{12}{5} \div \dfrac{9}{10} = \dfrac{\overset{4}{\cancel{12}}}{\underset{1}{\cancel{5}}} \times \dfrac{\overset{2}{\cancel{10}}}{\underset{3}{\cancel{9}}}$

$$= \dfrac{8}{3}$$

Rational expressions are divided the same way as rational numbers are divided. If possible, simplify by dividing numerator and denominator by common factors first.

Example 2

Simplify.

a) $\dfrac{2x^2}{-3} \div \dfrac{8x^3}{15}$

b) $\dfrac{6(a-1)}{a^2} \div \dfrac{3(a-1)}{a(a+2)}$

Solution

To divide, multiply the dividend by the reciprocal of the divisor then simplify.

a) $\dfrac{2x^2}{-3} \div \dfrac{8x^3}{15} = \dfrac{2x^2}{-3} \times \dfrac{15}{8x^3}$ Multiply by the reciprocal of the divisor.

$= \dfrac{\overset{1}{2x^2}}{\underset{-1}{-3}} \times \dfrac{\overset{5}{15}}{\underset{4}{8x^3}}$ Divide numerators and denominators by common factors.

$= \dfrac{5x^2}{-4x^3}$ Divide numerator and denominator by x^2.

$= \dfrac{-5}{4x}$

b) $\dfrac{6(a-1)}{a^2} \div \dfrac{3(a-1)}{a(a+2)} = \dfrac{6(a-1)}{a^2} \times \dfrac{a(a+2)}{3(a-1)}$ Multiply by the reciprocal of the divisor.

$= \dfrac{\overset{2}{6(a-1)}^{1}}{a^2} \times \dfrac{a(a+2)}{\underset{1}{3(a-1)}_{1}}$ Divide by common factors.

$= \dfrac{2a(a+2)}{a^2}$ Divide numerator and denominator by a.

$= \dfrac{2(a+2)}{a}$

In *Example 2a*, the negative rational expression may be written in any one of three equivalent forms.

$$\dfrac{-5}{4x} = -\dfrac{5}{4x} = \dfrac{5}{-4x}$$

It is usual to place the negative sign either with the numerator, or in front of the rational expression.

Factoring a polynomial is often an important step when simplifying a rational expression.

Example 3

Simplify.

a) $\dfrac{x^2 - x - 6}{x^2 + 8x + 15} \times \dfrac{x + 5}{x - 3}$

b) $\dfrac{6a^2 - 15a}{a^2 - a - 12} \div \dfrac{4a^2 - 25}{3a + 9}$

Solution

a) Factor the numerator. Factor the denominator. Divide the numerator and denominator by their common factors.

$$\dfrac{x^2 - x - 6}{x^2 + 8x + 15} \times \dfrac{x + 5}{x - 3} = \dfrac{\overset{1}{\cancel{(x - 3)}}(x + 2)}{(x + 3)\cancel{(x + 5)}_1} \times \dfrac{\cancel{(x + 5)}^1}{\cancel{(x - 3)}_1}$$

$$= \dfrac{x + 2}{x + 3}$$

b) To divide, multiply by the reciprocal of the divisor, then proceed as in part a.

$$\dfrac{6a^2 - 15a}{a^2 - a - 12} \div \dfrac{4a^2 - 25}{3a + 9} = \dfrac{6a^2 - 15a}{a^2 - a - 12} \times \dfrac{3a + 9}{4a^2 - 25}$$

$$= \dfrac{3a\cancel{(2a - 5)}^1}{(a - 4)\cancel{(a + 3)}_1} \times \dfrac{3\cancel{(a + 3)}^1}{{}_1\cancel{(2a - 5)}(2a + 5)}$$

$$= \dfrac{9a}{(a - 4)(2a + 5)}$$

Discuss

What are the restrictions on the variable in each part of *Example 3*?

2.4 Exercises

A

1. Simplify.

a) $\dfrac{3}{5} \times \dfrac{10a}{7}$

b) $\dfrac{x^2}{9} \times \dfrac{3}{x}$

c) $\dfrac{-2m}{15} \times \dfrac{3m}{4}$

d) $\dfrac{3b^2}{20} \times \dfrac{10}{7b}$

e) $\dfrac{-12t}{35} \times \dfrac{14}{3t}$

f) $\dfrac{4r^2}{9} \times \dfrac{3}{8r}$

g) $\dfrac{10x^3}{5} \times \dfrac{25}{2x}$

h) $5 \times \dfrac{a}{10b}$

2. Simplify.

a) $\dfrac{9b^2}{14} \div \dfrac{3b}{7}$

b) $\dfrac{16}{12a} \div \dfrac{8}{3a^2}$

c) $\dfrac{-6m}{5} \div \dfrac{2m}{25}$

d) $\dfrac{12a^3}{7} \div \dfrac{2a^2}{7b}$

e) $\dfrac{-20t}{3} \div \dfrac{4t^3}{12}$

f) $\dfrac{14r^2}{9} \div \dfrac{49}{3r}$

g) $\dfrac{6m}{49n^2} \div \dfrac{3}{7n}$

h) $2 \div \dfrac{3}{x}$

i) $\dfrac{2}{3} \div a$

3. Simplify.

a) $\dfrac{12x^2y}{25xy} \times \dfrac{10y}{3x}$

b) $\dfrac{4x}{5xy} \times \dfrac{15y}{16x^2}$

c) $\dfrac{30a^2b}{2ab} \times \dfrac{15ab^2}{10ab}$

d) $\dfrac{-15m^2n^5}{16mn^3} \div \dfrac{-25n^2}{2m^4}$

e) $\dfrac{3m^2n^3}{6mn^3} \div \dfrac{4m^2n}{8mn}$

f) $\dfrac{3ab}{52} \div \dfrac{9b^2}{13c}$

4. Knowledge/Understanding

a) Simplify.

i) $\dfrac{21}{8m} \times \dfrac{4}{7n}$

ii) $\dfrac{9x^2}{8y} \times \dfrac{24y^2}{3x}$

iii) $\dfrac{-16x^2}{9x} \times \dfrac{12x^3}{4x^2}$

iv) $\dfrac{14}{8b^3} \times \dfrac{-2b}{7}$

v) $\dfrac{5m^2}{12n} \div \dfrac{25m}{6}$

vi) $\dfrac{3ab}{52} \div \dfrac{9b^2}{13c}$

vii) $\dfrac{35}{16a} \div \dfrac{28}{4a^2}$

viii) $\dfrac{6x^3}{5x^2y} \div \dfrac{3}{10y^2}$

ix) $\dfrac{21u}{32} \div \dfrac{7u^3}{8p}$

b) Choose one product or quotient from part a. Write to explain how you would identify the restrictions on the variable(s).

B

5. Simplify.

a) $\dfrac{(3x)^2}{5xy} \times \dfrac{15y}{27x}$

b) $\dfrac{3a^2b^3}{2ab} \times \dfrac{(5ab)^2}{10ab}$

c) $\dfrac{15mn^2}{12mn} \times \dfrac{(2mn)^2}{10mn^3}$

d) $\dfrac{3x}{5y} \times \dfrac{4z}{9x} \times \dfrac{10y}{3x}$

e) $\dfrac{6a}{7b^2} \times \dfrac{14c^2}{9a^3} \div \dfrac{2c}{3a}$

f) $\dfrac{(3m)^2}{5n} \times \dfrac{8n}{6} \div \dfrac{18m}{10m^3}$

6. Thinking/Inquiry/Problem Solving
Each rational expression below is the product of two other rational expressions. For each, write what the two rational expressions might have been. Explain how you obtained your answers.

a) $\dfrac{1}{x}$

b) $\dfrac{x}{y}$

c) $\dfrac{3m}{-2n}$

d) $\dfrac{a}{2}$

e) $3b$

f) $\dfrac{-1}{abc}$

7. Communication
Assume each rational expression in exercise 6 is the quotient of two other rational expressions. For each, write what the other two rational expressions might have been. Explain how you obtained your answers.

8.
a) Simplify. Identify any restrictions on the variables.

i) $\dfrac{6x}{x+1} \times \dfrac{5(x+1)}{3x}$

ii) $\dfrac{2(a-3)}{15a} \times \dfrac{5a}{6(a-3)}$

iii) $\dfrac{9(x-2)}{x+1} \div \dfrac{3}{x+1}$

iv) $\dfrac{6s^2}{3(s-4)} \times \dfrac{12(s-4)}{2s}$

v) $\dfrac{4(t-3)}{7(t-2)} \div \dfrac{2}{14(2-t)}$

vi) $\dfrac{2(3-x)}{5x} \div \dfrac{6(x-3)}{10(x+1)}$

b) Choose one product and one quotient from part a. Write to explain how you identified the restrictions on the variable in the product. How did this process compare with the identification of restrictions on the variable in the quotient?

9. Simplify.

a) $\dfrac{x+y}{5x} \times \dfrac{10x}{3(x+y)}$

b) $\dfrac{5a^2b}{3(a-b)} \times \dfrac{9(a-b)}{25ab^3}$

c) $\dfrac{2y^3}{y^2-9} \times \dfrac{4y-12}{10y^2}$

d) $\dfrac{18a}{9a^2-12a} \div \dfrac{2ab}{9a^2-16}$

e) $\dfrac{14m-8}{10mn^2} \div \dfrac{7m-4}{25m^2n}$

f) $\dfrac{2x^2-18y^2}{4x^2-10} \div \dfrac{x-3y}{6x^2-15}$

g) $\dfrac{(2x)^3}{6(x-1)} \times \dfrac{x^2-1}{(3x)^2}$

h) $\dfrac{(5ab^3)^2}{(a+b)^3} \div \dfrac{(2a^2b)^3}{(a+b)^2}$

i) $\dfrac{(6mn)^2}{(n-m)^2} \times \dfrac{(n-m)^3}{(2mn)^3}$

10. Simplify.

a) $\dfrac{2n^2 + 6n}{3n - 6} \times \dfrac{3n^2 - 6n}{2n + 6}$

b) $\dfrac{4x^2 + 4x}{5x^2 + 10x} \times \dfrac{3x^2 + 6x}{6x^2 - 6x}$

c) $\dfrac{a^2 - a - 2}{a^2 + a - 6} \times \dfrac{a^2 + 5a + 6}{a^2 + a}$

d) $\dfrac{b^2 - b}{b^2 - 4b + 3} \times \dfrac{b^2 - 5b + 6}{b^2 + 4b}$

e) $\dfrac{c^2 - 1}{c^2 - 2c + 1} \times \dfrac{c^2 + 3c + 2}{c^2 + 2c + 1}$

f) $\dfrac{x^2 + 2x - 3}{x^2 + 4x + 3} \times \dfrac{x^2 - 4x + 4}{x^2 - 3x + 2}$

11. Simplify.

a) $\dfrac{3x^2 - 3x}{2x^2 + 2x} \div \dfrac{9x - 9}{4x + 8}$

b) $\dfrac{5e^2 - 10}{10e^2 + 10e} \div \dfrac{2e - 4}{3e + 3}$

c) $\dfrac{a^2 - 1}{a^2 + a - 2} \div \dfrac{a^2 - 2a - 3}{a^2 + 5a + 6}$

d) $\dfrac{n^2 + 3n - 10}{n^2 + 5n - 6} \div \dfrac{n^2 + 6n + 5}{n^2 + 7n + 6}$

e) $\dfrac{m^2 + m - 6}{m^2 + 5n + 4} \div \dfrac{m^2 + 4m + 3}{m^2 + 6m + 8}$

f) $\dfrac{c^2 - 4c + 4}{c^2 - 4} \div \dfrac{c^2 - 5c + 6}{c^2 + 5c + 6}$

✓ **12.** Simplify.

a) $\dfrac{9 - x^2}{x^2 - x - 20} \div \dfrac{x - 3}{x + 4}$

b) $\dfrac{a^2 - 25}{3 + a} \times \dfrac{a^2 + 5a + 6}{5 - a}$

c) $\dfrac{a^2 - 2a}{a^2 - a - 2} \times \dfrac{a^2 - 1}{a^2 - a}$

d) $\dfrac{a^2 + 2a - 8}{a^2 - 2a + 1} \div \dfrac{a^2 + 8a + 16}{a^2 + 3a - 4}$

e) $\dfrac{x^2 - 7x + 12}{x^2 + 7x + 12} \div \dfrac{x^2 - x - 12}{x^2 + x - 12}$

f) $\dfrac{m^2 - 8m + 7}{m^2 + 6m - 7} \times \dfrac{m^2 + 3m + 2}{m^2 - 5m - 14}$

13. Each rational expression below is the product of two other rational expressions. For each, write what the other two rational expressions might have been.

a) $\dfrac{1}{x + 1}$

b) $\dfrac{x - 2}{x + 2}$

c) $\dfrac{a}{a + b}$

d) $\dfrac{(x + y)^2}{x}$

14. Application Assume each rational expression in exercise 13 is the quotient of two other rational expressions. For each, write what the other two rational expressions might have been.

✓ **15.** Simplify.

a) $\dfrac{4x^2 - 10}{x - 3y} \times \dfrac{9y^2 - x^2}{6x^2 - 15}$

b) $\dfrac{a^2 - b^2}{4a + 2b} \times \dfrac{6a + 3b}{b - a}$

c) $\dfrac{6mn^2}{4m^2 - 9} \times \dfrac{2m - 3}{-18m^2n}$

d) $\dfrac{8mn}{4n^2 - m^2} \div \dfrac{4n^2}{3m - 6n}$

e) $\dfrac{9a^2 - 16b^2}{a + 2b} \div \dfrac{12ab - 9a^2}{6a + 12b}$

f) $\dfrac{3x^2 - 6xy}{4x + 20y} \div \dfrac{18xy - 9x^2}{3xy + 15y^2}$

C

16. Simplify.

a) $\dfrac{x + 3y}{x - 2y} \times \dfrac{x^2 - 4y^2}{x^2 - 9y^2} \div \dfrac{x + 2y}{x - 3y}$

b) $\dfrac{x + 3y}{x - 2y} \times \dfrac{4y^2 - x^2}{x^2 - 9y^2} \div \dfrac{x + 2y}{x - 3y}$

c) $\dfrac{(2a + 5b)^2}{3a - 4b} \times \dfrac{9a^2 - 16b^2}{4a^2 - 25b^2} \div \dfrac{3a + 4b}{2a - 5b}$

d) $\dfrac{(2a + 5b)^2}{3a - 4b} \times \dfrac{16b^2 - 9a^2}{4a^2 - 25b^2} \div \dfrac{3a + 4b}{2a - 5b}$

2.5 Adding and Subtracting Rational Expressions: Part I

Remember the steps to add two rational numbers:

- Determine a common denominator.
- Express each fraction as an equivalent fraction with this common denominator.
- Add the numerators. Write the sum over the common denominator.
- Simplify if possible.

For example, $\dfrac{-7}{6} + \dfrac{5}{9} = \dfrac{-7}{6} \times \dfrac{3}{3} + \dfrac{5}{9} \times \dfrac{2}{2}$ The lowest common denominator is 18.

$$= \dfrac{-21}{18} + \dfrac{10}{18}$$

$$= \dfrac{-21 + 10}{18}$$

$$= \dfrac{-11}{18}$$

Rational expressions are added and subtracted the same way as rational numbers are added and subtracted.

Example 1

Add or subtract, as indicated.

a) $\dfrac{5}{2a} + \dfrac{1}{3a}$ **b)** $\dfrac{3}{2m} + \dfrac{1}{5}$ **c)** $\dfrac{5}{8x} - \dfrac{7}{12x^2}$

Solution

a) $\dfrac{5}{2a} + \dfrac{1}{3a} = \dfrac{5}{2a} \times \dfrac{3}{3} + \dfrac{1}{3a} \times \dfrac{2}{2}$ The lowest common denominator is $6a$.

$$= \dfrac{15}{6a} + \dfrac{2}{6a}$$

$$= \dfrac{15 + 2}{6a}$$

$$= \dfrac{17}{6a}$$

b) $\dfrac{3}{2m} + \dfrac{1}{5} = \dfrac{3}{2m} \times \dfrac{5}{5} + \dfrac{1}{5} \times \dfrac{2m}{2m}$ The lowest common denominator is $10m$.

$$= \dfrac{15}{10m} + \dfrac{2m}{10m}$$

$$= \dfrac{15 + 2m}{10m}$$

Discuss

When we write an equivalent fraction, why must we multiply both the numerator and denominator by the same factor?

c) $\dfrac{5}{8x} - \dfrac{7}{12x^2} = \dfrac{5}{8x} \times \dfrac{3x}{3x} - \dfrac{7}{12x^2} \times \dfrac{2}{2}$ The lowest common denominator is $24x^2$.

$$= \dfrac{15x}{24x^2} - \dfrac{14}{24x^2}$$

$$= \dfrac{15x - 14}{24x^2}$$

Discuss

Suppose the common denominator $48x^2$ was used in *Example 1c*. Would you get the same result? Explain.

Example 2

Add or subtract, as indicated.

a) $-\dfrac{7x}{y} - \dfrac{3x}{5y^2}$
b) $\dfrac{x+2}{3x} - 1$
c) $m + \dfrac{2m}{n} - \dfrac{3+n}{m}$

Solution

a) $-\dfrac{7x}{y} - \dfrac{3x}{5y^2} = \dfrac{-7x}{y} \times \dfrac{5y}{5y} - \dfrac{3x}{5y^2}$ The lowest common denominator is $5y^2$.

$\qquad\qquad\qquad = \dfrac{-35xy}{5y^2} - \dfrac{3x}{5y^2}$

$\qquad\qquad\qquad = \dfrac{-35xy - 3x}{5y^2}$

b) $\dfrac{x+2}{3x} - 1 = \dfrac{x+2}{3x} - \dfrac{1}{1}$ Writing -1 as $-\dfrac{1}{1}$

$\qquad\qquad = \dfrac{x+2}{3x} - \dfrac{1}{1} \times \dfrac{3x}{3x}$ The lowest common denominator is $3x$.

$\qquad\qquad = \dfrac{x+2}{3x} - \dfrac{3x}{3x}$

$\qquad\qquad = \dfrac{x+2-3x}{3x}$

$\qquad\qquad = \dfrac{2-2x}{3x}$

c) $m + \dfrac{2m}{n} - \dfrac{3+n}{m} = \dfrac{m}{1} + \dfrac{2m}{n} - \dfrac{3+n}{m}$ Writing m as $\dfrac{m}{1}$

$\qquad\qquad\qquad = \dfrac{m}{1} \times \dfrac{mn}{mn} + \dfrac{2m}{n} \times \dfrac{m}{m} - \dfrac{3+n}{m} \times \dfrac{n}{n}$ The lowest common denominator is mn.

$\qquad\qquad\qquad = \dfrac{m^2n}{mn} + \dfrac{2m^2}{mn} - \dfrac{n(3+n)}{mn}$

$\qquad\qquad\qquad = \dfrac{m^2n + 2m^2 - n(3+n)}{mn}$

$\qquad\qquad\qquad = \dfrac{m^2n + 2m^2 - 3n - n^2}{mn}$

2.5 Exercises

A

1. Write each rational expression with a denominator of $36xy$.

a) $\dfrac{2}{9x}$
b) $\dfrac{5x}{12y}$
c) $\dfrac{-1x}{2}$
d) $\dfrac{11xy}{6}$
e) $\dfrac{-7y}{18xy}$

f) $\dfrac{-13}{9}$
g) $\dfrac{7}{xy}$
h) $\dfrac{11y}{-12x}$
i) $\dfrac{5xy}{-6y}$
j) $\dfrac{-11z}{9y}$

2. For each pair of rational expressions, write an equivalent pair with a common denominator.

a) $\dfrac{m}{2}, \dfrac{m}{5}$
b) $\dfrac{x}{3}, \dfrac{3}{x}$
c) $\dfrac{4}{3p}, \dfrac{-1}{p}$

d) $\dfrac{5}{6x}, \dfrac{2}{9}$
e) $\dfrac{2x}{3y}, \dfrac{x}{4z}$
f) $\dfrac{x+3}{2x}, \dfrac{x-5}{x^2}$

3. Simplify. State any restrictions on the variables.

a) $\frac{3}{x} + \frac{4}{x}$

b) $\frac{5}{2x} + \frac{3}{2x}$

c) $\frac{6}{7x} + \frac{5x}{7x}$

d) $\frac{3}{7m^2} + \frac{4}{7m^2}$

e) $\frac{3a}{4b} + \frac{a}{4b}$

f) $\frac{13x}{15y} + \frac{7x}{15y}$

g) $\frac{9x}{8y^2} + \frac{3x}{8y^2}$

h) $\frac{26a^2}{17ab} + \frac{11b^2}{17ab}$

4. Simplify.

a) $\frac{7}{x} - \frac{4}{x}$

b) $\frac{6}{5x} - \frac{4}{5x}$

c) $\frac{3}{2x^2} + \frac{5x}{2x^2}$

d) $\frac{7}{2m^3} - \frac{6m}{2m^3}$

e) $\frac{6x}{2y} - \frac{5x}{2y}$

f) $\frac{10a^2}{7b^3} + \frac{15a^2}{7b^3}$

g) $\frac{31m^2}{9mn} - \frac{19m^2}{9mn}$

h) $\frac{2}{11x^2} - \frac{14}{11x^2}$

B

✓ **5.** Simplify. State any restrictions on the variables.

a) $\frac{3a}{2} + \frac{5a}{3}$

b) $\frac{6}{5m} + \frac{3}{2m}$

c) $\frac{5x}{2} + \frac{7}{3x}$

d) $\frac{2}{5a} + \frac{3a}{7}$

e) $\frac{3a}{4a^2} + \frac{2}{3a}$

f) $\frac{5}{6x} + \frac{2}{3x^2}$

g) $\frac{3x}{2y} + \frac{2y}{3x}$

h) $\frac{7ab}{3c} + \frac{2}{a}$

i) $\frac{3}{4x} + \frac{5}{4y}$

✓ **6.** Simplify.

a) $\frac{2x}{3} - \frac{4x}{5}$

b) $\frac{2}{3a} - \frac{3}{4a}$

c) $\frac{5}{3a} - \frac{1}{4}$

d) $\frac{2}{3x} - \frac{4}{5x}$

e) $\frac{3}{4a} - \frac{7a}{4b}$

f) $\frac{3a}{7b} - \frac{5}{8b^2}$

g) $\frac{7ab}{5} - \frac{4}{a}$

h) $\frac{2}{3a} - \frac{5a}{11b}$

i) $\frac{3x}{2y} - \frac{7}{6y}$

7. Simplify.

a) $\frac{2x}{7} - \frac{4x}{5y}$

b) $-\frac{2}{5a^2} - \frac{3}{4a}$

c) $\frac{5}{3a} + \frac{1}{4b}$

d) $\frac{5y}{3x} - \frac{2}{5xy}$

e) $-\frac{1}{4a} + \frac{3a}{4b^2}$

f) $\frac{3a}{7b} - \frac{3a}{8b^2}$

g) $\frac{-8b}{5} - \frac{2b}{a}$

h) $\frac{2b}{7ab} - \frac{5a}{11b}$

i) $\frac{5x}{2y} - \frac{1}{6xy}$

✓ **8. Knowledge/Understanding** Simplify.

a) $\frac{3a}{10} - \frac{2a}{5} + \frac{7a}{2}$

b) $-\frac{6m}{12} + \frac{5m}{3} - \frac{7m}{4}$

c) $\frac{1}{2a} - \frac{3}{4a} + \frac{6}{5a}$

d) $-\frac{9}{6y} - \frac{2}{5y} + \frac{11}{4y}$

e) $\frac{2}{3m} - \frac{6}{5n} + \frac{3}{mn}$

f) $\frac{5}{x} - \frac{3}{y} + \frac{8}{3x}$

g) $-\frac{2}{5xy} + \frac{4}{5y} + \frac{1}{4y}$

h) $\frac{6}{5a} + \frac{6}{5b} + \frac{6}{5ab}$

i) $\frac{5}{3x} - \frac{3}{7y} - \frac{2}{11xy}$

✓ **9.** Simplify.

a) $\frac{a+2}{2} + \frac{a+3}{2}$

b) $\frac{a+2}{2} - \frac{a+3}{2}$

c) $\frac{2x+3}{x} + \frac{4x-5}{x}$

d) $\frac{2x+3}{x} - \frac{4x-5}{x}$

e) $\frac{2m-3n}{mn} + \frac{m-2n}{mn}$

f) $\frac{2m-3n}{mn} - \frac{m-2n}{mn}$

g) $\frac{3y-2}{2} + \frac{7-2y}{3}$

h) $\frac{-d-3}{6} - \frac{2d+5}{3}$

i) $\frac{4-x}{2} + \frac{2x-7}{4}$

j) $\frac{10-3b}{4} - \frac{2b+5}{3}$

k) $\frac{2n-9}{5} + \frac{10-3n}{10}$

l) $\frac{-3x+1}{4} - \frac{5x-2}{6}$

10. a) Simplify.

i) $\dfrac{3}{5} - \dfrac{2m}{3} + 4$

ii) $6 - \dfrac{5m + 1}{3}$

iii) $\dfrac{1 + 4b}{2a} - \dfrac{3}{4a} + 3$

iv) $\dfrac{9}{6y} - 5 + \dfrac{1 + y}{4y}$

v) $2 - \dfrac{1}{2n} + \dfrac{3 + m}{mn}$

vi) $\dfrac{x - 5}{x} - \dfrac{3}{y} + 2$

vii) $\dfrac{2p}{5q} - \dfrac{3q}{4r} - 4r$

viii) $\dfrac{3}{5a} + \dfrac{4}{5b} - 2$

ix) $\dfrac{5}{3x} - 3 - \dfrac{3}{5xy}$

b) Communication Choose one expression from part a. Write to explain how you simplified it.

11. Thinking/Inquiry/Problem Solving Write each rational expression as the sum of two rational expressions.

a) $\dfrac{2}{a}$

b) $\dfrac{3a}{4b}$

c) $\dfrac{1}{9ab}$

d) $\dfrac{3x}{4y^2}$

e) $\dfrac{8x - y}{4xy}$

12. Write each rational expression in exercise 11 as the difference of two rational expressions.

13. Simplify. State any restrictions on the variables.

a) $\dfrac{2a - 3}{2} + \dfrac{a + 1}{5}$

b) $\dfrac{x - 1}{6} - \dfrac{3x - 2}{2}$

c) $\dfrac{2x}{y} + \dfrac{5x - 2}{3y^2}$

d) $\dfrac{m^2 + 3}{m^2} + \dfrac{m - 1}{5}$

e) $\dfrac{a^2 - 2}{a} - \dfrac{a + 5}{7}$

f) $\dfrac{6x^2 - 1}{2x^2} - \dfrac{9x + 5}{3x}$

14. Application Remember the lens formula on page 95: $f = \dfrac{pq}{p + q}$.

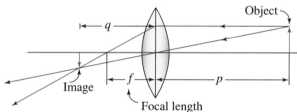

Object

Image

Focal length

Another way to write this formula is $\dfrac{1}{f} = \dfrac{1}{p} + \dfrac{1}{q}$.

a) Explain how one version of the formula is derived from the other version.

b) A zoom lens in a camera is used to take a picture of a flower. The flower is 60.0 cm in front of the lens. The distance between the lens and the film is 10.4 cm. Calculate the focal length of the lens.

15. Write as a sum or a difference of two rational expressions.

a) $\dfrac{12 - a}{3}$

b) $\dfrac{2x - 5}{10x}$

c) $\dfrac{x^2 + xy}{xy}$

d) $\dfrac{7x^2 + x + 1}{x}$

C

16. Simplify.

a) $\dfrac{\frac{1}{x} + 4}{\frac{1}{x} - 4}$

b) $\dfrac{4 - \frac{1}{x}}{4 + \frac{1}{x}}$

c) $\dfrac{x - \frac{1}{4}}{x + \frac{1}{4}}$

d) $\dfrac{\frac{2}{3x} + 2}{\frac{4}{3x} - 1}$

2.6 Adding and Subtracting Rational Expressions: Part II

We can use the methods of Section 2.5 to add and subtract rational expressions with denominators that are not monomials.

Example 1

Add or subtract as indicated.

a) $\dfrac{x+2}{x-1} - \dfrac{2x-3}{x-1}$

b) $\dfrac{2}{5} + \dfrac{3}{x+4}$

c) $m + \dfrac{2m}{m+n} - \dfrac{3}{n}$

Solution

a) Since the terms have a common denominator, the numerators can be combined directly.

$$\frac{x+2}{x-1} - \frac{2x-3}{x-1} = \frac{x+2-(2x-3)}{x-1}$$

$$= \frac{x+2-2x+3}{x-1}$$

$$= \frac{-x+5}{x-1}, \text{ or } \frac{5-x}{x-1}$$

Discuss

Why is it preferable to write the expression as $\frac{5-x}{x-1}$?

b) $\dfrac{2}{5} + \dfrac{3}{x+4} = \dfrac{2}{5} \times \dfrac{x+4}{x+4} + \dfrac{3}{x+4} \times \dfrac{5}{5}$ The common denominator is $5(x+4)$.

$$= \frac{2(x+4) + 3(5)}{5(x+4)}$$

$$= \frac{2x + 8 + 15}{5(x+4)}$$

$$= \frac{2x + 23}{5(x+4)}$$

c) $m + \dfrac{2m}{m+n} - \dfrac{3}{n} = \dfrac{m}{1} + \dfrac{2m}{m+n} - \dfrac{3}{n}$ Writing m as $\frac{m}{1}$

$$= \frac{m}{1} \times \frac{n(m+n)}{n(m+n)} + \frac{2m}{m+n} \times \frac{n}{n} - \frac{3}{n} \times \frac{m+n}{m+n}$$

The common denominator is $n(m+n)$.

$$= \frac{mn(m+n) + 2mn - 3(m+n)}{n(m+n)}$$

$$= \frac{m^2n + mn^2 + 2mn - 3m - 3n}{n(m+n)}$$

When the denominators are polynomials, you may be able to factor these polynomials to determine the lowest common denominator.

Example 2

Simplify.

a) $\dfrac{a+1}{a-3} - \dfrac{a-7}{a+2}$

b) $\dfrac{x}{2-x} - \dfrac{x}{x+2} + \dfrac{1}{x^2-4}$

c) $\dfrac{a}{a^2+5a-6} - \dfrac{2}{a^2+3a+2}$

Solution

a) $\dfrac{a+1}{a-3} - \dfrac{a-7}{a+2} = \dfrac{a+1}{a-3} \times \dfrac{a+2}{a+2} - \dfrac{a-7}{a+2} \times \dfrac{a-3}{a-3}$

The common denominator is $(a-3)(a+2)$.

$$= \dfrac{(a+1)(a+2) - (a-7)(a-3)}{(a-3)(a+2)}$$

$$= \dfrac{a^2 + 3a + 2 - (a^2 - 10a + 21)}{(a-3)(a+2)}$$

$$= \dfrac{a^2 + 3a + 2 - a^2 + 10a - 21}{(a-3)(a+2)}$$

$$= \dfrac{13a - 19}{(a-3)(a+2)}$$

b) $\dfrac{x}{2-x} - \dfrac{x}{x+2} + \dfrac{1}{x^2 - 4}$

Factor the third denominator $x^2 - 4 = (x-2)(x+2)$.

The first denominator $2 - x$ can be written as $-(x-2)$.

So, the first rational expression becomes $\dfrac{x}{-(x-2)}$ or $\dfrac{-x}{x-2}$.

The common denominator is $(x-2)(x+2)$.

$\dfrac{x}{2-x} - \dfrac{x}{x+2} + \dfrac{1}{x^2-4} = \dfrac{-x}{x-2} - \dfrac{x}{x+2} + \dfrac{1}{(x-2)(x+2)}$

$$= \dfrac{-x}{x-2} \times \dfrac{x+2}{x+2} - \dfrac{x}{x+2} \times \dfrac{x-2}{x-2} + \dfrac{1}{(x-2)(x+2)}$$

$$= \dfrac{-x(x+2) - x(x-2) + 1}{(x-2)(x+2)}$$

$$= \dfrac{-x^2 - 2x - x^2 + 2x + 1}{(x-2)(x+2)}$$

$$= \dfrac{-2x^2 + 1}{(x-2)(x+2)}$$

Discuss

Why did we write $\dfrac{x}{2-x}$ as $\dfrac{-x}{x-2}$? Could we have simplified without doing this? Explain.

c) Factor the denominators first.

$\dfrac{a}{a^2 + 5a + 6} - \dfrac{2}{a^2 + 3a + 2} = \dfrac{a}{(a+3)(a+2)} - \dfrac{2}{(a+2)(a+1)}$

The lowest common denominator is $(a+1)(a+2)(a+3)$.

$\dfrac{a}{a^2 + 5a + 6} - \dfrac{2}{a^2 + 3a + 2} = \dfrac{a}{(a+3)(a+2)} \times \dfrac{a+1}{a+1} - \dfrac{2}{(a+2)(a+1)} \times \dfrac{a+3}{a+3}$

$$= \dfrac{a(a+1) - 2(a+3)}{(a+3)(a+2)(a+1)}$$

$$= \dfrac{a^2 + a - 2a - 6}{(a+3)(a+2)(a+1)}$$

$$= \dfrac{a^2 - a - 6}{(a+3)(a+2)(a+1)}$$

The numerator can be factored.

$$= \dfrac{(a-3)(a+2)}{(a+3)(a+2)(a+1)}$$

Divide the numerator and denominator by $a+2$.

$$= \dfrac{a-3}{(a+3)(a+1)}$$

A

1. Simplify.

a) $\dfrac{2+x}{x-1} + \dfrac{4}{x-1}$

b) $\dfrac{a-5}{a+3} + \dfrac{2}{a+3}$

c) $\dfrac{m-4}{2m+1} + \dfrac{m+5}{2m+1}$

d) $\dfrac{4k+3}{3k-2} + \dfrac{6-2k}{3k-2}$

e) $\dfrac{6a-1}{a^2+3} - \dfrac{2a+5}{a^2+3}$

f) $\dfrac{3x+7}{x+5} - \dfrac{2x-1}{x+5}$

g) $\dfrac{k+3}{3k-1} + \dfrac{6-2k}{3k-1}$

h) $\dfrac{7m+5}{m^2+4} - \dfrac{2m-5}{m^2+4}$

i) $\dfrac{3a+50}{a-9} - \dfrac{2a-50}{a-9}$

2. Simplify.

a) $\dfrac{1}{x} + \dfrac{4}{x-1}$

b) $\dfrac{7}{a+5} + \dfrac{3}{a}$

c) $\dfrac{2}{y-4} - \dfrac{5}{y}$

d) $\dfrac{7}{a} - \dfrac{3}{a+2}$

e) $\dfrac{x}{2} - \dfrac{3}{x+2}$

f) $\dfrac{8}{a+3} - \dfrac{6}{5}$

g) $\dfrac{6}{m} - \dfrac{4}{m-1}$

h) $\dfrac{x}{x+4} - \dfrac{3}{x-1}$

i) $\dfrac{1}{a+8} - \dfrac{a}{5}$

3. Simplify.

a) $6 + \dfrac{2}{a-3}$

b) $\dfrac{6}{a+2} + 7$

c) $3 - \dfrac{5}{y+2}$

d) $\dfrac{4}{2m+1} - 5$

e) $\dfrac{6}{x-1} - x - 2$

f) $4 - \dfrac{1}{a+3} - a$

g) $3 + \dfrac{3}{3m+3}$

h) $\dfrac{2}{x-5} - 2x - 7$

i) $4a - \dfrac{3}{2a-3}$

B

4. Simplify.

a) $\dfrac{1}{x+3} + \dfrac{1}{x-3}$

b) $\dfrac{1}{x+3} - \dfrac{1}{x-3}$

c) $\dfrac{4}{a+2} + \dfrac{2}{a-3}$

d) $\dfrac{7}{2x+1} - \dfrac{3}{x-1}$

e) $\dfrac{5x}{x+2} + \dfrac{2x}{x+7}$

f) $\dfrac{3a}{a-5} - \dfrac{5a}{a+2}$

g) $\dfrac{5}{x+1} - \dfrac{3}{2x-1}$

h) $\dfrac{7x}{x-2} + \dfrac{2x}{x-7}$

i) $\dfrac{4m}{m+3} - \dfrac{3m}{m+2}$

5. Knowledge/Understanding Simplify.

a) $\dfrac{x+1}{x-3} + \dfrac{7}{x-2}$

b) $\dfrac{a+3}{a+2} - \dfrac{7}{a-4}$

c) $\dfrac{m+2}{m-1} + \dfrac{m+1}{m+3}$

d) $\dfrac{x+2}{x-1} - \dfrac{x+3}{x-5}$

e) $\dfrac{7}{2(a+1)} + \dfrac{3}{5(a-1)}$

f) $\dfrac{5}{2(x+1)} - \dfrac{2}{3(x-3)}$

g) $\dfrac{x-9}{2x+1} - \dfrac{2x-1}{x-1}$

h) $\dfrac{7+w}{4(w+1)} + \dfrac{1+3w}{2(w-1)}$

i) $\dfrac{5-a}{5(a-1)} - \dfrac{2+a}{3(a+4)}$

6. Simplify.

a) $\dfrac{x+2}{x-3} + \dfrac{8}{x-2}$

b) $\dfrac{a-3}{a+2} - \dfrac{6}{a-4}$

c) $\dfrac{m+2}{m-1} - \dfrac{m+1}{m+3}$

d) $\dfrac{x-2}{x+1} - \dfrac{x-3}{x+5}$

e) $\dfrac{a+8}{3(a+1)} + \dfrac{a-3}{4(a-1)}$

f) $\dfrac{a-5}{2(a+1)} - \dfrac{a+2}{a-9}$

g) $\dfrac{3x+2}{x+1} - \dfrac{4x+3}{x-2}$

h) $\dfrac{7m}{2(m-2)} + \dfrac{3m}{4(m+1)}$

i) $\dfrac{4x}{3(x+1)} - \dfrac{3x}{6(x-3)}$

7. Write each rational expression as the sum of two rational expressions.

a) $\dfrac{2}{x+1}$

b) $\dfrac{x+2}{x-6}$

c) $\dfrac{2b}{a+b}$

8. Communication Write each rational expression in exercise 7 as the difference of two rational expressions. Write to explain how you did this.

9. Add the rational expressions in each list. Extend each pattern for two more examples.

a) $\dfrac{1}{x} + \dfrac{1}{x+1}$

$\dfrac{1}{x+1} + \dfrac{1}{x+2}$

$\dfrac{1}{x+2} + \dfrac{1}{x+3}$

b) $\dfrac{1}{x+1} + \dfrac{2}{x+2}$

$\dfrac{2}{x+2} + \dfrac{3}{x+3}$

$\dfrac{3}{x+3} + \dfrac{4}{x+4}$

c) $\dfrac{1}{x(x-1)} + \dfrac{1}{x(x+1)}$

$\dfrac{1}{x(x-2)} + \dfrac{1}{x(x+2)}$

$\dfrac{1}{x(x-3)} + \dfrac{1}{x(x+3)}$

10. Thinking/Inquiry/Problem Solving Make up a pattern similar to each of those in exercise 9. Write to explain your patterns.

11. Simplify.

a) $\dfrac{5}{2x-2} + \dfrac{7}{3x-3}$

b) $\dfrac{5}{3x-12} - \dfrac{7}{4x-16}$

c) $\dfrac{2}{5x-10} + \dfrac{4}{2-x}$

d) $\dfrac{7}{6x-18} - \dfrac{2}{3-x}$

e) $\dfrac{5}{xy-x} + \dfrac{7}{2y-2}$

f) $\dfrac{6}{ab^2-b} + \dfrac{2}{3-3ab}$

g) $\dfrac{2x+3}{3x-4} - \dfrac{2x+7}{3x+4}$

h) $\dfrac{3-x}{x-2} + \dfrac{2x-5}{x+2} + 1$

i) $2 - \dfrac{x-1}{x+3} + \dfrac{x-1}{x-3}$

12. Simplify.

a) $\dfrac{3}{a-2} + \dfrac{4}{a+2}$

b) $\dfrac{7}{5-x} - \dfrac{3}{25-x^2}$

c) $\dfrac{2}{m^2-9} + \dfrac{4}{3-m}$

d) $\dfrac{3}{25-x^2} - \dfrac{4}{x-5}$

e) $\dfrac{2}{x-4} + \dfrac{5}{x^2-16}$

f) $\dfrac{5}{9a^2-4} - \dfrac{6}{3a+2}$

13. Application

a) Sketch each polygon. What is the measure of each angle in each polygon?

 i) equilateral triangle

 ii) square

 iii) regular pentagon

 iv) regular hexagon

 v) regular octagon

b) Use the method of part a. Develop a formula to determine the measure of each angle in a regular polygon with n sides.

c) What is the measure of each angle in a regular decagon (10 sides)?

14. Simplify.

a) $\dfrac{3}{x-1} + \dfrac{4}{x+1} + \dfrac{5}{x^2-1}$

b) $\dfrac{x}{x+2} - \dfrac{2x}{x-2} + \dfrac{3}{x^2-4}$

c) $\dfrac{m}{m+4} + \dfrac{3m}{m+3} - \dfrac{3m^2}{m^2+7m+12}$

d) $\dfrac{2n}{2n+1} - \dfrac{4n}{2n+3} - \dfrac{5}{4n^2+8n+3}$

e) $\dfrac{c+4}{c+7} - \dfrac{c+3}{c-2} + \dfrac{2c}{14-5c-c^2}$

f) $\dfrac{2m+3}{2m-1} + \dfrac{2m+1}{2m-3} + \dfrac{3m}{4m^2-8m+3}$

g) $\dfrac{1-2n}{2n-1} - \dfrac{2-5n}{2n-5} - \dfrac{3}{4n^2-12n+5}$

h) $\dfrac{3a+2}{2a+3} - \dfrac{2a}{a-6} + \dfrac{1}{18+9a-2a^2}$

15. Simplify.

a) $\dfrac{2a}{a^2 - 6a + 8} + \dfrac{7a}{a^2 - a - 12}$

b) $\dfrac{7x}{x^2 - x - 12} - \dfrac{4x}{x^2 + 2x - 3}$

c) $\dfrac{3b}{b^2 + 6b + 8} + \dfrac{2b}{b^2 + 2b - 8}$

d) $\dfrac{4m}{m^2 - 5m + 6} - \dfrac{6m}{m^2 + m - 6}$

e) $\dfrac{n}{n^2 - n - 20} + \dfrac{5n}{n^2 - 7n + 10}$

f) $\dfrac{2a}{a^2 + 9a + 8} - \dfrac{3a}{a^2 + 8a + 7}$

g) $\dfrac{6x}{x^2 - 3x - 10} + \dfrac{2x}{x^2 - 2x - 15}$

h) $\dfrac{4x}{x^2 + x - 12} - \dfrac{3x}{x^2 - 2x - 3}$

16. Simplify.

a) $\dfrac{x + 1}{x^2 - 3x - 10} + \dfrac{x - 1}{x^2 - 9x + 20}$

b) $\dfrac{a - 1}{a^2 + 8a + 15} - \dfrac{a - 2}{a^2 - 2a - 15}$

c) $\dfrac{x - 3}{x^2 - 9x + 20} + \dfrac{2x - 1}{x^2 - 7x + 12}$

d) $\dfrac{3x + 2}{36 - x^2} - \dfrac{x - 4}{x^2 - 8x + 12}$

e) $\dfrac{a - 6}{a^2 - 11a + 28} - \dfrac{a - 5}{a^2 - 8a + 7}$

f) $\dfrac{3a + 2}{a^2 + 10a + 21} + \dfrac{5a - 4}{15 + 2a - a^2}$

g) $\dfrac{2b - 5}{b^2 - 2b - 15} + \dfrac{3b}{b^2 + b - 30}$

h) $\dfrac{3 - 4x}{x^2 + 3x - 18} - \dfrac{2x + 3}{12 - x - x^2}$

17. Simplify.

a) $\dfrac{3}{2x^2 + x - 3} + \dfrac{4}{2x^2 + 5x + 3}$

b) $\dfrac{2}{3x^2 + 5x + 2} - \dfrac{5}{2x^2 + 3x + 1}$

c) $\dfrac{a}{2a^2 + 7a + 6} + \dfrac{2a}{2a^2 + 9a + 9}$

d) $\dfrac{-2n}{2n^2 - 5n - 3} - \dfrac{6n}{n^2 - 10n + 21}$

e) $\dfrac{4m}{2m^2 + 8m + 6} + \dfrac{3m}{3m^2 + 9m + 6}$

f) $\dfrac{5c}{3c^2 + 13c + 4} - \dfrac{2c}{2c^2 + 11c + 12}$

18. Simplify.

a) $\dfrac{3 - x}{2x^2 + 7x + 3} + \dfrac{2 + x}{x^2 + x - 6}$

b) $\dfrac{a - 4}{2a^2 + 4a + 2} - \dfrac{a + 5}{2a^2 + 3a + 1}$

c) $\dfrac{2c + 3}{2c^2 - 7c - 15} + \dfrac{2c - 1}{2c^2 - 11c + 5}$

d) $\dfrac{4 - 2m}{2m^2 - 8} - \dfrac{3 + m}{6 + 5m + m^2}$

e) $\dfrac{2x + 3}{6x^2 + 7x + 2} + \dfrac{3x + 2}{2x^2 + 5x + 2}$

f) $\dfrac{n + 3}{3n^2 + 7n + 2} - \dfrac{3 + n}{2n^2 - n - 10}$

19. Simplify.

a) $\dfrac{3x^2 + 6xy}{3x} - \dfrac{4y^2 - 2xy}{2y}$

b) $\dfrac{x^2 - 5xy + 6y^2}{x - 3y} - \dfrac{x^2 - xy - 12y^2}{x - 4y}$

c) $\dfrac{x^2 - 4xy - 21y^2}{3x - 21y} + \dfrac{x^2 + 2xy - 24y^2}{2x + 12y}$

d) $\dfrac{a - b}{a^2 + 2ab - 3b^2} + \dfrac{a + b}{a^2 - 2ab - 3b^2}$

C

20. Write each rational expression as the sum of two rational expressions.

a) $\dfrac{2x - 4}{x(x - 4)}$

b) $\dfrac{2x}{x^2 - y^2}$

c) $\dfrac{3x + 11}{(x + 3)(x + 4)}$

21. Suppose you extended the lists in exercise 9 upward. Determine the three previous expressions in each list. Predict each sum. Add the expressions to confirm your prediction.

1. Simplify.

a) $\dfrac{25}{12x^2y} \times \dfrac{3y^3}{10x}$

b) $\dfrac{64a^2b}{27b^2c} \div \dfrac{8b^2c}{9abc}$

c) $\dfrac{3x}{8y} \times \dfrac{4z}{9x} \times \dfrac{7y}{3x}$

d) $\dfrac{6a^2}{5b^2} \times \dfrac{10c^2}{15a^3} \div \dfrac{2bc}{3a}$

e) $\dfrac{6s^2}{3(s-4)} \times \dfrac{18(s-4)}{9s}$

f) $\dfrac{3(3-x)}{5x+5} \div \dfrac{9(x-3)}{10(x+1)}$

2. Simplify.

a) $\dfrac{x^2-25}{12x^3} \times \dfrac{9x}{2x^2+10x}$

b) $\dfrac{3a^2+7a}{16-a^2} \div \dfrac{14+6a}{3a+12}$

c) $\dfrac{9x^2+9x+2}{3x^2-x-2} \times \dfrac{3x^2-4x+1}{9x^2-1}$

d) $\dfrac{4x^2-1}{2x^2-5x+2} \div \dfrac{2x^2-x-1}{x^2-4}$

3. Simplify.

a) $\dfrac{2x^2-5x-3}{5x^2-45} \times \dfrac{2x^2-6x-36}{2x^2-11x-6}$

b) $\dfrac{3x^2-5x-2}{2x^2-12x+16} \times \dfrac{3x^2-24x+48}{9x^2-1}$

c) $\dfrac{2a^2+a-10}{5a^3+15a^2} \div \dfrac{4a^2-25}{2a^2+a-15}$

d) $\dfrac{4x^2-12x+9}{2x^2-x-3} \div \dfrac{x^2-2x+1}{4x^2-4}$

4. Simplify.

a) $\dfrac{3}{2a} + \dfrac{4}{6a}$

b) $\dfrac{5}{m} + \dfrac{2}{m+3}$

c) $\dfrac{7a}{10} - \dfrac{3a}{5} + \dfrac{5a}{2}$

d) $\dfrac{8}{5y} - \dfrac{2}{3y} + \dfrac{9}{4y}$

e) $\dfrac{2}{3xy} - \dfrac{3}{4y} - \dfrac{4}{5y}$

f) $\dfrac{5}{3x} - \dfrac{6}{5y} - \dfrac{7}{9xy}$

5. Simplify. State any restrictions on the variable.

a) $\dfrac{5}{a+1} + \dfrac{a+2}{a-3}$

b) $\dfrac{4}{3x+1} - \dfrac{7}{x-1}$

c) $\dfrac{x+2}{2x+1} - \dfrac{2x+1}{2x-1}$

d) $\dfrac{6+m}{4(m+1)} + \dfrac{1+5m}{2(m-1)}$

e) $\dfrac{y-5}{2(y+7)} - \dfrac{y+2}{y-3}$

f) $\dfrac{2}{x^2-4} + \dfrac{1}{x^2-x-2}$

How Much Time Does Extra Speed Save?

George was driving along Highway 401 at 120 km/h. He was stopped by a police officer. "Why are you driving so fast?" asked the officer. "I want to save time," said George. "How much time do you save by breaking the speed limit?" asked the police officer. "I'm travelling 500 km today, and the speed limit is 100 km/h," replied George. "If I drive at the speed limit, it would take 5 hours. If I drive 20 km/h faster, that's 20% more speed. So it would take 20% less time. That's a whole hour."

Is George right?

Formulating Questions

This is the problem we want to investigate.

Suppose the speed limit is 100 km/h and you travel 500 km. How much time do you save when you break the speed limit by a certain amount?

Representing the Time Saved in Mathematical Form

Suppose we increase the speed by x km/h.
Then the speed is $(100 + x)$ km/h.

The time to travel 500 km at this speed is $\dfrac{500}{100 + x}$ hours.

Let t hours represent the time saved. Then,

$$t = 5 - \frac{500}{100 + x}$$

$$= \frac{(500 + 5x) - 500}{100 + x}$$

$$= \frac{5x}{100 + x}$$

This equation expresses the time saved as a function of the speed increase. To determine the time saved when travelling at 120 km/h, substitute $x = 20$ to obtain $\dfrac{100}{100 + 20} = \dfrac{5}{6}$. The time saved is $\dfrac{5}{6}$ of an hour, or 50 min.

The graph of the function $t = \dfrac{5x}{100 + x}$ for $0 \le x \le 60$ is shown at the right. It shows that for a speed increase of 20 km/h, the time saved is less than one hour.

If you think George is right, what do you think of these arguments?

- Suppose he drives at 160 km/h, which is 60% more speed. So, it would take 60% less time. That's only 2 h.
- Suppose he drives at 200 km/h, which is 100% more speed. So, it would take 100% less time, or no time at all!

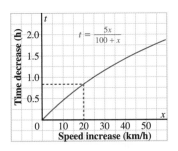

Interpreting Information and Forming Conclusions

To see why George's reasoning is wrong, look at this formula:

$$\text{speed} \times \text{time} = \text{distance}$$

At 100 km/h: $100 \times 5 = 500$

If the speed is larger, the time must be smaller to make the product 500. At 120 km/h, the speed is 20% larger. That's $\frac{1}{5}$ larger. We can write the speed as $100 \times \left(1 + \frac{1}{5}\right)$. George thinks the time is $\frac{1}{5}$ smaller. If so, we can write the time as $5 \times \left(1 - \frac{1}{5}\right)$. But these don't have a product of 500.

$$100 \times \left(\tfrac{6}{5}\right) \times 5 \times \left(\tfrac{4}{5}\right) \neq 500$$

To make the product 500, we need $\frac{5}{6}$ instead of $\frac{4}{5}$.

$$100 \times \left(\tfrac{6}{5}\right) \times 5 \times \left(\tfrac{5}{6}\right) = 500$$

This shows that the time can be written as $5 \times \left(1 - \frac{1}{6}\right)$.

An increase in speed by $\frac{1}{5}$ will cut George's time by only $\frac{1}{6}$.

Therefore, George saves $\frac{1}{6} \times 5 \text{ h} = 50 \text{ min}$.

The above example illustrates a general principle that involves two quantities with a constant product. To discover this principle, let the quantities be A and B. Suppose A is increased by a fraction r, and we want to know the corresponding fractional decrease in B. Let s represent this fractional decrease. Then A becomes $A(1 + r)$ and B becomes $B(1 - s)$.

Now use the fact that the product is constant.

$$A(1 + r) \times B(1 - s) = AB$$

Solve for s. Divide each side by AB.

$$(1 + r)(1 - s) = 1$$

$$1 - s = \frac{1}{1 + r}$$

$$s = 1 - \frac{1}{1 + r}$$

$$s = \frac{r}{1 + r}$$

Reflecting on the Reasonableness of Results

The formula $s = \dfrac{r}{1 + r}$ expresses the fractional decrease in terms of the fractional increase. Since the denominator is greater than 1, we know that $s < r$.

Notice the connection to a difference of squares. If George is right, the product $\left(1 + \frac{1}{5}\right)\left(1 - \frac{1}{5}\right)$ has to equal 1. However, we know that it equals $1 - \frac{1}{25}$.

The awesome power of algebra

We solved the numerical example by inspection, by recognizing that the fraction $\frac{5}{6}$ was needed instead of $\frac{4}{5}$. We won't be able to do this in other situations. Therefore, we use A and B (which don't even have to represent speed and time) and introduce s as an unknown. Then we form an equation and solve it for s.

The expressions $A(1 + r)$ and $B(1 - s)$ are examples of the multiplier principles for growth and decay, respectively.

We have now found the general principle we wanted. We might call it the *constant product principle*:

Suppose two varying quantities have a constant product. When r is the fractional increase in one quantity, the fractional decrease in the other quantity is $s = \dfrac{r}{1+r}$.

This principle will be useful in some of the problems that follow. But it is not the principle by itself that is important. Recognize that the method used to determine this relationship can be used in other situations. The method applies to any problem in which two quantities are related and we want to know how a fractional change in one quantity affects the other quantity. See problems 8 and 10.

The graph of $s = \dfrac{r}{1+r}$ is shown below. Notice that it lies below the line $s = r$. This tells us that the fractional decrease in one quantity is always less than the fractional increase in the other.

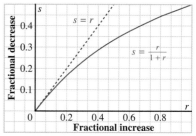

Problems

1. Use the constant product principle to determine how much time George saves by driving 500 km at 120 km/h instead of 100 km/h.

2. Suppose George drives at 110 km/h.
   a) How much time will he save when he drives 500 km at this speed instead of at 100 km/h?
   b) Is the answer to part a one-half the answer to the problem on page 118? Explain.

3. Suppose George drives at 80 km/h.
   a) How much more time would it take him to travel 500 km at this speed than at 100 km/h?
   b) Does driving at 20 km/h below the speed limit take the same amount of extra time as the time saved by driving at 20 km/h above the speed limit? Explain.

4. As I am driving along the highway at 80 km/h, a car passes me in the left lane. I estimate that I will be in the next town in 10 min. How many minutes before I get there will the car that passed me arrive in this town when it is travelling at each speed?
   a) 100 km/h   b) 120 km/h

5. Suppose you drive to work along country roads. Each morning you leave home at 8:30 and arrive at work at 9:00. However, today you are late and do not leave until 8:35. By how much will you have to increase your speed to get to work at 9:00?

Selecting Strategies, Resources, Technology, and Tools

You can use the constant product principle to solve many of these problems, or you can reason them out using a method similar to that at the bottom of page 118.

To use the constant product principle:
• Identify two quantities that have a constant product.
• Determine the fractional change in one quantity.
• Use the equation to determine the fractional change in the other quantity.

Fractional changes can be expressed as fractions or as percents.

6. Each time I stop at the gas station I put exactly $20 worth of gas into my car.

    a) This week the gas prices have risen by 5%. Does this mean that I will get 5% less gas for my $20? Explain.

    b) How much gas will I get?

    c) Suppose gas prices rise by a fraction r. What is the effect on the amount of gas my $20 will buy?

7. One share of the stock of a certain company is worth $120. After a disappointing earnings report is released, the value drops to $90. That is a decrease of $30, or 25%.

    a) Suppose the price now increases by 25%. Would the share be worth $120 again? Explain.

    b) What percent increase is needed to get the price back to $120?

    c) Suppose the price of a share decreases by a fraction r. What fractional increase is needed to get the price back to its original price?

8. A and B are two quantities that satisfy the equation $\frac{A}{B} = 100$. Suppose A is increased by 20%. What is the corresponding change in B?

Challenge Problems

9. On page 120, the graph of the function $s = \frac{r}{1+r}$ is shown for $0 \le r \le 1$.

    a) Find out as much as you can about the graph for other values of r.

    b) Interpret the results in terms of the constant product principle, where possible.

10. A cylindrical can is designed to hold a volume of 1000 cm^3.

    a) Suppose the radius is increased by 25%. What is the corresponding percent decrease in the height so the volume is still 1000 cm^3?

    b) Suppose the radius is increased by a fraction p. What is the effect on the height?

    c) Suppose the height is increased by a fraction q. What is the effect on the radius?

11. In a relay race, each team has two sprinters. They run the same distance one after the other. Suppose there are two teams, A and B. The sprinters in team A run at the same speed. In team B, the sprinters run at different speeds. One sprinter runs faster than the A team by a fraction s. The other sprinter runs slower than the A team by the same fraction s. Which team will win the race, and by how much?

Notice how problems 8 and 10 are similar to the problems you solved using the constant product principle.

- In problem 8, what would be a corresponding constant quotient principle?
- What would be the corresponding principle in problem 10?

Algebra Tools

- The distributive law:

$a(x + y + z) = ax + ay + az$

$(a + b)(x + y + z) = ax + ay + az + bx + by + bz$

- A rational expression is written as $\frac{p}{q}$, where p and q are polynomials, and $q \neq 0$.

- A rational expression is not defined when its denominator is 0. Values of the variable that would make the denominator 0 are called non-permissible values.

- A simplified rational expression is defined only for the values of the variables for which the original expression was defined.

- To simplify a rational expression: factor both the numerator and denominator, then divide the numerator and denominator by their common factors. See pages 96–98.

- To multiply two rational expressions: multiply the numerators, multiply the denominators, and simplify. See pages 103, 105.

- To divide two rational expressions: multiply the dividend by the reciprocal of the divisor. See pages 104, 105.

- To add or subtract two rational expressions: determine the lowest common denominator, create equivalent expressions with that denominator, then add or subtract the numerators as indicated. Write the sum, or difference, of the numerators over the common denominator. See pages 112, 113.

2.1

1. Simplify.

a) $(4x^3 - 2x^2 + 5x - 1) + (-2x^3 + 7x^2 - x + 4)$

b) $(5x^4 + 3x^2 - 8x - 6) + (-3x^4 + x^3 + 4x + 2)$

c) $(4x^2 - 2x + 1) + (3x^2 + x - 6)$

d) $(5x^2y - 3xy + 2y^2) + (-2x^2y + xy - 4y^2)$

2. Simplify.

a) $(5x^2 + 3x + 7) - (4x^2 + 6x + 5)$

b) $(6y^3 - 3y^2 + 7y - 2) - (4y^3 - 4y^2 - 2y + 5)$

c) $(4x^2 - 2xy + 3y^2) - (3x^2 - 5xy - y^2)$

d) $(a^2b^2 + 5a^3b - 3ab^3) - (-2a^2b^2 - 3a^3b + ab^3)$

3. Simplify.

a) $(3x^2 + 17xy) - (12x^2 - 3xy)$

b) $(3m^2 - 5mn) - (3mn - 7n^2)$

c) $2x(x + y) - 3x(2x - 3y)$

d) $2a(3a - 5b) - a(2b + 3a)$

e) $3xy(x - 2y) - 3x(2xy + 3y^2) - y(2x^2 + 5xy)$

f) $5m(3mn - 2n^2) - 2(m^2n - 15mn^2) + 5n(-3mn - 5m^2)$

4. Simplify.

a) $6(2x^2 - 5x) - 14(3x - x^2) + 3(x - x^2)$

b) $-7(c - 3d + 5e) + 4(2c - 11d - 3e) - 5(3c - 7d + 2e)$

c) $7m(2m - 5n + 3) + 2m(-3m + 9n - 4)$

d) $4x^2(5x - 2y - 8) - 3x^2(4x - 8y - 2)$

5. Simplify.

a) $(2x - 4)(x + 3)$ b) $(5x + 2)(x + 4)$

c) $(2m - 3)^2$ d) $(4a + 1)^2$

e) $(2x - 5)(2x^2 - 7x - 4)$ f) $(3y + 4)(8y^2 + 3y - 7)$

2.2 6. Evaluate each rational expression for $x = 2$.

a) $\dfrac{x + 1}{5 - x}$ b) $\dfrac{x^2 + x - 3}{x + 1}$ c) $\dfrac{2x + 3}{2x - 3}$

d) $\dfrac{5x^2 - 3x + 1}{x^2 - 25}$ e) $\dfrac{x - 3}{x^2 + x - 12}$ f) $\dfrac{x^2 + 5x + 6}{x^2 + 7x + 10}$

7. In exercise 6, state any restrictions on the values of x.

2.3 8. Simplify.

a) $\dfrac{50a^4b}{15a^3}$ b) $\dfrac{6m + 3}{3}$ c) $\dfrac{40x^2 - 8x}{20x}$

d) $\dfrac{12ab - 4b^2}{-6ab}$ e) $\dfrac{10xy}{5x^2y - 15xy}$ f) $\dfrac{-3m^3n}{6m^2n^2 + 2mn^2}$

9. Simplify. State any restrictions on the variables.

a) $\dfrac{12 - 24y}{6y - 3}$ b) $\dfrac{x^2 - 9}{7x^2 - 21x}$ c) $\dfrac{x^2 - x - 12}{x^2 - 16}$

d) $\dfrac{12 - 3a^2}{a^2 - 5a + 6}$ e) $\dfrac{m^2 - 7m + 12}{m^2 - 5m + 4}$ f) $\dfrac{6x - x^2}{x^2 - 4x - 12}$

2.4 10. Simplify.

a) $\dfrac{5a^3}{4} \times \dfrac{8}{5a}$ b) $\dfrac{-12mn}{9} \times \dfrac{3}{2m}$ c) $\dfrac{14x^2y}{15} \times \dfrac{9}{2x^3y^4}$

d) $\dfrac{6}{(3x)^2} \times \dfrac{(2x^2)^3}{12x}$ e) $6 \times \dfrac{7}{15b}$ f) $\dfrac{12a^2}{5b} \times 20b^3$

11. Simplify.

a) $\dfrac{12}{5a^3} \div \dfrac{4}{15a}$

b) $\dfrac{-6xy}{7} \div \dfrac{2xy^2}{21}$

c) $\dfrac{(3a)^2}{4m} \div \dfrac{2a^3}{8m^2}$

d) $\dfrac{7a}{12} \div \dfrac{(2a^2)^3}{-6a}$

e) $\dfrac{1}{3x} \div 4x$

f) $12b^3 \div \dfrac{3b}{2}$

12. Simplify.

a) $\dfrac{x^2 - 5x}{3x^2} \times \dfrac{x + 5}{x^2 - 25}$

b) $\dfrac{7}{a^2 + 6a + 9} \times \dfrac{a^2 - 9}{14a}$

c) $\dfrac{3m^2 - 4m - 7}{6m^2 + 6m} \times \dfrac{3m}{3m - 7}$

d) $\dfrac{2a^2 + 12a}{a - 5} \times \dfrac{a^2 - 4a - 5}{a + 6}$

e) $\dfrac{3x^2 - 6x}{x^2 - 7x + 10} \times \dfrac{x - 5}{12x^2}$

f) $\dfrac{4 - m^2}{m - 3} \times \dfrac{m + 2}{m^2 - 5m + 6}$

13. Simplify.

a) $\dfrac{a^2 + 3a}{a^2 - 2a - 3} \div \dfrac{a^2 - 9}{a^2 + a}$

b) $\dfrac{5x^3}{4x^2 - 1} \div \dfrac{15x^4}{12x^2 - 6x}$

c) $\dfrac{5 - m}{m + 2} \div \dfrac{m^2 - 25}{m^2 + 7m + 10}$

d) $\dfrac{2x^2}{x + 6} \div \dfrac{x^2 - 5x}{x^2 + x - 30}$

e) $\dfrac{a^2 + 9a + 18}{12a^2b} \div \dfrac{a^2 - 2a - 15}{3a^2 - 15a}$

f) $\dfrac{a^2 + ab}{a^2 + 3ab + 2b^2} \div \dfrac{a^2 + 2ab + b^2}{a^2 + 2ab}$

2.5 **14.** Simplify.

a) $\dfrac{3}{4a} + \dfrac{7}{4a}$

b) $\dfrac{5}{x} + \dfrac{3}{4x}$

c) $\dfrac{2}{6} + \dfrac{4}{3m}$

d) $\dfrac{4x}{3} - \dfrac{3x}{4} + \dfrac{x}{8}$

e) $\dfrac{4}{3a} + \dfrac{3}{4a} - \dfrac{5}{4a}$

f) $\dfrac{5}{7b} - \dfrac{3}{14b^2} + \dfrac{2}{b}$

15. Simplify.

a) $\dfrac{x + 1}{x} + \dfrac{2x - 3}{x}$

b) $\dfrac{3x - 1}{2} - \dfrac{2x - 2}{3}$

c) $\dfrac{a - 2}{4a} + \dfrac{6a - 1}{5}$

d) $\dfrac{x + 3}{4x} + \dfrac{5x - 1}{6x}$

e) $\dfrac{2a^2 - 2}{a} - \dfrac{a + 5}{4}$

f) $\dfrac{6m^2 - 1}{6m^2} + \dfrac{5m - 2}{9m}$

2.6 **16.** Simplify.

a) $\dfrac{5}{a} + \dfrac{4}{a - 2}$

b) $\dfrac{5}{m + 5} + \dfrac{2}{m}$

c) $\dfrac{2}{x - 1} - \dfrac{4}{x}$

d) $3 + \dfrac{1}{m - 2}$

e) $\dfrac{4}{a + 3} - 5$

f) $6 - \dfrac{2}{y + 1}$

17. Simplify.

a) $\dfrac{3}{4x - 2} + \dfrac{5}{6x - 3}$

b) $\dfrac{6}{ab - a} - \dfrac{2}{3b - 3}$

c) $\dfrac{4}{mn^2 - n} + \dfrac{7}{5 - 5mn}$

d) $\dfrac{2}{9 - x^2} + \dfrac{5}{x - 3}$

e) $\dfrac{2}{4a^2 - 25} - \dfrac{3}{2a + 5}$

f) $\dfrac{5}{x - 2} - \dfrac{3}{4 - x^2} + \dfrac{1}{2 + x}$

18. Simplify.

a) $\dfrac{3x}{x^2 - 4x + 3} - \dfrac{5}{x - 3}$

b) $\dfrac{7}{x - 4} - \dfrac{4x}{x^2 + 3x - 28}$

c) $\dfrac{3x}{2x^2 + 5x - 12} + \dfrac{2}{4x^2 - 9}$

d) $\dfrac{x}{3x - 1} - \dfrac{x - 1}{3x + 2}$

Self-Test

1. Simplify.

   a) $(3m - 2n + 6n^2) + (2m - 3n^2)$ **b)** $2a(a + b^2) - 3(a^2 - 5ab^2)$

   c) $(5x + 2y)(x - 3y)$ **d)** $(a + 2)(a^2 - 2a + 4)$

2. **Knowledge/Understanding** For what values of the variable(s) is each rational expression not defined?

   a) $\dfrac{5}{3xy}$ **b)** $\dfrac{x - 2}{5x(x - 2)}$ **c)** $\dfrac{12x}{x^2 - 8x + 7}$ **d)** $\dfrac{x + 3}{y^2 + 2}$

3. Evaluate each expression in exercise 2 for $x = 3$ and $y = -2$.

4. Simplify.

   a) $\dfrac{9ab}{12a^2}$ **b)** $\dfrac{9x^2 - 4}{3x + 2}$ **c)** $\dfrac{x^2 - 36}{x^2 + 3x - 18}$ **d)** $\dfrac{60 - 15x^2}{5x^2 - 5x - 10}$

5. **Thinking/Inquiry/Problem Solving** Choose one rational expression from exercise 4.

   a) Write the expression as the sum of two rational expressions with different denominators.

   b) Write the expression as the difference of two rational expressions with different denominators.

6. Simplify.

   a) $\dfrac{4a + 3}{a + 1} \times \dfrac{3a + 3}{8a + 6}$ **b)** $\dfrac{7t - 21}{12t - 12} \div \dfrac{42 - 3t}{3t}$ **c)** $\dfrac{x^2 - 16}{9x^3} \times \dfrac{12x^2}{5x - 20}$

7. **Communication** Simplify. Identify any restrictions on the variables. Write to explain the significance of the restrictions.

   a) $\dfrac{a^2 - 2a - 3}{2a + 1} \div \dfrac{a^2 - 1}{2a^2 - a - 1}$ **b)** $\dfrac{16x^2 - 9}{4x^2 - 9x - 9} \times \dfrac{6x^2 - 12x - 18}{9 - 12x}$

   c) $\dfrac{2}{x^2 + x - 12} + \dfrac{5}{9 - x^2}$ **d)** $\dfrac{a - 3}{a^2 - a} - \dfrac{a + 5}{a^2 + 2a - 3}$

8. Each rational expression below is the product of two other rational expressions. For each, write what the two rational expressions might have been. Explain how you obtained your answers.

   a) $\dfrac{3}{x}$ **b)** $\dfrac{5b}{6}$ **c)** $\dfrac{2}{m(m + 1)}$

9. Suppose each rational expression in exercise 8 is the sum of two other rational expressions with different denominators. For each, write what the two other rational expressions might have been. Explain how you obtained your answers.

10. **Application** In an electrical circuit, two resistances x ohms and y ohms are connected in parallel. The total resistance, z ohms, is given by the formula $\frac{1}{z} = \frac{1}{x} + \frac{1}{y}$.

a) Solve the formula for z.

b) Two resistances in parallel are 10 ohms and 12 ohms. What is the total resistance?

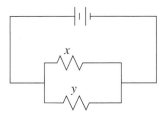

Assessment Tasks

1. I have 30 m of fencing and wish to enclose a rectangular sheep pen. One pen could have length 10 m and width 5 m. However, I would prefer the area of the pen to be as large as possible.

a) Analyse how the area of the enclosure depends on the width of the pen. Illustrate your analysis with suitable diagrams, tables, graphs, and algebra.

b) The side-wall of a barn could form one side of the sheep pen. Describe the effect on the area enclosed of using the side-wall in this way.

2. a) Simplify each sum.

i) $\dfrac{1}{2 \times 3} + \dfrac{1}{3 \times 4} + \dfrac{1}{4 \times 5}$

ii) $\dfrac{1}{3 \times 4} + \dfrac{1}{4 \times 5} + \dfrac{1}{5 \times 6}$

iii) $\dfrac{1}{4 \times 5} + \dfrac{1}{5 \times 6} + \dfrac{1}{6 \times 7}$

b) Describe any patterns in part a.

c) Show that any sum similar to those in part a will fit the patterns.

3. The *arithmetic mean* of two positive numbers is one-half the sum of the numbers. The *harmonic mean* of two numbers is the reciprocal of the mean of their reciprocals. For example, the arithmetic mean of 5 and 7 is $\frac{5+7}{2} = 6$. The harmonic mean of 5 and 7 is $\left(\frac{5^{-1} + 7^{-1}}{2} \right)^{-1} = \frac{35}{6}$, which is less than the arithmetic mean. Show that the harmonic mean of two distinct positive numbers, $a - x$ and $a + x$, is always less than the arithmetic mean.

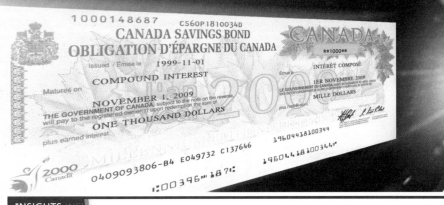

INSIGHTS INTO A RICH PROBLEM

Canada Savings Bonds (CSBs) are a common form of investment. When you own a CSB, you can redeem it at any time for its face value plus accumulated interest.

At the end of this chapter, you will learn about other kinds of bonds that cannot be redeemed before their maturity date. Instead, they can be bought and sold in the financial marketplace. This means that the value of these bonds change daily. You will use geometric series to calculate the value of these bonds.

Curriculum Expectations

By the end of this chapter, you will:

- Derive the formulas for compound interest and present value, the amount of an ordinary annuity, and the present value of an ordinary annuity, using the formulas for the nth term of a geometric sequence and the sum of the first n terms of a geometric series.

- Solve problems involving compound interest and present value.

- Solve problems involving the amount and the present value of an ordinary annuity.

- Demonstrate an understanding of the relationships between simple interest, arithmetic sequences, and linear growth.

- Demonstrate an understanding of the relationships between compound interest, geometric sequences, and exponential growth.

- Analyse the effects of changing the conditions in long-term savings plans.

- Describe the manner in which interest is calculated on a mortgage and compare this with the method of interest compounded monthly and calculated monthly.

- Generate amortization tables for mortgages, using spreadsheets or other appropriate software.

- Analyse the effects of changing the conditions of a mortgage.

- Communicate the solutions to problems and the findings of investigations with clarity and justification.

Necessary Skills

1. New: Simple Interest

Interest is a fee charged for the use of money. For example, suppose you buy a $100 savings certificate from a bank that pays 5% interest per year. During the year, the bank "rents" your money and uses it for other investments. When you cash your certificate at the end of the year, you receive $100 plus $5 interest.

Take Note

> ### *Simple Interest*
>
> Simple interest is calculated using this formula:
>
> $$I = Prt$$
>
> *I* is the interest in dollars.
> *P* is the principal, the money borrowed, in dollars.
> *r* is the annual interest rate expressed as a decimal.
> *t* is the time in years.
>
> The amount, *A* dollars, is the sum of the principal, *P* dollars, and the interest, *I* dollars.
>
> $$A = P + I$$

Simple interest is used only for time periods of 1 year, or less.

Example 1

A bank account pays annual interest of 3%. On April 30, the balance was $578.24. On May 25, the account was closed. Calculate the interest that should be credited to the account in May before closing the account.

Solution

Use the formula $I = Prt$.

Substitute $P = 578.24$, $r = 0.03$, $t = \frac{25}{365}$.

$$I = (578.24)(0.03)\left(\frac{25}{365}\right)$$

$$\doteq 1.19$$

The interest is $1.19.

Each year, the federal government sells a new issue of Canada Savings Bonds (CSBs). Each bond may be held for an agreed period of years, at an interest rate guaranteed not to fall below that stated at the time of purchase. You cannot deposit or withdraw money from the bond during this time. However, you may redeem it for cash at any time.

Example 2

Felix bought a $500 regular interest Canada Savings Bond. A regular interest CSB pays simple interest annually. The interest rate for Felix's bond is 5% per year. He plans to keep the bond until it matures in 8 years.

a) Determine the interest at the end of the first year. Calculate the total interest accumulated at the end of each year. Write the data in a table.

b) Graph the data in part a.

c) What type of growth does accumulated simple interest illustrate?

d) How does the accumulated simple interest relate to an arithmetic sequence?

Solution

a) Use the formula $I = Prt$. Substitute $P = 500$, $r = 0.05$, $t = 1$.
$$I = Prt$$
$$= (500)(0.05)(1)$$
$$= 25$$
The interest at the end of the first year is $25.

The interest earned each year is $25.

Year	Interest ($)	Total interest accumulated ($)
1	25	25
2	25	50
3	25	75
4	25	100
5	25	125
6	25	150
7	25	175
8	25	200

b) Plot *Year* horizontally and *Total interest accumulated* vertically.

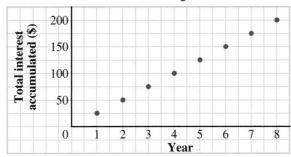

Interest Accumulated on a Regular Interest CSB

c) In the table, the total interest accumulated increases by a constant amount, $25, each year. The points on the graph lie on a straight line. Thus, accumulated simple interest illustrates linear growth.

d) The accumulated interest increases by $25 each year. The yearly accumulated interest is an arithmetic sequence with first term 25 and common difference 25; that is, 25, 50, 75, 100 … .

Exercises

1. Determine each missing item in the table.

	Interest ($)	Principal ($)	Annual interest rate (%)	Time (months)
a)		200	5	4
b)		387	5.3	8
c)	55		6.8	5
d)	20.33	813		6
e)	246.38	4500	7.3	
f)		893.47	6.24	11

2. Determine the interest on $715 at an annual rate of 6.2% for 10 months.

3. How many days will $800 have to be invested at 7% annually to earn $13.50?

4. At what annual interest rate will $555 earn $17.11 in 5 months?

5. A credit card company charges an annual interest rate of 18% on the unpaid balance of an account. Calculate the amount that must be paid to the company when a balance of $726.40 is paid 15 days late.

6. Determine the amount when $458 is invested at 6.5% annually for 4 months.

7. Sun bought a $100 regular interest CSB that matures in 8 years. It earns interest at 6.5% annually.

   a) Draw a graph to show the total interest accumulated until maturity.

   b) What type of growth does the graph represent?

   c) How is simple interest related to arithmetic sequences and linear growth?

2. Review: Solving Equations

Example

Solve for x.

a) $3 + x = \dfrac{5x}{4}$ **b)** $ax - 5 = c$

Solution

a)

$$3 + x = \frac{5x}{4}$$

$$3 + x - x = \frac{5x}{4} - x \qquad \text{Subtracting } x \text{ from each side}$$

$$3 = x\left(\frac{5}{4} - 1\right) \qquad \text{Collecting like terms}$$

$$3 = x\left(\frac{1}{4}\right) \qquad \text{Simplifying}$$

$$3 \times 4 = x\left(\frac{1}{4}\right) \times 4 \qquad \text{Multiplying each side by 4}$$

$$x = 12$$

b)

$$ax - 5 = c$$

$$ax - 5 + 5 = c + 5 \qquad \text{Adding 5 to each side}$$

$$ax = c + 5$$

$$\frac{ax}{a} = \frac{c + 5}{a} \qquad \text{Dividing each side by } a$$

$$x = \frac{c + 5}{a}$$

Exercises

1. Solve each equation for x.

   a) $8 = 7x$ **b)** $6 = \dfrac{7x}{4}$ **c)** $5(x - 2) = 4(2x + 1)$

   d) $x - \dfrac{1}{4}x = 15$ **e)** $a + 4x = d$ **f)** $h - gx = -2$

   g) $x^2 = 5$ **h)** $x^2 = 2$ **i)** $Ax^2 = b$

3. Review: Geometric Series

Remember these results from Chapter 1.

The series $a + ar + ar^2 + ar^3 + ar^4 + \cdots$ is geometric with the nth term ar^{n-1}.

The sum of the first n terms is $S_n = \dfrac{a(r^n - 1)}{r - 1}$, $r \neq 1$.

Example

Determine the sum of the first 7 terms of this geometric series.

$100 + 100(0.05) + 100(0.05)^2 + 100(0.05)^3 + \cdots$.

Solution

The first term, a, is 100.

The common ratio r is $\dfrac{100(0.05)}{100} = 0.05$.

Substitute $a = 100$, $r = 0.05$, and $n = 7$ into $S_n = \dfrac{a(r^n - 1)}{r - 1}$.

$S_7 = \dfrac{100(0.05^7 - 1)}{0.05 - 1}$ Use a calculator.

$\doteq 105.26$

The sum of the first 7 terms of the series is approximately 105.26.

Exercises

1. Determine each indicated sum. Write each answer to 4 decimal places where necessary.

a) $3 + 3(0.1) + 3(0.1)^2 + \cdots$; 15 terms   b) $0.3 + 0.3(24) + 0.3(24)^2 + \cdots$; 9 terms

c) $4 + 8 + 16 + \cdots$; 8 terms   d) $5 + 1 + 0.2 + 0.04 + \cdots$; 9 terms

4. Review: Using a Calculator to Evaluate Expressions

When you use a calculator:

- Record all the data that you input as well as the result.
- Make sure you press the correct keys.
- Learn to use the special calculator functions you need.
- Apply the order of operations correctly.

  For example, remember that $\dfrac{35}{4 \times 7} = 35 \div 4 \div 7$.

- Use calculator memory to store intermediate results.
- Estimate to check calculator results.
- Round only after the answer is obtained.

Recall that the keystrokes are for the TI-30X IIS calculator.

Example 1

Use a calculator to evaluate. Write each answer to 3 decimal places.

a) $\dfrac{2.1 + 3.8}{5.7}$ b) $(1 + 0.0375)^6$ c) $\dfrac{7.2 \times 3.6 \times 9.8}{4.4 \times 5.9}$

Solution

a) $\dfrac{2.1 + 3.8}{5.7}$

Calculate the sum, 2.1 + 3.8, before you divide by 5.7. As you input the numbers, place brackets around this sum.

Key in: (2.1 + 3.8) ÷ 5.7 (ENTER =) to display 1.035087719

To 3 decimal places, $\dfrac{2.1 + 3.8}{5.7} \doteq 1.035$

b) $(1 + 0.0375)^6$

Add 1 + 0.0375 mentally to get 1.0375.

Key in: 1.0375 (^) 6 (ENTER =) to display 1.247178548

To 3 decimal places, $(1 + 0.0375)^6 \doteq 1.247$

c) $\dfrac{7.2 \times 3.6 \times 9.8}{4.4 \times 5.9}$

Remember to divide the numerator by 4.4, then divide by 5.9.

Key in: 7.2 (×) 3.6 (×) 9.8 (÷) 4.4 (÷) 5.9 (ENTER =) to display 9.784899846

To 3 decimal places, $\dfrac{7.2 \times 3.6 \times 9.8}{4.4 \times 5.9} \doteq 9.785$

Example 2

Evaluate. Write each answer to 2 decimal places.

a) $A = 1345(1.076)^{24}$ b) $P = \dfrac{476.93}{(1 + 0.088)^{15}}$ c) $S = \dfrac{3400(1.058^{13} - 1)}{1.058 - 1}$

Solution

a) $A = 1345(1.076)^{24}$

Key in: 1345 (×) 1.076 (^) 24 (ENTER =) to display 7802.194925

$A \doteq 7802.19$

b) $P = \dfrac{476.93}{(1 + 0.088)^{15}}$

Key in: 476.93 (÷) 1.088 (^) 15 (ENTER =) to display 134.5926088

$P \doteq 134.59$

c) $S = \dfrac{3400(1.058^{13} - 1)}{1.058 - 1}$

Calculate $1.058 - 1$ mentally as 0.058, then divide by this number.

Key in: 3400 $\boxed{(}$ 1.058 $\boxed{\wedge}$ 13 $\boxed{-}$ 1 $\boxed{)}$ $\boxed{\div}$ 0.058 $\boxed{\text{ENTER} \atop =}$ to display 63380.65113

$S \doteq 63\ 380.65$

In some exercises, you may need to solve for the variable first.

Example 3

Solve for R. Write the answer to 2 decimal places.

$5000 = \dfrac{R(1.0433^8 - 1)}{1.0433 - 1}$

Solution

$5000 = \dfrac{R(1.0433^8 - 1)}{1.0433 - 1}$

Simplify the denominator.

$5000 = \dfrac{R(1.0433^8 - 1)}{0.0433}$

Multiply each side by 0.0433.

$5000(0.0433) = R(1.0433^8 - 1)$

Divide each side $1.0433^8 - 1$.

$\dfrac{5000(0.0433)}{1.0433^8 - 1} = R$

To evaluate, place brackets around the denominator.

Key in: 5000 $\boxed{\times}$ 0.0433 $\boxed{\div}$ $\boxed{(}$ 1.0433 $\boxed{\wedge}$ 8 $\boxed{-}$ 1 $\boxed{)}$ $\boxed{\text{ENTER} \atop =}$ to display 536.2920754

$R \doteq 536.29$

Exercises

1. Evaluate each expression. Write each answer to 1 decimal place.

a) $\dfrac{6.3 + 8.7 - 11.0}{5.4 - 6.1 + 3.8}$ **b)** $(1 + 0.047)^9$ **c)** $\dfrac{6.3 \times 3.5 \times 4.1}{2.5 \times 5.9 \times 8.3}$

2. Evaluate. Write each answer to 2 decimal places.

a) $A = 285.58(1.0566)^{13}$ **b)** $P = \dfrac{6789.76}{(1 + 0.049)^8}$ **c)** $S = \dfrac{6700(1.062^9 - 1)}{1.062 - 1}$

3. Solve for R. Write each answer to 2 decimal places.

a) $30\ 000 = \dfrac{R(1.062^{16} - 1)}{1.062 - 1}$ **b)** $93\ 000 = \dfrac{R(1 - 1.05^{-10})}{0.05}$

3.1 Compound Interest: Amount and Present Value

In this chapter, you will examine some current banking, investment, and business practices, and explore how these practices can affect you, the customer. Most calculations in this chapter involve interest rates, and these can change frequently. However, we shall make the following assumptions throughout this chapter to allow you to focus on the mathematics.

- Interest rates are constant in each problem, unless stated otherwise.

- Income taxes are not considered.

- No other deposits or withdrawals are made.

When you deposit money in a bank account, you lend money to the bank. In return, the bank pays you *interest*, which is money paid for the use of your money. Consider interest that is paid annually. In the second year of an investment, interest is earned not only on the principal, but also on the first year's interest. When interest is earned on interest, we say the interest *compounds*; hence, the term *compound interest*.

Suppose you open a bank account and deposit a principal of $1000. The interest rate is 6% per annum, compounded annually. What is the amount after 10 years?

Since the interest rate is 6% per annum, the amount increases by 6% each year. From Chapter 1, recall the multiplier principle. We use it to calculate the amount after each year. To increase the amount by 6% is the same as multiplying it by 1.06.

1st year:	$1000(1.06)$ $= \$1060.00$
2nd year:	$1000(1.06)^2 = \$1123.60$
3rd year:	$1000(1.06)^3 \doteq \$1191.02$
$\vdots$	$\vdots$
10th year:	$1000(1.06)^{10} \doteq \$1790.85$

The amount after 10 years is $1790.85.

In the example above, the principal is $1000, the interest rate is 6% or 0.06, and the multiplier is $1 + 0.06$, or 1.06. The yearly amounts form a geometric sequence with common ratio 1.06.

A similar pattern occurs for other principals and other interest rates. In general, suppose a principal of P dollars is invested at an interest rate of i per annum, compounded annually. The multiplier is $1 + i$. The yearly amounts form the geometric sequence: $P(1 + i)$, $P(1 + i)^2$, $P(1 + i)^3$, ... We use this pattern to determine that the amount A after n years is given by the formula $A = P(1 + i)^n$.

Example 1

Lauren deposited $1000 in an investment savings account. The annual interest rate is 4.25% compounded annually. Determine the amount after 7 years.

Solution

The time diagram illustrates this situation.

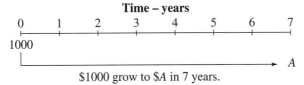

Time – years

$1000 grow to $A in 7 years.

Use the formula for amount. Substitute $P = 1000$, $i = 0.0425$, $n = 7$.

$A = P(1 + i)^n$
$= 1000(1.0425)^7$
$\doteq 1338.24$

The amount after 7 years is $1338.24.

Example 2

Nicholas opened an investment savings account. The interest rate is $5\frac{3}{4}\%$ per annum, compounded annually. He wants the amount to be $5000 in 8 years. What principal should he deposit now?

Solution

Let P represent the principal.
The time diagram illustrates this situation.

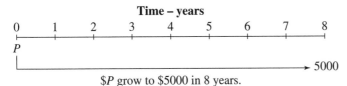

Time – years

$P grow to $5000 in 8 years.

Use the formula for amount. Substitute $A = 5000$, $i = 0.0575$, $n = 8$.

$A = P(1 + i)^n$
$5000 = P(1.0575)^8$

Solve for P.

$P = \dfrac{5000}{(1.0575)^8}$ Key in: 5000 ÷ 1.0575 ^ 8 ENTER
$\doteq 3196.88$

Nicholas should deposit $3196.88.

In *Example 2*, the principal of $3196.88 is called the *present value* of $5000 in 8 years. Present value calculations occur frequently in financial mathematics. To determine a formula for present value, we solve the formula $A = P(1 + i)^n$ for P.

$$A = P(1 + i)^n$$

Divide each side by $(1 + i)^n$.

$$P = \frac{A}{(1 + i)^n}$$

Take Note

Compound Interest for Annual Compounding

Formula for amount

$$A = P(1 + i)^n$$

Formula for present value

$$P = \frac{A}{(1 + i)^n}$$

P is the money invested (the principal).

A is the amount.

i is the interest rate for the compounding period, expressed as a decimal.

n is the number of compounding periods.

Since the calculation of the amount uses a multiplier, the amount grows exponentially.

To remember the formulas for amount and present value, visualize a time diagram that represents the growth of $100 earning compound interest at an annual interest rate i, compounded annually.

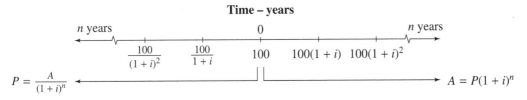

Present value

- Move to the left.
- Divide by $(1 + i)$ for each year.
- The present value of $100 due in n years is $\frac{100}{(1 + i)^n}$.

Amount

- Move to the right.
- Multiply by $(1 + i)$ for each year.
- The amount of $100 after n years is $100(1 + i)^n$.

Example 3

What interest rate, compounded annually, is required for a $200 investment to amount to $250 in 4 years?

Solution

The time diagram illustrates this situation.

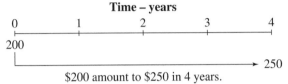

Time – years

$200 amount to $250 in 4 years.

Use the formula for amount. Substitute $A = 250$, $P = 200$, $n = 4$.

$$A = P(1 + i)^n$$
$$250 = 200(1 + i)^4$$
$$(1 + i)^4 = \frac{250}{200}$$
$$(1 + i)^4 = 1.25$$

Take the 4th root of each side; that is, raise each side to the exponent $\frac{1}{4}$.

$$\left[(1 + i)^4\right]^{\frac{1}{4}} = 1.25^{\frac{1}{4}}$$
$$1 + i = 1.25^{\frac{1}{4}}$$
$$1 + i \doteq 1.057\ 371\ 263$$
$$i \doteq 0.057\ 371\ 263$$

Express the interest rate as a percent.
$0.057\ 371\ 263 \doteq 5.74\%$

The interest rate is approximately 5.74% per annum, compounded annually.

3.1 Exercises

A

1. Use the formula $A = P(1 + i)^n$. Calculate A for each set of values.

  a) $P = \$500$, $i = 0.04$, $n = 3$ **b)** $P = \$1000$, $i = 0.04$, $n = 3$

  c) $P = \$500$, $i = 0.08$, $n = 3$ **d)** $P = \$500$, $i = 0.04$, $n = 6$

 2. Calculate the amount. Each interest rate is per annum, compounded annually.

  a) $500 invested for 8 years at 6%

  b) $800 invested for 10 years at 7.5%

  c) $1000 invested for 5 years at 5.75%

  d) $750 invested for 12 years at 6.25%

3. Use the formula $P = \dfrac{A}{(1 + i)^n}$. Calculate P for each set of values.

a) $A = \$1000$, $i = 0.035$, $n = 5$ **b)** $A = \$2000$, $i = 0.035$, $n = 5$

c) $A = \$1000$, $i = 0.07$, $n = 5$ **d)** $A = \$1000$, $i = 0.035$, $n = 10$

 4. Calculate the present value. Each interest rate is per annum, compounded annually.

a) $1000 in 9 years at 5%   **b)** $1200 in 4 years at 6.75%

c) $2500 in 8 years at 5.5%   **d)** $10 000 in 12 years at 8.25%

Exercises 5 to 13 refer to *Example 1* or *Example 2*, page 136.

B

 5. Refer to *Example 1*. Determine the amount in each case.

a) The principal is twice as great, $2000.

b) The interest rate is twice as great, 8.5%.

c) The time period is twice as long, 14 years.

6. In which part(s) of exercise 5 is the amount twice as great as the amount in *Example 1*? Explain.

7. Refer to *Example 2*. Determine the present value in each case.

a) The amount is twice as great, $10 000.

b) The interest rate is twice as great, $11\frac{1}{2}\%$.

c) The time period is twice as long, 16 years.

8. In which part(s) of exercise 7 is the present value twice as great as the present value in *Example 2*? Explain.

9. In *Example 1*, Lauren deposited $1000 into an investment account with an annual interest rate of 4.25% compounded annually. This graph shows the amounts in the account for up to 50 years.

a) Estimate the amount Lauren would have after each time.

    i) 10 years   **ii)** 20 years   **iii)** 30 years

    iv) 40 years   **v)** 50 years

b) Estimate how long it would take to save each amount.

    i) $1500   **ii)** $2000   **iii)** $3000

c) Describe how the amount grows as the number of years increases.

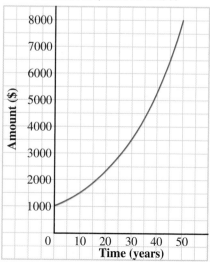

Amount of $1000 at 4.25%

d) Describe how the graph would change in each case.

    i) The interest rate is greater than 4.25%.

    ii) The amount deposited is greater than $1000.

e) For part d) i, one student suggested that, if the principal was $1500, the new graph would be the image of the original graph after a vertical translation of $500. Was the student correct? Explain.

10. In *Example 2*, Nicholas invests money into an account that pays 5.75% interest per annum, compounded annually. The graph below shows the principal he needs to deposit for this principal to amount to $5000 for different numbers of years.

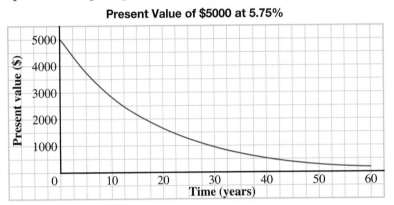

Present Value of $5000 at 5.75%

a) Estimate the principal Nicholas needs to deposit to have $5000 after each time.

    i) 10 years   **ii)** 20 years   **iii)** 30 years

    iv) 40 years   **v)** 50 years   **vi)** 60 years

b) Estimate the time it takes for each principal to amount to $5000.

    i) $1500   **ii)** $2000   **iii)** $3000

c) Describe how the present value changes as the number of years increases.

d) Describe how the graph would change in each case.

    i) The interest rate is greater than 5.75%.

    ii) The amount is greater than $5000.

11. Compare the graphs in exercises 9 and 10. Explain why one graph goes up to the right and the other goes down to the right.

12. Start a new spreadsheet. Enter the data shown below in all cells except D5. These data are from *Example 1*. In cell D5, enter the formula =D2*(1+D3)^D4. The computer displays the amount shown below. Compare this result with *Example 1*.

	A	B	C	D
1	Calculating Amount			
2	Principal		P	1,000.00
3	Annual interest rate		i	4.25%
4	Number of years		n	7
5	Amount		A	1,338.24

Use your spreadsheet to solve each problem.

a) Determine the amount after 7 years for each interest rate.

   i) 3%   **ii)** 5%   **iii)** 6.75%   **iv)** 9.25%

   Change the interest rate back to 4.25% before you continue.

b) Determine the amount at 4.25% per annum, compounded annually, after each time.

   i) 2 years   **ii)** 4 years   **iii)** 10 years   **iv)** 15 years

13. Use the spreadsheet in exercise 12 to solve each problem.

a) Suppose you invest $400 at 5.5% per annum, compounded annually. What is the amount after 7 years?

b) Suppose $750 will grow to $2000 in 10 years. What interest rate do you need?

c) Suppose $2000 grows to $5000 at 8% per annum, compounded annually. How many years does it take?

d) Choose either part b or part c. Write to explain how you solved the problem.

14. A $1000 Guaranteed Investment Certificate (GIC) has an annual interest rate of 6.5% compounded annually. Determine its value after each time.

a) 4 years   **b)** 6 years   **c)** 8 years

15. A trust company offers GICs at 7.25% per annum, compounded annually, to mature in 6 years. Determine the maturity value of each certificate.

a) $250   **b)** $500   **c)** $1000

16. The interest rate on a GIC may vary and depend on the term of the investment. Use the information in the advertisement. The interest rates are per annum, compounded annually.

a) Determine the value of each GIC after the specified time.

   i) a $1000 one-year GIC   **ii)** a $2500 two-year GIC

   iii) a $5000 three-year GIC **iv)** a $10 000 four-year GIC

   v) a $100 000 five-year GIC

b) Why does the interest rate vary with the term?

GIC Rates	
5 years	6.5%
4 years	6.25%
3 years	5.75%
2 years	5.5%
1 year	4.75%
ABC Bank	

17. Use the information in the advertisement for exercise 16. What principal should you invest today to obtain each amount?

a) $3980 in 5 years   **b)** $2850 in 3 years

c) $10 400 in 1 year   **d)** $5460 in 2 years

18. Knowledge/Understanding Suppose you want an amount of $5000 in 10 years. What principal should you invest today at an annual rate of 6.25% compounded annually?

19. A parent wants to invest money now to amount to $8000 in 4 years when her daughter starts university. What principal must be invested now at each annual interest rate, compounded annually, to provide this amount?

   a) 3%   **b)** 4%   **c)** 5%   **d)** 6%   **e)** 7%

✓ **20. a)** Would you rather have $1000 today or $2000 five years from now? Explain.

   b) Would you rather have $1000 today or $4000 ten years from now? Explain.

   c) Would you rather have $1000 today or $16 000 twenty years from now? Explain.

   d) What interest rates correspond to the situations in parts a and b?

21. In exercise 20, do you think the answer to part d might cause you to change your answers to parts a, b, or c? Explain.

22. Communication Write to explain the difference between simple interest and compound interest. Use examples to illustrate your explanation.

23. A person donated $1 000 000 to a hospital. The money was to be invested for 6 years. After this time, the amount was to be used to help pay for a planned addition to the hospital. The hospital invested the funds at 8% per annum, compounded annually. What amount would be available in 6 years?

✓ **24.** Suppose you want to deposit enough money today into an investment account so you will have $1 000 000 in 50 years. Suppose the account pays 7% per annum, compounded annually. How much would you need to deposit?

25. About how many years will it take a principal to double when invested at each annual interest rate, compounded annually?

   a) 5%   **b)** 6%   **c)** 7%   **d)** 8%   **e)** 9%

26. At what annual interest rate, compounded annually, will a principal double in each time?

   a) 4 years   **b)** 8 years   **c)** 12 years   **d)** 16 years   **e)** 20 years

27. Application The 50¢ Bluenose is one of Canada's most famous postage stamps. In 1929, it could be bought at the post office for 50¢. In 2000, a superb copy was sold at an auction for $529. What annual interest rate corresponds to an investment of 50¢ in 1929 that grows to $529 in 2000?

Stamp reproduced courtesy of Canada Post Corporation

28. The formula $A = P(1 + i)^n$ contains four quantities P, A, i, and n. Write to explain how you can determine one of these quantities when you know the other three quantities.

✓ **29.** This graph shows the number of years required for money to double when invested at different interest rates.

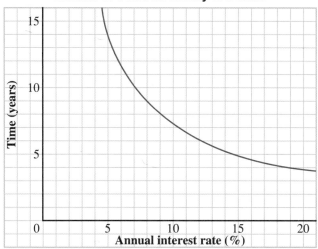

Number of Years for Money to Double

a) About how long does it take money to double when invested at each rate?
   i) 10%   ii) 15%

b) What interest rate would double an investment in each time?
   i) 6 years   ii) 10 years

30. Karl has $125 in his account, which pays 6.4% per annum, compounded annually. After the 3rd year, he deposits an additional $200. How much will Karl have in his account after 5 years?

31. Melissa has $2200 in her trust account, which pays 5.15% per annum, compounded annually. After 2 years, she withdraws $200. One year later, she deposits $1000. How much will she have after 5 years?

32. Ravi has $775 in his account, which pays 5.25% per annum, compounded annually. After the 3rd year, the interest rate increases to 6.25%. How much will he have after 5 years?

 33. Thinking/Inquiry/Problem Solving Sue-Lang has $3750 in her account, which pays annual interest of 5.5%, compounded annually. After one year, the interest rate decreases to 5%. Two years later, the rate increases to 6%.

a) How much will Sue-Lang have in her account after 5 years?

b) The *effective* interest rate is the constant rate that would result in the same growth at the end of the given period. What is the effective interest rate Sue-Lang earned during the 5 years?

34. Use the formula for the nth term of a geometric sequence, $t_n = ar^{n-1}$, to derive the formula for amount, $A = P(1 + i)^n$.

3.2　Compound Interest: Other Compounding Periods

Interest is often calculated more frequently than once a year. For example, interest may be calculated every 6 months. We say the *compounding period* is 6 months.

When an interest rate is quoted, it is an annual rate. So, we delete the words "per annum" when describing an interest rate.

Semi-annual compounding

Suppose you open an investment account and deposit $1000. The interest rate is 6% compounded semi-annually. How much will be in the account after 10 years?

Compounded semi-annually means that interest is calculated and added to the principal two times each year. A rate of *6% compounded semi-annually* means you will receive 3% interest every 6 months.

We can use the multiplier principle to calculate the amount after every 6 months.

1st 6 months:	$1000(1.03) $= \$1030.00$
next 6 months:	$1000(1.03)^2 = \$1060.90$
next 6 months:	$1000(1.03)^3 \doteq \$1092.73$
$\vdots$	$\vdots$
10th year:	$1000(1.03)^{20} \doteq \$1806.11$

There will be $1806.11 in the account after 10 years.

We could have used the compound interest formula $A = P(1 + i)^n$ to determine this amount. Substitute $P = 1000$, $i = 0.03$, and $n = 20$.

$$A = 1000(1.03)^{20}$$
$$\doteq 1806.11$$

When interest is compounded semi-annually, there are 2 interest calculations each year. The interest rate for each 6-month period is $\frac{1}{2}$ the annual rate. The number of compounding periods is $2 \times$ the number of years.

Monthly compounding

Suppose you open an investment account and deposit $1000. The interest rate is 6% compounded monthly. How much will be in the account after 10 years?

Compounded monthly means that interest is calculated every month.
6% compounded monthly means that you will receive $\frac{6}{12}\% = 0.5\%$ interest every month. In 10 years, there are 10×12, or 120 compounding periods.

Use the formula $A = P(1 + i)^n$. Substitute $P = 1000$, $i = 0.005$, and $n = 120$.

$$A = 1000(1.005)^{120}$$
$$\doteq 1819.40$$

There will be $1819.40 in the account after 10 years.

When interest is compounded monthly, there are 12 interest calculations per year. The interest rate each month is $\frac{1}{12}$ the annual rate. The number of compounding periods is $12 \times$ the number of years.

Take Note

Compound Interest Formula

Recall the formulas $A = P(1 + i)^n$ and $P = \frac{A}{(1 + i)^n}$:

A is the amount, in dollars.

P is the principal, in dollars.

i is the interest rate for each compounding period, expressed as a decimal.

n is the number of compounding periods.

Amounts and present values can be found for any compounding periods, including weekly or daily.

Example 1

Sophie put $2500 into a Registered Retirement Savings Plan (an RRSP) that earns $7\frac{1}{2}\%$ compounded semi-annually. Determine the amount after 8 years.

Solution

Use the formula for amount.

The interest rate per compounding period is $\frac{7.5\%}{2} = 3.75\%$.

Substitute $P = 2500$, $i = 0.0375$, $n = 8 \times 2 = 16$.

$$A = P(1 + i)^n$$
$$= 2500(1.0375)^{16}$$
$$\doteq 4505.57$$

The amount after 8 years is $4505.57.

Example 2

What principal should be invested today to have \$10 000 after 6 years?
The interest rate is 5% compounded monthly.

Solution

Use the formula for present value. Substitute $A = 10\ 000$, $i = \frac{0.05}{12}$, $n = 6 \times 12 = 72$.

$$P = \frac{A}{(1 + i)^n}$$

$$= \frac{10\ 000}{\left(1 + \frac{0.05}{12}\right)^{72}}$$

Key in: 10000 $\div$ (1 + 0.05 $\div$
12) ^ 72 ENTER

$$\doteq 7412.80$$

A principal of \$7412.80 should be invested today.

3.2 Exercises

1. Use the formula $A = P(1 + i)^n$. Calculate A for each set of values.

    a) $P = \$100$, $i = 0.03$, $n = 10$ **b)** $P = \$200$, $i = 0.04$, $n = 8$

    c) $P = \$250$, $i = 0.025$, $n = 4$ **d)** $P = \$150$, $i = 0.0575$, $n = 7$

2. Calculate the amount.

    a) \$350 invested for 5 years at 6% compounded annually

    b) \$225 invested for 4 years at 5% compounded semi-annually

    c) \$570 invested for 6 years at 4.5% compounded quarterly

3. Use the formula $P = \frac{A}{(1 + i)^n}$. Calculate P for each set of values.

    a) $A = \$1500$, $i = 0.05$, $n = 12$ **b)** $A = \$2360$, $i = 0.06$, $n = 10$

    c) $A = \$3475$, $i = 0.055$, $n = 8$ **d)** $A = \$4572$, $i = 0.0325$, $n = 5$

4. Calculate the present value.

    a) \$5000 in 10 years at 5% compounded annually

    b) \$6000 in 8 years at 4% compounded semi-annually

    c) \$10 000 in 7 years at $4\frac{1}{4}$% compounded monthly

5. The interest is compounded semi-annually. Determine each amount.

    a) \$480 for 5 years at 6%   **b)** \$300 for 8 years at 5%

    c) \$550 for 7 years at 6.5%   **d)** \$1500 for 10 years at $4\frac{3}{4}$%

6. The interest is compounded monthly. Determine each amount.

  a) $250 for 4 years at 6% **b)** $500 for 7 years at 4%

  c) $750 for 3 years at 5.25% **d)** $4000 for 9 years at $7\frac{1}{2}$%

  e) $450 for 2 years at $4\frac{1}{4}$% **f)** $980 for 3 years at $5\frac{1}{8}$%

7. Determine the interest on $1000 after 1 year at each rate.

  a) 4.5% compounded semi-annually **b)** 4.5% compounded monthly

8. Calculate the amount after $250 are invested for 3 years at each rate.

  a) 5% compounded monthly **b)** 5% compounded semi-annually

9. Determine the principal that should be deposited today to amount to $1000 in 3 years at each rate.

  a) 4.5% compounded semi-annually **b)** 4.5% compounded monthly

10. Knowledge/Understanding Determine the interest rate for a principal of $150 to amount to $275 in 8 years with interest compounded semi-annually.

11. On May 1, 2001, Marcie deposited $500 in a term deposit that pays 4% compounded semi-annually. On May 1, 2002, she deposited another $500. There are no further deposits and no withdrawals. Determine the amount in Marcie's account on May 1, 2003.

12. Application This table shows the growth of a $6000 RRSP.

  a) Graph the data.

  b) Describe the growth of this RRSP investment.

  c) Estimate the time required for the RRSP to amount to $15 000.

  d) Estimate the amount after 7 years.

Time (years)	Amount ($)
0	6000.00
1	6375.00
2	6773.44
3	7196.78
4	7646.58
5	8124.49

13. What principal invested today at $3\frac{1}{2}$% compounded semi-annually will amount to $2500 in 6 years?

14. Suppose you deposit $1000 in an investment account for one year at 6%. How much more money will you receive if the investment is:

  a) compounded semi-annually instead of annually?

  b) compounded quarterly instead of semi-annually?

  c) compounded monthly instead of quarterly?

15. Mark plans to invest $500 in a GIC for 2 years. He has a choice of two plans:
Plan A: 6.75% compounded annually
Plan B: 6.60% compounded monthly

What will the GIC be worth after 2 years for each plan?

16. **Communication** Use the result of exercise 15. Explain why a lower annual interest rate may result in a greater amount.

17. Andrea plans to invest $750 in a GIC for 3 years. She has a choice of two plans:

    Plan A: 7.5% compounded annually
    Plan B: 7.5% compounded quarterly

    a) Which plan provides more interest? How do you know?

    b) How much more interest will Andrea receive under this plan?

18. Trevor borrowed $500 from his uncle and paid it back after 3 years. His uncle charged 3% compounded quarterly. How much did Trevor pay his uncle?

19. Maya plans to invest $3000 for 5 years. She wants at least $4000 after 5 years. What interest rate compounded semi-annually does she require?

20. Start a new spreadsheet. Enter the text in column A and in row 5. These data are from *Example 1*. Enter the data shown in cells C2, C3, and C4. Enter these formulas in cells C6, D6, E6, and F6:

    C6: =C2*(1+C3)^C4
    D6: =C2*(1+C3/2)^(C4*2)
    E6: =C2*(1+C3/4)^(C4*4)
    F6: =C2*(1+C3/12)^(C4*12)

    The computer displays the values shown below. Compare this result with *Example 1*.

	A	B	C	D	E	F
1	Calculating Amount					
2	Principal		2,500.00			
3	Annual interest rate		7.50%			
4	Number of years		8			
5	Type of compounding		Annual	Semi-annual	Quarterly	Monthly
6	Amount		4,458.69	4,505.57	4,530.06	4,546.80

Use your spreadsheet to solve each problem.

a) Suppose you invest $1000 for 5 years at 6.5% compounded quarterly. What is the amount?

b) Suppose you invest $2000 at 4.25% compounded monthly. How many years will it take to amount to $3000?

c) Suppose you want to accumulate $10 000 in 12 years in an investment account that pays 5.75% compounded semi-annually. How much do you need to deposit now?

21. Use the spreadsheet in exercise 20. The spreadsheet shows the amount of $2500.00 after 8 years at 7.50% interest with different compounding periods. What <u>interest rate</u>, compounded annually, gives approximately the same amount as each interest rate?

a) 7.5% compounded semi-annually

b) 7.5% compounded quarterly

c) 7.5% compounded monthly

22. Determine, to the nearest half-year, how long it will take $100 to amount to $500 at $6\frac{1}{2}$% compounded semi-annually.

23. Determine, to the nearest month, how long it will take $300 to amount to $1000 at 5% compounded monthly.

24. **Thinking/Inquiry/Problem Solving** Shabir makes regular contributions to his RRSP, starting on January 1. Which investment schedule would you recommend and why?

a) On the first day of each month, invest $100 at 8.5% compounded monthly.

b) On January 1 and July 1, invest $600 at 8.5% compounded semi-annually.

25. Determine how long it takes money to double in each situation.

a) 7% compounded semi-annually

b) $5\frac{1}{4}$% compounded semi-annually

c) $8\frac{1}{2}$% compounded monthly

26. Banks use computers to calculate daily interest. They could use the same technology to calculate interest for compounding periods of 1 hour or even 1 second. Use a graphing calculator to investigate whether there would be any advantage to this. Enter these formulas, which calculate the amount for 1 day, 1 hour, and 1 second, for $100 invested at 6% interest.

Y1 = 100(1 + .06/365)^(365X)
Y2 = 100(1 + .06/365/24)^(365*24X)
Y3 = 100(1 + .06/365/24/3600)^(365*24*3600X)

Press [2nd] [WINDOW] for TBLSET. Select values of X that are multiples of 5. Display the tables of values that correspond to these functions.

a) Compare the amounts after 35 years when interest is calculated by the day, the hour, and the second.

b) How do these amounts compare with the amount of $100 invested at 6% compounded monthly?

c) Suggest reasons why financial institutions rarely offer interest compounded hourly or by the minute.

1. **a)** Suppose you invest $500 at 7.5% compounded annually. What is the amount after 9 years?

   b) Suppose $750 grows to $1800 in 9 years. What is the annual interest rate?

   c) Suppose $3000 grows to $9000 at 8% compounded annually. How many years does it take?

2. Calculate the amount.

   a) $600 invested for 11 years at 6.2% compounded annually

   b) $1800 invested for 9 years at 7.25% compounded annually

3. Calculate the present value of each amount.

   a) $1000 in 8 years at 5.5% compounded annually

   b) $1500 in 5 years at 8.75% compounded annually

4. Suppose the interest is compounded semi-annually. Determine each amount.

   a) $3000 for 10 years at 6%   **b)** $1500 for 9 years at $3\frac{3}{4}\%$

5. Suppose the interest is compounded monthly. Determine each amount.

   a) $750 for 3 years at 5.25%   **b)** $2000 for 9.5 years at $7\frac{1}{2}\%$

6. A $1000 GIC pays interest at 6.38% compounded annually. Determine the value of the GIC after 8 years.

7. Suppose you want to accumulate $5000 in 10 years. How much would you need to invest today at 5.87% compounded annually?

8. Determine the interest rate necessary for $1500 to amount to $2075 in 6 years with interest compounded semi-annually.

9. What principal invested today at 6.22% compounded semi-annually will amount to $2500 in 10 years?

10. Mei-Lin borrowed $800 from her aunt and paid it back in a lump sum after 2 years. Her aunt charged 4% interest compounded monthly. How much did Mei-Lin pay her aunt?

11. Suppose you invest $1000 at 5.5% compounded semi-annually. How many years will it take to amount to $3000?

3.3 The Amount of an Annuity

Suppose you make regular deposits into an account. You deposit $1000 at the end of each year into an account that pays 6% compounded annually. What will the amount be after 10 years?

The time diagram illustrates this situation. The amount of each deposit after 10 years is shown at the right. The amount after 10 years is the sum of these amounts.

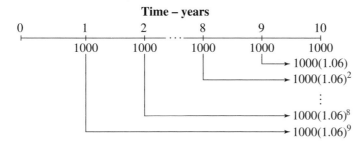

The amount after 10 years is:

$1000 + 1000(1.06) + 1000(1.06)^2 + \ldots + 1000(1.06)^9$

This is a geometric series with 10 terms, where the first term is 1000 and the common ratio is 1.06.

To calculate the amount, use the formula from Chapter 1 for the sum of the first *n* terms of a geometric series.

$$S = \frac{a(r^n - 1)}{r - 1}$$

Substitute $a = 1000$, $r = 1.06$, $n = 10$.

$$S = \frac{1000(1.06^{10} - 1)}{1.06 - 1}$$

$$= \frac{1000(1.06^{10} - 1)}{0.06}$$

$$\doteq 13\ 180.79$$

Key in: 1000 (1.06 ^ 10 − 1)
÷ 0.06 ENTER =

After 10 years, the amount will be $13 180.79.

The series of deposits shown above is called an *annuity*. An annuity is a series of equal deposits made at equal time intervals. When the deposits are made at the end of each time interval, the annuity is called an *ordinary annuity*. The total value of all the deposits at the end of the last time interval is called the *amount* of the annuity. The compounding period is the time between deposits.

For all annuities in this chapter, the deposit is made at the end of each period unless stated otherwise.

To obtain a formula for the amount of an annuity, use the time diagram below.

  R dollars represents the regular deposit.
  i represents the interest rate per period.
  n represent the number of periods.

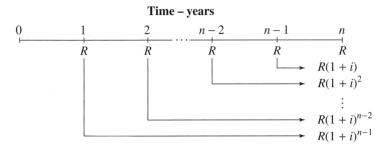

The amount, A, of all the deposits after n periods is:

$A = R + R(1 + i) + R(1 + i)^2 + \ldots + R(1 + i)^{n-1}$

Use the formula for the sum of the first n terms of a geometric series.

$$S = \frac{a(r^n - 1)}{r - 1}$$

Substitute $S = A$, $a = R$, $r = 1 + i$.

$$A = \frac{R[(1 + i)^n - 1]}{(1 + i) - 1}$$

$$= \frac{R[(1 + i)^n - 1]}{i}$$

After n periods, the amount will be $\dfrac{R[(1 + i)^n - 1]}{i}$ dollars.

Take Note

Amount of an Ordinary Annuity

A deposit R is made at the end of each period for n periods.
The deposits earn interest at a rate i per period.
The amount of these deposits at the end of the nth period is:

$$A = \frac{R[(1 + i)^n - 1]}{i}$$

A is the amount of the annuity.

This formula can only be used when:

- The deposit interval is the same as the compounding period.
- A deposit is made at the end of each compounding period.

Example 1

Suppose you deposit $250 every 6 months into an investment account that pays 4.5% compounded semi-annually. What is the amount of these regular deposits after 3 years?

Solution

The time diagram illustrates this situation.

Time – years

```
0          1          2          3
+----+----+----+----+----+----+
   250  250  250  250  250  250

   ──────────────────────────────► A
```

Regular deposits of $250 grow to $A in 3 years.

Discuss

This is a simplified time diagram. Compare it with the time diagram on page 152. Which conveys more information? Explain.

Use the formula for the amount of an ordinary annuity.

$$A = \frac{R[(1 + i)^n - 1]}{i}$$

Substitute $R = 250$, $i = \frac{0.045}{2} = 0.0225$, $n = 2 \times 3 = 6$.

$$A = \frac{250(1.0225^6 - 1)}{0.0225}$$

$$\doteq 1586.95$$

After 3 years, the amount is $1586.95.

Example 2

Suppose you begin a savings program to have $2500 after 5 years. You make a regular deposit every 6 months into an investment account that pays 5.5% compounded semi-annually. Calculate the regular deposit.

Solution

The time diagram illustrates this situation.

Time – years

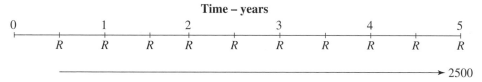

Regular deposits of $R grow to $2500 in 5 years.

Use the formula for the amount of an ordinary annuity.

$$A = \frac{R[(1 + i)^n - 1]}{i}$$

Substitute $A = 2500$, $i = \frac{0.055}{2} = 0.0275$, $n = 2 \times 5 = 10$.

$$2500 = \frac{R(1.0275^{10} - 1)}{0.0275}$$

Solve for R.

$$R = \frac{(2500)(0.0275)}{1.0275^{10} - 1}$$

$$\doteq 220.60$$

The regular deposit is \$220.60.

Discuss

The formula for amount can also be written

$$A = R\left[\frac{(1 + i)^n - 1}{i}\right].$$

Repeat the solution using this form. Which form is easier? Explain.

3.3 Exercises

1. Use the formula $A = \frac{R[(1 + i)^n - 1]}{i}$. Calculate A for each set of values.

a) $R = \$500$, $i = 0.04$, $n = 8$ b) $R = \$1000$, $i = 0.04$, $n = 8$

c) $R = \$500$, $i = 0.08$, $n = 8$ d) $R = \$500$, $i = 0.04$, $n = 16$

 2. Calculate the amount of each annuity. The interest compounds annually.

a) \$100 deposited every year for 6 years at 5%

b) \$200 deposited every year for 5 years at 4.5%

c) \$300 deposited every year for 8 years at $4\frac{1}{4}\%$

d) \$350 deposited every year for 3 years at $5\frac{3}{4}\%$

3. Use the formula $A = \frac{R[(1 + i)^n - 1]}{i}$. Calculate R for each set of values.

a) $A = \$2500$, $i = 0.03$, $n = 6$ b) $A = \$3000$, $i = 0.05$, $n = 10$

c) $A = \$2750$, $i = 0.045$, $n = 7$ d) $A = \$1800$, $i = 0.0325$, $n = 9$

 4. Calculate the regular deposit for each annuity.

a) \$5000 in 8 years at 5% compounded annually

b) \$6000 in 7 years at 6% compounded semi-annually

c) \$4000 in 4 years at 4.5% compounded quarterly

d) \$3000 in 5 years at 3.75% compounded monthly

Exercises 5 to 11 refer to *Example 1* or *Example 2*, pages 153, 154.

B

5. Refer to *Example 1*. Determine the amount in each case.

   a) The deposits are twice as great, $500.

   b) The interest rate is twice as great, 9%.

   c) The time period is twice as long, 6 years.

6. In which part(s) of exercise 5 is the amount twice as great as the amount in *Example 1*? Explain.

7. Refer to *Example 2*. Determine the regular deposit in each case.

   a) The amount is twice as great, $5000.

   b) The interest rate is twice as great, 11% compounded semi-annually.

   c) The time period is twice as long, 10 years.

8. In which part(s) of exercise 7 is the regular deposit twice as great as the regular deposit in *Example 2*? Explain.

9. In *Example 1*, you deposit $250 every 6 months into an investment account that pays 4.5% compounded semi-annually. The graph below shows the amounts in the account for up to 60 years.

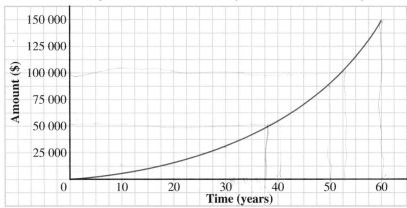

$250 every 6 months at 4.5% Compounded Semi-annually

   a) Estimate the amount you would have after each time.

i) 10 years	**ii)** 20 years	**iii)** 30 years
iv) 40 years	**v)** 50 years	**vi)** 60 years

   b) Estimate how long it would take to save each amount.

i) $50 000	**ii)** $100 000	**iii)** $150 000

   c) Describe how the amount grows as the number of years increases.

   d) Describe how the graph would change in each case.
   i) The interest rate is greater than 4.5%.
   ii) The regular deposit is greater than $250.

10. Start a new spreadsheet. Enter the text in column A and the symbols in column C. Enter the data shown in cells D2, D3, D4, and D5. These data are from *Example 1*. Enter these formulas in cells D6, D7, and D8:

D6: =D3/D4
D7: =D4*D5
D8: =D2*((1+D6)^D7−1)/D6

The computer displays the amount shown below in cell D8. Compare this result with *Example 1*.

	A	B	C	D
1	Calculating the Amount of an Annuity			
2	Regular deposits		R	250.00
3	Annual interest rate			4.50%
4	Compounding periods per year			2
5	Number of years			3
6	Interest rate per period		i	2.25%
7	Number of periods		n	6
8	Amount		A	1,586.95

Use your spreadsheet to solve each problem.

What's wrong?

a) Determine the amount after 3 years for each interest rate.
  i) 4.5% compounded monthly   **ii)** 4.5% compounded annually
  iii) 7.25% compounded monthly   **iv)** 9.75% compounded quarterly
  Change the interest rate back to 4.5% compounded semi-annually.

b) Determine the amount after each time at 4.5% compounded semi-annually.
  i) 2 years   **ii)** 4 years   **iii)** 10 years   **iv)** 15 years
  Change the number of years back to 3 before you continue.

11. Use the spreadsheet in exercise 10. Suppose you want an amount of $5000. You could do this in different ways.

a) You could increase the regular deposit. What regular deposit is needed to produce an amount of $5000?

Change the regular deposit back to $250 before you continue.

b) You could increase the time. How many years are needed to produce an amount of $5000?

12. Knowledge/Understanding A deposit of $2000 is made at the end of every year for 8 years at 7.5% compounded annually. Calculate the amount of the annuity after 8 years.

13. A deposit of $100 is made at the end of every six months for 5 years at 6% compounded semi-annually. Calculate the amount of the annuity after 5 years.

14. David deposits $50 at the end of each month for 5 years in an investment account that pays 6% compounded monthly. Calculate the amount in the account after 5 years.

15. Consider these three annuities.

Annuity A: $400 per month for 5 years at 6% compounded monthly
Annuity B: $200 per month for 10 years at 6% compounded monthly
Annuity C: $100 per month for 20 years at 6% compounded monthly

The total of all the regular deposits is the same for each annuity.

a) Predict which annuity has the greatest amount; or are all the amounts the same? Explain.

b) Carry out calculations to confirm your prediction in part a.

16. Application One month after their twins were born, Mr. and Mrs. Deepstra deposited $25 to open an account that pays 6% compounded monthly. The parents deposit $25 each month. What is the amount on the twins' birthday after each time?

a) 10 years   **b)** 15 years   **c)** 20 years

17. Suppose you begin a savings program to have $1000 after 4 years. You can obtain 6.5% compounded semi-annually in an investment account. How much should you deposit every 6 months?

18. What regular deposit must be made at the end of each year in an account that pays 7% compounded annually, to have an amount of $2000 after 8 years?

19. What regular deposit would you have to invest at the end of every 6 months for the next 10 years to amount to $5000 at each interest rate?

a) 5.4% compounded semi-annually

b) 7.6% compounded semi-annually

20. A company plans to replace its computers in 3 years. It estimates it will cost $50 000. To prepare for the expense, the company invests monthly in an account that pays 4.5% interest compounded monthly. What monthly deposit should the company make to ensure it has $50 000 in 3 years?

21. Suppose you deposit $1000 into an investment account each year for 10 years, then leave the amount on deposit for another 30 years. The money earns an average return of 7% compounded annually. How much will be in the account after 40 years?

22. Suppose you deposit $500 at the end of each 6-month period in an account that pays 6% compounded semi-annually. What will the amount be after 8 years?

23. Communication A contest winner is given the choice of receiving $1 000 000 today or $80 000 in annual payments over 20 years, starting one year from today. Which is the better choice? Make a recommendation, then justify it.

Comparing long-term investment strategies

✓ **24.** Martha and Randy are both 25 years old. They save for their retirement years using these strategies.

Martha: Saves $1000 at the end of each year for 40 years.
Randy: Waits 20 years. Then saves $5000 at the end of each year for 20 years.

a) What is the total amount each person plans to save?

b) Assume each investment pays 8% compounded annually. Who will have the greater amount at age 65?

c) In part b, would it be possible for the other person to have the greater amount if the interest rate was different from 8%? Explain.

25. Thinking/Inquiry/Problem Solving Dave and Milena have different long-term investment strategies.

Dave: Deposits $1000 at the end of each year for 10 years in an account. Then he leaves the money to earn interest for another 20 years.
Milena: Waits 10 years. Then she deposits $1000 at the end of each year for 20 years.

Which is the better plan? Explain.

26. Suppose you deposit the same principal into an investment account at the end of each year. You want the amount to be $1 000 000.

a) Suppose you did this for 50 years, and the interest rate is 7% compounded annually. How much would you have to deposit each year?

b) Suppose you did this for 50 years, and you deposit $5000 each year. What interest rate would you need?

c) Suppose you deposit $5000 each year, and the interest rate is 7% compounded annually. How many years would it take?

C

27. Suppose you deposit $500 every six months in an account that pays 6.4% compounded semi-annually. About how many years will it take to amount to $20 000?

28. Suppose you deposit $500 every six months in an investment account for 10 years. What interest rate will you need to have an amount of $15 000?

29. a) Suppose you deposit $1000 at the beginning of each year into an account that pays 6% compounded annually. What will the amount be after 10 years?

b) The annuity in part a is an example of an *annuity due* because the payments are made at the beginning of each compounding period. Determine a formula for the amount of an annuity due of R dollars per period after n periods at an interest rate i per period.

3.4 The Present Value of an Annuity

Suppose you have promised to pay your niece an annuity of $300 at the end of each year for the next 10 years. You open an account that pays 7% compounded annually. You deposit enough money today so you can withdraw $300 at the end of each year for the next 10 years. How much money do you need to deposit now?

The time diagram illustrates this situation. Use the formula for present value, $P = \dfrac{A}{(1 + i)^n}$. The present value of each deposit is shown at the left. The money you need to deposit now is the sum of these present values.

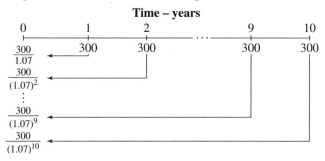

The money you need to deposit now is:

$$\frac{300}{1.07} + \frac{300}{(1.07)^2} + \frac{300}{(1.07)^3} + \ldots + \frac{300}{(1.07)^9} + \frac{300}{(1.07)^{10}}$$

This is a geometric series with first term $\dfrac{300}{1.07}$ and common ratio $\dfrac{1}{1.07}$.

Instead of using this series, it is simpler to reverse the order of the terms.

$$\frac{300}{(1.07)^{10}} + \frac{300}{(1.07)^9} + \ldots + \frac{300}{(1.07)^3} + \frac{300}{(1.07)^2} + \frac{300}{1.07}$$

This is a geometric series with first term $\dfrac{300}{(1.07)^{10}}$ and common ratio 1.07.

Use the formula for the sum of the first n terms of a geometric series.

$$S = \frac{a(r^n - 1)}{r - 1}$$

Substitute $a = \dfrac{300}{(1.07)^{10}}$, $r = 1.07$, $n = 10$.

$$S = \frac{300}{(1.07)^{10}} \times \frac{1.07^{10} - 1}{1.07 - 1}$$

$$= \frac{300(1.07^{10} - 1)}{(1.07)^{10}(0.07)}$$

Key in: 300 (1.07 ^ 10 – 1)
÷ 1.07 ^ 10 ÷ 0.07 ENTER

$$\doteq 2107.07$$

The money you need to deposit now is $2107.07.
This amount is the present value of the annuity.

To obtain a formula for the present value of an ordinary annuity, use the time diagram that follows.

R represents the regular payment in dollars.
i represents the interest rate per period.
n represents the number of periods.

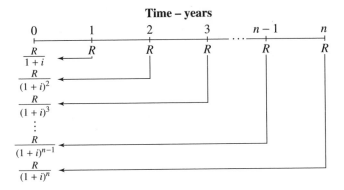

The present value, P, of all the payments is:

$$P = \frac{R}{(1+i)^n} + \frac{R}{(1+i)^{n-1}} + \frac{R}{(1+i)^{n-2}} + \ldots + \frac{R}{(1+i)^2} + \frac{R}{1+i}$$

Use the formula for the sum of the first n terms of a geometric series.

$$S = \frac{a(r^n - 1)}{r - 1}$$

Substitute $S = P$, $a = \dfrac{R}{(1+i)^n}$, $r = 1 + i$.

$$P = \frac{R}{(1+i)^n} \times \frac{(1+i)^n - 1}{(1+i) - 1}$$

$$= \frac{R[(1+i)^n - 1]}{i(1+i)^n}$$

$$= \frac{R}{i} \times \left[\frac{(1+i)^n - 1}{(1+i)^n}\right]$$

$$= \frac{R}{i} \times \left[\frac{(1+i)^n}{(1+i)^n} - \frac{1}{(1+i)^n}\right]$$

$$= \frac{R}{i} \times [1 - (1+i)^{-n}]$$

$$= \frac{R[1 - (1+i)^{-n}]}{i}$$

The present value of the annuity is $\dfrac{R[1 - (1+i)^{-n}]}{i}$ dollars.

Take Note

Present Value of an Ordinary Annuity

A payment R is withdrawn from an account at the end of each period for n periods.

The account earns interest at a rate i per period. The amount required in the account at the beginning of the first period is:

$$P = \frac{R[1 - (1+i)^{-n}]}{i}$$

P is the present value of the annuity.

This formula can only be used when:

- The payment interval is the same as the compounding period.
- A payment is made at the end of each compounding period.

Example 1

Suppose you have an investment account that pays 5.5% compounded semi-annually. You wish to withdraw $350 every 6 months for 3 years. What is the present value of this annuity? That is, how much do you need to have in the account now?

Solution

The time diagram illustrates this situation.

Time – years

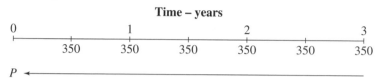

The present value of the annuity is $P.

Use the formula for the present value of an ordinary annuity.

$$P = \frac{R[1 - (1 + i)^{-n}]}{i}$$

Substitute $R = 350$, $i = \frac{0.055}{2} = 0.0275$, $n = 2 \times 3 = 6$.

$$P = \frac{350(1 - 1.0275^{-6})}{0.0275}$$

Key in: 350 (1 – 1.0275 ^ (-)

6) ÷ 0.0275 ENTER =

$$\doteq 1911.83$$

The present value of the annuity is $1911.83; that is, you need to have $1911.83 in the account now.

Example 2

Sue needs to borrow $7500 to purchase a used car. The car dealer arranges with a finance company to lend Sue the money at 2.9% compounded monthly for 3 years. What will Sue's monthly payment be?

Solution

Sue needs the money now to pay for the car.
The time diagram illustrates this situation.

Time – years

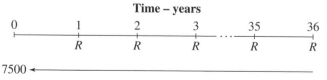

The present value of the payments is $7500.

Use the formula for the present value of an ordinary annuity. Determine R.

$$P = \frac{R[1 - (1 + i)^{-n}]}{i}$$

Substitute $P = 7500$, $i = \frac{0.029}{12}$, $n = 3 \times 12 = 36$.

$$7500 = \frac{R\left[1 - \left(1 + \frac{0.029}{12}\right)^{-36}\right]}{\frac{0.029}{12}}$$

Solve for R.

$$R = \frac{(7500)(0.029)}{12\left[1 - \left(1 + \frac{0.029}{12}\right)^{-36}\right]}$$

$\doteq 217.78$

Key in: 7500 $\boxed{\times}$ 0.029 $\boxed{\div}$ 12 $\boxed{\div}$
$\boxed{(}$ 1 $\boxed{-}$ $\boxed{(}$ 1 $\boxed{+}$ 0.029 $\boxed{\div}$ 12
$\boxed{)}$ $\boxed{\wedge}$ $\boxed{(-)}$ 36 $\boxed{)}$ $\boxed{\text{ENTER}}$ $\boxed{=}$

Sue's monthly payment is $217.78.

3.4 Exercises

1. Use the formula $P = \frac{R[1 - (1 + i)^{-n}]}{i}$. Calculate P for each set of values.

   a) $R = \$500$, $i = 0.04$, $n = 8$

   b) $R = \$1000$, $i = 0.04$, $n = 8$

   c) $R = \$500$, $i = 0.08$, $n = 8$

   d) $R = \$500$, $i = 0.04$, $n = 16$

2. Calculate the present value of each annuity.

   a) A payment of $400 every year for 6 years at 5% compounded annually

   b) A payment of $600 every 6 months for 4 years at 3% compounded semi-annually

   c) A payment of $750 every 3 months for 5 years at $4\frac{1}{2}\%$ compounded quarterly

   d) A payment of $200 every month for 3 years at $3\frac{1}{4}\%$ compounded monthly

3. Use the formula $P = \frac{R[1 - (1 + i)^{-n}]}{i}$. Calculate R for each set of values.

   a) $P = \$5000$, $i = 0.05$, $n = 12$

   b) $P = \$6500$, $i = 0.07$, $n = 24$

   c) $P = \$8250$, $i = 0.0125$, $n = 36$

   d) $P = \$4236$, $i = 0.0225$, $n = 15$

4. Calculate the regular payment for each annuity. The payment period is the same as the compounding period.

   a) A loan of $10 000 at 5% compounded annually for 4 years
   b) A loan of $15 000 at 4% compounded semi-annually for 8 years
   c) A loan of $20 000 at 3.5% compounded quarterly for 5 years
   d) A loan of $25 000 at 6.25% compounded monthly for 10 years

B

Exercises 5 to 12 refer to *Example 1* or *Example 2*, pages 161, 162.

5. Refer to *Example 1*. Determine the present value in each case.

   a) The withdrawals are twice as great, $700.
   b) The interest rate is twice as great, 11%.
   c) The time period is twice as long, 6 years.

6. In which part(s) of exercise 5 is the present value twice as great as the present value in *Example 1*? Explain.

 7. Refer to *Example 2*. Determine the monthly payment in each case.

   a) The amount borrowed is twice as great, $15 000.
   b) The interest rate is twice as great, 5.8% compounded monthly.
   c) The time period is twice as long, 6 years.

 8. In which part(s) of exercise 7 is the monthly payment twice as great as the payment in *Example 2*? Explain.

9. In *Example 1*, you withdraw $350 every 6 months from an account that pays 5.5% compounded semi-annually. The graph below shows the amounts in the account for up to 60 years.

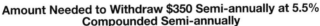

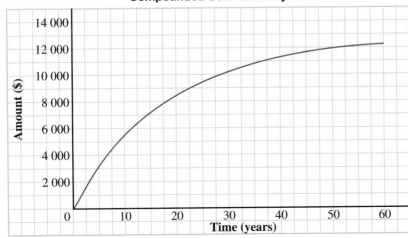

a) Estimate the amount you would need to do this for each time.

    i) 10 years   **ii)** 20 years   **iii)** 30 years

    iv) 40 years   **v)** 50 years   **vi)** 60 years

b) Estimate how long you could do this for each amount.

    i) $5000   **ii)** $7500   **iii)** $10 000

c) Describe how the amount grows as the number of years increases.

d) Describe how the graph would change in each case.

    i) The interest rate is greater than 5.5%.

    ii) The regular withdrawal is greater than $350.

10. Compare the graph in exercise 9 with the graph in Section 3.3, exercise 9. Explain why the graphs go up to the right in different ways.

11. Compare the graph in exercise 9 with the graph in Section 3.1, exercise 10. Explain why one graph goes up to the right and the other goes down to the right.

12. Start a new spreadsheet. Enter the text in column A and the symbols in column C. Enter the data shown in cells D2, D3, D4, and D5. The data are from *Example 1*. Enter these formulas in cells D6, D7, and D8:

    D6: =D3/D4

    D7: =D4*D5

    D8: =D2*(1−(1+D6)^−D7)/D6

The computer displays the present value shown below in cell D8. Compare this result with *Example 1*.

	A	B	C	D
1	Calculating the Present Value of an Annuity			
2	Regular payments		R	350.00
3	Annual interest rate			5.50%
4	Compounding periods per year			2
5	Number of years			3
6	Interest rate per period		i	2.75%
7	Number of periods		n	6
8	Present value		P	1,911.83

Use your spreadsheet to solve each problem.

a) Determine the present value for each interest rate.

    i) 5.5% compounded monthly   **ii)** 5.5% compounded annually

    iii) 8.65% compounded monthly   **iv)** 9.08% compounded quarterly

    Change the interest rate back to 5.5% compounded semi-annually before you continue.

b) Determine the present value for each time.

    i) 2 years   **ii)** 4 years   **iii)** 10 years   **iv)** 15 years

    Change the number of years back to 3 before you continue.

13. Knowledge/Understanding Calculate the present value of an annuity of $7500 invested every year for 12 years at 6.75% compounded annually.

14. Calculate the present value of an annuity of $500 invested every six months for 8 years at 8.25% compounded semi-annually.

15. Consider these three annuities.

Annuity A: $400 per month for 5 years at 6% compounded monthly
Annuity B: $200 per month for 10 years at 6% compounded monthly
Annuity C: $100 per month for 20 years at 6% compounded monthly

The total of all the payments is the same for each annuity.

a) Which annuity has the greatest present value, or are all the present values the same? Explain.

b) Carry out calculations to confirm your prediction in part a.

16. Application Mr. Singh's life savings total $300 000. He plans to use this money to purchase an annuity earning interest at 6.75% compounded semi-annually. This will provide him with equal semi-annual payments for 20 years. The first payment is 6 months from the date of purchase. How much is each semi-annual payment?

17. Communication Suppose you win a lottery. You have two choices for receiving the money:

Choice 1: $50 000 at the end of each year for 20 years
Choice 2: $500 000 now

Which is the better choice? Justify your decision.

18. Thinking/Inquiry/Problem Solving Suppose you deposit $1200 into an investment account that pays 6.5% compounded semi-annually. You plan to make equal withdrawals every 6 months for 5 years. The balance will become 0 when the last withdrawal is made. How much can you withdraw every 6 months?

C

19. Refer to the calculations on pages 159, 160.

a) Find a different way to determine the sum of the present values of the deposits.

b) Use your method to develop the formula for the present value of an annuity.

20. Sue has $4000 to invest in an annuity. She wants to receive payments of $1000 at the end of each year for the next 5 years. What interest rate must she obtain?

21. a) Suppose you wish to withdraw $1000 at the beginning of each year from an account that pays 6% compounded annually. You want to be able to do this for 10 years. What is the present value of this annuity?

b) The annuity in part a is an annuity due. Determine a formula for the present value of an annuity due of R dollars per period for n periods at an interest rate i per period.

1. Use the formula $A = \frac{R[(1 + i)^n - 1]}{i}$. Calculate A for each set of values.

   a) $R = \$800$, $i = 0.05$, $n = 10$

   b) $R = \$1000$, $i = 0.06$, $n = 9$

2. Calculate the amount of each annuity.

   a) A principal of $150 is invested at the end of each year for 15 years at 4.8% compounded annually.

   b) A principal of $400 is invested at the end of every 6 months for 7.5 years at 6.2% compounded semi-annually.

3. Suppose you deposit $324 every 6 months into an investment account that pays 4.9% compounded semi-annually. How much will you have after 5 years?

4. Suppose you begin a savings program to have $8000 after 7 years. You plan to make regular deposits every 6 months into an investment account that pays 5.8% compounded semi-annually. Calculate the regular deposit.

5. Use the formula $P = \frac{R[1 - (1 + i)^{-n}]}{i}$. Calculate P for each set of values.

   a) $R = \$400$, $i = 0.04$, $n = 9$

   b) $R = \$1000$, $i = 0.08$, $n = 11$

6. Calculate the present value of each annuity.

   a) A payment of $2000 is withdrawn at the end of each year for 10 years. The principal is invested at 6.4% compounded annually.

   b) A payment of $350 is withdrawn at the end of each month for 5 years. The principal is invested at 6% compounded monthly.

7. Suppose you have an investment account that pays 4.5% compounded semi-annually. You wish to withdraw $360 every 6 months for 4 years. How much do you need to have in the account now?

8. Rosina borrowed $12 500 to purchase her new car. The finance company offered her a loan at 4.8% compounded monthly for 3 years. What is Rosina's monthly payment?

9. Dimitri deposits $50 at the end of each month for 5 years in an investment account that pays 6% compounded monthly. Calculate the amount in the account after 5 years.

10. What deposit must be made at the end of each year in an account that pays 7.6% compounded annually to have $16 000 after 8 years?

3.5 Mortgages

Most people who buy a home require a loan called a *mortgage*. A mortgage is similar to other loans but is repaid over a longer time called the *amortization period*. During this period, some of the conditions of the mortgage may change. For example, the original interest rate may apply for only 3 years. In this section, we will assume that the interest rate is constant for the entire amortization period unless stated otherwise.

Canadian law requires that mortgage interest rates be compounded semi-annually. For example, a mortgage rate of 8% means "8% compounded semi-annually." Since the payments are usually made monthly, the payment interval is not the same as the compounding period. We must allow for this discrepancy when we do calculations that involve mortgage interest rates.

Converting a semi-annual rate to a monthly rate

To convert a mortgage rate of 8% compounded semi-annually to a monthly rate, consider these time diagrams.

Interest rate i every month

Time – months

$1 grows to $1(1 + i)^6$ in 6 months.

Interest rate 8%, or 4% every 6 months

Time – years

```
0                                    0.5
1
```

$1 grows to $1(1.04)$ in 0.5 years.

Since the two amounts are equal:

$$(1 + i)^6 = 1.04$$

Take the 6th root of each side.

$$\left[(1 + i)^6\right]^{\frac{1}{6}} = 1.04^{\frac{1}{6}}$$

$$1 + i = 1.04^{\frac{1}{6}}$$

$$1 + i \doteq 1.006\ 558\ 197$$

$$i \doteq 0.006\ 558\ 197$$

$$\doteq 0.655\ 819\ 7\%$$

Therefore, 8% compounded semi-annually is equivalent to 0.655 819 7% every month.

Example 1

Rita buys a home. She needs a mortgage of $100 000. The bank offers Rita a 25-year mortgage at 8.5%. What is the monthly payment?

Solution

A mortgage rate of 8.5% means 8.5% compounded semi-annually.

The semi-annual rate is $\frac{0.085}{2} = 0.0425$.

Let i represent the monthly rate. Calculate the monthly rate.

Consider the amount of $1 after 6 months at each rate.

Since the two rates are equivalent, the amounts after 6 months are equal.

$$(1 + i)^6 = 1.0425$$

Take the 6th root of each side.

$$1 + i = 1.0425^{\frac{1}{6}}$$
$$i = 1.0425^{\frac{1}{6}} - 1$$
$$\doteq 0.006\ 961\ 062$$

The monthly interest rate is about 0.696 106 2%.

The time diagram illustrates this situation. Since $25 \times 12 = 300$, the amortization period is 300 months.

Time – months

The present value of the payments is $100 000.

Use the formula for the present value of an ordinary annuity.

$$P = \frac{R[1 - (1 + i)^{-n}]}{i}$$

Solve for R.

$$R = \frac{Pi}{1 - (1 + i)^{-n}}$$

Substitute $P = 100\ 000$, $i = 0.006\ 961\ 062$, $n = 25 \times 12 = 300$.

$$R = \frac{(100\ 000)(0.006\ 961\ 062)}{1 - (1.006\ 961\ 062)^{-300}}$$
$$\doteq 795.36$$

The monthly payment is $795.36.

The monthly payment on a loan or mortgage depends on three factors:
- the principal
- the interest rate
- the amortization period

Example 2

Calculate the total interest paid on the mortgage in *Example 1*.

Solution

There are 300 monthly payments of $795.36.

The total of the 300 payments is $300 \times \$795.36 = \$238\ 608$.

The total interest paid is $\$238\ 608 - \$100\ 000 = \$138\ 608$.

Example 3

How much is still owing on the mortgage in *Example 1* after the first 3 years?

Solution

Let P represent the amount still owing; that is, the present value of the remaining payments.

Since 3 years have elapsed, the number of months remaining is $300 - (3 \times 12) = 264$.

The time diagram illustrates this situation.

Time – months

0	1	2	3	...	263	264
	795.36	795.36	795.36	...	795.36	795.36

$P \leftarrow$ ——————————————— ... ——————

The present value of the 264 remaining payments is P.

Use the formula for the present value of an ordinary annuity.

$$P = \frac{R[1 - (1 + i)^{-n}]}{i}$$

Substitute $R = 795.36$, $i = 0.006\ 961\ 062$, $n = 264$.

$$P = \frac{(795.36)(1 - 1.006\ 961\ 062^{-264})}{0.006\ 961\ 062}$$

$$\doteq 95\ 954.62$$

The amount still owing after the first 3 years is $95 954.62.

Discuss

Why is the amount still owing not $264 \times \$795.36$?

A

1. Calculate the equivalent monthly rate. Each interest rate is compounded semi-annually.

   a) 6%   **b)** 6.5%   **c)** 7%   **d)** 7.75%   **e)** 8.33%

 2. **Knowledge/Understanding** Determine the monthly payment for each mortgage.

   a) $120 000 at 6.5%, over 20 years

   b) $60 000 at 5.75%, over 10 years

   c) $90 000 at 8%, over 25 years

3. How much is still owing on each mortgage in exercise 2 after each time?

   a) 1 year   **b)** 2 years   **c)** 3 years   **d)** 4 years

B

Exercises 4 to 11 refer to *Examples 1* and *2*, pages 168, 169.

 4. To reduce the monthly payment, the bank offers Rita a 30-year mortgage.

   a) Repeat the solution of *Example 1*, replacing 25 years with 30 years. What is the monthly payment?

   b) Repeat the solution of *Example 2*, replacing 300 payments with 360 payments. What is the total interest paid?

5. To reduce the interest costs, Rita has a 20-year mortgage.

   a) Repeat the solution of *Example 1*, replacing 25 years with 20 years. What is the monthly payment?

   b) Repeat the solution of *Example 2*, replacing 300 payments with 240 payments. What is the total interest paid?

6. Suppose Rita shops around for a better interest rate. A trust company offers her a 25-year mortgage at 8.25%.

   a) Calculate the monthly payment.

   b) What is the total interest paid for this mortgage?

7. Suppose Rita waits for a month. The interest rate has increased to 8.75%.

   a) Calculate the monthly payment.

   b) What is the total interest paid for this mortgage?

8. The graph below shows how the monthly payment for Rita's mortgage in *Example 1* depends on the amortization period.

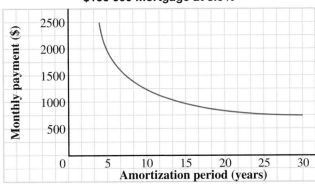

$100 000 Mortgage at 8.5%

a) Estimate the monthly payment for each amortization period.

   i) 5 years   **ii)** 10 years   **iii)** 15 years

   iv) 20 years   **v)** 25 years   **vi)** 30 years

b) Describe how the monthly payment changes as the amortization period changes.

c) Describe how the graph would change in each case.
   i) The interest rate is greater than 8.5%.
   ii) The mortgage is greater than $100 000.

9. Use your answers to exercise 8a. Estimate the total interest paid for each amortization period.

10. Start a new spreadsheet. Enter the text shown below in column A. Enter the data shown in cells C2, C3, and C4. Format cell C5 to report a percent to 7 decimal places. The data are from *Example 1*. Enter these formulas in cells C5 and C6:
C5: =(1+C3/2)^(1/6)−1
C6: =C2*C5/(1−(1+C5)^(−12*C4))
The computer will calculate the equivalent monthly rate and the monthly payment. Compare this result with Rita's mortgage in *Example 1*.

	A	B	C
1	Calculating Mortgage Payments		
2	Principal		100,000.00
3	Annual interest rate		8.50%
4	Amortization period (years)		25
5	Equivalent monthly rate		0.6961062%
6	Monthly payment		795.36

Use your spreadsheet to solve each problem.

a) Determine the monthly payment for each amortization period.

    i) 5 years   **ii)** 10 years   **iii)** 15 years

    iv) 20 years   **v)** 25 years   **vi)** 30 years

    Change the amortization period back to 25 years before you continue.

b) Determine the monthly payment for each interest rate.

    i) 8%   **ii)** 8.25%   **iii)** 8.75%   **iv)** 9%

    Change the interest rate back to 8.5% before you continue.

11. Use the spreadsheet in exercise 10. Suppose Rita can afford to make monthly payments of $850.

    a) Determine an amortization period that provides a monthly payment of approximately $850.

    b) Suppose Rita chooses this amortization period. How much interest would she save?

12. Ryan bought a home. He needs a mortgage of $125 000. The bank offers him a 25-year mortgage at 7.75%.

    a) Calculate the monthly payment.

    b) Calculate the total interest paid on this mortgage.

    c) How much is still owing on this mortgage after the first 3 years?

13. Helen bought a home. She needs a mortgage of $175 000. The bank offers her a 20-year mortgage at 8.4%.

    a) Calculate the monthly payment.

    b) Calculate the total interest paid on this mortgage.

    c) How much is still owing on this mortgage after the first 3 years?

14. Tony bought a home. He needs a mortgage of $140 000. The bank offers an interest rate of 8.25%. Calculate the monthly payment for each amortization period.

    a) 25 years   **b)** 20 years   **c)** 15 years

15. Kyo applies for a mortgage of $82 000, amortized over 20 years. The bank currently offers these mortgage rates. After the specified term has expired, the mortgage must be renegotiated at a new interest rate.

1-year term	5.25%
2-year term	6.00%
3-year term	6.50%
4-year term	6.75%
5-year term	7.00%

    a) Calculate the monthly payment for each term.

        i) 1 year   **ii)** 3 years   **iii)** 5 years

    b) Suggest some reasons to choose a 5-year term instead of a 1-year term.

16. **Application** In the early 1980s, interest rates soared to over 20%. To understand the devastating effect this had on some homeowners, consider a family with a mortgage of $75 000 amortized over 25 years. Calculate the monthly payment for each interest rate.

    a) 7%   b) 12%   c) 20%

17. **Communication** Why do you think Canadian law requires that mortgage interest rates be compounded semi-annually?

18. **Thinking/Inquiry/Problem Solving** Refer to *Example 1*. Suppose you were able to invest the $795.36 monthly payment instead of paying it to the bank. Assume you could obtain the same interest rate as the mortgage compounded semi-annually.

    a) What would the amount be after 25 years?

    b) What is the present value of the amount?

19. A family moves into its new home. The $90 000 mortgage is amortized over 25 years at 7.5% for a 3-year term.

    a) Calculate the monthly mortgage payment.

    b) At the end of the 3-year term, interest rates increase by 1%. The family renews its mortgage at current rates. Calculate the new monthly payment.

C

20. Mike estimates that he can afford a monthly mortgage payment of $575. Current interest rates are 6.75%.

    a) Calculate the mortgage Mike could afford for each amortization period.

       i) 15 years   ii) 20 years   iii) 25 years

    b) What other factors should Mike consider before he assumes the mortgage?

21. Refer to *Example 1*. How much interest was paid during each time period?

    a) the first year   b) the first 5 years

    c) the last year   d) the last 5 years

22. A mortgage, M dollars, is amortized over n years, at an interest rate of j, compounded semi-annually. Show that the amount still owing, P dollars, after k years is given by the formula $P = M\left(\dfrac{r^{2n} - r^{2k}}{r^{2n} - 1}\right)$, where $r = 1 + \dfrac{j}{2}$.

3.6 Investigate: Using the TVM Solver on a Graphing Calculator

The TI-83 graphing calculator can carry out financial calculations. It has a feature called the TVM (Time Value of Money) Solver. When interest is paid on a principal, the amount changes with time. This change is the time value of money.

To access the TVM Solver on the TI-83, press
2nd   x⁻¹   ENTER . This screen appears.

To access the TVM Solver on the TI-83 Plus,
press APPS 1 1.

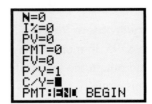

The variables represent these quantities:

> N: total number of payments
> I%:   annual interest rate as a percent
> PV: present value
> PMT: payment each period
> FV: future value, or amount
> P/Y: number of payments per year
> C/Y: number of compounding periods per year

The calculator displays either positive or negative values for PV, PMT, and FV. A positive value indicates the amount is earned. A negative value indicates the amount is invested.

When you make a payment on a loan, PMT is negative. When you calculate the amount of an investment, the principal is the present value, and PV is negative.

When you input four of the first five quantities, the calculator can provide the fifth. The five examples that follow demonstrate this. In each case, to input the known quantities use the arrow and ENTER keys.

1. Solve for N (the number of payments).

To buy a new car, you take out a loan of $10 593.30. You can afford a payment of $238 per month. The finance company charges an annual interest rate of 3.75% compounded monthly. How many payments must you make?

Enter the values shown, below left, in the TVM Solver.

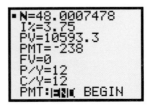

The payment will be made at the end of a payment period, so the word END should be highlighted.

To find the number of payments, move the cursor to the row for N, then press ALPHA ENTER to obtain the second screen at the bottom of page 174.

You must make 48 payments. That is one payment each month for 4 years.

2. Solve for I (the interest rate).

A certain college program will cost $20 000. You can save $288.50 per month for the next 5 years and hope to have the money for the course saved at that time. What annual interest rate, compounded monthly, must you obtain?

Enter the values shown, below left, in the TVM Solver.

Move the cursor to the row for I%. Press ALPHA ENTER to obtain the screen above right.

You must obtain an annual interest rate of at least 5.75% compounded monthly.

3. Solve for PV (the present value).

You plan to buy a car. You can afford payments of $525 per month. The interest rate is 6.25% compounded monthly. The finance company offers the loan for 2 years. How much can you afford to borrow?

Enter the values shown, below left, in the TVM Solver.

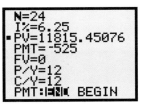

Move the cursor to the row for PV. Press ALPHA ENTER to obtain the screen above right.

You can afford to borrow $11 815.45.

4. Solve for PMT (the payment).

You want to buy a house. You have a 30-year mortgage of $100 000 at 8% compounded monthly. What is the monthly payment?

Enter the values shown, below left, in the TVM Solver.

 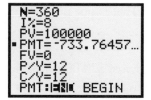

Move the cursor to the row for PMT. Press [ALPHA] [ENTER] to obtain the screen above right.

The monthly payment is $733.76.

5. Solve for FV (the future value or amount).

You invest $6500. The bank offers an interest rate of 8.25% compounded annually. What will the amount be in 7 years?

Enter the values shown, below left, in the TVM Solver.

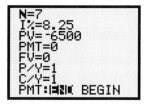 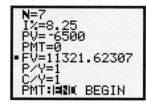

Move the cursor to the row for FV. Press [ALPHA] [ENTER] to obtain the screen above right.

The amount will be $11 321.62.

3.6 Exercises

Use the TVM Solver to complete these exercises.

1. To buy a used car, you take out a loan for $4500. You can afford payments of $180 per month. The interest rate on the loan is 9.5% compounded monthly. How many payments do you make?

2. A three-year college program costs $9500. You can save $150 per month for the next 4 years. What annual interest rate, compounded monthly, will provide the money you need?

3. You want to buy a car. You can afford monthly payments of $425. The car dealership is keen to reduce its inventory, so it offers loans at 3.5% compounded monthly. The loan is for 3 years. How much can you afford to borrow?

4. Suppose you buy a house. You have a 25-year mortgage of $150 000 at 7% compounded monthly. What is your monthly payment?

5. Suppose you win $10 000 in a lottery. You invest $7500. The interest rate is 6.25% compounded annually. What will your investment be worth in 6 years?

6. How much money would you have to invest today, at 6.5% compounded semi-annually, for the investment to accumulate to $7500 in 3 years?

7. Marge wants to buy a car for $14 700 (price includes tax). She plans to finance the car over a four-year period. She estimates that she can afford monthly car payments of $350.

   a) What interest rate allows her to purchase this car?

   b) Is this realistic? Explain.

8. How long will it take $400 to accumulate to $1000 at 6.75% compounded semi-annually?

9. Joe deposits $100 at the end of each month into a savings account that pays 6% compounded monthly.

   a) Investigate the growth of Joe's annuity. Copy and complete this table.

Investment period (years)	1	5	10	15	20	25	30	35	40
Accumulated amount ($)									

   b) Graph these data with *Investment period* on the horizontal axis.

   c) Copy and complete this table.

Investment period (years)	1	5	10	15	20	25	30	35	40
Amount invested ($)									

   d) Plot these data on the grid for part b.

   e) Compare the two sets of data on the graph. Explain why it is advantageous to begin investing early.

3.7 Amortization Tables

Remember the mortgage from *Example 1*, page 168. The payments for this mortgage are displayed in the spreadsheet on page 179. The spreadsheet shows the first 18 payments and the last 18 payments. A table of mortgage payments is called an *amortization table*.

Constructing the amortization table

Start a new spreadsheet document.

- Enter the text in cells A1 down to A6.
- Enter the data in cells C2, C3, and C4.
- Enter these formulas in cells C5 and C6:
    - C5: $=(1+C3/2)\char`\^(1/6)-1$
    - C6: $=\text{ROUND}(C2*C5/(1-(1+C5)\char`\^(-12*C4)),2)$
- Format these cells as follows:
    - C2: numbers to 2 decimal places
    - C3: percents to 2 decimal places
    - C4: numbers to 0 decimal places
    - C5: percents to 7 decimal places
- Enter the headings in row 8.
- Enter these formulas in row 9:
    - A9: $=0$ D9: $=C2$
- Enter these formulas in row 10:
    - A10: $=A9+1$ B10: $=\text{ROUND}(\$C\$5*D9,2)$
    - C10: $=\$C\$6-B10$ D10: $=D9-C10$
- Format cells B10, C10, and D10 to show numbers to 2 decimal places.
- For a 25-year mortgage, use the Fill Down command to copy the formulas in row 10 down to row 309.

To see the top part and the bottom part of the spreadsheet at the same time:

- At the top of the vertical scroll bar, point to the split box and drag it down to create two parts of the spreadsheet.
- In the bottom part, drag the vertical scroll box down until row 309 becomes visible.
- Adjust the split line and the scroll box until your spreadsheet is similar to that on page 179.

If necessary, consult the spreadsheet manual or Help file for further information.

Amortization Table

	A	B	C	D
1	Calculating Mortgage Payments			
2	Principal		100,000.00	
3	Annual interest rate		8.50%	
4	Amortization period (years)		25	
5	Equivalent monthly rate		0.6961062%	
6	Monthly payment		795.36	
7				
8	Payment	Interest	Principal	Balance
9	0			100,000.00
10	1	696.11	99.25	99,900.75
11	2	695.42	99.94	99,800.81
12	3	694.72	100.64	99,700.17
13	4	694.02	101.34	99,598.83
14	5	693.31	102.05	99,496.78
15	6	692.60	102.76	99,394.02
16	7	691.89	103.47	99,290.55
17	8	691.17	104.19	99,186.36
18	9	690.44	104.92	99,081.44
19	10	689.71	105.65	98,975.79
20	11	688.98	106.38	98,869.41
21	12	688.24	107.12	98,762.29
22	13	687.49	107.87	98,654.42
23	14	686.74	108.62	98,545.80
24	15	685.98	109.38	98,436.42
25	16	685.22	110.14	98,326.28
26	17	684.46	110.90	98,215.38
27	18	683.68	111.68	98,103.70
⋮	⋮	⋮	⋮	⋮
292	283	93.39	701.97	12,713.37
293	284	88.50	706.86	12,006.51
294	285	83.58	711.78	11,294.73
295	286	78.62	716.74	10,577.99
296	287	73.63	721.73	9,856.26
297	288	68.61	726.75	9,129.51
298	289	63.55	731.81	8,397.70
299	290	58.46	736.90	7,660.80
300	291	53.33	742.03	6,918.77
301	292	48.16	747.20	6,171.57
302	293	42.96	752.40	5,419.17
303	294	37.72	757.64	4,661.53
304	295	32.45	762.91	3,898.62
305	296	27.14	768.22	3,130.40
306	297	21.79	773.57	2,356.83
307	298	16.41	778.95	1,577.88
308	299	10.98	784.38	793.50
309	300	5.52	789.84	3.66

Interpreting the amortization table

Part of each payment is interest and the rest reduces the principal. For example, in the first month:

- The interest is 0.696 106 2% of $100 000 ≐ $696.11.
- The principal is reduced by $795.36 − $696.11 = $99.25.
- The balance at the end of the month is $100 000.00 − $99.25 = $99 900.75.

Similarly, in the 5th month:

- The interest is 0.696 106 2% of the balance at the end of the 4th month:
  0.696 106 2% of $99 598.83 = 0.006 961 062 × $99 598.83 ≐ $693.31
- The principal is reduced by $795.36 − $693.31 = $102.05.
- The balance at the end of the month is $99 598.83 − $102.05 = $99 496.78.

Each year, the interest payments decrease and the principal payments increase. The mortgage is paid off at the end of 25 years.

3.7 Exercises

For exercises 1 to 12, you do not need a computer. For exercises 13 to 26, you do need a computer.

B

1. **Knowledge/Understanding** Choose one row in the top part of the spreadsheet on page 179. Use a calculator to verify the calculations.

2. Choose one row in the bottom part of the spreadsheet. Use a calculator to verify the calculations.

3. How does the interest paid during the first few months compare with the principal paid? Explain.

4. How does the interest paid during the last few months compare with the principal paid? Explain.

5. **Communication** Explain why the interest payments decrease each month and the principal payments increase.

6. **Thinking/Inquiry/Problem Solving** Consider the first 12 months of the mortgage.

   a) Estimate the total paid against the principal during the first 12 months.

   b) Estimate the total interest paid during the first 12 months.

7. Consider the last 12 months of the mortgage.

    a) Estimate the total paid against the principal during the last 12 months.

    b) Estimate the total interest paid during the last 12 months.

8. Application The *total cost* of a mortgage is the sum of all the mortgage payments.

    a) Calculate the total cost of the mortgage.

    b) Use the result of part a to determine the total interest paid during the 25 years.

9. The formulas in cells C5 and C6 are given on page 178. Explain why these formulas are correct.

10. Explain why the amount in cell D309 is not 0.00.

11. This graph shows the monthly interest payments and payments against the principal for the mortgage in the spreadsheet on page 179. Use the graph to complete this exercise.

Interest and Principal Payments

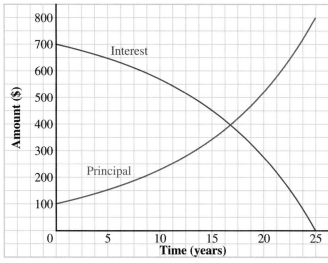

a) Explain why the *Interest* graph goes down when the *Principal* graph goes up.

b) What is the significance of the point where the two graphs intersect?

c) Visualize a horizontal line through the point where the two graphs intersect. Explain why one graph is the reflection of the other graph in this line.

12. This graph shows the balance of the mortgage in the spreadsheet on page 179. Use the graph to answer each question.

a) What is the balance after each time?

i) 5 years **ii)** 10 years **iii)** 15 years **iv)** 20 years

b) How long does it take until one-half the principal has been repaid?

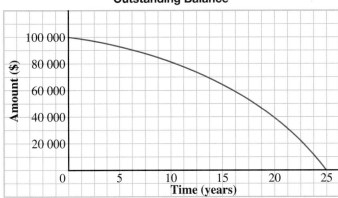

Outstanding Balance

If you have not already done so, follow the steps on page 178 to create the spreadsheet on page 179.

13. a) Click on cell B310. Enter the formula =SUM(B10:B309) to calculate the total interest paid.

b) Click on cell C310. Enter the formula =SUM(C10:C309) to calculate the total principal paid.

c) Explain why the answer in part b is not exactly $100 000.

14. Scroll down the spreadsheet until the numbers in the *Interest* and *Principal* columns are approximately the same. How long does it take until more than one-half the monthly payment is used to reduce the principal?

Investigating the effect of changing the interest rate

15. Complete this exercise to investigate the effect on the monthly payment when you change the interest rate.

a) Copy this table. Complete the table by changing the percent in cell C3.

$100 000 amortized over 25 years

Interest rate	6%	7%	8%	9%	10%
Monthly payment					

b) Calculate the differences in the monthly payments. Does an increase of 1% in the interest rate always have the same effect on the monthly payment? Explain.

16. Complete this exercise to investigate the effect on the total interest paid when you change the interest rate.

a) Copy this table. Complete the table by changing the percent in cell C3.

$100 000 amortized over 25 years

Interest rate	6%	7%	8%	9%	10%
Total interest paid					

b) Calculate the differences in the total interest paid. Does an increase of 1% in the interest rate always have the same effect on the total interest paid? Explain.

17. In the early 1980s, interest rates soared to 20% or more. Suppose the interest rate on this mortgage was 20%.

a) Determine the monthly payment.

b) How much of the first month's payment is interest? How much is used to reduce the principal?

c) What is the total interest paid on the mortgage?

Investigating ways to reduce interest costs

Banks and trust companies can suggest strategies to reduce the interest costs of a mortgage. In the following exercises, you will investigate some of these strategies. Before you complete the exercises, add another column to the spreadsheet as follows.

- Add the heading shown in cells E8 and E9.
- Enter these formulas in column E:
    E10: =B10
    E11: =E10+B11
- Use the Fill Down command to copy the formula in E11 down to row 309.

	A	B	C	D	E
1	Calculating Mortgage Payments				
2	Principal		100,000.00		
3	Annual interest rate		8.50%		
4	Amortization period (years)		25		
5	Equivalent monthly rate		0.6961062%		
6	Monthly payment		795.36		
7					
8	Payment	Interest	Principal	Balance	Total
9	0			100,000.00	Interest

Shorten the amortization period.

✓ **18.** Suppose the amortization period is 20 years instead of 25 years.

The answers to these problems do not have to be exact to the nearest cent.

    a) Change the number in cell C4 to 20. What is the new monthly payment?

    b) Scroll down the spreadsheet to the row that corresponds to the 240th payment. The balance should be approximately 0.
      i) What is the total interest paid?
      ii) How much interest is saved by choosing a 20-year amortization instead of a 25-year amortization?

19. Repeat exercise 18, using an amortization period of 15 years.

Note: Change the number in cell C4 to 25 before you continue.

Increase the monthly payments.

✓ **20.** Suppose the monthly payments are increased by $25.

    a) Click on cell C6 and enter 820.36.

    b) Scroll down the spreadsheet to the row where the balance is closest to 0.
      i) What is the total interest paid?
      ii) How much interest is saved when you increase the payments by $25?
      iii) How many years does it take to repay the mortgage?

21. Repeat exercise 20, increasing the payments by $50.

Note: Click on cell C6 and reenter the formula from page 178 before you continue.

Make a lump sum payment.

✓ **22.** Suppose an additional $1000 can be repaid at the end of the first year.

    a) Click on cell C21 and enter 1107.12.

    b) Scroll down the spreadsheet to the row where the balance is closest to 0.
      i) What is the total interest paid?
      ii) How much interest is saved?
      iii) How many years does it take to repay the mortgage?

23. Repeat exercise 22, but repay an additional $5000 at the end of the first year.

Note: Copy the formula in cell C20 to cell C21 to restore the spreadsheet.

Make more frequent payments.

To complete the following exercise, you will need to make major changes to your spreadsheet. You should save your spreadsheet and make a copy of it for use here.

Follow these steps to change the spreadsheet.

- Insert two new rows above the table, as shown. Enter the new text in cells A7 and A8.

- In cell C7, enter the following formula to calculate the weekly interest rate.
  C7: =(1+C3/2)^(1/26)−1
  Format cell C7 to show percents to 7 decimal places.

- Banks and trust companies usually divide the monthly payment by 4 to calculate the weekly payment. Enter this formula in cell C8:
  C8: =C6/4

- Enter these new formulas in cells B12 and C12:
  B12: =ROUND(C7*D11,2)
  C12: =C8−B12

- Use the Fill Down command to copy the formulas in cells A12, B12, C12, and D12 down as many rows as you need until the balance becomes as close to 0 as possible.

- Use the Fill Down command to copy the formula in cell E13 down as far as you did in the preceding step.

	A	B	C	D	E
1	Calculating Mortgage Payments				
2	Principal		100,000.00		
3	Annual interest rate		8.50%		
4	Amortization period (years)		25		
5	Equivalent monthly rate		0.6961062%		
6	Monthly payment		795.36		
7	Equivalent weekly rate		0.1602116%		
8	Weekly payment		198.84		
9					
10	Payment	Interest	Principal	Balance	Total
11	0			100,000.00	Interest

 24. Suppose payments are made weekly instead of monthly.

    a) What is the total interest cost?

    b) How much interest is saved?

    c) How many years and months does it take to repay the mortgage?

25. Explain why the weekly payment strategy results in much greater savings in interest costs than any previous strategy.

26. A person has many factors to consider when he or she decides on a mortgage. Suggest some ways to reduce the total interest you pay on a mortgage. Describe their advantages and disadvantages.

The interest rate for a mortgage is unlikely to be constant for the entire amortization period. Although the rate may change, the effect of repaying some of the principal as illustrated by these problems will be the same. You can save much interest by doing this, especially in the early years of a mortgage.

Self-Check 3.5 – 3.7

1. Calculate the equivalent monthly rate. Each interest rate is compounded semi-annually.

   a) 6%   b) 7.75%   c) 8.33%

2. Determine the monthly payment for each mortgage.

   a) $120 000 at 6.5%, over 20 years   b) $60 000 at 5.75%, over 10 years

3. Bernard bought a home and requires a mortgage of $120 000. The bank offers him a 25-year mortgage at 8.3%. What is the monthly payment?

4. Colleen bought a condominium and requires a mortgage of $90 000. A trust company offers her a 25-year mortgage at 8.12%.

   a) Calculate the monthly payment.   b) What is the total interest for this mortgage?

5. Marta bought a home and requires a mortgage of $145 000. The bank offers her a 25-year mortgage at 7.95%.

   a) Calculate the monthly payment.

   b) Calculate the total interest paid on this mortgage.

   c) How much is still owing on this mortgage after the first 3 years?

6. Walter bought a home and requires a mortgage of $130 000. The bank offers an interest rate of 8.55%. Calculate the monthly payment for each amortization period.

   a) 25 years   b) 20 years

7. A family moves into its new home. The $100 000 mortgage is amortized over 25 years at 7.6% for a 3-year term.

   a) Calculate the monthly mortgage payment.

   b) At the end of the 3-year term, interest rates increased by 1%. The family renews its mortgage at current rates. Calculate the new monthly payment.

8. For mortgage payments:

   a) How does the interest paid during the first few months compare with the principal paid? Explain.

   b) How does the interest paid during the last few months compare with the principal paid? Explain.

   c) Explain why the interest payments decrease each month while the principal payments increase each month.

9. Explain the effect of each action on the size of the regular payment and the total interest paid.

   a) Reduce the amortization period.   b) Increase the monthly payments.

   c) Make a lump sum payment.   d) Make more frequent payments.

Where Did the $314 Come From?

My aunt Brenda is introducing me to investing. I have a $1000 regular interest Canada Savings Bond that pays 6% interest. I receive $60 interest each year, and I can redeem the bond at any time and get my $1000 back.

"I have a different kind of bond," said Brenda. "I invested $5000 in it 2 years ago. It pays 7% compounded semi-annually, so I get $175 interest every 6 months."

"Your investment is better than mine because the interest rate is higher," I said.

"That's right," said Brenda, "and my last monthly statement says that it is now worth about $5314."

"But you invested $5000. Where did the $314 come from?"

> Governments and large corporations often borrow millions of dollars to finance special projects. Since it is difficult to find a single financial institution prepared to lend this much money, the government or corporation may issue bonds. These are purchased by many small lenders as an investment.

Formulating Questions

This is the problem we want to investigate.

Why is Brenda's bond worth $5314?

Representing the Value of the Bond in Mathematical Form

Brenda's bond was issued by a gas company. It has these features:

- Face value $5000
- Interest rate   7% compounded semi-annually
- Term   10 years

Unlike a Canada Savings Bond, this bond cannot be redeemed at any time. It can only be redeemed at the end of the 10-year term.

> The semi-annual interest payments are:
> $5000 \times \frac{0.07}{2} = \$175$.

The bond is a guarantee by the gas company to pay interest payments of $175 every 6 months for 10 years, plus the repayment of the face value of $5000 on the stated maturity date. Brenda cannot redeem her bond for its face value until the maturity date. However, since an open market for bonds exists, she may sell her bond at fair market value.

Anyone who buys Brenda's bond will receive the $5000 at the end of the 10-year term, plus the remaining semi-annual payments of $175. These payments reflect an interest rate of 7%. If interest rates had gone down to 6% since the bond was issued, there would be an increased demand for her bond. Investors would be willing to pay more than $5000 for it.

> **Selecting Strategies, Resources, Technology, and Tools**
>
> We can represent these amounts on a time diagram, then apply the principles of compound interest from earlier sections of this chapter.

Consider the time diagram below. The amounts shown in blue have already been paid to Brenda, and can be ignored. We consider the remaining interest payments and the face value.

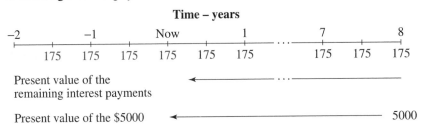

Time – years

-2		-1		Now		1		…	7		8
175	175	175	175	175	175				175	175	175

Present value of the
remaining interest payments

Present value of the $5000   5000

Brenda's bond earns 7% interest at a time when general interest rates are 6%. We calculate the present value of the amounts on the diagram at 6%.

The present value of the remaining interest payments is:

$$\frac{R[1 - (1 + i)^{-n}]}{i} = \frac{175(1 - 1.03^{-16})}{0.03}$$

$$\doteq 2198.19$$

The present value of the $5000 is:

$$\frac{A}{(1 + i)^n} = \frac{5000}{1.03^{16}}$$

$$\doteq 3115.83$$

The total present value is $2198.19 + $3115.83 = $5314.02.

The value $5314 accounts for the fact that the bond continues to earn interest at 7%, when general interest rates are 6%. That is, if someone buys the bond, he or she pays up front for the difference in yield. We say that a price of $5314.02 yields a return of 6%. This rate is called the *yield rate*.

This explains why Brenda's bond is worth $5314. The $314 is the additional amount an investor would pay to own a 7% bond in a 6% economy.

In these calculations we are using an interest rate of 6% compounded semi-annually. Suppose we use 7% compounded semi-annually. What would the total present value be?

Interpreting Information and Forming Conclusions

We can repeat the above calculations for any annual yield rate y, compounded semi-annually. The total present value of the remaining interest payments and the $5000 face value is:

$$P = \frac{175\left[1 - \left(1 + \frac{y}{2}\right)^{-16}\right]}{\frac{y}{2}} + \frac{5000}{\left(1 + \frac{y}{2}\right)^{16}} \qquad ①$$

Equation ① represents the price of the bond to yield a rate y compounded semi-annually. The graph of the function is shown on page 189 for $0.04 \leq y \leq 0.10$. The prices for yield rates of 6% and 7% are shown.

Suppose Brenda's bond had an interest rate different from 7% when she bought it. Only one number in equation ① would be different. Which number is this? How would the number be calculated?

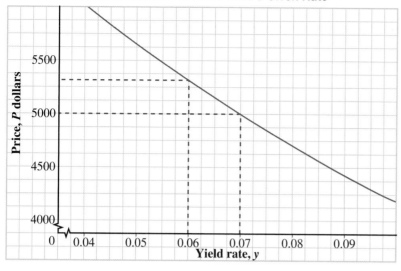

Price of Brenda's Bond to Yield a Given Rate

Price, *P* dollars (vertical axis): 4000, 4500, 5000, 5500

Yield rate, *y* (horizontal axis): 0, 0.04, 0.05, 0.06, 0.07, 0.08, 0.09

Reflecting on the Reasonableness of Results

Explain why each statement is reasonable.
- When interest rates go down, the price of a bond goes up.
- When interest rates go up, the price of a bond goes down.

Bond prices are listed in the financial pages of newspapers. Typical listings are shown in the table below. Each price is for a bond with a face value of $100. "Coupon" refers to the interest rate of the bond. Half this rate is paid every 6 months.

Problems

1. Refer to the calculations on page 188.

　a) Repeat the calculations to determine the price of the bond to yield a return of 8%.

　b) Use the graph above to check your result.

2. Look at the Westcoast Energy bond below.

　a) Use the information in columns 2, 3, and 5 to calculate the price of the bond. Compare your answer with the price in the listing.

　b) Prepare an entry for the listing in the newspaper for December 16 of the current year, assuming that the yield rate is 7.64%.

In problem 2, why can we use the method on page 188 to calculate the price of the Westcoast Energy bond, but not the other bonds?

Financial institutions earn money by buying and selling bonds. Their charges are factored into the price and yield rate.
The prices of these bonds change daily. What will happen to the price of any of these bonds as its maturity date approaches? Explain.

CANADIAN BONDS			December 16, 2000	
Issuer	**Coupon**	**Maturity**	**Price**	**Yield**
B C	5.700	Jun 18/29	94.31	6.12
B C	6.350	Jun 18/31	103.17	6.12
Canada	14.000	Oct 01/06	141.55	5.50
Canada	10.750	Oct 01/09	135.98	5.52
Canada	9.750	Jun 01/21	148.37	5.71
Ontario	10.875	Jan 10/01	100.40	3.61
Rogers Cable	8.750	Jul 15/07	98.00	9.16
Royal Bank	6.400	Aug 15/05	101.73	5.97
Westcoast Energy	6.750	Dec 15/27	95.01	7.17

Problems 2 to 6, and 10 refer to the bond listings on page 189.

3. Look at the three Canada bonds in the listings on page 189.

   a) Explain why the price of each bond is much higher than the prices of the other bonds.

   b) Explain why the 14% bond has a lower price than the 9.75% bond.

4. The Ontario bond has a higher coupon rate than two of the Canada bonds. Explain why its price is much lower.

5. The two British Columbia bonds yield 6.12%. Explain why the price of one bond is less than $100 and the price of the other bond is more than $100.

6. The Rogers Cable bond has the highest yield. What would happen to its price if the yield rate were lower?

In all problems, make these assumptions unless stated otherwise:
• Interest is compounded semi-annually.
• Interest is paid every 6 months.

7. I have agreed to lend my cousin $10 000. She will pay me 12 monthly instalments of $60, then repay the $10 000 at the end of one year. Since my money is now in a bank account that pays 6% interest compounded monthly, I think the deal with my cousin is a better deal. Am I right? If so, how much more will I receive from my cousin than from the bank?

In the newspaper in which the listings on page 189 appeared, about 150 different bonds were listed. Many more bonds were priced higher than $100 than lower. Suggest a reason for this.

8. You want to give your sister's new baby boy some money. You suggest these options:

   • 40 semi-annual payments of $100 up to his 20th birthday, and $1000 on his 21st birthday

   • $2500 now, which your sister can invest how she likes

   Your sister estimates that her money can earn 6% compounded semi-annually over the next 21 years. Which option should she choose?

Challenge Problems

9. Equation ① defines P as a function of y, but this equation is not defined when $y = 0$. The graph of P for $0 \leq y \leq 0.15$ is shown at the right. It suggests that a value of P does exist when $y = 0$. Determine this value of P, and explain its significance.

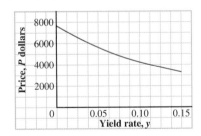

10. Choose one bond from the listing on page 189. Prepare a listing for the entry in today's newspaper, assuming the price of the bond is $105.25. Make any other necessary assumptions.

Financial Tools

Simple Interest

- Simple interest is usually earned for time periods no greater than 1 year.
  Accumulated simple interest illustrates linear growth.
  Yearly accumulated interest forms an arithmetic sequence.
- The simple interest is $I = Prt$.
  P is the principal in dollars.
  r is the annual interest rate expressed as a decimal.
  t is the time in years.
- The amount is $A = P + I$.

Compound Interest

- Compound interest is interest earned on interest. It represents exponential growth.
  The yearly amounts form a geometric sequence.
- The amount is $A = P(1 + i)^n$.
- The present value is $P = \dfrac{A}{(1 + i)^n}$.
  n is the number of compounding periods.
  i is the interest rate per compounding period, expressed as a decimal.

Annuities

- An annuity is a series of regular deposits or payments. The interest is
  compounded just before each deposit or payment is made. A deposit or
  payment is made at the end of each compounding period.
- An annuity can be regular deposits into an account.
- An annuity can be the withdrawal of regular payments from an account.
- The amount of an annuity is $A = \dfrac{R[(1 + i)^n - 1]}{i}$, where R is the regular deposit or
  payment, in dollars.
- The present value of an annuity (before payments begin) is $P = \dfrac{R[1 - (1 + i)^{-n}]}{i}$,
  where R is the regular payment, in dollars.

Mortgages

- A mortgage involves the present value of an annuity. A mortgage is a loan
  secured by real property as collateral.
- The amortization period of a mortgage is the time during which payments are
  made to repay the mortgage.

Review Exercises

- A mortgage rate is quoted with interest compounded semi-annually, but it must be converted to an equivalent rate that corresponds to the time between regular payments.
- An amortization table lists the details of each payment in a mortgage. See page 179.

3.1

1. a) Suppose you invest $800 at 4.3% compounded annually. What is the amount after 7 years? $A = 800 (1+.043)^7 = 1074.19$

b) Suppose $1350 grows to $1800 in 9 years. What is the interest rate compounded annually?

c) Suppose $4000 grows to $9500 at 7.6% compounded annually. How many years does it take?

2. Calculate the amount.

a) $700 invested for 14 years at 7.5% compounded annually $A = 700(1+0.075)^{14} = 1926.71$

b) $2300 invested for 12 years at 6.25% compounded annually

c) $1500 invested for 9 years at 8.33% compounded annually

3. Calculate the present value of each amount.

a) $1000 due in 8 years at 5.5% compounded annually

b) $1500 due in 5 years at 8.75% compounded annually

c) $7700 due in 12 years at 9.8% compounded annually

4. Suppose you want to accumulate $8000 in 10 years. How much would you need to invest today at an annual rate of 6.05%?

3.2

5. Suppose interest is compounded semi-annually. Determine each amount.

a) $8000 for 12 years at 8%

b) $900 for 14 years at $5\frac{3}{8}$%

c) $750 for 9.5 years at 7.6%

d) $4344 for 6 years at 3.41%

6. Suppose interest is compounded monthly. Determine each amount.

a) $380 for 4 years at 5%

b) $5000 for 8.5 years at $7\frac{1}{2}$%

c) $2900 for 15 years at 6.9%

d) $388 for 20 years at 12%

7. A $1000 GIC has an annual interest rate of 6.46%. Determine its value after 10 years.

8. Determine the interest rate necessary for $1000 to accumulate to $2500 in 9 years with interest compounded semi-annually.

9. What principal invested today at 6.73% compounded semi-annually will ⌐mount to $5000 in 9 years?

10. Cheung borrowed $500 from his uncle and paid it back in a lump sum after 3 years. His uncle charged 4% interest compounded quarterly. How much did Cheung pay his uncle?

11. Suppose you invest $10 000 at 6.5% compounded semi-annually. How many years will it take to amount to $50 000?

3.3   **12.** Use the formula $A = \dfrac{R[(1 + i)^n - 1]}{i}$. Calculate A for each set of values.

a) $R = \$800$, $i = 0.05$, $n = 10$ b) $R = \$1000$, $i = 0.06$, $n = 9$

c) $R = \$250$, $i = 0.075$, $n = 20$

13. Calculate the amount of each annuity.

a) A principal of $1050 is invested at the end of each year for 16 years at 5.4% compounded annually.

b) A principal of $450 is invested at the end of every 6-month period for 10 years at 7.2% compounded semi-annually.

c) A principal of $234 is invested at the end of every 6-month period for 12 years at 6.83% compounded semi-annually.

14. Suppose you deposit $423 at the end of every 6 months into an investment account that pays 5.8% compounded semi-annually. What is the amount after 7 years?

3.4   **15.** Use the formula $P = \dfrac{R[1 - (1 + i)^{-n}]}{i}$. Calculate P for each set of values.

a) $R = \$1200$, $i = 0.05$, $n = 10$ b) $R = \$760$, $i = 0.082$, $n = 9$

c) $R = \$1000$, $i = 0.057$, $n = 6$

16. Calculate the present value of each annuity.

a) A payment of $400 is withdrawn at the end of each year for 10 years. The principal is invested at 6.5% compounded annually.

b) A payment of $377 is withdrawn at the end of each month for 6 years. The principal is invested at 5.7% compounded monthly.

c) A payment of $450 is withdrawn at the end of each month for 8 years. The principal is invested at 7.6% compounded monthly.

17. Suppose you begin a savings program to have $9500 after 6 years. You plan to make regular deposits every 6 months into an investment account that pays 5.7% compounded semi-annually. Calculate each regular deposit.

18. Suppose you have an investment account that pays 7.45% compounded semi-annually. You wish to withdraw $360 every 6 months for 4 years. How much do you need to have in the account now?

19. Nicole borrowed $10 500 to purchase her new car. The car dealership offered her a loan at 8.8% compounded monthly for 3 years. What is Nicole's monthly payment?

20. Colin deposits $114 at the end of each month for 6 years in an account that pays 6.5% compounded monthly. Calculate the amount after 6 years.

21. What principal must be deposited at the end of each year in an account that pays 5.8% compounded annually to amount to $18 000 after 14 years?

3.5 22. Calculate the equivalent monthly rate. Each interest rate is compounded semi-annually.

   a) 8%   b) 10%   c) 12%   d) 5.6%   e) 6.85%   f) 8.74%

23. Determine the monthly payment for each mortgage.

   a) $140 000 at 7.4%, over 25 years   b) $95 000 at 6.87%, over 25 years

   c) $110 000 at 8.1%, over 20 years

24. Pierre has bought a home and requires a mortgage of $118 000. The bank offers him a 25-year mortgage at 8.7%. What is the monthly payment?

25. Emma has bought a condominium and requires a mortgage of $97 000. A trust company offers her a 25-year mortgage at 7.92%.

   a) Calculate the monthly payment.

   b) What is the total interest paid on this mortgage?

26. Kwaw has bought a home and requires a mortgage of $133 000. The bank offers him a 25-year mortgage at 8.07%.

   a) Calculate the monthly payment.

   b) Calculate the total interest paid on this mortgage.

   c) How much is still owing on this mortgage after the first 3 years?

27. Mina has bought a home and requires a mortgage of $143 000. The bank offers an interest rate of 8.45%. Calculate the monthly payment for each amortization period.

   a) 25 years   b) 20 years

28. A family moves into its new home. The $125 000 mortgage is amortized over 25 years at 7.77% for a 3-year term.

   a) Calculate the monthly mortgage payment.

   b) At the end of the 3-year term, interest rates increase by 1.5%. The family renews its mortgage at current rates. Calculate the new monthly payment.

Self-Test

1. a) What is the amount after you invest $1100 at 5.7% compounded annually for 10 years?

   b) What is the annual interest rate required for $1450 to grow to $1800 in 8 years?

   c) How many years does it take for $3000 to grow to $6400 at 7.1% compounded annually?

2. A table similar to that below appeared in a magazine. Suppose another row is added to the table for 50 years. Calculate the amounts in this row.

The Magic of Compound Interest
Value of an annual investment of $1,000

Years	6%	8%	10%	12%
10	13,180.79	14,486.56	15,937.42	17,548.74
20	36,785.59	45,761.96	57,275.00	72,052.44
30	79,058.19	113,283.21	164,494.02	241,332.68
40	154,761.97	259,056.52	442,592.56	767,091.42

3. Calculate the present value of each amount. The interest compounds annually.

   a) $3000 in 12 years at 7.1%   b) $834.56 in 8 years at 9.08%

4. A principal of $650 is invested at the end of each year for 14 years at 6.4% compounded annually. Calculate the amount of the annuity.

5. A payment of $345 is withdrawn at the end of each month for 6 years. The principal is invested at 6.6% compounded monthly. Calculate the present value of the annuity.

6. Determine the monthly payment for each mortgage.

   a) $125 000 at 7.2%, over 25 years   b) $180 000 at 8.2%, over 20 years

7. **Knowledge/Understanding** A $1000 GIC has an annual interest rate of 5.89%. Determine its value after 10 years.

8. **Communication** Suppose you deposit $255 at the end of every 6 months into an account that pays 6.4% compounded semi-annually. How much will you have after 8 years? Write to explain how you calculated the amount.

9. Determine the interest rate necessary for $1000 to amount to $1800 in 6 years with interest compounded semi-annually.

10. How many years will it take $10 000 to amount to $50 000? The money is invested at 5.5% compounded semi-annually.

11. Suppose you have an investment account that pays 6.63% compounded semi-annually. You plan to withdraw $500 every 6 months for 5 years. How much do you need to have in the account now?

12. **Application** To buy a new car, you borrow $14 800 at 6.8% compounded monthly for 3 years. What are your monthly payments?

13. An account pays 6.9% compounded annually. How much must be deposited at the end of each year to obtain $20 000 after 15 years?

14. A home was purchased with a mortgage of $130 000. The bank offered a 25-year mortgage at 8.4%. What was the monthly payment?

15. A home was purchased, and a mortgage of $99 000 was required. The bank offered a 25-year mortgage at 7.9%.

   a) Calculate the monthly payment.

   b) Calculate the total interest paid on this mortgage.

   c) How much is still owing on this mortgage after the first 3 years?

Assessment Tasks

1. Suppose you have bought a new home and take a 25-year mortgage at 6% compounded semi-annually. You have $10 000 in a bank account that pays 6% compounded monthly. You must decide whether to reduce your mortgage by $10 000 and so reduce your monthly mortgage payments.

   a) How much lower would your monthly mortgage payments be if you reduced your mortgage by $10 000?

   b) Should you use the $10 000 to reduce your mortgage or leave it in your account? What difference would the decision make to your financial situation after 25 years?

2. Suppose you have three aunts who together decided to give you $1000 annually for the first 21 years of your life. The first gift is given on your first birthday, and the last on your 21st birthday. Assume an interest rate of 6% compounded annually.

   a) What is the value of the annuity on the day of your birth?

   b) The eldest aunt will make the first 7 payments, the second aunt will make the next 7 payments, and the youngest aunt will make the last 7. How much should each aunt have at the date of your birth to ensure she can meet her obligations?

   c) Verify your answers to part b.

Quadratic Functions and Complex Numbers

4

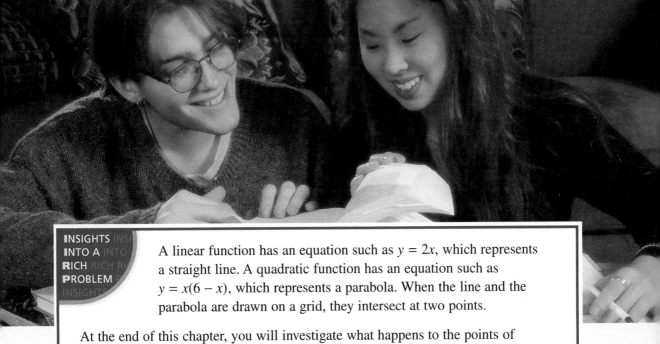

INSIGHTS INTO A RICH PROBLEM

A linear function has an equation such as $y = 2x$, which represents a straight line. A quadratic function has an equation such as $y = x(6 - x)$, which represents a parabola. When the line and the parabola are drawn on a grid, they intersect at two points.

At the end of this chapter, you will investigate what happens to the points of intersection when the line is moved parallel to itself. You will investigate this problem both geometrically and algebraically, then compare the results. You will also investigate similar problems involving a line and other curves.

Curriculum Expectations

By the end of this chapter, you will:

- Determine the maximum or minimum value of a quadratic function whose equation is given in the form $y = ax^2 + bx + c$, using the algebraic method of completing the square.

- Identify the structure of the complex number system and express complex numbers in the form $a + bi$, where $i^2 = -1$.

- Determine the real or complex roots of quadratic equations, using an appropriate method, and relate the roots to the x-intercepts of the graph of the corresponding function.

- Add, subtract, multiply, and divide complex numbers in rectangular form. (Functions and Relations)

- Explain mathematical processes, methods of solution, and concepts clearly to others.

- Communicate solutions to problems … clearly and concisely, orally and in writing ….

- Demonstrate the correct use of mathematical language, symbols, visuals, and conventions.

1. Review: The Quadratic Function $y = ax^2 + bx + c$

When the equation of a quadratic function has the form $y = ax^2 + bx + c$, the constants used to sketch a graph of the function are not obvious. The equation must be converted to the form $y = a(x - p)^2 + q$.

Example 1

a) Write the equation $y = x^2 - 14x + 38$ in the form $y = a(x - p)^2 + q$.

b) Graph the function.

Solution

a) $y = x^2 - 14x + 38$

The coefficient of x^2 is 1; so $a = 1$.
Complete the square for $y = x^2 - 14x + 38$.
Add and subtract the square of one-half
the coefficient of x; that is, $\left(\dfrac{-14}{2}\right)^2 = 49$

$y = x^2 - 14x + 49 - 49 + 38$

Write the first 3 terms as a perfect square.
$y = (x - 7)^2 - 11$

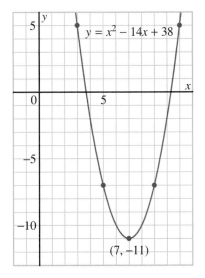

b) To graph the function, use the vertex, and two other points and their reflections in the axis of symmetry.

From the equation, the vertex has coordinates $(7, -11)$.
Substitute $x = 5$ in $y = x^2 - 14x + 38$
$$y = 5^2 - 14(5) + 38$$
$$= -7$$
Substitute $x = 3$ in $y = x^2 - 14x + 38$
$$y = 3^2 - 14(3) + 38$$
$$= 5$$

Two points on the parabola are $(5, -7)$ and $(3, 5)$.
Reflect each point in the axis of symmetry $x = 7$.
Two other points on the graph are $(9, -7)$ and $(11, 5)$.
Plot these points, then join them with a smooth curve.

Example 2

a) Write the equation $y = -x^2 + 3x + 2$ in the form $y = a(x - p)^2 + q$.

b) Graph the function.

Solution

a) $y = -x^2 + 3x + 2$

The coefficient of x^2 is -1; so $a = -1$.
Complete the square for $y = -x^2 + 3x + 2$.
Remove -1 as a common factor for the first 2 terms.
$y = -1(x^2 - 3x) + 2$

Within the brackets, add and subtract the square of $\frac{1}{2}(-3)$;
that is, $\left(-\frac{3}{2}\right)^2 = \frac{9}{4}$

$y = -1\left(x^2 - 3x + \frac{9}{4} - \frac{9}{4}\right) + 2$

Write the first 3 terms in the brackets as a perfect square.
Multiply the 4th term in the brackets by -1.

$y = -1\left(x^2 - 3x + \frac{9}{4}\right) + \frac{9}{4} + 2$

$\quad = -1\left(x - \frac{3}{2}\right)^2 + \frac{9}{4} + \frac{8}{4}$

$\quad = -\left(x - \frac{3}{2}\right)^2 + \frac{17}{4}$

b) To graph the function, use the vertex, and two other points
and their reflections in the axis of symmetry.

From the equation, the vertex has coordinates $\left(\frac{3}{2}, \frac{17}{4}\right)$.

Substitute $x = 0$ in $y = -x^2 + 3x + 2$
$\qquad\qquad y = -0^2 + 3(0) + 2$
$\qquad\qquad\quad = 2$

Substitute $x = -1$ in $y = -x^2 + 3x + 2$
$\qquad\qquad y = -(-1)^2 + 3(-1) + 2$
$\qquad\qquad\quad = -2$

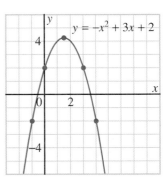

Two points on the parabola are $(0, 2)$ and $(-1, -2)$.

Reflect each point in the axis of symmetry $x = \frac{3}{2}$.

Two other points on the graph are $(3, 2)$ and $(4, -2)$.
Plot these points, then join them with a smooth curve.

Exercises

1. Write each equation in the form $y = (x - p)^2 + q$.

   a) $y = x^2 + 4x + 1$ b) $y = x^2 + 6x + 10$ c) $y = x^2 - 8x - 5$

   d) $y = x^2 - 3x + 2$ e) $y = x^2 - 5x - 5$ f) $y = x^2 + 7x + 10$

2. Write each equation in the form $y = a(x - p)^2 + q$.

   a) $y = -x^2 + 6x + 8$ b) $y = -x^2 - 10x + 1$ c) $y = -x^2 - 4x - 3$

   d) $y = -x^2 - 3x - 7$ e) $y = -x^2 - 5x + 4$ f) $y = -x^2 + x - 8$

3. Write each equation in the form $y = a(x - p)^2 + q$. Sketch a graph of each equation.

   a) $y = x^2 + 2x + 7$ b) $y = -x^2 - 2x - 6$ c) $y = x^2 + 6x - 1$

   d) $y = -x^2 - 3x - 8$ e) $y = -x^2 + 5x - 2$ f) $y = x^2 - x - 5$

2. Review: Number Systems

In grade 9, you learned about these number systems.

The natural numbers are the positive whole numbers.
$N = \{1, 2, 3, \ldots\}$
With natural numbers, you can solve equations such as $x + 7 = 10$.

The whole numbers are the natural numbers and 0.
$W = \{0, 1, 2, \ldots\}$
With whole numbers, you can solve equations such as $x + 7 = 7$.

The integers are the positive and negative whole numbers.
$I = \{\ldots, -2, -1, 0, 1, 2, \ldots\}$
With integers, you can solve equations such as $x + 10 = 7$.

A rational number is a number that can be written as a fraction, where the numerator and denominator are integers, and the denominator is not 0. The set of rational numbers is denoted by Q.

Some examples of rational numbers are $\frac{3}{4}, -\frac{10}{3}, \frac{-9}{-5}, 1.46, -3.\overline{2}, -5$.
With rational numbers, you can solve equations such as $2x = 3$.

An irrational number is a number that cannot be written as a fraction. In decimal form, an irrational number neither terminates nor repeats. The set of irrational numbers is denoted by $\overline{Q}$.

Some examples of irrational numbers are π, $\sqrt{2}$, $\cos 30°$, $5.462\ 798\ \dots$.
With irrational numbers, you can solve equations such as $x^2 = 5$.

The real numbers are all the rational and irrational numbers; that is, all the numbers that can be expressed in decimal form. The set of real numbers is denoted by R.

This diagram illustrates how the sets of numbers are related.

Real numbers, R

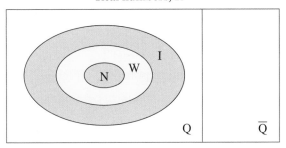

Exercises

1. List three examples for each type of number.

a) Whole number   b) Rational number   c) Real number

d) Integer   e) Irrational number   f) Natural number

2. To which number system(s) does each number belong?

a) 48   b) 3.48   c) $-\dfrac{5}{9}$ d) $\sin 45°$ e) $\sqrt{625}$

f) 0   g) –8   h) $\sqrt{36}$ i) π j) $\sqrt{5}$

3. Draw a diagram similar to that above. Insert these numbers correctly in the diagram:

$10,\ -4.37,\ \dfrac{3}{4},\ \sqrt{10},\ \tan 30°,\ \sqrt{81},\ 0,\ \pi,\ -6,\ 3.721\ 486\ \dots,\ 4.\overline{13}$

3. Review: Intercepts and Zeros

Remember that an x-intercept of the graph of a function is the x-coordinate of the point where the graph intersects the x-axis.

Similarly, the y-intercept is the y-coordinate of the point where the graph intersects the y-axis.

Necessary Skills

Example 1

Determine each y-intercept.

a) $2x - 3y = 6$

b) $y = x^2 + x - 6$

Solution

To determine the y-intercept, substitute $x = 0$, then solve for y.

a) $2x - 3y = 6$

Substitute $x = 0$.

$$\begin{aligned} 2(0) - 3y &= 6 \\ -3y &= 6 \\ y &= -2 \end{aligned}$$

The y-intercept is –2.

b) $y = x^2 + x - 6$

Substitute $x = 0$.

$$\begin{aligned} y &= 0^2 + 0 - 6 \\ &= -6 \end{aligned}$$

The y-intercept is –6.

Example 2

Determine the x-intercept(s).

a) $2x - 3y = 6$

b) $y = x^2 + x - 6$

Solution

To determine the x-intercept, substitute $y = 0$, then solve for x.

a) $2x - 3y = 6$

Substitute $y = 0$.

$$\begin{aligned} 2x - 3(0) &= 6 \\ 2x &= 6 \\ x &= 3 \end{aligned}$$

The x-intercept is 3.

b) $y = x^2 + x - 6$

Substitute $y = 0$, then solve for x.

$0 = x^2 + x - 6$

$0 = (x - 2)(x + 3)$

Either $x - 2 = 0$ or $x + 3 = 0$

$x = 2$ $\qquad$ $x = -3$

The x-intercepts are 2 and –3.

Example 3

Use the results of *Examples 1* and *2* to sketch a graph of each function.

a) $2x - 3y = 6$ **b)** $y = x^2 + x - 6$

Solution

a) $2x - 3y = 6$

From *Examples 1* and *2*, the graph passes through $(0, -2)$ and $(3, 0)$.

Plot these points on a grid, then join them with a straight line.

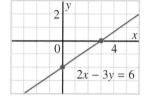

b) $y = x^2 + x - 6$

From *Examples 1* and *2*, the graph passes through $(0, -6)$, $(2, 0)$, and $(-3, 0)$.

Plot these points on a grid, then join them with a smooth curve.

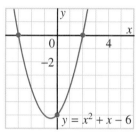

In *Example 3*, remember that the *x*-intercepts of the graph of a function are the *zeros* of the function.

That is, the linear function $2x - 3y = 6$ has a zero of 3.
The quadratic function $y = x^2 + x - 6$ has zeros 2 and –3.

Exercises

1. Determine the *x*- and *y*-intercepts. Use the intercepts to sketch a graph of each function.

  a) $y = -2x + 8$ **b)** $3x + 4y = 12$ **c)** $4x - 9y + 36 = 0$

  d) $y = x^2 + 4x - 5$ **e)** $y = -x^2 + 9x - 18$ **f)** $y = x^2 + 8x + 16$

2. Determine each *y*-intercept.

  a) $y = 3x - 7$ **b)** $5x - 7y = 35$ **c)** $y = x^2 - 5x + 2$

  d) $y = 2x^2 - 3x + 5$ **e)** $y = 81 - x^2$ **f)** $y = 4x^2 + 16$

3. Determine the *x*-intercept(s).

  a) $y = 3x - 8.1$ **b)** $7.2x + 3.7y = 2.7$ **c)** $y = x^2 + 7x + 12$

  d) $y = 16x^2 - 24x + 9$ **e)** $y = 10x^2 - 19x - 56$ **f)** $y = 121 + x^2$

Necessary Skills

4. New: Multiplying and Dividing Radicals

A positive number such as 3 has two square roots, because there are two different numbers that satisfy the equation $x^2 = 3$. One number is positive and the other negative. The positive square root is denoted by $\sqrt{3}$. This expression is an example of a *radical*. In this chapter, you will multiply and divide radicals.

We can tell that $\sqrt{4} \times \sqrt{9} = \sqrt{36}$ because the left side equals 2×3 and the right side equals 6. But what about $\sqrt{3} \times \sqrt{5}$? To show that $\sqrt{3} \times \sqrt{5} = \sqrt{15}$, use a calculator:

$$\sqrt{3} \times \sqrt{5} \doteq 1.732\ 050\ 808 \times 2.236\ 067\ 977$$
$$\doteq 3.872\ 983\ 346$$
$$\sqrt{15} \doteq 3.872\ 983\ 346$$

We cannot be certain that $\sqrt{3} \times \sqrt{5} = \sqrt{15}$ because we used decimal approximations. To prove that $\sqrt{3} \times \sqrt{5} = \sqrt{15}$, square each expression.

Left side:

$$(\sqrt{3} \times \sqrt{5})^2 = \sqrt{3} \times \sqrt{5} \times \sqrt{3} \times \sqrt{5}$$
$$= \sqrt{3} \times \sqrt{3} \times \sqrt{5} \times \sqrt{5}$$
$$= 3 \times 5$$
$$= 15$$

Right side:

$$(\sqrt{15})^2 = \sqrt{15} \times \sqrt{15}$$
$$= 15$$

Since the left side equals the right side, we conclude that $\sqrt{3} \times \sqrt{5} = \sqrt{15}$. The following properties can be justified in the same way, by squaring each side, then simplifying.

Take Note

Multiplication and Division Properties of Radicals

$$\sqrt{a} \times \sqrt{b} = \sqrt{a \times b} \qquad (a \geq 0, b \geq 0)$$

$$\frac{\sqrt{a}}{\sqrt{b}} = \sqrt{\frac{a}{b}} \qquad (a \geq 0, b > 0)$$

These properties can also be used in reverse. For example, consider $\sqrt{20}$. Notice that 20 has 4 as a perfect-square factor. Therefore, we can write:

$$\sqrt{20} = \sqrt{4 \times 5}$$
$$= \sqrt{4} \times \sqrt{5}$$
$$= 2\sqrt{5}$$

The expression $2\sqrt{5}$ is an example of a *mixed radical*.

To determine whether a radical can be expressed as a mixed radical, look for a factor that is a perfect square.

Example 1

Simplify.

a) $\sqrt{3} \times \sqrt{10}$

b) $\dfrac{\sqrt{42}}{\sqrt{3}}$

Solution

a) $\sqrt{3} \times \sqrt{10} = \sqrt{30}$

b) $\dfrac{\sqrt{42}}{\sqrt{3}} = \sqrt{14}$

Example 2

Express as a mixed radical, if possible.

a) $\sqrt{18}$ **b)** $\sqrt{30}$ **c)** $\sqrt{32}$

Solution

a) 18 has 9 as a perfect-square factor.
$$\sqrt{18} = \sqrt{9} \times \sqrt{2}$$
$$= 3\sqrt{2}$$

b) Since 30 does not have a perfect-square factor, $\sqrt{30}$ cannot be expressed as a mixed radical.

c) 32 has two perfect-square factors, 4 and 16.
$$\sqrt{32} = \sqrt{4} \times \sqrt{8}$$
$$= 2\sqrt{8}$$
or
$$\sqrt{32} = \sqrt{16} \times \sqrt{2}$$
$$= 4\sqrt{2}$$

In *Example 2c*, there are two ways to write $\sqrt{32}$ as a mixed radical. We say that $4\sqrt{2}$ is in *simplest form* because the number under the radical sign has no perfect-square factor.

Exercises

1. Multiply or divide.

a) $\sqrt{5} \times \sqrt{2}$ **b)** $\sqrt{7} \times \sqrt{6}$ **c)** $\dfrac{\sqrt{21}}{\sqrt{3}}$ **d)** $\dfrac{\sqrt{30}}{\sqrt{6}}$

2. Express as a mixed radical in simplest form, if possible.

a) $\sqrt{8}$ **b)** $\sqrt{12}$ **c)** $\sqrt{27}$ **d)** $\sqrt{35}$ **e)** $\sqrt{40}$ **f)** $\sqrt{50}$

g) $\sqrt{60}$ **h)** $\sqrt{63}$ **i)** $\sqrt{72}$ **j)** $\sqrt{75}$ **k)** $\sqrt{80}$ **l)** $\sqrt{200}$

3. In exercise 2, most of the radicals can be expressed as mixed radicals.

a) Write a different radical that can be expressed as a mixed radical.

b) Only the radical in exercise 2d cannot be expressed as a mixed radical. Write another radical that cannot be expressed as a mixed radical.

4.1 Maximum or Minimum Value of a Quadratic Function

Remember that the equation of a quadratic function has the form $y = ax^2 + bx + c$. The graph of a quadratic function is a parabola. The y-coordinate of the vertex of the parabola is either the maximum value of the function, or its minimum value.

Recall that for $y = ax^2 + bx + c$

When $a > 0$, the parabola opens up and the function has a minimum value.
When $a < 0$, the parabola opens down and the function has a maximum value.

Another form of the equation of a quadratic function is $y = a(x - p)^2 + q$.
In this form, the coordinates of the vertex are identified as (p, q).

Maximum value
$y = ax^2 + bx + c$
$\quad a < 0$
or,
$y = a(x - p)^2 + q$
$\quad a < 0$

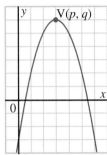

Minimum value
$y = ax^2 + bx + c$
$\quad a > 0$
or,
$y = a(x - p)^2 + q$
$\quad a > 0$

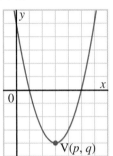

When the equation of a quadratic function is given in the form $y = ax^2 + bx + c$, we complete the square to write the equation in the form $y = a(x - p)^2 + q$.

Example 1

a) Write the equation $y = 2x^2 - 10x + 9$ in the form $y = a(x - p)^2 + q$.

b) Graph the function.

Solution

a) $y = 2x^2 - 10x + 9$

Remove 2 as a common factor for the first 2 terms.
$y = 2(x^2 - 5x) + 9$

Within the brackets, add and subtract the square of one-half the coefficient of x.

That is, add and subtract $\left(\frac{5}{2}\right)^2 = \frac{25}{4}$.

$y = 2\left(x^2 - 5x + \frac{25}{4} - \frac{25}{4}\right) + 9$

Write the first 3 terms in the brackets as a perfect square.
Multiply the 4th term in the brackets by 2, then remove it from the brackets.

$$y = 2\left(x^2 - 5x + \frac{25}{4}\right) - \frac{25}{2} + 9$$

$$y = 2\left(x - \frac{5}{2}\right)^2 - \frac{25}{2} + \frac{18}{2}$$

$$y = 2\left(x - \frac{5}{2}\right)^2 - \frac{7}{2}$$

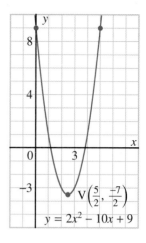

$y = 2x^2 - 10x + 9$

b) Plot the vertex $\left(\frac{5}{2}, -\frac{7}{2}\right)$.

From the equation $y = 2x^2 - 10x + 9$, the y-intercept is 9.
Plot the point $(0, 9)$.
Reflect this point in the axis of symmetry $x = \frac{5}{2}$.
Plot the point $(5, 9)$.
Draw a smooth curve through the plotted points.

Example 2

Without sketching the graph, determine the maximum or minimum value of the function $y = -\frac{1}{2}x^2 - 3x + 1$.

Solution

Since the coefficient of x^2 is negative, the parabola opens down and the function has a maximum value. To determine the maximum value, write the equation of the function in the form $y = a(x - p)^2 + q$.
Complete the square for $y = -\frac{1}{2}x^2 - 3x + 1$.

Remove $-\frac{1}{2}$ as a common factor for the first 2 terms.
To remove $-\frac{1}{2}$ as a factor of -3, divide -3 by $-\frac{1}{2}$; that is, multiply -3 by -2.
$$y = -\frac{1}{2}(x^2 + 6x) + 1$$

Within the brackets, add and subtract $\left(\frac{6}{2}\right)^2 = 9$.
$$y = -\frac{1}{2}(x^2 + 6x + 9 - 9) + 1$$

Write the first 3 terms in the brackets as a perfect square.
Multiply the 4th term in the brackets by $-\frac{1}{2}$, then remove it from the brackets.
$$y = -\frac{1}{2}(x^2 + 6x + 9) + \frac{9}{2} + 1$$

$$y = -\frac{1}{2}(x + 3)^2 + \frac{11}{2}$$

The maximum value of the function is $\frac{11}{2}$.

Here is an alternative method to determine the maximum or minimum value without sketching the graph. Consider the function in *Example 2*.

$$y = -\frac{1}{2}x^2 - 3x + 1$$

The vertex of the graph of $y = -\frac{1}{2}x^2 - 3x + 1$ is 1 unit above the vertex of the graph of $y = -\frac{1}{2}x^2 - 3x$. The graphs are drawn as an illustration, and are not part of the solution.

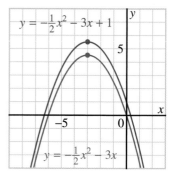

Determine the zeros of $y = -\frac{1}{2}x^2 - 3x$ by substituting $y = 0$.

$$-\frac{1}{2}x^2 - 3x = 0$$

Solve by factoring.

$$x\left(-\frac{1}{2}x - 3\right) = 0$$

$x = 0$ or $-\frac{1}{2}x - 3 = 0$

$$-\frac{1}{2}x = 3$$

$$x = -6$$

The equation of the axis of symmetry is $x = \frac{-6 + 0}{2}$; that is, $x = -3$.
The x-coordinate of the vertex of each graph is -3.

Substitute $x = -3$ in $y = -\frac{1}{2}x^2 - 3x + 1$

$$y = -\frac{1}{2}(-3)^2 - 3(-3) + 1$$

$$= -\frac{9}{2} + 9 + 1$$

$$= \frac{11}{2}$$

The maximum value of the function is $\frac{11}{2}$.

We can use the maximum or minimum value of a function to solve problems.

Example 3

A ball is thrown vertically upward from the balcony of an apartment building. The ball falls to the ground. The height of the ball, h metres, above the ground after t seconds is given by the function $h = -5t^2 + 15t + 45$.

a) Determine the maximum height of the ball.

b) How long does it take the ball to reach its maximum height?

c) How high is the balcony?

Solution

a) $h = -5t^2 + 15t + 45$

To determine the maximum height, complete the square to write the function in the form $h = a(t - p)^2 + q$.
$$h = -5t^2 + 15t + 45$$

Remove -5 as a common factor for the first 2 terms.
$$h = -5(t^2 - 3t) + 45$$

Within the brackets, add and subtract the square of one-half the coefficient of t. That is, add and subtract $\left(\frac{3}{2}\right)^2 = \frac{9}{4}$.
$$h = -5\left(t^2 - 3t + \frac{9}{4} - \frac{9}{4}\right) + 45$$

Write the first 3 terms in the brackets as a perfect square. Multiply the 4th term in the brackets by -5.
$$h = -5\left(t^2 - 3t + \frac{9}{4}\right) + 11.25 + 45$$
$$h = -5\left(t - \frac{3}{2}\right)^2 + 56.25$$

Compare this equation with $h = -a(t - p)^2 + q$.

The coordinates of the vertex are $\left(\frac{3}{2}, 56.25\right)$, or (1.5, 56.25).

The maximum height of the ball is the h-coordinate of the vertex, which is 56.25 m.

Discuss

Why did we write $\pm\frac{9}{4}$ in the brackets, instead of ±2.25?

b) The time for the ball to reach its maximum height is the t-coordinate of the vertex, which is 1.5 s.

c) When the ball leaves the balcony, $t = 0$.

Substitute $t = 0$ in $h = -5t^2 + 15t + 45$.
$$h = -5(0)^2 + 15(0) + 45$$
$$= 45$$

The balcony is 45 m high.

Discuss

How does the path of the ball compare with the graph below?

We can use a graphing calculator to check the results of *Example 3*.
Input $h = -5t^2 + 15t + 45$ as $y = -5x^2 + 15x + 45$.

Press [Y=]. Input [(-)] 5 [X,T,θ,n] [x²] [+] 15 [X,T,θ,n] [+] 45.

Press [WINDOW]. Input Xmin $= -1$, Xmax $= 6$, Xscl $= 1$, Ymin $= -10$, Ymax $= 70$, Yscl $= 10$.

Press [GRAPH] to display this screen.

To determine the coordinates of the vertex, press [2nd] [TRACE] for CALC. Then press **4** for **maximum**.

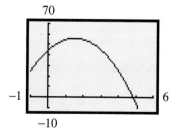

Use the arrow keys to move the cursor to the left of the maximum point. Press ENTER. Move the cursor to the right of the maximum point. Press ENTER ENTER.
The coordinates are displayed: X = 1.4999996 Y = 56.25

These coordinates are the time in seconds to reach the maximum height, and the maximum height in metres.

For the height of the balcony, press [2nd] [TRACE] for CALC. Then press **1** for **value**. Input 0 [ENTER], and the y-intercept is displayed: Y = 45.

This is the height of the balcony in metres.

4.1 Exercises

1. For each function, state its maximum or minimum value and identify which it is.

a) $y = (x + 4)^2 - 3$
b) $y = \frac{1}{4}(x - 3)^2 + 5$
c) $y = -0.5(x - 1)^2 + 2$

d) $y = 3\left(x + \frac{1}{2}\right)^2 - 1$
e) $y = -(x - 2)^2$
f) $y = -x^2 + 16$

2. For each quadratic function:

    i) State the maximum or minimum value of y, and identify which it is.
    ii) State the corresponding value of x.

a) $y = (x + 2)^2 - 4$
b) $y = -\frac{1}{2}(x + 3)^2 - 2$
c) $y = -3(x + 1)^2 + 3$

d) $y = -(x - 1)^2 - 10$
e) $y = 0.4x^2 + 6$
f) $y = -2(x + 4)^2$

3. Write each equation in the form $y = a(x - p)^2 + q$.

a) $y = x^2 - 6x + 8$
b) $y = x^2 + 10x + 9$
c) $y = x^2 + 4x - 7$

d) $y = x^2 - 2x + 1$
e) $y = x^2 + 5x - 3$
f) $y = x^2 + x - 2$

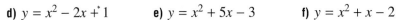

4. Write each equation in the form $y = a(x - p)^2 + q$.

a) $y = 2x^2 + 6x - 7$
b) $y = 3x^2 + 6x - 8$
c) $y = -3x^2 - 9x + 8$

d) $y = -2x^2 + 8x + 4$
e) $y = 4x^2 + 4x + 2$
f) $y = -4x^2 - 8x + 1$

5. Write each equation in the form $y = a(x - p)^2 + q$.

a) $y = 2x^2 + 5x - 1$
b) $y = 3x^2 - 4x + 6$
c) $y = -2x^2 - 3x - 6$

d) $y = -3x^2 + 5x - 4$
e) $y = 4x^2 + 6x - 3$
f) $y = -4x^2 - 10x + 1$

6. Knowledge/Understanding Write each equation in the form $y = a(x - p)^2 + q$. Determine the maximum or minimum value of each function.

a) $y = 2x^2 - 12x + 15$
b) $y = 3x^2 - 6x + 8$
c) $y = 2x^2 - 10x + 20$

d) $y = -x^2 - 6x + 5$
e) $y = -5x^2 + 40x - 3$
f) $y = -4x^2 - 24x + 6$

7. Write each equation in the form $y = a(x - p)^2 + q$.

   a) $y = \frac{1}{2}x^2 + 3x + 2$ **b)** $y = \frac{1}{3}x^2 - 2x + 1$ **c)** $y = -\frac{1}{4}x^2 + x - 3$

   d) $y = -\frac{1}{2}x^2 + 6x - 2$ **e)** $y = -\frac{1}{3}x^2 - 4x + 6$ **f)** $y = \frac{1}{10}x^2 + 2x + 4$

8. Write each equation in the form $y = a(x - p)^2 + q$, then sketch its graph.

   a) $y = x^2 - 2x - 3$ **b)** $y = -x^2 + 6x + 8$ **c)** $y = -2x^2 + 12x - 16$

   d) $y = 3x^2 - 24x + 36$ **e)** $y = -\frac{1}{2}x^2 + 2x - 3$ **f)** $y = \frac{1}{3}x^2 - 4x + 7$

9. Without sketching the graph, determine the maximum or minimum value of each function, state which it is, and state the corresponding x-value.

   a) $y = x^2 - 8x + 21$ **b)** $y = -x^2 + 2x - 6$ **c)** $y = -4x^2 - 32x - 50$

   d) $y = 2x^2 - 8x - 5$ **e)** $y = \frac{1}{10}x^2 - 5x + \frac{1}{4}$ **f)** $y = -\frac{1}{3}x^2 + 9x - \frac{7}{4}$

10. Write an equation of a quadratic function that satisfies each set of conditions.

   a) The function has a minimum value of 6 at $x = 4$.

   b) The function has a minimum value of -3 at $x = 5$.

   c) The function has a maximum value of 10 at $x = -2$.

   d) The parabola is congruent to $y = 3x^2$, and has a minimum value of 7.

   e) The parabola is congruent to $y = -x^2$, and has a maximum value of -3.

11. Are there other possible equations for quadratic functions that satisfy each set of conditions in exercise 10? If so, give an example for each part of this exercise.

12. **Communication** Suppose the coordinates of the vertex of a parabola are known. What additional information is needed to write the equation of the parabola? Explain.

13. **Application** A stone is thrown into the air from a bridge over a river. The stone falls into the river. The height of the stone, h metres, above the river t seconds after the stone is thrown is given by $h = -5t^2 + 10t + 7$.

   a) Determine the maximum height of the stone above the river.

   b) How long does it take the stone to reach its maximum height?

   c) How high is the bridge above the river?

14. **Thinking/Inquiry/Problem Solving** In an electrical circuit, the voltage, V volts, as a function of time, t minutes, is given by $V = 12 - 9t + 2t^2$. Determine the greatest and least values of voltage during the first 5 min. When do these values occur?

In Chapter 2, you solved quadratic equations such as $x^2 + 3x + 2 = 0$, when you determined non-permissible values of the variable for certain rational expressions. You used factoring to solve these equations. However, many quadratic equations cannot be solved by factoring.

The general quadratic equation has the form $ax^2 + bx + c = 0$, where $a \neq 0$. In grade 10, you used the following formula to solve this equation.

Take Note

Quadratic Formula

The real roots of the quadratic equation $ax^2 + bx + c = 0$, $a \neq 0$, are

$x = \dfrac{-b \pm \sqrt{b^2 - 4ac}}{2a}$, where $b^2 - 4ac \geq 0$.

The expression, $b^2 - 4ac$, is the *discriminant* of the quadratic equation.

Since this formula was not proved in grade 10, we will prove it below. We will use the method of completing the square.

Consider $ax^2 + bx + c = 0$.
Remove a as a common factor for the first 2 terms.
$$a(x^2 + \frac{b}{a}x) + c = 0$$

Within the brackets, add and subtract the square of one-half the coefficient of x.
That is, add and subtract $\left(\dfrac{b}{2a}\right)^2 = \dfrac{b^2}{4a^2}$.
$$a\left(x^2 + \frac{b}{a}x + \frac{b^2}{4a^2} - \frac{b^2}{4a^2}\right) + c = 0$$

Write the first 3 terms in the brackets as a perfect square.
Multiply the 4th term in the brackets by a, then remove it from the brackets.
$$a\left(x^2 + \frac{b}{a}x + \frac{b^2}{4a^2}\right) - \frac{b^2}{4a} + c = 0$$
$$a\left(x + \frac{b}{2a}\right)^2 - \frac{b^2}{4a} + c = 0$$

Isolate the binomial square, then simplify the right side.
$$a\left(x + \frac{b}{2a}\right)^2 = \frac{b^2}{4a} - c$$
$$a\left(x + \frac{b}{2a}\right)^2 = \frac{b^2 - 4ac}{4a}$$
$$\left(x + \frac{b}{2a}\right)^2 = \frac{b^2 - 4ac}{4a^2}$$

Take the square root of each side. This step is valid only if $b^2 - 4ac \geq 0$.

$$x + \frac{b}{2a} = \pm\sqrt{\frac{b^2 - 4ac}{4a^2}}$$

Use the division property of radicals.

$$x + \frac{b}{2a} = \pm\frac{\sqrt{b^2 - 4ac}}{2a}$$

Solve for x, then simplify the right side.

$$x = \frac{-b}{2a} \pm \frac{\sqrt{b^2 - 4ac}}{2a}$$

$$x = \frac{-b \pm \sqrt{b^2 - 4ac}}{2a}$$

That is, $x = \dfrac{-b + \sqrt{b^2 - 4ac}}{2a}$ or $x = \dfrac{-b - \sqrt{b^2 - 4ac}}{2a}$

Taken together, these two roots form the quadratic formula.

Example 1

Solve, then check. Write the answers to 4 decimal places where necessary.

a) $2x^2 + 5x - 3 = 0$ **b)** $9x^2 - 12x = -2$ **c)** $x^2 + 6x + 11 = 0$

Solution

a) $2x^2 + 5x - 3 = 0$

Use the quadratic formula.

$$x = \frac{-b \pm \sqrt{b^2 - 4ac}}{2a}$$

Substitute $a = 2$, $b = 5$, $c = -3$.

$$x = \frac{-5 \pm \sqrt{5^2 - 4(2)(-3)}}{2(2)}$$

$$x = \frac{-5 \pm \sqrt{25 + 24}}{4}$$

$$x = \frac{-5 \pm \sqrt{49}}{4}$$

$$x = \frac{-5 \pm 7}{4}$$

$$x = \frac{-5 + 7}{4} \qquad \text{or} \qquad x = \frac{-5 - 7}{4}$$

$$= \frac{1}{2} \qquad\qquad\qquad\qquad = -3$$

Discuss

What other method could you have used to solve this equation? Explain.

Check.

Substitute each value for x in the equation.

$2x^2 + 5x - 3 = 0$

When $x = \frac{1}{2}$

Left side $= 2\left(\frac{1}{2}\right)^2 + 5\left(\frac{1}{2}\right) - 3$

$\qquad = \frac{1}{2} + \frac{5}{2} - 3$

$\qquad = 0$

$\qquad =$ Right side

When $x = -3$

Left side $= 2(-3)^2 + 5(-3) - 3$

$\qquad = 18 - 15 - 3$

$\qquad = 0$

$\qquad =$ Right side

The solution is correct.

b) $9x^2 - 12x = -2$

Rearrange the equation so the right side is 0.

$9x^2 - 12x + 2 = 0$

Use the quadratic formula.

$x = \dfrac{-b \pm \sqrt{b^2 - 4ac}}{2a}$

Substitute $a = 9$, $b = -12$, $c = 2$.

$x = \dfrac{12 \pm \sqrt{(-12)^2 - 4(9)(2)}}{2(9)}$

$x = \dfrac{12 \pm \sqrt{72}}{18}$

$x = \dfrac{12 + \sqrt{72}}{18}$ or $x = \dfrac{12 - \sqrt{72}}{18}$

$\quad \doteq 1.1381$ $\doteq 0.1953$

Check.

Substitute each value for x in the equation.

$9x^2 - 12x = -2$

When $x = 1.1381$

Left side $= 9(1.1381)^2 - 12(1.1381)$

$\qquad \doteq -1.9998$

$\qquad \doteq -2$

$\qquad =$ Right side

When $x = 0.1953$

Left side $= 9(0.1953)^2 - 12(0.1953)$

$\qquad \doteq -2.0003$

$\qquad \doteq -2$

$\qquad =$ Right side

To 3 decimal places, the left side equals the right side.

The solution is correct.

Discuss

In the check for part b, why did the right side not equal the left side in each solution? Explain.

c) $x^2 + 6x + 11 = 0$

Use the quadratic formula.
$$x = \frac{-b \pm \sqrt{b^2 - 4ac}}{2a}$$

Substitute $a = 1$, $b = 6$, $c = 11$.
$$x = \frac{-6 \pm \sqrt{6^2 - 4(1)(11)}}{2(1)}$$

$$x = \frac{-6 \pm \sqrt{-8}}{2}$$

Since $\sqrt{-8}$ is not defined as a real number, this equation has no real roots.

We can use a graphing calculator to illustrate the results of *Example 1*.

The screens show the graphs of the three quadratic functions that correspond to the given equations.

The dotted curve is the graph of $y = 2x^2 + 5x - 3$, which intersects the x-axis at $x = \frac{1}{2}$ and $x = -3$.

The thick curve is the graph of $y = 9x^2 - 12x + 2$, which intersects the x-axis at $x \doteq 1.1$ and $x \doteq 0.2$.

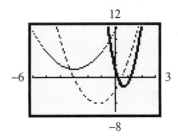

The thin curve is the graph of $y = x^2 + 6x + 11$, which does not intersect the x-axis.

Remember that the zeros of a quadratic function are the x-intercepts of its graph.

Since the graph of a quadratic function is a parabola with a vertical axis of symmetry, the graph has two different x-intercepts, two equal x-intercepts, or no x-intercepts, as shown on the next page.

Similarly, a quadratic equation has two different real roots, two equal real roots, or no real roots.

We can use the quadratic formula, $x = \frac{-b \pm \sqrt{b^2 - 4ac}}{2a}$, to determine the nature of the roots of the general quadratic equation $ax^2 + bx + c = 0$, $a \neq 0$.

Consider how the quadratic formula applies to these three equations:
$x^2 - 8x + 12 = 0$, $x^2 - 8x + 16 = 0$, $x^2 - 8x + 20 = 0$

$x^2 - 8x + 12 = 0$

$x = \dfrac{8 \pm \sqrt{64 - 48}}{2}$

$x = \dfrac{8 \pm \sqrt{16}}{2}$ ———— Positive

The roots are

$\dfrac{8 + 4}{2}$, or 6

and $\dfrac{8 - 4}{2}$, or 2 ———— Two different real roots

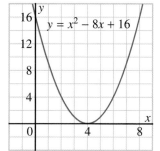

The parabola intersects the x-axis at two points.

$x^2 - 8x + 16 = 0$

$x = \dfrac{8 \pm \sqrt{64 - 64}}{2}$

$x = \dfrac{8 \pm \sqrt{0}}{2}$ ———— Zero

The roots are

$\dfrac{8 + 0}{2}$, or 4

and $\dfrac{8 - 0}{2}$, or 4 ———— Two equal real roots

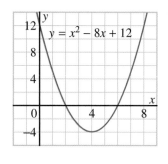

The parabola intersects the x-axis at one point.

$x^2 - 8x + 20 = 0$

$x = \dfrac{8 \pm \sqrt{64 - 80}}{2}$

$x = \dfrac{8 \pm \sqrt{-16}}{2}$ ———— Negative

The roots are not defined as ———— No real roots
real numbers.

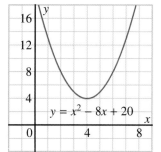

The parabola does not intersect the x-axis.

We can use the quadratic formula to solve problems that involve quadratic functions.

Example 2

A flare is fired upward from the deck of a ship. The flare hits the water. The height of the flare, h metres, above the water after t seconds is given by the function $h = -4.9t^2 + 98t + 8$.

a) Determine the maximum height of the flare.

b) How long does it take the flare to reach its maximum height?

c) When does the flare hit the water?

d) How high is the deck of the ship above the water?

Solution

a) $h = -4.9t^2 + 98t + 8$

To determine the maximum height, complete the square.

$h = -4.9\left(t^2 - \frac{98t}{4.9}\right) + 8$

$h = -4.9(t^2 - 20t) + 8$

$h = -4.9(t^2 - 20t + 100 - 100) + 8$

$h = -4.9(t^2 - 20t + 100) + 490 + 8$

$h = -4.9(t - 10)^2 + 498$

The maximum height of the ball is 498 m.

b) From part a, the time to reach the maximum height is 10 s.

c) The flare hits the water when its height is zero; that is, $h = 0$.

Substitute $h = 0$ in $h = -4.9t^2 + 98t + 8$.

$0 = -4.9t^2 + 98t + 8$

Solve for t. Use the quadratic formula $t = \frac{-b \pm \sqrt{b^2 - 4ac}}{2a}$.

Substitute $a = -4.9$, $b = 98$, $c = 8$.

$t = \frac{-98 \pm \sqrt{98^2 - 4(-4.9)(8)}}{2(-4.9)}$

$t = \frac{-98 \pm \sqrt{9760.8}}{-9.8}$

$t \doteq \frac{-98 \pm 98.7968}{-9.8}$

Multiply the numerator and denominator by -1.

$t \doteq \frac{98 \pm 98.7968}{9.8}$

Ignore the negative root because time cannot be negative.

$t \doteq \frac{98 + 98.7968}{9.8}$

$\doteq 20.08$

The flare hits the water after about 20 s.

Discuss

How could you complete part c using the equation in its completed square form?

d) The flare leaves the deck when $t = 0$.

Substitute $t = 0$ in $h = -4.9t^2 + 98t + 8$.

$h = -4.9(0)^2 + 98(0) + 8$

$= 8$

The deck is 8 m above the water.

4.2 Exercises

 1. Match each equation with the graph of a corresponding function shown below. Use the graph to solve each equation.

a) $x^2 + 9 = -6x$ **b)** $7x = 10 + x^2$ **c)** $2x = x^2 + 3$

d) $x^2 + x = 2$ **e)** $x^2 + 10 = 6x$ **f)** $4x + 5 = x^2$

i)
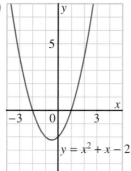
$y = x^2 + x - 2$

ii)
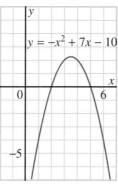
$y = -x^2 + 7x - 10$

iii)
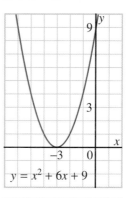
$y = x^2 + 6x + 9$

iv)
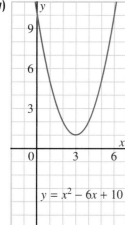
$y = x^2 - 6x + 10$

v)
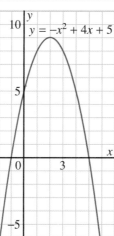
$y = -x^2 + 4x + 5$

vi)
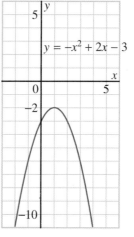
$y = -x^2 + 2x - 3$

2. Solve by factoring.

a) $x^2 - 7x + 12 = 0$ **b)** $m^2 - 9m + 8 = 0$ **c)** $x^2 + 4x + 4 = 0$

d) $a^2 - 5a - 24 = 0$ **e)** $x^2 - 36 = 0$ **f)** $y^2 - 144 = 0$

3. Solve.

a) $x^2 = 25$ **b)** $d^2 = 6$ **c)** $k^2 - 12 = 0$

d) $9x^2 - 2 = 0$ **e)** $(x - 1)^2 = 16$ **f)** $(a + 2)^2 = 3$

4. Solve, then check where possible.

a) $x^2 + 2x - 24 = 0$ **b)** $n^2 - 6n + 5 = 0$ **c)** $x^2 - 6x + 4 = 0$

d) $x^2 + 4x + 2 = 0$ **e)** $18x + 5 = -9x^2$ **f)** $4a^2 = 3 - 16a$

B

5. **Knowledge/Understanding** Solve.

   a) $x^2 + 5x + 6 = 0$ b) $a^2 - 9a + 14 = 0$ c) $m^2 + 7m = 12$

   d) $5x^2 + 14 = 8x$ e) $2k^2 - 13k + 10 = 0$ f) $4x^2 + 10x + 3 = 0$

6. **Communication**

   a) Solve each equation.

   i) $x^2 - 4x - 5 = 0$ ii) $x^2 - 4x + 4 = 0$ iii) $x^2 - 4x + 9 = 0$

   b) On the same grid, graph a function that corresponds to each quadratic equation in part a. Explain how the roots of each quadratic equation relate to the graphs.

7. Determine the roots of each equation to 2 decimal places. Check by using a graphing calculator to graph a corresponding function.

   a) $2b^2 - 13b + 10 = 0$ b) $2z^2 - 7z + 4 = 0$ c) $3x^2 - x - 5 = 0$

   d) $2a^2 - 9a - 1 = 0$ e) $5t^2 - 3t + 1 = 0$ f) $2y^2 + 5y + 4 = 0$

8. Solve.

   a) $x^2 - 14x + 33 = 0$ b) $y^2 + 7y - 18 = 0$ c) $6x^2 - 7x - 3 = 0$

   d) $2m^2 + 5m - 3 = 0$ e) $x^2 - 4x = 0$ f) $2m^2 - m = 0$

9. **Thinking/Inquiry/Problem Solving**

   a) Solve.

   i) $4x^2 + 20x + 10 = 0$ ii) $4x^2 + 20x + 21 = 0$ iii) $4x^2 + 20x + 25 = 0$

   b) Examine the pattern in the equations in part a. What part of the equation changes? How is this change reflected in the graph of a corresponding function? Determine an equation that has the same pattern and has no real solutions.

10. Solve, then check.

    a) $m^2 - 2m - 15 = 0$ b) $t^2 + 12t + 32 = 0$ c) $3x^2 + 7x + 4 = 0$

    d) $2x^2 - 9x - 5 = 0$ e) $4x^2 - 4x - 3 = 0$ f) $4m^2 - 9m + 5 = 0$

11. Solve.

    a) $3x^2 + 5x + 1 = 0$ b) $2k^2 + 3k - 8 = 0$ c) $5x^2 - x + 2 = 0$

    d) $3x^2 + 4x + 7 = 0$ e) $4a^2 + 12a + 9 = 0$ f) $4x^2 - 24x + 36 = 0$

12. State which equations in exercise 11 have:

    a) 2 different real roots   b) 2 equal real roots   c) no real roots

13. Determine the roots of each equation to 2 decimal places.

a) $5x^2 + 6x - 1 = 0$　　b) $2c^2 - 6c - 1 = 0$　　c) $3m^2 + 2m = 7$

d) $4r^2 + 2r = 3$　　e) $3p^2 - 6p + 1 = 0$　　f) $2a^2 - 6a + 1 = 0$

14. Use a graphing calculator. Solve each quadratic equation. Explain how the graphs of corresponding functions account for the differences in the roots of the equations.

a) $4x^2 - 4x - 3 = 0$　　　　　　b) $4x^2 - 4x - 1 = 0$

c) $4x^2 - 4x + 1 = 0$　　　　　　d) $4x^2 - 4x + 3 = 0$

15. Application The height of an infield fly ball, h metres, t seconds after it is hit is given by the formula $h = 1.5 + 30t - 4.9t^2$.

a) Determine the maximum height of the ball.

b) How long does it take the ball to reach its maximum height?

c) How long does it take the ball to reach the ground?

d) How high is the ball when it is hit?

16. a) Solve each equation.

　i) $x^2 - 6x + 9 = 0$　　　　　　ii) $x^2 + 10x + 25 = 0$

　iii) $4x^2 - 12x + 9 = 0$　　　　iv) $4x^2 + 20x + 25 = 0$

b) All the equations in part a have 2 equal real roots. Under what conditions does a quadratic equation have 2 equal real roots?

c) Without solving, determine which equations have 2 equal real roots.

　i) $2x^2 + 5x - 1 = 0$　　　　　ii) $x^2 - 4x + 4 = 0$

　iii) $x^2 - 7x + 9 = 0$　　　　　iv) $9x^2 - 6x + 1 = 0$

17. a) Solve each equation.

　i) $x^2 - 5x + 7 = 0$　　　　　　ii) $-3x^2 + 7x - 11 = 0$

　iii) $2x^2 + 5x + 6 = 0$　　　　　iv) $3x^2 - 7x + 10 = 0$

b) All the equations in part a have no real roots. Under what conditions does a quadratic equation have no real roots?

c) Without solving, determine which equations have no real roots.

　i) $5x^2 + 4x + 1 = 0$　　　　　ii) $3x^2 - 8x + 7 = 0$

　iii) $6x^2 - 5x - 3 = 0$　　　　　iv) $12x^2 - 19x + 7 = 0$

C

18. Consider the quadratic equation $x^2 - bx + 4 = 0$. For what values of b does each solution occur?

a) 2 different real roots　　b) 2 equal real roots　　c) no real roots

1. Write each equation in the form $y = a(x - p)^2 + q$.

a) $y = x^2 - 5x + 9$

b) $y = 2x^2 + 4x + 7$

c) $y = -2x^2 - 6x + 1$

d) $y = 2x^2 - 3x - 2$

e) $y = \frac{1}{2}x^2 + 2x - 5$

f) $y = -\frac{1}{3}x^2 - x + 4$

2. Write each equation in the form $y = a(x - p)^2 + q$.

a) $y = x^2 - 10x + 11$

b) $y = 2x^2 + 12x - 9$

c) $y = -x^2 + 4x + 1$

d) $y = -2x^2 - 7x + 6$

e) $y = \frac{1}{10}x^2 - 2x + 3$

f) $y = -\frac{1}{4}x^2 - 5x - 1$

3. For each quadratic function in exercise 2, state its maximum or minimum value and the corresponding value of x.

4. Write an equation of a quadratic function that has a maximum value of 6 at $x = -3$.

5. Solve each equation by factoring.

a) $x^2 + 7x + 12 = 0$

b) $4m^2 - 12m + 9 = 0$

c) $4a^2 - 12a + 5 = 0$

d) $3x^2 + 13x + 4 = 0$

e) $6a^2 - 11a - 10 = 0$

f) $2x^2 - 7x - 15 = 0$

6. Solve each equation by using the quadratic formula.

a) $x^2 - 9 = -8x$

b) $2b^2 + 4b + 3 = 0$

c) $-2x^2 + 5x + 7 = 0$

d) $4a^2 - 11a + 1 = 0$

e) $3a^2 - 2a = 2$

f) $2x^2 + 3x + 4 = 0$

7. Solve each equation.

a) $x^2 + 25 = 0$

b) $a^2 + 2a + 3 = 0$

c) $4(x - 3)^2 = -7$

d) $5x^2 + 2x + 1 = 0$

e) $-3x^2 - 2x + 7 = 0$

f) $\frac{1}{2}x^2 - 3x - 6 = 0$

8. Use a graphing calculator. Solve each quadratic equation. Explain how the graphs of corresponding functions account for the differences in the roots of the equations.

a) $x^2 + 10x + 15 = 0$

b) $x^2 + 10x + 20 = 0$

c) $x^2 + 10x + 25 = 0$

d) $x^2 + 10x + 30 = 0$

4.3 Introduction to Complex Numbers

In Section 4.2, we discovered that some quadratic equations have no real roots. When we attempt to solve one of these equations using the quadratic formula, we encounter the square root of a negative number. The square root of a negative number is not defined as a real number. However, we can extend the number system to include the square roots of negative numbers.

Consider these examples that involve the number systems you reviewed in Necessary Skills, page 200.

- The equation $x + 3 = 0$ has no solution in the set of natural numbers. But it does have a solution, $x = -3$, in the set of integers.
- The equation $2x + 1 = 0$ has no solution in the set of integers. But it does have a solution, $x = -\frac{1}{2}$, in the set of rational numbers.
- The equation $x^2 - 2 = 0$ has no solution in the set of rational numbers. But it has two solutions, $x = \pm\sqrt{2}$, in the set of irrational numbers.
- The equation $x^2 + 1 = 0$ has no solution in the set of real numbers.

We can extend the number system even further to have a solution for the equation $x^2 + 1 = 0$. We define a new number i with the property that $i^2 = -1$. Then, i is a square root of -1. We now have two square roots of -1 because $-i$ will also have a square of -1:

$$\begin{aligned}(-i)^2 &= [(-1)(i)]^2 \\ &= (-1)^2(i)^2 \\ &= (1)(-1) \\ &= -1\end{aligned}$$

The number i is not a real number. It is not meaningful to say that $\sqrt{-1}$ is the positive square root of -1 because only real numbers can be positive. The symbol $\sqrt{-1}$ could mean either of the two numbers, i or $-i$. Therefore, we define $\sqrt{-1} = i$. Similarly, we define $\sqrt{-4} = 2i$, $\sqrt{-9} = 3i$, and so on. These definitions extend to other numbers of the form $\sqrt{-k}$.

Take Note

Definition of $\sqrt{-k}$

- We define the number i such that $i^2 = -1$.
- We define $\sqrt{-1} = i$.
- When $k > 0$, we define $\sqrt{-k} = \sqrt{k}i$. This is the *principal* square root of $-k$. Thus, the two square roots of $-k$ are $\pm\sqrt{-k} = \pm\sqrt{k}i$.

Example 1

Simplify.

a) $\sqrt{-36}$ **b)** $\sqrt{-12}$ **c)** $(7i)^2$ **d)** i^3

Solution

Use the definition of $\sqrt{-k}$.

a) $\sqrt{-36} = \sqrt{36}i$
$\qquad\quad\; = 6i$

b) $\sqrt{-12} = \sqrt{12}i$
$\qquad\qquad\; = 2\sqrt{3}i$

c) $(7i)^2 = 7^2 \times i^2$
$\qquad\;\; = 49(-1)$
$\qquad\;\; = -49$

d) $i^3 = i^2 \times i$
$\qquad\; = -1(i)$
$\qquad\; = -i$

In *Example 1b*, we could write $(2\sqrt{3})i$ to avoid confusion with $2\sqrt{3i}$.

We can use the definition of $\sqrt{-k}$ to solve a quadratic equation whose solution leads to the square root of a negative number.

Example 2

Solve each equation.

a) $x^2 + 9 = 0$ **b)** $x^2 + 5 = 0$ **c)** $4x^2 + 7 = 0$ **d)** $(x - 2)^2 = -25$

Solution

a) $x^2 + 9 = 0$
$\qquad x^2 = -9$
$\qquad x = \pm\sqrt{-9}$
$\qquad x = \pm 3i$

b) $x^2 + 5 = 0$
$\qquad x^2 = -5$
$\qquad x = \pm\sqrt{-5}$
$\qquad x = \pm\sqrt{5}i$

c) $4x^2 + 7 = 0$
$\qquad x^2 = \dfrac{-7}{4}$
$\qquad x = \pm\sqrt{\dfrac{-7}{4}}$
$\qquad x = \pm\dfrac{\sqrt{7}i}{2}$

d) $(x - 2)^2 = -25$
$\qquad x - 2 = \pm\sqrt{-25}$
$\qquad x - 2 = \pm 5i$
$\qquad x = 2 \pm 5i$

All the roots of the equations in *Example 2* have the form $a + bi$, where a and b are real numbers and $i^2 = -1$. These are examples of *complex numbers*.

Complex Numbers

- An expression of the form $a + bi$, where a and b are real numbers and $i^2 = -1$, is a *complex number*.
- The set of complex numbers includes the real numbers, since any real number x can be written in the form $x + 0i$.

We can use complex numbers to determine the roots of any quadratic equation. This means that the restriction $b^2 - 4ac \geq 0$ in the statement of the quadratic formula on page 212 can be removed (see exercise 16).

Example 3

Solve, then check.

a) $x^2 - 6x + 13 = 0$ **b)** $x^2 + x + 1 = 0$

Solution

a) $x^2 - 6x + 13 = 0$

Use the quadratic formula, $x = \dfrac{-b \pm \sqrt{b^2 - 4ac}}{2a}$.

Substitute $a = 1$, $b = -6$, $c = 13$.

$$x = \frac{-(-6) \pm \sqrt{(-6)^2 - 4(1)(13)}}{2(1)}$$

$$= \frac{6 \pm \sqrt{-16}}{2}$$

$$= \frac{6 \pm 4i}{2}$$

$$= \frac{2(3 \pm 2i)}{2}$$

$$= 3 \pm 2i$$

The roots of the equation are $3 + 2i$ and $3 - 2i$.

Check.

When $x = 3 + 2i$,

Left side $= x^2 - 6x + 13$

     $= (3 + 2i)^2 - 6(3 + 2i) + 13$

     $= 9 + 12i + 4i^2 - 18 - 12i + 13$

     $= -9 + 4(-1) + 13$

     $= 0$

Right side $= 0$

When $x = 3 - 2i$,

Left side $= x^2 - 6x + 13$

     $= (3 - 2i)^2 - 6(3 - 2i) + 13$

     $= 9 - 12i + 4i^2 - 18 + 12i + 13$

     $= -9 + 4(-1) + 13$

     $= 0$

Right side $= 0$

Both roots are correct.

b) $x^2 + x + 1 = 0$

Use the quadratic formula, $x = \dfrac{-b \pm \sqrt{b^2 - 4ac}}{2a}$.

Substitute $a = 1$, $b = 1$, $c = 1$.

$$x = \frac{-1 \pm \sqrt{1^2 - 4(1)(1)}}{2}$$

$$= \frac{-1 \pm \sqrt{-3}}{2}$$

$$= \frac{-1 \pm \sqrt{3}i}{2}$$

$$= -\frac{1}{2} \pm \frac{\sqrt{3}}{2}i$$

The roots of the equation are $-\frac{1}{2} + \frac{\sqrt{3}}{2}i$ and $-\frac{1}{2} - \frac{\sqrt{3}}{2}i$.

Check.

When $x = -\frac{1}{2} + \frac{\sqrt{3}}{2}i$,

Left side $= x^2 + x + 1$

$$= \left(-\frac{1}{2} + \frac{\sqrt{3}}{2}i\right)^2 + \left(-\frac{1}{2} + \frac{\sqrt{3}}{2}i\right) + 1$$

$$= \frac{1}{4} + 2\left(-\frac{1}{2}\right)\left(\frac{\sqrt{3}}{2}i\right) + \left(\frac{\sqrt{3}}{2}i\right)^2 - \frac{1}{2} + \frac{\sqrt{3}}{2}i + 1$$

$$= \frac{1}{4} - \frac{\sqrt{3}}{2}i + \frac{3}{4}i^2 - \frac{1}{2} + \frac{\sqrt{3}}{2}i + 1$$

$$= \frac{1}{4} - \frac{3}{4} - \frac{1}{2} + 1$$

$$= 0$$

Right side $= 0$

When $x = -\frac{1}{2} - \frac{\sqrt{3}}{2}i$,

Left side $= x^2 + x + 1$

$$= \left(-\frac{1}{2} - \frac{\sqrt{3}}{2}i\right)^2 + \left(-\frac{1}{2} - \frac{\sqrt{3}}{2}i\right) + 1$$

$$= \frac{1}{4} + 2\left(-\frac{1}{2}\right)\left(-\frac{\sqrt{3}}{2}i\right) + \left(-\frac{\sqrt{3}}{2}i\right)^2 - \frac{1}{2} - \frac{\sqrt{3}}{2}i + 1$$

$$= \frac{1}{4} + \frac{\sqrt{3}}{2}i + \frac{3}{4}i^2 - \frac{1}{2} - \frac{\sqrt{3}}{2}i + 1$$

$$= \frac{1}{4} - \frac{3}{4} - \frac{1}{2} + 1$$

$$= 0$$

Right side $= 0$

Both roots are correct.

Look at the roots of the equations in *Example 3*.

The roots of $x^2 - 6x + 13 = 0$ are $3 + 2i$ and $3 - 2i$.

The roots of $x^2 + x + 1 = 0$ are $-\dfrac{1}{2} + \dfrac{\sqrt{3}}{2}i$ and $-\dfrac{1}{2} - \dfrac{\sqrt{3}}{2}i$.

In each case, the roots differ only in the sign of the term containing i. Two complex numbers with this property are called *conjugates*. The complex roots of a quadratic equation always occur in conjugate pairs.

We can now modify the quadratic formula so that it applies to complex roots.

Take Note

Quadratic Formula

The roots of the quadratic equation $ax^2 + bx + c = 0$, $a \neq 0$, are

$$x = \frac{-b \pm \sqrt{b^2 - 4ac}}{2a}$$

When $b^2 - 4ac > 0$, there are two different real roots.

When $b^2 - 4ac = 0$, there are two equal real roots.

When $b^2 - 4ac < 0$, there are two complex roots that are conjugates.

4.3 Exercises

A

1. Simplify.

   a) $\sqrt{-4}$ b) $\sqrt{-25}$ c) $\sqrt{-49}$ d) $\sqrt{-2}$

   e) $\sqrt{-5}$ f) $\sqrt{-8}$ g) $\sqrt{-18}$ h) $\sqrt{-72}$

2. Simplify.

   a) $(3i)^2$ b) $(5i)^2$ c) $(\sqrt{6}i)^2$ d) $(2\sqrt{3}i)^2$

   e) i^2 f) i^3 g) i^4 h) i^5

3. Classify each number as an integer, a rational number, an irrational number, a real number, and/or a complex number. A number can belong to more than one set.

   a) $\dfrac{5}{2}$ b) $\sqrt{3}$ c) -4 d) $5i$

   e) $6 - 2i$ f) 0 g) π h) $\dfrac{3\sqrt{2}}{5}i$

   i) $3.4\overline{7}$ j) $-\dfrac{3}{4}$ k) $2.716\,347\ldots$ l) $-4i$

4. Which pairs of complex numbers are conjugates?

a) $1 + i$, $1 - i$

b) $2 + 3i$, $3 - 2i$

c) $3 - 5i$, $3 + 5i$

d) $4 - 2i$, $2 + i$

e) $3 + 4i$, $4i - 3$

f) $2 + \sqrt{3}i$, $2 - \sqrt{3}i$

B

5. Solve each equation. Write the roots in the form bi, where b is a real number.

a) $x^2 + 25 = 0$

b) $x^2 + 12 = 0$

c) $3x^2 + 27 = 0$

d) $2x^2 + 32 = 0$

e) $3x^2 + 60 = 0$

f) $9 + 4x^2 = 0$

6. Solve each equation.

a) $x^2 - 16 = 0$

b) $x^2 + 16 = 0$

c) $x^2 - 6 = 0$

d) $x^2 + 6 = 0$

e) $4x^2 - 25 = 0$

f) $4x^2 + 25 = 0$

g) $4x^2 - 16 = 0$

h) $4x^2 + 16 = 0$

i) $4x^2 - 11 = 0$

j) $4x^2 + 11 = 0$

7. Knowledge/Understanding Solve.

a) $x^2 - 2x + 2 = 0$

b) $x^2 + 4x + 5 = 0$

c) $x^2 + 2x + 3 = 0$

d) $x^2 + x + 2 = 0$

e) $-x^2 + 5x - 7 = 0$

f) $1 - 4x + 2x^2 = 0$

8. Communication

a) Show that both $2i$ and $-2i$ are the roots of the equation $x^2 + 4 = 0$.

b) Without solving the equation, what are the roots of the equation $x^2 + 36 = 0$? Explain.

9. Solve, then check.

a) $x^2 - 2x + 5 = 0$

b) $x^2 + 4x - 7 = 0$

c) $3x^2 - 4x + 2 = 0$

d) $-3x^2 + 2x - 2 = 0$

e) $2 - 4x + 7x^2 = 0$

f) $x^2 - x + 2 = 0$

10. Solve, then check.

a) $x^2 + x - 12 = 0$

b) $2a^2 - 11a + 5 = 0$

c) $2a^2 + 5a - 1 = 0$

d) $2m^2 + 2m + 1 = 0$

e) $k^2 - 6k + 9 = 0$

f) $x^2 + 2x + 4 = 0$

11. Consider the product $\sqrt{-2} \times \sqrt{-3}$. When we use the definition of $\sqrt{-k}$ to simplify this product, we obtain $\sqrt{2}i \times \sqrt{3}i = \sqrt{6}i^2 = -\sqrt{6}$. When we use the multiplication property of radicals to simplify the product, we obtain $\sqrt{(-2)(-3)} = \sqrt{6}$.

a) Which answer is correct?

b) Explain why the other answer is not correct.

12. **Application** Since a complex number has two parts, it can be plotted as a point on a coordinate grid. For example, on the diagram, point A represents the complex number $3 + 4i$. The horizontal axis is the *real axis* and the vertical axis the *imaginary axis*.

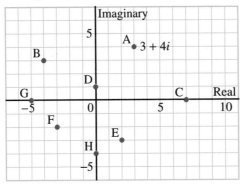

a) Copy the diagram on grid paper.

b) Write the complex number for each point on the grid.

c) Choose any complex number on the grid. How would you define the opposite of this complex number? Plot the point for the opposite number. How are the two points related?

13. Draw a grid similar to that in exercise 12. Plot each complex number on the grid.

a) $5 - 3i$ b) $6i$ c) 2 d) $\frac{5}{2}i$

e) $-1 - i$ f) $\frac{11}{2}$ g) $2 + 3i$ h) $-\sqrt{5}i$

14. **Thinking/Inquiry/Problem Solving**

a) Simplify i^2, i^3, i^4, i^5, i^6.

b) Describe any patterns in the results of part a.

c) Graph the results of part a on a grid, as in exercise 12. Include the points that correspond to i^0 and i^1. Explain how the algebraic and geometric results are related.

d) Use the result of part a to simplify i^{12}, i^{21}, i^{30}, and i^{59}.

15. Solve, then check.

a) $x^2 + ix + 2 = 0$ b) $x^2 + ix - 2 = 0$

16. Refer to the proof of the quadratic formula on pages 212, 213. Look at the line where we take the square root of each side. From this point on, the solution should be divided into two cases. In Case 1, we assume that $b^2 - 4ac \geq 0$ as shown in the text. In Case 2, we assume $b^2 - 4ac < 0$. Complete the solution for Case 2.

In Section 4.3, we defined a complex number as an expression of the form $a + bi$, where a and b are real numbers and $i^2 = -1$. When we checked the solutions of the equation $x^2 - 6x + 13 = 0$ in *Example 3*, page 224, we simplified $(3 + 2i)^2$ and $-6(3 + 2i)$ using the rules of algebra. However, these rules were established for real numbers, and we need to ensure they apply to complex numbers. We will define operations with complex numbers so these rules do apply.

Addition, Subtraction, and Multiplication of Complex Numbers

Suppose we have two complex numbers, such as $5 + 3i$ and $2 - 4i$. The way to add and subtract them is to use the rules of algebra.

$$(5 + 3i) + (2 - 4i) = 5 + 3i + 2 - 4i$$
$$= 5 + 2 + 3i - 4i$$
$$= 7 - i$$
$$(5 + 3i) - (2 - 4i) = 5 + 3i - 2 + 4i$$
$$= 5 - 2 + 3i + 4i$$
$$= 3 + 7i$$

The way to multiply the numbers is to use the rules of algebra, and $i^2 = -1$.

$$(5 + 3i)(2 - 4i) = 10 - 20i + 6i - 12i^2$$
$$= 10 - 14i - 12(-1)$$
$$= 10 - 14i + 12$$
$$= 22 - 14i$$

To add, subtract, and multiply complex numbers this way requires us to define these operations as follows. Each result is a complex number.

Let $z_1 = a_1 + b_1 i$ and $z_2 = a_2 + b_2 i$ be any two complex numbers.
We define: $z_1 + z_2 = (a_1 + a_2) + (b_1 + b_2)i$
$$z_1 - z_2 = (a_1 - a_2) + (b_1 - b_2)i$$
$$z_1 z_2 = (a_1 a_2 - b_1 b_2) + (a_1 b_2 + a_2 b_1)i$$

Take Note

Operations with Complex Numbers

To add, subtract, and multiply complex numbers, use the rules of algebra and $i^2 = -1$.

Example 1

Simplify.

a) $(12 - 3i) - 3(5 + 2i)$

b) $i(4 - 5i)$

c) $(2 - 3i)(5 + 2i)$

d) $(1 + 2i)(1 - 2i)$

Solution

a) $(12 - 3i) - 3(5 + 2i) = 12 - 3i - 15 - 6i$

$$= -3 - 9i$$

b) $i(4 - 5i) = 4i - 5i^2$

$$= 4i - 5(-1)$$

$$= 5 + 4i$$

c) $(2 - 3i)(5 + 2i) = 10 + 4i - 15i - 6i^2$

$$= 10 - 11i - 6(-1)$$

$$= 16 - 11i$$

d) $(1 + 2i)(1 - 2i) = 1 - 2i + 2i - 4i^2$

$$= 1 - 4(-1)$$

$$= 5$$

The result in *Example 1d* is a real number. Since the set of complex numbers includes the set of real numbers, we sometimes obtain real numbers when we operate with complex numbers.

Division of Complex Numbers

Remember how division and multiplication are related. For example, we know that $\frac{12}{3} = 4$ because $3 \times 4 = 12$. We use the same principle to define division of complex numbers. First, we will consider the case where the divisor is a complex number of the form di.

Case 1. Dividing by di

Consider dividing 12 by $3i$. When we use the above principle, $\frac{12}{3i}$ is the number that results in 12 when it is multiplied by $3i$.

Let $\qquad \dfrac{12}{3i} = z$

Then $\qquad (3i)(z) = 12$

By inspection, z must be $-4i$.

Therefore, $\qquad \dfrac{12}{3i} = -4i$

The quotient $-4i$ is not negative. The sign "–" in $-4i$ means that this is the opposite of $4i$.

A more efficient way to obtain the same result is to multiply $\frac{12}{3i}$ by $\frac{i}{i}$. Since this equals 1, the value of the expression is not changed.

$$\frac{12}{3i} = \frac{12}{3i} \times \frac{i}{i}$$

$$= \frac{12i}{3i^2}$$

$$= \frac{12i}{-3}$$

$$= -4i$$

Note that multiplying $\frac{12}{3i}$ by $\frac{i}{i}$ makes the denominator a real number, -3.

Example 2

Simplify.

a) $\frac{1}{i}$

b) $\frac{2 - 3i}{-4i}$

Solution

Multiply each expression by $\frac{i}{i}$, then simplify.

a) $\frac{1}{i} = \frac{1}{i} \times \frac{i}{i}$

$\phantom{a)\ \frac{1}{i}} = \frac{i}{i^2}$

$\phantom{a)\ \frac{1}{i}} = \frac{i}{-1}$

$\phantom{a)\ \frac{1}{i}} = -i$

b) $\frac{2 - 3i}{-4i} = \frac{2 - 3i}{-4i} \times \frac{i}{i}$

$\phantom{b)\ \frac{2 - 3i}{-4i}} = \frac{2i - 3i^2}{-4i^2}$

$\phantom{b)\ \frac{2 - 3i}{-4i}} = \frac{2i - 3(-1)}{-4(-1)}$

$\phantom{b)\ \frac{2 - 3i}{-4i}} = \frac{2i + 3}{4}$

$\phantom{b)\ \frac{2 - 3i}{-4i}} = \frac{3}{4} + \frac{2}{4}i$

$\phantom{b)\ \frac{2 - 3i}{-4i}} = \frac{3}{4} + \frac{1}{2}i$

Take Note

Dividing by di

To simplify $\frac{a + bi}{di}$, multiply by $\frac{i}{i}$.

Now we will consider the case where the divisor is a complex number of the form $c + di$.

Case 2. Dividing by c + di

Consider dividing $3 + 2i$ by $1 - 2i$.

We want to simplify $\dfrac{3 + 2i}{1 - 2i}$.

The result should be a complex number $a + bi$ so that $(1 - 2i)(a + bi) = 3 + 2i$. Although it is possible to determine a and b by expanding the left side, there is a more efficient way to obtain the same result. This is similar to the method in Case 1.

Remember that when we multiplied $\dfrac{12}{3i}$ by $\dfrac{i}{i}$, the denominator became a real number. We want the same thing to occur with $\dfrac{3 + 2i}{1 - 2i}$. That is, we want to multiply the numerator and denominator by an expression so the denominator becomes a real number. Remember also that when complex numbers arise in the solution of a quadratic equation, they do so in conjugate pairs such as $1 + 2i$ and $1 - 2i$, which differ only in the sign of the term containing i. The product of these numbers is a real number. Therefore, if we multiply $\dfrac{3 + 2i}{1 - 2i}$ by $\dfrac{1 + 2i}{1 + 2i}$, its value remains the same and the denominator becomes a real number. We do this in *Example 3*.

Example 3

Simplify $\dfrac{3 + 2i}{1 - 2i}$.

Solution

Multiply the expression by $\dfrac{1 + 2i}{1 + 2i}$.

$$\frac{3 + 2i}{1 - 2i} = \frac{3 + 2i}{1 - 2i} \times \frac{1 + 2i}{1 + 2i}$$

$$= \frac{(3 + 2i)(1 + 2i)}{(1 - 2i)(1 + 2i)}$$

$$= \frac{3 + 8i + 4i^2}{1 - 4i^2}$$

$$= \frac{3 + 8i - 4}{1 + 4}$$

$$= \frac{-1 + 8i}{5}$$

$$= -\frac{1}{5} + \frac{8}{5}i$$

Take Note

Dividing by c + di

To simplify $\dfrac{a + bi}{c + di}$, multiply by $\dfrac{c - di}{c - di}$.

A

1. Simplify.

   a) $(4 + i) + (5 - 4i)$ b) $(3 + 2i) - (1 + 5i)$

   c) $(6 - 2i) + (5 + 4i)$ d) $(7 + 5i) - (9 - i)$

   e) $4(2 + 3i) + 2(1 - 6i)$ f) $-(6 - i) + 3(2 + 2i)$

2. Simplify.

   a) $3(4 + i) - 2(5 - 4i)$ b) $4(3 + 2i) - 6(1 + 5i)$

   c) $(7 + 5i) + i(9 - i)$ d) $(5 - 6i) + 2i(3 + 4i)$

   e) $3i(3 + 2i) - i(6 - 3i)$ f) $2i(5 - i) - 3i(6 + 2i)$

3. Simplify.

   a) $(2 + i)(2 - i)$ b) $(4 - 3i)(4 + 3i)$ c) $(1 + 2i)(3 + 4i)$

   d) $(5 - 3i)(2 + 4i)$ e) $(1 + i)^2$ f) $(7 - 4i)^2$

4. Refer to the definitions of $z_1 + z_2$, $z_1 - z_2$, and z_1z_2 on page 229.

   a) What special cases occur when $b_1 = b_2 = 0$?

   b) Explain why $z_1z_2 = (a_1a_2 - b_1b_2) + (a_1b_2 + a_2b_1)i$.

5. On page 231, we multiplied $\frac{12}{3i}$ by $\frac{i}{i}$. Explain why $\frac{i}{i} = 1$.

6. Simplify.

   a) $\frac{6}{3i}$ b) $\frac{20}{4i}$ c) $\frac{7}{4i}$ d) $\frac{6}{9i}$

   e) $\frac{1}{-6i}$ f) $\frac{1}{-3i}$ g) $\frac{9}{-3i}$ h) $\frac{6}{-2i}$

B

7. Simplify.

   a) $\frac{3 + 4i}{2i}$ b) $\frac{3 - 4i}{2i}$ c) $\frac{4 + 3i}{2i}$ d) $\frac{4 - 3i}{2i}$

   e) $\frac{5 + i}{-4i}$ f) $\frac{6 - 2i}{3i}$ g) $\frac{2 + 7i}{-4i}$ h) $\frac{-10 - 3i}{6i}$

8. A geometric sequence has first term 1 and common ratio i.

   a) Write the first 8 terms of the sequence in simplest form.

   b) Determine each term of the sequence in part a.

   i) t_{21} ii) t_{42} iii) t_{59} iv) t_{80}

   c) When you know the term number, how can you determine its value?

9. **Communication** Multiply each complex number by its conjugate. What do you notice about the results? Explain.

a) $2 + i$

b) $3 - i$

c) $-4 + 3i$

d) $-5 - 2i$

e) $\frac{1}{2} + i$

f) $\frac{1}{4} + \frac{1}{2}i$

g) $\sqrt{2} + i$

h) $\frac{1}{2} - \frac{\sqrt{3}}{2}i$

10. Consider two complex numbers that are not conjugates. Is it possible for the product of these complex numbers to be a real number? If your answer is yes, give an example. If it is no, explain why not.

11. For each part of exercise 9, add the complex number and its conjugate. What do you notice about the results? Explain.

12. Consider two complex numbers that are not conjugates. Is it possible for the sum of these complex numbers to be a real number? If your answer is yes, give an example. If it is no, explain why not.

 13. **Knowledge/Understanding** Simplify.

a) $2i(3 - 5i)$

b) $2i(-4i - 5)$

c) $(2 - 7i)(5 + 3i)$

d) $(7 + 2i)(5 - 4i)$

e) $(6 + 3i)(2 + 5i)$

f) $(2 - 3i)(7 - 2i)$

g) $6i(5 - i)^2$

h) $3i(2 + 5i)^2$

14. Simplify.

a) $i(3 - 2i) - 5i(7 + 3i)$

b) $2i(4 + 6i) + 3i(5 - 2i)$

c) $(2 - i)(2 + i) + (2 - i)^2$

d) $(3 + 2i)(3 + i) + (4 - 3i)^2$

e) $(2 + \sqrt{6}i)^2$

f) $(3 - \sqrt{2}i)^2$

g) $(1 + i)^3$

h) $(1 - i)^3$

 15. Simplify.

a) $\dfrac{1 + 2i}{1 + i}$

b) $\dfrac{2 + 3i}{1 + 2i}$

c) $\dfrac{1 + i}{1 - i}$

d) $\dfrac{4 - i}{2 + i}$

e) $\dfrac{6 - 2i}{3 + 4i}$

f) $\dfrac{5 - 2i}{3 + 2i}$

g) $\dfrac{26}{3 - 2i}$

h) $\dfrac{20}{2 + 4i}$

i) $\dfrac{15i}{2 + 5i}$

j) $\dfrac{-2i}{7 + 3i}$

k) $\dfrac{5i}{2 - 6i}$

l) $\dfrac{-3 - 2i}{1 - 2i}$

16. a) How would you define the reciprocal of a complex number?

b) Determine the reciprocal of each complex number.

i) $2i$

ii) $1 + 2i$

iii) $1 - 2i$

iv) $4 - 3i$

c) Find a number whose reciprocal equals its opposite.

17. Thinking/Inquiry/Problem Solving The complex numbers in exercise 16b parts ii and iii are conjugates.

 a) Write two other conjugate complex numbers, then determine their reciprocals.

 b) Explain how you could use conjugates to determine the reciprocal of a complex number. Illustrate your explanation with an example.

18. Is it possible for the quotient of two complex numbers to be a real number? If your answer is yes, give an example. If it is no, explain why not.

19. Write the terms of each geometric sequence as complex numbers in the form $a + bi$.

 a) $5 + 2i$, $(5 + 2i)i$, $(5 + 2i)i^2$, $(5 + 2i)i^3$, $(5 + 2i)i^4$

 b) $1 + 6i$, $(1 + 6i)i$, $(1 + 6i)i^2$, $(1 + 6i)i^3$, $(1 + 6i)i^4$

 c) $4 - i$, $(4 - i)i$, $(4 - i)i^2$, $(4 - i)i^3$, $(4 - i)i^4$

20. Application In 4.3 Exercises, exercise 12, you learned that a complex number can be plotted as a point on a grid. We can use a grid to give a geometric meaning to multiplying by i, and to $i^2 = -1$.

 a) Choose one geometric sequence from exercise 19, then plot the terms on a coordinate grid.

 b) Describe the geometric effect of multiplying by i.

 c) Describe the geometric meaning of $i^2 = -1$.

C

21. Solve for a and b.
$a + bi = (5 - 2i)^2$

22. Determine all the roots of each equation.

 a) $x^4 = 1$ b) $x^2 = i$

23. On page 232, we observed that $\dfrac{3 + 2i}{1 - 2i}$ should be a complex number $a + bi$, so that $(1 - 2i)(a + bi) = 3 + 2i$. Expand the product on the left side of this equation, and continue the solution to determine a and b.

24. The complex numbers $z_1 = a_1 + b_1 i$ and $z_2 = a_2 + b_2 i$ are given. On page 229, we defined $z_1 + z_2$, $z_1 - z_2$, and $z_1 z_2$. Write a similar definition for $\dfrac{z_1}{z_2}$.

1. Simplify.

   a) $\sqrt{-81}$ b) $\sqrt{-82}$ c) $\sqrt{-100}$ d) $\sqrt{-10}$

   e) $(4i)^2$ f) $(-4i)^2$ g) $\left(\sqrt{5}i\right)^2$ h) $\left(-\sqrt{5}i\right)^2$

2. Solve each quadratic equation.

   a) $x^2 + 2x + 3 = 0$ b) $3x^2 - x + 2 = 0$

   c) $-4x^2 - 2x - 1 = 0$ d) $2x^2 - 7x + 7 = 0$

   e) $\frac{1}{2}x^2 - 2x + 5 = 0$ f) $\frac{1}{5}x^2 + 3x - 20 = 0$

3. Solve, then check.

   a) $x^2 + 2x + 2 = 0$ b) $x^2 - 3x + 6 = 0$

   c) $2x^2 + 6x + 9 = 0$ d) $3x^2 + x + 5 = 0$

   e) $10x^2 - 3x + 1 = 0$ f) $2x^2 - 5x + 4 = 0$

Functions and Relations

4. Simplify.

   a) $(5 + 2i) + (10 + 12i)$ b) $(5 - 2i) + (2 - 5i)$

   c) $(-5 - 2i) + (6 - 7i)$ d) $(-5 + 2i) + (-9 + 6i)$

5. Simplify.

   a) $(7 + 2i) - (4 + 6i)$ b) $(7 - 2i) - (4 - 6i)$

   c) $(-7 - 2i) - (-3 + 8i)$ d) $(-7 + 2i) - (-1 + i)$

6. Simplify.

   a) $3i(6 - 5i)$ b) $(3 + 2i)(4 - 7i)$

   c) $(6 - i)^2$ d) $(-4 + 7i)(1 - 8i)$

7. Simplify.

   a) $\sqrt{-6} \times \sqrt{-24}$ b) $\left(\sqrt{-8}\right)^2$ c) $\frac{15}{3i}$

   d) $\frac{39}{2 - 3i}$ e) $\frac{6 - 5i}{1 + i}$ f) $\frac{5 + 2i}{3 + 4i}$

8. Write the reciprocal of each complex number.

   a) $3i$ b) $2 + 3i$ c) $3 - 4i$

Parabolas and Lines

The graphs of the parabola $y = x(6 - x)$ and the line $y = 2x$ are shown at the right.

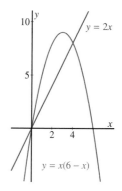

Formulating Questions

We will investigate the following problem.

Suppose we move the line $y = 2x$ parallel to itself. How will the number of intersections with the parabola $y = x(6 - x)$ change?

We will investigate the problem both algebraically and geometrically, then compare the results.

Representing the Intersections in Mathematical Form

We begin by finding the points of intersection of the parabola and the line. The graph suggests that we will find two intersection points, the origin and one around $x = 4$.

To distinguish the line and the parabola, we will use y_P for points on the parabola and y_L for points on the line:

$$y_P = x(6 - x) \qquad ①$$
$$y_L = 2x \qquad ②$$

For any value of x, y_P is the height of the parabola at that x, and y_L is the height of the line. At any point where the parabola and the line intersect, these heights are equal. Therefore, we want the values of x for which:

$$y_P = y_L$$

This gives us the following equation that we can solve for x.

$$x(6 - x) = 2x$$
$$6x - x^2 = 2x$$
$$x^2 - 4x = 0$$
$$x(x - 4) = 0$$

We get two solutions, $x = 0$ and $x = 4$. That's what we expect from the graph, because these are the x-coordinates of the two points of intersection. We could determine their y-coordinates, but we will not do this because we are only interested in the number of points of intersection.

Scan along the x-axis and consider the values of x. For any value, we can calculate two y-values, one for the parabola (this is y_P) and one for the line (this is y_L).

What do you think of this solution?
$$x(6 - x) = 2x$$
Divide each side by x.
$$6 - x = 2$$
$$x = 4$$
This gives one point of intersection. We lost the other point when we divided each side by x, because this step is only valid when $x \neq 0$. The case when $x = 0$ has to be considered separately.

Moving the line geometrically

Suppose the line moves parallel to itself. How does the number of intersections between the line and the parabola change? The diagram suggests the following conjecture:

One of the lines intersects the parabola at one point, where the line just touches the curve. We say that the line is a *tangent* to the parabola. Each line below the tangent intersects the parabola at two different points. Each line above the tangent does not intersect the parabola.

Moving the line algebraically

Since all the lines have slope 2, we can represent them by this general equation:

$$y_L = 2x + b$$

For each value of b, we want to find the points of intersection with the parabola $y_P = x(6 - x)$. We equate the y-expressions:

$$y_P = y_L$$
$$x(6 - x) = 2x + b$$
$$6x - x^2 = 2x + b$$

Collect all terms on the left side, then combine like terms.

$$-x^2 + 4x - b = 0$$

We want the coefficient of x^2 to be positive (we can arrange this with an equation, but not with a function).

$$x^2 - 4x + b = 0$$

This equation corresponds to the equation on page 237 that we solved by factoring. We use the quadratic formula to solve the equation above.

$$x = \frac{4 \pm \sqrt{16 - 4b}}{2}$$
$$x = \frac{4 \pm \sqrt{4(4 - b)}}{2}$$
$$x = 2 \pm \sqrt{4 - b}$$

These are the x-coordinates of the point(s) of intersection of the parabola and the line for each value of b.

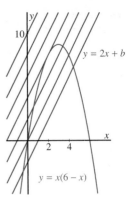

This graph shows the parabola $y = x(6 - x)$ and some members of the family of lines $y = 2x + b$. The symbol b is called a *parameter*. Each value of b corresponds to one line of the family. We want to know how the number of intersections with the parabola changes as the value of b changes.

Parameters often have a physical or geometric interpretation. Here, b represents the y-intercept of each line.

The solutions of $ax^2 + bx + c = 0$ are:
$x = \frac{-b \pm \sqrt{b^2 - 4ac}}{2a}$
To solve
$x^2 - 4x + b = 0$,
substitute 1 for a,
-4 for b, and b for c.
Notice that the two bs are not the same.

Interpreting Information and Forming Conclusions

Notice that b occurs in the discriminant, $4 - b$. That is good, because this expression discriminates among the different numbers of solutions for x.

    < 4, the discriminant is positive, and there are 2 solutions.
    $= 4$, the discriminant is 0, and there is only 1 solution.
    > 4, the discriminant is negative, and there are no solutions.

4 QUADRATIC FUNCTIONS AND COMPLEX NUMBERS

Reflecting on the Reasonableness of the Results

This proves our geometric conjecture. It tells us that lower lines have two intersections, that higher lines have no intersections, and there is one line between them that has only one intersection. Our geometric conjecture also tells us which lines they are. To determine the equation of the tangent, substitute $b = 4$ into the equation of the family, $y = 2x + b$. The result is $y = 2x + 4$. All of this matches what we see in the diagram.

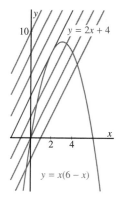

Problems

1. Graph the parabola $y = x^2$ and the line $y = 4x$. The line intersects the parabola twice. Visualize the family of lines with slope 4. How many intersections does each line have with the parabola?

   a) Study your graph and make a conjecture that answers the question.

   b) Represent the family of lines algebraically, then prove your conjecture. Illustrate your solution with a diagram.

2. a) Graph the parabola $y = (x + 1)^2 + 1$, and some members of the family of lines with slope -2.

   b) Represent this family of lines algebraically.

   c) Determine the number of intersections of the line and the parabola. Illustrate your solution with a diagram.

3. The graphs of the curve $y = \dfrac{1}{x}$ and the line $y = -4x$ are shown at the right. The line does not intersect the curve. Visualize the family of lines parallel to $y = -4x$. How many intersections does each line have with the curve?

   a) Study the graph, then make a conjecture that answers the question.

   b) Represent the family of lines algebraically, then prove your conjecture.

4. Graph the parabola $y = x^2$ and some members of the family of parabolas $y = -(x - 1)^2 + k$.

   a) Make a conjecture about all the possible intersections.

   b) Use the equations to prove your conjecture.

   c) For what value(s) of k are the curves tangent to each other?

Problems 5 and 6 refer to the problem on page 237. To solve these problems, use the three graphs in the margin on the next page.

Selecting Strategies, Resources, Technology, and Tools

To create graphs like those above and below, use a spreadsheet or graphing software. Some programs, such as *Graphmatica*, can produce graphs of families of lines or curves with one command.

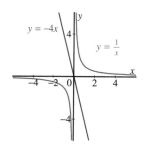

5. Instead of moving the line parallel to itself, we could rotate it about the origin. This creates a family of lines where the slope m is a parameter.

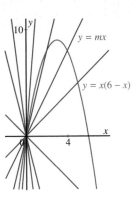

  a) Study the graph at the right and make a conjecture that answers this question. How many intersections does each line have with the parabola?

  b) Use the equations to prove your conjecture.

  c) What is the equation of the line that is tangent to the parabola?

6. The second and third graphs at the right illustrate other possibilities for the situation on page 237. Each graph shows a family of parabolas. The equation of the family appears below the graph. Choose one graph.

  a) Describe the family of parabolas.

  b) Make a conjecture that answers this question. How many intersections does each parabola have with the line?

  c) Use the equations to prove your conjecture.

  d) What is the equation of the parabola that is tangent to the line?

  e) On the diagram, all the parabolas open down. Parabolas that open up are also members of the family. How are these parabolas affected by your analysis?

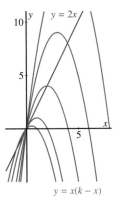

Challenge Problems

7. Graph the circle $x^2 + y^2 = 2$ and some members of the family of lines $y = -x + b$.

  a) Make a conjecture about all the possible intersections.

  b) Use the equations to prove your conjecture.

8. Graph the circle $x^2 + y^2 = 1$ and some members of the family of parabolas $y = x^2 + k$.

  a) Make a conjecture about all the possible intersections.

  b) Use the equations to prove your conjecture.

  c) Write a summary of your results. Illustrate your results on a diagram large enough to show all the possible intersections clearly.

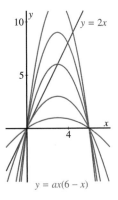

9. In terms of the parameter a, when does this system of equations have 0, 1, 2, 3, 4, or 5 solutions?

$$y^2 = x^2$$
$$(x - a)^2 + y^2 = 1$$

Algebra Tools

- A quadratic function in the form $y = ax^2 + bx + c$ can be changed to the form $y = a(x - p)^2 + q$ by completing the square. See page 207 for an example.
- The graph of a quadratic function in the form $y = a(x - p)^2 + q$ is a parabola with vertex (p, q) and axis of symmetry $x = p$. The parabola opens up when $a > 0$ and opens down when $a < 0$.
- The zeros of the quadratic function $y = ax^2 + bx + c$ are the real roots of the quadratic equation $ax^2 + bx + c = 0$. The zeros are the x-intercepts of the graph.
- The quadratic formula states that the roots of the quadratic equation $ax^2 + bx + c = 0$, $a \neq 0$, are $x = \frac{-b \pm \sqrt{b^2 - 4ac}}{2a}$.

  When $b^2 - 4ac > 0$, there are two different real roots.

  When $b^2 - 4ac = 0$, there are two equal real roots.

  When $b^2 - 4ac < 0$, there are two complex roots that are conjugates.
- In the complex number system, the number i is defined so that $i^2 = -1$.
- An expression of the form $a + bi$, where a and b are real numbers and $i^2 = -1$, is a complex number. When $b = 0$, then $a + bi$ is a real number.
- Two complex numbers that differ only in the sign of the term containing i are conjugates; for example, $3 + 2i$ and $3 - 2i$.

Functions and Relations

- To add, subtract, and multiply complex numbers, use the rules of algebra and $i^2 = -1$.
- To simplify $\frac{a + bi}{di}$, multiply by $\frac{i}{i}$. To simplify $\frac{a + bi}{c + di}$, multiply by $\frac{c - di}{c - di}$.

4.1

1. For each quadratic function:

   i) Write it in the form $y = a(x - p)^2 + q$.
   ii) Identify the coordinates of the vertex.
   iii) Identify the equation of the axis of symmetry.
   iv) Identify the zeros of the function.
   v) Sketch the graph.

   a) $y = \frac{1}{2}x^2 + 4x - 5$ **b)** $y = -\frac{1}{3}x^2 - 8x + 12$ **c)** $y = 2x^2 + 4x - 6$

   d) $y = 3x^2 - 12x + 9$ **e)** $y = -x^2 + 6x - 5$ **f)** $y = -2x^2 - 4x + 6$

2. Without sketching the graph, determine the maximum or minimum value of each function, state whether it is a maximum or minimum, and write the corresponding x-value.

   a) $y = 3x^2 + 42x + 147$ b) $y = -2x^2 + 12x - 14$ c) $y = -x^2 + x - 1$

3. A rock is thrown into the air from a bridge and falls to the water below. The height of the ball, h metres, relative to the water t seconds after being thrown is given by $h = -5t^2 + 20t + 15$.

   a) Determine the maximum height of the rock above the water.

   b) How long does it take the rock to reach the maximum height?

   c) After how many seconds does the rock hit the water?

4.2 4. Solve each quadratic equation.

   a) $a^2 - 8a + 15 = 0$ b) $x^2 - 13x + 30 = 0$ c) $2a^2 + 15 = 13a$

   d) $2 + 5x = 3x^2$ e) $2m^2 + 12m = -10$ f) $x^2 - 6x + 10 = 0$

4.3 5. Simplify.

   a) $\sqrt{-16}$ b) $\sqrt{-36}$ c) $\sqrt{-48}$ d) $\sqrt{-12}$ e) $(5i)^2$

   f) $(7i)^2$ g) $(-\sqrt{3}i)^2$ h) $(\sqrt{5}i)^2$ i) i^4 j) i^3

6. Solve, then check.

   a) $x^2 + 14x + 40 = 0$ b) $x^2 - 8x + 12 = 0$ c) $x^2 - 6x - 14 = 0$

   d) $x^2 + 2x - 5 = 0$ e) $x^2 - 2x + 5 = 0$ f) $x^2 + 12x + 45 = 0$

Functions and Relations

4.4 7. Simplify.

   a) $(6 + 2i) + (3 - 4i)$ b) $(9 - 7i) - (2 + 3i)$ c) $6i(2 + 3i)$

   d) $4i(7 - 2i)$ e) $(4 - 3i)(5 + 2i)$ f) $(6 + i)(5 - i)$

   g) $(2 + 5i)^2$ h) $(3 - 7i)^2$ i) $(7 - 2i)(7 + 2i)$

8. Simplify.

   a) $\dfrac{15}{5i}$ b) $\dfrac{16}{8i}$ c) $\dfrac{5 - 2i}{3i}$ d) $\dfrac{6 + 3i}{2i}$

   e) $\dfrac{20}{4 + 2i}$ f) $\dfrac{5}{2 - 3i}$ g) $\dfrac{1 + i}{1 - i}$ h) $\dfrac{2 - 3i}{5 + 2i}$

9. Determine the reciprocal of each number.

   a) i b) $-2i$ c) $2 + i$ d) $4 - 3i$

Self-Test

1. **Knowledge/Understanding** Write each quadratic function in the form $y = a(x - p)^2 + q$.

   a) $y = 2x^2 - 8x + 18$

   b) $y = 3x^2 + 11x + 4$

   c) $y = -2x^2 + 10x - 12$

   d) $y = \frac{1}{2}x^2 - 3x - 7$

2. For each function in exercise 1, state:

   i) the maximum or minimum value of the function

   ii) whether it is a maximum or minimum

   iii) the x-value where this maximum or minimum occurs

3. **Application** A ball is thrown into the air from a building and falls to the ground below. The height of the ball, h metres, relative to the ground t seconds after being thrown is given by $h = -5t^2 + 30t + 35$.

   a) Determine the maximum height of the ball above the ground.

   b) How long does it take the ball to reach the maximum height?

   c) After how many seconds does the ball hit the ground?

4. **Communication** To solve each equation below, examine the graph of a corresponding function. Write to explain how each graph and equation are related.

   a) $x^2 - 2x - 3 = 0$

   b) $x^2 = 4x - 4$

   c) $x^2 + x + 1 = 0$

   i)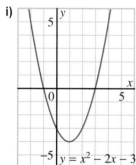
   $y = x^2 - 2x - 3$

   ii)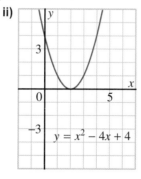
   $y = x^2 - 4x + 4$

   iii)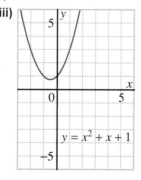
   $y = x^2 + x + 1$

5. Solve each quadratic equation.

   a) $9x^2 - 16 = 0$

   b) $x^2 - 5 = 0$

   c) $3x^2 + 21 = 0$

   d) $a^2 = a + 20$

   e) $2k^2 - 5k = 3$

   f) $9x^2 + 30x + 25 = 0$

6. Solve, then check.

   a) $x^2 + 144 = 0$

   b) $(a - 2)^2 = 6$

   c) $(k + 1)^2 = -9$

   d) $x^2 + 2x + 2 = 0$

   e) $2x^2 - 3x + 5 = 0$

   f) $2x^2 + 2x - 3 = 0$

7. Simplify.

a) $\sqrt{-25}$
b) $\sqrt{-12}$
c) $(6i)^2$
d) $(-2i)^3$

8. Thinking/Inquiry/Problem Solving Determine the sum and product of the roots of the quadratic equation $ax^2 + bx + c = 0$.

Functions and Relations

9. Simplify.

a) $(3 + i) - (2 + 5i) + (6 - 4i)$
b) $2i(5 - 6i)$
c) $(6 + 7i)(6 - 7i)$
d) $(4 - 3i)^2$

10. Simplify.

a) $\sqrt{-7} \times \sqrt{-7}$
b) $\dfrac{5 - 3i}{2i}$
c) $\dfrac{13}{1 + 5i}$
d) $\dfrac{2 - i}{2 + i}$

11. Determine the reciprocal of each number.

a) $5i$
b) $4 - 3i$

Assessment Tasks

1. For each value of t, the equation $y = x^2 - 2tx$ defines a parabola.

a) On the same grid, draw the parabolas for $t = 0, \pm1$, and ±2.

b) Let t represent time. For each value of t, we have a parabola; as time proceeds, the parabola moves. You will investigate the path followed by the vertex of the parabola.
   i) Determine the coordinates of the vertex in terms of t.
   ii) Describe the path of the vertex as t changes. Determine the equation of this path, then graph it on the grid in part a.

2. A U-shaped trough is made from a piece of sheet metal 20 cm wide. Equal widths of x centimetres are bent up on either side. The cross section is a rectangle without a top. The *carrying capacity* of the trough is defined as the area A square centimetres of this rectangle.

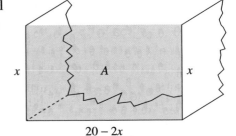

a) Is a carrying capacity of 40 cm^2 possible? If so, what is the corresponding value of x?

b) Repeat part a for a carrying capacity of 80 cm^2.

c) What is the maximum carrying capacity of the trough? What is the corresponding value of x?

d) Show that the problem of whether a given value of A is possible reduces to the mathematical problem of whether a certain quadratic equation has real roots. Explain your reasoning. Solve this quadratic equation, then determine the possible values of A. What is the nature of the roots of the quadratic equation at the point of maximum capacity in part c?

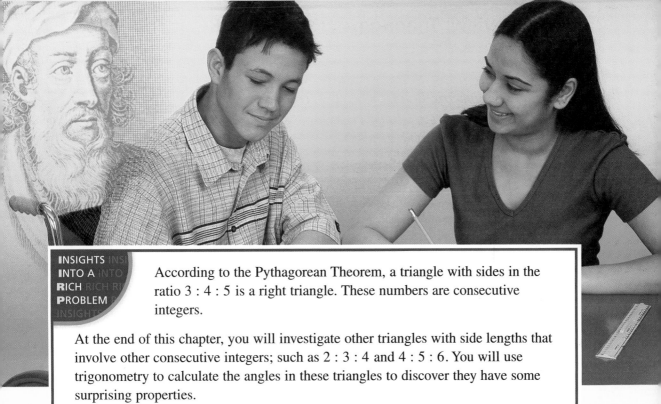

INSIGHTS INTO A RICH PROBLEM

According to the Pythagorean Theorem, a triangle with sides in the ratio 3 : 4 : 5 is a right triangle. These numbers are consecutive integers.

At the end of this chapter, you will investigate other triangles with side lengths that involve other consecutive integers; such as 2 : 3 : 4 and 4 : 5 : 6. You will use trigonometry to calculate the angles in these triangles to discover they have some surprising properties.

Curriculum Expectations

By the end of this chapter, you will:

- Determine the sine, cosine, and tangent of angles greater than 90°, using a suitable technique, and determine two angles that correspond to a given single trigonometric function value.

- Solve problems in two dimensions and three dimensions involving right triangles and oblique triangles, using the primary trigonometric ratios, the cosine law, and the sine law (including the ambiguous case).

- Define the term *radian measure*.

- Describe the relationship between radian measure and degree measure.

- Represent, in applications, radian measure in exact form as an expression involving π and in approximate form as a real number.

- Determine the exact values of the sine, cosine, and tangent of the special angles $0, \frac{\pi}{6}, \frac{\pi}{4}, \frac{\pi}{3}, \frac{\pi}{2}$ and their multiples less than or equal to 2π.

- Prove simple identities, using the Pythagorean identity, $\sin^2 x + \cos^2 x = 1$, and the quotient relation, $\tan x = \frac{\sin x}{\cos x}$.

- Solve linear and quadratic trigonometric equations on the interval $0 \le x \le 2\pi$.

- Demonstrate facility in the use of radian measure in solving equations.

Necessary Skills

1. Review: Trigonometric Ratios in Right Triangles

Remember the primary trigonometric ratios in a right triangle.

Take Note

Trigonometric Ratios in a Right Triangle

$$\sin A = \frac{\text{length of side opposite } \angle A}{\text{length of hypotenuse}}$$

$$\cos A = \frac{\text{length of side adjacent to } \angle A}{\text{length of hypotenuse}}$$

$$\tan A = \frac{\text{length of side opposite } \angle A}{\text{length of side adjacent to } \angle A}$$

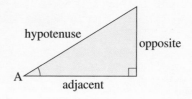

To *solve* a right triangle means to determine all unknown side and angle measures.

The calculator keys are for the TI-30X IIS. If your calculator is different, refer to its manual.

Example

Solve $\triangle ABC$, given $AC = 4.0$ cm, $BC = 1.5$ cm, and $\angle B = 90°$.

Solution

Use the Pythagorean Theorem to determine AB.

$$AC^2 = AB^2 + BC^2$$
$$4.0^2 = AB^2 + 1.5^2$$
$$AB^2 = 16 - 2.25$$
$$\quad\ = 13.75$$
$$AB = \sqrt{13.75}$$
$$\quad\ \doteq 3.7081$$

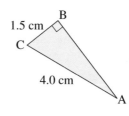

AB is approximately 3.7 cm.

Use the sine ratio to determine $\angle A$.

$$\sin A = \frac{\text{opposite}}{\text{hypotenuse}}$$

$$\quad\ = \frac{1.5}{4.0}$$ Key in: 1.5 ⌈÷⌉ 4 ⌈ENTER =⌉

$$\quad\ = 0.375$$ Then key in: ⌈2nd⌉ ⌈SIN⌉ ⌈2nd⌉ ⌈(-)⌉ ⌈ENTER =⌉

$$\angle A \doteq 22.0243°$$

$\angle A$ is approximately $22°$.

Use the angle sum of a triangle to determine $\angle C$.

Since $\angle B = 90°$, and $\angle A + \angle B + \angle C = 180°$,

then $\angle A + \angle C = 90°$

$\angle C \doteq 90° - 22°$

$\doteq 68°$

$\angle C$ is approximately $68°$.

Discuss

Explain the use of the keys [2nd] [⊢].

What other ways could you have solved △ABC?

Exercises

1. Determine the measure of $\angle A$ in each triangle.

a)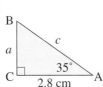

b)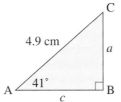

c)

2. Determine the length of side a in each triangle.

a)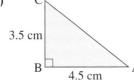

b)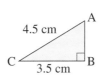

c)

3. Choose one part of exercise 2. Determine the length of side c in two different ways.

4. Solve each triangle.

a)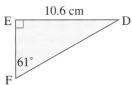

b)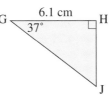

c)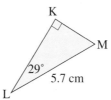

d)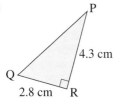

e)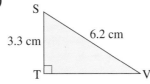

Necessary Skills

5. Solve each △ABC. In each triangle, ∠B = 90°

    a) $c = 4.8$ cm, $a = 2.3$ cm   **b)** $c = 11.4$ cm, $b = 13.7$ cm

    c) $a = 5.2$ cm, $b = 8.4$ cm   **d)** ∠A = 43°, $a = 2.3$ cm

    e) ∠A = 32°, $c = 5.6$ cm   **f)** ∠A = 71°, $b = 9.3$ cm

2. Review: The Sine Law in Acute Triangles

Remember the Sine Law in an acute triangle.

Take Note

Sine Law

$$\frac{\sin A}{a} = \frac{\sin B}{b} = \frac{\sin C}{c}$$

or, $\dfrac{a}{\sin A} = \dfrac{b}{\sin B} = \dfrac{c}{\sin C}$

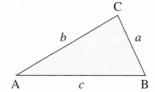

To use the Sine Law, we need to know:

- the measures of two sides and one non-included angle, or

- the measures of two angles and one side

Example 1

In △HJK, ∠J = 75°, HJ = 8.3 cm, and HK = 10.4 cm; calculate the measure of ∠K to the nearest degree.

Solution

Use the Sine Law.

$$\frac{\sin K}{k} = \frac{\sin J}{j}$$

Substitute the known measures.

$$\frac{\sin K}{8.3} = \frac{\sin 75°}{10.4}$$

Multiply each side by 8.3.

$\sin K = \dfrac{8.3 \sin 75°}{10.4}$ Key in: 8.3 [SIN] 75 [)] [÷] 10.4 [ENTER]

    $\doteq 0.770\ 88$ Then key in: [2nd] [SIN] [2nd] [(-)] [ENTER =]

  ∠K $\doteq 50°$

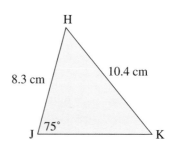

Discuss

An alternative key sequence to determine ∠K is [2nd] [SIN] 8.3 [SIN] 75 [)] [÷] 10.4 [)] [ENTER =]. Which sequence do you prefer? Explain.

Example 2

In △DEF, ∠D = 46°, ∠E = 59°, and DE = 9.8 cm; calculate the length of DF.

Solution

To use the Sine Law, we need to know the measure of an angle and its opposite side. First, calculate the measure of ∠F.

Use the sum of the angles in a triangle to calculate ∠F.

$$\angle F = 180° - 46° - 59°$$
$$= 75°$$

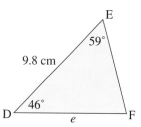

Use the Sine Law.

$$\frac{e}{\sin E} = \frac{f}{\sin F}$$

$$\frac{e}{\sin 59°} = \frac{9.8}{\sin 75°}$$

Multiply each side by sin 59°.

$$e = \frac{9.8 \sin 59°}{\sin 75°}$$

Key in: 9.8 [SIN] 59 [ )] [÷] [SIN] 75 [ENTER =]

$$\doteq 8.6966$$

The length of DF is approximately 8.7 cm.

Exercises

1. Determine the measure of ∠A in each triangle.

a)

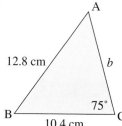

b)

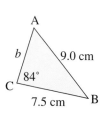

c)

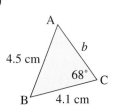

2. In exercise 1, determine the length of side *b* in each triangle.

3. Determine the length of side a in each triangle.

a)

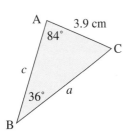

A
84°
3.9 cm
C
c
36°
a
B

b)

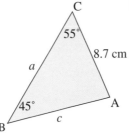

C
55°
8.7 cm
a
45°
c
A
B

c)

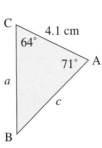

C
64°
4.1 cm
71° A
a
c
B

4. In exercise 3, determine the length of side c in each triangle.

5. Solve each triangle.

a)

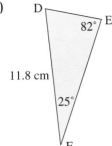

D
82°
E
11.8 cm
25°
F

b)

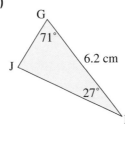

G
71°
6.2 cm
J
27°
H

c)

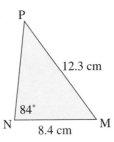

P
12.3 cm
84°
N
8.4 cm
M

6. Solve each triangle.

a) $\triangle$PQR with $\angle$P = 33°, $\angle$R = 71°, q = 13.5 cm

b) $\triangle$STU with $\angle$T = 82°, s = 9.4 cm, t = 12.8 cm

c) $\triangle$VWX with $\angle$V = 41°, $\angle$X = 88°, v = 14.3 cm

3. Review: The Cosine Law in Acute Triangles

Remember the Cosine Law in an acute triangle.

Take Note

Cosine Law

$$a^2 = b^2 + c^2 - 2bc \cos A$$

or, $b^2 = a^2 + c^2 - 2ac \cos B$

or, $c^2 = a^2 + b^2 - 2ab \cos C$

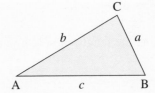

C
b
a
A
c
B

To use the Cosine Law, we need to know:

• the measures of two sides and their included angle, or

• the measures of three sides

Example 1

In $\triangle$CDE, $\angle$C = 56°, CE = 4.7 cm, and CD = 8.5 cm; calculate the length of DE.

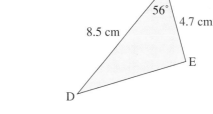

Solution

Use the Cosine Law.
$$c^2 = d^2 + e^2 - 2de \cos C$$

Substitute the known measures.

$c^2 = 4.7^2 + 8.5^2 - 2(4.7)(8.5)\cos 56°$ Key in: 4.7 $\boxed{x^2}$ $\boxed{+}$ 8.5 $\boxed{x^2}$ $\boxed{-}$ 2

$\boxed{\times}$ 4.7 $\boxed{\times}$ 8.5 $\boxed{\cos}$ 56 $\boxed{\text{ENTER}}$

$ \doteq 49.660\ 487$ Then key in: $\boxed{\text{2nd}}$ $\boxed{x^2}$ $\boxed{\text{2nd}}$ $\boxed{(-)}$ $\boxed{\text{ENTER}}$

$c \doteq 7.047$

The length of DE is approximately 7.0 cm.

Example 2

In $\triangle$GHJ, GH = 8.1 cm, GJ = 5.9 cm, and HJ = 9.2 cm; calculate the measure of $\angle$G to 1 decimal place.

Solution

Use the Cosine Law.
$$g^2 = h^2 + j^2 - 2hj \cos G$$

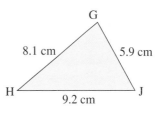

Substitute the known measures, then solve for cos G.
$$9.2^2 = 5.9^2 + 8.1^2 - 2(5.9)(8.1)\cos G$$
$$9.2^2 - 5.9^2 - 8.1^2 = -2(5.9)(8.1)\cos G$$

Divide each side by $-2(5.9)(8.1)$.
$$\frac{9.2^2 - 5.9^2 - 8.1^2}{-2(5.9)(8.1)} = \cos G$$
$$\cos G \doteq 0.165\ 097$$
$$\angle G \doteq 80.497°$$

The measure of $\angle$G is approximately 80.5°.

Exercises

1. Determine the length of side *a* in each triangle.

a)

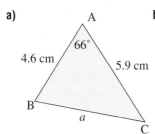

b)

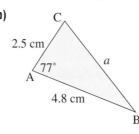

c)

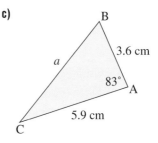

2. In exercise 1, determine the measures of ∠B and ∠C in each triangle. Which law will you use? Justify your answer.

3. Determine the measure of ∠A in each triangle.

a)

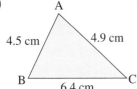

b)

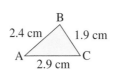

c)

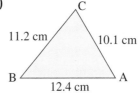

4. In exercise 3, determine the measures of ∠B and ∠C in each triangle. Which law will you use? Justify your answer.

5. Solve each triangle.

a)

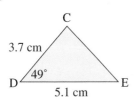

b)

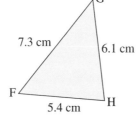

c)

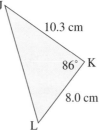

6. Solve each triangle.

   a) △BCD with $b = 10.2$ cm, $c = 9.4$ cm, $d = 3.1$ cm

   b) △EFG with ∠F = 71°, $g = 9.6$ cm, $e = 12.5$ cm

   c) △HJK with $h = 23.0$ cm, $j = 24.0$ cm, $k = 25.0$ cm

7. Do the Cosine Law and Sine Law apply to right triangles? Explain your answer and include examples.

5.1 The Sine and Cosine of an Obtuse Angle

We have used trigonometry to solve problems that involve triangles, but none of those triangles has contained an obtuse angle. Before we can solve problems that involve obtuse triangles, we need to define the trigonometric ratios of an obtuse angle.

The trigonometric ratios have been defined as ratios of the side lengths of a right triangle. Since a right triangle does not contain obtuse angles, trigonometric ratios of obtuse angles have no meaning according to these definitions. We shall redefine the trigonometric ratios in a way that applies to both acute and obtuse angles. The new definitions involve a coordinate grid.

Draw a semicircle with centre O(0, 0) and radius 1 unit. Let P(x, y) be any point on this semicircle in Quadrant I. Let A be the point (1, 0). Join OP, and let $\angle POA = \theta$. Construct PN perpendicular to the x-axis, to form right $\triangle PON$.

In $\triangle PON$, $\angle PON = \theta$, and OP = 1
Use the definitions of the cosine and sine ratios.

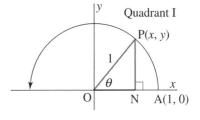

$\cos \theta = \dfrac{ON}{OP} = \dfrac{ON}{1} = x$ (the first coordinate of P)

$\sin \theta = \dfrac{NP}{OP} = \dfrac{NP}{1} = y$ (the second coordinate of P)

We redefine $\cos \theta$ as the first coordinate of P, and $\sin \theta$ as the second coordinate of P. These definitions are consistent with the right-triangle definitions because we used the right-triangle definitions to obtain them.

Suppose P rotates to Quadrant II, where OP = 1 and $\angle POA = \theta$ is an obtuse angle. We define $\cos \theta$ as the first coordinate of P, and $\sin \theta$ as the second coordinate of P.

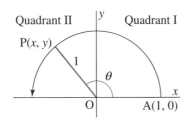

Definitions of the Cosine and Sine of an Angle between 0° and 180°

Point P is a point on a semicircle with centre O(0, 0) and radius 1 unit.
Point A has coordinates (1, 0), and ∠POA = θ.
The following definitions are valid when 0° ≤ θ ≤ 180°.

In these definitions, the radius OP must be 1 unit.

We define: cos θ is the first coordinate of P.
sin θ is the second coordinate of P.

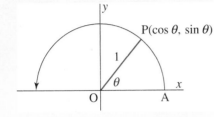
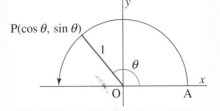

Special cases:

$$\cos 0° = 1 \qquad \cos 90° = 0 \qquad \cos 180° = -1$$
$$\sin 0° = 0 \qquad \sin 90° = 1 \qquad \sin 180° = 0$$

With these definitions, it does not matter whether P is in Quadrant I or II. It does not matter whether θ is acute or obtuse. In Quadrant I, θ is acute. In Quadrant II, θ is obtuse.

Finding sines and cosines of obtuse angles

To determine the sine and cosine of an obtuse angle, use a calculator.

For example, to determine sin 144° and cos 144°:

Key in: [SIN] 144 [ENTER] to display 0.587785252
Key in: [COS] 144 [ENTER] to display −0.809016994

Rounded to 4 decimal places: sin 144° = 0.5878 and cos 144° = −0.8090
Sin 144° is positive, but cos 144° is negative.

Finding angles with given sines and cosines

To determine an angle when its sine or cosine is known, use a calculator.
Care must be taken in some situations, as *Example 1* shows.

Example 1

For each equation, determine the value(s) of θ to the nearest degree. Assume that 0° ≤ θ ≤ 180°. Draw a diagram to explain what each equation means.

a) cos θ = 0.8 **b)** cos θ = −0.8 **c)** sin θ = 0.8

Solution

In each case, draw a semicircle with centre O(0, 0) and radius 1 unit.

a) $\cos\theta = 0.8$

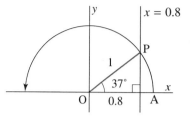

Key in: [2nd] [COS] 0.8 [ENTER ＝] to display 36.86989765
Hence, $\theta \doteq 37°$

Draw a vertical line at $x = 0.8$, to meet the semicircle at P.
Join PO. $\cos\theta = 0.8$ means that θ is the angle where the
x-coordinate of P is 0.8.

b) $\cos\theta = -0.8$

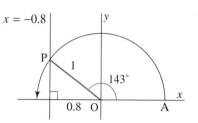

Key in: [2nd] [COS] [(-)] 0.8 [ENTER ＝] to display 143.1301024
Hence, $\theta \doteq 143°$

Draw a vertical line at $x = -0.8$, to meet the semicircle at P.
$\cos\theta = -0.8$ means that θ is the angle where the
x-coordinate of P is −0.8.

c) $\sin\theta = 0.8$

Key in: [2nd] [SIN] 0.8 [ENTER ＝] to display 53.13010235
Hence, $\theta \doteq 53°$

Draw a horizontal line at $y = 0.8$, to meet the semicircle at P. Since this
line intersects the semicircle at two points, there are two possible positions
for P. Each position corresponds to an angle θ so that $\sin\theta = 0.8$. One
angle θ is acute, and the other is obtuse.

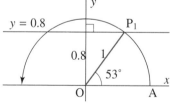
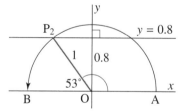

The calculator displays only one value of θ, for the acute angle. This is
approximately 53°. Since the calculator cannot display two different results
for the same keystrokes, use the 53° angle to determine the other angle.

Points P_1 and P_2 are symmetrically placed on either side of the y-axis.
This means that $\angle P_2OB = 53°$
Hence, $\angle P_2OA = 180° - 53° = 127°$
Therefore, when $\sin\theta = 0.8$, then $\theta \doteq 53°$ or $\theta \doteq 127°$

$\sin\theta = 0.8$ means that θ is the angle where the y-coordinate of P is 0.8.
Since there are two positions for P, there are two values of θ.

In *Example 1*, note that the keystrokes ⟨2nd⟩ ⟨SIN⟩ represent ⟨SIN⁻¹⟩. Similarly, ⟨2nd⟩ ⟨COS⟩ represent ⟨COS⁻¹⟩.

In *Example 1c*, the equation $\sin \theta = 0.8$ has two solutions. Since the second solution was obtained by subtracting the first from $180°$, the two solutions have a sum of $180°$. You will obtain similar results for any other equation that is similar to $\sin \theta = 0.8$.

Take Note

Sine of Obtuse Angles

Any equation of the form $\sin \theta = k$, where $0° \leq \theta \leq 180°$, has two solutions for θ.

To determine these solutions:

- Use the ⟨SIN⁻¹⟩ key to obtain one solution.
- Subtract the first solution from $180°$ to obtain the second solution.

Example 2

Given that $0° \leq \theta \leq 180°$, determine the value(s) of θ, to 1 decimal place.
a) $\cos \theta = 0.5329$ **b)** $\cos \theta = -0.5329$ **c)** $\sin \theta = 0.5329$

Solution

a) $\cos \theta = 0.5329$

The positive cosine indicates that the angle is acute.
Key in: ⟨2nd⟩ ⟨COS⟩ 0.5329 ⟨ENTER⟩ to display 57.79839364
$\theta \doteq 57.8°$

b) $\cos \theta = -0.5329$

The negative cosine indicates that the angle is obtuse.
Key in: ⟨2nd⟩ ⟨COS⟩ ⟨(-)⟩ 0.5329 ⟨ENTER⟩ to display 122.2016064
$\theta \doteq 122.2°$

c) $\sin \theta = 0.5329$

The positive sine indicates that the angle could be acute or obtuse.
Key in: ⟨2nd⟩ ⟨SIN⟩ 0.5329 ⟨ENTER⟩ to display 32.20160636

There are two solutions:
$\theta \doteq 32.2°$ $\theta \doteq 180° - 32.2° = 147.8°$

Discuss

How could you use a calculator to check the answers?

Relating sines and cosines

The diagrams on page 254 are repeated below, with perpendiculars drawn from P(cos θ, sin θ) to the *x*-axis.

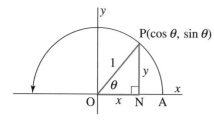
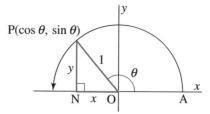

On each diagram, $\triangle$ONP is a right triangle with hypotenuse 1 unit and legs *x* units and *y* units. According to the Pythagorean Theorem, $x^2 + y^2 = 1$.

Since $x = \cos \theta$ and $y = \sin \theta$, this means that:

$$(\cos \theta)^2 + (\sin \theta)^2 = 1$$

For any θ, the sum of the squares of the sine and cosine is 1.

Since the expressions $(\cos \theta)^2$ and $(\sin \theta)^2$ occur frequently, we write them as $\cos^2 \theta$ and $\sin^2 \theta$. Thus, $\cos^2 \theta + \sin^2 \theta = 1$

The result above is called the *Pythagorean identity*. An identity is an equation that is satisfied for all values of the variable for which the equation is defined.

Discuss

In the second diagram above, *x* is negative. Does this affect the result that $\cos^2 \theta + \sin^2 \theta = 1$? Explain.

Take Note

Pythagorean Identity

$$\cos^2 \theta + \sin^2 \theta = 1$$

5.1 Exercises

A

1. Determine the sine and cosine of each angle to 4 decimal places.

  a) 0°   **b)** 10°   **c)** 19°   **d)** 27°   **e)** 35°

  f) 46°   **g)** 63°   **h)** 77°   **i)** 81°   **j)** 90°

2. Determine the sine and cosine of each angle to 4 decimal places.

  a) 120°   **b)** 165°   **c)** 121°   **d)** 96°   **e)** 158°

  f) 143°   **g)** 101°   **h)** 180°   **i)** 132°   **j)** 176°

3. a) Predict whether each value will be positive or negative. Sketch each angle on coordinate axes.

 i) $\sin 98°$ **ii)** $\sin 113°$ **iii)** $\cos 62°$

 iv) $\cos 143°$ **v)** $\cos 92°$ **vi)** $\sin 49°$

 b) For part a, write to explain how you predicted which values are negative.

4. Determine the sine and cosine of each angle to 3 decimal places. Then sketch each angle on coordinate axes. Show the coordinates of the endpoint of the 1-unit line segment that forms that angle with the positive x-axis.

 a) $110°$ **b)** $95°$ **c)** $138°$ **d)** $73°$ **e)** $142°$

 f) $35°$ **g)** $172°$ **h)** $54°$ **i)** $129°$ **j)** $151°$

B

5. Knowledge/Understanding Each angle θ is between $0°$ and $180°$. Solve each equation. Which equations result in two different values for θ?

 a) $\sin \theta = 0.7071$ **b)** $\cos \theta = -0.5$ **c)** $\sin \theta = 0.9269$

 d) $\cos \theta = -0.7071$ **e)** $\sin \theta = 0.8660$ **f)** $\cos \theta = -1$

 g) $\sin \theta = \frac{3}{4}$ **h)** $\cos \theta = \frac{3}{4}$ **i)** $\cos \theta = -\frac{3}{4}$

6. Communication For exercise 5, write to explain why there are two values of θ for some equations, and only one value of θ for other equations.

7. Given that $0° \le \theta \le 180°$, determine the value(s) of θ.

 a) $\sin \theta = 0.9063$ **b)** $\cos \theta = 0.5736$ **c)** $\cos \theta = -0.7321$

 d) $\sin \theta = 0.4283$ **e)** $\sin \theta = 0.5726$ **f)** $\cos \theta = -0.3747$

 g) $\sin \theta = \frac{1}{2}$ **h)** $\cos \theta = \frac{1}{2}$ **i)** $\cos \theta = -\frac{1}{2}$

 j) $\sin \theta = \frac{2}{3}$ **k)** $\sin \theta = \frac{1}{4}$ **l)** $\cos \theta = -\frac{5}{6}$

8. Select two parts from exercise 7, one that involves a sine and one that involves a cosine. Write to explain how you decided the number of possible angles, and how you found them.

9. Verify that $\cos^2 \theta + \sin^2 \theta = 1$ for each angle θ.

 a) $30°$ **b)** $72°$ **c)** $115°$ **d)** $164°$

10. Application

 a) Determine the sine and cosine of each angle.

  i) $30°$ **ii)** $45°$ **iii)** $60°$

 b) Describe how some of the sines and cosines in part a are related. Use diagrams to illustrate your explanation.

11. Angle θ is acute.

    a) $\sin \theta = 0.7$; calculate $\cos \theta$ to 3 decimal places.

    b) $\cos \theta = 0.3$; calculate $\sin \theta$ to 3 decimal places.

12. Angle θ is obtuse.

    a) $\sin \theta = 0.2$; calculate $\cos \theta$ to 3 decimal places.

    b) $\cos \theta = -0.6$; calculate $\sin \theta$ to 3 decimal places.

13. Angle θ is between $0°$ and $180°$.

    a) $\sin \theta = 0.25$; calculate $\cos \theta$ to 3 decimal places.

    b) $\cos \theta = 0.65$; calculate $\sin \theta$ to 3 decimal places.

14. On a grid, draw a semicircle centre O, radius 1 unit. Label points A(1, 0), B(−1, 0), and C(0, 1).

    a) Use the diagram to determine each pair of ratios.

       i) $\cos 0°$, $\sin 0°$ **ii)** $\cos 90°$, $\sin 90°$ **iii)** $\cos 180°$, $\sin 180°$

    b) Use a calculator to check the results of part a. Explain how the ratios in each pair are related.

15. a) Determine the sine and cosine of each angle.

       i) $0°$ **ii)** $20°$ **iii)** $40°$ **iv)** $60°$ **v)** $80°$

       vi) $100°$ **vii)** $120°$ **viii)** $140°$ **ix)** $160°$ **x)** $180°$

    b) Identify pairs of angles that have the same sine. How are the angles related?

    c) Use the angle pairs you identified in part b. How are the cosines of the angles in each pair related?

    d) What can you conclude about the sines and cosines of acute and obtuse angles?

16. Thinking/Inquiry/Problem Solving Use the results of exercise 15a.

    a) Investigate the relationship between the sine and cosine of complementary acute angles. Write a result that you think is true for every acute angle θ, then use a diagram to explain why your result is true.

    b) Use a table to summarize the relationships among the trigonometric ratios of an angle θ and its complementary and supplementary angles.

17. The trigonometric ratios were defined on page 246 for acute angles in a right triangle. On page 253, the sine and cosine of an acute angle were defined as the coordinates of a point P(x, y) that is 1 unit from the origin in Quadrant I. Explain why the two definitions are equivalent.

5.2 The Cosine Law and Sine Law in Obtuse Triangles

In Necessary Skills, pages 248–252, you reviewed the Sine Law and Cosine Law in acute triangles. Now that we have defined the sines and cosines of obtuse angles, we can apply these laws to solve problems that involve any triangle.

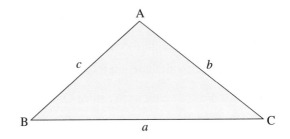

Sine Law

$$\frac{\sin A}{a} = \frac{\sin B}{b} = \frac{\sin C}{c}$$

or, $\quad \dfrac{a}{\sin A} = \dfrac{b}{\sin B} = \dfrac{c}{\sin C}$

Cosine Law

$$a^2 = b^2 + c^2 - 2bc \cos A$$
or, $\quad b^2 = a^2 + c^2 - 2ac \cos B$
or, $\quad c^2 = a^2 + b^2 - 2ab \cos C$

Take Note

Sine and Cosine Ratios of Angles between 0° and 180°

For $0° \leq \theta \leq 90°$

- $\sin \theta$ is positive
- $\cos \theta$ is positive

For $90° < \theta \leq 180°$

- $\sin \theta$ is positive
- $\cos \theta$ is negative

Example 1

In $\triangle ABC$, $AB = 2.8$ cm, $\angle ABC = 119°$, and $BC = 2.7$ cm; determine the length of CA.

Solution

Since we know two sides and their included angle, use the Cosine Law.

$b^2 = a^2 + c^2 - 2ac \cos B$
$\quad = 2.7^2 + 2.8^2 - 2(2.7)(2.8) \cos 119°$

Key in: 2.7 $\boxed{x^2}$ $\boxed{+}$ 2.8 $\boxed{x^2}$ $\boxed{-}$ 2 $\boxed{\times}$ 2.7 $\boxed{\times}$ 2.8 $\boxed{\cos}$ 119 $\boxed{\text{ENTER}}$
$b^2 \doteq 22.460\ 321\ 46$

Then key in: $\boxed{\text{2nd}}$ $\boxed{x^2}$ $\boxed{\text{2nd}}$ $\boxed{(-)}$ $\boxed{\text{ENTER}}$
$\quad b \doteq 4.739$

CA is approximately 4.7 cm.

Discuss

Solve the equation for *b* before using the calculator. Which keystrokes would you then use?

Example 2

A bridge, AB, is to be built across a river.
The points B and C are 49.4 m apart,
∠ACB = 34.1°, and ∠ABC = 42.6°.
How long will the bridge be?

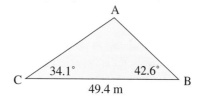

Solution

Since we know two angles and one side, use the Sine Law.

To use the Sine Law, we need the measure of the angle opposite BC.
Use the sum of the angles in a triangle.

$$\angle A = 180° - 34.1° - 42.6°$$
$$= 103.3°$$

Use the Sine Law.

$$\frac{c}{\sin C} = \frac{a}{\sin A}$$

$$\frac{c}{\sin 34.1°} = \frac{49.4}{\sin 103.3°}$$ Multiply each side by sin 34.1°.

$$c = \frac{49.4 \sin 34.1°}{\sin 103.3°}$$

Key in: 49.4 [SIN] 34.1 [ )] [÷]
[SIN] 103.3 [ENTER =]

$$\doteq 28.4589$$

The bridge will be about 28.5 m long.

Discuss

In the keystrokes, why did we include
[ )] after 34.1?

The Ambiguous Case

Suppose we are given these dimensions of △ABC:
$a = 3$ cm, $c = 5$ cm, and $\angle A = 30°$.

When we attempt to draw this triangle, we see that two different triangles can
be drawn with these measurements.

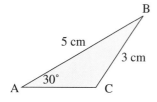
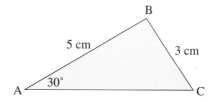

Since we are given two sides and the non-included angle, we use the Sine Law
to solve the triangle. As we do so, we need to calculate the measures in
both triangles.

Example 3

In △ABC, $c = 5$ cm, $a = 3$ cm, and $\angle A = 30°$; for each possible △ABC,

  i) Determine sin C.

  ii) Calculate the measure of $\angle C$ to 2 decimal places.

  iii) Determine the length of AC to 1 decimal place.

a)

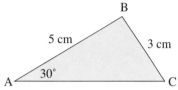

b)

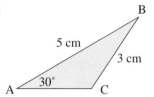

Solution

a) Use the Sine Law.

  i) $\dfrac{\sin C}{c} = \dfrac{\sin A}{a}$

  $\dfrac{\sin C}{5} = \dfrac{\sin 30°}{3}$

  $\sin C = \dfrac{5 \sin 30°}{3}$

  $\doteq 0.8333$

  ii) Use the $\boxed{\text{SIN}^{-1}}$ key.

  $\angle C \doteq 56.4427°$

  $\angle C$ is approximately $56.44°$.

  iii) First calculate $\angle B$.

  $\angle B = 180° - 30° - 56.44°$

  $\doteq 93.56°$

  Use the Sine Law
  to determine b.

  $\dfrac{b}{\sin B} = \dfrac{a}{\sin A}$

  $\dfrac{b}{\sin 93.56°} = \dfrac{3}{\sin 30°}$

  $b = \dfrac{3 \sin 93.56°}{\sin 30°}$

  $\doteq 5.988$

  AC is approximately 6.0 cm.

b) Use the Sine Law.

  i) $\dfrac{\sin C}{c} = \dfrac{\sin A}{a}$

  $\dfrac{\sin C}{5} = \dfrac{\sin 30°}{3}$

  $\sin C = \dfrac{5 \sin 30°}{3}$

  $\doteq 0.8333$

  ii) From part a) ii, $\angle C \doteq 56.44°$

  But, from the triangle, $\angle C$ is obtuse.

  So, $\angle C \doteq 180° - 56.44°$

  $\doteq 123.56°$

  iii) First calculate $\angle B$.

  $\angle B \doteq 180° - 30° - 123.56°$

  $\doteq 26.44°$

  Use the Sine Law
  to determine b.

  $\dfrac{b}{\sin B} = \dfrac{a}{\sin A}$

  $\dfrac{b}{\sin 26.44°} = \dfrac{3}{\sin 30°}$

  $b = \dfrac{3 \sin 26.44°}{\sin 30°}$

  $\doteq 2.6716$

  AC is approximately 2.7 cm.

The word "ambiguous" means "more than one meaning." In *Example 3*, △ABC is ambiguous because two different triangles can be drawn with the given measurements.

When you use the Sine Law to solve a triangle, always sketch the triangle to check whether it is ambiguous.

A

1. Calculate the length of AC in each triangle.

a)

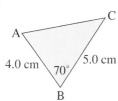

b)

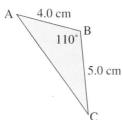

c)

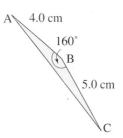

2. Calculate the length of PQ in each triangle.

a)

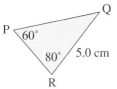

b)

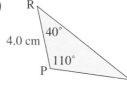

c)

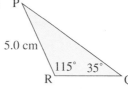

3. Calculate the measure of ∠A in each triangle.

a)

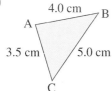

b)

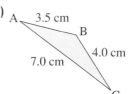

c)

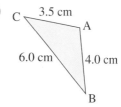

4. Calculate the measure of ∠P in each triangle.

a)

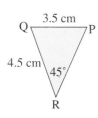

b)

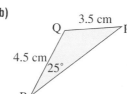

c)

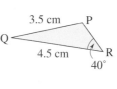

B

✓

5. Solve each triangle.

a)

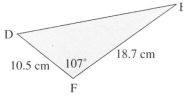

b)

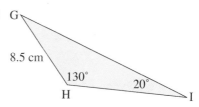

c)

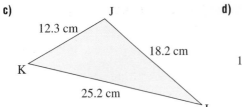

d)

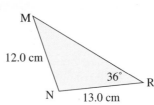

6. Knowledge/Understanding For each $\triangle ABC$, two sides and a non-included angle are given. Determine two possible measures for $\angle C$ and for AC.

a) AB = 3.2 cm, $\angle A = 28°$, BC = 2.4 cm

b) AB = 9.4 cm, $\angle A = 47°$, BC = 8.6 cm

7. Draw $\triangle ABC$ with $\angle B = 90°$. What happens to the length of AC in each situation below? Use the triangle and the Cosine Law to explain.

a) Suppose $\angle B$ is increased, but sides AB and BC stay the same.

b) Suppose $\angle B$ is decreased, but sides AB and BC stay the same.

8. Solve each triangle.

a) $\triangle ABC$ in which AB = 10.3 cm, BC = 14.4 cm, and CA = 23.0 cm

b) $\triangle EDF$ in which $\angle E = 38°$, $\angle F = 48°$, and $f = 15.8$ cm

c) $\triangle GHJ$ in which $\angle G = 61°$, $h = 5.3$ cm, and $j = 3.1$ cm

d) $\triangle KMN$ in which MN = 12.5 cm, KM = 9.6 cm, and $\angle M = 42°$

e) $\triangle PQR$ in which QR = 28.5 cm, RP = 23.6 cm, and $\angle P = 72°$

f) $\triangle STU$ in which ST = 6.8 cm, TU = 3.5 cm, and $\angle S = 22°$

9. Solve $\triangle PQR$ in which PQ = 8.6 cm, $\angle Q = 122°$, and QR = 9.2 cm.

10. Solve $\triangle ABC$ in which AB = 4.4 cm, $\angle B = 141°$, and AC = 7.9 cm.

11. Application A tunnel is to be built through a hill to connect points A and B in a straight line (below left). Point C is chosen to be visible from both A and B. Measurements are taken, and $\angle C = 98.5°$, CA = 2.92 km, and CB = 3.68 km. Calculate the length of AB.

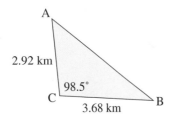

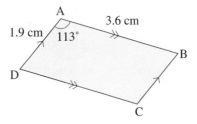

12. Determine the length of each diagonal in parallelogram ABCD (above right).

13. Three circles with radii 3 cm, 4 cm, and 5 cm touch each other externally. Calculate the measures of the angles of the triangle formed by joining the centres of the circles.

Note: From now on, you may need to use the Pythagorean Theorem, the sine, cosine or tangent ratio in a right triangle, or the Sine Law, or the Cosine Law to complete each exercise.

14. Two sides of a parallelogram measure 8.0 cm and 10.0 cm. The longer diagonal measures 15.5 cm.

a) Determine the measures of the angles of the parallelogram.

b) Determine the length of the other diagonal.

15. A rectangular prism has length 10 cm, width 8 cm, and height 5 cm.

a) Calculate the length of the diagonal shown in red. This is a body diagonal.

b) Calculate the measure of angle θ.

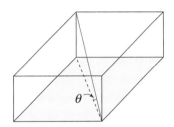

16. Thinking/Inquiry/Problem Solving The sides of a quadrilateral, in order, are 2.96 cm, 3.75 cm, 3.49 cm, and 3.06 cm. The angle between the first two sides is 121.1°. Calculate the measures of the other three angles.

17. Communication Two angles in a triangle measure 24° and 38°. The longest side is 24 cm longer than the shortest side. Write to explain how you would determine the length of the shortest side.

18. A square pyramid has a base with side length 10.5 cm (below left). The slant height of the pyramid is 19.5 cm.

a) Calculate the height of the pyramid.

b) Calculate the angle θ between one face and the base.

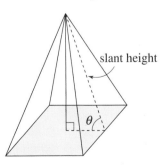

slant height

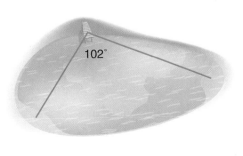

102°

19. Two small beaches are on opposite sides of a lake (above right). The distances from a dock at one end of the lake to the beaches are 1.2 km and 890 m. Determine the distance between the beaches.

20. A cylinder (below left) has radius 4.8 cm and height 9.2 cm. What is the radius of the smallest possible sphere that can enclose the cylinder?

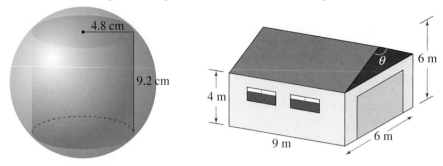

21. For the garage (above right), calculate the angle θ between the sloping sections of the roof.

✓ **22.** A circular ring with radius 20 cm is suspended from a point vertically above its centre by six cords. Each cord is 80 cm long. The cords are attached at equally spaced intervals around the ring.

a) Calculate the angle between each cord and the vertical.

b) Calculate the angle between two adjacent cords.

c) How far above the ring is the point where the six cords are joined?

C

23. Each of three people on level ground measures the angle of elevation of a balloon, B, as 71° (below left). The balloon is 64.0 m high. The angle between the lines of sight from a person at P to the people at Q and R is 82°. Calculate the distance QR.

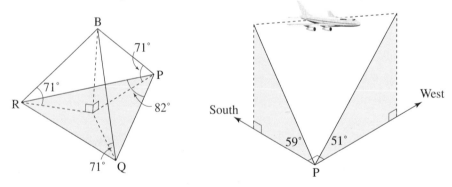

24. An airplane travels in a straight line at an average speed of 850 km/h at a constant height over level ground (above right). It is due south of a point P on the ground from which its angle of elevation is 59°. Ten seconds later, it is due west of P at an angle of elevation of 51°. Calculate the height of the airplane.

25. Refer to the triangles in *Example 3*. Use the Cosine Law to calculate the two possible lengths of AC.

1. Determine the sine and cosine of each angle.

a) 84°   **b)** 171.2°   **c)** 97°   **d)** 134.3°

2. Explain the relationship between the Pythagorean Theorem and the identity $\sin^2 \theta + \cos^2 \theta = 1$.

3. Determine the value of x in each triangle.

a)
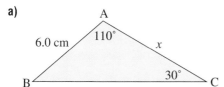

b)
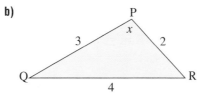

4. Explain why $\cos 20° > \cos 50°$. Use a diagram in your explanation.

5. Suppose you are given △ABC, in which AB = BC = 5 cm; AC = 8 cm, and ∠ABC = 110°. Explain what is wrong with this information.

6. Solve each triangle.

a)
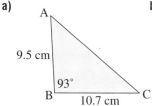

b)
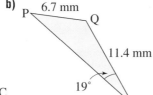

c)
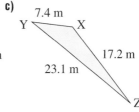

7. Solve △ABC in which BC = 6.0 cm, AC = 4.0 cm, and ∠ABC = 30°.

8. Solve △ABC in which AB = 4.1 cm, ∠ABC = 139°, and AC = 7.5 cm.

9. In △KPM, KP = 32.0 cm, ∠P = 29°, and KM = 27.0 cm. Calculate two possible values for PM.

10. A radar station is tracking two ships. At noon, the ships are 5.0 km and 7.0 km from the radar station. The angle between the lines of sight to the ships is 110°. How far apart are the ships at noon?

11. A parallelogram has vertices A(3, 3), B(8, 0), C(1, –6), and D(–4, –3). Calculate the length of each diagonal.

12. The dimensions of the base of a rectangular pyramid are 10.0 cm by 7.0 cm. The length of each edge is 16.0 cm. Sketch the pyramid, then calculate its height.

5.3 Angles in Standard Position

Up to now, we have used trigonometry to solve triangles. For this purpose, we require values of $\cos\theta$ and $\sin\theta$ where $0° < \theta < 180°$. In Chapter 6, we will use trigonometric functions to model quantities that vary periodically. To do this, we require values of $\cos\theta$ and $\sin\theta$ that are not restricted to $0° < \theta < 180°$. In this section, we will define angles in standard position, for any value of θ.

Point $P(x, y)$ is a point that moves around a circle with centre $O(0, 0)$ and radius 1 unit. This circle is called the *unit circle*. Point P starts at $A(1, 0)$ on the x-axis. For any position of P, an angle θ represents the amount of rotation about the origin. We say that the angle θ is in *standard position*, where OA is the *initial arm* and OP the *terminal arm*.

When $\theta > 0$, the rotation   When $\theta < 0$, the rotation
is counterclockwise.   is clockwise.

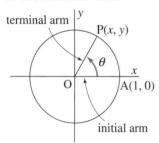
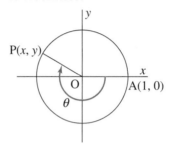

When P moves around the circle, the motion is repeated after P has rotated 360°. When any angle θ is given, we can always determine other angles for which the position of P is the same. All these angles are in standard position.

Given an angle of 50°   … add 360°,   … add 360° again,
                             $50° + 360° = 410°$ $410° + 360° = 770°$

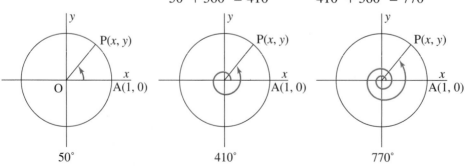

| 50° | 410° | 770° |

The angles above are in standard position, and have the same terminal arm. For this reason, they are called coterminal angles. When an angle is in standard position, other angles that are coterminal with it can be found by adding or subtracting multiples of 360°.

Coterminal Angles

Point P moves around a unit circle.

- Two or more angles in standard position are *coterminal angles* when the position of P is the same for each angle.
- When an angle has measure θ degrees, then the measure of any coterminal angle is $(\theta + 360n)$ degrees, where n is an integer.

Example 1

For each angle:

a) $\theta = 140°$ **b)** $\theta = -40°$

    i) Draw the angle θ in standard position.
    ii) Determine two other angles coterminal with θ. Illustrate each angle with a diagram.
    iii) Write an expression to represent any angle coterminal with θ.

Solution

a) i) $140°$ **ii)** $140° + 360° = 500°$ $140° - 360° = -220°$

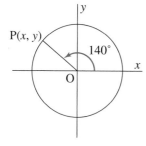
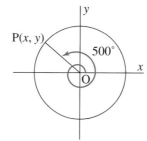
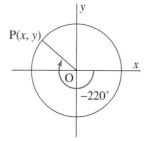

    iii) Any angle coterminal with $140°$ is represented by $(140 + 360n)$ degrees, where n is an integer.

b) i) $-40°$ **ii)** $-40° + 360° = 320°$ $-40° - 360° = -400°$

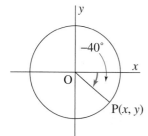
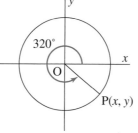
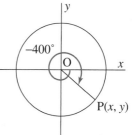

    iii) Any angle coterminal with $-40°$ is represented by $(-40 + 360n)$ degrees, where n is an integer.

Example 2

Suppose P has rotated –830° about O(0, 0) from A(1, 0).

a) How many rotations have been made?

b) In which quadrant is P located?

c) Draw a diagram to show the position of P.

Solution

a) P has made a clockwise rotation of 830°. Since a complete rotation is 360°, divide 830 by 360 to obtain $830 \div 360 \doteq 2.3056$.
Since the result is between 2 and 3, P has made 2 complete rotations around the circle, and part of a third rotation.

b) Two complete rotations amount to 2(360°), or 720°. The additional rotation beyond 720° is $830° - 720° = 110°$.
Since $90° < 110° < 180°$, P is in Quadrant III.

c)

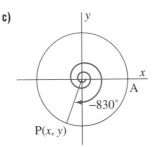

5.3 Exercises

A

1. For each angle in standard position, determine θ in degrees.

a)

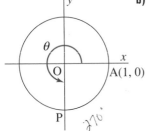

b)

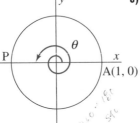

c)

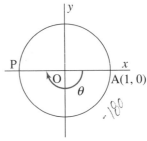

2. Sketch each angle θ in standard position.

a) $\theta = 70°$ **b)** $\theta = -110°$ **c)** $\theta = -155°$ **d)** $\theta = 220°$

e) $\theta = 90°$ **f)** $\theta = -45°$ **g)** $\theta = 120°$ **h)** $\theta = -270°$

3. **Knowledge/Understanding** For each part of exercise 2, determine two angles that are coterminal with θ.

4. For each angle θ in standard position, determine two other angles that are coterminal with θ.

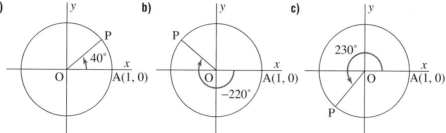

a)   b)   c)

5. Determine two angles that are coterminal with each angle θ.

a) $\theta = 180°$ b) $\theta = 90°$ c) $\theta = -60°$ d) $\theta = 360°$

6. **Communication** Choose one angle from exercise 5. Write to explain how you determined two coterminal angles.

7. Point P is on the terminal arm of an angle θ in standard position. Suppose P has rotated 440°.

a) How many rotations have been made?

b) In which quadrant is P located?

c) Draw a diagram to show the position of P.

8. Repeat exercise 7 for each angle of rotation for P.

a) 380°   b) −460°   c) 760°   d) −900°

9. Sketch each angle θ in standard position.

a) $\theta = 500°$ b) $\theta = 650°$ c) $\theta = -300°$ d) $\theta = -80°$

10. Write an expression to represent any angle coterminal with each angle θ.

a) $\theta = -45°$ b) $\theta = 150°$ c) $\theta = 240°$ d) $\theta = -30°$

e) $\theta = 180°$ f) $\theta = -45°$ g) $\theta = 450°$ h) $\theta = -80°$

11. **Application** An angle θ is in standard position on a coordinate grid. Point P(−3, −4) is on the terminal arm of θ. Determine the measure of θ.

12. **Thinking/Inquiry/Problem Solving** Angle θ is in standard position on a coordinate grid. The terminal arm of θ is in Quadrant II on the line with equation $3y + 2x = 0$. Determine the measure of angle θ.

5.4 Trigonometric Functions of Angles in Standard Position

In Section 5.1, we defined $\cos \theta$ and $\sin \theta$ for $0° \leq \theta \leq 180°$. In Chapter 6, we will use trigonometry to model quantities that vary periodically. To do this, we need definitions of $\cos \theta$ and $\sin \theta$ for any value of θ, not just those between $0°$ and $180°$. We will now extend the previous definitions.

Visualize a point P rotating around the unit circle, and forming an angle θ in standard position. For any position of P on the unit circle, we define:

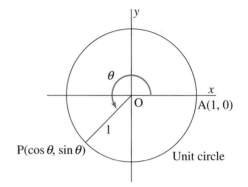

$\cos \theta$ is the first coordinate of P.

$\sin \theta$ is the second coordinate of P.

$\tan \theta = \dfrac{\sin \theta}{\cos \theta}$, where $\cos \theta \neq 0$

When P is in Quadrants I or II, the definitions of $\cos \theta$ and $\sin \theta$ are the same as those in Section 5.1.

When P is in Quadrant I, $\theta = \angle PON$, which is an acute angle. According to the definitions in Necessary Skills, page 246,

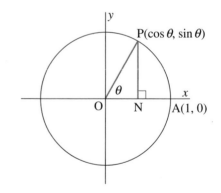

$$\tan \theta = \tan \angle PON$$

$$= \frac{\text{length of side opposite } \angle PON}{\text{length of side adjacent to } \angle PON}$$

$$= \frac{\text{second coordinate of P}}{\text{first coordinate of P}}$$

$$= \frac{\sin \theta}{\cos \theta}, \text{ where } \cos \theta \neq 0$$

Hence, the right-triangle definition of the tangent of an angle is a special case of the new definition.

As P rotates around the circle, the values of $\cos \theta$, $\sin \theta$, and $\tan \theta$ change periodically. You can use a calculator to determine these values for any given angle. Some typical values are illustrated on the next page.

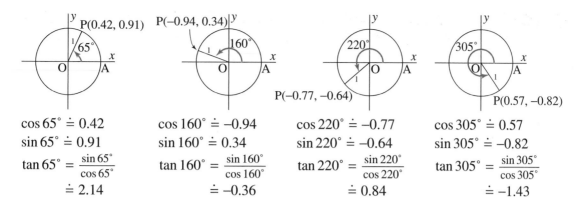

$\cos 65° \doteq 0.42$

$\sin 65° \doteq 0.91$

$\tan 65° = \dfrac{\sin 65°}{\cos 65°}$

$\doteq 2.14$

$\cos 160° \doteq -0.94$

$\sin 160° \doteq 0.34$

$\tan 160° = \dfrac{\sin 160°}{\cos 160°}$

$\doteq -0.36$

$\cos 220° \doteq -0.77$

$\sin 220° \doteq -0.64$

$\tan 220° = \dfrac{\sin 220°}{\cos 220°}$

$\doteq 0.84$

$\cos 305° \doteq 0.57$

$\sin 305° \doteq -0.82$

$\tan 305° = \dfrac{\sin 305°}{\cos 305°}$

$\doteq -1.43$

Special cases of these definitions occur when the terminal arm coincides with an axis. In these cases, the angles are multiples of 90°.

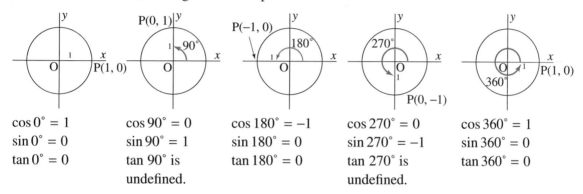

$\cos 0° = 1$

$\sin 0° = 0$

$\tan 0° = 0$

$\cos 90° = 0$

$\sin 90° = 1$

$\tan 90°$ is undefined.

$\cos 180° = -1$

$\sin 180° = 0$

$\tan 180° = 0$

$\cos 270° = 0$

$\sin 270° = -1$

$\tan 270°$ is undefined.

$\cos 360° = 1$

$\sin 360° = 0$

$\tan 360° = 0$

Recall that a function is a rule that gives a single output for every valid input number. We say that $\cos \theta$, $\sin \theta$, and $\tan \theta$ are *trigonometric functions* of θ because we can use the following definitions to determine a value for each expression for any angle θ.

Take Note

Trigonometric Functions of an Angle in Standard Position

$P(x, y)$ represents any point on the unit circle and θ is the measure of an angle in standard position.

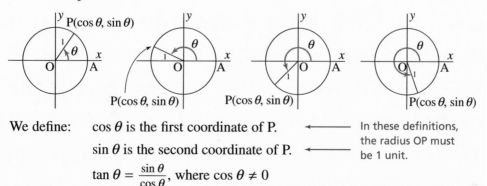

We define: $\cos \theta$ is the first coordinate of P. ⟵

$\sin \theta$ is the second coordinate of P. ⟵

In these definitions, the radius OP must be 1 unit.

$\tan \theta = \dfrac{\sin \theta}{\cos \theta}$, where $\cos \theta \neq 0$

Example 1

Determine the sine, cosine, and tangent of each angle to 2 decimal places.
Draw a diagram to illustrate each angle.

a) $70°$ **b)** $170°$ **c)** $250°$ **d)** $310°$

Solution

Use a calculator.

a) $\sin 70° \doteq 0.94$
$\cos 70° \doteq 0.34$
$\tan 70° \doteq 2.75$

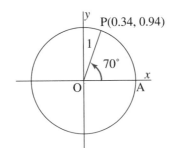

b) $\sin 170° \doteq 0.17$
$\cos 170° \doteq -0.98$
$\tan 170° \doteq -0.18$

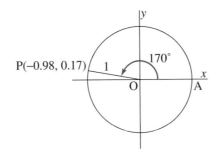

c) $\sin 250° \doteq -0.94$
$\cos 250° \doteq -0.34$
$\tan 250° \doteq 2.75$

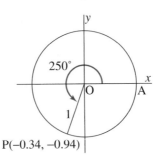

d) $\sin 310° \doteq -0.77$
$\cos 310° \doteq 0.64$
$\tan 310° \doteq -1.19$

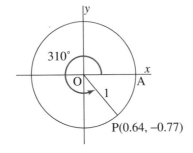

Discuss

The values of each trigonometric function are positive in some quadrants and negative in others. For each function, how can you remember in which quadrant it is positive, and in which it is negative?

As P rotates around the circle, past 360°, the same coordinates are encountered again. Hence, in *Example 1*, there are infinitely many angles that have the same sine as 70°, the same cosine as 250°, and the same tangent as 310°.

These values are also equal to sin 70°.
sin (70° + 360°), or sin 430°
sin (430° + 360°), or sin 790°

These values are also equal to cos 250°.
cos (250° + 360°), or cos 610°
cos (610° + 360°), or cos 970°

These values are also equal to tan 310°.
tan (310° + 360°), or tan 670°
tan (670° + 360°), or tan 1030°

We now consider how to determine an angle when its sine, cosine, or tangent is given.

An equation, such as $\sin \theta = 0.2$, $\cos \theta = -0.3$, and $\tan \theta = 0.4$, has infinitely many solutions. Each solution is an angle in standard position with its terminal arm in one of four quadrants. The table below illustrates the sign of each trigonometric function value in each quadrant.

	Quadrant I	Quadrant II	Quadrant III	Quadrant IV
$\sin \theta$	+	+	−	−
$\cos \theta$	+	−	−	+
$\tan \theta$	+	−	+	−

Example 2

Determine two angles between 0° and 360° that have each trigonometric function value. Write the angles to the nearest degree.

a) $\sin \theta = 0.72$ **b)** $\cos \theta = 0.39$ **c)** $\tan \theta = 2.73$

Solution

a) $\sin \theta = 0.72$

Since $\sin \theta$ is positive, θ lies in Quadrant I or II.
Key in: (2nd) (SIN) 0.72 (ENTER) to display 46.05448044
$\theta \doteq 46°$

The angle in Quadrant I is approximately 46°.
Another value of θ can be determined by combining the diagrams of angles in Quadrants I and II.
By symmetry, the angle in Quadrant II is
$180° - 46° = 134°$
Two angles are approximately 46° and 134°.

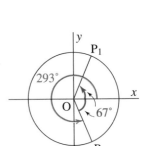

b) $\cos \theta = 0.39$

Since $\cos \theta$ is positive, θ lies in Quadrant I or IV.
Key in: (2nd) (COS) 0.39 (ENTER) to display 67.0455006
$\theta \doteq 67°$

The angle in Quadrant I is approximately 67°.
Combine the diagrams for Quadrants I and IV.
By symmetry, the angle in Quadrant IV is $360° - 67° = 293°$
Two angles are approximately 67° and 293°.

c) $\tan \theta = 2.73$

Since $\tan \theta$ is positive, θ lies in Quadrant I or III.

Key in: (2nd) (TAN) 2.73 (ENTER) to display 69.88219898
$\theta \doteq 70°$

The angle in Quadrant I is approximately 70°.
Combine the diagrams for Quadrants I and III.
By symmetry, the angle in Quadrant III is
$180° + 70° = 250°$
Two angles are approximately 70° and 250°.

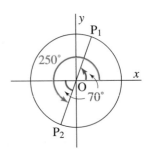

Discuss

For each of $\sin \theta$, $\cos \theta$, and $\tan \theta$, what are two other values of θ that have the same trigonometric function value?

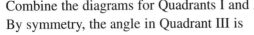

The results of *Example 2* can be summarized.

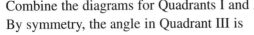

Solving sin θ = k, cos θ = k, and tan θ = k

- When $\sin \theta = k$, two values of θ that satisfy this equation are θ and $180° - \theta$.

- When $\cos \theta = k$, two values of θ that satisfy this equation are θ and $360° - \theta$.

- When $\tan \theta = k$, two values of θ that satisfy this equation are θ and $180° + \theta$.

Example 3

Determine two angles between 0° and 360° that have each trigonometric function value. Write the angles to the nearest degree.

a) $\sin \theta = -0.45$ b) $\cos \theta = -0.76$ c) $\tan \theta = -3.42$

Solution

a) $\sin \theta = -0.45$

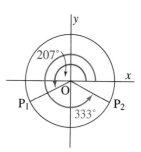

Since $\sin \theta$ is negative, θ lies in Quadrant III or IV.
Key in: [2nd] [SIN] [(−)] 0.45 [ENTER] to display −26.74368395
$\theta \doteq -27°$

One angle is approximately −27°.
However, this angle is not between 0° and 360°.
To obtain the angle in Quadrant IV, add 360°.
$\theta = -27° + 360°$
   $= 333°$

To obtain the angle in Quadrant III, subtract −27° from 180°.
$\theta = 180° - (-27°)$
   $= 207°$
Two angles are approximately 207° and 333°.

b) $\cos \theta = -0.76$

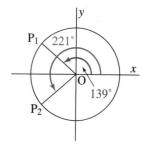

Since $\cos \theta$ is negative, θ lies in Quadrant II or III.
Key in: [2nd] [COS] [(−)] 0.76 [ENTER] to display 139.4641979
$\theta \doteq 139°$

The angle in Quadrant II is approximately 139°.
To obtain the angle in Quadrant III, subtract 139° from 360°.
$\theta = 360° - 139°$
   $= 221°$
Two angles are approximately 139° and 221°.

c) $\tan \theta = -3.42$

Since $\tan \theta$ is negative, θ lies in Quadrant II or IV.
Key in: 2nd TAN (−) 3.42 ENTER to display −73.70120362
$\theta \doteq -74°$

One angle is approximately −74°.
This angle is not between 0° and 360°.
To obtain the angle in Quadrant IV, add 360°.
$\theta = -74° + 360°$
$\quad = 286°$
To obtain the angle in Quadrant II, add −74° to 180°.
$\theta = -74° + 180°$
$\quad = 106°$
Two angles are approximately 106° and 286°.

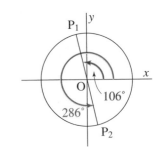

5.4 Exercises

A

1. In each diagram, determine $\sin \theta$, $\cos \theta$, and $\tan \theta$.

a) 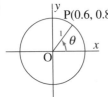 **b)** 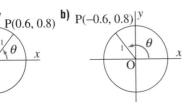 **c)** 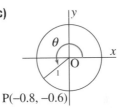 **d)**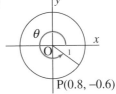

2. Determine each value to 3 decimal places.

a) $\sin 63°$	**b)** $\cos 63°$	**c)** $\tan 63°$
d) $\sin 151°$	**e)** $\cos 151°$	**f)** $\tan 151°$
g) $\sin 227°$	**h)** $\cos 227°$	**i)** $\tan 227°$
j) $\sin 302°$	**k)** $\cos 302°$	**l)** $\tan 302°$

3. a) Determine each value.

i) $\sin 0°$	**ii)** $\cos 0°$	**iii)** $\tan 0°$
iv) $\sin 90°$	**v)** $\cos 90°$	**vi)** $\tan 90°$
vii) $\sin 180°$	**viii)** $\cos 180°$	**ix)** $\tan 180°$
x) $\sin 270°$	**xi)** $\cos 270°$	**xii)** $\tan 270°$
xiii) $\sin 360°$	**xiv)** $\cos 360°$	**xv)** $\tan 360°$

b) From the results in part a, explain why the tangent function values of two angles are undefined.

4. Determine each value to 3 decimal places.

a) tan 48°

b) sin 57°

c) cos 71°

d) sin 157°

e) tan 148°

f) cos 171°

g) cos 278°

h) sin 257°

i) tan 248°

j) sin 357°

k) tan 338°

l) cos 321°

5. Knowledge/Understanding For each expression below:

　i) Determine its value to 3 decimal places.

　ii) Determine two other angles that have the same trigonometric
　　　function value.

a) sin 47°

b) cos 56°

c) tan 33°

d) sin 108°

e) cos 162°

f) tan 154°

g) sin 189°

h) cos 211°

i) tan 254°

j) sin 325°

k) cos 294°

l) tan 281°

6. Without using a calculator, determine whether each quantity is positive or
negative. Explain your answer.

a) sin 282°

b) cos 156°

c) tan 230°

d) tan 139°

e) sin 141°

f) cos 312°

7. Communication Suppose point P starts at A(1, 0) and makes one complete
rotation counterclockwise around the unit circle. Describe how the values of
each trigonometric function change as θ increases from 0° to 360°.

a) sin θ

b) cos θ

c) tan θ

8. Determine an angle between 0° and 90° that has each trigonometric function
value. Write the angle to the nearest degree.

a) tan θ = 2.3

b) sin θ = 0.3

c) cos θ = 0.7

d) sin θ = 0.6

e) cos θ = 0.2

f) tan θ = 0.8

9. Determine an angle between 90° and 180° that has each trigonometric
function value. Write the angle to the nearest degree.

a) sin θ = 0.42

b) tan θ = −0.35

c) cos θ = −0.58

d) tan θ = −1.25

e) cos θ = −0.45

f) sin θ = 0.75

10. Determine an angle between 180° and 270° that has each trigonometric
function value. Write the angle to the nearest degree.

a) cos θ = −0.82

b) tan θ = 2.21

c) sin θ = −0.57

d) tan θ = 0.66

e) cos θ = −0.21

f) sin θ = −0.45

11. Determine an angle between 270° and 360° that has each trigonometric function value. Write the angle to the nearest degree.

a) $\tan \theta = -0.83$ b) $\cos \theta = 0.74$ c) $\sin \theta = -0.19$

d) $\tan \theta = -4.75$ e) $\sin \theta = -0.69$ f) $\cos \theta = 0.35$

12. Determine two angles between 0° and 360° that have each trigonometric function value. Write the angles to the nearest degree.

a) $\cos \theta = 0.42$ b) $\sin \theta = 0.29$ c) $\tan \theta = 1.37$

d) $\sin \theta = 0.82$ e) $\cos \theta = 0.73$ f) $\tan \theta = 2.48$

13. Determine two angles between 0° and 360° that have each trigonometric function value. Write the angles to the nearest degree.

a) $\sin \theta = -0.47$ b) $\tan \theta = -0.92$ c) $\cos \theta = -0.91$

d) $\sin \theta = -0.85$ e) $\cos \theta = -0.29$ f) $\tan \theta = -5.7$

14. Thinking/Inquiry/Problem Solving The graphing calculator screens below show squares whose vertices lie on a unit circle with centre O(0, 0). The measurements at the bottom left of each screen refer to the vertex marked with the cursor. They show the corresponding angle in standard position, in degrees, and the x-coordinate to the nearest thousandth. The y-coordinate of the vertex is in the middle, at the bottom of the screen. For each square:

　i) Write the coordinates of each vertex.

　ii) Write the angles in standard position, in degrees, corresponding to each vertex.

　iii) Write the cosine and the sine of each angle in part ii.

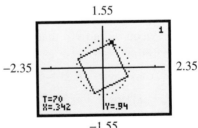

a)　　1.55

b)　　1.55

15. Use the diagram in exercise 14a. Determine each pair of values.

a) $\cos 150°$ and $\sin 150°$ b) $\cos 330°$ and $\sin 330°$

c) $\cos 60°$ and $\sin 60°$ d) $\cos 240°$ and $\sin 240°$

16. Use the diagram in exercise 14b. Determine each pair of values.

a) $\cos 110°$ and $\sin 110°$ b) $\cos 290°$ and $\sin 290°$

c) $\cos 20°$ and $\sin 20°$ d) $\cos 200°$ and $\sin 200°$

17. The point R(2, 6) lies on the terminal arm of an angle θ in standard position. Determine the value of each trigonometric function to 3 decimal places.

   a) $\sin \theta$ **b)** $\cos \theta$ **c)** $\tan \theta$

18. The point S(–3, –5) lies on the terminal arm of an angle θ in standard position. Determine the value of each trigonometric function to 3 decimal places.

   a) $\sin \theta$ **b)** $\cos \theta$ **c)** $\tan \theta$

19. The terminal arm of an angle θ lies in Quadrant IV on the line with equation $5x + 12y = 0$. Determine the value of each trigonometric function.

   a) $\sin \theta$ **b)** $\cos \theta$ **c)** $\tan \theta$

20. Application The angle θ is in Quadrant I, and $\cos \theta = \dfrac{3}{5}$.

   a) On a grid, draw a diagram to show the angle in standard position and a point Q on its terminal arm.

   b) Sketch a circle on which Q lies. What is the radius of this circle?

   c) Calculate $\sin \theta$.

   d) Determine possible coordinates for Q.

21. The angle θ is in Quadrant II, and $\cos \theta = -\dfrac{3}{5}$.

   a) On a grid, draw a diagram to show the angle in standard position and a point D on its terminal arm.

   b) Sketch a circle on which D lies. What is the radius of this circle?

   c) Calculate $\sin \theta$.

   d) Determine possible coordinates for D.

22. The angle θ is in Quadrant III and $\sin \theta = -\dfrac{2}{\sqrt{5}}$. A point E lies on the terminal arm. Determine possible coordinates for E.

23. The angle θ is in Quadrant IV and $\tan \theta = -\dfrac{12}{5}$. A point F lies on the terminal arm. Determine possible coordinates for F.

24. You can use a calculator to determine the sine, the cosine, or the tangent of any angle in standard position. Determine the largest angle your calculator will accept.

C

25. Triangle CBO has vertices C(–3, 0), B(–3, –7), and O(0, 0). A circle, radius 1 unit, centre O(0, 0), intersects OB at P. Point A has coordinates (1, 0). Angle AOP is θ.

   a) Determine the coordinates of P, then use the coordinates to determine $\sin \theta$ and $\cos \theta$.

   b) Compare the values of $\sin \theta$ and $\cos \theta$ with those you would obtain by using the lengths of the sides of $\triangle$CBO. What do you notice?

5.5 Sine, Cosine, and Tangent of Special Angles

When you use a calculator to determine trigonometric function values, the results are approximate to 9 decimal places. These values are accurate enough for most purposes. For some special angles, exact values can be determined from geometric relationships.

Angle 45° and its multiples

This diagram shows a unit circle and the angle 45° in standard position.

Since $\angle PON = 45°$ and PN is perpendicular to OA, then $\triangle PON$ is a right isosceles triangle.

Then, ON = NP

Use the Pythagorean Theorem in $\triangle PON$.

$$ON^2 + NP^2 = OP^2$$
$$2ON^2 = 1$$
$$ON^2 = \frac{1}{2}$$
$$ON = \frac{1}{\sqrt{2}}$$

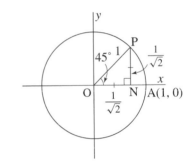

So, $NP = ON = \frac{1}{\sqrt{2}}$

The coordinates of P are $\left(\frac{1}{\sqrt{2}}, \frac{1}{\sqrt{2}}\right)$.

Hence, $\cos 45° = \frac{1}{\sqrt{2}}$ and $\sin 45° = \frac{1}{\sqrt{2}}$

$$\tan 45° = \frac{\frac{1}{\sqrt{2}}}{\frac{1}{\sqrt{2}}}$$
$$= 1$$

We can determine the sine, cosine, and tangent of any multiple of 45° by drawing the right isosceles triangle in different positions. This triangle is called a 45-45-90 triangle.

Example 1

Determine cos 135°, sin 135°, and tan 135°.

Solution

Draw a diagram.

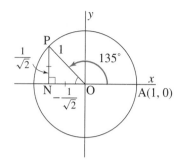

Since ∠POA = 135°, then ∠PON = 45°

△PON is a 45-45-90 triangle with sides $\frac{1}{\sqrt{2}}$, $\frac{1}{\sqrt{2}}$, and 1.

Since P is in Quadrant II, cos 135° is negative, sin 135° is positive, and tan 135° is negative.

Hence, cos 135° $= -\dfrac{1}{\sqrt{2}}$

$\qquad$ sin 135° $= \dfrac{1}{\sqrt{2}}$

$\qquad$ tan 135° $= -1$

Discuss

How could you check the results?

In *Example 1*, ∠PON is called the reference angle. A *reference angle* is the acute angle between the terminal arm and the *x*-axis.

Angle 30° and its multiples

This diagram shows a unit circle and the angle 30° in standard position.

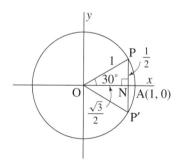

Since ∠PON = 30° and PN is perpendicular to OA, then △PON is a 30-60-90 triangle.

By reflecting △PON in the *x*-axis, an equilateral △POP′ is formed, in which ∠POP′ = ∠OPP′ = ∠OP′P = 60°. N is the midpoint of PP′.

Hence, P′N = NP = $\frac{1}{2}$

Use the Pythagorean Theorem in △PON to determine the length of ON.

$$ON^2 + NP^2 = OP^2$$
$$ON^2 + \frac{1}{4} = 1$$
$$ON^2 = \frac{3}{4}$$
$$ON = \frac{\sqrt{3}}{2}$$

The coordinates of P are $\left(\dfrac{\sqrt{3}}{2}, \dfrac{1}{2}\right)$.

Hence, $\cos 30° = \dfrac{\sqrt{3}}{2}$, $\sin 30° = \dfrac{1}{2}$, and $\tan 30° = \dfrac{\frac{1}{2}}{\frac{\sqrt{3}}{2}}$

$$= \dfrac{1}{2} \times \dfrac{2}{\sqrt{3}}$$

$$= \dfrac{1}{\sqrt{3}}$$

To determine the sine, cosine, and tangent of 60°, reflect the 30-60-90 triangle in the line $y = x$.

By symmetry, $\angle POA = 60°$

The coordinates of P are $\left(\dfrac{1}{2}, \dfrac{\sqrt{3}}{2}\right)$.

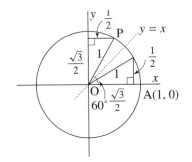

Hence, $\cos 60° = \dfrac{1}{2}$, $\sin 60° = \dfrac{\sqrt{3}}{2}$, and $\tan 60° = \dfrac{\frac{\sqrt{3}}{2}}{\frac{1}{2}}$

$$= \sqrt{3}$$

The trigonometric function values of special angles are summarized below.

Take Note

Sine, Cosine, and Tangent of Special Angles

Values for 30° and 60°

Remember the sides of a 30-60-90 triangle are $1, \dfrac{1}{2}, \dfrac{\sqrt{3}}{2}$.

Remember that sines and cosines of 30° and 60° involve $\dfrac{1}{2}$ and $\dfrac{\sqrt{3}}{2}$.

Memorize $\sin 30° = \dfrac{1}{2}$; then $\cos 30° = \dfrac{\sqrt{3}}{2}$.

For 60°, interchange the values:

$\sin 60° = \dfrac{\sqrt{3}}{2}$ and $\cos 60° = \dfrac{1}{2}$.

For a tangent value, divide the sine value by the cosine value, where possible.

Values for 45°

Remember the sides of a 45-45-90 triangle are $1, \dfrac{1}{\sqrt{2}}, \dfrac{1}{\sqrt{2}}$.

Remember that $\sin 45° = \cos 45° = \dfrac{1}{\sqrt{2}}$.

Values for 0° and 90°

Use the coordinates of the points (1, 0) and (0, 1).

Remember that $\cos \theta$ is the first coordinate and $\sin \theta$ is the second coordinate.

So, $\cos 0° = 1$, $\sin 0° = 0$; and $\cos 90° = 0$, $\sin 90° = 1$

By drawing the 30-60-90 triangle in different positions, we can determine the cosine, sine, and tangent of any multiple of 30° and 60°.

Example 2

Determine cos 240°, sin 240°, and tan 240°.

Solution

Draw a diagram.

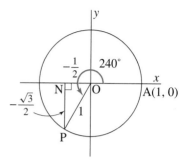

The reference angle is ∠PON = 240° − 180° = 60°.

△PON is a 30-60-90 triangle with sides $\frac{1}{2}$, 1, and $\frac{\sqrt{3}}{2}$.

Since P is in Quadrant III, both cos 240° and
sin 240° are negative, while tan 240° is positive.

Hence, cos 240° $= -\frac{1}{2}$, sin 240° $= -\frac{\sqrt{3}}{2}$, and tan 240° $= \sqrt{3}$

The trigonometric function values of 45° and 30° and their multiples are either
$0, \pm\frac{1}{2}, \pm 1$, or simple expressions that involve radicals. These are not the only
angles whose trigonometric function values can be expressed in this way.
Other examples occur in the exercises.

5.5 Exercises

A

1. a) Draw a diagram to show each angle in standard position.

    i) 225°   **ii)** 210°   **iii)** 315°   **iv)** 240°

    v) 150°   **vi)** 120°   **vii)** 135°   **viii)** 300°

  b) State the reference angle for each angle in part a.

2. Knowledge/Understanding State each exact value.

    a) sin 45°   **b)** sin 135°   **c)** sin 225°   **d)** sin 315°

    e) sin 30°   **f)** sin 150°   **g)** sin 210°   **h)** sin 330°

    i) sin 60°   **j)** sin 120°   **k)** sin 240°   **l)** sin 300°

3. Repeat exercise 2, replacing each sine with tangent.

4. Repeat exercise 2, replacing each sine with cosine.

B

5. Communication What is the advantage of using geometric relationships
instead of a calculator to determine trigonometric function values of
special angles?

6. Application

    a) Triangle ABC is a 45-45-90 triangle. Verify that
$$\sin 2A + \sin 2B + \sin 2C = 4\sin A \sin B \sin C$$

    b) Determine whether the equation in part a holds for each triangle.

       i) a 30-60-90 triangle   **ii)** an equilateral triangle

7. Thinking/Inquiry/Problem Solving Notice that $\sin 45° = \frac{1}{\sqrt{2}} \times \frac{\sqrt{2}}{\sqrt{2}} = \frac{\sqrt{2}}{2}$.
So, we may write $\sin 45° = \frac{\sqrt{2}}{2}$ and $\sin 60° = \frac{\sqrt{3}}{2}$. Look at the numbers in these expressions. The denominators are the same and the numbers under the radical signs are 2 and 3.

    a) Find out if this is part of a pattern that includes the values of $\sin 0°$, $\sin 30°$, and $\sin 90°$.

    b) Find a similar pattern for cosines.

    c) Find a pattern that involves $\tan 30°$, $\tan 45°$, and $\tan 60°$. Describe the pattern.

8. The graphing calculator screens below show regular polygons whose vertices lie on a unit circle with centre O(0, 0). For each regular polygon:

    i) Write the coordinates of each vertex.
    ii) Write the angles in standard position that correspond to each vertex.
    iii) Write the cosine, the sine, and the tangent of each angle in part ii.

a)

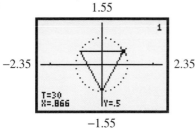

b)

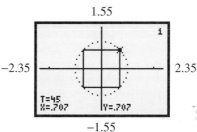

c)

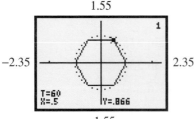

d)

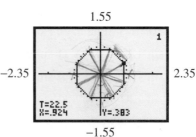

9. Evaluate each expression. Do not use a calculator.

    a) $\sin 30° + \cos 30°$ **b)** $\sin 60° + \tan 30°$ **c)** $\sin 120° + \cos 120°$

    d) $\sin 300° + \tan 225°$ **e)** $\cos 135° + \tan 60°$ **f)** $\tan 150° + \cos 330°$

10. Use a calculator to verify each result.

    a) $\cos 15° = \frac{\sqrt{6} + \sqrt{2}}{4}$ **b)** $\cos 22.5° = \frac{\sqrt{2 + \sqrt{2}}}{2}$ **c)** $\cos 36° = \frac{\sqrt{5} + 1}{4}$

1. Sketch each angle in standard position.

a) $\theta = 50°$ b) $\theta = 240°$ c) $\theta = 130°$

d) $\theta = -60°$ e) $\theta = -120°$ f) $\theta = 510°$

2. Determine two angles that are coterminal with each angle θ.

a) $\theta = 270°$ b) $\theta = 75°$ c) $\theta = 150°$ d) $\theta = -120°$

3. For each expression below:

  i) Determine its value to 3 decimal places.

  ii) Determine three other angles that have the same trigonometric function value.

a) $\sin 24°$ b) $\cos 72°$ c) $\tan 38°$

d) $\sin 137°$ e) $\cos 97°$ f) $\tan 146°$

g) $\sin 230°$ h) $\cos 266°$ i) $\tan 198°$

j) $\sin 304°$ k) $\cos 293°$ l) $\tan 320°$

4. Without using a calculator, determine whether each quantity is positive or negative. Explain your answer.

a) $\sin 274°$ b) $\cos 98°$ c) $\tan 241°$

d) $\cos 165°$ e) $\sin 352°$ f) $\tan 174°$

5. Determine an angle between $90°$ and $180°$ that has each trigonometric function value. Write the angle to the nearest degree.

a) $\sin \theta = 0.82$ b) $\tan \theta = -0.62$ c) $\cos \theta = -0.75$

6. Determine the angles between $0°$ and $360°$ that have each trigonometric function value. Write each angle to the nearest degree.

a) $\cos \theta = 0.46$ b) $\sin \theta = -0.24$ c) $\tan \theta = 1.64$

7. State each exact value.

a) $\cos 150°$ b) $\cos 210°$ c) $\cos 225°$

d) $\tan 330°$ e) $\tan 120°$ f) $\sin 150°$

8. a) Show that $\sin 30° + \sin 30° \neq \sin 60°$.

  b) Show that $\cos 30° + \cos 60° \neq \cos 90°$.

  c) Show that $\tan 45° + \tan 45° \neq \tan 90°$.

9. Explain how you could use an isosceles right triangle to determine the exact values of $\cos 45°$, $\sin 45°$, and $\tan 45°$.

5.6 Radian Measure

Remember that a degree is a unit of angle measure defined by using 360° for a complete rotation. On a calculator, you will notice another unit of angle measure called a radian. In many situations, radians are more useful than degrees. After you learn what a radian is, and how it is related to degrees, we will explain why it is a useful unit for angle measure.

Investigation

What Is a Radian?

You will use a calculator to determine how many degrees there are in one radian. Instructions for the TI-83 Plus and TI-30X IIS calculators are given. Other calculators have similar features, but they may be accessed differently. Consult your manual if necessary.

On the TI-83 Plus calculator

1. To find what one radian is, use a calculator to enter one radian, then convert it to degrees. Follow these steps.

   a) Make sure your calculator is in degree mode. Use the MODE menu to do this.

   b) Press 1 [2nd] [APPS] 3 to display 1^r.

   c) Press [ENTER]. The number of degrees will be displayed.

On the TI-30X IIS calculator

1. To find what one radian is, use a calculator to enter one radian, then convert it to degrees. Follow these steps.

   a) Press [DRG]. Use [▶] if necessary to underline DEG. Press [ENTER]. The calculator is in degree mode.

   b) Press 1 [°' "] then [▶] until r for radians is underlined. Do not clear the display.

   c) Press [ENTER] [ENTER] to display the angle in degrees equal to one radian.

2. How many degrees are there in one radian?

3. You should have found that one radian is slightly less than 60°. So 3 radians are slightly less than 180°. That is, 180° is a little more than 3 radians.

   a) What number is a little more than 3 and has something to do with circles?

   b) Use your calculator to convert 90° to radians. What is 180° in radians? Does the result confirm your answer to part a?

A radian is a unit, different from a degree, for measuring angles. In the *Investigation*, you should have found that one radian is approximately 57.295 78°. Instructions for converting radians to degrees were programmed into a calculator's processor chip using the following definition, which was established before calculators were invented.

Radian Measure

One *radian* is the measure of an angle subtended at the centre of a circle by an arc equal in length to the radius of the circle.

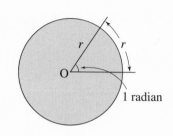

1 radian

Consider equilateral △ABC with rigid sides AB and BC. There is a hinge at B, and side AC is flexible.

Push point A down slightly so that AC bends outward and forms part of a circle, centred at B.

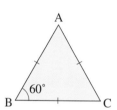

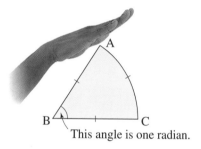

This angle is one radian.

One radian is slightly less than 60°.
Hence, 3 radians are slightly less than 180°.
That is, 180° is slightly more than 3 radians.

In the formulas for the circumference and area of a circle, remember $\pi \doteq 3.1416$. It turns out that 180° is π radians and we can show this as follows.

Angle ABC is the same fraction of a complete rotation as arc AC is of the circumference.

$$\frac{\angle ABC}{360°} = \frac{\text{arc AC}}{\text{circumference}}$$

$$\frac{1 \text{ radian}}{360°} = \frac{r}{2\pi r}$$

Multiply each side by 360°.

$$1 \text{ radian} = \frac{180°}{\pi}$$

Multiply each side by π.

$$\pi \text{ radians} = 180°$$

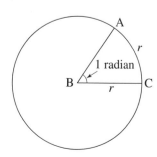

Since π radians = 180°, 2π radians = $2 \times 180°$
$$= 360°$$

Similarly,

$$\frac{\pi}{2} \text{ radians} = \frac{180°}{2}$$
$$= 90°$$

$$\frac{\pi}{4} \text{ radians} = \frac{180°}{4}$$
$$= 45°$$

$$\frac{\pi}{3} \text{ radians} = \frac{180°}{3}$$
$$= 60°$$

$$\frac{\pi}{6} \text{ radians} = \frac{180°}{6}$$
$$= 30°$$

These results are summarized below.

Take Note

Angle Measures in Degrees and Radians

Degrees	0°	45°	90°	135°	180°		360°
Radians	0	$\frac{\pi}{4}$	$\frac{\pi}{2}$	$\frac{3\pi}{4}$	π	$\cdots$	2π

Degrees	0°	30°	60°	90°	120°	150°	180°		360°
Radians	0	$\frac{\pi}{6}$	$\frac{\pi}{3}$	$\frac{\pi}{2}$	$\frac{2\pi}{3}$	$\frac{5\pi}{6}$	π	$\cdots$	2π

π radians are 180° and this fact is used to convert between angle measures.

Example 1

Express each angle to 2 decimal places.

a) 4 radians in degrees

b) 138° in radians

Solution

a) π radians = 180°

$$1 \text{ radian} = \frac{180°}{\pi}$$

$$4 \text{ radians} = 4\left(\frac{180°}{\pi}\right)$$

$$\doteq 229.18°$$

b) 180° = π radians

$$1° = \frac{\pi}{180} \text{ radians}$$

$$138° = 138\left(\frac{\pi}{180}\right) \text{ radians}$$

$$\doteq 2.41 \text{ radians}$$

In *Example 1a*, the number of degrees is much greater than the number of radians. We multiplied 4 by $\frac{180°}{\pi}$, which makes the number larger. In part b, the number of radians is much less than the number of degrees. We multiplied 138 by $\frac{\pi}{180}$, which makes the number smaller.

We can use radian measure to derive a formula that relates the length of an arc of a circle to the radius and the angle subtended by the arc at the centre.

Let a represent the length of an arc that subtends an angle θ radians at the centre of a circle with radius r. The ratio of the arc length to the circumference is equal to the ratio of the angle at the centre to a complete rotation. That is,

$$\frac{\text{arc length}}{\text{circumference}} = \frac{\text{angle at centre}}{2\pi}$$

$$\frac{a}{2\pi r} = \frac{\theta}{2\pi}$$

$$a = r\theta$$

Take Note

The Arc Length of a Circle

The arc length a subtended by an angle θ radians in a circle with radius r is given by the formula:

$a = r\theta$

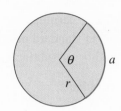

If degree measure had been used to develop the arc length formula, we would have obtained the formula $a = \frac{\pi}{180}r\theta$ for arc length. When radian measure is used, the formula is simpler. Other formulas that involve angles in mathematics also become simpler when radians are used instead of degrees. One of these occurs in exercise 21. Hence, radian measure is useful because it simplifies formulas that involve angles. Also, it is customary to use radian measure when we apply trigonometric functions to model quantities that vary periodically.

Example 2

A circle has radius 6.5 cm. Calculate the length of an arc of this circle subtended by each angle. Express each length to the nearest tenth of a centimetre.

a) 2.3 radians b) $75°$

Solution

a) Use the formula $a = r\theta$.

$$a = (6.5)(2.3)$$
$$= 14.95$$

The arc length is approximately 15.0 cm.

b) To use the formula $a = r\theta$, the angle must be in radians.

$$180° = \pi \text{ radians}$$
$$1° = \frac{\pi}{180} \text{ radians}$$
$$75° = 75\left(\frac{\pi}{180}\right) \text{ radians}$$
$$\doteq 1.309 \text{ radians}$$

Substitute in the formula $a = r\theta$.

$$a \doteq (6.5)(1.309)$$
$$\doteq 8.5085$$

The arc length is approximately 8.5 cm.

Angles in standard position with the same terminal arm are coterminal angles. When an angle measured in radians is in standard position, other angles that are coterminal with it can be found by adding or subtracting multiples of 2π.

Begin with an angle of $\frac{\pi}{4}$ radians …

… add 2π radians,
$$\frac{\pi}{4} + 2\pi = \frac{9\pi}{4}$$

… add 2π radians again,
$$\frac{9\pi}{4} + 2\pi = \frac{17\pi}{4}$$

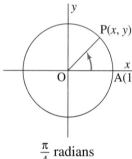

$\frac{\pi}{4}$ radians

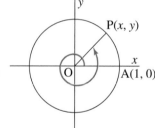

$\frac{9\pi}{4}$ radians

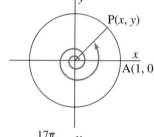

$\frac{17\pi}{4}$ radians

Take Note

Coterminal Angles Measured in Radians

When an angle has measure θ radians, then the measure of any coterminal angle is $(\theta + 2n\pi)$ radians, where n is an integer.

5.6 Exercises

A

 1. Convert to radians. Express each angle in terms of π.

a) 30°   **b)** 60°   **c)** 90°   **d)** 120°   **e)** 150°   **f)** 180°

g) 210°   **h)** 240°   **i)** 270°   **j)** 300°   **k)** 330°   **l)** 360°

2. Convert to radians. Express each angle in terms of π.

a) $45°$ **b)** $135°$ **c)** $225°$ **d)** $315°$

✓ **3.** Convert to degrees.

a) $\dfrac{\pi}{6}$ radians   **b)** $\dfrac{2\pi}{6}$ radians   **c)** $\dfrac{3\pi}{6}$ radians   **d)** $\dfrac{4\pi}{6}$ radians

e) $\dfrac{5\pi}{6}$ radians   **f)** $\dfrac{6\pi}{6}$ radians   **g)** $\dfrac{\pi}{4}$ radians   **h)** $\dfrac{2\pi}{4}$ radians

i) $\dfrac{3\pi}{4}$ radians   **j)** $\dfrac{4\pi}{4}$ radians   **k)** $\dfrac{5\pi}{4}$ radians   **l)** $\dfrac{6\pi}{4}$ radians

4. Determine how many radians there are in each rotation.

a) one full turn   **b)** one-half turn   **c)** one-quarter turn

5. Sketch each angle in standard position. Determine two angles that are coterminal with each angle.

a) $\dfrac{\pi}{6}$ radians   **b)** $\dfrac{\pi}{4}$ radians   **c)** $\dfrac{\pi}{3}$ radians   **d)** $\dfrac{\pi}{2}$ radians

e) $\dfrac{2\pi}{3}$ radians   **f)** $\dfrac{5\pi}{6}$ radians   **g)** $\dfrac{4\pi}{3}$ radians   **h)** $\dfrac{5\pi}{3}$ radians

✓ **6.** Determine two angles that are coterminal with each angle.

a) $\dfrac{3\pi}{4}$ radians   **b)** $\dfrac{5\pi}{4}$ radians   **c)** $\dfrac{7\pi}{4}$ radians   **d)** $\dfrac{11\pi}{6}$ radians

e) $\dfrac{7\pi}{6}$ radians   **f)** $\dfrac{3\pi}{2}$ radians   **g)** π radians   **h)** 2π radians

B

✓ **7. Knowledge/Understanding** Convert to radians. Express each angle to 2 decimal places.

a) $105° \times \dfrac{\pi}{180}$ **b)** $220°$ **c)** $57.3°$ **d)** $131°$ **e)** $82°$ **f)** $45°$

g) $64°$ **h)** $23.1°$ **i)** $140°$ **j)** $60°$ **k)** $\dfrac{180°}{\pi}$ **l)** $\dfrac{90°}{\pi}$

✓ **8.** Convert to degrees. Express each angle to 1 decimal place.

a) 3 radians $\times \dfrac{180}{\pi}$ **b)** 4 radians   **c)** 2.1 radians   **d)** 1.6 radians

e) 0.5 radians   **f)** 1.2 radians   **g)** 6.6 radians   **h)** 2π radians

✓ **9.** Convert to degrees.

a) $\dfrac{\pi}{2}$ radians   **b)** $\dfrac{11\pi}{6}$ radians   **c)** $\dfrac{2\pi}{3}$ radians   **d)** $\dfrac{7\pi}{6}$ radians

e) $\dfrac{5\pi}{3}$ radians   **f)** $\dfrac{3\pi}{2}$ radians   **g)** $\dfrac{7\pi}{4}$ radians   **h)** $\dfrac{9\pi}{4}$ radians

10. Communication

a) Choose an angle in degrees. Write to explain how to convert degrees to radians.

b) Choose a different angle in radians. Write to explain how to convert radians to degrees.

11. Sketch each angle in standard position.

    a) $\frac{9\pi}{2}$ radians   b) $-\pi$ radians   c) $\frac{3\pi}{2}$ radians   d) $-\frac{5\pi}{2}$ radians

    e) $-\frac{5\pi}{4}$ radians   f) $\frac{10\pi}{3}$ radians   g) -2π radians   h) $-\frac{2\pi}{3}$ radians

12. Determine the length of the arc that subtends each angle at the centre of a circle with radius 4.0 cm.

    a) 2.5 radians   b) 3.2 radians   c) 1.7 radians

    d) 6.2 radians   e) 4.5 radians   f) 0.9 radians

13. Determine the length of the arc of a circle, radius 15.0 cm, that subtends each angle at the centre.

    a) 130°   b) 70°   c) 100°   d) 155°

    e) 210°   f) 90°   g) 330°   h) 300°

14. a) Write an expression for each distance from A to B.

    i) along the segment AB

    ii) along the circular arc from A to B

    b) How many times as long as the straight-line distance is the distance along the circular arc from A to B?

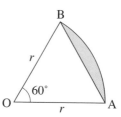

15. Determine the angle at the centre of a circle, radius 6.0 cm, for each arc length. Express each answer in degrees and radians.

    a) 3.0 cm   b) 7.0 cm   c) 12.5 cm   d) 16.4 cm

16. The area of a circle is 38.0 cm². Determine the length of one-quarter of the circumference.

17. The hypotenuse of an isosceles right triangle is the chord of a circle. The legs of the triangle are radii of the circle. The length of the chord is 8 cm. What is the length of the arc subtended by this chord?

18. **Application** The moon travels in a nearly circular orbit around Earth. The radius of the orbit is approximately 384 400 km. The moon orbits Earth once every 27.3 days.

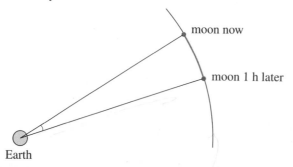

a) Consider two positions of the moon at times 1 h apart. What is the measure, in radians, of the angle subtended at Earth?

b) About how far does the moon travel in 1 h in its orbit around Earth?

19. **Thinking/Inquiry/Problem Solving** When an object moves in a circle, its *angular velocity* is the angle per unit of time through which it rotates about the centre.

a) A bicycle wheel has diameter 60 cm. Determine its angular velocity, in radians per second, when the bicycle travels at 20 km/h.

b) Write an expression for the angular velocity, in radians per second, for a bicycle wheel with diameter d centimetres when the bicycle travels at x kilometres per hour.

20. Santa's Village is in Bracebridge, Ontario. It is advertised as being halfway between the Equator and the North Pole; that is, at a latitude of 45°. Geographers use lines of latitude to measure how far a place is from the Equator, as shown in the diagram. Determine the shortest distance from Bracebridge to the North Pole. The radius of Earth is 6378 km.

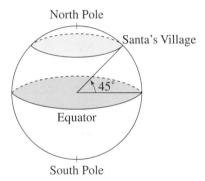

C

21. **a)** Derive a formula for the area, A, of a sector of a circle with radius, r, formed by an angle θ radians.

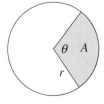

b) Derive a similar formula when the measure of the angle is in degrees.

c) Explain how the results of parts a and b justify the use of radian measure instead of degree measure.

5.7 Trigonometric Functions of Angles in Radians

In Chapter 6, we will use trigonometric functions to model quantities that vary periodically. Although it is possible to do this using angles in degrees, it is customary to use angles in radians. Therefore, in this section we will work with trigonometric functions of angles in radians instead of degrees. The only difference from previous work is that the angles are in radians.

It is usual to omit the word "radians" when we refer to an angle in radians. For example, when we refer to an angle of 2.4, it is understood that the angle is in radians. From now on, when the unit of an angle is not given, the angle is in radians.

Here are some typical trigonometric function values of θ in radians.

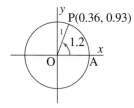
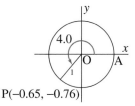
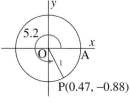

$\cos 1.2 \doteq 0.36$	$\cos 2.7 \doteq -0.90$	$\cos 4.0 \doteq -0.65$	$\cos 5.2 \doteq 0.47$
$\sin 1.2 \doteq 0.93$	$\sin 2.7 \doteq 0.43$	$\sin 4.0 \doteq -0.76$	$\sin 5.2 \doteq -0.88$
$\tan 1.2 \doteq 2.57$	$\tan 2.7 \doteq -0.47$	$\tan 4.0 \doteq 1.16$	$\tan 5.2 \doteq -1.89$

The diagrams above review the sign of each trigonometric function value in each quadrant. We use these signs to determine the possible measures of an angle in radians, when a trigonometric function value is given.

Example 1

Determine two angles between 0 and 2π that have each trigonometric function value. Write the angles to 2 decimal places.

a) $\sin \theta = 0.37$ **b)** $\cos \theta = 0.54$ **c)** $\tan \theta = 2.49$

Solution

Make sure the calculator is in radian mode.

a) $\sin \theta = 0.37$

Since $\sin \theta$ is positive, θ lies in Quadrant I or II.
Key in: 2nd SIN 0.37 ENTER to display 0.379009021
$\theta \doteq 0.38$

The angle in Quadrant I is approximately 0.38.
Consider angle θ in Quadrants I and II.

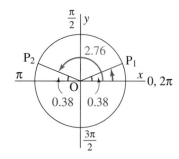

By symmetry, the angle in Quadrant II is $\pi - 0.38 \doteq 2.76$
The two angles are approximately 0.38 and 2.76.

b) $\cos \theta = 0.54$

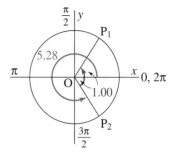

Since $\cos \theta$ is positive, θ lies in Quadrant I or IV.
Key in: (2nd) (COS) 0.54 (ENTER) to display 1.000359217
$\theta \doteq 1.00$

The angle in Quadrant I is approximately 1.00.
Consider angle θ in Quadrants I and IV.

By symmetry, the angle in Quadrant IV is $2\pi - 1.00 \doteq 5.28$
The two angles are approximately 1.00 and 5.28.

c) $\tan \theta = 2.49$

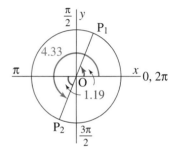

Since $\tan \theta$ is positive, θ lies in Quadrant I or III.
Key in: (2nd) (TAN) 2.49 (ENTER) to display 1.188905868
$\theta \doteq 1.19$

The angle in Quadrant I is approximately 1.19.
Consider angle θ in Quadrants I and III.

By symmetry, the angle in Quadrant III is $\pi + 1.19 \doteq 4.33$
The two angles are approximately 1.19 and 4.33.

The results of *Example 1* can be summarized.

Take Note

Solving sin θ = k, cos θ = k, and tan θ = k

- When $\sin \theta = k$, and θ is in radians, two values of θ that satisfy the equation are θ and $\pi - \theta$.
- When $\cos \theta = k$, and θ is in radians, two values of θ that satisfy the equation are θ and $2\pi - \theta$.
- When $\tan \theta = k$, and θ is in radians, two values of θ that satisfy the equation are θ and $\pi + \theta$.

Example 2

Determine two angles between 0 and 2π that have each trigonometric function value. Write the angles to 2 decimal places.

a) $\sin \theta = -0.68$ **b)** $\cos \theta = -0.42$ **c)** $\tan \theta = -1.85$

Solution

Make sure the calculator is in radian mode.

a) $\sin \theta = -0.68$

Since $\sin \theta$ is negative, θ lies in Quadrant III or IV.
Key in: [2nd] [SIN] [(−)] 0.68 [ENTER] to display −0.747762635
$\theta \doteq -0.75$

One angle is approximately −0.75.
However, the angle is not between 0 and 2π.

To obtain the angle in Quadrant IV, add 2π.
$\theta = -0.75 + 2\pi$
$\quad \doteq 5.54$

To obtain the angle in Quadrant III, subtract −0.75 from π.
$\theta = \pi - (-0.75)$
$\quad \doteq 3.89$

The two angles are approximately 3.89 and 5.54.

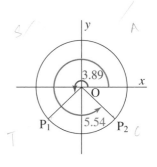

b) $\cos \theta = -0.42$

Since $\cos \theta$ is negative, θ lies in Quadrant II or III.
Key in: [2nd] [COS] [(−)] 0.42 [ENTER] to display 2.004241647
$\theta \doteq 2.00$

The angle in Quadrant II is approximately 2.00.
To obtain the angle in Quadrant III, subtract 2.00 from 2π.
$\theta = 2\pi - 2.00$
$\quad \doteq 4.28$

The two angles are approximately 2.00 and 4.28.

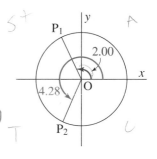

c) $\tan \theta = -1.85$

Since $\tan \theta$ is negative, θ lies in Quadrant II or IV.
Key in: [2nd] [TAN] [(−)] 1.85 [ENTER] to display −1.075244653
$\theta \doteq -1.08$

One angle is approximately −1.08. This angle is not
between 0 and 2π. To obtain the angle in Quadrant IV,
add 2π.
$\theta = -1.08 + 2\pi$
$\quad \doteq 5.21$

To obtain the angle in Quadrant II, add −1.08 to π.
$\theta = \pi - 1.08$
$\quad \doteq 2.07$

The two angles are approximately 2.07 and 5.21.

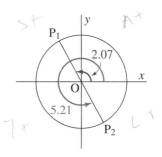

Discuss

How can you check
the results?

Remember, from Section 5.5, that we determined the trigonometric function values for certain special angles. In that section, the angles were expressed in degrees. We can also express the angles in radians, with the following results.

Take Note

Sine, Cosine, and Tangent of Special Angles in Radians

Values for $\frac{\pi}{6}$ and $\frac{\pi}{3}$

Remember that $\frac{\pi}{6} = 30°$, so $\sin\frac{\pi}{6} = \frac{1}{2}$ and $\cos\frac{\pi}{6} = \frac{\sqrt{3}}{2}$.

For $\frac{\pi}{3}$, interchange the values:

$\sin\frac{\pi}{3} = \frac{\sqrt{3}}{2}$ and $\cos\frac{\pi}{3} = \frac{1}{2}$.

For a tangent value, divide the sine value by the cosine value, where possible.

Values for $\frac{\pi}{4}$

Remember that $\frac{\pi}{4} = 45°$, so $\sin\frac{\pi}{4} = \cos\frac{\pi}{4} = \frac{1}{\sqrt{2}}$.

Values for 0 and $\frac{\pi}{2}$

Use the coordinates of the points (1, 0) and (0, 1).

Remember that $\cos\theta$ is the first coordinate and $\sin\theta$ is the second coordinate.

So, $\cos 0 = 1$, $\sin 0 = 0$; and $\cos\frac{\pi}{2} = 0$, $\sin\frac{\pi}{2} = 1$

Example 3

Determine $\sin\frac{11\pi}{6}$, $\cos\frac{11\pi}{6}$, and $\tan\frac{11\pi}{6}$.

Solution

Draw a diagram.

The reference angle is $\angle PON = 2\pi - \frac{11\pi}{6} = \frac{\pi}{6}$.

$\triangle PON$ is a 30-60-90 triangle with sides $\frac{1}{2}$, 1, and $\frac{\sqrt{3}}{2}$.

Since P is in Quadrant IV, both $\sin\frac{11\pi}{6}$ and $\tan\frac{11\pi}{6}$ are negative, while $\cos\frac{11\pi}{6}$ is positive.

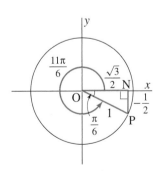

Hence, $\sin\frac{11\pi}{6} = -\frac{1}{2}$

$\cos\frac{11\pi}{6} = \frac{\sqrt{3}}{2}$

$\tan\frac{11\pi}{6} = -\frac{1}{\sqrt{3}}$

A

1. Determine each value to 3 decimal places.

   a) $\sin 1.3$ b) $\cos 0.9$ c) $\tan 0.6$

   d) $\tan 2.6$ e) $\sin 1.9$ f) $\cos 2.8$

   g) $\cos 3.6$ h) $\tan 4.1$ i) $\sin 4.3$

   j) $\sin 5.1$ k) $\tan 5.7$ l) $\cos 5.3$

2. Determine the sine, cosine, and tangent of each angle to 3 decimal places, where possible.

   a) 0 b) $\dfrac{\pi}{2}$ c) π d) $\dfrac{3\pi}{2}$ e) 2π

3. State each exact value.

   a) $\sin \dfrac{\pi}{3}$ b) $\tan \dfrac{\pi}{4}$ c) $\cos \dfrac{\pi}{3}$

   d) $\tan \dfrac{\pi}{3}$ e) $\sin \dfrac{\pi}{6}$ f) $\cos \dfrac{\pi}{4}$

   g) $\sin \dfrac{\pi}{4}$ h) $\tan \dfrac{\pi}{6}$ i) $\cos \dfrac{\pi}{6}$

   j) $\cos \pi$ k) $\tan 0$ l) $\sin \dfrac{\pi}{2}$

B

4. For each expression below:

   i) Determine its value to 3 decimal places.

   ii) Determine two other angles that have the same trigonometric function value. Write the angles to 3 decimal places.

   a) $\sin 2.3$ b) $\tan 3.6$ c) $\cos 4.8$

   d) $\cos 1.7$ e) $\sin 5.9$ f) $\tan 0.9$

5. **Knowledge/Understanding** Determine two angles between 0 and 2π that have each trigonometric function value. Write the angles to 2 decimal places.

   a) $\sin \theta = 0.71$ b) $\tan \theta = 2.98$ c) $\cos \theta = 0.34$

   d) $\tan \theta = 1.72$ e) $\cos \theta = 0.90$ f) $\sin \theta = 0.23$

6. Determine two angles between 0 and 2π that have each trigonometric function value. Write the angles to 2 decimal places.

   a) $\tan \theta = -1.80$ b) $\cos \theta = -0.62$ c) $\sin \theta = -0.54$

   d) $\tan \theta = -0.98$ e) $\sin \theta = -0.15$ f) $\cos \theta = -0.33$

7. State each exact value.

a) $\cos \dfrac{5\pi}{6}$ b) $\sin \dfrac{11\pi}{6}$ c) $\tan \dfrac{4\pi}{3}$

d) $\sin \dfrac{7\pi}{6}$ e) $\cos \dfrac{4\pi}{3}$ f) $\tan \dfrac{11\pi}{6}$

g) $\tan \dfrac{5\pi}{6}$ h) $\sin \dfrac{3\pi}{4}$ i) $\cos \dfrac{2\pi}{3}$

8. State each exact value.

a) $\sin \dfrac{7\pi}{4}$ b) $\cos \dfrac{11\pi}{6}$ c) $\tan \dfrac{2\pi}{3}$

d) $\cos \dfrac{7\pi}{6}$ e) $\sin \dfrac{5\pi}{6}$ f) $\tan \dfrac{7\pi}{6}$

g) $\sin \dfrac{2\pi}{3}$ h) $\cos \dfrac{3\pi}{4}$ i) $\sin \dfrac{4\pi}{3}$

j) $\cos \dfrac{7\pi}{4}$ k) $\tan \dfrac{3\pi}{4}$ l) $\tan \dfrac{7\pi}{4}$

9. **Communication** State the exact value of the sine, cosine, and tangent of each angle. Write to explain how you determined each value.

a) $\dfrac{5\pi}{4}$ b) $\dfrac{5\pi}{6}$ c) $\dfrac{5\pi}{3}$

10. Determine two angles between 0 and 2π that have each trigonometric function value. Write the angles to 2 decimal places.

a) $\sin \theta = \dfrac{1}{2}$ b) $\sin \theta = -\dfrac{\sqrt{3}}{2}$

c) $\tan \theta = 1$ d) $\tan \theta = -\sqrt{3}$

e) $\sin \theta = -\dfrac{1}{\sqrt{2}}$ f) $\cos \theta = -1$

11. **Application** A table has the shape of a regular octagon of side length 1.2 m. The table seats 8 people, one at the centre of each side.

a) Calculate the distance between 2 people seated opposite each other at the table.

b) What is the area of a circular cloth that overhangs the table by 5 cm?

12. **Thinking/Inquiry/Problem Solving**

a) Use a calculator to determine the values of θ in radians for which $\sin \theta = \tan \theta = \theta$ to:

i) 1 decimal place ii) 2 decimal places iii) 3 decimal places

b) Explain why $\sin \theta \doteq \tan \theta \doteq \theta$ for small values of θ.

5.8 Trigonometric Equations

An equation that involves one or more trigonometric ratios of a variable is a
trigonometric equation.

These are trigonometric equations.

$3 \sin \theta + \cos \theta = 0$

$\theta + \sin \theta = 2$

$3 \sin^2 \theta + 2 \cos \theta - 1 = 0$

These are not trigonometric equations.

$2x + 5 \tan 4 = 1.5$

$x^3 - \cos \pi = 0$

Example 1

Solve the equation $\sin \theta = \dfrac{\sqrt{3}}{2}$ for $0 \le \theta \le 2\pi$.

Solution

$\sin \theta = \dfrac{\sqrt{3}}{2}$

Since $\sin \theta$ is positive, θ is in Quadrant I or II.

Since $\sin \dfrac{\pi}{3} = \dfrac{\sqrt{3}}{2}$, $\theta = \dfrac{\pi}{3}$ is the angle in Quadrant I.

To determine the angle in Quadrant II, subtract $\dfrac{\pi}{3}$ from π.

$\theta = \pi - \dfrac{\pi}{3}$

$\quad = \dfrac{2\pi}{3}$

The solutions are $\theta = \dfrac{\pi}{3}$ and $\dfrac{2\pi}{3}$.

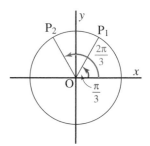

Example 2

Solve the equation $\cos \theta = -\dfrac{1}{\sqrt{2}}$ for $0 \le \theta \le 2\pi$.

Solution

$\cos \theta = -\dfrac{1}{\sqrt{2}}$

Since $\cos \theta$ is negative, θ is in Quadrant II or III.

Since $\cos \dfrac{\pi}{4} = \dfrac{1}{\sqrt{2}}$, the solution involves multiples of $\dfrac{\pi}{4}$.

From the diagram,

in Quadrant II: $\theta = \pi - \dfrac{\pi}{4}$

$\qquad\qquad = \dfrac{3\pi}{4}$

in Quadrant III: $\theta = \pi + \dfrac{\pi}{4}$

$\qquad\qquad = \dfrac{5\pi}{4}$

The solutions are $\theta = \dfrac{3\pi}{4}$ and $\dfrac{5\pi}{4}$.

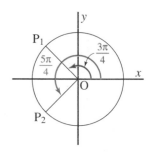

Discuss

How could you check
the solutions?

The trigonometric equations in *Examples 1* and *2* are linear. We can also solve quadratic trigonometric equations.

Example 3

Solve the equation $2 \sin^2 \theta - \sin \theta - 1 = 0$ for $0 \le \theta \le 2\pi$.

Solution

The equation $2 \sin^2 \theta - \sin \theta - 1 = 0$ is similar to the quadratic equation $2m^2 - m - 1 = 0$.

The left side of the equation factors: $(2m + 1)(m - 1) = 0$

Similarly, $2 \sin^2 \theta - \sin \theta - 1 = 0$ can be factored as

$$(2 \sin \theta + 1)(\sin \theta - 1) = 0$$

Either $2 \sin \theta + 1 = 0$ or $\sin \theta - 1 = 0$

$\qquad\qquad 2 \sin \theta = -1 \qquad\qquad\qquad \sin \theta = 1$

$\qquad\qquad\quad \sin \theta = -\dfrac{1}{2} \qquad$ Since $\sin \dfrac{\pi}{2} = 1$, one solution is $\theta = \dfrac{\pi}{2}$.

Since $\sin \theta$ is negative,
θ is in Quadrant III or IV.

Since $\sin \dfrac{\pi}{6} = \dfrac{1}{2}$, the solution
involves multiples of $\dfrac{\pi}{6}$.

From the diagram,

in Quadrant III: $\theta = \pi + \dfrac{\pi}{6}$

$\qquad\qquad = \dfrac{7\pi}{6}$

in Quadrant IV: $\theta = 2\pi - \dfrac{\pi}{6}$

$\qquad\qquad = \dfrac{11\pi}{6}$

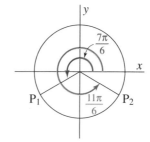

The solutions are $\theta = \dfrac{\pi}{2}, \dfrac{7\pi}{6}$, and $\dfrac{11\pi}{6}$.

Recall the Pythagorean identity: $\sin^2 \theta + \cos^2 \theta = 1$.
This identity may be used to simplify a quadratic trigonometric equation.

Example 4

Solve the equation $6 \sin^2 \theta - \cos \theta - 4 = 0$ for $0 \le \theta \le 2\pi$.

Solution

$6 \sin^2 \theta - \cos \theta - 4 = 0$

Rearrange the Pythagorean identity: $\sin^2 \theta = 1 - \cos^2 \theta$

Substitute for $\sin^2 \theta$ in the equation.
$$6(1 - \cos^2 \theta) - \cos \theta - 4 = 0$$
$$6 - 6\cos^2 \theta - \cos \theta - 4 = 0$$
$$-6\cos^2 \theta - \cos \theta + 2 = 0$$
Multiply by -1.
$$6\cos^2 \theta + \cos \theta - 2 = 0$$
Factor.
$$(3\cos \theta + 2)(2\cos \theta - 1) = 0$$

Either $3\cos \theta + 2 = 0$ or $2\cos \theta = 1$
$$3\cos \theta = -2 \qquad\qquad\qquad \cos \theta = \frac{1}{2}$$
$$\cos \theta = -\frac{2}{3}$$

Since $\cos \theta$ is negative, θ is in Quadrant II or III.

Key in: [2nd] [COS] [(-)] 2 [÷] 3 [ENTER =] to display 2.300523983

$\theta \doteq 2.30$

The angle in Quadrant II is approximately 2.3.

Since $\cos \theta$ is positive, θ is in Quadrant I or IV.

Since $\cos \frac{\pi}{3} = \frac{1}{2}$, $\theta = \frac{\pi}{3}$ is the angle in Quadrant I.

To obtain the angle in Quadrant III, subtract 2.3 from 2π.

$$\theta \doteq 2\pi - 2.3$$
$$\doteq 3.98$$

To obtain the angle in Quadrant IV, subtract $\frac{\pi}{3}$ from 2π.

$$\theta = 2\pi - \frac{\pi}{3}$$
$$= \frac{5\pi}{3}$$

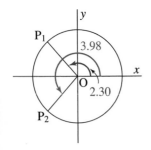

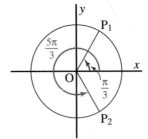

Discuss

At the top of the page, why did we substitute for $\sin^2 \theta$? Could we have substituted for $\cos \theta$ instead? Explain.

The exact solutions are $\theta = \frac{\pi}{3}$ and $\frac{5\pi}{3}$; the approximate solutions are θ is 2.30 and 3.98.

A

1. Solve each equation for $0 \le \theta \le 2\pi$.

a) $\sin \theta = 0$ b) $\cos \theta = 0$ c) $\tan \theta = 0$

d) $\sin \theta = 1$ e) $\cos \theta = 1$ f) $\tan \theta = 1$

2. Solve each equation for $0 \le \theta \le 2\pi$.

a) $\cos \theta = \dfrac{\sqrt{3}}{2}$ b) $\sin \theta = \dfrac{1}{2}$ c) $\tan \theta = \sqrt{3}$

d) $\sin \theta = \dfrac{1}{\sqrt{2}}$ e) $\cos \theta = \dfrac{1}{\sqrt{2}}$ f) $\tan \theta = \dfrac{1}{\sqrt{3}}$

3. Solve each equation for $0 \le \theta \le 2\pi$.

a) $\cos \theta = -\dfrac{1}{2}$ b) $\sin \theta = -\dfrac{1}{\sqrt{2}}$ c) $\tan \theta = -\dfrac{1}{\sqrt{3}}$

d) $\sin \theta = -\dfrac{\sqrt{3}}{2}$ e) $\sin \theta = -1$ f) $\tan \theta = -\sqrt{3}$

g) $\tan \theta = -1$ h) $\cos \theta = -1$ i) $\cos \theta = -\dfrac{\sqrt{3}}{2}$

B

4. Solve each equation for $0 \le \theta \le 2\pi$.

a) $\cos \theta = \dfrac{1}{4}$ b) $\sin \theta = \dfrac{3}{4}$ c) $\tan \theta = 3$

d) $\sin \theta = \dfrac{3}{5}$ e) $\cos \theta = \dfrac{1}{5}$ f) $\tan \theta = \dfrac{2}{3}$

g) $\tan \theta = 4$ h) $\cos \theta = \dfrac{3}{4}$ i) $\sin \theta = \dfrac{1}{4}$

5. Knowledge/Understanding Solve each equation for $0 \le \theta \le 2\pi$.

a) $\tan \theta = -3$ b) $\cos \theta = -\dfrac{2}{3}$ c) $\sin \theta = -\dfrac{1}{3}$

d) $\cos \theta = -\dfrac{4}{5}$ e) $\tan \theta = -\dfrac{3}{4}$ f) $\sin \theta = -\dfrac{2}{5}$

g) $\sin \theta = -\dfrac{3}{4}$ h) $\tan \theta = -\dfrac{5}{4}$ i) $\cos \theta = -\dfrac{1}{4}$

6. Communication

a) Solve the equation $\tan \theta = 2$ for $0 \le \theta \le 2\pi$.

b) Explain why there is no real number θ that satisfies either $\sin \theta = 2$ or $\cos \theta = 2$.

7. Solve each equation for $0 \le \theta \le 2\pi$.

a) $(\sin \theta - 1)(\sin \theta + \dfrac{1}{2}) = 0$ b) $(\cos \theta + \dfrac{1}{\sqrt{2}})(\cos \theta + \dfrac{1}{2}) = 0$

c) $(\tan \theta - 1)(\tan \theta + \sqrt{3}) = 0$ d) $(\cos \theta - \dfrac{\sqrt{3}}{2})(\cos \theta - 1) = 0$

e) $(\sin \theta + \dfrac{1}{\sqrt{2}})(\sin \theta - \dfrac{\sqrt{3}}{2}) = 0$ f) $(\tan \theta + 1)(\tan \theta - \dfrac{1}{\sqrt{3}}) = 0$

8. Factor each expression.

a) $\cos^2 x + 2\cos x$

b) $\sin^2 x + 5\sin x + 6$

c) $2\sin^2 x + \sin x - 6$

d) $3\cos^2 x - 2\cos x - 1$

e) $2\cos^2 x - 7\cos x + 3$

f) $6\sin^2 x + \sin x - 1$

9. Solve each equation for $0 \leq \theta \leq 2\pi$.

a) $\cos^2 \theta + 2\cos \theta = 0$

b) $\sin^2 \theta + 5\sin \theta + 6 = 0$

c) $2\sin^2 \theta + \sin \theta - 6 = 0$

d) $3\cos^2 \theta - 2\cos \theta - 1 = 0$

e) $2\cos^2 \theta - 7\cos \theta + 3 = 0$

f) $6\sin^2 \theta + \sin \theta - 1 = 0$

✓ **10.** Solve each equation for $0 \leq \theta \leq 2\pi$.

a) $\sin^2 \theta - \sin \theta = 0$

b) $\cos^2 \theta + \cos \theta = 0$

c) $2\sin^2 \theta + \sin \theta - 1 = 0$

d) $2\sin^2 \theta - \sin \theta - 1 = 0$

e) $\cos^2 \theta + 3\cos \theta + 2 = 0$

f) $\sin^2 \theta + 2\sin \theta - 3 = 0$

g) $2\cos^2 \theta + 3\cos \theta + 1 = 0$

h) $2\cos^2 \theta - 3\cos \theta + 1 = 0$

i) $\sin^2 \theta + 3\sin \theta + 2 = 0$

j) $\sin^2 \theta + 5\sin \theta + 6 = 0$

k) $4\cos^2 \theta - 4\cos \theta + 1 = 0$

l) $4\sin^2 \theta - 1 = 0$

✓ **11.** Solve each equation for $0 \leq \theta \leq 2\pi$.

a) $\tan^2 \theta - \tan \theta = 0$

b) $\tan^2 \theta + \tan \theta = 0$

c) $\tan^2 \theta - 1 = 0$

d) $\tan^2 \theta - (\sqrt{3} + 1)\tan \theta + \sqrt{3} = 0$

e) $2\tan^2 \theta = 3\tan \theta - 1$

f) $3\tan^2 \theta = 2\tan \theta + 4$

12. Application Write a trigonometric equation that has each given root.

a) $\theta = 0$

b) $\theta = \dfrac{\pi}{6}$

c) $\theta = \dfrac{\pi}{2}$

d) $\theta = \dfrac{\pi}{3}$

e) $\theta = \dfrac{\pi}{4}$

f) $\theta = \dfrac{3\pi}{4}$

13. Thinking/Inquiry/Problem Solving Write a trigonometric equation that has each pair of roots.

a) $\theta = \dfrac{\pi}{6}, \dfrac{\pi}{2}$

b) $\theta = \dfrac{\pi}{3}, \dfrac{\pi}{4}$

c) $\theta = \dfrac{\pi}{4}, \dfrac{3\pi}{4}$

✓ **14.** Solve each equation for $0 \leq \theta \leq 2\pi$.

a) $2\sin \theta = 1 - \cos^2 \theta$

b) $2\cos \theta = 1 - \sin^2 \theta$

c) $\cos^2 \theta - \sin^2 \theta = 1$

d) $\sin^2 \theta - \cos^2 \theta = 1$

e) $2\cos^2 \theta - \sin \theta - 1 = 0$

f) $4\sin^2 \theta + 4\cos \theta = 5$

✓ **15.** Solve each equation for $0 \leq \theta \leq 2\pi$.

a) $6\cos^2 \theta + \sin \theta - 4 = 0$

b) $6\sin^2 \theta + \cos \theta - 5 = 0$

c) $2\cos^2 \theta - \sin \theta - 2 = 0$

d) $18\sin^2 \theta + 3\cos \theta - 17 = 0$

e) $3\cos \theta \sin^2 \theta - \cos \theta = 0$

f) $4\sin \theta \cos^2 \theta = 2\sin \theta$

5.9 Trigonometric Identities

From page 257, recall the definition of an identity: an equation that is true for all values of the variable for which both sides of the equation are defined.

Here are examples of algebraic identities.

$2x + 3x = 5x$

$(x + 1)(x - 1) = x^2 - 1$

The left side of the identity equals the right side for all permissible values of x.

Previously, you encountered the Pythagorean identity: $\cos^2 \theta + \sin^2 \theta = 1$

The definition of $\tan \theta$ is called the *quotient identity*: $\tan \theta = \dfrac{\sin \theta}{\cos \theta}$, $\cos \theta \neq 0$

We can use the Pythagorean identity and the quotient identity to prove other identities.

To prove an identity, we show that each side of the identity simplifies to the same expression.

Example

Prove the identity $1 - \sin^2 \theta = \dfrac{\sin^2 \theta}{\tan^2 \theta}$.

Solution

$1 - \sin^2 \theta = \dfrac{\sin^2 \theta}{\tan^2 \theta}$

Use the Pythagorean identity on the left side.

Use the definition of $\tan \theta$ on the right side.

Restrict the values of θ to those for which $\tan \theta$ is defined, and $\tan \theta \neq 0$.

Left side	Reason
$1 - \sin^2 \theta = \cos^2 \theta$	Pythagorean identity

Discuss

Why are there restrictions on the value of θ?

Right side	Reason
$\dfrac{\sin^2 \theta}{\tan^2 \theta} = \dfrac{\sin^2 \theta}{\frac{\sin^2 \theta}{\cos^2 \theta}}$	Quotient identity, $\tan \theta \neq 0$
$= \sin^2 \theta \times \dfrac{\cos^2 \theta}{\sin^2 \theta}$	To divide by a fraction, invert then multiply.
$= \cos^2 \theta$	Divide numerator and denominator by $\sin^2 \theta$, $\sin \theta \neq 0$.

Since both sides simplify to the same expression, the identity is proved.

A

✓ **1.** Prove each identity.

a) $\sin \theta = \tan \theta \cos \theta$

b) $\cos \theta = \dfrac{\sin \theta}{\tan \theta}$

2. Explain how an identity is different from an equation.

✓ **3.** Prove each identity.

a) $\dfrac{1}{\sin \theta}(1 + \sin \theta) = 1 + \dfrac{1}{\sin \theta}$

b) $\sin \theta\left(1 + \dfrac{1}{\sin \theta}\right) = 1 + \sin \theta$

c) $\cos \theta\left(\dfrac{1}{\cos \theta} - 1\right) = 1 - \cos \theta$

d) $\dfrac{\sin \theta}{\cos \theta \tan \theta} = 1$

B

✓ **4. Knowledge/Understanding** Prove each identity.

a) $\tan^2 \theta = \dfrac{1 - \cos^2 \theta}{\cos^2 \theta}$

b) $\sin \theta \tan \theta = \dfrac{1 - \cos^2 \theta}{\cos \theta}$

c) $\dfrac{\sin \theta}{1 + \cos \theta} = \dfrac{1 - \cos \theta}{\sin \theta}$

d) $1 - \tan \theta = -\tan \theta\left(1 - \dfrac{1}{\tan \theta}\right)$

5. Prove each identity.

a) $\sin \theta \tan \theta + \dfrac{1}{\cos \theta} = \dfrac{\sin^2 \theta + 1}{\cos \theta}$

b) $\dfrac{1 + \cos \theta}{1 - \cos \theta} = \dfrac{1 + \frac{1}{\cos \theta}}{\frac{1}{\cos \theta} - 1}$

c) $\dfrac{1 + \sin \theta}{1 - \sin \theta} = \dfrac{\frac{1}{\sin \theta} + 1}{\frac{1}{\sin \theta} - 1}$

d) $\left(\dfrac{1}{\cos \theta} + \tan \theta\right)(1 - \sin \theta) = \cos \theta$

✓ **6.** Prove each identity.

a) $\dfrac{\sin^2 \theta}{\tan^2 \theta} = 1 - \sin^2 \theta$

b) $\dfrac{1}{\sin^2 \theta} - 1 = \dfrac{\cos^2 \theta}{\sin^2 \theta}$

c) $\sin^2 \theta = \dfrac{\tan^2 \theta}{1 + \tan^2 \theta}$

d) $\sin \theta + \dfrac{\cos \theta}{\tan \theta} = \dfrac{1}{\cos \theta \tan \theta}$

✓ **7. Application**

a) Prove this identity.
$$\sin \theta + \cos \theta = \sin \theta \cos \theta\left(\dfrac{1}{\sin \theta} + \dfrac{1}{\cos \theta}\right)$$

b) Predict a similar identity for the expression $\sin \theta + \tan \theta$, then prove it is correct.

c) Establish another identity, similar to those in parts a and b.

8. a) Prove this identity.
$$\tan^2 \theta = \left(\dfrac{1}{\cos \theta} - 1\right)\left(\dfrac{1}{\cos \theta} + 1\right)$$

b) Predict a similar identity for $\dfrac{1}{\tan^2 \theta}$, then prove it is correct.

9. Prove each identity.

a) $(1 + \tan^2 \theta)(1 - \cos^2 \theta) = \tan^2 \theta$

b) $\left(1 + \dfrac{1}{\tan^2 \theta}\right)(1 - \sin^2 \theta) = \dfrac{1}{\tan^2 \theta}$

10. Prove each identity.

a) $\tan \theta + \dfrac{1}{\tan \theta} = \dfrac{1}{\sin \theta \cos \theta}$

b) $\dfrac{1}{\cos^2 \theta} + \dfrac{1}{\sin^2 \theta} = \dfrac{1}{\sin^2 \theta \cos^2 \theta}$

c) $\dfrac{1}{\sin^2 \theta} + \dfrac{1}{\cos^2 \theta} = \left(\tan \theta + \dfrac{1}{\tan \theta}\right)^2$

d) $\sin^2 \theta = \cos \theta \left(\dfrac{1}{\cos \theta} - \cos \theta\right)$

11. **Communication** Prove the identity $\dfrac{\cos \theta}{1 + \sin \theta} + \dfrac{\cos \theta}{1 - \sin \theta} = \dfrac{2}{\cos \theta}$.

Write to explain why the identity is not true for $\theta = \dfrac{\pi}{2}$ and $\dfrac{3\pi}{2}$.

12. a) Prove the identity $\dfrac{1}{1 + \sin \theta} + \dfrac{1}{1 - \sin \theta} = \dfrac{2}{\cos^2 \theta}$.

b) Establish a similar identity for $\dfrac{1}{1 + \cos \theta} + \dfrac{1}{1 - \cos \theta}$.

13. Prove each identity.

a) $\dfrac{1 + \sin \theta}{\cos \theta} = \dfrac{\cos \theta}{1 - \sin \theta}$

b) $\dfrac{1 + \sin \theta + \cos \theta}{1 - \sin \theta + \cos \theta} = \dfrac{1 + \sin \theta}{\cos \theta}$

14. Prove each identity.

a) $(\cos \theta - \sin \theta)^2 = 1 - 2 \sin \theta \cos \theta$

b) $\cos^4 \theta - \sin^4 \theta = \cos^2 \theta - \sin^2 \theta$

c) $\dfrac{\tan^2 \theta}{1 + \tan^2 \theta} = \sin^2 \theta$

d) $\dfrac{\tan \theta + \cos \theta}{\sin \theta} = \dfrac{1}{\cos \theta} + \dfrac{\cos \theta}{\sin \theta}$

15. **Thinking/Inquiry/Problem Solving** Determine an identity (different from any in these exercises) that involves all 3 trigonometric ratios.

a) Verify your identity numerically.

b) Prove your identity algebraically.

c) Write to explain how you found the identity.

C

16. Prove the identity $\dfrac{1 - \sin \theta}{1 + \sin \theta} = \tan \theta + \dfrac{1}{\cos \theta}$.

1. Convert to radians. Express each angle in terms of π.

   a) $15°$ **b)** $105°$ **c)** $40°$ **d)** $310°$

2. Convert to degrees.

   a) $\dfrac{2\pi}{3}$ radians   **b)** $\dfrac{\pi}{8}$ radians

   c) $\dfrac{7\pi}{4}$ radians   **d)** $\dfrac{11\pi}{6}$ radians

3. Determine the length of the arc that subtends each angle at the centre of a circle, radius 3.0 cm.

   a) 2.4 radians   **b)** 3.9 radians   **c)** $195°$ **d)** $320°$

4. State each exact value.

   a) $\cos \dfrac{\pi}{6}$ **b)** $\sin \dfrac{7\pi}{6}$ **c)** $\tan \dfrac{5\pi}{3}$

   d) $\sin \dfrac{9\pi}{4}$ **e)** $\cos \dfrac{4\pi}{3}$ **f)** $\tan \dfrac{11\pi}{2}$

5. Explain how you know that $\dfrac{7\pi}{6}$ is in Quadrant III.

6. Determine two angles between 0 and 2π that have each trigonometric ratio. Write the angles to 2 decimal places.

   a) $\tan \theta = 1.84$ **b)** $\sin \theta = 0.49$ **c)** $\cos \theta = 0.08$

   d) $\sin \theta = -0.25$ **e)** $\cos \theta = -0.63$ **f)** $\tan \theta = -2.40$

7. Solve each equation for $0 \le \theta \le 2\pi$.

   a) $\cos \theta = \dfrac{2}{5}$ **b)** $\tan \theta = 1$

   c) $\sin \theta = -\dfrac{4}{5}$ **d)** $(2 \cos \theta + \sqrt{3})(\cos \theta - 1) = 0$

   e) $\sin \theta \left(\sin \theta - \dfrac{1}{\sqrt{2}} \right) = 0$ **f)** $(\tan \theta - 1)(\tan \theta + \sqrt{3}) = 0$

8. Solve each equation for $0 \le \theta \le 2\pi$.

   a) $2 \sin^2 \theta + \sin \theta - 1 = 0$ **b)** $4 \cos^2 \theta - 1 = 0$

   c) $\sin^2 \theta + 2 \sin \theta - 3 = 0$ **d)** $3 \tan^2 \theta - 2\sqrt{3} \tan \theta + 1 = 0$

   e) $\cos^2 \theta - 2 \cos \theta + 1 = 0$ **f)** $\sin^2 \theta + 4 \sin \theta + 2 = 0$

9. Prove each identity.

   a) $\tan \theta + \dfrac{1}{\tan \theta} = \dfrac{1}{\sin \theta \cos \theta}$ **b)** $\dfrac{\sin \theta}{1 + \cos \theta} + \dfrac{1 + \cos \theta}{\sin \theta} = \dfrac{2}{\sin \theta}$

   c) $\tan \theta + \dfrac{\cos \theta}{1 + \sin \theta} = \dfrac{1}{\cos \theta}$ **d)** $\dfrac{\tan \theta - \sin \theta}{\sin^3 \theta} = \dfrac{1}{\cos \theta(1 + \cos \theta)}$

10. Is $\sin \theta = \cos \theta$ an identity? Explain.

The 2-3-4 Triangle

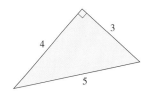

Since $3^2 + 4^2 = 5^2$, a triangle with sides 3, 4, and 5 satisfies the Pythagorean Theorem, and contains an angle of 90°. Any triangle whose side lengths are in the ratio 3 : 4 : 5 is similar to this triangle. All these similar triangles are called *3-4-5 triangles*. We represent these lengths on a diagram without units, as shown. For example, all the triangles with the following side lengths are 3-4-5 triangles, and this diagram represents all of them.

$$3 \text{ cm}, \quad 4 \text{ cm}, \quad 5 \text{ cm}$$
$$6 \text{ cm}, \quad 8 \text{ cm}, \quad 10 \text{ cm}$$
$$1.5 \text{ m}, \quad 2.0 \text{ m}, \quad 2.5 \text{ m}$$

Property of a 3-4-5 triangle

A 3-4-5 triangle is a right triangle.

Formulating Questions

The numbers 3, 4, and 5 are consecutive integers. Other triangles can have sides that are consecutive integers. Here are the problems we shall investigate.

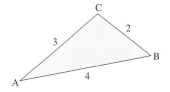

- Do the angles in a 2-3-4 triangle have any special properties?

- What other problems does this bring to mind, and what results can we find?

Representing the Angles in Mathematical Form

The diagram (above right) shows △ABC with sides 2, 3, and 4. We can calculate the angles using the Cosine Law three times.

$$a^2 = b^2 + c^2 - 2bc \cos A$$
$$2^2 = 3^2 + 4^2 - 2(3)(4) \cos A$$
$$\cos A = \frac{9 + 16 - 4}{24}$$
$$= \frac{7}{8}$$
$$A \doteq 28.955\,024\,37°$$

$$b^2 = a^2 + c^2 - 2ac \cos B$$
$$3^2 = 2^2 + 4^2 - 2(2)(4) \cos B$$
$$\cos B = \frac{4 + 16 - 9}{16}$$
$$= \frac{11}{16}$$
$$B \doteq 46.567\,463\,44°$$

$$c^2 = a^2 + b^2 - 2ab \cos C$$
$$4^2 = 2^2 + 3^2 - 2(2)(3) \cos C$$
$$\cos C = \frac{4 + 9 - 16}{12}$$
$$= -\frac{1}{4}$$
$$C \doteq 104.477\,512\,2°$$

For simplicity, we omit the angle signs on ∠A, ∠B, and ∠C.
The angles are approximately 29°, 47°, and 104°, but no special property
is evident. Let us calculate the ratios of these angles, dividing the larger
angle by the smaller angle each time:

$$\frac{B}{A} = \frac{46.567\ 463\ 44°}{28.955\ 024\ 37°} \doteq 1.608\ 268\ 8$$

$$\frac{C}{B} = \frac{104.477\ 512\ 2°}{46.567\ 463\ 44°} \doteq 2.243\ 573\ 2$$

$$\frac{C}{A} = \frac{104.477\ 512\ 2°}{28.955\ 024\ 37°} \doteq 3.608\ 268\ 8$$

The decimals in two of the ratios are the same. This could be a
coincidence, but it is more likely that there is an underlying pattern.
Since the third ratio is 2 more than the first ratio, we write:

$$2 + \frac{B}{A} = \frac{C}{A}$$

Multiply each side by A.

$$2A + B = C$$

This equation illustrates a simple relationship among the angles of a
2-3-4 triangle.

Property of a 2-3-4 triangle

The angles in a 2-3-4 triangle have this property:

$2 \times$ (smallest angle) + (middle angle) = (largest angle)

This property has not
been proved here. Can
you explain why? For a
proof of the property,
see problem 9.

Interpreting Information and Forming Conclusions

Our success in finding an angle property for a 2-3-4 triangle
suggests that we might look for similar properties in other
triangles with consecutive integer sides. See problems 1 and 2.

The sides of each triangle in problems 1 and 2 are in arithmetic
sequence. This suggests that we might investigate triangles with
sides in geometric sequence. See problems 6 and 8.

In the problem on page 311, we started with a side property and
developed an angle property. This suggests that we could start
with an angle property and try to develop a side property. The
angles could be in arithmetic sequence (problems 4a, 7) or in
geometric sequence (problem 5).

In problems 1 and 2, you will determine relationships among
angles in a triangle. In any triangle, we know that the angles are
always related: their sum is 180°. In each problem, you will
determine a relationship different from this.

*Selecting Strategies,
Resources,
Technology,
and Tools*

- You could use the
  Cosine Law 3 times,
  as on page 311.
  What other ways are
  there to determine
  the 3 angles?
- You could use a
  scientific calculator to
  do the calculations.
- You could set up a
  spreadsheet to solve
  a triangle when 3
  sides are known.
- You could construct
  the triangles, then
  make accurate
  measurements to
  confirm the results.

1. a) Determine the angles in a 4-5-6 triangle (below left).

   b) Find out whether any angles are related. Describe how these angles are related.

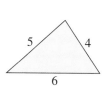 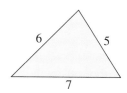 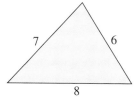

2. a) Determine the angles in a 5-6-7 triangle and in a 6-7-8 triangle (above middle and right).

   b) In one of these triangles, the three angles are related. Describe how they are related.

   c) Compare the angles in the 6-7-8 triangle with the angles in the 2-3-4 triangle on page 311. What do you notice?

The relationship in problem 2c is the key to proving the angle property of a 2-3-4 triangle. See problem 9.

3. A mathematician who read the problem about the 2-3-4 triangle and the results of problems 1 and 2 wrote the comments in the margin.

   a) Read the comments. Then explain each statement.
   i) "The Sine Law gives us $3 \sin A = 2 \sin B$."
   ii) "The relationship $2A + B = C$ gives us $3A + 2B = 180$."
   iii) "$3A + 2B = 180$ means that $\sin 3A = \sin 2B$."

   b) Verify that the values of A and B on page 311 satisfy these equations:
   $$3 \sin A = 2 \sin B$$
   $$\sin 3A = \sin 2B$$

4. a) The 30°-60°-90° triangle is a right triangle with angles in arithmetic sequence. Explain why there is no other right triangle with angles in arithmetic sequence.

   b) The 3-4-5 triangle is a right triangle with sides in arithmetic sequence. Explain why there is no other right triangle with sides in arithmetic sequence.

5. The right triangle shown has angles in geometric sequence.

   a) Write two equations that relate a and r. Solve the equations. Use the results to determine the angles in degrees.

   b) In this triangle, the first term of the sequence corresponds to the smallest angle. Suppose the first term corresponds to the right angle. Would you get the same triangle or a different triangle? Explain.

"The integer sided triangle stuff is awesome. I've never seen anything like it before. I can hardly believe those results, but they certainly hold. It has that 'irresistible' quality to it. Just playing with the 2-3-4 triangle, I observe that the Sine Law gives us:
   $3 \sin A = 2 \sin B$,
and the relationship $2A + B = C$ gives us
   $3A + 2B = 180$,
which means that
   $\sin 3A = \sin 2B$.
Huh?!! That's quite a stunner right there."

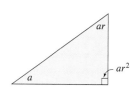

6. The right triangle shown has sides in geometric sequence.

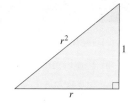

a) Write an equation for r. Solve the equation. Use the result to determine the angles in degrees.

b) In this triangle, the first term of the sequence corresponds to the shorter leg of the triangle. Suppose the first term corresponds to the hypotenuse. Would you get the same triangle or a different triangle? Explain.

7. The 45°-60°-75° triangle has angles in arithmetic sequence. In △ABC, AB = 1, ∠A = 45°, and ∠B = 60°. Without using a calculator, find exact expressions for:

a) the lengths of AC and BC

b) sin 75°, cos 75°, and tan 75°

c) sin 15°, cos 15°, and tan 15°

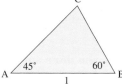

Since the trigonometric ratios of 45° and 60° involve $\sqrt{2}$ and $\sqrt{3}$, we expect the answers in problem 7 to involve $\sqrt{2}$ and $\sqrt{3}$.

Challenge Problems

8. When a, ar, and ar^2 represent the side lengths of a triangle, we can divide them by a to obtain a similar triangle with sides 1, r, and r^2. We call this a 1-r-r^2 triangle.

a) Explain why there are some values of r that do not correspond to triangles.

b) For what values of r is it possible to have a 1-r-r^2 triangle? Illustrate your solution with some examples.

9. In the diagram, CD = CB = 6, DB = 3, and AD = 4.

a) **i)** Prove that AC = 8.

ii) Prove that CD bisects ∠ACB.

b) Explain why the results in part a prove the following properties.

i) In a 6-7-8 triangle,
(smallest angle) + $\frac{1}{2}$(middle angle) = (largest angle)

ii) In a 2-3-4 triangle,
2(smallest angle) + (middle angle) = (largest angle)

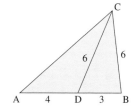

10. In the diagram, BC = 4, AC = 5, AB = 6, and point D is on AB so that AD = CD.

a) **i)** Prove that AD = $\frac{10}{3}$.

ii) Prove that ∠DCB = ∠A.

b) Explain why these results prove this property: In a 4-5-6 triangle, the largest angle is double the smallest angle.

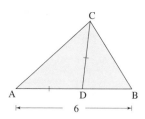

Trigonometry Tools

Sine Law

$$\frac{\sin A}{a} = \frac{\sin B}{b} = \frac{\sin C}{c}$$

or, $\quad\dfrac{a}{\sin A} = \dfrac{b}{\sin B} = \dfrac{c}{\sin C}$

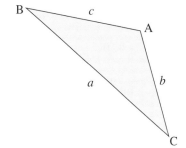

Cosine Law

$$a^2 = b^2 + c^2 - 2bc \cos A$$

or, $\quad b^2 = a^2 + c^2 - 2ac \cos B$

or, $\quad c^2 = a^2 + b^2 - 2ab \cos C$

Radians and Degrees

Radians and degrees are related by π radians $= 180°$.

Converting from degrees to radians:
There are fewer radians than degrees.
Multiply by $\dfrac{\pi}{180}$.

Converting from radians to degrees:
There are more degrees than radians.
Multiply by $\dfrac{180}{\pi}$.

Definitions of sin θ, cos θ, and tan θ

Point P is any point on the unit circle and θ is the measure of an angle in standard position.

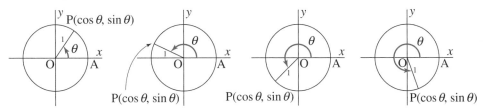

cos θ is the first coordinate of P.

sin θ is the second coordinate of P.

$\tan \theta = \dfrac{\sin \theta}{\cos \theta}$, where $\cos \theta \neq 0$

θ can be in degrees or in radians.

Trigonometric Functions of an Angle θ

	Quadrant I	Quadrant II	Quadrant III	Quadrant IV
sin θ	+	+	−	−
cos θ	+	−	−	+
tan θ	+	−	+	−

Trigonometric Identities

The Pythagorean identity: $\sin^2 \theta + \cos^2 \theta = 1$

The quotient identity: $\tan \theta = \dfrac{\sin \theta}{\cos \theta}$, $\cos \theta \neq 0$

Sine, Cosine, and Tangent of Special Angles

θ	$0°, 0$	$30°, \frac{\pi}{6}$	$45°, \frac{\pi}{4}$	$60°, \frac{\pi}{3}$	$90°, \frac{\pi}{2}$
$\sin \theta$	0	$\frac{1}{2}$	$\frac{1}{\sqrt{2}}$	$\frac{\sqrt{3}}{2}$	1
$\cos \theta$	1	$\frac{\sqrt{3}}{2}$	$\frac{1}{\sqrt{2}}$	$\frac{1}{2}$	0
$\tan \theta$	0	$\frac{1}{\sqrt{3}}$	1	$\sqrt{3}$	undefined

5.1

1. Predict whether each value will be positive or negative. Sketch each angle on a coordinate grid.

    a) $\tan 167°$ **b)** $\sin 99°$ **c)** $\cos 132°$

2. Given that $0° \leq \theta \leq 180°$, determine the value(s) of θ to 1 decimal place.

    a) $\cos \theta = 0.4772$ **b)** $\tan \theta = -0.2272$ **c)** $\sin \theta = 0.5476$

    d) $\tan \theta = 1.6191$ **e)** $\sin \theta = 0.3486$ **f)** $\cos \theta = -0.5577$

3. Angle θ is obtuse.

    a) $\tan \theta = -0.4452$; calculate $\sin \theta$ to 4 decimal places.

    b) $\sin \theta = 0.9707$; calculate $\cos \theta$ to 4 decimal places.

5.2

4. A regular tetrahedron ABCD has edge length 2 cm (below left). Calculate the angle between AD and the face BCD.

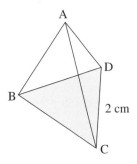

2 cm

5. The hour hand of a clock is 5 cm long and the minute hand is 6 cm long (bottom right, page 316). Calculate the distance between the ends of the hands at 5 o'clock.

6. Solve each triangle.

   a) $\triangle ABC$ in which $BC = 62.5$ cm, $\angle A = 112°$, and $\angle C = 42°$

   b) $\triangle PQR$ in which $QR = 42.2$ cm, $PQ = 21.2$ cm, and $\angle P = 100.5°$

   c) $\triangle XYZ$ in which $XY = 31$ mm, $XZ = 52$ mm, and $\angle X = 33°$

7. Triangle ABC has area 30 cm², $AC = 9$ cm, and $BC = 7$ cm. Calculate the measure of $\angle ACB$ and the largest possible length of AB.

5.3   **8.** Sketch each angle θ in standard position, then write a coterminal angle.

   a) $\theta = 170°$ **b)** $\theta = 293°$ **c)** $\theta = -30°$ **d)** $\theta = -320°$

   e) $\theta = 450°$ **f)** $\theta = 600°$ **g)** $\theta = -370°$ **h)** $\theta = 200°$

5.4   **9.** Determine two angles between 0° and 360° that have each trigonometric function value. Write the angle to the nearest degree.

   a) $\sin \theta = 0.42$ **b)** $\cos \theta = -0.31$ **c)** $\tan \theta = 3.46$

10. The point $P(4, -15)$ lies on the terminal arm of an angle θ in standard position. Determine each trigonometric function value to 3 decimal places.

   a) $\sin \theta$ **b)** $\cos \theta$ **c)** $\tan \theta$

11. The terminal arm of an angle θ lies in Quadrant II on the line with equation $4x + 3y = 0$. Determine each trigonometric function value.

   a) $\sin \theta$ **b)** $\cos \theta$ **c)** $\tan \theta$

5.5   **12.** State each exact value. Do not use a calculator.

   a) $\cos 135°$ **b)** $\tan 225°$ **c)** $\sin 210°$ **d)** $\dfrac{1}{\tan 60°}$

13. Simplify each expression. Do not use a calculator.

   a) $\sin 30° + \cos 60°$ **b)** $\tan 45° + \tan 225°$ **c)** $\sin 240° + \cos 300°$

14. Use a calculator to verify each result.

   a) $\sin 67.5° = \sqrt{\dfrac{1 + \sqrt{2}}{2\sqrt{2}}}$ **b)** $\tan 195° = \dfrac{\sqrt{3} - 1}{\sqrt{3} + 1}$

5.6   **15.** Convert to radians. Express each angle in terms of π.

   a) $30°$ **b)** $225°$ **c)** $315°$ **d)** $210°$

16. Convert to degrees. Express each angle to 1 decimal place.

a) 2 radians **b)** 0.6 radians **c)** 5.4 radians **d)** $\frac{\pi}{7}$

17. An arc of a circle, centre O, subtends an angle of 1.5 radians at the centre. Determine the ratio of the length of arc AB to the length of line segment AB.

5.7 **18.** For each expression below:

  i) Determine its exact value.
  ii) Determine two other angles that have the same trigonometric function value.

a) $\sin \frac{2\pi}{3}$ **b)** $\cos \frac{7\pi}{4}$ **c)** $\tan \frac{5\pi}{6}$

19. Determine two angles between 0 and 2π that have each trigonometric function value. Write the angles to 2 decimal places.

a) $\cos \theta = 0.82$ **b)** $\tan \theta = 1.42$ **c)** $\sin \theta = 0.43$

d) $\sin \theta = -0.51$ **e)** $\cos \theta = -0.21$ **f)** $\tan \theta = -2.61$

5.8 **20.** Solve each equation for $0 \le \theta \le 2\pi$.

a) $7 \cos \theta = 3$ **b)** $5 \sin \theta - 1 = 0$ **c)** $\tan \theta + \sqrt{3} = 0$

21. Solve each equation for $0 \le \theta \le 2\pi$. Give exact answers where possible.

a) $(2 \cos \theta - 1)(\cos \theta + \frac{1}{\sqrt{3}}) = 0$ **b)** $(\tan \theta - 1)(\tan \theta + \sqrt{3}) = 0$

c) $\left(\sin \theta + \frac{1}{\sqrt{2}} \right)\left(\sin \theta - \frac{\sqrt{3}}{2} \right) = 0$ **d)** $(2 \cos \theta + \sqrt{3})(\tan \theta + 1) = 0$

22. Solve each equation for $0 \le \theta \le 2\pi$.

a) $\sin \theta - 2 \sin^2 \theta = 0$ **b)** $2 \cos^2 \theta - 3 \cos \theta - 2 = 0$

c) $3 \tan^2 \theta - \tan \theta = 0$ **d)** $8 \sin^2 \theta - 6 \sin \theta + 1 = 0$

23. Solve each equation for $0 \le \theta \le 2\pi$.

a) $2 \cos^2 \theta = 1 - \sin \theta$ **b)** $\cos \theta + 1 - 2 \sin^2 \theta = 0$

c) $5 \cos^2 \theta - 12 \sin \theta + 6 = 0$ **d)** $5 - 6 \sin^2 \theta - \cos \theta = 0$

5.9 **24.** Prove each identity.

a) $(\sin \theta + \cos \theta)^2 = 1 + 2 \sin \theta \cos \theta$ **b)** $\frac{1}{\cos \theta} - \tan \theta \sin \theta = \cos \theta$

c) $\sin^2 \theta \left(1 + \frac{1}{\tan^2 \theta} \right) = 1$ **d)** $\frac{\cos \theta}{1 + \sin \theta} - \frac{1}{\cos \theta} = -\tan \theta$

25. Prove each identity.

a) $\frac{\tan \theta - \sin \theta}{\sin^3 \theta} = \frac{1}{\cos \theta (1 + \cos \theta)}$ **b)** $\tan^2 \theta \cos^2 \theta + \frac{\sin^2 \theta}{\tan^2 \theta} = 1$

Self-Test

1. **Knowledge/Understanding** Angle θ is obtuse, and $\cos \theta = -0.7593$.
   Determine $\sin \theta$ and $\tan \theta$.

2. Solve each triangle.

   a)

   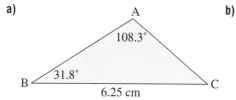

   A
   108.3°
   31.8°
   B
   6.25 cm
   C

   b)

   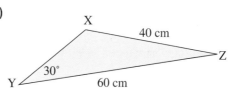

   X
   40 cm
   30°
   Y
   60 cm
   Z

3. Sketch each angle in standard position, then write two coterminal angles.
   a) 309°   b) 148°   c) −54°

4. Convert each angle in exercise 3 to radians.

5. **Application** The terminal arm of an angle θ lies in Quadrant III on the line
   with equation $5x - 2y = 0$.
   a) Sketch a diagram to illustrate the angle θ.
   b) Determine the exact value of each trigonometric function of θ.
   c) Calculate θ to the nearest degree.

6. Solve each equation for $0 \le \theta \le 2\pi$.
   a) $\tan \theta = 0.24$ b) $2 \sin \theta - 3 = 0$
   c) $\sin \theta(3 - 4\cos^2 \theta) = 0$ d) $(1 + 2 \sin \theta)(2 + \sin \theta) = 0$

7. **Thinking/Inquiry/Problem Solving** To get around an obstruction, an oil
   pipeline is constructed in two straight sections, one 3.675 km long and the
   other 4.765 km long. The sections are joined so the angle between the
   sections is 168°. How much more pipe is necessary due to the obstruction?

8. **Communication** A decorative glass panel is
   surrounded by a metal frame. The panel is
   made of two congruent circular sectors and
   an isosceles triangle. Write to explain how
   you would calculate the length of the
   metal frame.

   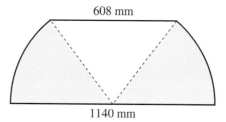

   608 mm
   1140 mm

9. Explain how you could use an equilateral triangle with side length 2 units to
   demonstrate the exact values of the trigonometric functions of 30° and 60°.

10. Solve each equation for $0 \leq \theta \leq 2\pi$.

a) $2\sin^2\theta - \sin\theta - 1 = 0$

b) $\sin^2\theta = 2\cos\theta - 2$

c) $2\cos^2\theta - \sin\theta + 1 = 0$

d) $\tan^2\theta + 2\tan\theta - 5 = 0$

11. Prove each identity.

a) $\dfrac{1 + \sin\theta}{\tan\theta} = \cos\theta + \dfrac{1}{\tan\theta}$

b) $\left(\tan\theta + \dfrac{1}{\tan\theta}\right)^2 = \dfrac{1}{\cos^2\theta} + \dfrac{1}{\sin^2\theta}$

c) $\dfrac{\sin^2\theta - 1}{\cos^2\theta - 1} = \dfrac{1}{\sin^2\theta} - 1$

d) $\dfrac{1}{1 - \sin\theta} + \dfrac{1}{1 + \sin\theta} = \dfrac{2}{\cos^2\theta}$

12. A radar scanner rotates at a speed of 30 revolutions per minute. Express its rotation in:

a) degrees per second

b) radians per second

Assessment Tasks

1. Triangle ABC has side lengths AB = 4, BC = 3, and $\angle$A = 30°.

a) Use the Cosine Law to calculate the length of AC.

b) Use the Sine Law to calculate the length of AC.

c) Draw a diagram to explain your answers to parts a and b. Which method of calculation is easier? Explain.

2. To 4 decimal places,

$\cos 10° = 0.9848 = \sin 100°$
$\cos 20° = 0.9397 = \sin 110°$
$\cos 30° = 0.8660 = \sin 120°$

From these results, we could conjecture that $\cos\theta = \sin(\theta + 90°)$.
Is this always true? Is it sometimes true?
Investigate the conjecture. Write a report of your findings.

3. On the same grid, sketch the circle $x^2 + y^2 = 25$ and the line $y = 10 - 2x$.
Label the points of intersection A and B. Calculate the length of the arc AB.

Graphing Trigonometric Functions

INSIGHTS INTO A RICH PROBLEM

There are many physical phenomena that can be modelled by sine or cosine functions. One example we use throughout the chapter is a weight attached to a spring. For convenience, we assume the weight oscillates indefinitely. In reality, forces such as friction and air resistance cause the oscillations to decrease over time.

At the end of this chapter, you will consider the effect of these forces and determine the equation of motion of a damped spring.

Curriculum Expectations

By the end of this chapter, you will:

- Sketch the graphs of $y = \sin x$ and $y = \cos x$, and describe their periodic properties.

- Determine, through investigation, using graphing calculators or graphing software, the effect of simple transformations on the graphs and equations of $y = \sin x$ and $y = \cos x$.

- Determine the amplitude, period, phase shift, domain, and range of sinusoidal functions whose equations are given in the form $y = a \sin (kx + d) + c$ or $y = a \cos (kx + d) + c$.

- Sketch the graphs of simple sinusoidal functions.

- Write the equation of a sinusoidal function, given its graph and given its properties.

- Sketch the graph of $y = \tan x$; identify the period, domain, and range of the function; and explain the occurrence of asymptotes.

- Determine, through investigation, the periodic properties of various models of sinusoidal functions drawn from a variety of applications.

- Explain the relationship between the properties of a sinusoidal function and the parameters of its equation, within the context of an application, and over a restricted domain.

- Predict the effects on the mathematical model of an application involving sinusoidal functions when the conditions in the application are varied.

- Pose and solve problems related to models of sinusoidal functions drawn from a variety of applications, and communicate the solutions with clarity and justification, using appropriate mathematical forms.

- Communicate solutions to problems and to findings of investigations clearly and concisely, orally and in writing … .

- Use graphing technology effectively.

1. Review: Transformations of Quadratic Functions

Remember how the graph of $y = a(x - p)^2 + q$ is related to the graph of $y = x^2$.

$x - p = 0$ is the axis of symmetry.

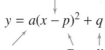

$$y = a(x - p)^2 + q$$

Congruent to the parabola $y = ax^2$

Coordinates of the vertex are (p, q).

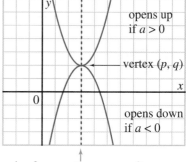

opens up if $a > 0$

vertex (p, q)

opens down if $a < 0$

axis of symmetry $x - p = 0$, or $x = p$

Example

Sketch the graph of $y = 0.5(x - 4)^2 - 3$.

Solution

$y = 0.5(x - 4)^2 - 3$

Plot the vertex, $(4, -3)$.

Draw the axis of symmetry, $x = 4$.

Determine the y-intercept.

Substitute $x = 0$.

$y = 0.5(0 - 4)^2 - 3$

$\quad = 0.5(16) - 3$

$\quad = 5$

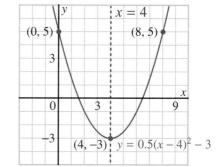

The y-intercept is 5. By symmetry, a third point on the parabola is $(8, 5)$.

Plot the points $(0, 5)$ and $(8, 5)$.

Draw a smooth curve through these points and the vertex.

In the *Example*, the graph of $y = 0.5(x - 4)^2 - 3$ is the *image* of the graph of $y = x^2$ after a transformation.

Exercises

1. Sketch the graph of each function.

a) $y = (x - 2)^2 - 4$ **b)** $y = 2(x + 4)^2 - 2$ **c)** $y = -(x + 4)^2 + 1$

d) $y = -(x - 6)^2 + 4$ **e)** $y = 0.5(x - 3)^2 - 5$ **f)** $y = -0.5(x - 3)^2 - 5$

2. Describe the transformation(s) that would transform the graph of $y = x^2$ to the graph of each function.

a) $y = 3x^2$ **b)** $y = -x^2$ **c)** $y = -0.5x^2$

d) $y = (x + 1)^2 - 2$ **e)** $y = 2(x - 3)^2 + 4$ **f)** $y = -2(x - 3)^2 + 4$

2. New: The Domain and Range of a Function

The use of some calculator keys illustrates the concept of a function. When you press ⬜, then enter 7.5 (the input number), the calculator displays 2.738612788 (the output number). But when you press ⬜, then enter –4, the calculator displays an error message. The input numbers must be *valid*. For the square-root function $y = \sqrt{x}$, the valid input numbers are the values of x so that $x \geq 0$. The output numbers are the values of y so that $y \geq 0$.

Take Note

Definitions of the Domain and Range of a Function

A *function* is a rule that gives a single output number for every valid input number.

The set of valid input numbers is the *domain* of the function.

The set of output numbers is the *range* of the function.

Example

a) Graph the function $y = (x - 2)^2$.

b) State the domain and range of the function.

Solution

a) The equation $y = a(x - p)^2 + q$ represents a parabola with vertex (p, q).
Therefore, $y = (x - 2)^2$ represents a parabola with vertex $(2, 0)$.
Substitute $x = 0$ to obtain another point on the parabola, $(0, 4)$.
By symmetry, a third point on the parabola is $(4, 4)$.
Use these points to graph the parabola.

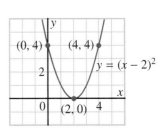

b) We can substitute any real number for x into the equation.
So, the domain of the function is the set of all real numbers.
The calculated values of y will be either 0 or positive.
So, the range is the set of all non-negative real numbers, $y \geq 0$.

In this book, all functions involve the set of real numbers. Functions that involve complex numbers occur in university-level mathematics.

Take Note

Visualizing the Domain and Range of a Function

Consider the graph of a function and visualize its shadows on the coordinate axes.

The shadow on the horizontal axis corresponds to the domain.

The shadow on the vertical axis corresponds to the range.

Exercises

1. State the domain and range of each function.

a)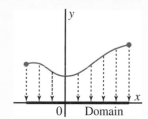

b)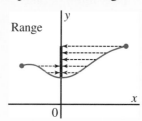

c)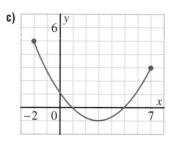

2. Sketch the graph of each function. State its domain and range.

a) $y = x + 2$
b) $y = 2 - x$
c) $y = x^2 + 2$

d) $y = (x + 2)^2$
e) $y = (x - 3)^2 + 1$
f) $y = -(x - 3)^2 + 1$

3. Determine the domain and range of each function.

a) $y = x^2$ **b)** $y = x^2 - 4$ **c)** $y = (x - 2)^2 - 3$

d) $y = 0.5x^2 + 6$ **e)** $y = 6 - x^2$ **f)** $y = -2(x + 1)^2 + 4$

4. A rectangle has perimeter 20 cm.

a) Write an equation to express its length as a function of its width.

b) What are the domain and range of the function?

5. For each triangle, express y as a function of x. What are the domain and range of each function?

a)

b)

3. New: Independent and Dependent Variables

Consider the equation of a function such as $y = x^2 + 5$. We use this equation to determine values of y when values of x are given. Since the value of y depends on the value of x, we call y the dependent variable. Since we can substitute any value of x in the equation of the function, we call x the independent variable.

Take Note

Independent and Dependent Variables

A function is a rule that gives a single output number for every valid input number.

The variable that represents input numbers is the *independent* variable (the domain).

The variable that represents output numbers is the *dependent* variable (the range).

Exercises

1. Identify the independent variable and the dependent variable for each function.

a) $y = 5x - 2x^2$ **b)** $A = 1000(1.06)^n$

c) $P = \dfrac{5000}{(1 + i)^{10}}$ **d)** $V = \dfrac{4}{3}\pi r^3$

e) $P = 3l$ **f)** $y = -(x + 1)^2 + 5$

2. Identify the independent variable and the dependent variable for each function.

a)

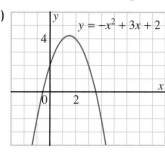

b)

$y = -x^2 + 3x + 2$

c)

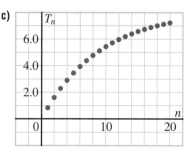

d) Revenue from Manufacturing Canoes

e) Invest $1000 Per Year for 40 Years

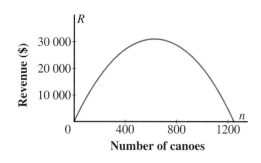
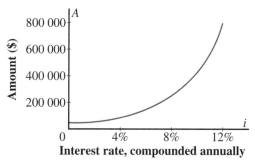

f) Ontario Teachers by Age, 2000

g) Height of a Bouncing Ball

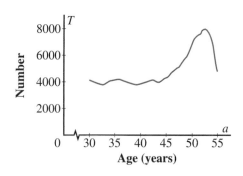
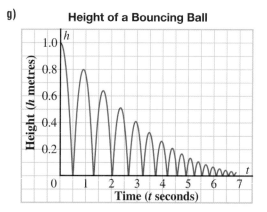

4. New: Absolute Value

On the number line below, each of the numbers –4 and 4 is located 4 units from 0. We say that each number has an absolute value of 4. The absolute value of a number is its distance from 0 on a number line.

We write: $|-4| = 4$ and $|4| = 4$.

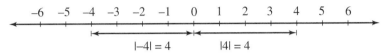

The definition of the absolute value of a number depends on whether the number is positive or negative.

Take Note

Definition of Absolute Value

If a number is positive or zero, its *absolute value* is the number itself.

If $x \geq 0$, then $|x| = x$

If a number is negative, its *absolute value* is the opposite number.

If $x < 0$, then $|x| = -x$

Example 1

Simplify.

a) $|12|$

b) $|-7|$

Solution

a) The absolute value of a positive number is the number itself.
   $|12| = 12$

b) The absolute value of a negative number is the opposite number.
   $|-7| = 7$

Example 2

Mark on a number line all the values of x that satisfy each inequality.

a) $|x| \le 5$ **b)** $|x| > 4$

Solution

a) $|x| \le 5$

The absolute value of x is less than or equal to 5; that is, x lies between −5 and 5, inclusive.

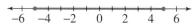

The solid dots at −5 and 5 indicate that they are part of the solution.

b) $|x| > 4$

The absolute value of x is greater than 4; that is, x is greater than 4 or less than −4.

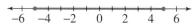

The open dots at −4 and 4 indicate that they are not part of the solution.

Discuss

How can you check the solutions?

In *Example 2a*, we can write $|x| \le 5$ as $-5 \le x \le 5$.
In *Example 2b*, we can write $|x| > 4$ as $x > 4$ or $x < -4$.

Exercises

1. Simplify.

   a) $|-9|$ **b)** $|4.2|$ **c)** $|-100|$ **d)** $|15|$ **e)** $|-3.14|$

2. Mark on a number line all the values of x that satisfy each equation.

   a) $|x| = 6$ **b)** $|x| = 3$ **c)** $|x - 1| = 3$ **d)** $|x| = x$

3. Mark on a number line all the values of x that satisfy each inequality.

   a) $|x| < 1$ **b)** $|x| > 2$ **c)** $|x| \le 3$ **d)** $|x| \ge x$

In this chapter, we will investigate a certain type of change that occurs frequently in the world around us. Trigonometry provides a new set of tools for modelling quantities that change in a regular way.

Swinging pendulum

The photograph shows a pendulum in a clock. The graph shows how the distance from the pendulum bob to the central position (when the pendulum is vertical) changes as the bob swings back and forth.

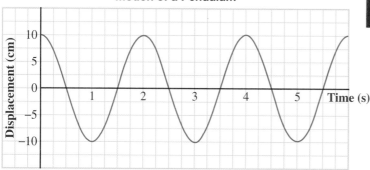

Motion of a Pendulum

Hours of sunlight

Each year, days grow longer as summer approaches, only to shorten as winter begins. The number of hours of sunlight follows a regular pattern, as the graph of hours of sunlight in Windsor demonstrates. The day number 0 represents January 1.

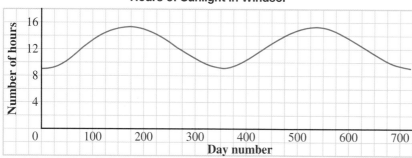

Hours of Sunlight in Windsor

Ocean tides

An ocean tide is another example of a natural event that repeats in a regular and predictable way. The graph shows how the depth of the water varies during a typical 24-h period at Hopewell Cape, NB, which is on the Bay of Fundy.

Tides at Hopewell Cape, NB, February 21, 22, 2001

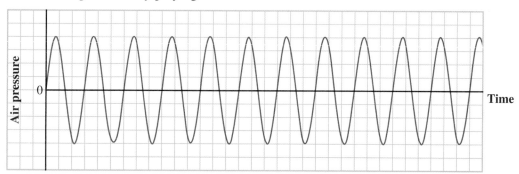

Musical notes

Each note in the musical scale has its own frequency. The graph shows the sound wave generated by playing middle C.

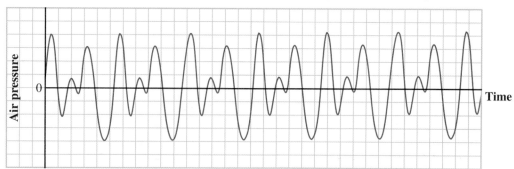

This graph shows the wave that results from playing middle C and G at the same time. This motion is also periodic, although each cycle is more complex.

The graphs in this section suggest the meaning of a *periodic function*.

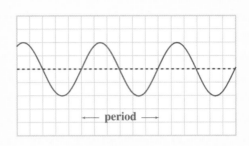

Take Note

Definition of a Periodic Function

The graph of a periodic function repeats in a regular way.
The green part of the graph represents one *cycle*.
The length of one cycle, measured along the horizontal axis, is the *period* of the function.

period

6.1 Exercises

A

1. Use the graph on page 329 that models the motion of a pendulum bob.

   a) What is the maximum distance from the rest position?

   b) What is the period of the motion? What does the period represent?

   c) At what times is the bob 5 cm from the rest position?

   d) For how long during each cycle is the bob more than 5 cm from the rest position?

2. Use the graph on page 329 that shows the number of hours of sunlight in Windsor.

   a) Estimate the number of hours of sunlight on each date.
      i) February 2   ii) July 31   iii) October 31

   b) Estimate the dates when each number of hours of sunlight occurs.
      i) 10 h   ii) 13 h   iii) 15 h

B

3. **Communication** Places in Northern Ontario, such as Timmins, have longer days in the summer and shorter days in the winter than places in Southern Ontario. This is because Northern Ontario is farther from the equator.

   a) Describe, in general terms, how the graph of the number of hours of sunlight in Timmins would be different from the graph for Windsor.

   b) How would the graphs be the same?

   c) What differences would there be in the graphs of sunlight hours for cities that are closer to the equator?

4. **Thinking/Inquiry/Problem Solving** Suppose you lived on the equator. Sketch a graph to show how the daily number of hours of sunlight vary during the year.

5. Use the graph on page 330 that shows the tides at Hopewell Cape, NB.

   a) What is the period of the graph?

   b) How shallow is the water at low tide?

   c) A different location has less extreme tides. How would the graph of the tides at this location differ from the graph for Hopewell Cape?

6. Application Use the graph of a middle C sound wave on page 330. The *frequency* of the sound is the number of cycles that occur in one second. The frequency of middle C is 256 cycles per second (called hertz, abbreviated to Hz).

   a) What is the period of the function on the graph?

   b) Describe a simple relationship between period and frequency.

   c) The graph represents a very small fraction of one second. How wide should the graph be to represent one second in the horizontal direction on the same scale?

7. Knowledge/Understanding These graphs were produced by *Graphmatica*. Determine whether each function is periodic.

   i) If a function is periodic, estimate its period.
   ii) If a function is not periodic, explain why.

a)

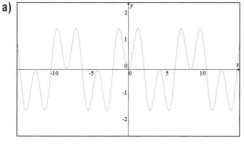

b)

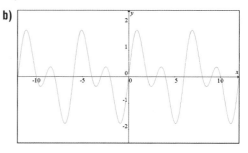

c)

d)

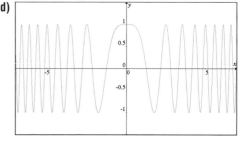

e)

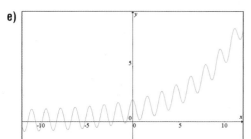

f)

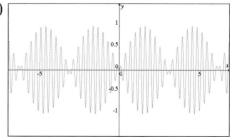

We shall define two functions $y = \cos x$ and $y = \sin x$, where x is the measure of an angle in radians. x and y are the independent and dependent variables in these equations. When we write an ordered pair (x, y), it represents the coordinates of a point on the graph of one of these functions.

Take Note

Definitions of cos x and sin x

Point P is on the circle with centre O(0, 0) and radius 1 unit.

Point A has coordinates $(1, 0)$, and $\angle POA = x$ radians.

We define:

$\cos x$ is the first coordinate of P.

$\sin x$ is the second coordinate of P.

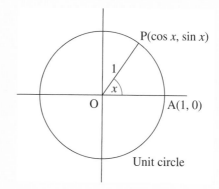

A point that moves around a circle is an example of periodic motion because the point returns to its previous positions on each successive rotation. Visualize a point P that rotates around the unit circle, starting at A(1, 0). As the angle of rotation, x radians, increases, $\sin x$ and $\cos x$ change in a regular and periodic way.

Graphing the function $y = \sin x$

Suppose x starts at 0 and increases to π. Then $\sin x$ changes as follows.

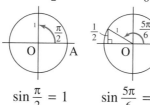

$x = 0$ $x = \dfrac{\pi}{6}$ $x = \dfrac{\pi}{2}$ $x = \dfrac{5\pi}{6}$ $x = \pi$

$\sin 0 = 0$ $\sin \dfrac{\pi}{6} = \dfrac{1}{2}$ $\sin \dfrac{\pi}{2} = 1$ $\sin \dfrac{5\pi}{6} = \dfrac{1}{2}$ $\sin \pi = 0$

We use these results to graph $y = \sin x$ for $0 \le x \le \pi$. Notice the pattern in the plotted points.

Starting at $(0, 0)$, go 1 right 1 up, then 2 right 1 up, then 2 right 1 down, then 1 right 1 down. Draw a smooth curve through these points.

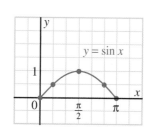

Suppose x continues from π to 2π. Then $\sin x$ changes as follows.

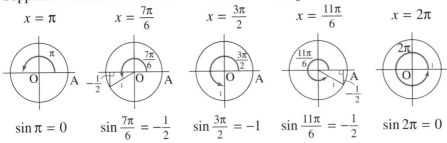

| $x = \pi$ | $x = \dfrac{7\pi}{6}$ | $x = \dfrac{3\pi}{2}$ | $x = \dfrac{11\pi}{6}$ | $x = 2\pi$ |

$$\sin \pi = 0 \qquad \sin \frac{7\pi}{6} = -\frac{1}{2} \qquad \sin \frac{3\pi}{2} = -1 \qquad \sin \frac{11\pi}{6} = -\frac{1}{2} \qquad \sin 2\pi = 0$$

We use these results to sketch the graph of $y = \sin x$ for $\pi \le x \le 2\pi$. The pattern continues. Starting at $(\pi, 0)$, go 1 right 1 down, then 2 right 1 down, then 2 right 1 up, then 1 right 1 up. There are 9 plotted points in all. A graph created using these points is called a *9-point sketch*.

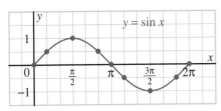

As x continues beyond 2π, P rotates around the circle again, and the same values of $\sin x$ are encountered. Hence, the graph can be continued to the right. Similarly, the graph can be continued to the left, corresponding to a rotation in the clockwise direction. The patterns in the graph repeat every 2π in each direction. The period of this function is 2π.

Graphing the function $y = \cos x$

Suppose x starts at 0 and increases to π. Then $\cos x$ changes as follows.

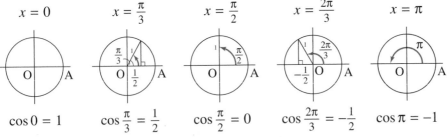

| $x = 0$ | $x = \dfrac{\pi}{3}$ | $x = \dfrac{\pi}{2}$ | $x = \dfrac{2\pi}{3}$ | $x = \pi$ |

$$\cos 0 = 1 \qquad \cos \frac{\pi}{3} = \frac{1}{2} \qquad \cos \frac{\pi}{2} = 0 \qquad \cos \frac{2\pi}{3} = -\frac{1}{2} \qquad \cos \pi = -1$$

We use these results to sketch the graph of $y = \cos x$ for $0 \le x \le \pi$. We use a similar pattern as before.

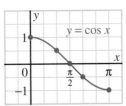

Suppose x continues from π to 2π. Then $\cos x$ changes as follows.

$x = \pi$ $x = \dfrac{4\pi}{3}$ $x = \dfrac{3\pi}{2}$ $x = \dfrac{5\pi}{3}$ $x = 2\pi$

$\cos \pi = -1$ $\cos \dfrac{4\pi}{3} = -\dfrac{1}{2}$ $\cos \dfrac{3\pi}{2} = 0$ $\cos \dfrac{5\pi}{3} = \dfrac{1}{2}$ $\cos 2\pi = 1$

We use these results to sketch the graph of $y = \cos x$ for $\pi \le x \le 2\pi$. The pattern continues as before, completing the 9-point sketch.

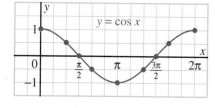

As x continues beyond 2π, P rotates around the circle again, and the same values of $\cos x$ are encountered. Hence, the graph can be continued to the right. Similarly, the graph can be continued to the left, corresponding to a rotation in the clockwise direction. The patterns in the graph repeat every 2π in each direction. The period of this function is 2π.

Take Note

Properties of the Functions $y = \sin x$ and $y = \cos x$

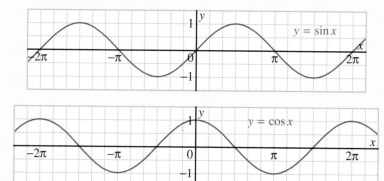

Period: 2π

Maximum value of y: 1   Minimum value of y: -1
Domain: all real numbers   Range: $-1 \le y \le 1$

For $y = \sin x$:   For $y = \cos x$:

x-intercepts: $0, \pm\pi, \pm2\pi, \ldots$ x-intercepts: $\pm\dfrac{\pi}{2}, \pm\dfrac{3\pi}{2}, \pm\dfrac{5\pi}{2}, \ldots$

y-intercept: 0 y-intercept: 1

Since the graphs of $y = \sin x$ and $y = \cos x$ look like waves, we use sine and cosine functions in applications that involve quantities that change periodically. To do this, we work with functions when their maximum and minimum values are different from 1 and −1, and their periods are different from 2π. We begin with the graphs on page 335, then expand or compress them in vertical or horizontal directions, and change their positions relative to the axes. When these changes are made to the graphs, corresponding changes occur in the equations. In Sections 6.3 and 6.4, we will investigate how the changes in the equations are related to the changes in the graphs.

6.2 Exercises

A

1. In these diagrams, graphs of $y = \sin x$ were started using different scales. Copy each graph onto grid paper, then extend it for the number of cycles indicated. Use a 9-point sketch to plot points for the graph, adjusted to fit the scales.

   a) 2 cycles   **b)** 2 cycles   **c)** 1 cycle

   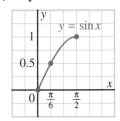 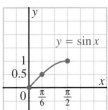 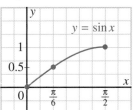

2. In these diagrams, graphs of $y = \cos x$ were started using different scales. Copy each graph onto grid paper, then extend it for the number of cycles indicated. Use a 9-point sketch, adjusted to fit the scales.

   a) 2 cycles   **b)** 2 cycles   **c)** 4 cycles

   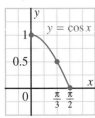 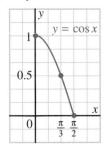 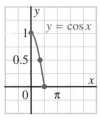

3. **a)** Explain why the graph of $y = \sin x$ is shaped like a wave.

   b) Explain why the graph of $y = \cos x$ has the same shape as the graph of $y = \sin x$.

B

Note: Make sure your calculator is in radian mode.

4. Use a calculator to determine each pair of values. Draw a unit circle diagram to explain the meaning of the results.

a) $\sin 0.5$ and $\cos 0.5$ b) $\sin 1$ and $\cos 1$

c) $\sin 2$ and $\cos 2$ d) $\sin 2.8$ and $\cos 2.8$

e) $\sin 4.3$ and $\cos 4.3$ f) $\sin 10$ and $\cos 10$

g) $\sin(-0.5)$ and $\cos(-0.5)$ h) $\sin(-3.7)$ and $\cos(-3.7)$

5. Graph $y = \sin x$ using the window $-2 \le x \le 7.4$ and $-3.1 \le y \le 3.1$.

a) Trace along the curve and observe how y changes. Move the cursor as close to π as possible. What happens to the value of y?

b) While Trace mode is active, press $\boxed{\text{2nd}}$ $\boxed{\frown}$ $\boxed{\text{ENTER}}$ to move the cursor to the point where $x = \pi$. Is the value of y what you expected?

c) Repeat part b. Move the cursor to: $\dfrac{\pi}{2}, \dfrac{3\pi}{2}, 2\pi$.

d) On the same screen, graph $y = \cos x$. Then repeat parts a to c.

e) Use your knowledge of special angles to predict the coordinates of the first point where the two graphs intersect. Use a calculator to confirm your prediction.

6. In exercise 5, find out what happens when you use the window $-2\pi \le x \le 2\pi$ and $-1.5 \le y \le 1.5$. What are the advantages and disadvantages of the two different windows?

7. Knowledge/Understanding For the function $y = \sin x$:

a) What is the maximum value of y? For what values of x does this occur?

b) What is the minimum value of y? For what values of x does this occur?

c) What are the domain and range of the function?

d) What are the x-intercepts of the graph?

e) What is the y-intercept of the graph?

f) What is the period?

8. Repeat exercise 7 for the function $y = \cos x$.

9. Thinking/Inquiry/Problem Solving Suppose a value of x is given. Describe a rule to determine whether $\sin x$ is greater than $\cos x$, equal to $\cos x$, or less than $\cos x$. Illustrate your rule with some examples.

10. The graphing calculator screen (below left) shows the coordinates of one point on the graph of $y = \sin x$, to the nearest thousandth. Use only the information on the screen. Write the coordinates of three other points on the graph that have the same y-coordinate as this point.

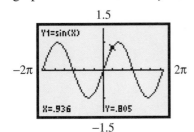

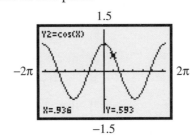

11. The graphing calculator screen (above right) shows the coordinates of one point on the graph of $y = \cos x$, to the nearest thousandth. Repeat exercise 10 for this screen.

12. Choose either exercise 10 or 11. Explain how you determined the coordinates.

13. **Communication** Compare the graphs of the functions $y = \sin x$ and $y = \cos x$. In what ways are they similar? In what ways are they different? Explain the similarities and the differences. Use examples to illustrate your explanations.

14. Graph $y = \sin x$. Draw a vertical line at $x = \frac{\pi}{2}$. This line cuts the first "hoop" of the graph into two symmetrical parts. Use the definition of $\sin x$ to explain why this symmetry is expected.

15. **Application** Suppose you do not realize your graphing calculator is in degree mode, and you use it to graph $y = \sin x$ for $-2 \le x \le 7.4$ and $-3.1 \le y \le 3.1$.

   a) Predict what the graph would look like.

   b) Use a graphing calculator to check your prediction.

16. a) Use the Mode menu to display numbers to 3 decimal places. Graph $y = \sin x$ for $-2\pi \le x \le 2\pi$ and $-1.5 \le y \le 1.5$. Trace to the point where $x = 1.069$. Observe the corresponding value of y.

   b) Predict some other values of x that produce the same value of y. Trace to these points to verify your predictions.

17. a) Graph $y = \cos x$ using the graphing window in exercise 16. Trace to the point where $x = 1.069$. Observe the corresponding value of y.

   b) Predict some other values of x that produce the same value of y. Trace to these points to verify your predictions.

c) Compare your answers in part b and exercise 16b. Explain why some *x*-coordinates are the same and why some are different.

18. Suppose the angle *x* is in degrees instead of radians.

   a) How would the graph of $y = \sin x$ on page 335 change?

   b) Is the function $y = \sin x$, where *x* is in degrees, the same as the function $y = \sin x$, where *x* is in radians? Explain.

19. Compare the two graphs in exercises 10 and 11. The *x*-coordinates of the indicated points are the same.

   a) How are the *y*-coordinates of these points related? Explain.

   b) Is the relationship you identified in part a true for all points with the same *x*-coordinate on the two graphs, or only for some points? Explain.

C

20. a) Graph $y = \sin x$ for $-4.7 \le x \le 4.7$ and $-3.1 \le y \le 3.1$. Use the zoom feature to enlarge the part of the graph that contains the origin. Zoom in enough times until the visible part of the graph looks like a straight line.

   b) Use Trace and the arrow keys to move the cursor along the graph. What do you notice about the coordinates of the points on the graph? Use the definition of $\sin x$ to explain.

   c) What other properties does the function $y = \sin x$ have that are not included on page 335?

21. Determine the solution of each system of equations.

   a) $y = \sin x$
      $y = x$

   b) $y = \cos x$
      $y = x$

   c) $y = \sin x$
      $y = \cos x$

22. The diagram at the right shows part of the graph of $y = \cos x$. Write a convincing argument why this graph is not part of a parabola.

23. Use the diagram in exercise 22.

   a) A chord is drawn at height 0.5. How long is the chord?

   b) Chords are drawn at heights 0.25 and 0.75. Calculate their lengths.

   c) The length of a chord is a function of its height.
      i) Graph the function.
      ii) Is the function sinusoidal? Explain.

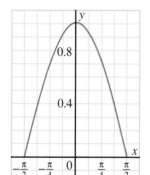

6.3 Graphing Sinusoidal Functions: Part I

The sine and cosine functions are tools for modelling quantities that change periodically. However, we need to transform these functions to match real data. For either function, we can change the graph and the equation so the maximum and minimum values, and the period, correspond to the quantities in the situation. In this section and Section 6.4, you will investigate the effects of certain transformations on $y = \sin x$ and $y = \cos x$. These functions and the functions that result from the transformations are *sinusoidal functions*.

Investigation

Transforming $y = \sin x$ and $y = \cos x$: Part I

The graphs of $y = \sin x$ and $y = \cos x$ are shown below. You will graph other related equations on the same screen. You will explain how the changes in the graphs are related to the changes in the equations.

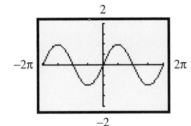
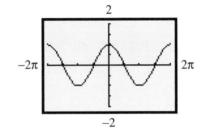

Comparing $y = a \sin x$ with $y = \sin x$, and $y = a \cos x$ with $y = \cos x$

1. Graph the function $y = \sin x$ using the window settings shown in the screens above.

2. a) Graph the function $y = 2 \sin x$ on the same screen.

   b) Describe how the graphs of $y = 2 \sin x$ and $y = \sin x$ are related. Explain this relationship.

   c) Repeat part a, using numbers other than 2 in the equation. Use both positive and negative numbers, including those between −1 and 1. Are the results what you expected? Explain.

3. Repeat exercises 1 and 2 using cosine functions.

4. What effect does changing the value of a have on the graphs of $y = a \sin x$ and $y = a \cos x$? Explain.

Comparing *y* = *sin x* + *c* with *y* = *sin x*, and *y* = *cos x* + *c* with *y* = *cos x*

5. Clear all graphs, then graph the function $y = \sin x$.

6. a) Graph the function $y = \sin x + 1$ on the same screen.

   b) Describe how the graphs of $y = \sin x + 1$ and $y = \sin x$ are related. Explain this relationship.

   c) Repeat part a, using numbers other than 1 in the equation. Use both positive and negative numbers, including those between –1 and 1. Are the results what you expected? Explain.

7. Repeat exercises 5 and 6 using cosine functions.

8. What effect does changing the value of c have on the graphs of $y = \sin x + c$ and $y = \cos x + c$? Explain.

Comparing *y* = *sin* (*x* – *d*) with *y* = *sin x*, and *y* = *cos* (*x* – *d*) with *y* = *cos x*

9. Clear all graphs, then graph the function $y = \sin x$.

10. a) Graph the function $y = \sin\left(x - \dfrac{\pi}{3}\right)$ on the same screen.

   b) Describe how the graphs of $y = \sin\left(x - \dfrac{\pi}{3}\right)$ and $y = \sin x$ are related. Explain this relationship.

   c) Repeat part a, using numbers other than $\dfrac{\pi}{3}$ in the equation. Use both positive and negative numbers. Are the results what you expected? Explain.

11. Repeat exercises 9 and 10 using cosine functions.

12. What effect does changing the value of d have on the graphs of $y = \sin(x - d)$ and $y = \cos(x - d)$? Explain.

In the *Investigation*, you made certain changes to the equations $y = \sin x$ and $y = \cos x$, and found what happened to the graphs. The results are summarized on the following pages.

The amplitude of a sinusoidal function

The coefficient a in $y = a \sin x$ or $y = a \cos x$ has the effect shown below. The number $|a|$ is the *amplitude*. It represents the distance from any maximum or minimum point to the x-axis.

Take Note

Graphs of y = a sin x and y = a cos x

The graphs of $y = a \sin x$ and $y = a \cos x$ are the images of the graphs of $y = \sin x$ and $y = \cos x$, respectively, under a vertical expansion or compression. When $a < 0$, there is also a reflection in the x-axis.

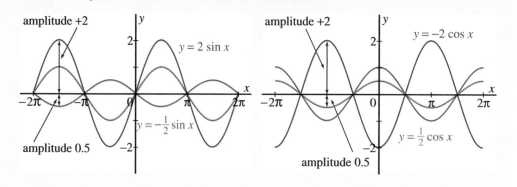

A weight moving up and down at the bottom of a spring is an example of periodic motion. The maximum distance of the weight from the rest position is the amplitude of the motion.

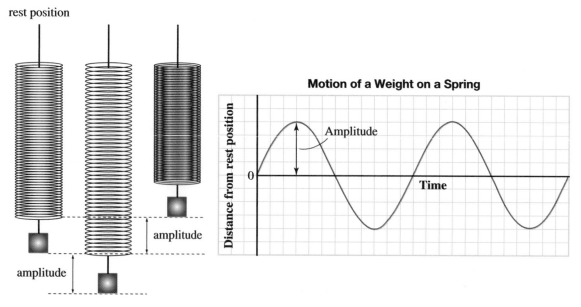

The vertical displacement of a sinusoidal function

The constant term c in $y = \sin x + c$ or $y = \cos x + c$ has the effect shown below. The number c is the *vertical displacement*. It represents the distance the graph has been translated vertically.

Graphs of $y = \sin x + c$ and $y = \cos x + c$

The graphs of $y = \sin x + c$ and $y = \cos x + c$ are the images of the graphs of $y = \sin x$ and $y = \cos x$, respectively, under a vertical translation of c units.

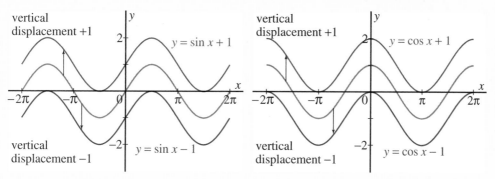

A weight on a spring illustrates vertical displacement. A graph of the height of the weight above the floor against time is sinusoidal. The vertical displacement of the motion is equal to the mean height of the weight above the floor.

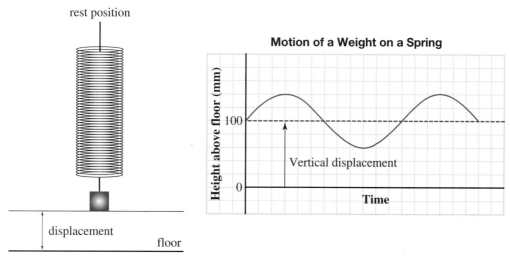

Example 1

a) Graph the function $y = 2 \sin t + 3$ over two cycles.

b) State the amplitude, the vertical displacement, and the period of the function.

Solution

a) Graph $y = \sin t$, then expand it vertically by a factor of 2. This produces the image $y = 2 \sin t$. Then translate the image 3 units up.

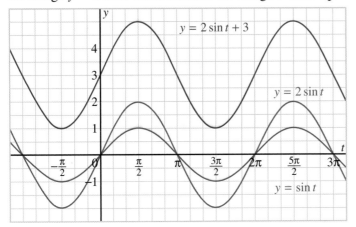

b) From the graph, the amplitude is 2. The vertical displacement is 3. The period is 2π.

In *Example 1*, the maximum value of the function is 5, and the minimum value is 1. The amplitude is one-half the distance from the minimum to the maximum, measured vertically. For this function, the amplitude is $\frac{1}{2}(5 - 1)$, or 2.

The phase shift of a sinusoidal function

The constant term d in $y = \sin(x - d)$ or $y = \cos(x - d)$ has the effect shown below. The number d is the *phase shift*. It represents the distance the graph has been translated horizontally.

Take Note

Graphs of $y = \sin(x - d)$ and $y = \cos(x - d)$

The graphs of $y = \sin(x - d)$ and $y = \cos(x - d)$ are the images of the graphs of $y = \sin x$ and $y = \cos x$, respectively, under a horizontal translation of d units.

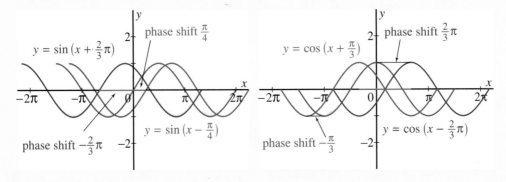

A weight on a spring can illustrate phase shift when time is not measured from the rest position.

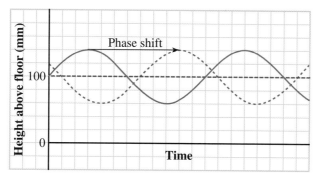

Take Note

Phase Shift of y = sin (x − d) and y = cos (x − d)

To determine the phase shift of $y = \sin(x - d)$, let $x - d = 0$, then solve for x. The phase shift of a sine function is the x-coordinate of a point where the sine cycle begins.

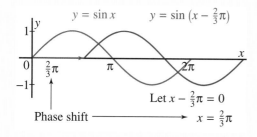

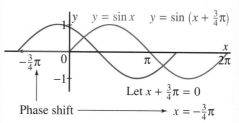

To determine the phase shift of $y = \cos(x - d)$, let $x - d = 0$, then solve for x. The phase shift of a cosine function is the x-coordinate of a maximum point.

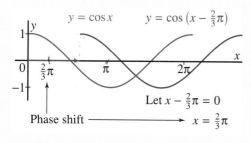

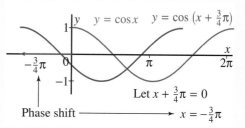

Example 2

Graph the function $y = \frac{1}{2}\cos\left(x + \frac{\pi}{3}\right) - \frac{3}{2}$ over 2 cycles. State the vertical displacement, the amplitude, and the phase shift.

Solution

Graph $y = \cos x$, then compress it vertically by a factor of $\frac{1}{2}$ to obtain the image $y = \frac{1}{2}\cos x$. Then translate the image $\frac{\pi}{3}$ units left and $\frac{3}{2}$ units down.

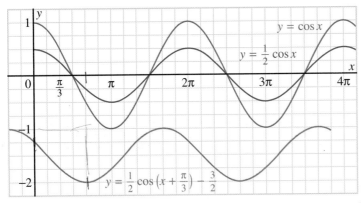

The vertical displacement is $-\frac{3}{2}$, the amplitude is $\frac{1}{2}$, and the phase shift is $-\frac{\pi}{3}$.

Example 3

A sinusoidal curve is shown below. For the function defined by this curve:

a) Write two different cosine equations.

b) Write two different sine equations.

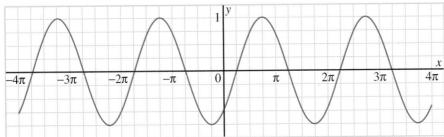

Solution

The graph could be a cosine function, with its phase shift from the y-axis to any maximum point. The graph could also be a sine function, with its phase shift from the origin to any point where the sine cycle begins on the x-axis.

a) The horizontal distances from the y-axis to the maximum points on either side of the y-axis are $\frac{3\pi}{4}$ and $-\frac{5\pi}{4}$. Hence, these are two possible phase shifts for a cosine function. The corresponding equations are $y = \cos\left(x - \frac{3\pi}{4}\right)$ and $y = \cos\left(x + \frac{5\pi}{4}\right)$.

b) Two points where the sine cycle begins on the x-axis are $\left(\frac{\pi}{4}, 0\right)$ and $\left(-\frac{7\pi}{4}, 0\right)$. Hence, two possible phase shifts for a sine function are $\frac{\pi}{4}$ and $-\frac{7\pi}{4}$. The corresponding equations are $y = \sin\left(x - \frac{\pi}{4}\right)$ and $y = \sin\left(x + \frac{7\pi}{4}\right)$.

6.3 Exercises

A

1. The graph of $y = \cos x$ is transformed as described. The equation of its image has the form $y = a\cos(x - d) + c$. Determine a, c, and d for each transformation.

a) Translate the graph 3 units up.

b) Translate the graph $\frac{\pi}{2}$ units left.

c) Expand the graph vertically by a factor of 2, then translate it 3 units down.

2. The graph of $y = \sin x$ is transformed as described. The equation of its image has the form $y = a\sin(x - d) + c$. Determine a, c, and d for each transformation.

a) Compress the graph vertically by a factor of $\frac{1}{2}$, then translate it 3 units down.

b) Expand the graph vertically by a factor of 2, then translate it $\frac{\pi}{3}$ units left and 2 units down.

3. Explain the difference between translating a graph up and expanding it vertically.

B

4. Consider a sinusoidal function of the form $y = a\sin(x - d) + c$. Write to explain how its graph will change for each change described.

a) The sign of a is changed and c is increased by 2.

b) d is increased by $\frac{3\pi}{4}$ and c is increased by 3.

c) a is doubled, d is decreased by $\frac{\pi}{3}$, and c is increased by 1.

d) a is halved, d is decreased by $\frac{\pi}{4}$, and c is decreased by 4.

5. Explain the difference between amplitude and vertical displacement. Use examples to illustrate your explanation.

6. In *Example 3*, how can you determine the points where the sine cycle begins on the *x*-axis?

7. **a)** Can the *x*-coordinate of any maximum point on the graph of a cosine function be taken as the phase shift? Explain.

   b) Can the *x*-coordinate of any point where the graph of a sine function intersects the *x*-axis be taken as the phase shift? Explain.

8. The screen (below left) shows the graphs of $y = \cos x + c$ for $c = -3, -2, -1, 0, 1, 2,$ and 3. The coordinates of one point on one graph are shown on the screen. Write the coordinates of the points on the other graphs on the screen that have the same *x*-coordinate as this point.

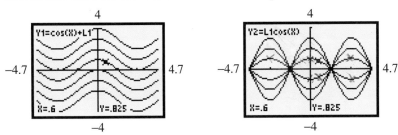

9. The screen (above right) shows the graphs of $y = a \cos x$ for $a = -3, -2, -1, 0, 1, 2,$ and 3. The coordinates of one point on one graph are shown on the screen. Write the coordinates of the points on the other graphs on the screen that have the same *x*-coordinate as this point.

10. **a)** Use the graphing window in exercise 8. Graph $y = \sin x + c$ for $c = -3, -2, -1, 0, 1, 2,$ and 3. Trace to the point on the graph of $y = \sin x$ where $x = 0.6$. Record the corresponding value of *y*.

    b) Predict the coordinates of a point on each of the other graphs that has the same value of *x*. Trace to these points to verify your predictions.

11. Repeat exercise 10, using $y = a \sin x$ for $a = -3, -2, -1, 0, 1, 2,$ and 3.

12. In *Example 2*, the vertical compression was applied before the translations. Could the translations be applied before the vertical compression? Explain.

13. **Communication** Explain why the graph of a sinusoidal function can have more than one equation. Use an example to illustrate your explanation.

14. The screen shows the graphs of $y = \cos(x - d)$ for $d = -2, -1, 0, 1,$ and 2. The coordinates of one point on one graph are shown. Write the coordinates of one point on each of the other graphs with the same *y*-coordinate as this point.

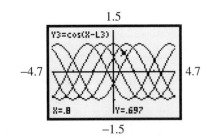

15. For each list, predict what the graphs of the equations would look like. Use a graphing calculator to check your predictions.

a) $y = 3\cos x + 3$
   $y = 2\cos x + 2$
   $y = \cos x + 1$

b) $y = 3\sin x - 3$
   $y = 2\sin x - 2$
   $y = \sin x - 1$

16. A sinusoidal function is graphed below.

a) The function can be considered as a sine function. Determine two possible values for the phase shift. What is the equation of the function for each phase shift?

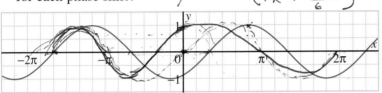
$y = \sin\left(x + \dfrac{5\pi}{3}\right)$ $y = \sin\left(x - \dfrac{\pi}{3}\right)$

b) The function can also be considered as a cosine function. Determine two possible values for the phase shift. What is the equation of the function for each phase shift?

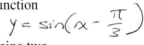
$y = \cos\left(x + \dfrac{7\pi}{6}\right)$ $y = \cos\left(x - \dfrac{5\pi}{6}\right)$

17. Knowledge/Understanding Each function below is sinusoidal. For each graph, state:

   i) an equation of the function
   ii) the amplitude
   iii) a possible phase shift
   iv) the maximum value of y, and the values of x for which it occurs
   v) the minimum value of y, and the values of x for which it occurs
   vi) the vertical displacement
   vii) the domain and range

a)

b)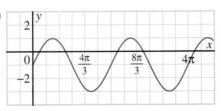

c)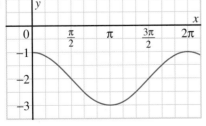

d)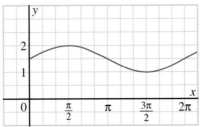

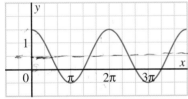

18. Graph each function over two cycles. Determine its domain and range, its phase shift, its amplitude, and its maximum and minimum values.

a) $y = 5 \sin x$

b) $y = 3 \cos x$

c) $h = 0.25 \sin e + 4$

d) $y = 2 \cos x - 3$

e) $y = 4 \sin x - 2$

f) $y = 1.5 \cos x + 3$

g) $y = \frac{1}{2} \sin x - 1$

h) $s = 2 + 2 \sin t$

i) $f = 1 + 3.5 \cos g$

19. Graph each function over two cycles. Determine its domain and range, its phase shift, its amplitude, and its maximum and minimum values.

a) $y = \sin\left(x - \frac{\pi}{4}\right)$

b) $y = \sin\left(x - \frac{4\pi}{3}\right)$

c) $y = 2 \sin\left(x + \frac{5\pi}{6}\right)$

d) $y = 3 \cos\left(x - \frac{\pi}{6}\right) + 3$

e) $y = 2 \cos\left(x + \frac{5\pi}{3}\right) - 2$

f) $y = 5 \cos\left(x - \frac{7\pi}{6}\right) + 2$

20. Choose either the function $y = a \sin(x - d) + c$ or the function $y = a \cos(x - d) + c$. Explain how changing the values of a, c, and d in the equation of the function affects its graph.

21. For the function $y = a \sin x + c$, explain how you can determine its maximum and minimum values, and the corresponding values of x.

22. Repeat exercise 21 for the function $y = a \cos x + c$.

23. **Application** Suppose M and m represent the maximum and minimum values, respectively, of a sinusoidal function. Write formulas in terms of M and m for:

a) the amplitude

b) the vertical displacement

c) the range

24. **Thinking/Inquiry/Problem Solving**

a) Graph the function $y = \cos\left(x - \frac{\pi}{2}\right)$. Visualize other functions you have graphed in this section. What conclusion can you make?

b) Determine the values of d for which the graph of $y = \cos(x - d)$ coincides with the graph of $y = \sin x$.

25. a) Graph the function $y = \sin\left(x - \frac{\pi}{2}\right)$. Visualize other functions you have graphed in this section. What conclusion can you make?

b) Determine the values of d for which the graph of $y = \sin(x - d)$ coincides with the graph of $y = \cos x$.

26. A function is given by the equation $y = 2 \sin\left(x + \frac{\pi}{2}\right)$. Explain why you might prefer to rewrite it using cosine instead of sine.

C

27. Determine the equation of a function of the form $y = \sin x + p$ whose graph just touches the x-axis. How many such functions are there? Explain.

1. The graph shows how the time of sunset at Saskatoon varies during a 2-year period. The times are from a 24-h clock, in hours and decimals of hours.

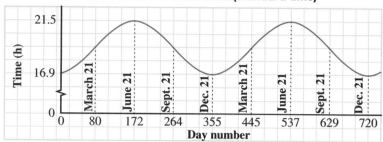

Time of sunset at Saskatoon (standard time)

a) Estimate the time of sunset on each date.
   i) February 2   ii) July 25   iii) October 30

b) Estimate the dates when the sun sets at each time.
   i) 8 P.M.   ii) 7 P.M.   iii) 6 P.M.

2. The graph (below left) represents data collected on the bird population in a certain wilderness area over a period of 5 years.

a) Estimate the period of the graph.

b) Estimate the minimum and maximum bird population each year.

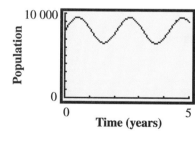

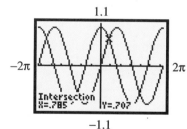

3. The graphing calculator screen (above right) shows the coordinates of one point of intersection of the graphs $y = \sin x$ and $y = \cos x$, to the nearest thousandth. Use the information on the screen. Write the coordinates of the other points of intersection of the graphs on this screen.

4. The graph of $y = \cos x$ is transformed. The equation of its image has the form $y = a \cos (x - d) + c$. Determine a, c, and d for each transformation.

a) Translate the graph 5 units down.   b) Translate the graph $\frac{\pi}{6}$ units right.

c) Expand the graph vertically by a factor of 2.

5. Graph the function $y = 2 \cos \left(x - \frac{\pi}{3}\right) + 1$ over 2 cycles. Determine the domain and range, phase shift, amplitude, and maximum and minimum values.

6.4 Graphing Sinusoidal Functions: Part II

In this section, you will continue the investigation of Section 6.3 to make other changes to the equations $y = \sin x$ and $y = \cos x$. Remember that the period of a periodic function is the length of one cycle, measured along the horizontal axis.

Investigation

Transforming $y = \sin x$ and $y = \cos x$: Part II

Comparing $y = \sin bx$ with $y = \sin x$, and $y = \cos bx$ with $y = \cos x$

1. Graph the function $y = \sin x$ using the window settings $-2\pi \leq x \leq 2\pi$.

2. **a)** Graph the function $y = \sin 2x$ on the same screen.

   b) Describe how the graphs of $y = \sin 2x$ and $y = \sin x$ are related. Explain this relationship.

   c) What is the period of the function $y = \sin 2x$? How is it related to the period of $y = \sin x$?

3. Repeat exercise 2, using the equation $y = \sin \frac{1}{2}x$.

4. Repeat exercise 2, using four other coefficients of x. Use positive coefficients that are both greater than 1 and less than 1. Are the results what you expected?

5. Repeat exercises 2 to 4, using cosine functions.

6. What effect does changing the value of b have on the graphs of $y = \sin bx$ and $y = \cos bx$? Explain.

In the *Investigation*, you made certain changes to the equations $y = \sin x$ and $y = \cos x$, and found what happened to the graphs. The results are summarized below.

The period of a sinusoidal function

The coefficient b in $y = \sin bx$ or $y = \cos bx$ has the effect shown below. The number b represents the factor by which the graph has been compressed or expanded horizontally.

Take Note

Graphs of y = sin bx and y = cos bx

The graphs of $y = \sin bx$ and $y = \cos bx$ are the images of the graphs of $y = \sin x$ and $y = \cos x$, respectively, under a horizontal compression or expansion.

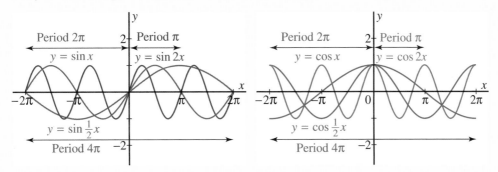

The motion of a weight on a spring illustrates the period. The period is the time for one complete cycle, such as the time for the weight to move from its maximum length to its rest position to its minimum length, to its rest position, then back to its maximum length.

Motion of a Weight on a Spring

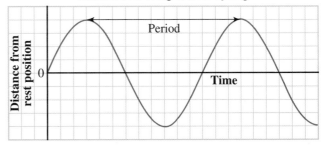

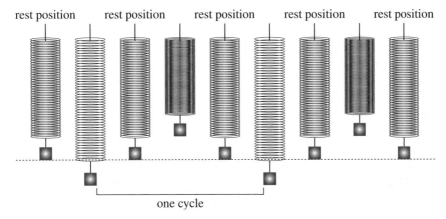

Period of y = sin bx and y = cos bx

When $b > 1$, there is a horizontal compression. The period is less than 2π.

For example, when $b = 3$, there is a compression by a factor of $\frac{1}{3}$.

The period of $y = \sin 3x$ is $\frac{1}{3}$ the period of $y = \sin x$.

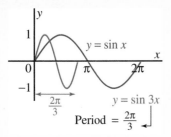

When $0 < b < 1$, there is a horizontal expansion. The period is greater than 2π.

For example, when $b = \frac{1}{2}$, there is an expansion by a factor of 2.

The period of $y = \sin \frac{1}{2}x$ is 2 times the period of $y = \sin x$.

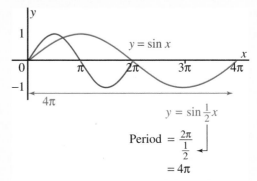

Similarly, the period of $y = \cos 3x$ is $\frac{1}{3}$ the period of $y = \cos x$.

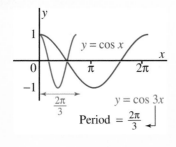

Similarly, the period of $y = \cos \frac{1}{2}x$ is 2 times the period of $y = \cos x$.

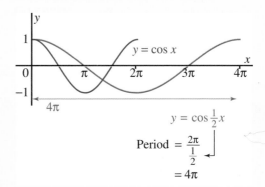

In general, the period of $y = \sin bx$ and $y = \cos bx$ is $\frac{2\pi}{b}$, $b > 0$.

The general form for the sinusoidal function in this text is $y = a \sin b(x - d) + c$. In this form, we can easily identify the phase shift as d.

On page 321, the general form is given as $y = a \sin(kx + d) + c$. To determine the phase shift when the function is in this form, remove k as a common factor from $kx + d$; that is, $y = a \sin k\left(x + \frac{d}{k}\right) + c$. The phase shift is $-\frac{d}{k}$.

½ period of
y = sinx

Example 1

a) Graph the function $y = \sin 2x + 3$ over two complete cycles.

b) State the vertical displacement, the phase shift, the period, and the amplitude.

c) State the domain and range.

Solution

a) Graph $y = \sin x$. Compress the graph horizontally by a factor of $\frac{1}{2}$ to obtain the graph of $y = \sin 2x$. Then translate the image 3 units up.

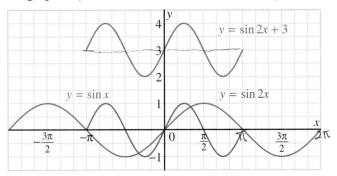

b) The vertical displacement is 3, the phase shift is 0, the period is π, and the amplitude is 1.

c) The domain is the set of real numbers. The range is the set of real numbers between 2 and 4, inclusive.

Example 2

a) Graph the function $y = -2\cos 3(x - \pi)$ over two complete cycles.

b) State the vertical displacement, the phase shift, the period, and the amplitude.

c) State the domain and range.

Solution

a) To graph $y = -2\cos x$, reflect the graph of $y = 2\cos x$ in the x-axis. Compress the graph horizontally by a factor of $\frac{1}{3}$ to obtain the graph of $y = -2\cos 3x$. Then translate the image π units right.

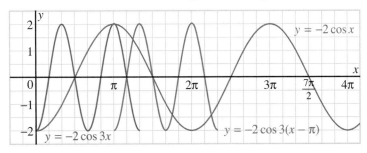

b) The vertical displacement is 0, the phase shift is π, the period is $\frac{2\pi}{3}$, and the amplitude is 2.

c) The domain is the set of real numbers. The range is the set of real numbers between –2 and 2 inclusive.

In *Examples 1* and *2*, we graphed several functions on the same grid to obtain the graph of the required function. To graph only the required function without showing any of the preliminary graphs, we begin with a sketch.

Example 3

Graph the function $y = 3\sin 2\left(x - \frac{\pi}{3}\right) + 4$ over two complete cycles.

Solution

The function $y = 3\sin 2\left(x - \frac{\pi}{3}\right) + 4$ has: amplitude 3; period $\frac{2\pi}{2}$, or π; phase shift $\frac{\pi}{3}$; and vertical displacement 4.

Sketch a sinusoidal curve on plain paper.

Step 1. Use the phase shift. This is $\frac{\pi}{3}$, and it is the x-coordinate of a point where the sine curve begins its cycle. Mark this on the sketch.

Step 2. Use the period. This is π. The point at the end of the cycle is π units to the right of the first point. Its x-coordinate is $\frac{\pi}{3} + \pi = \frac{4\pi}{3}$. Mark this on the sketch.

Step 3. One-quarter of the period is $\frac{\pi}{4}$. The x-coordinate of the first maximum point is $\frac{\pi}{3} + \frac{\pi}{4} = \frac{7\pi}{12}$. Mark this on the sketch, then change the other x-coordinates to have the same denominator, 12. They become $\frac{4\pi}{12}$ and $\frac{16\pi}{12}$.

Step 4. Think of an arithmetic sequence of 5 terms, beginning with $\frac{4\pi}{12}, \frac{7\pi}{12}$, and ending with $\frac{16\pi}{12}$. The x-coordinate of the halfway point is $\frac{10\pi}{12}$, and the x-coordinate of the minimum point is $\frac{13\pi}{12}$. Mark these on the sketch.

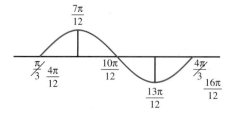

Transfer the sketch to grid paper.

Step 5. Draw x- and y-axes, where 12 squares along the x-axis represent π. Each square in this direction represents $\frac{\pi}{12}$. The vertical displacement is 4. Draw a horizontal line through 4 on the y-axis. Plot the point where the sine curve begins its cycle, $\left(\frac{4\pi}{12}, 4\right)$. The amplitude is 3. Plot the maximum point, $\left(\frac{7\pi}{12}, 7\right)$. Plot the halfway point, $\left(\frac{10\pi}{12}, 4\right)$. Plot the minimum point, $\left(\frac{13\pi}{12}, 1\right)$. Plot the endpoint of the cycle, $\left(\frac{16\pi}{12}, 4\right)$.

Step 6. Use the pattern in the plotted points to draw some corresponding points for the next cycle. Draw a smooth curve through the plotted points.

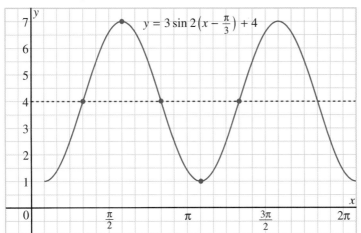

$$y = 3\sin 2\left(x - \frac{\pi}{3}\right) + 4$$

Discuss

We can write
$$y = 3\sin 2\left(x - \frac{\pi}{3}\right) + 4$$
as
$$y = 3\sin\left(2x - \frac{2\pi}{3}\right) + 4.$$
Which form is better? Explain.

6.4   Exercises

A

✓ **1.** Write the equation of a sine curve that has each period.

  a) 2π b) π c) $\frac{\pi}{2}$ d) $\frac{2\pi}{3}$

✓ **2.** For each graph, write an equation in the form $y = \sin bx$, then identify the period.

  a) 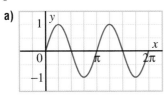   b)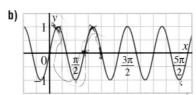

c)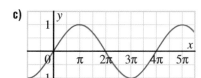

d)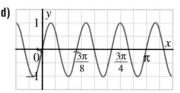

3. "The period of a sinusoidal function is the distance between two consecutive maximum points." Do you agree with this statement? Give reasons for your answer.

B

 4. Four different transformations of the graph of $y = \cos x$ are described below. The equation of each image has the form $y = a \cos b(x - d) + c$. Determine a, b, c, and d for each transformation.

   a) Compress the graph horizontally by a factor of $\frac{1}{2}$.

   b) Expand the graph horizontally by a factor of 5.

   c) Compress the graph horizontally by a factor of $\frac{1}{3}$, then expand it vertically by a factor of 4.

   d) Expand the graph horizontally by a factor of 2, expand it vertically by a factor of 3, then translate it $\frac{\pi}{3}$ units right.

5. Consider a sinusoidal function of the form $y = a \sin b(x - d) + c$. Explain how the resulting graph will be related to the original graph for each change described.

   a) b is doubled.

   b) b is halved.

   c) a and b are both doubled, and c is decreased by 2.

   d) a is tripled, b is halved, c is increased by 4, and d is increased by $\frac{\pi}{6}$.

 6. a) Graph each set of functions on the same grid for $-\pi \leq x \leq \pi$.

   i) $y = \sin 2x$ $y = \sin x$ $y = \sin \frac{1}{2}x$

   ii) $y = \cos 3x$ $y = \cos x$ $y = \cos \frac{1}{3}x$

   b) Describe the effect on the graph of $y = \sin bx$ as b varies.

   c) Describe the effect on the graph of $y = \cos bx$ as b varies.

7. Graph each function, then state its amplitude and period.

   a) $y = 2 \sin 2x$ b) $y = 3 \sin \frac{1}{2}x$ c) $y = -\frac{1}{2} \sin 3x$

   d) $y = 4 \cos \frac{1}{2}x$ e) $y = 5 \cos 2x$ f) $y = \frac{1}{3} \cos 3x$

8. Communication Explain why increasing the value of a in the equation $y = a \sin bx$ expands the graph vertically, but increasing the value of b compresses the graph horizontally. Assume $a > 0$ and $b > 0$. Include some graphs in your explanation.

9. Each function below is sinusoidal. For each graph, state:

    i) the amplitude   **ii)** the period   **iii)** a possible phase shift
    iv) the maximum value of y, and the values of x for which it occurs
    v) the minimum value of y, and the values of x for which it occurs
    vi) the vertical displacement   **vii)** the domain and range

a)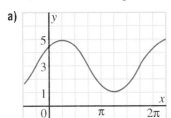

b)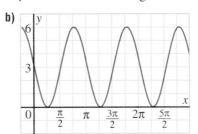

c)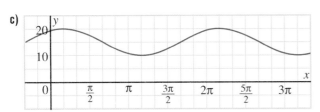

10. Write an equation to represent each function in exercise 9.

11. Knowledge/Understanding Consider the function $y = 2 \cos 2\left(x - \frac{\pi}{3}\right) + 4$.

    a) State the phase shift, the period, the vertical displacement, and the amplitude.

    b) Graph the function over two complete cycles.

    c) What are the domain and range of the function?

12. Repeat exercise 11 for each function.

    a) $y = 3 \sin 2\left(x - \frac{\pi}{4}\right) + 3$ **b)** $y = 5 \cos 3(x - \pi)$

    c) $y = 2 \sin 3\left(x - \frac{\pi}{2}\right)$ **d)** $y = 2.5 \cos\left(x - \frac{2\pi}{3}\right)$

    e) $y = 0.5 \cos 4\left(x + \frac{\pi}{4}\right)$ **f)** $y = 4 \sin 3\left(x - \frac{\pi}{2}\right) + 4$

    g) $y = -3 \cos 2\left(x + \frac{\pi}{6}\right) - 6$ **h)** $y = 4 \sin 3\left(x - \frac{\pi}{6}\right) + 2$

13. Consider the function $y = 2 \sin\left(2x + \frac{\pi}{3}\right)$.

    a) State the phase shift, the period, the vertical displacement, and the amplitude.

    b) Graph the function over two complete cycles.

    c) What are the domain and range of the function?

14. Repeat exercise 13 for each function.

a) $y = 5\cos\left(2x - \frac{\pi}{2}\right)$ 　　　　 **b)** $y = 3\cos\left(2x + \frac{\pi}{2}\right)$

c) $y = 2\sin(2x - \pi)$ 　　　　 **d)** $y = 2\sin\left(3x + \frac{\pi}{2}\right)$

15. Refer to exercise 2. For each graph, write an equation of the form $y = \cos b(x - d)$.

16. Thinking/Inquiry/Problem Solving These graphs were produced by *Graphmatica*. Each pattern shows the graphs of 10 sinusoidal functions. For each pattern, write a set of equations that could be used to make a similar pattern.

a)

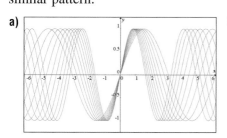

b)

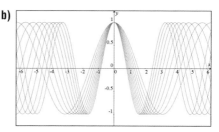

17. Describe what happens to the graph of each function.

a) $y = a\cos 3\left(x - \frac{\pi}{6}\right) + 4$, as a varies

b) $y = 2\cos b\left(x - \frac{\pi}{6}\right) + 4$, as b varies

c) $y = 2\cos 3(x - d) + 4$, as d varies

d) $y = 2\cos 3\left(x - \frac{\pi}{6}\right) + c$, as c varies

18. Application

a) Determine the period of the function $y = \cos 2\pi x$. Then graph the function over two complete cycles.

b) Repeat part a for each function.

　　i) $y = \cos\frac{2\pi}{2}x$ 　　　　　　 **ii)** $y = \cos\frac{2\pi}{3}x$

c) Describe the graph of $y = \cos\frac{2\pi}{p}x$, where p is any real number.

19. Repeat exercise 18 using sine functions.

20. The screen shows the graphs of $y = \cos bx$ for $b = 2$, 1, and 0.5. The coordinates of one point on one graph are shown. Write the coordinates of a point on each of the other graphs with the same y-coordinate as this point.

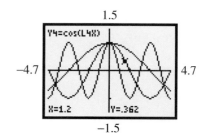

21. a) Use the same window settings as in exercise 20. Graph $y = \sin bx$ for $b = 2$, 1, and 0.5. Trace to the point on the graph of $y = \sin x$ that has x-coordinate 0.8. Record the y-coordinate.

b) Predict the coordinates of a point on each of the other graphs that has the same y-coordinate as the point in part a. Trace to these points to verify your predictions.

22. Consider the function defined by $y = \cos^2 x$.

a) Sketch a graph of this function.

b) Explain why the function is periodic, then determine its period.

c) Determine the maximum and minimum values of the function, and some values of x for which they occur.

d) This function is sinusoidal. Given this information, use the results of part c to write a sinusoidal formula for $\cos^2 x$.

e) Write a similar formula for $\sin^2 x$.

23. a) Two of these equations represent the same function. Which two are they?

   i) $y = 3 \sin 2\left(x - \dfrac{\pi}{2}\right)$ **ii)** $y = 3 \cos 2x$

   iii) $y = 3 \cos 2\left(x + \dfrac{\pi}{4}\right)$ **iv)** $y = 3 \sin 2(x - \pi)$

b) Suppose you are given two equations of the form $y = a \sin b(x - d)$. Describe how you could tell, just by looking at the numbers in the equations, whether they represent the same function.

c) Repeat part b, where one equation has the form $y = a \sin b(x - d)$ and the other equation has the form $y = a \cos b(x - d)$.

d) Create another set of four equations similar to those in part a, where only two equations represent the same function but it is not obvious at first which ones they are.

24. Consider the function $y = a \sin b(x - d) + c$, where $a > 0$.

a) Write an expression for the maximum value of y. For what values of x does this occur?

b) Write an expression for the minimum value of y. For what values of x does this occur?

25. Repeat exercise 24 for the function $y = a \cos b(x - d) + c$, where $a > 0$.

6.5 Applications of Sinusoidal Functions

In the preceding sections, the horizontal axis of each graph of a sinusoidal function was scaled in terms of the irrational number π. These scales are not useful in applications, such as those in Section 6.1, where the horizontal axis is usually marked in time intervals. In this section, we will modify the equations of sinusoidal functions so the horizontal axis is marked with whole numbers.

A weight is supported by a spring. The weight rests 50 cm above a tabletop. The weight is pulled down 25 cm and released at time $t = 0$. This creates a periodic up-and-down motion. It takes 1.6 s for the weight to return to the low position each time.

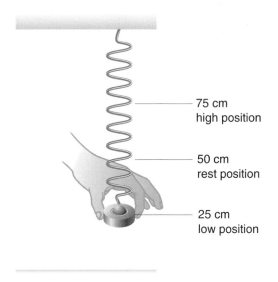

75 cm
high position

50 cm
rest position

25 cm
low position

We sketch a graph of the height of the weight above the tabletop against time, then show the coordinates of some maximum and minimum points and the rest position. Since the initial position of the weight is (0, 25), and its period is 1.6 s, the first maximum is (0.8, 75) and the second minimum is (1.6, 25).

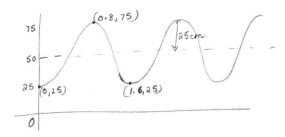

The mean height is 50 cm and the amplitude is 25 cm. We transfer the information on the sketch to grid paper.

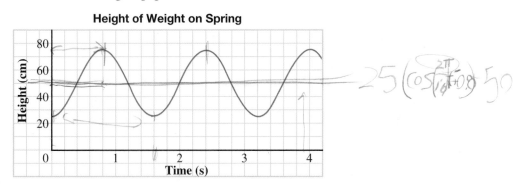

Height of Weight on Spring

Let h metres represent the height of the weight above the tabletop after t seconds. Since we know the position of the first maximum, we use a cosine function to describe the motion.

The equation of the function has the form $h = a \cos b(t - d) + c$.

The amplitude, a, is 25.

The phase shift, d, is 0.8.

The vertical displacement, c, is 50 cm.

Then, the equation of the function is $h = 25 \cos b(t - 0.8) + 50$, where b is to be determined.

In this equation, the period is $\frac{2\pi}{b}$. The period of the motion is 1.6 s.

Therefore, $\frac{2\pi}{b} = 1.6$

$$2\pi = 1.6b$$

$$b = \frac{2\pi}{1.6}$$

Discuss

Why do we not simplify $\frac{2\pi}{1.6}$ and write it as $\frac{\pi}{0.8}$?

The equation of the function is $h = 25 \cos \frac{2\pi}{1.6}(t - 0.8) + 50$.

Notice the meaning of the numbers in this equation.

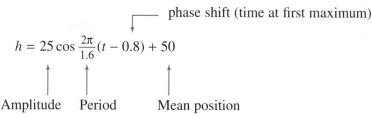

phase shift (time at first maximum)

$$h = 25 \cos \frac{2\pi}{1.6}(t - 0.8) + 50$$

Amplitude   Period   Mean position

When we write this equation, we assume the relationship between the height of the weight and time is sinusoidal. It can be shown that this is true.

Take Note

The General Cosine Function

$$y = a \cos \frac{2\pi}{b}(x - d) + c$$

$|a|$ is the amplitude.

b is the period, $b > 0$

d is the phase shift (the x-coordinate of the first maximum).

c is the vertical displacement.

When we work with sinusoidal functions, π must occur either on the graph or in the equation. To have the horizontal axis marked with whole numbers, π must occur in the equation.

Example 1

Write two other equations for the function $h = 25 \cos \frac{2\pi}{1.6}(t - 0.8) + 50$.
Use a cosine for one function and a sine for the other function.

Solution

For another cosine function, use a different phase shift. Since
$0.8 \text{ s} + 1.6 \text{ s} = 2.4 \text{ s}$, the second maximum occurs when $t = 2.4 \text{ s}$.

Another equation is $h = 25 \cos \frac{2\pi}{1.6}(t - 2.4) + 50$.

For a sine function, the cycle starts when $h = 50 \text{ cm}$ and $t = 0.4 \text{ s}$.

Another equation is $h = 25 \sin \frac{2\pi}{1.6}(t - 0.4) + 50$.

Example 2

Use the equation of the function $h = 25 \cos \frac{2\pi}{1.6}(t - 0.8) + 50$.

a) Calculate the height of the weight above the tabletop after 3.0 s.

b) Determine one of the times when the height of the weight is 60 cm.

Solution

Make sure your calculator is in radian mode.

Using a graphing calculator

a) Use the window shown in the screen below.
Graph the function above.
Key in: [Y=] 25 [COS] 2 [2nd]
[^] [(] [X,T,θ,n] [−] 0.8 [)]
[÷] 1.6 [)] [+] 50 [GRAPH]

Press [TRACE] 3 [ENTER].

After 3.0 s, the mass is approximately 32.3 cm above the tabletop.

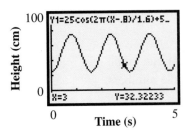

Using a scientific calculator

a) Substitute $t = 3$ in the equation.
$$h = 25 \cos \frac{2\pi}{1.6}(3 - 0.8) + 50$$
$$\doteq 32.322\ 330\ 47$$
After 3.0 s, the mass is approximately 32.3 cm above the tabletop.

b) Substitute $h = 60$ in the equation, then solve for t.
$$25 \cos \frac{2\pi}{1.6}(t - 0.8) + 50 = 60$$
$$25 \cos \frac{2\pi}{1.6}(t - 0.8) = 10$$
$$\cos \frac{2\pi}{1.6}(t - 0.8) = \frac{10}{25}$$
To find a number whose cosine is $\frac{10}{25}$, use [2nd] [COS] for [COS⁻¹].
Key in: [2nd] [COS] 10 [÷] 25
[ENTER =] to display 1.159279481.

b) Graph $y = 60$ on the same screen. Activate the intersect feature. Key in: [2nd] [TRACE] **5**. Move the cursor to the left of one intersection point. Press [ENTER]. Move the cursor to the right of the point. Press [ENTER] [ENTER].

The mass is 60 cm above the tabletop at approximately 2.10 s.

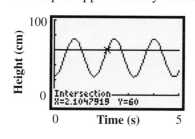

Hence,

$$2\pi\frac{(t - 0.8)}{1.6} \doteq 1.159\ 279\ 481$$

$$t - 0.8 \doteq \frac{1.159\ 279\ 481 \times 1.6}{2\pi}$$

$$t \doteq 1.095\ 208\ 096$$

The mass is 60 cm above the tabletop at approximately 1.10 s.

Discuss

Why do the two methods produce different answers for part b?

In summer, the sun sets later than it does in winter. The time of the sunset can be important information for some people including parents, environmentalists, and film-makers. The latest sunsets occur around June 21 (the 172nd day of the year), and the earliest ones occur around December 21 (the 355th day of the year).

Sunset times at Parry Sound on these dates in 2001 are given in the table.

Date	Day of the year	Sunset time (standard time)
June 21	172	20.18 h
December 21	355	16.68 h

You can use these data to write an equation for the time of the sunset at Parry Sound on any day of the year.

Example 3

Determine an equation for the time of the sunset at Parry Sound on the nth day of the year.

Solution

Sketch the sinusoidal curve.
Mark one maximum point (172, 20.18).
Mark the next minimum point (355, 16.68).

The mean sunset time is $\dfrac{20.18\ h + 16.68\ h}{2} = 18.43\ h$.

This is the vertical displacement.

The amplitude is $\dfrac{20.18\ h - 16.68\ h}{2} = 1.75\ h$.

The period is 365 days.

Since we know the coordinates of the first maximum point, use a cosine function. The phase shift is the n-coordinate of the first maximum point, 172.

Show this information on the rough sketch.

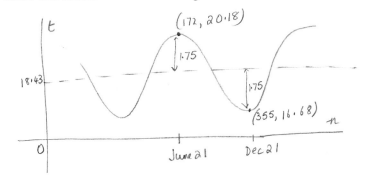

An equation for the time of the sunset at Parry Sound on the nth day of the year is

$$t = 1.75 \cos \frac{2\pi}{365}(n - 172) + 18.43$$

We can use the equation in *Example 3* to calculate the time of the sunset on any day of the year, or to calculate the day(s) when the sun sets at a particular time (see exercise 12). When we write the equation in *Example 3*, we assume the variation in the times of the sunset is sinusoidal. This is reasonable because sunsets are caused by the motion of Earth in its orbit around the sun. The variation in the times of the sunset is caused by Earth's axis being tilted with respect to the plane of the orbit.

6.5 Exercises

A

1. State the amplitude, period, phase shift, and vertical displacement for each function.

a) $y = 2 \cos \frac{2\pi}{5}(x - 3) + 4$

b) $y = 6 \cos \frac{2\pi}{3}(x - 1) + 10$

c) $y = 12 \cos \frac{2\pi}{6}(x - 1) + 12$

d) $y = 15 \cos \frac{2\pi}{100}(x - 30) + 75$

2. Identify the period of each function. Then write its equation in the form $y = \cos \dfrac{2\pi}{p}x$.

a)
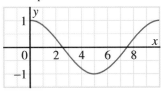

b)
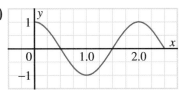

c)
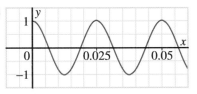

d)
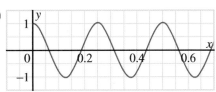

B

3. Each function below is sinusoidal. For each graph, state:

    i) the amplitude   **ii)** the period   **iii)** a possible phase shift

    iv) the maximum value of y, and 4 values of x for which it occurs

    v) the minimum value of y, and 4 values of x for which it occurs

    vi) the range   **vii)** the vertical displacement

a)
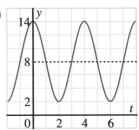

b)
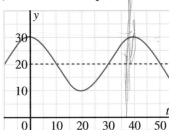

4. Write an equation to represent each function in exercise 3.

5. Write an equation for each function in the form $y = a\cos \dfrac{2\pi}{p}x + c$.

a)

b)
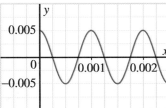

c)
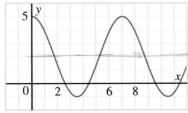

d)
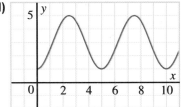

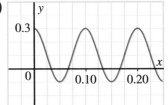

6. Choose one graph and its equation from exercise 5. Pose a problem for which the graph and/or its equation is required in the solution of the problem. Solve the problem you posed.

7. **Communication** Refer to the graph on page 362 and the equation on page 363 that show the height of the weight on a spring as a function of time. Describe how the graph and the equation would change in each case.

   a) The mean position is 60 cm above the tabletop.

   b) The weight is pulled down 20 cm.

   c) It takes 2.0 s for the weight to return to the low position each time.

8. **Application** Towers and skyscrapers appear to be rigid, but they are designed to sway with the wind. Suppose you are standing on the glass floor of the CN Tower, which is 342 m above the ground. The graph shows how your horizontal position might change during a strong wind.

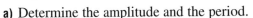
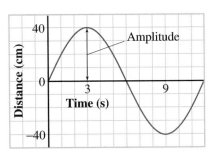

   a) Determine the amplitude and the period.

   b) Write an equation for the function.

   c) Suppose you are standing in the Sky Pod, which is 447 m above the ground. Describe how the graph and the equation would be different.

   d) Pose a problem about the motion of the CN Tower. Solve the problem you posed.

9. **Knowledge/Understanding** The volume of air in the lungs during normal breathing is a sinusoidal function of time. Suppose a person's lungs contain from 2200 mL to 2800 mL of air during normal breathing. Suppose a normal breath takes 4 s, and that time $t = 0$ s corresponds to a minimum volume.

   a) Let V millilitres represent the volume of air in the person's lungs. Draw a graph of V against t for 20 s.

   b) State the period, amplitude, phase shift, and vertical displacement.

   c) Write an equation for the function.

   d) Describe how the graph and the equation would change in each case.
      i) The person breathes more rapidly.
      ii) The person takes bigger breaths.

10. Thinking/Inquiry/Problem Solving The pedals of an exercise bicycle are mounted on a bracket whose centre is 30 cm above the floor. Each pedal is 18 cm from the centre of the bracket. Assume the bicycle is pedalled at 60 cycles per minute. The centre of the bracket is 100 cm from a wall in front of the bicycle.

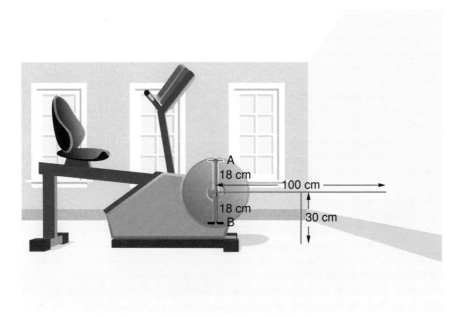

Four sinusoidal functions are involved in this situation:

    height of pedal A above the floor   ①
    height of pedal B above the floor   ②
    distance from pedal A to the wall   ③
    distance from pedal B to the wall   ④

Assume pedal A starts at the top when $t = 0$.

a) **i)** Graph functions ① and ② on the same grid for the first few cycles.
  ii) Write the equations of functions ① and ②.
 iii) Describe how the graphs and equations are related.

b) Repeat part a using functions ③ and ④.

c) Choose either function ① or function ③. Describe how its graph and equation are related.

11. Refer to *Example 2*. Suppose your calculator is in degree mode.

a) How would you modify the equation $h = 25 \cos \frac{2\pi}{1.6}(t - 0.8) + 50$ to obtain the correct answers to parts a and b?

b) Check your answer to part a by repeating the solution of *Example 2* with your modified equation.

12. In *Example 3*, the equation $t = 1.75 \cos \dfrac{2\pi}{365}(n - 172) + 18.43$ describes the time of the sunset at Parry Sound on the nth day of the year. Use this equation.

a) Calculate the time of the sunset on August 1 (the 212th day of the year).

b) Determine one of the dates when the sun sets at 6 P.M.

c) Pose a problem about the times of sunset in Parry Sound. Solve the problem you posed.

13. On page 329, there is a graph that shows the number of hours of sunlight in Windsor. This graph is repeated below.

Hours of Sunlight in Windsor

a) The maximum number of hours of sunlight is 15.3 h, and occurs on June 21 (day 172). The minimum number of hours of sunlight is 9.1 h, and occurs on December 21 (day 355). Use this information. Determine the period, amplitude, phase shift, and vertical displacement.

b) Write an equation for the function.

c) Use the equation to calculate the number of hours of sunlight on April 1 (day 91).

d) Determine a day when there are 14 h of sunlight.

14. The table shows the minimum and maximum number of hours of sunlight in Dryden, Ontario.

Date	Day of the year	Hours of sunlight
June 21	172	15.7
December 21	355	8.1

a) Determine an equation for the number of hours of sunlight on the nth day of the year.

b) Graph the equation.

c) Predict the number of hours of sunlight on February 10 (day 41).

d) Predict a day when there are 14 h of sunlight.

e) Pose a problem about the number of hours of sunlight in Dryden. Solve the problem you posed.

15. The world's highest tides occur at the Bay of Fundy. The following data for Hopewell Cape, NB, a popular tourist location, were obtained from the Internet. These data were used to draw the graph on page 330.

Date	Time	Height	
February 21, 2001	10:54 A.M.	11.43 m	High tide
	5:53 P.M.	2.12 m	Low tide
	11:19 P.M.	11.21 m	High tide
February 22, 2001	5:50 A.M.	2.34 m	Low tide
	11:34 A.M.	11.71 m	High tide

The maximum heights are not the same, nor are the minimum heights. The data are not exactly sinusoidal. Therefore, to use a sinusoidal function to describe the data, you need to make some changes to the data so they are sinusoidal. These changes can be done in different ways.

a) Use the data to predict the height at 3 P.M. on February 21.

b) Describe how you changed the data.

c) Complete part a in a different way, and compare the results.

d) In parts a and c, you created two possible equations for the graph on page 330. Would it matter which equation is used to draw the graph? Explain.

16. Pistons in a car engine move up and down many times each second. The graph shows how the height varies with time for the pistons in a 6-cylinder engine.

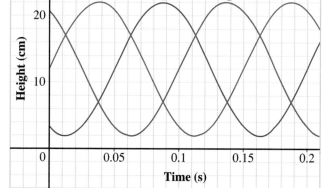

a) Determine an equation for each graph.

b) The *frequency* of the periodic motion is the reciprocal of the period. Determine the frequency.

c) The graph describes the motion of all 6 cylinders. Suggest why there are only 3 curves on the graph.

d) Choose one graph. Describe how the speed of the piston changes.

e) Determine the maximum speed of the piston, and the times when it occurs.

6.6 Graphing the Tangent Function

In Chapter 5, we defined $\tan \theta = \frac{\sin \theta}{\cos \theta}$, where θ represents the measure of an angle in standard position. Therefore, when x is in radians, $\tan x = \frac{\sin x}{\cos x}$. This expression is not useful for graphing the function $y = \tan x$ because we would have to divide $\sin x$ by $\cos x$ for every value of x. Although that can be done by computers, it is difficult to visualize the result. We need a way to express $\tan x$ that makes it possible to visualize its graph without having to think about dividing $\sin x$ by $\cos x$.

We express $\tan x$ using the independent variable only once. This makes it easier to visualize the graph of $y = \tan x$.

Visualize a point P that rotates around a unit circle, with centre O(0, 0). Point A has coordinates (1, 0), and point P has coordinates $(\cos x, \sin x)$, where x represents the measure of $\angle AOP$ in radians. Draw a vertical line through A. This line is a *tangent* to the circle because it meets the circle at only one point. Let Q(1, k) be the point where the line through O and P intersects the tangent.

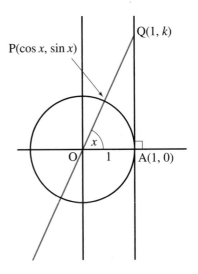

Since P and Q lie on the same line through O(0, 0), the slopes of OQ and OP are equal.

Therefore, $\qquad \dfrac{k}{1} = \dfrac{\sin x}{\cos x}$

$\qquad\qquad\quad k = \tan x$

Take Note

Coordinate Property of tan x

Point P is on the unit circle, with centre O(0, 0).

Point A has coordinates (1, 0) and $\angle POA = x$ radians.

Q is the point where OP intersects the vertical line through A.

Then, $\tan x$ is the second coordinate of Q.

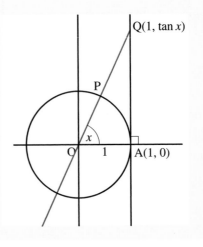

Determine each value to 4 decimal places. Draw a diagram to explain its meaning.

a) tan 1.2

b) tan 2.3

Solution

Make sure the calculator is in radian mode.

a) tan 1.2 $\doteq$ 2.5722

This means that when ∠AOP is 1.2 radians (about 69°), the line through O and P intersects the tangent at A(1, 0) at the point with coordinates (1, 2.5722). The slope of OP is 2.5722.

b) tan 2.3 $\doteq$ −1.1192

This means that when ∠AOP is 2.3 radians (about 132°), the line through O and P intersects the tangent at A(1, 0) at the point with coordinates (1, −1.1192). The slope of OP is −1.1192.

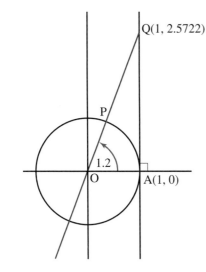

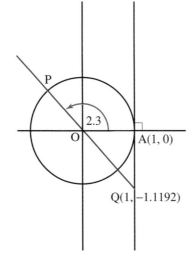

Discuss

The word "tangent" may refer to a trigonometric function or to a line that meets a circle at one point. When you read the word "tangent", how do you know to which it refers?

Graphing the function $y = \tan x$

Suppose x starts at 0 and increases to π. Then $\tan x$ changes as follows.

$x = 0$

$\tan x = 0$

As x increases from 0 to $\frac{\pi}{4}$, $\tan x$ increases from 0 to 1.

$x = \frac{\pi}{4}$

$\tan x = 1$

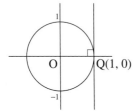

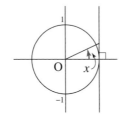

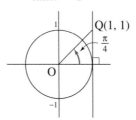

As *x* increases from $\frac{\pi}{4}$ to $\frac{\pi}{2}$, tan *x* continues to increase.

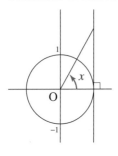

$x = \frac{\pi}{2}$

tan $\frac{\pi}{2}$ is undefined.

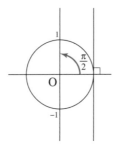

As *x* increases from $\frac{\pi}{2}$ to $\frac{3\pi}{4}$, tan *x* increases to -1.

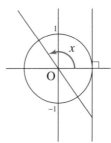

$x = \frac{3\pi}{4}$

tan *x* = -1

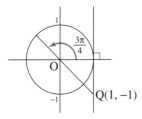

As *x* increases from $\frac{3\pi}{4}$ to π, tan *x* increases from -1 to 0.

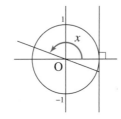

$x = \pi$

tan *x* = 0

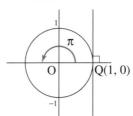

We use these results to sketch the graph of *y* = tan *x* for $0 \le x \le \pi$. No value is plotted for tan *x* when $x = \frac{\pi}{2}$. We say that tan $\frac{\pi}{2}$ is undefined. As *x* continues beyond π, the line OP intersects the tangent at A at the same locations as before, and the same values of tan *x* are encountered. Hence, the graph can be continued to the right. Similarly, the graph can be continued to the left, corresponding to a rotation in the counterclockwise direction.

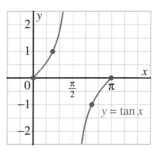

Suppose $x < \frac{\pi}{2}$. As *x* increases and comes closer and closer to $\frac{\pi}{2}$, the graph comes closer and closer to the line $x = \frac{\pi}{2}$, but never reaches this line.

Suppose $x > \frac{\pi}{2}$. As *x* decreases and comes closer and closer to $\frac{\pi}{2}$, the graph comes closer and closer to the line $x = \frac{\pi}{2}$, but never reaches this line.

For these reasons, the line $x = \frac{\pi}{2}$ is called an *asymptote*.

The graph of *y* = tan *x* has asymptotes $x = \pm\frac{\pi}{2}$, $x = \pm\frac{3\pi}{2}$, $x = \pm\frac{5\pi}{2}$, ...

Take Note

Properties of the Function *y* = tan *x*

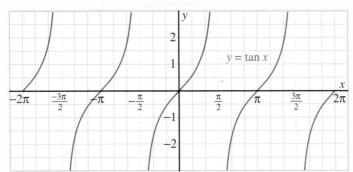

Period: π

Domain: all real numbers except $\pm\frac{\pi}{2}$, $\pm\frac{3\pi}{2}$, …

Range: all real numbers

x-intercepts: 0, ±π, ±2π, …

y-intercept: 0

Asymptotes: $x = \pm\frac{\pi}{2}$, $x = \pm\frac{3\pi}{2}$, $x = \pm\frac{5\pi}{2}$, …

6.6) Exercises

A

1. Explain why each statement is true.

   a) The function *y* = tan *x* is periodic.

   b) The period of the function *y* = tan *x* is not the same as the period of the functions *y* = cos *x* and *y* = sin *x*.

   c) Tan *x* is not defined for all values of *x*.

 2. In these diagrams, graphs of *y* = tan *x* were started using different scales. Copy each graph onto grid paper, then extend it for two cycles.

a)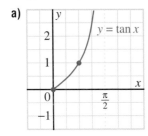

b)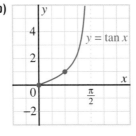

c)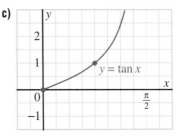

B

3. Determine each value. Draw a diagram to explain the meaning of each result.

a) $\tan 2.7$ **b)** $\tan 3.9$ **c)** $\tan(-1.25)$ **d)** $\tan(-4.0)$

e) $\tan 2\pi$ **f)** $\tan \dfrac{3\pi}{4}$ **g)** $\tan \dfrac{5\pi}{4}$ **g)** $\tan\left(-\dfrac{\pi}{2}\right)$

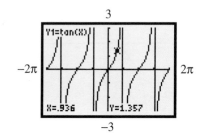

4. The graphing calculator screen shows the coordinates of one point on the graph of $y = \tan x$. Use only the information on the screen. Write the coordinates of three other points on the graph of $y = \tan x$ that have the same y-coordinate as this point.

5. Compare the y-coordinate in the screen in exercise 4 with the y-coordinates in the screens on page 338. Write to explain how the three y-coordinates are related.

6. Communication Compare the graph of $y = \tan x$ with the graph of $y = \sin x$. Explain the similarities and the differences. Use examples to illustrate your explanations.

7. Knowledge/Understanding For the function $y = \tan x$:

a) Why are there no maximum or minimum values?

b) What are the domain and range of the function?

c) What are the x-intercepts of the graph?

d) What is the y-intercept of the graph?

e) What is the period?

8. Describe and account for any symmetry in the graph of $y = \tan x$.

9. Thinking/Inquiry/Problem Solving

When $0 < x < \dfrac{\pi}{2}$, which is greater, $\sin x$ or $\tan x$? Explain your answer in two different ways.

10. Application A rocket is launched vertically upward. From an observation station 100 m away, the angle of elevation of the rocket is measured as it rises.

a) Write the height of the rocket as a function of the angle of elevation, using appropriate variables.

b) Graph the function in part a for reasonable angles of elevation.

c) For what heights do you think the graph is useful? Explain.

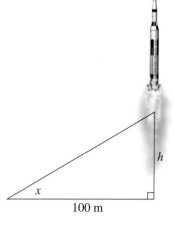

11. Graph $y = \tan x$ using the window $-4.7 \le x \le 4.7$ and $-3.1 \le y \le 3.1$.

a) Trace along the curve and observe how y changes. Move the cursor as close to $\frac{\pi}{2}$ as possible. What happens to the value of y?

b) While Trace mode is active, press [2nd] [^] [÷] 2 [ENTER] to move the cursor to the point where $x = \frac{\pi}{2}$. Is the result what you expected? Explain.

c) Repeat part b, moving the cursor to: $\frac{\pi}{4}$, $\frac{3\pi}{4}$, and $-\frac{\pi}{2}$.

12. a) Use the Mode menu to display numbers to 3 decimal places. Graph $y = \tan x$ using the window $-2\pi \le x \le 2\pi$ and $-1.5 \le y \le 1.5$. Trace to the point where $x = 1.069$. Observe the corresponding value of y.

b) Predict some other values of x that produce the same value of y. Trace to these points to verify your predictions.

13. a) Use grid paper. Graph $y = \sin x$ and $y = 2 \cos x$ on the same axes for $0 \le x \le 2\pi$.

b) Use a graphing calculator to make the same graph.

c) Use Trace and Zoom or the intersect feature to determine all solutions to the equation $\sin x = 2 \cos x$ between 0 and 2π.

d) Find a way to check your results.

14. A long straight wall runs north and south. A powerful searchlight is mounted 20 m west of the wall and rotates counterclockwise (viewed from above) with one rotation every 10 s. This is a double searchlight, which casts a beam both backward and forward. At time $t = 0$, the light beam is perpendicular to the wall and illuminates a spot, A, on the wall.

a) Sketch a diagram to illustrate this situation.

b) Determine an equation for the distance, d metres, of the illuminated spot from A after t seconds.

c) Graph the function in part b.

C

15. Refer to exercise 18 in Section 6.2. Suppose the angle x is in degrees instead of radians.

a) How would the graph of $y = \tan x$ on page 375 change?

b) Is the function $y = \tan x$ (where x is in degrees) the same as the function $y = \tan x$ (where x is in radians)? Explain.

c) For values of x close to 0, how do the values of x, $\sin x$, and $\tan x$ compare?

1. Consider the function $y = 4 \sin 2\left(x - \frac{\pi}{4}\right) + 5$.

  a) State the phase shift, period, vertical displacement, and amplitude.

  b) Graph the function over two complete cycles.

  c) What are the domain and range of the function?

2. Determine the phase shift and the period of each function, then draw its graph.

  a) $y = \sin(2x - \pi)$ **b)** $y = 2 \cos(3x - \pi) + 1$

  c) $y = 2 \cos(3x - \pi) + 4$ **d)** $y = 5 \sin(4x + \pi) - 3$

3. The graphing calculator screen shows the coordinates of one point on the graph of $y = \sin \frac{\pi}{2} x$. Use the information on the screen. Write the coordinates of four other points on the graph that have the same y-coordinate as this point.

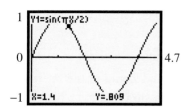

4. This graph shows how the voltage, V volts, varies with time, t seconds, for the electricity provided to an electrical appliance.

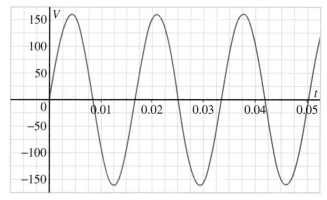

  a) Identify the period and amplitude of the function.

  b) What is the peak (maximum) voltage?

  c) Write an equation to describe the graph.

5. Use the Mode menu of a graphing calculator to display numbers to 3 decimal places. Graph $y = \tan x$, using the window $-2\pi \le x \le 2\pi$, $-3 \le y \le 3$. Trace to the point where $x = \frac{\pi}{6}$. Note the corresponding y-coordinate. Predict other values of x that produce the same value of y.

The Equation of a Damped Spring

A small weight is attached to the bottom of a spring. A vertical ruler is fastened so when the weight is pulled down and released, the oscillations can be measured with the ruler.

Representing the Height of the Weight in Mathematical Form

We can determine an equation for the height of the weight as a function of time. Let y centimetres represent the height of the weight from its equilibrium (rest) position after t seconds.

We can sketch a graph that illustrates the motion of the weight over time by making the weight oscillate and plotting some ordered pairs (t, y). For convenience, we take $t = 0$ at a point when the weight is at its equilibrium position and rising.

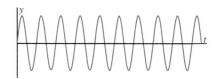

The graph looks like a sine function, and in Sections 6.3 and 6.4 we assumed that the variation in the height of the weight is sinusoidal. We need calculus to prove this. However, an experiment can be performed that makes our choice of a sinusoidal function plausible.

A bicycle wheel is placed vertically. A small stick is tied to the rim, perpendicular to the wheel, and the wheel is rotated. A light source is placed in the plane of the wheel to cast a shadow of the wheel on a wall. What you see on the wall is a vertical line (the wheel) and a horizontal bar (the stick) moving up and down. We ignore the wheel and consider the motion of the shadow of the stick. It reverses direction at the top and bottom. Now consider the oscillating spring. The comparison is quite striking. *It is exactly the same motion!*

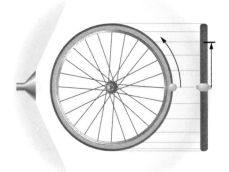

We could use a sine or cosine function to model the height of the weight. In this case, our choice for $t = 0$ makes it more convenient to use the sine function. The equation has the form $y = a \sin \frac{2\pi}{b} t$, where a is the amplitude and b is the period.

In one experiment, these parameters were measured as $a = 60$ cm and $b = 2.1$ s. The equation is $y = 60 \sin \frac{2\pi}{2.1} t$.

Measuring a and b

The weight was pulled down 60 cm from its equilibrium position, then released. Thus, $a = 60$. Ten complete cycles were timed and they took 21 s. This gives a period of 2.1 s per cycle; so $b = 2.1$.

Reflecting on the Reasonableness of the Results

The equation above accurately models the oscillations of the weight for only a short period of time. It assumes the amplitude of the oscillations remains constant. In reality, the oscillations gradually die down, and the 60 should be replaced with smaller numbers. This is the phenomenon of *damping* — the effect of frictional forces that rob the system of energy.

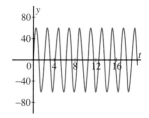

Formulating Questions

1. How can we model the decrease in amplitude due to the effects of friction?

2. What is the equation of the damped spring?

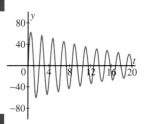

Selecting Strategies, Resources, Technology, and Tools

An equation that accounts for damping will have amplitude that decreases with time.

The standard theory of the damped spring predicts a multiplicative decrease in amplitude; that is, the amplitude decreases at a constant percent rate. For example, if a decreases by 10% in the first minute, it will decrease by another 10% in the second minute, another 10% in the third minute, and so on.

Since we are measuring time in seconds, we need a as a function of t in seconds. This means that we need to determine the *one-second* decrease in amplitude. It is difficult to directly measure the decrease over such a short interval of time. Instead, we measure the decrease in amplitude over a longer period of time and calculate the one-second multiplier from it.

Suppose in the first 10 min, we measure a change in amplitude from 60 cm to 8 cm. We can calculate the one-second decrease in amplitude as follows.

Let k be the one-second multiplier.
Originally the amplitude is 60 cm.
After 1 s, the amplitude is $60k$ cm.
After 2 s, the amplitude is $60k^2$ cm.
After 3 s, the amplitude is $60k^3$ cm.

$\vdots \qquad\qquad \vdots$

After t s, the amplitude is $60k^t$ cm.

What about the period?

How does it change as the amplitude changes? For example, does the period decrease as the amplitude decreases?

According to the theory of the damped spring, the period is constant. It is independent of the amplitude. This can be verified experimentally by timing 10 oscillations at different amplitudes.

t (s)	a (cm)
0	60
$\vdots$	$\vdots$
600	8

This gives a multiplier of $\frac{8}{60}$ over a period of 600 s.

The amplitude can be represented by the equation $a = 60k^t$.

To determine k, substitute $a = 8$ and $t = 600$.

$$8 = 60k^{600}$$

$$k^{600} = \frac{8}{60}$$

$$k = \left(\frac{8}{60}\right)^{\frac{1}{600}}$$

$$\doteq 0.996\ 65$$

Thus, an equation for the amplitude as a function of time is $a = 60(0.996\ 65)^t$.

Interpreting Information and Forming Conclusions

Here is the equation that models the height, y centimetres, of the weight from its equilibrium position after t seconds.

$$y = a \sin \frac{2\pi}{b}t$$

initial   one-second
amplitude multiplier

$$y = 60(0.996\ 65)^t \sin \frac{2\pi}{2.1}t$$

period

exponential   periodic
function   function

A sketch of the graph for the 10-min period of the experiment is shown below.

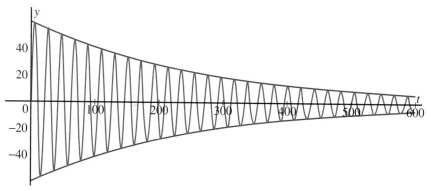

In addition to the height, y, of the weight, we have also plotted the amplitude functions $a = \pm 60(0.996\ 65)^t$. These curves enclose the points on the graph of the height function. As t increases, $\sin \frac{2\pi}{2.1}t$ oscillates between -1 and 1; therefore, y oscillates between $-a$ and a. The result is a sine curve with an exponentially decaying amplitude.

A quantity whose original amount is repeatedly multiplied by a number between 0 and 1 is said to exhibit *exponential decay*. The equation that represents this decay is an example of an *exponential function*. You will study exponential functions in grade 12.

The equation of the damped spring is the product of 2 functions: an exponential function and a periodic function.

This graph is not exactly the graph of the equation of the damped spring.

If we drew the real graph, it would be a grey blur because, in 600 s, the spring oscillates 286 times (2.1 s/oscillation). For this graph, we multiplied the period by 10 so, in 600 s, we have only 28.6 oscillations. That allows us to show the up and down motion more easily. Remember, the accurate graph has 10 oscillations for every one shown.

Problems

1. A damped spring with a weight on one end makes 3 cycles in 2 s. The oscillation starts (at $t = 0$) with amplitude 40 cm. After 5 min, the amplitude has decreased to 20 cm. Determine the equation of the height of the weight, y centimetres, after t seconds under each condition.

   a) The weight starts at its equilibrium position ($y = 0$) and is rising.

   b) The weight starts at its lowest point ($y = -40$).

2. A damped spring with a weight on one end has a period of 4 s. Suppose the oscillation has initial amplitude 50 cm and is reduced by 10% each second. The weight starts at its equilibrium position ($y = 0$) and is rising.

   a) Determine the equation of the height of the weight, y centimetres, after t seconds.

   b) Draw a graph of y against t for 3 cycles. Begin by drawing the amplitude curve and its negative. As a guide, plot the points at which the sine function has values 1 or –1. These are the points at which the y-graph meets either the amplitude curve or its negative.

   c) Calculate the height of the weight at $t = 2.5$ s. Mark this point on the graph.

Challenge Problems

3. a) Determine an equation for the oscillatory curve graphed at the right. The amplitude curves are parabolas with vertices $(10, 0)$.

   b) Using trial and error, find all the times at which $y = -60$. Use the graph as a guide.

4. An arm OA has length 1 unit and rotates counterclockwise about O with a period of 40 s. At the same time, a spherical ball moves at a constant speed back and forth along the arm between O and A. The ball takes 10 s to go from O to A and back to O again. Suppose at $t = 0$, the ball starts at O and the arm is horizontal with A to the right of O.

   a) Sketch the trajectory of the ball for one complete period of the motion.

   b) Suppose the origin of a coordinate system is at O. Determine equations for the x- and y-coordinates of the centre of the ball as functions of time.

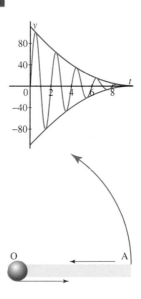

Trigonometric Function Tools

The Sine, Cosine, and Tangent Functions

Point P is on the unit circle, with centre O(0, 0).

Point A has coordinates (1, 0), and $\angle POA = x$ radians.

Q is the point where OP intersects the vertical line through A.

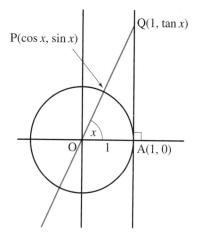

We define: $\cos x$ is the first coordinate of P.

$\sin x$ is the second coordinate of P.

$\tan x$ is the second coordinate of Q.

Properties of $y = \sin x$, $y = \cos x$, and $y = \tan x$

	$y = \sin x$	$y = \cos x$	$y = \tan x$
Period	2π	2π	π
Maximum value of y	1	1	–
Minimum value of y	-1	-1	–
Domain	all real numbers	all real numbers	all real numbers except $\pm\frac{\pi}{2},\ \pm\frac{3\pi}{2},\ \ldots$
Range	$-1 \le y \le 1$	$-1 \le y \le 1$	all real numbers
x-intercepts	$0, \pm\pi, \pm 2\pi, \ldots$	$\pm\frac{\pi}{2},\ \pm\frac{3\pi}{2},\ \pm\frac{5\pi}{2}, \ldots$	$0, \pm\pi, \pm 2\pi, \ldots$
y-intercept	0	1	0
Asymptotes	–	–	$x = \pm\frac{\pi}{2},\ x = \pm\frac{3\pi}{2},\ x = \pm\frac{5\pi}{2}, \ldots$

Graphing a Sinusoidal Function

- The amplitude

  The graphs of $y = a \sin x$ and $y = a \cos x$ are the images of the graphs of $y = \sin x$ and $y = \cos x$, respectively, under a vertical expansion or compression. When $a < 0$, there is also a reflection in the x-axis. See page 342 for the graphs.

Review Exercises

- **The vertical displacement**

  The graphs of $y = \sin x + c$ and $y = \cos x + c$ are the images of the graphs of $y = \sin x$ and $y = \cos x$, respectively, under a vertical translation of c units. See page 343 for the graphs.

- **The phase shift**

  The graphs of $y = \sin(x - d)$ and $y = \cos(x - d)$ are the images of the graphs of $y = \sin x$ and $y = \cos x$, respectively, under a horizontal translation of d units. See page 344 for the graphs.

- **The period**

  The graphs of $y = \sin bx$ and $y = \cos bx$ are the images of the graphs of $y = \sin x$ and $y = \cos x$, respectively, under a horizontal compression or expansion. See page 353 for the graphs.

The General Cosine Function

$$y = a\cos\frac{2\pi}{b}(x - d) + c$$

$|a|$ is the amplitude.

b is the period, $b > 0$.

d is the phase shift (the x-coordinate of the first maximum).

c is the vertical displacement.

6.1   **1.** Use this graph.

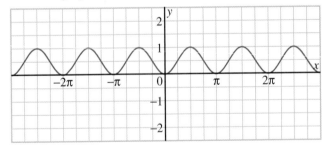

a) What is the maximum value of y?

b) What is the minimum value of y?

c) What is the period of the function?

2. Is this graph periodic? Give reasons for your answer.

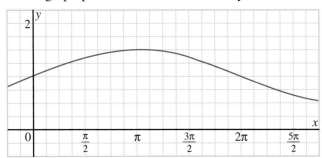

3. Sunspots are dark spots that appear from time to time on the surface of the sun. This graph shows how the number of sunspots varied from 1944 to 1998.

Monthly Mean Sunspot Numbers, 1944–1998

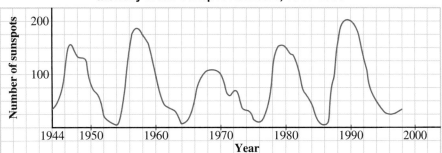

The graph shows that sunspot activity increases and decreases at approximately regular intervals. Estimate the average number of years between the times when there is a maximum number of sunspots.

6.2 **4. a)** On grid paper, sketch $y = \cos x$ for $-2\pi \le x \le 2\pi$.

b) State: the maximum value of y; the minimum value of y; the domain and range; the x-intercepts; the y-intercept; and the period.

5. a) Graph the functions $y = \sin x$ and $y = \cos x$ on the same grid or screen for $0 \le x \le 2\pi$.

b) How are the two graphs related?

c) What is the period of each function?

d) What are the coordinates of the points of intersection?

6. How many times does the graph of $y = \sin x$ intersect the x-axis on the interval $-5\pi \le x \le 5\pi$? Explain how you determined your answer.

6.3 **7.** Sketch a graph of each function, then write a second equation that describes the function.

a) $y = \cos x - 2$ **b)** $y = 2 \sin \left(x - \frac{\pi}{2}\right)$ **c)** $y = 3 \cos \left(x + \pi\right) + 1$

8. Match each graph below with its equation.

i) $y = \sin \left(x + \frac{\pi}{3}\right)$ **ii)** $y = \sin \left(x - \frac{\pi}{2}\right)$ **iii)** $y = \sin \left(x - \frac{\pi}{6}\right)$ **iv)** $y = \sin \left(x + \frac{\pi}{4}\right)$

a)

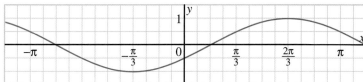

b)

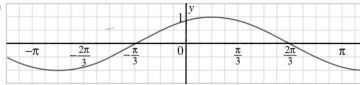

c)

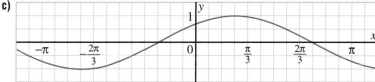

d)

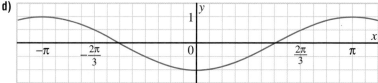

9. For each graph in exercise 8, write a second equation to describe it.

10. Match each graph below with its equation.

i) $y = 2 \sin \left(x + \frac{\pi}{3}\right)$ **ii)** $y = \sin 2x + 2$ **iii)** $y = 2 \sin \left(x - \frac{\pi}{3}\right) + 1$

a)

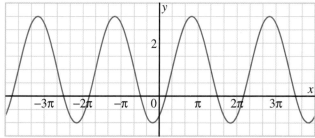

b)

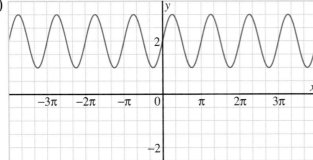

c)

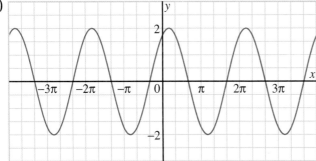

11. Graph each function over two cycles. Determine its domain and range, its phase shift, its amplitude, and its maximum and minimum values.

   a) $y = 2.5 \cos x$
   b) $y = 3.5 \cos x - 2$
   c) $y = 1.5 + 3 \sin x$

   d) $y = \cos\left(x + \frac{\pi}{4}\right)$
   e) $y = 3 \sin\left(x - \frac{5\pi}{6}\right)$
   f) $y = 4 \sin\left(x - \frac{\pi}{6}\right) - 1$

6.4 12. State the amplitude, the period, and the phase shift for each function.

   a) $y = -\sin 2\left(x + \frac{\pi}{4}\right)$
   b) $y = 2 \cos 3\left(x + \frac{\pi}{6}\right)$

13. Graph each function, then state its amplitude and period.

   a) $y = 3 \sin 2x$
   b) $y = 2 \cos \frac{1}{3}x$
   c) $y = \frac{1}{2} \sin 3x$

14. Consider the function $y = 3 \sin 2\left(x + \frac{\pi}{2}\right) - 1$.

   a) State the phase shift, period, vertical displacement, and amplitude.

   b) Graph the function over two complete cycles.

   c) What are the domain and range of the function?

15. Repeat exercise 14 for each function.

   a) $y = 2 \cos 3\left(x - \frac{\pi}{4}\right) + 2$
   b) $y = 0.5 \sin\left(x + \frac{\pi}{3}\right)$

   c) $y = 3 \sin 2\left(x + \frac{3\pi}{4}\right) - 1$
   d) $y = 4 \cos 3\left(x - \frac{7\pi}{6}\right) + 1$

16. Describe what happens to the graph of each function.

 a) $y = a\sin 2\left(x - \frac{\pi}{4}\right) - 1$, as a varies

 b) $y = 3\sin b\left(x - \frac{\pi}{3}\right) + 1$, as b varies

 c) $y = 2\sin 3(x - d) - 1$, as d varies

 d) $y = 4\sin 2\left(x - \frac{\pi}{6}\right) + c$, as c varies

17. On June 21, the 172nd day of the year, a certain town in Ontario has 15.58 h of daylight. On December 21, the 355th day, the town has 8.45 h of daylight.

 a) Determine an equation for the number of hours of daylight on the nth day of the year.

 b) Use the equation to predict the number of hours of daylight on each date.

  i) March 21   **ii)** August 10   **iii)** September 21

18. On a typical day at an ocean port, the water has a maximum depth of 18 m at 6:00 A.M. The minimum depth of 9 m occurs 6.8 h later. Write an equation of the form $h = a\cos b(t - d) + c$ to describe the relationship between the depth of the water and time.

19. Technicians often use oscilloscopes to display graphs of voltage against time. The display may be sinusoidal. A microphone was connected to the oscilloscope, and the voltage, V volts, recorded as a tuning fork was sounded for t seconds. The graph shows the display that might result.

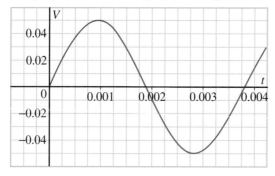

 a) Estimate the period.

 b) The frequency of the tuning fork is the reciprocal of the period. Estimate the frequency of the tuning fork.

 c) Write an equation that describes the graph.

6.6 **20.** Explain why the graph of $y = \tan x$ has asymptotes.

 21. Graph $y = \tan x$ for the interval $-6\pi \le x \le 0$.

Self-Test

1. The graphing calculator screen shows the coordinates of point A on the graph of $y = \sin x$. Point B has the same y-coordinate as point A. Determine the x-coordinate of point B.

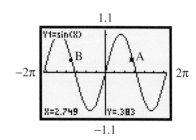

2. **Knowledge/Understanding** Three points P, Q, and R lie on the graph of $y = \sin x$. The x-coordinate of Q is $\frac{3\pi}{4}$. Determine the *exact* coordinates of P, Q, and R.

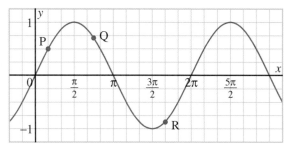

3. **Application** Determine the coordinates of the points of intersection of the graphs of $y = \frac{\pi}{4}$ and $y = \sin 2x$, when $0 \le x \le 2\pi$.

4. Consider the function $y = \cos 2\left(x + \frac{\pi}{2}\right) - 1$.

   a) State the phase shift, period, vertical displacement, and amplitude.

   b) Graph the function over two complete cycles.

   c) What are the domain and range of the function?

5. People get on a Ferris wheel at the bottom. The graph shows how a person's height above the ground changes during the first two rotations of the ride.

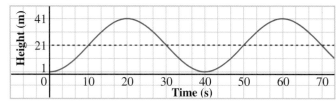

   a) Write an equation that expresses a person's height above the ground, h metres, as a function of time, t seconds.

   b) Calculate the person's height after 15 s.

   c) What is the radius of the Ferris wheel?

6. A water wheel, with radius 7 m, has 1 m submerged. The wheel rotates at 6 revolutions per hour. Time is measured from when point P, on the rim of the wheel, is at its maximum height above the surface of the water.

   a) Graph the distance, d metres, of the point P above the surface of the water during one complete revolution.

   b) Determine an equation that describes d as a function of time, t hours.

   c) How far is P above the water after 8 min?

7. **Thinking/Inquiry/Problem Solving** A tsunami is a fast-moving ocean wave caused by an underwater earthquake. The water first goes down from its normal level, rises an equal distance above its normal level, then returns to its normal level. The period is about 15 min. A tsunami with an amplitude of 10 m approached a pier where the normal depth of water was 9 m.

   a) Assume the depth of water varied sinusoidally with time as the tsunami passed the pier. Predict the depth of water at each time after the tsunami first reached the pier.
   i) 2 min   ii) 4 min   iii) 12 min

   b) According to this model, what will the minimum depth of water be? Explain what this means in terms of the pier.

8. Graph the function $y = \tan x$ for $-\pi \le x \le \pi$. Plot and list the coordinates of 5 points on the graph that have exact values.

9. **Communication** Explain how to determine the number of x-intercepts of the graph $y = \sin bx$ for $-2\pi \le x \le 2\pi$.

Assessment Tasks

1. A bicycle has wheels with radius 30 cm. The bicycle moves along the road at a speed of 6 m/s.

   a) Determine the period of rotation of the tire; that is, the time required for the tire to make one complete revolution.

   b) The outside of the tire has a speck of paint on it. Determine an equation for the height, y metres, of the speck above the road as a function of time, t seconds. Assume the speck is at its highest point when $t = 0$.

   c) Sketch the graph of y against t.

2. A person is riding on a Ferris wheel that turns at a constant speed. The lowest point of the wheel is at ground level. Another person is standing at the side of the wheel on a platform 4 m above the ground. She notes the times that the person on the wheel is at the same level as she. The intervals between two successive times are alternately 6 s and 18 s.

   a) What is the period of the rotation of the Ferris wheel?

   b) What is the radius of the wheel?

**INSIGHTS
INTO A
RICH
PROBLEM**

In earlier grades, and in Chapter 4, you studied quadratic functions.

At the end of this chapter, you will investigate a quartic function. You will use the inverse of a function.

Curriculum Expectations

By the end of this chapter, you will:

- Solve first-degree inequalities and represent the solutions on number lines.

- Define the term *function*.

- Demonstrate facility in the use of function notation for substituting into and evaluating functions.

- Determine, through investigation, the properties of the functions defined by $f(x) = \sqrt{x}$ and $f(x) = \frac{1}{x}$.

- Explain the relationship between a function and its inverse, using examples drawn from linear and quadratic functions, and from the functions $f(x) = \sqrt{x}$ and $f(x) = \frac{1}{x}$.

- Represent inverse functions, using function notation, where appropriate.

- Represent transformations of the functions defined by $f(x) = x$, $f(x) = x^2$, $f(x) = \sqrt{x}$, $f(x) = \sin x$, and $f(x) = \cos x$, using function notation.

- Describe, by interpreting function notation, the relationship between the graph of a function and its image under one or more transformations.

- State the domain and range of transformations of the functions defined by $f(x) = x$, $f(x) = x^2$, $f(x) = \sqrt{x}$, $f(x) = \sin x$, and $f(x) = \cos x$.

- Use graphing technology effectively.

1. New: The Vertical Line Test

Remember that a function is a rule that gives a *single* output number for every valid input number. One word is italicized to emphasize an important part of this definition. For each input number, there must be only one output number.

Now consider this rule. When you determine the square root of the input number, the result is the output number. We make a table of values and draw the graph.

x	y
0	0
1	±1
4	±2
9	±3

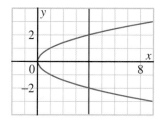

This rule is not a function because each of several input numbers has two output numbers. For example, the input number 4 has two output numbers, 2 and –2. The points (4, 2) and (4, –2) lie on a vertical line.

In general, when an input number has more than one output number, the points that represent these ordered pairs lie on a vertical line. So, when a vertical line intersects a graph at two or more points, the graph does not represent a function. For this reason, a vertical line test can be used to determine whether a graph represents a function.

Take Note

Vertical Line Test for a Function

When a graph is given, visualize a vertical line moving across the graph.

If the vertical line never intersects the graph in more than one point, the graph represents a function.

If the vertical line intersects the graph in more than one point, the graph does not represent a function.

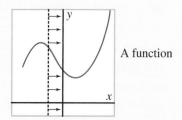

A function

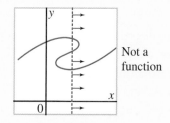

Not a function

The equation for the rule above is $y = \pm\sqrt{x}$, or $y^2 = x$, where x is an input number and y is an output number. We can tell from the equation that, when the input number is 4, there are two output numbers, 2 and –2. Therefore, there is an equation test for a function that is the algebraic equivalent of the vertical line test.

Take Note

Equation Test for a Function

If there are no values of x that produce more than one value of y when substituted into the equation, the equation represents a function.

If a value of x can be found that produces more than one value of y, the equation does not represent a function.

Example

Does the equation $x^2 + y^2 = 25$ represent a function? Explain.

Solution

$x^2 + y^2 = 25$

Substitute $x = 0$. Then $y^2 = 25$, so $y = \pm 5$

There are two values of y for this value of x.
The equation does not represent a function.

Exercises

1. Is it possible to have a function whose graph is a circle? Explain.

2. State whether each graph represents a function. Explain.

a)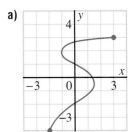

b)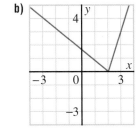

c)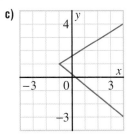

d)

Sales

e)

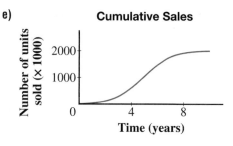

Cumulative Sales

f)

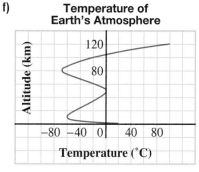

Temperature of Earth's Atmosphere

g)

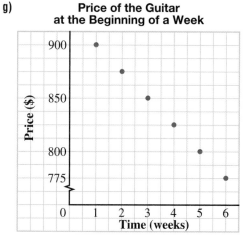

Price of the Guitar at the Beginning of a Week

3. State whether each equation represents a function. Explain.

a) $y = 5x - 2$ **b)** $y = 2(x - 3)^2 + 2$ **c)** $y^2 = -x$

d) $A = 4\pi r^2$ **e)** $x^2 - y^2 = 0$ **f)** $d = \dfrac{10}{t}$

2. New: Solving Linear Inequalities

In an *inequality*, the "greater than" sign or the "less than" sign is used to relate two expressions.

Consider the inequality: $2 < 6$

Suppose we
     add 4 to each side: $6 < 10$
     subtract 4 from each side: $-2 < 2$
     multiply each side by 2: $4 < 12$
     divide each side by 2: $1 < 3$

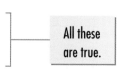

All these are true.

Suppose we
     multiply each side by –2: $-4 < -12$
     divide each side by –2: $-1 < -3$

Both these are *false*.

The results on page 394 suggest that the rules for solving linear inequalities are the same as those for solving linear equations, with this exception:

Take Note

Solving a Linear Inequality

When both sides of an inequality are multiplied or divided by a negative number, the inequality sign must be reversed.

Example

Solve each inequality. Illustrate the solution on a number line.

a) $x + 6 < 3 - 2x$

b) $2(x + 1) \leq -2 + 3x$

Solution

a) $x + 6 < 3 - 2x$
$x + 2x < 3 - 6$
$3x < -3$
Divide each side by 3.
$x < -1$

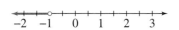

The open dot at −1 indicates that it is not part of the solution.

b) $2(x + 1) \leq -2 + 3x$
$2x + 2 \leq -2 + 3x$
$2x - 3x \leq -2 - 2$
$-x \leq -4$
Multiply each side by −1, and reverse the inequality sign.
$x \geq 4$

Discuss

How could you complete part b without multiplying by −1?

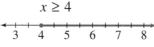

The solid dot at 4 indicates that it is part of the solution.

Exercises

1. Solve each inequality.

  a) $2x + 1 \leq 9$ **b)** $3 - x > 5$ **c)** $5 - 2x < -3 + 2x$

  d) $5n + 2 \geq 8 - 3n$ **e)** $3(x - 1) < 2 - x$ **f)** $2(c + 4) \leq -(5 - c)$

2. Solve each inequality. Illustrate the solution on a number line.

  a) $3x - 5 \leq 1$ **b)** $1 - 2x < 7$ **c)** $4x - 5 \geq 6x + 3$

  d) $k + 2 > 8 + 3k$ **e)** $2(x - 3) \leq 5x + 6$ **f)** $-2(3 - n) > 3(n + 2)$

In previous grades and previous chapters of this book, you encountered certain types of functions. The graphs of these functions have characteristic shapes. By transforming the graphs in certain ways, we can use them to model real situations.

Linear Functions

The graph of the simplest linear function, $y = x$, is a straight line with slope 1 through the origin. By changing the slope and the vertical intercept, we can use a linear function to model situations that involve fixed and variable costs.

Remember that the set of possible input numbers is the domain of the function. The set of output numbers is the range of the function.

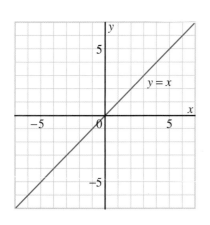

Yearbook Printing Costs up to 1500 Copies

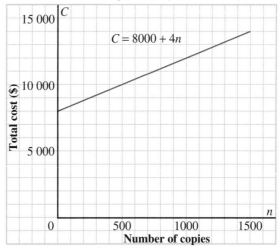

For the function $y = x$
Domain: all real numbers
Range: all real numbers

For $C = 8000 + 4n$
Domain: $0 \leq n \leq 1500$ → y
Range: $8000 \leq C \leq 14\,000$ → x

Quadratic Functions

The graph of the simplest quadratic function, $y = x^2$, is a parabola with vertex O(0, 0) and the y-axis as its axis of symmetry. By transforming the graph, we can use it to model situations that involve projectiles.

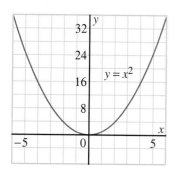

Height of Falling Object

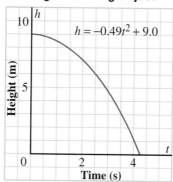

For the function $y = x^2$

Domain: all real numbers

Range: $y \geq 0$

For $h = -0.49t^2 + 9.0$

Domain: $0 \leq t \leq 4.2$

Range: $0 \leq h \leq 9$

Sinusoidal Functions

By transforming the graph of $y = \cos x$, we can use a cosine function to model quantities that change periodically.

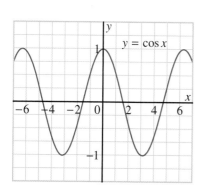

Number of Hours of Daylight in Ottawa During a 2-Year Period

For the function $y = \cos x$

Domain: all real numbers

Range: $-1 \leq y \leq 1$, or $|y| \leq 1$

For $h = 3.4 \cos \dfrac{2\pi}{365}(n - 172) + 12.2$

Domain: $0 \leq n \leq 730$

Range: $8.8 \leq h \leq 15.6$

The following *Example* illustrates another function whose graph has a characteristic shape.

Example

a) Graph the function $y = \sqrt{25 - x^2}$.

b) Describe the graph and account for its shape.

c) Determine the domain and range of the function.

Solution

a) *Using a graphing calculator*

Since the number under a square root sign cannot be negative, $25 - x^2$ cannot be negative. The possible values of x are from -5 to 5. The possible values of y are from 0 to 5. Use window settings $-9 \leq x \leq 9$, $-6 \leq y \leq 6$. Enter the equation $Y1 = \sqrt{(25-X^2)}$.

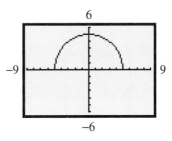

Using grid paper

Make a table of values, plot the points, then draw a smooth curve through them.

x	y
0	5
±3	4
±4	3
±5	0

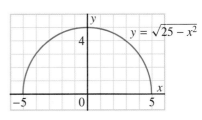

b) The graph appears to be a semicircle. To determine whether it is a semicircle, consider any point $P(x, y)$ on the graph. The coordinates of P satisfy the equation.

$$y = \sqrt{25 - x^2}$$

Square each side.

$$y^2 = 25 - x^2$$
$$x^2 + y^2 = 25$$

Take the positive square root of each side.

$$\sqrt{x^2 + y^2} = 5$$

This equation states that the length of OP is 5 units. That is, P lies on a circle with centre O and radius 5. Since $y \geq 0$, all points on the graph must be on or above the x-axis. Hence, the graph is a semicircle.

c) From the graph

Domain: $-5 \leq x \leq 5$, or $|x| \leq 5$

Range: $0 \leq y \leq 5$

The *Example* suggests that the graph of the function $y = \sqrt{a - x^2}$, where a is constant, is a semicircle. In the exercises of this section and Section 7.2, you will investigate other functions that have graphs with characteristic shapes.

A

1. Refer to the graph on page 396 that shows the yearbook printing costs.

   a) In the equation $C = 8000 + 4n$, explain what the numbers 8000 and 4 represent.

   b) Describe how the graph would change if the numbers 8000 and 4 were to change.

   c) Does the graph of the function have a maximum point and a minimum point? Explain.

2. Refer to the graph on page 397 that shows the height of a falling object.

   a) What was the initial height of the object?

   b) How long did it take for the object to hit the ground?

   c) Describe how the graph would change if the initial height were different.

3. **Knowledge/Understanding** Refer to the graph on page 397 that shows the number of hours of daylight in Ottawa.

   a) i) Determine the greatest number of hours of daylight.
      ii) Determine the least number of hours of daylight.
     iii) Determine the mean number of hours of daylight.

   b) Explain the effect of each number in the equation
      $h = 3.4 \cos \dfrac{2\pi}{365}(n - 172) + 12.2$, in relation to amplitude, period, phase shift, and vertical displacement.

   c) A location farther south than Ottawa has a lesser variation in the number of hours of daylight. Describe how the graph would change if it was drawn for this location.

B

The Absolute Value Function $y = |x|$

If you have a graphing calculator, complete exercises 4 and 6.
If you do not have a graphing calculator, complete exercises 5 and 6.

4. Set the graphing window so that $-4.7 \le x \le 4.7$ and $-1.5 \le y \le 4.7$.

   a) To enter the equation Y1 = |X|: press ⟨ Y= ⟩; to enter the absolute-value expression, press ⟨ MATH ⟩ ⟨ ▶ ⟩ **1** ⟨ X,T,θ,n ⟩ ⟨) ⟩. Graph the function $y = |x|$.

   b) Trace to display the coordinates of points on the graph. Use both positive and negative values of x.

   c) Enter the equation Y2 = X to graph the functions $y = |x|$ and $y = x$ on the same screen.

   d) Graph $y = |x|$ and $y = x$ on grid paper.

5. a) Make a table of values for the function $y = |x|$, using both positive and negative values of x. Then graph the function on grid paper.

b) Graph the function $y = x$ on the same grid.

 6. Communication Summarize the properties of the function $y = |x|$ as follows.

a) Describe the domain and range of the function.

b) Explain how the graph of $y = |x|$ is related to the graph of $y = x$.

c) Does the graph of $y = |x|$ have any of these characteristics? Explain.
  i) lines of symmetry
  ii) maximum or minimum points
  iii) asymptotes

The Functions $y = \sqrt{a - x^2}$

 7. a) Graph these functions on the same screen.

    i) $y = \sqrt{16 - x^2}$ **ii)** $y = \sqrt{9 - x^2}$ **iii)** $y = \sqrt{4 - x^2}$
    iv) $y = \sqrt{1 - x^2}$ **v)** $y = \sqrt{-x^2}$

b) Describe how the graph of $y = \sqrt{a - x^2}$ changes as a varies. Include the special case where $a = 0$.

c) What happens when $a < 0$?

The Functions $y = \sqrt{a + x^2}$

 8. Application

a) Graph these functions on the same screen.

    i) $y = \sqrt{16 + x^2}$ **ii)** $y = \sqrt{9 + x^2}$ **iii)** $y = \sqrt{4 + x^2}$
    iv) $y = \sqrt{1 + x^2}$ **v)** $y = \sqrt{x^2}$ **vi)** $y = \sqrt{-1 + x^2}$
    vii) $y = \sqrt{-4 + x^2}$ **viii)** $y = \sqrt{-9 + x^2}$ **ix)** $y = \sqrt{-16 + x^2}$

b) Describe how the graph of $y = \sqrt{a + x^2}$ changes as a varies. Include the case where $a = 0$, and the cases where $a < 0$.

 9. Thinking/Inquiry/Problem Solving Graph the function $y = \sqrt[3]{25 - x^2}$. Describe how the graph of this function is similar to, and different from, the graph of the function in the *Example*; that is, $y = \sqrt{25 - x^2}$.

 C

10. Functions whose equations have the form $y = x^a$, where a is constant, are *power functions*.

a) Graph these power functions on the same screen, for $x \geq 0$.
    i) $y = x^{0.5}$ **ii)** $y = x^{0.75}$ **iii)** $y = x^{1.0}$
    iv) $y = x^{1.5}$ **v)** $y = x^{2.0}$ **vi)** $y = x^{2.5}$

b) Describe how the graph of $y = x^a$ changes as a varies, when $a > 0$ and $x \geq 0$.

7.2 Function Notation

In algebra, symbols such as x and y are used to represent numbers.
To represent functions, we use notation such as $f(x)$ and $g(x)$.

For example, we write $f(x) = x^2 + 2x - 8$.

The notation $f(x)$ is read "f of x", or "f at x." It means that the expression that follows contains x as a variable. The notation $f(5)$ means "substitute 5 for every x in the expression."

$$f(x) = x^2 + 2x - 8$$

$$f(5) = 5^2 + 2(5) - 8$$
$$= 25 + 10 - 8$$
$$= 27$$

Example 1

Given $f(x) = 2x^2 - 3x + 1$, determine each value.

a) $f(3)$ b) $f(-3)$ c) $f\left(\frac{1}{3}\right)$ d) $f(\sqrt{3})$

Solution

a) $f(x) = 2x^2 - 3x + 1$
$f(3) = 2(3)^2 - 3(3) + 1$
$\quad = 18 - 9 + 1$
$\quad = 10$

b) $f(x) = 2x^2 - 3x + 1$
$f(-3) = 2(-3)^2 - 3(-3) + 1$
$\quad = 18 + 9 + 1$
$\quad = 28$

c) $f(x) = 2x^2 - 3x + 1$
$f\left(\frac{1}{3}\right) = 2\left(\frac{1}{3}\right)^2 - 3\left(\frac{1}{3}\right) + 1$
$\quad = \frac{2}{9} - 1 + 1$
$\quad = \frac{2}{9}$

d) $f(x) = 2x^2 - 3x + 1$
$f(\sqrt{3}) = 2(\sqrt{3})^2 - 3\sqrt{3} + 1$
$\quad = 2(3) - 3\sqrt{3} + 1$
$\quad = 6 - 3\sqrt{3} + 1$
$\quad = 7 - 3\sqrt{3}$
$\quad \doteq 7 - 3(1.7321)$
$\quad \doteq 1.804$

We can use function notation to substitute algebraic expressions for the variable.

Example 2

Given the function $f(x) = x^2 + 1$, determine each expression.

a) $f(n)$ **b)** $f(2x)$ **c)** $f(x - 2)$ **d)** $f\left(\frac{1}{x}\right), x \neq 0$

Solution

a) $f(x) = x^2 + 1$
$f(n) = n^2 + 1$

b) $f(x) = x^2 + 1$
$f(2x) = (2x)^2 + 1$
$= 4x^2 + 1$

c) $f(x) = x^2 + 1$
$f(x - 2) = (x - 2)^2 + 1$
$= x^2 - 4x + 5$

d) $f(x) = x^2 + 1$
$f\left(\frac{1}{x}\right) = \left(\frac{1}{x}\right)^2 + 1$
$= \frac{1}{x^2} + 1$
$= \frac{1 + x^2}{x^2}, x \neq 0$

Example 3

A function is defined by $f(x) = \frac{6x}{x^2 + 1}$.

a) Graph the function.

b) What are the domain and range of the function?

Solution

Write the equation in the form $y = \frac{6x}{x^2 + 1}$.

a) Input the function, set the window, then graph the function.

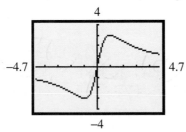

Discuss

The graph shows only $-4.7 \leq x \leq 4.7$. How do we know that the domain is the set of all real numbers?

How do we know that the range is $|y| \leq 3$?

b) In the equation, we can substitute any real number for x.
So, the domain is the set of all real numbers.
From the graph, the range is $-3 \leq y \leq 3$, or $|y| \leq 3$.

The equation for a function can be written using "$y =$" or "$f(x) =$"; as illustrated in *Example 3*. We use both ways in this book.
We can use function notation to represent a function in the form $y = f(x)$.
This is useful when there is no equation that relates the variables (see exercise 9).

Properties of the Function $f(x) = \sqrt{x}$
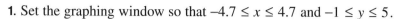

If you have a graphing calculator, complete exercises 1 and 3.
If you do not have a graphing calculator, complete exercises 2 and 3.

1. Set the graphing window so that $-4.7 \le x \le 4.7$ and $-1 \le y \le 5$.

   a) Enter the equation Y1 = $\sqrt{X}$, then graph the function $f(x) = \sqrt{x}$.

   b) Trace to display the coordinates of points on the graph. Record these coordinates.

   c) Enter the equation Y2 = X^2. Graph the functions $f(x) = \sqrt{x}$ and $f(x) = x^2$ on the same screen.

   d) Graph $f(x) = \sqrt{x}$ and $f(x) = x^2$ on grid paper. Use the coordinates of some of the points you found by tracing.

2. a) Make a table of values for the function $f(x) = \sqrt{x}$, then graph the function on grid paper.

   b) Graph the function $f(x) = x^2$ on the same grid.

3. Summarize the properties of the function $f(x) = \sqrt{x}$ as follows.

   a) Describe the domain and range of the function.

   b) Does the graph of $f(x) = \sqrt{x}$ have any of these characteristics? Explain.
   i) lines of symmetry
   ii) maximum or minimum points
   iii) asymptotes

   c) Explain how the graph of $f(x) = \sqrt{x}$ is related to the graph of $f(x) = x^2$.

Properties of the Function $f(x) = \dfrac{1}{x}$

If you have a graphing calculator, complete exercises 1, 3, and 4.
If you do not have a graphing calculator, complete exercises 2, 3, and 4.

1. Set the graphing window so that $-4.7 \le x \le 4.7$ and $-3.1 \le y \le 3.1$.

   a) Enter the equation Y1 = 1/X, then graph the function $f(x) = \dfrac{1}{x}$.

   b) Trace to display the coordinates of points on the graph. Trace along both parts of the graph. Record the coordinates. Check that some of these coordinates satisfy the equation $f(x) = \dfrac{1}{x}$.

   c) Trace to the point where $x = 0$ appears at the bottom of the screen. What happens to the y-coordinate at this point? Explain.

d) The graph appears to have two parts, called *branches*. Predict whether these two branches are connected. To verify your prediction, turn off the axes as follows. Press 2nd ZOOM for FORMAT. Choose AxesOff, press ENTER, then press GRAPH. Turn the axes back on before you continue.

e) Enter the equation Y2 = X. Graph the functions $f(x) = \frac{1}{x}$ and $f(x) = x$ on the same screen.

f) Graph $f(x) = \frac{1}{x}$ and $f(x) = x$ on grid paper. Use the coordinates of some of the points you found by tracing.

2. a) Make a table of values for the function $f(x) = \frac{1}{x}$, then graph the function on grid paper. Since there is no y-value when $x = 0$, the table of values is divided into two separate parts. Your graph will also have two separate parts.

b) Graph the function $f(x) = x$ on the same grid.

3. Suppose x is a negative number that is much less than 0, such as −100.

a) How does the value of $\frac{1}{x}$ compare with the value of x? Explain.

b) Visualize the values of x increasing from left to right in the table of values, or along the graph. What happens to the value of $\frac{1}{x}$ in each case?
   i) when x increases to −1
   ii) when x increases from −1 to 0
   iii) when x increases from 0 to 1
   iv) when x increases to a relatively large value, such as 100

4. Summarize the properties of the function $f(x) = \frac{1}{x}$ as follows.

a) Describe the domain and range of the function.

b) Does the graph of $f(x) = \frac{1}{x}$ have any of these characteristics? Explain.
   i) lines of symmetry
   ii) maximum or minimum points
   iii) asymptotes

c) Explain how the graph of $f(x) = \frac{1}{x}$ is related to the graph of $f(x) = x$.

7.2   Exercises

1. Given $f(x) = 2x - 1$, determine each value.

  a) $f(4)$ **b)** $f(10)$ **c)** $f(0.5)$ **d)** $f(0)$ **e)** $f(-2)$

2. Given $g(x) = x^2 + x$, determine each value.

  a) $g(10)$ **b)** $g(4)$ **c)** $g(-3)$ **d)** $g(-0.1)$ **e)** $g(0)$

3. Given $h(x) = 3x^2 + 2x - 1$, determine each value.

a) $h(10)$ **b)** $h(-10)$ **c)** $h(5)$ **d)** $h(-1)$ **e)** $h(0)$

4. For each function, determine $f(2), f(2.5)$, and $f\left(\frac{1}{2}\right)$.

a) $f(x) = x$ **b)** $f(x) = x^2$ **c)** $f(x) = \sqrt{x}$

d) $f(x) = \dfrac{1}{x}$ **e)** $f(x) = \sin x$ **f)** $f(x) = \cos x$

5. Knowledge/Understanding For each function, determine $g(-1)$, $g(0.5)$, and $g(-0.5)$.

a) $g(x) = 10 - x$ **b)** $g(x) = x^2 + 4x$ **c)** $g(x) = 5(x - 1)$

d) $g(x) = (x + 1)(x - 3)$ **e)** $g(x) = \dfrac{1}{x}$ **f)** $g(x) = 4^x$

6. Measurement formulas can be written using function notation. For example, the formula for the circumference of a circle with radius r can be written as $C(r) = 2\pi r$.

a) Determine each value.

     i) $C(10)$ **ii)** $C(5)$ **iii)** $C(2.5)$ **iv)** $C(1)$

b) Let $A(r)$ represent the area of a circle with radius r. Write a formula for $A(r)$.

c) Determine each value.

     i) $A(10)$ **ii)** $A(5)$ **iii)** $A(2.5)$ **iv)** $A(1)$

7. Communication In an expression such as $a(x - 2)$, both a and x are variables. This expression can be expanded using the distributive law to obtain $ax - 2a$.

a) In *Example 2c*, why did we not write $fx - 2f$?

b) How can you tell that $a(x - 2)$ means $ax - 2a$, but $f(x - 2)$ does not mean $fx - 2f$?

B

8. For each function, determine $f(0), f\left(\frac{\pi}{4}\right)$, and $f\left(\frac{\pi}{2}\right)$.

a) $f(x) = \sin x$ **b)** $f(x) = \cos x$ **c)** $f(x) = \sin 2x$

d) $f(x) = \cos\left(x + \dfrac{\pi}{4}\right)$ **e)** $f(x) = \sin\left(\dfrac{\pi}{2} - x\right)$ **f)** $f(x) = \sin^2 x + \cos^2 x$

9. For each graph of $y = f(x)$, determine $f(-2), f(1)$, and $f(3)$.

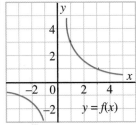

10. For each graph in exercise 9, solve the equation $f(x) = 2$.

11. Graph each function. State its domain and range.

a) $f(x) = 3x - 5$ b) $f(x) = x^2 - 4$ c) $f(x) = |x|$

d) $f(x) = \dfrac{1}{x}$ e) $f(x) = \sin x$ f) $f(x) = \sqrt{x}$

12. Graph each function. State its domain and range.

a) $f(x) = \dfrac{1}{2}x - 1$ b) $f(x) = 0.5x^2 + 1$ c) $f(x) = (x - 2)^2 + 1$

d) $f(x) = (x + 3)(x - 5)$ e) $f(x) = \sqrt{9 - x^2}$ f) $f(x) = \sqrt{2x}$

13. Given $f(x) = 2x + 5$, determine each expression.

a) $f(r)$ b) $f(2x)$ c) $f(-x)$

d) $f(x - 2)$ e) $f(x^2)$ f) $f\left(\dfrac{1}{x}\right)$

14. Given $g(x) = x^2 - 3x + 1$, determine each expression.

a) $g(x + 1)$ b) $g(x + 2)$ c) $g(x + 3)$

d) $g(2x)$ e) $g(3x)$ f) $g(-x)$

15. Given the function $f(x) = \dfrac{x^2 + 1}{x}$, $x \neq 0$, determine each expression.

a) $f(n)$ b) $f(2x)$ c) $f(x - 2)$

d) $f(1 - x)$ e) $f(x^2)$ f) $f\left(\dfrac{1}{x}\right)$

16. Given $f(x) = 2x - 1$ and $g(x) = 3x$, determine each expression.

a) $f(g(x))$ b) $g(f(x))$ c) $f(f(x))$

17. a) Determine a function $f(x)$ so that $f(3) = 6$.

   b) Determine a different function $g(x)$ so that $g(3) = 6$.

18. a) Determine a function $f(x)$ so that $f(1) = 2$ and $f(2) = 5$.

   b) Determine a different function $g(x)$ so that $g(1) = 2$ and $g(2) = 5$.

19. Determine two different functions $f(x)$ and $g(x)$ so that $f(0) = 4$ and $g(1) = 5$.

20. Given $f(x) = 5 - 2x$, determine x for each value of $f(x)$.

a) 5   b) -1 c) 7

21. **Application** Remember that the symbol t_n was defined in Chapter 1 to represent the general term of a sequence. For example, the arithmetic sequence 1, 3, 5, 7, ... has general term $t_n = 2n - 1$. The symbol t_n is a variation of function notation, because there is little difference between writing t_n and $t(n)$. However, when we use t_n, we know we are dealing with a sequence.

a) Graph the first few terms of the sequence $t_n = 2n - 1$.

b) Graph the function defined by $t(n) = 2n - 1$, where n is a real number.

c) Use the definition of a function to explain why any arithmetic sequence can be considered to be a function.

d) Can any geometric sequence be considered to be a function? Explain.

22. Consider the function $f(x) = \dfrac{x}{1 + x}$.

a) Evaluate each expression.

i) $f(2)$ ii) $f\left(\dfrac{1}{2}\right)$ iii) $f(2) + f\left(\dfrac{1}{2}\right)$

iv) $f(3)$ v) $f\left(\dfrac{1}{3}\right)$ vi) $f(3) + f\left(\dfrac{1}{3}\right)$

b) Predict the value of $f(n) + f\left(\dfrac{1}{n}\right)$. Show that your prediction is correct.

c) For what values of n is the result in part b true?

23. Consider the function $f(x) = mx + b$. Determine m and b in each case.

a) The graph of the function has slope $\dfrac{2}{5}$, and $f(5) = -1$.

b) The graph of the function has y-intercept 2, and $f(2) = 8$.

c) The graph of the function has y-intercept -3, and $f(-2) = -3$.

24. a) The *identity function*, $i(x)$, is a special case of a linear function. It is defined by $i(x) = x$.

i) Evaluate $i(3)$, $i(4.5)$, and $i(-2.7)$.
ii) Graph the identity function $i(x)$.

b) The *constant function* is another special case of a linear function. For example, we can define the function $f(x)$ to be equal to 5 for every value of x.

i) Evaluate $f(2), f(-3.4)$, and $f(5.6)$.
ii) Graph the constant function $f(x)$.

25. Thinking/Inquiry/Problem Solving

a) A function $f(x)$ with the property $f(-x) = f(x)$ is an *even function*.
i) Find two examples of even functions, then sketch their graphs.
ii) What special property does the graph of an even function have? Why does it have this property?

b) A function $f(x)$ with the property $f(-x) = -f(x)$ is an *odd function*.
i) Find two examples of odd functions, then sketch their graphs.
ii) What special property does the graph of an odd function have? Why does it have this property?

26. A function $y = f(x)$ is defined to be periodic if there is a number p so that $f(x + p) = f(x)$ for all values of x in the domain. Use this definition to show that the functions $y = \sin x$ and $y = \cos x$ are periodic.

1. Solve each inequality. Illustrate the solution on a number line.

a) $3a - 5 \geq 2a + 4$

b) $2(c + 1) \leq 3(4 - c)$

c) $-4(1 - 2n) > 5 - 2n$

d) $4 - 3x < 5x - 4$

e) $6m - 3(4 + m) > 0$

f) $1 + 3(2x - 5) \leq 2(x + 1) - 1$

2. a) Graph the function $y = 3x - 2$.

b) Describe the graph and account for its shape.

c) Determine the domain and range of the function.

3. a) Graph the function $y = 2(x - 3)^2 + 5$. $\bigcup$ shifted right 3 up 5

b) Describe the graph and account for its shape.

c) Determine the domain and range of the function.

4. a) Graph the function $y = \sqrt{16 - x^2}$.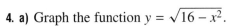

b) Describe the graph and account for its shape.

c) Determine the domain and range of the function.

5. a) Graph the function $y = \sqrt{16 + x^2}$. left 16

b) Describe the graph and account for its shape.

c) Determine the domain and range of the function.

6. Given $f(x) = 3x + 1$, determine each value.

a) $f(1)$ **b)** $f(-1)$ **c)** $f(0)$ **d)** $f(\sqrt{2})$ **e)** $f(-\sqrt{2})$

7. Given $g(x) = 2x^2 - 5$, determine each value.

a) $g(0)$ **b)** $g(0.5)$ **c)** $g(-0.5)$ **d)** $g(\sqrt{3})$ **e)** $g(-\sqrt{3})$

8. Given $h(x) = -x^2 + 4x - 1$, determine each value.

a) $h(0)$ **b)** $h(0.25)$ **c)** $h(-0.25)$ **d)** $h(\sqrt{5})$ **e)** $h(-\sqrt{5})$

9. Given $g(x) = 2(x - 3)(x^2 - 1)$, determine each value.

a) $g(3)$ **b)** $g(4)$ **c)** $g(-1)$ **d)** $g(0)$ **e)** $g(10)$

10. Determine $f(x - 3)$ for each function.

a) $f(x) = -3x + 1$

b) $f(x) = x^2 - 2x + 5$

c) $f(x) = \sin x$

d) $f(x) = \cos x$

e) $f(x) = \dfrac{1}{x}$

f) $f(x) = \sqrt{x}$

11. The function $y = f(x)$ has $f(6) = 2$ and $f(3) = -4$.

a) Sketch a graph of $y = f(x)$.

b) Is the graph unique? Explain.

7.3 Transforming Functions

In grade 10, you found that when you change the equation $y = x^2$, its graph has corresponding changes. Similarly, in Chapter 6, you found that when you change the equations $y = \sin x$ or $y = \cos x$, their graphs have corresponding changes. These kinds of changes occur with all functions.

Translating Graphs of Functions

Remember how the graph of $y = (x - 5)^2 + 2$ is related to the graph of $y = x^2$.

$$y = (x - 5)^2 + 2$$

Translate 2 units up.

Translate 5 units right.

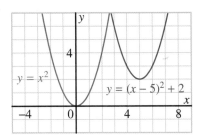

This equation can be written as follows:

$$y - 2 = (x - 5)^2$$

Replacing x with $x - 5$ translates the graph 5 units right.
Replacing y with $y - 2$ translates the graph 2 units up.

A similar relationship occurs for any function $y = f(x)$.

$$y = f(x + 1) - 3$$

Translate 3 units down.

Translate 1 unit left.

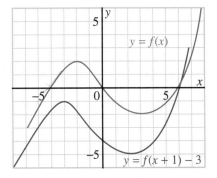

This equation can be written as follows:

$$y + 3 = f(x + 1)$$

Replacing x with $x + 1$ translates the graph 1 unit left.
Replacing y with $y + 3$ translates the graph 3 units down.

Compressing and Expanding Graphs of Functions

Remember how the graph of $y = \frac{1}{2} \cos 3x$ is related to the graph of $y = \cos x$.

$$y = \frac{1}{2} \cos 3x$$

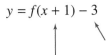

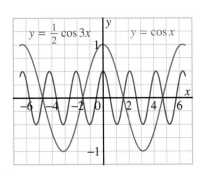

Compress horizontally by a factor of $\frac{1}{3}$.

Compress vertically by a factor of $\frac{1}{2}$.

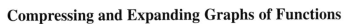

This equation can be written as follows:

$$2y = \cos 3x$$

Replacing x with $3x$ compresses the graph horizontally.
Replacing y with $2y$ compresses the graph vertically.

A similar relationship occurs for any function $y = f(x)$.

$$y = 2f\left(\tfrac{1}{3}x\right)$$

Expand horizontally by a factor of 3.

Expand vertically by a factor of 2.

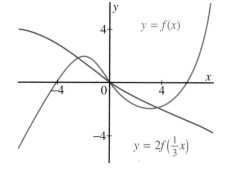

This equation can be written as follows:

$$\tfrac{1}{2}y = f\left(\tfrac{1}{3}x\right)$$

Replacing x with $\tfrac{1}{3}x$ expands the graph horizontally.

Replacing y with $\tfrac{1}{2}y$ expands the graph vertically.

Reflecting Graphs of Functions

Remember how the graph of $y = (x - 5)^2 + 2$ is related
to the graph of $y = (-x - 5)^2 + 2$, or $y = (x + 5)^2 + 2$.

$$y = (-x - 5)^2 + 2$$

Reflect in the y-axis.

Replacing x with $-x$ reflects the graph in the y-axis.

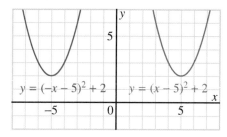

Similarly, remember how the graph of $y = (x - 5)^2 + 2$
is related to the graph of $-y = (x - 5)^2 + 2$,
or $y = -(x - 5)^2 - 2$.

$$-y = (x - 5)^2 + 2$$

Reflect in the x-axis.

Replacing y with $-y$ reflects the graph in the x-axis.

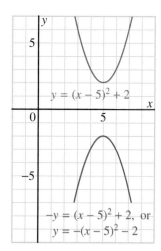

Transformations Applied to $y = f(x)$

- Vertical translation of k units
  Replace y with $y - k$ for the image equation $y - k = f(x)$.
  When $k > 0$, the translation is up.
  When $k < 0$, the translation is down.

- Horizontal translation of k units
  Replace x with $x - k$ for the image equation $y = f(x - k)$.
  When $k > 0$, the translation is to the right.
  When $k < 0$, the translation is to the left.

- Reflection in the y-axis
  Replace x with $-x$ for the image equation $y = f(-x)$.

- Reflection in the x-axis
  Replace y with $-y$ for the image equation $-y = f(x)$, or $y = -f(x)$.

- Vertical expansion or compression
  Replace y with ky for the image equation $ky = f(x)$, or $y = \frac{1}{k}f(x)$.
  When $0 < k < 1$, there is an expansion.
  When $k > 1$, there is a compression.
  When $k < 0$, there is also a reflection in the x-axis.

- Horizontal expansion or compression
  Replace x with kx for the image equation $y = f(kx)$.
  When $0 < k < 1$, there is an expansion.
  When $k > 1$, there is a compression.
  When $k < 0$, there is also a reflection in the y-axis.

Example 1

Consider the function $f(x) = \sin x$.

a) Graph the function for $-2\pi \le x \le 2\pi$.

b) Graph the image of $f(x) = \sin x$ under a translation of $\frac{\pi}{3}$ units right.

c) Write the equation of the image function $g(x)$.

d) What are the domain and range of the image function?

Solution

a), b) Remember the graph of $y = \sin x$ from Chapter 6. Choose the
maximum and minimum points, and the intercepts. Move each point
$\frac{\pi}{3}$ units right. Join the points with a smooth curve.

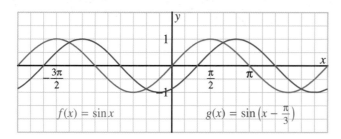

$f(x) = \sin x$

$g(x) = \sin\left(x - \frac{\pi}{3}\right)$

c) For the image equation, in $f(x) = \sin x$, replace x with $x - \frac{\pi}{3}$.

The equation of the image function is $g(x) = \sin\left(x - \frac{\pi}{3}\right)$.

d) The domain of the image function is the set of all real numbers.
The range of the image function is $-1 \le y \le 1$.

Example 2

The function $f(x) = \sqrt{x}$ is given.

a) Graph the function $f(x)$.

b) On the same grid, graph the function $g(x) = \sqrt{2x}$.

c) Describe how the graph of $g(x)$ is related to the graph of $f(x)$.

d) What are the domain and range of the function $g(x)$?

Solution

a), b) Remember the graph of $y = \sqrt{x}$ from
Section 7.2, *Investigation 1*.
Plot the points $(9, 3), (4, 2), (1, 1)$,
$(0, 0)$. Join the points with a smooth curve.

Multiply each x-coordinate by $\frac{1}{2}$ to get the
corresponding points for $y = \sqrt{2x}$:
$(4.5, 3), (2, 2), (0.5, 1), (0, 0)$
Plot the points, then join them with a smooth curve.

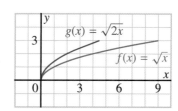

c) The graph of $g(x) = \sqrt{2x}$ is compressed horizontally by
a factor of $\frac{1}{2}$ relative to the graph of $f(x) = \sqrt{x}$.

d) The domain of $g(x)$ is the set of all non-negative real numbers.
The range of $g(x)$ is the set of all non-negative real numbers.

Discuss

What is meant by
"non-negative real
numbers"?

Examples 1 and *2* involve the functions $f(x) = \sin x$ and $f(x) = \sqrt{x}$, which you
investigated in Chapter 6 and Section 7.2, respectively. Transformations can be
applied to any function with similar results.

A

1. Refer to the translation at the top of page 409: translate 5 units right and 2 units up. Write the equation of the image function if we had started with each function below instead of $y = x^2$.

   a) $y = \sqrt{x}$ **b)** $y = |x|$ **c)** $y = \cos x$

   d) $y = x$ **e)** $y = \sin x$ **f)** $y = f(x)$

2. Refer to the transformation at the bottom of page 409: compress vertically a factor of $\frac{1}{2}$ and horizontally by a factor of $\frac{1}{3}$. Write the equation of the transformed function if we had started with each function below instead of $y = \cos x$.

   a) $y = \sqrt{x}$ **b)** $y = \sin x$ **c)** $y = x^2$

   d) $y = x$ **e)** $y = |x|$ **f)** $y = f(x)$

3. Explain each statement.

   a) On the first graph on page 409, subtracting 5 from x (which makes x smaller) moves the graph right (which makes x larger).

   b) On the last graph on page 409, multiplying x by 3 (which makes x larger) compresses the graph horizontally (which makes x smaller).

4. Use transformations to describe how the graph of the second function compares to the graph of the first function.

   a) $f(x) = x$ **b)** $f(x) = \sqrt{x}$ **c)** $f(x) = \cos x$

   $g(x) = x - 3$ $g(x) = \sqrt{x - 3}$ $g(x) = \cos(x - 3)$

   d) $f(x) = \sin x$ **e)** $f(x) = x^2$ **f)** $y = f(x)$

   $g(x) = \sin 3x$ $g(x) = 9x^2$ $y = f(3x)$

5. **Knowledge/Understanding** Suppose you make these changes to the equation of a function. Use transformations to describe what happens to the graph.

   a) Replace x with $x - 4$. **b)** Replace y with $y - 1$.

   c) Replace x with $3x$. **d)** Replace y with $2y$.

   e) Replace x with $\frac{1}{2}x$. **f)** Replace y with $\frac{1}{2}y$.

   g) Replace x with $-2x$. **h)** Replace y with $-2y$.

   i) Replace x with $x + 3$. **j)** Replace y with $y + 2$.

6. Suppose you make these changes to the graph of a function $y = f(x)$. Write the equation of the image function.

a) Translate 2 units right.

b) Translate 5 units down.

c) Compress by a factor of $\frac{1}{3}$ horizontally.

d) Expand by a factor of 2 horizontally.

e) Expand by a factor of 4 vertically.

f) Compress by a factor of $\frac{1}{2}$ vertically.

g) Compress horizontally by a factor of $\frac{1}{2}$, then reflect in the y-axis.

h) Expand vertically by a factor of 5, then reflect in the x-axis.

7. Refer to *Example 1* on page 411. Repeat this example for each function below.

a) $f(x) = \cos x$ **b)** $f(x) = 2\cos x$ **c)** $f(x) = 2\sin x$

8. Refer to *Example 2* on page 412. Repeat this example for each function below.

a) $f(x) = x^2$ **b)** $f(x) = \sin x$ **c)** $f(x) = x$

9. a) Use transformations to describe how the graph of the second function compares to the graph of the first function.

i) $y = x$ **ii)** $y = x^2$ **iii)** $y = \sqrt{x}$
  $y = 2x + 3$ $y = 2x^2 + 3$ $y = 2\sqrt{x} + 3$

b) For each pair of functions in part a, write the equations of another pair of functions that are related in the same way.

10. Graph the functions in each list on the same grid.

a) $y = x$ **b)** $y = x^2$ **c)** $y = \sqrt{x}$
  $y = x - 3$ $y = (x - 3)^2$ $y = \sqrt{x} - 3$
  $y = x + 3$ $y = (x + 3)^2$ $y = \sqrt{x} + 3$

11. a) Graph the function $f(x) = \cos x$.

b) Use transformations to describe how the graph of $g(x) = \cos\left(x - \frac{\pi}{6}\right)$ is related to the graph of $f(x) = \cos x$.

c) Graph the function $g(x) = \cos\left(x - \frac{\pi}{6}\right)$.

d) State the domain and range of the function $g(x)$.

e) Describe the symmetry of the graph of the function $g(x)$.

12. **Communication** The equation of a function does not have to be written in a form beginning with $y =$. For example, the equation $x + y = 1$ defines a linear function whose graph is shown below. Describe what happens to the graph when you make each change to its equation, then graph the image function.

a) Replace x with $2x$.
b) Replace y with $2y$.
c) Replace x with $-2x$.
d) Replace y with $-2y$.
e) Replace x with $x - 3$.
f) Replace y with $y - 3$.
g) Replace x with $\frac{1}{2}x$.
h) Replace y with $\frac{1}{3}y$.

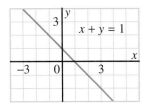

13. Consider the function $f(x) = 2x + 1$.

a) Graph the function $f(x)$.

b) On the same grid, graph the function $g(x) = f(x - 3)$.

c) Describe how the graph of $g(x)$ is related to the graph of $f(x)$.

14. Consider the function $f(x) = \sin x$.

a) Graph the function $f(x)$.

b) On the same grid, graph the function $g(x) = f\left(x + \frac{\pi}{4}\right)$.

c) Describe how the graph of $g(x)$ is related to the graph of $f(x)$.

15. Graph each function $f(x)$. On the same grid, graph the function $g(x) = f(2x)$. Describe how the graph of $g(x)$ is related to the graph of $f(x)$.

a) $f(x) = x - 1$
b) $f(x) = \sqrt{x + 4}$
c) $f(x) = \cos x$

16. Suppose the graph of a function $y = f(x)$ is given. Describe how the graph of each function is related to the graph of $y = f(x)$.

a) $y = f(x - 1)$
b) $y = f(x) - 4$
c) $y = f(x + 9) - 2$
d) $y = -f(x)$
e) $y = 4f(x)$
f) $y = f(4x)$
g) $y = f(-5x)$
h) $y = 3f(2x)$

17. a) Graph the function $f(x) = \cos x$.

b) Use the graph of this function as a guide. Graph the functions $y = f(-x)$ and $y = -f(x)$.

c) Explain why one graph in part b coincides with the graph of $y = f(x)$.

d) Graph the function $y = f(2x)$.

18. a) Graph the function $y = \sqrt{x}$.

b) Determine the equation of the image of $y = \sqrt{x}$ in each case.

i) Its graph is compressed horizontally by a factor of $\frac{1}{4}$.

ii) Its graph is expanded vertically by a factor of 2.

c) Compare the results in part b. Explain how it is possible that the same image graph can be obtained by two different transformations.

d) Give an example of a graph whose images would not be the same under the two transformations in part b.

19. a) Graph the function $y = x(x - 4)$ on grid paper.

b) Graph the image of the function in part a under a translation 3 units right and 3 units up.

c) Write the equation of the image in part b in each form:

i) $y = (x - a)(x - b)$ ii) $y = (x - c)^2 + d$

d) What information does each form of the equation in part c tell you about the image function?

✓ 20. a) Graph the function $f(x) = x(x - 6)$ on grid paper.

b) Write the equations of the functions $y = f(2x)$ and $y = f\left(\frac{1}{2}x\right)$.

c) On the same grid as in part a, graph the functions $y = f(2x)$ and $y = f\left(\frac{1}{2}x\right)$.

✓ 21. Refer to the graph on page 396 that shows yearbook printing costs as a function of the number of copies. On this graph, the equation has the form $y = 8000 + 4x$. Describe how this graph can be obtained by transforming the graph of the function $y = x$.

✓ 22. Refer to the graph on page 397 that shows the height of a falling object as a function of time. On this graph, the equation has the form $y = -0.49x^2 + 9.0$. Describe how this graph can be obtained by transforming the graph of the function $y = x^2$.

23. **Application** At an interest rate i percent, the principal P dollars that must be invested now to have $100 in one year is $P = \dfrac{100}{1 + i}$.

a) Explain why this equation is correct.

b) Describe how the graph of $P = \dfrac{100}{1 + i}$ compares to the graph of $P = \dfrac{1}{i}$.

✓ 24. **Thinking/Inquiry/Problem Solving** One curve in each pattern below is on page 412. Write a set of equations that could be used to make each pattern.

a)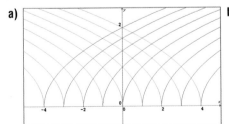

b)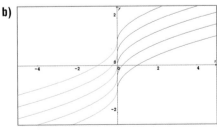

25. A simple pendulum is a weight suspended by thread. The period of the pendulum is the time it takes to swing back and forth once. The approximate period, T seconds, of a simple pendulum with length, L metres, is given by the formula $T = 2\sqrt{L}$.

a) Graph the function for reasonable values of L.

b) What are the domain and range of the function in part a?

26. When money is invested at an annual interest rate i, the approximate number of years, n, it takes to double in value is given by $n = \frac{72}{i}$.

a) Graph the function for reasonable values of i.

b) What are the domain and range of the function in part a?

c) Explain how the function in part a is related to the function $y = \frac{1}{x}$.

27. Write to explain each transformation.

a) Changing the value of c in the equation of a function $y = f(x - c)$ translates its graph to the left or the right. Include an explanation of how you can tell which direction it moves.

b) Replacing x with $-x$ in the equation of a function $y = f(x)$ reflects the graph in the y-axis. Include some graphs to illustrate your explanation.

c) Changing the value of b in the equation of a function $y = f(bx)$ expands or compresses the graph. Include an explanation of how you can tell whether there is an expansion or a compression.

C

28. Find two different examples of a function that produces the same image when its graph is reflected in the y-axis as it does when its graph is reflected in the x-axis. Use the equation of each function to show that the two images are the same.

29. a) Graph the function $f(x) = \sqrt{3 - x}$.

b) Write to explain how you graphed the function in part a.

c) Describe what happens to the graph of a function $y = f(x)$ when x is replaced with $k - x$.

30. A function $f(x)$ has the following property. When its graph is translated 3 units right and 2 units up, the image graph coincides with the graph of $f(x)$.

a) Find an example of a function with this property.

b) How many functions are there with this property? Explain.

31. a) Graph the function $f(x) = \sqrt{25 - x^2}$.

b) Expand the graph in part a by a factor of 2 horizontally and vertically. Determine the equation of the image function in two different ways.

c) Show that the two equations you obtained in part b are the same.

7.4 Combining Transformations of Functions

Vertical Expansion and Translation

Consider the function $y = \sqrt{x}$. We will apply two vertical transformations to this function: a vertical expansion by a factor of 2, and a translation 3 units up.

We apply the vertical expansion first, then the translation.

Start with $y = \sqrt{x}$.

Expand vertically by a factor of 2.
The equation becomes $y = 2\sqrt{x}$.

Translate 3 units up.
The equation becomes $y = 2\sqrt{x} + 3$.

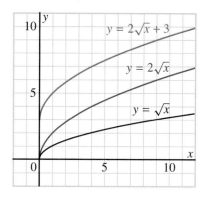

Horizontal Compression and Translation

Consider the function $y = \sqrt{x}$ again. We will apply two horizontal transformations to this function: a horizontal compression by a factor of $\dfrac{1}{2}$, and a translation 3 units left.

We apply the horizontal compression first, then the translation.

Start with $y = \sqrt{x}$.

Compress horizontally by a factor of $\dfrac{1}{2}$.
The equation becomes $y = \sqrt{2x}$.

Translate 3 units left.
The equation becomes $y = \sqrt{2(x + 3)}$.

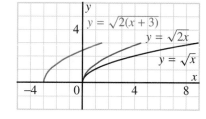

In each of the above situations, the result would have been different if the translation had been applied first.

Example

Use transformations to sketch a graph of each function.

a) $y = 3(x + 6)$ **b)** $y = 3x + 6$

Solution

a) $y = 3(x + 6)$

Start with $y = x$.

Compress $y = x$ by a factor of $\frac{1}{3}$ horizontally.

The equation becomes $y = 3x$.

Translate $y = 3x$ left 6 units.

The equation becomes $y = 3(x + 6)$.

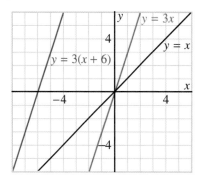

b) $y = 3x + 6$

Rewrite the equation in a form similar to that in part a.

$y = 3x + 6$ can be written as $y = 3(x + 2)$.

Compress $y = x$ by a factor of $\frac{1}{3}$ horizontally.

The equation becomes $y = 3x$.

Translate $y = 3x$ left 2 units.

The equation becomes $y = 3(x + 2)$.

This is the graph of $y = 3x + 6$.

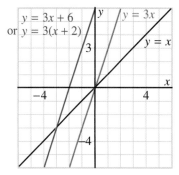

7.4 Exercises

Ⓐ

1. Refer to the vertical expansion and translation on page 418: expand vertically by a factor of 2, then translate 3 units up. Write the equation of the image function if we had started with each function below instead of $y = \sqrt{x}$.

  a) $y = x$ **b)** $y = x^2$ **c)** $y = \sin x$ **d)** $y = \cos x$ **e)** $y = f(x)$

2. Refer to the horizontal expansion and translation on page 418: compress horizontally by a factor of $\frac{1}{2}$, then translate 3 units left. Write the equation of the image function if we had started with each function below instead of $y = \sqrt{x}$.

  a) $y = x$ **b)** $y = x^2$ **c)** $y = \sin x$ **d)** $y = \cos x$ **e)** $y = f(x)$

3. Use transformations to describe how the graph of the second function compares to the graph of the first function.

  a) $f(x) = x^2$ **b)** $f(x) = \sqrt{x}$ **c)** $f(x) = \cos x$

     $g(x) = (x + 4)^2 - 1$ $g(x) = \sqrt{x + 4} - 1$ $g(x) = \cos(x + 4) - 1$

d) $f(x) = \sin x$
$g(x) = 2\sin 3x$

e) $f(x) = \sqrt{x}$
$g(x) = 2\sqrt{3x}$

f) $y = f(x)$
$y = 2f(3x)$

✓ **4. Knowledge/Understanding** Suppose the graph of a function is given. Describe what happens to the graph when you make each change to its equation.

a) Replace x with $3x$, then replace x with $x - 2$.

b) Replace x with $x - 2$, then replace x with $3x$.

c) Replace x with $-x$, then replace x with $x + 4$.

d) Replace x with $x + 4$, then replace x with $-x$.

5. Suppose you make these changes to the graph of a function $y = f(x)$. Write the equation of the image function.

a) Translate 3 units right and 7 units up.

b) Translate 4 units left and 2 units down.

c) Compress by a factor of $\frac{1}{2}$ horizontally and by a factor of $\frac{1}{3}$ vertically.

d) Expand by a factor of 3 horizontally and compress by a factor of $\frac{1}{2}$ vertically.

B

6. Graph the functions in each list on the same grid.

a) $y = x$
$y = 2x$
$y = 2(x + 6)$

b) $y = x^2$
$y = (2x)^2$
$y = [2(x + 6)]^2$

c) $f(x) = \sqrt{x}$
$f(x) = \sqrt{2x}$
$f(x) = \sqrt{2(x + 6)}$

✓ **7.** Refer to the *Example* on pages 418, 419. Sketch a graph of each function.

a) $y = \sqrt{3(x + 6)}$ **b)** $y = \sqrt{3x + 6}$ **c)** $y = |3(x + 6)|$

d) $y = |3x + 6|$ **e)** $y = [3(x + 6)]^2$ **f)** $y = 3(x + 6)^2$

✓ **8.** Refer to the vertical expansion and translation on page 418. Write the equation of the image function when the vertical translation is applied before the vertical expansion.

✓ **9.** Refer to the horizontal compression and translation on page 418. Write the equation of the image function when the horizontal translation is applied before the horizontal compression.

10. This screen shows the graphs of $y = \sqrt{x}$ and $y = \sqrt{4x + 8}$.

a) Describe how the graph of the second function is related to the graph of the first function.

b) Sketch graphs to verify your answer in part a.

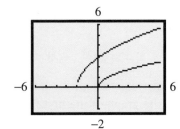

11. This screen shows the graphs of $y = |x|$ and $y = 3|x - 5| + 1$.

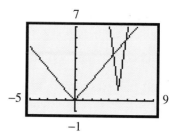

a) Describe how the graph of the second function is related to the graph of the first function.

b) Sketch graphs to verify your answer in part a.

 12. Communication

a) Graph the functions $y = x^2$ and $y = \left[\frac{1}{2}(x - 4)\right]^2$.

b) Describe how the graph of the second function is related to the graph of the first function.

c) State the domain and range of each function.

13. Repeat exercise 12, using each pair of functions.

a) $y = \sqrt{x}$ and $y = \sqrt{2x - 5}$

b) $f(x) = \sin x$ and $g(x) = \sin 2x - 1$

 14. The graph below shows these two functions:

$f(x) = \cos x$ and $g(x) = 2 \cos\left(x - \frac{\pi}{3}\right) + 1$

a) Explain how the graph of $g(x)$ is related to the graph of $f(x)$.

b) State the domain and range of $g(x)$.

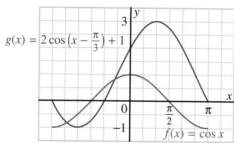

15. The equation $x + y = 1$ defines a linear function whose graph is shown on page 415. Describe what happens to the graph when you make each change to its equation. Determine the slope and the y-intercept of the graph of each image function.

a) Replace x with $2x$, then replace x with $x - 3$.

b) Replace y with $2y$, then replace y with $y - 3$.

c) Replace x with $2x$ and y with $3y$, then replace x with $x - 1$ and y with $y - 2$.

d) Replace x with $\frac{1}{2}x$ and y with $3y$, then replace x with $x + 3$ and y with $y - 4$.

16. Refer to the graph on page 397 that shows the number of hours of daylight in Ottawa. The equation is $h = 3.4 \cos \frac{2\pi}{365}(n - 172) + 12.2$. Describe how this graph can be obtained by transforming the graph of the function $h = \cos n$.

17. Application A ball was thrown upward and allowed to fall. A stroboscopic picture of the ball was taken. Measurements from the picture were used to model the height of the ball, h metres, as a function of time, t seconds. The result is shown in the graph below left. The equation of the parabola of best fit for these data is $h = -4.89t^2 + 8.09t$.

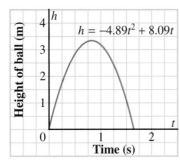
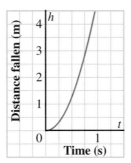

The graph is translated so the maximum point moves to the origin. Then the graph is reflected in the horizontal axis. The result (above right) can be used to model the distance an object falls, d metres, as a function of time, t seconds.

a) Determine the coordinates of the maximum point on the first graph.

b) Use the equation of the first function to predict the equation of the second function.

18. Water dripped steadily from a burette. A stroboscopic picture of the falling droplets was taken. Measurements from the picture were used to model the distance a droplet falls, d metres, as a function of time, t seconds. The equation of the parabola of best fit for these data is $d = 4.8t^2 + 0.04t$.

a) Compare this equation with your answer to exercise 17b. In what ways are the equations similar? In what ways are they different?

b) Explain why the equations are different.

19. Thinking/Inquiry/Problem Solving Suppose you are given the equation of a function that involves horizontal translations and expansions or compressions. Write to explain how you can tell whether the translation is applied first or whether the expansion or compression is applied first. Use examples to illustrate your explanation.

C

20. In the lumber industry, logs are measured in imperial units. Various methods are used to estimate the volume of lumber that can be obtained from a log. One method is as follows.
    - Subtract 4 inches from the diameter of the log.
    - Square the result.
    - Multiply by the length of the log in feet.

    The result is an estimate of the volume of the log in units called board feet.

    a) Write an equation to express the volume, V board feet, of a log as a function of its diameter, d inches, and its length, L feet.

    b) Write the equations of the functions that correspond to logs with lengths 12 feet, 16 feet, and 20 feet.

    c) Graph the functions in part b on the same grid for $26 \leq d \leq 36$.

    d) Write to explain how the graphs are related.

21. a) Graph the function $y = \sqrt{25 - x^2}$ and its image after each transformation.
    i) Translate 3 units right.
    ii) Translate 2 units up.
    iii) Translate 3 units right and 2 units up.

    b) Write the equation of each image function.

    c) State the domain and range of the function and each image.

22. a) Graph the function $y = \sqrt{25 - x^2}$ and its image after each transformation.
    i) Compress horizontally by a factor of $\frac{1}{2}$.
    ii) Expand horizontally by a factor of 2.
    iii) Compress vertically by a factor of $\frac{1}{2}$.
    iv) Expand vertically by a factor of 2.

    b) Write the equation of each image function.

    c) State the domain and range of the function and each image.

23. When we apply horizontal expansions or compressions and translations to the graph of a function $y = f(x)$, we write equations such as $y = f(2x - 5)$ or $y = f(2(x - 5))$, depending on which transformation is applied first. However, when we apply vertical expansions or compressions and translations, we usually write equations such as $y = 3f(x) + 4$.

    a) In $y = 3f(x) + 4$, in which order are the two transformations applied? Explain.

    b) Write the equation that corresponds to the other order of applying the transformations.

7.5 The Inverse of a Function

Variables are used in two different ways in mathematics — in applications and conventionally. In applications, the variables have meanings that come from the context and we choose them to reflect those meanings. Conventionally, we use the variables x and y. We treat x as the independent variable (plotted horizontally) and y as the dependent variable (plotted vertically).

Using Variables in Applications

This equation expresses the distance, d metres, that an object falls from rest in t seconds. Recall this equation from Chapter 1, page 67.

$$d = 4.9t^2 \qquad ①$$

This equation is useful when we know the time and need to determine the distance the object falls. When we know the distance and need to determine the time, we solve the equation for t.

$$d = 4.9t^2$$
$$t^2 = \frac{d}{4.9} \qquad ②$$

Take the positive square root of each side.

$$t = \sqrt{\frac{d}{4.9}} \qquad ③$$

In equation ②, both d and t are assumed to be positive. Since $d \geq 0$, we can take the square root of the right side. Since $t \geq 0$, we only want the positive square root.

Equation ③ expresses the time as a function of the distance. It is the *inverse* of equation ①. The graphs below represent these two functions.

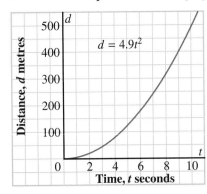

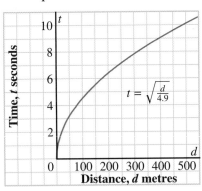

The two functions provide the same information. When we use function ①, we think of d depending on t. In the equation, we substitute a value for t, then calculate d. On the graph, we locate t on the horizontal axis, then move up to the curve and over to the vertical axis to determine d. We complete a similar process with function ③, but we think of t depending on d.

When we use variables in applications, each variable has a physical meaning and has a name (such as t or d) that makes sense. The variables help keep track of what the equations and graphs mean.

Using Variables Conventionally

In mathematics, we use the variables x and y that may have no physical meaning. For example, consider this linear function.

$$y = 3x + 2 \qquad ④$$

We can solve this equation for x as we solved equation ① for t.

$$3x = y - 2$$
$$x = \frac{y - 2}{3} \qquad ⑤$$

These equations are graphed below. The graph of equation ⑤, below right, has x plotted vertically and y plotted horizontally.

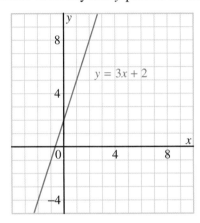 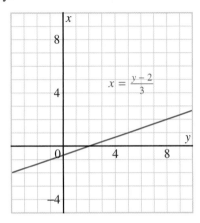

If we were using these variables in applications, we would use equation ⑤ as the inverse of equation ④. But when we use variables conventionally, we always think of y as depending on x. The x is always the independent variable. It appears on the right side of the equation and is plotted horizontally. The y is always the dependent variable. It appears on the left side of the equation and is plotted vertically. We accomplish this by interchanging x and y in equation ⑤ so that it becomes:

$$y = \frac{x - 2}{3} \qquad ⑥$$

When we use variables conventionally, equation ⑥ is the inverse of equation ④. The graphs of these equations are shown. Interchanging x and y permits us to graph the function $y = 3x + 2$ and its inverse $y = \frac{x - 2}{3}$ on the same grid. The graphs illustrate a property of the two functions. Their graphs are reflections of each other in the line $y = x$. The proof of this property is left to the exercises (see exercise 25).

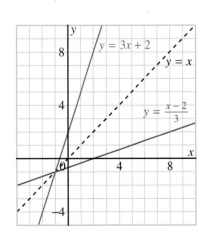

This interchange of variables is not meaningful when we use them in applications. It does not make sense to interchange t and d in equation ③, and it does not make sense to draw the two graphs on page 424 on the same grid.

Determining the Inverse of a Function

Given the equation of the function:

When the variables are used in applications:

> Solve the equation for the variable on the right side.

When the variables are used conventionally:

> Solve the equation for x in terms of y.
> Then interchange x and y.

Given the graph of the function:

Hold the paper by the top right and bottom left corners.

Flip the paper. The graph you see through the paper is the graph of the inverse.

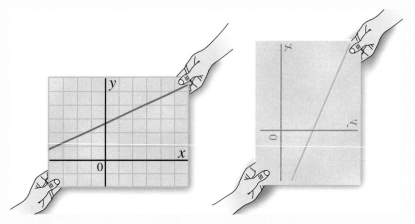

Alternatively, reflect the graph in the line $y = x$.

Example 1

Determine the inverse of the function $y = -5x + 2$.

Solution

Solve the equation for x.

$$y = -5x + 2$$
$$5x = -y + 2$$
$$x = \frac{-y + 2}{5}$$

Interchange x and y. The equation of the inverse is $y = \frac{-x + 2}{5}$.

In *Example 1*, we can write the given function using function notation $f(x)$. Since the inverse is also a function, we can write it using function notation. The symbol $f^{-1}(x)$ represents the inverse function. We write:

$$f(x) = -5x + 2$$
$$f^{-1}(x) = \frac{-x + 2}{5}$$

Example 2

Consider the function $f(x) = \frac{1}{x - 2}$.

a) Determine the inverse of $f(x)$.

b) Graph $y = f(x)$ and its inverse on the same grid.

c) Explain why the inverse is a function. Write its equation using function notation.

d) State the domain and range of $f(x)$ and $f^{-1}(x)$.

Solution

a) Let $y = \frac{1}{x - 2}$, where $x \neq 2$.

Solve the equation for x.

$$y = \frac{1}{x - 2}$$
$$y(x - 2) = 1$$
$$xy - 2y = 1$$
$$xy = 1 + 2y$$
$$x = \frac{1 + 2y}{y} \qquad (y \neq 0)$$

Interchange x and y. The equation of the inverse is $y = \frac{1 + 2x}{x}, x \neq 0$.

b) To graph $y = \frac{1}{x - 2}$, visualize the graph of $y = \frac{1}{x}$.

The graph of $y = \frac{1}{x - 2}$ is 2 units right of $y = \frac{1}{x}$.

To graph the inverse, reflect the graph of $y = \frac{1}{x - 2}$ in the line $y = x$.

c) The inverse is a function because its graph satisfies the vertical line test.

The equation of the inverse function is $f^{-1}(x) = \frac{1 + 2x}{x}$.

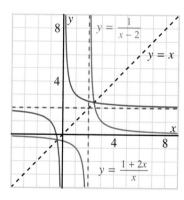

d) From the graph:

For $f(x)$:   Domain: all real numbers except 2
               Range: all real numbers except 0

For $f^{-1}(x)$: Domain: all real numbers except 0
               Range: all real numbers except 2

Discuss

Why is $x = 2$ not in the domain of $y = \frac{1}{x - 2}$?

Why is $y = 0$ not in the range of $y = \frac{1}{x - 2}$?

In *Example 2*, the domain of $f(x)$ is the range of $f^{-1}(x)$. Similarly, the range of $f(x)$ is the domain of $f^{-1}(x)$.

Note that $f^{-1}(x)$ is a notation for the inverse function of $f(x)$. The notation $f^{-1}(x)$ does *not* mean $\dfrac{1}{f(x)}$.

Example 3

Consider the function $f(x) = x^2 + 2$.

a) Determine the inverse of $f(x)$.

b) Graph $y = f(x)$ and its inverse on the same grid.

c) Is the inverse of $f(x)$ a function? Explain.

Solution

a) Let $y = x^2 + 2$.

Solve the equation for x.
$$y = x^2 + 2$$
$$x^2 = y - 2$$
$$x = \pm\sqrt{y - 2}$$
Interchange x and y. The equation of the inverse is $y = \pm\sqrt{x - 2}$.

b) To graph $y = x^2 + 2$, visualize the graph of $y = x^2$. The graph of $f(x) = x^2 + 2$ is 2 units above it.

To graph the inverse, reflect the graph of $y = x^2 + 2$ in the line $y = x$.

c) The inverse is not a function because its graph fails the vertical line test.

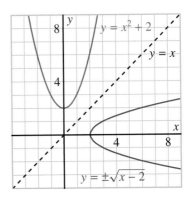

Example 3 shows that the inverse of a function is not necessarily a function. For this reason, we cannot use the notation $f^{-1}(x)$ to represent the inverse of the function in *Example 3*. However, by restricting the domain of $f(x)$, we can define related functions whose inverses are functions. Suppose we define the functions $g(x)$ and $h(x)$ as follows:
$$g(x) = x^2 + 2, \ x \geq 0$$
$$h(x) = x^2 + 2, \ x \leq 0$$

The graph of $g(x)$ is the part of the graph of $y = x^2 + 2$ to the right of the y-axis. Its inverse is $y = \sqrt{x - 2}$. The inverse of $g(x)$ is a function, $g^{-1}(x) = \sqrt{x - 2}$.

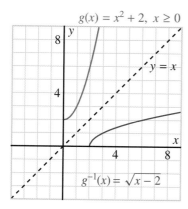

$g(x) = x^2 + 2, \ x \geq 0$

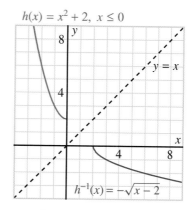

$h(x) = x^2 + 2, \ x \leq 0$

The graph of $h(x)$ is the part of the graph of $y = x^2 + 2$ to the left of the y-axis. Its inverse is $y = -\sqrt{x - 2}$. The inverse of $h(x)$ is a function, $h^{-1}(x) = -\sqrt{x - 2}$.

Now that we know how to determine the inverse of a function, we can make a precise definition. Recall that a function is defined as a rule that gives a single output number for every valid input number.

For the function $d = 4.9t^2$, $t \geq 0$, on page 424, the input numbers are the times and the output numbers are the distances. For the inverse $t = \sqrt{\frac{d}{4.9}}$, $d \geq 0$, the input numbers are the distances and the output numbers are the times. The input numbers for the inverse are the output numbers for the original function, and vice versa.

The same is true for all the functions on pages 425 to 428. Consider the function $y = x^2 + 2$ in *Example 3*. The input numbers are the real numbers and the output numbers are the real numbers greater than or equal to 2. For the inverse $y = \pm\sqrt{x - 2}$, the input numbers are the output numbers of the original function, and vice versa.

Take Note

Definition of the Inverse of a Function

- A function is a rule that gives a single output number for every valid input number.

- The inverse of a function is the rule obtained by reversing the roles of the input and output numbers.

A

1. Measurement formulas contain variables used in applications. Determine the inverse of each function.

   a) The diameter of a circle: $d = 2r$

   b) The circumference of a circle: $C = \pi d$

   c) The area of a circle: $A = \pi r^2$

   d) The surface area of a sphere: $A = 4\pi r^2$

   e) The volume of a sphere: $V = \frac{4}{3}\pi r^3$

2. Suppose you are given two functions whose variables are used in applications. How could you tell whether one function is the inverse of the other in each case?

   a) You are given the equations of the functions.

   b) You are given the graphs of the functions.

✓ 3. Determine the inverse of each function.

   a) $f(x) = x + 4$ b) $f(x) = 2x - 1$ c) $f(x) = 3x$

   d) $f(x) = 1 - x$ e) $f(x) = \frac{1}{2}x + 5$ f) $f(x) = \frac{2}{3}x + 1$

✓ 4. Determine the inverse of each function.

   a) $f(x) = x^2$ b) $f(x) = x^2 - 2$ c) $f(x) = 3 - x^2$

   d) $f(x) = 3x^2 + 2$ e) $f(x) = \frac{1}{2}x^2 - 1$ f) $f(x) = 5 - 2x^2$

✓ 5. Use examples to explain your answer to each question.

   a) Is the inverse of a linear function a linear function?

   b) Is the inverse of a quadratic function a quadratic function?

✓ 6. **Communication** Suppose you are given two functions whose variables are used conventionally. How could you tell whether one function is the inverse of the other in each case?

   a) You are given the equations of the functions.

   b) You are given the graphs of the functions.

✓ 7. a) Determine the inverse of each function in each list.

   i) $f(x) = x$ ii) $f(x) = -x$ iii) $f(x) = x$ iv) $f(x) = x + 1$
   $f(x) = x + 1$ $f(x) = 1 - x$ $f(x) = 2x$ $f(x) = 2x + 2$
   $f(x) = x + 2$ $f(x) = 2 - x$ $f(x) = 3x$ $f(x) = 3x + 3$
   $f(x) = x + 3$ $f(x) = 3 - x$ $f(x) = 4x$ $f(x) = 4x + 4$

   b) Choose one list from part a. Explain how you could use patterns to find the inverses.

8. a) Determine the inverse of each function in each list.

i) $f(x) = x^2$ **ii)** $f(x) = \dfrac{1}{x}$ **iii)** $f(x) = \dfrac{1}{x}$ **iv)** $f(x) = \dfrac{1}{x}$

$f(x) = (x - 1)^2$ $f(x) = \dfrac{1}{2x}$ $f(x) = \dfrac{1}{x + 1}$ $f(x) = \dfrac{1}{x} + 1$

$f(x) = (x - 2)^2$ $f(x) = \dfrac{1}{3x}$ $f(x) = \dfrac{1}{x + 2}$ $f(x) = \dfrac{1}{x} + 2$

$f(x) = (x - 3)^2$ $f(x) = \dfrac{1}{4x}$ $f(x) = \dfrac{1}{x + 3}$ $f(x) = \dfrac{1}{x} + 3$

b) Choose one list from part a. Explain how you could use patterns to find the inverses.

9. Knowledge/Understanding Two functions are described in words. Is each function the inverse of the other? Explain.

a) Multiply by 3, then add 2.   Subtract 2, then divide by 3.

b) Multiply by 4, then add 1.   Divide by 4, then subtract 1.

c) Add 2, then multiply by 5.   Subtract 2, then divide by 5.

d) Add 7, then multiply by 4.   Divide by 4, then subtract 7.

e) Add 1, then take the reciprocal.   Take the reciprocal, then subtract 1.

f) Multiply by 2, then take the reciprocal.   Take the reciprocal, then divide by 2.

10. Each graph is a reflection of the other in the line $y = x$. Write the equation of each coloured graph.

a)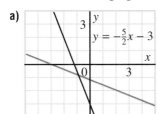

b)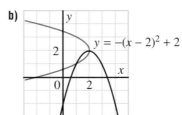

11. Use the definition of a function and suitable examples to explain your answer to each question.

a) Does every function have an inverse?

b) Is the inverse of every function also a function?

12. Six examples of functions whose variables are used in applications are given. Determine the inverse of each function and describe it in words.

a) The cost C dollars to print n copies of a school yearbook is given by the formula $C = 8000 + 4n$.

b) When an object 9 m above the ground falls, its height after t seconds is given by the formula $h = -0.49t^2 + 9$.

c) When you are h kilometres above the ground, the approximate distance, d kilometres, to the horizon is given by the formula $d = 113\sqrt{h}$.

d) An approximate formula for converting degrees Celsius to degrees Fahrenheit is $F = 2C + 30$.

e) The exact formula for converting degrees Celsius to degrees Fahrenheit is $F = \frac{9}{5}C + 32$.

f) The *period*, T, of a planet is the number of Earth days for it to travel once around the sun. For a planet whose mean distance from the sun is d million kilometres, the period is given by the formula $T \doteq 0.2d^{\frac{3}{2}}$.

13. Consider the function $f(x) = x^2$.

a) Determine the inverse of $f(x)$.

b) Graph $y = f(x)$ and its inverse on the same grid.

c) Is the inverse a function? Explain.

14. Consider the function $g(x) = \sqrt{x}$.

a) Determine the inverse of $g(x)$.

b) Graph $y = g(x)$ and its inverse on the same grid.

c) Is the inverse a function? Explain.

15. Determine the inverse of each function.

a) $f(x) = x - 4$ **b)** $f(x) = -3x$ **c)** $f(x) = \frac{1}{2}x + 7$

d) $g(x) = \frac{1}{1-x}$ **e)** $g(x) = \frac{1}{x+1}$ **f)** $h(x) = \frac{3}{x}$

16. Determine the inverse of each function. Graph the function, its inverse, and $y = x$ on the same grid. State the domain and range of the inverse. State whether the inverse is a function.

a) $y = 2x + 3$ **b)** $y = 10 - x$ **c)** $y = x^2 - 4$

d) $f(x) = (x - 1)^2$ **e)** $f(x) = \frac{6}{x}$ **f)** $g(x) = \sqrt{x - 2}$

17. Determine the inverse of each function. Explain why each inverse is a function. Write the inverse using function notation.

a) $f(x) = 4x - 7$ **b)** $f(x) = 5 - x$ **c)** $f(x) = 8 - 3x$

d) $f(x) = \frac{2}{x}$ **e)** $f(x) = \frac{1}{x+3}$ **f)** $f(x) = \sqrt{x+1}$

18. Thinking/Inquiry/Problem Solving Explain your answer to each part.

a) Find a function that is equal to its own inverse function.

b) How many different functions are there that are equal to their own inverse function? Explain.

19. Restrict the domain of each function so its inverse is a function. Graph the function and its inverse.

a) $y = x^2 - 1$ **b)** $y = 2x^2 + 3$ **c)** $y = (x - 1)^2$

d) $f(x) = (x + 2)^2 + 1$ **e)** $f(x) = (x - 4)(x + 2)$ **f)** $f(x) = x^2 - 4x + 3$

20. **Application** A scientific calculator has a key labelled "$\sin^{-1}$", associated with the ⌜SIN⌝ key. This gives values for a function called the inverse of the sine function, represented by $\sin^{-1} x$.

   a) Use a calculator to determine some values of $\sin^{-1} x$.

   b) Graph the function $y = \sin^{-1} x$.

   c) Explain how the graph of $y = \sin^{-1} x$ is related to the graph of $y = \sin x$.

   d) What are the domain and range of the function $y = \sin^{-1} x$?

21. a) Graph the function $f(x) = \cos x$, for $-2\pi \le x \le 2\pi$.

   b) Write the equation of the inverse of the function in part a. Graph the inverse on the same grid. Is the inverse a function? Explain.

22. Follow these steps to graph a function and its inverse on the TI-83 Plus.

   • Input a function as Y1 in the Y= list.

   • Define the viewing window. For accurate results, the length : width ratio of the screen should be about 3 : 2.

   • Press ⌜2nd⌝ ⌜PRGM⌝ for DRAW. Then press **8** ⌜VARS⌝ ⌜▶⌝ **1 1**. "DrawInv Y1" will appear on the screen. Press ⌜ENTER⌝.

   Practise graphing a function and its inverse from the exercises in this section.

C

23. Choose one part of exercise 15. Determine $f(f^{-1}(x))$ and $f^{-1}(f(x))$. Explain the result.

24. Refer to *Example 2*.

   a) Show that the equation of the inverse can be written as $y = \dfrac{1}{x} + 2$.

   b) Visualize the graph of $y = \dfrac{1}{x}$ drawn on the same grid. When this graph is translated 2 units right, it becomes the given function. When the graph of $y = \dfrac{1}{x}$ is translated 2 units up, it becomes the inverse function. Is this just a coincidence, or are the graphs of a function and its inverse always related this way? Explain.

25. On page 425, the graphs of $y = 3x + 2$ and its inverse, $y = \dfrac{x-2}{3}$, are reflections of each other in the line $y = x$. You can prove this property as follows.

   a) Draw the graph on page 425. Let P(a, b) be any point on the graph of $y = 3x + 2$. Let Q be the corresponding point on the graph of the inverse.

   b) What are the coordinates of Q? Explain.

   c) Prove that the line $y = x$ bisects PQ at right angles. Explain why this proves that the graphs are reflections of each other in the line $y = x$.

1. Consider the function $f(x) = \cos x$.

   a) Graph the function for $-2\pi \le x \le 2\pi$.

   b) Graph the image of $f(x)$ under a translation of $\frac{\pi}{4}$ units left.

   c) Write the equation of the image function $g(x)$.

   d) What are the domain and range of the image function?

2. Consider the function $f(x) = \sqrt{x}$.

   a) Graph the function $f(x)$.

   b) On the same grid, graph the function $g(x) = \sqrt{\frac{1}{2}x}$.

   c) Describe how the graph of $g(x)$ is related to the graph of $f(x)$.

   d) What are the domain and range of $f(x)$ and $g(x)$?

3. Suppose you make these changes to the equation of a function. Describe what happens to each graph.

   a) Replace x with $x + 3$.   b) Replace y with $y - 2$.

   c) Replace x with $2x$.   d) Replace y with $4y$.

   e) Replace x with $\frac{1}{3}x$.   f) Replace y with $\frac{1}{5}y$.

   g) Replace x with $-3x$.   h) Replace y with $-3y$.

4. Consider the function $f(x) = x^2$.

   a) Graph the function $f(x)$.

   b) On the same grid, graph the function $g(x) = -2(x + 3)^2 - 4$.

   c) Describe how the graph of $g(x)$ is related to the graph of $f(x)$.

   d) What are the domain and range of $f(x)$ and $g(x)$?

5. Suppose the graph of a function is given. Describe what happens to the graph when you make each change to its equation.

   a) Replace x with $2x$, then replace x with $x + 1$.

   b) Replace x with $x + 1$, then replace x with $2x$.

   c) Replace x with $-2x$, then replace x with $x - 1$.

   d) Replace x with $x - 1$, then replace x with $-2x$.

6. Determine the inverse of each function. Graph the function and its inverse on the same grid. State whether the inverse is a function.

   a) $y = -2x + 7$ b) $y = 2x^2 - 3x + 1$ c) $f(x) = 2\sqrt{x - 1} + 4$

7. a) State the domain and range of each function in exercise 6.

   b) State the domain and range of the inverse of each function in exercise 6.

Inverting a Quartic Function

A quartic polynomial has degree 4. The graph of the quartic function $y = (x^2 - 1)^2$ and its inverse are shown below. The graph of the inverse is the reflection of the original graph in the line $y = x$; a point (a, b) on the original graph corresponds to a point (b, a) on the inverse.

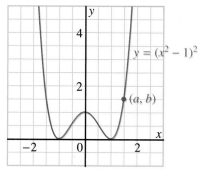
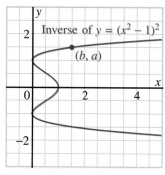

Although $y = (x^2 - 1)^2$ is a function, its inverse is not. For a function, each value of x gives a unique value of y. On the graph of the inverse, each value of x between 0 and 1 has *four* corresponding values of y. Two of these values are positive, while the other two are negative. Since the graph is symmetrical about the x-axis, the negative values are the opposites of the positive values.

Taken as a whole, the graph of the inverse is not a function. However, if we break the graph into the four pieces shown in colour, each individual piece is a function. We can call these four pieces "functional pieces." These functional pieces are labelled from top to bottom as $f(x)$, $g(x)$, $h(x)$, and $k(x)$.

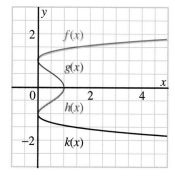

Formulating Questions

Here is the problem we want to investigate.

What are the equations of the functional pieces in the graph of the inverse of the quartic function $y = (x^2 - 1)^2$?

Selecting Strategies, Resources, Technology, and Tools

It seems reasonable to assume that the equations of the functional pieces are related to the equation of the inverse. So, we begin there.

Representing the Inverse in Algebraic Form

Recall that the equation of the inverse is found as follows:

- Solve the original equation for x.

- Then interchange x and y.

The original equation is $y = (x^2 - 1)^2$.

Rearrange the equation.

$$(x^2 - 1)^2 = y$$

Solve for x. Remember that, by definition, the square roots of a^2 are $\pm a$.

$$x^2 - 1 = \pm\sqrt{y}$$
$$x^2 = 1 \pm \sqrt{y}$$
$$x = \pm\sqrt{1 \pm \sqrt{y}}$$

Interchange x and y.

$$y = \pm\sqrt{1 \pm \sqrt{x}}$$

The equation of the inverse is $y = \pm\sqrt{1 \pm \sqrt{x}}$.

Reflecting on the Reasonableness of Results

We take square roots twice, each time being careful to insert the $\pm$ signs. We want 4 expressions, one for each functional piece.

We now have a general expression for the inverse. In fact, we have *four* expressions. There are two $\pm$ signs and we have two choices for each, for a total of four choices. These four expressions correspond to the four functional pieces of the inverse function.

Interpreting Information and Forming Conclusions

How do we match each expression with its corresponding functional piece? There are several ways to do this. Here is one possibility.

- The top two functional pieces are positive; that is, they lie above the *x*-axis. So, they must use the first (outside) + sign.
  The top branch will use both the + signs.
  Thus, $f(x) = +\sqrt{1 + \sqrt{x}}$ and $g(x) = +\sqrt{1 - \sqrt{x}}$

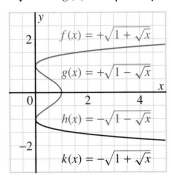

- The bottom two functional pieces are reflections of the top two functional pieces in the *x*-axis.
  Since $f(x) = +\sqrt{1 + \sqrt{x}}$, its reflection has equation $k(x) = -\sqrt{1 + \sqrt{x}}$.
  Therefore, $h(x) = -\sqrt{1 - \sqrt{x}}$

> When working with functions, take every chance you get to make connections between the information provided by the graph and the information provided by the equation. The interaction between geometry and algebra provides insight that may not be apparent by considering the graph and equation separately.

Problems

1. State the domain and range of each functional piece in the inverse of $y = (x^2 - 1)^2$.

2. Investigate other connections between the graph and equation of $y = (x^2 - 1)^2$.

   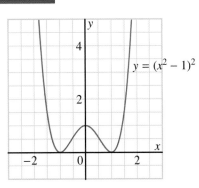

   a) The graph intersects the *x*-axis at $x = \pm 1$. How could you have obtained this information from the equation?

   b) The graph is always above the *x*-axis. How could you have predicted this from the equation?

   c) The graph is symmetrical about the *y*-axis; that is, on both sides of the *y*-axis, the height of the graph is the same at the same distance from the *y*-axis. Why is this?

3. Graph the function $y = x^2 - 4$.

   a) Determine its inverse both graphically and algebraically.

   b) Determine the equation for each functional piece of the inverse graph.

   c) Specify the domain in each case, then match each functional piece with its equation.

4. Repeat exercise 3, using the function $y = x^2 - 2x$.

5. The function $y = \dfrac{1}{x^2 - 4}$ is graphed at the right.

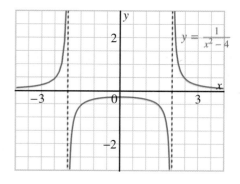

  a) Determine its inverse both graphically and algebraically.

  b) Determine the equation for each functional piece of the graph of the inverse.

  c) For each functional piece in part b, specify its domain, then match the functional piece with its equation.

Challenge Problems

6. a) Draw the graph of $y = (x^2 - 1)^2$ translated 1 unit to the right.

  b) Determine the equation of the image graph.

  c) Determine the inverse of the image function, both graphically and algebraically, then identify the functional pieces of the inverse.

  d) Are the functional pieces identical to those of the inverse of $y = (x^2 - 1)^2$ translated 1 unit up? Explain.

7. Repeat exercise 5, using the function $y = \dfrac{2x}{x^2 - 1}$ graphed at the right. Simplify the equation of the inverse as much as possible. It seems reasonable to assume that there will be three functional pieces for the inverse. Identify these pieces, then determine their equations.

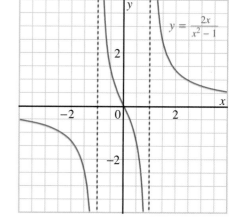

8. By any method, make a careful drawing of the graph of $x^{\frac{2}{3}} + y^{\frac{2}{3}} = 1$. Note that the expression on the left side of the equation is defined for both negative and positive values of x and y.

  a) There are many types of symmetry exhibited by the graph. Describe all of them.

  b) Solve the equation for y as a function of x.

  c) Determine the inverse both graphically and algebraically. Identify all functional pieces of the inverse.

  d) State the domain of each functional piece, then determine its equation.

Review Exercises

Mathematics Toolkit

Function Tools

- Vertical Line Test
  If a vertical line drawn on a graph never meets more than one point on the graph, the graph represents a function.

- Equation Test
  If there are no values of x that produce more than one value of y when substituted into an equation, the equation represents a function.

- The inverse of a function is the rule obtained by reversing the roles of the input and output numbers.

- Transformations applied to $y = f(x)$

  Vertical translation of k units
  Replace y with $y - k$ for the image equation $y - k = f(x)$.
  When $k > 0$, the translation is up. $+$
  When $k < 0$, the translation is down. $-$

  Horizontal translation of k units
  Replace x with $x - k$ for the image equation $y = f(x - k)$.
  When $k > 0$, the translation is to the right. $+$
  When $k < 0$, the translation is to the left. $-$

  Reflection in the y-axis
  Replace x with $-x$ for the image equation $y = f(-x)$.

  Reflection in the x-axis
  Replace y with $-y$ for the image equation $-y = f(x)$, or $y = -f(x)$.

  Vertical expansion or compression
  Replace y with ky for the image equation $ky = f(x)$, or $y = \frac{1}{k}f(x)$.
  When $0 < k < 1$, there is an expansion.
  When $k > 1$, there is a compression.
  When $k < 0$, there is also a reflection in the x-axis.

  Horizontal expansion or compression
  Replace x with kx for the image equation $y = f(kx)$.
  When $0 < k < 1$, there is an expansion.
  When $k > 1$, there is a compression.
  When $k < 0$, there is also a reflection in the y-axis.

NS 1. Solve each inequality. Illustrate the solution on a number line.

    a) $3x + 5 < 5x + 10$ **b)** $2(a + 3) \leq -3(1 - a)$

    c) $-(2n + 5) < -(5n - 1)$ **d)** $-3(x - 2) + 5 \geq 2(4 - x) - 1$

    e) $\frac{1}{2}(a - 1) + 3 > \frac{1}{3}(1 - a) + 2$ **f)** $-3 + 4(2x - 1) > -2(2 + 3x) + 4$

7.1 2. **a)** Graph the function $y = \sqrt{x + 2}$.

    b) Describe the domain and range of the function.

    c) Does the graph of $y = \sqrt{x + 2}$ have any of these characteristics? Explain.
        i) lines of symmetry   **ii)** maximum or minimum points
        iii) asymptotes

3. In a study of wind speeds near a large city, it was found that wind speed increases with height above the ground. The wind speed is represented by v metres per second at a height h metres. The equations that express v as a function of h are given.

    i) In the downtown core: $v = 0.5\sqrt{h}$, $0 \leq h \leq 500$
    ii) In the suburbs: $v = 0.6\sqrt{h}$, $0 \leq h \leq 350$
    iii) In nearby rural areas: $v = 0.7\sqrt{h}$, $0 \leq h \leq 200$

    a) Sketch the graphs of these functions on the same grid.

    b) What are the domain and range of each function?

7.2 4. Given $f(x) = -2x^2 + 3x - 7$, determine each value.

    a) $f(0)$ **b)** $f(1)$ **c)** $f(-1)$ **d)** $f(\frac{1}{2})$ **e)** $f(-0.5)$

5. For each function, determine $f(3), f(\frac{1}{3})$, and $f(\sqrt{3})$. Write each answer to 3 decimal places where necessary.

    a) $f(x) = 3x - 1$ **b)** $f(x) = -x^2 + 2$ **c)** $f(x) = \sqrt{x + 1}$

    d) $f(x) = \dfrac{1}{x + 1}$ **e)** $f(x) = \cos x$ **f)** $f(x) = \sin x$

6. Graph each function. State its domain and range.

    a) $f(x) = \frac{1}{3}x + 2$ **b)** $f(x) = -2x^2 + 5$ **c)** $f(x) = 2(x + 1)^2 - 4$

    d) $f(x) = \sqrt{x - 1}$ **e)** $f(x) = \dfrac{1}{x - 1}$ **f)** $f(x) = \cos x - 1$

7. Given $f(x) = 3x^2 - x - 1$, determine each expression.

    a) $f(a)$ **b)** $f(-2a)$ **c)** $f(a + 1)$ **d)** $f(a^2)$ **e)** $f(\sqrt{a})$

8. Sketch a graph of $f(x) = \sqrt{x}$.

    a) State the domain and range of $f(x)$.

    b) Explain how $f(x)$ is related to $g(x) = x^2$.

9. Sketch a graph of $f(x) = \dfrac{1}{x}$.

a) State the domain and range of $f(x)$.

b) Explain how $f(x)$ is related to $g(x) = x$.

7.3 **10. a)** Graph the functions $f(x) = |x|$ and $g(x) = |x - 3|$ on the same grid.

b) Describe how the graph of $g(x) = |x - 3|$ is related to the graph of $f(x) = |x|$.

c) State the domain and range of the function $g(x) = |x - 3|$.

11. After two years at an interest rate i percent compounded annually, a principal of $500 amounts to A dollars, where $A = 500(1 + i)^2$.

a) Describe how the graph of A against i compares to the graph of $y = x^2$.

b) State the domain and range of the function $A = 500(1 + i)^2$.

12. The approximate distance, d kilometres, to the horizon is given by the formula $d = 113\sqrt{h}$, where h kilometres is your height above the ground. Describe how the graph of this function can be obtained by transforming the graph of the function $y = \sqrt{x}$.

13. A cup of instant coffee is made with boiling water, then allowed to stand for 2 h. A thermometer with both Celsius and Fahrenheit scales is placed in the water. The graph shows how the Celsius temperature decreases during this time. The formula $F = 1.8C + 32$ relates the two temperatures.

a) Describe how a graph of the temperature in degrees Fahrenheit is related to the graph shown.

b) Copy the graph onto grid paper. Draw the corresponding graph for temperatures in degrees Fahrenheit on the same grid.

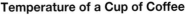

Temperature of a Cup of Coffee

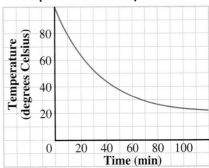

7.4 **14.** Graph these functions on the same grid. Explain how each function is related to $y = x$.

a) $y = x$ 　　　　b) $y = 3x$ 　　　　c) $y = 3(x - 2)$

d) $y = 3(x - 2) + 1$ 　　e) $y = 3(-x - 2) + 1$ 　　f) $-y = 3(x - 2) + 1$

15. Graph these functions on the same grid. Explain how each function is related to $y = x^2$.

a) $y = x^2$ 　　　　b) $y = 2x^2$ 　　　　c) $y = 2(x + 3)^2$

d) $y = 2(x + 3)^2 - 4$ 　e) $y = 2(-x + 3)^2 - 4$ 　f) $-y = 2(x + 3)^2 - 4$

Review Exercises

16. Graph these functions on the same grid. Explain how each function is related to $f(x) = \sqrt{x}$.

a) $f(x) = \sqrt{x}$

b) $g(x) = \sqrt{2x}$

c) $g(x) = 2\sqrt{x}$

d) $g(x) = \sqrt{2(x-3)}$

e) $g(x) = 2\sqrt{x-3}$

f) $g(x) = -2\sqrt{x-3}$

17. Graph these functions on the same grid. Explain how each function is related to $f(x) = \sin x$.

a) $f(x) = \sin x$

b) $g(x) = 2\sin x$

c) $g(x) = \sin 2x$

d) $g(x) = 2\sin(x-1)$

e) $g(x) = \sin 2(x-1)$

f) $g(x) = 2\sin x - 1$

18. Consider the function $f(x) = \cos x$.

a) Graph the function for $-2\pi \le x \le 2\pi$.

b) On the same grid, graph the function $g(x) = \frac{1}{2}\cos\left(x + \frac{\pi}{6}\right) + 2$.

c) Describe how the graph of $g(x)$ is related to the graph of $f(x)$.

d) What are the domain and range of $f(x)$ and $g(x)$?

7.5 **19.** Determine the inverse of each function.

a) $y = 2x + 5$

b) $y = (x-1)^2 + 4$

c) $y = 3x^2 + 4x - 5$

d) $f(x) = -\sqrt{x+2} - 3$

e) $g(x) = \dfrac{2}{x+1}$

f) $g(x) = \dfrac{2}{x} + 1$

20. Consider the function $f(x) = (x-3)^2 + 2$.

a) Determine the inverse of $f(x)$.

b) Graph $y = f(x)$ and its inverse on the same grid.

c) Is the inverse a function? Explain.

21. For each function below:

i) Determine its inverse.

ii) Graph the function and its inverse on the same grid.

iii) State the domain and range of the function.

iv) State the domain and range of the inverse.

v) State whether the inverse is a function.

vi) If the inverse is not a function, describe how to restrict the domain of $f(x)$ so the inverse is a function.

a) $f(x) = \frac{1}{2}x - 1$ **b)** $f(x) = 2(x+2)^2 + 2$ **c)** $f(x) = 2\sqrt{x+2} - 2$

1. a) Determine a function $f(x)$ so that $f(4) = 3$.

   b) Determine a different function $g(x)$ so that $g(4) = 3$.

   c) Determine a function $h(x)$ so that $h(0) = -2$ and $h(3) = 5$.

2. Knowledge/Understanding

   a) Graph the function $f(x) = \cos x$ for $-2\pi \le x \le 2\pi$.

   b) On the same grid, graph the function $g(x) = f\left(x - \frac{\pi}{3}\right)$.

   c) Describe how the graph of $g(x)$ is related to the graph of $f(x)$.

   d) State the domain and range of $f(x)$ and $g(x)$.

3. Thinking/Inquiry/Problem Solving Every linear function has an equation of the form $y = mx + b$.

   a) Does every linear function have an inverse that is also a function?

   b) Explain your answer to part a both algebraically and graphically.

4. a) Graph the function $f(x) = \sqrt{x}$ and its image after this transformation: expand horizontally by a factor of 2, then compress vertically by a factor of $\frac{1}{2}$.

   b) Write the equation of the image function $g(x)$.

   c) State the domain and range of $f(x)$ and $g(x)$.

5. Communication The notation for the inverse of a function contains the symbol "–". The meaning of this symbol is different from the meanings you have encountered previously.

   a) List as many different meanings as you can for the symbol "–". Illustrate each meaning with an example.

   b) For each example, explain how you can tell which meaning is intended.

6. a) Determine the inverse of the function $f(x) = -2x^2 + 5$.

   b) Graph $f(x)$ and its inverse on the same grid.

   c) State the domain and range of $f(x)$ and of its inverse.

   d) State whether the inverse is a function.

   e) If the inverse is not a function, describe how to restrict the domain of $f(x)$ so its inverse is a function.

7. **Application** A hole is punched in the side of a cylindrical water tank and water begins to flow out. The hole is punched at time $t = 0$ min. The volume of water in the tank, V litres, at any time t when water is flowing out is given by $V = t^2 - 16t + 100$.

a) How much water is in the tank at the beginning?

b) How long does it take to empty the tank?

c) How much water flows out of the tank and how much is left inside?

d) Determine a formula for the time t when the tank has a given volume V. State the domain and range of this function.

Assessment Tasks

1. Copy the table below. It has the values of $f(x)$ for all whole-number values of x between 1 and 10. The four blank columns refer to different transformations of $f(x)$. The fifth column refers to the inverse of $f(x)$. Use the information in the $f(x)$ column. Complete as much of the other columns as possible.

x	f(x)	f(x+1)	f(2x)	f(3x−2)	3f(x)−2	f⁻¹(x)
1	1					
2	3					
3	5					
4	7					
5	9					
6	8					
7	6					
8	4					
9	2					
10	0					

2. Make two copies of the graph of $y = f(x)$ on grid paper.

a) On one copy, sketch the graph of $y = f(2x)$.

b) On the other copy, draw the graph of $y = f(x - 1)$.

c) Solve each equation as accurately as you can. Mark each solution on the appropriate diagram.

i) $f(x) = f(2x)$

ii) $f(x) = f(x - 1)$

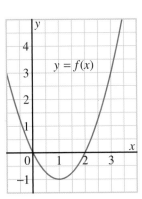

1. Describe the similarities and differences between arithmetic sequences and geometric sequences.

2. Simplify without using a calculator.

    a) $4^{\frac{3}{2}}$

    b) $125^{-\frac{2}{3}}$

    c) $\left(16^{-\frac{3}{5}}\right)^{-\frac{10}{3}}$

3. The 2nd term of an arithmetic sequence is 41 and the 6th term is 68.2. Determine the first 5 terms of the arithmetic sequence.

4. The 2nd term of a geometric sequence is 6 and the 3rd term is 9. Determine the first 5 terms of the geometric sequence.

5. Solve each equation.

    a) $32^{2x+11} = 27^{x-5}$

    b) $7^{3x+1} = 49^{7-2x}$

6. Determine the sum of each series.

    a) $49 + 47 + 45 + \cdots - 21$

    b) $4 - 12 + 36 + \cdots - 8748$

7. An arithmetic series has a first term of $3q$ and a common difference of $8p$. Derive a formula for the sum of the first s terms.

8. The first term of a geometric series is 10. The fifth term is 160. Determine the fourth term.

9. Expand, then simplify.

    a) $(3p - 5)(p + 2)^2$

    b) $(5x - 1)^2 + 4(2x - 1)(9x + 1)$

10. Simplify. State any restrictions on the variables.

    a) $\dfrac{y^2 - 5y - 24}{y^2 - 10y + 16}$

    b) $\dfrac{3x - 2}{6x} - \dfrac{4 - x}{x - 1}$

11. Simplify.

    a) $\dfrac{3x - 5y}{9x^2 - 25y^2} \times \dfrac{3x + 5y}{9x - 7y}$

    b) $\dfrac{(5x + 8y)^2}{x - 5y} \div \dfrac{25x^2 - 64y^2}{x^2 - 25y^2}$

12. Simplify.

    a) $\dfrac{4x}{2x^2 + 8x + 6} - \dfrac{3x}{3x^2 + 9x + 6}$

    b) $\dfrac{2x - 5}{8x^2 - 14x - 15} + \dfrac{3x + 1}{9x^2 - 3x - 2}$

13. Explain the differences between a mortgage and an ordinary annuity.

14. Suppose you invest $1000 at 7.2% for 12 years. Calculate the amount of your investment for each compounding period.

    a) annually

    b) semi-annually

    c) monthly

15. Suppose you invest $3500 at 6.2% compounded semi-annually. What is the minimum number of six-month periods needed for your investment to double?

16. Suppose you start a savings plan and deposit $400 every six months. Your money earns 6.3% compounded semi-annually. What amount will be in your savings account after 9 years?

17. What regular deposit must be made at the end of each year in an account that pays 5.7% compounded annually, to have an amount of $25 000 after 15 years?

18. Calculate the monthly payment for a $140 000 mortgage at 7.5% amortized over 25 years.

19. A 20-year mortgage of $85 000 is available at 8.1% to help pay for a new condominium.

a) Calculate the monthly payment.

b) Calculate the total interest paid on this mortgage.

c) How much is still owing on this mortgage after the first 3 years?

20. Write each equation in the form $y = a(x - p)^2 + q$.

a) $y = 2x^2 - 12x + 3$
 b) $y = -\frac{1}{3}x^2 + 8x + 2$

21. For each function in exercise 20, state whether it has a maximum or a minimum value, then state what that maximum or minimum value is.

22. Use the quadratic formula to solve each equation. Leave the roots in radical form.

a) $x^2 - 5x + 2 = 0$
 b) $3x^2 + 6x - 2 = 0$

23. Determine the roots of each equation to 3 decimal places.

a) $5x^2 + 5x - 2 = 0$
 b) $3w^2 - 8w + 3 = 0$

24. Simplify.

a) i^3
 b) $\sqrt{-50}$
 c) $\sqrt{-54}$

25. Solve each equation.

a) $z^2 - 2z + 5 = 0$
 b) $3z^2 + 2z + 1 = 0$

26. A triangle has a base of $(4 - x)$ cm and a height of $(2x + 3)$ cm.

a) What is the maximum area of the triangle?

b) What value of x will produce that maximum area?

27. (Functions and Relations) Simplify.

a) $4(7 + i) - 9(5 - 7i)$

b) $(5 + 3i)(4 - 8i)$

28. (Functions and Relations) Simplify.

a) $\dfrac{2 + 3i}{9 - 3i}$

b) $2i(3 - 5i)^2$

29. (Functions and Relations) Calculate the sum of the first 5 terms of this geometric series: $2, 6i, -18, \dots$.

30. Solve $\triangle ABC$ in which $AB = 22.3$ cm, $BC = 26.8$ cm, and $\angle ABC = 113°$.

31. The point $Q(-2, -5)$ lies on the terminal arm of an angle θ in standard position. Determine the values of $\sin \theta$, $\cos \theta$, and $\tan \theta$ to 3 decimal places.

32. Determine the exact value of $\sin \dfrac{5\pi}{4} - \cos \dfrac{11\pi}{6}$.

33. In a fishing boat, as cable is wrapped around a drum a net is pulled in. The drum is 120 cm in diameter. The drum turns at 5 revolutions per minute. At what speed, in metres per second, is the net being pulled in?

34. Solve this equation for $0 \le \theta \le \pi$, to 3 decimal places:
$$2 \sin^2 \theta - 4 \cos \theta - 1 = 0$$

35. Prove each identity.

a) $\dfrac{-\cos^2 \theta}{\sin \theta + 1} = \sin \theta - 1$

b) $\dfrac{1}{\cos^2 \theta(\tan^2 \theta)} + \dfrac{\tan^2 \theta}{\sin^2 \theta} = \dfrac{1}{\sin^2 \theta \cos^2 \theta}$

36. a) Determine the acute angle between the line $2x + 3y = 6$ and the y-axis.

b) Determine the acute angle between the line $y = 2x - 1$ and the x-axis.

37. Given that $y = f(x)$ is periodic, describe the basic characteristics of $f(x)$.

38. Graph $y = 2 \sin \dfrac{x}{2}$ for $-2\pi \le x \le 2\pi$. Label the coordinates of maximum and minimum points, and points of intersection with the x-axis.

39. Graph each pair of functions on the same grid for $-2\pi \le x \le 2\pi$.

a) $y = \cos x$, $y = 2 \cos x + 1$

b) $y = \sin x$, $y = 0.5 \sin \left(x - \dfrac{\pi}{3}\right)$

40. Graph each function for $-2\pi \le x \le 2\pi$, then state its amplitude and period.

a) $y = 2.5 \cos 2x - 0.5$

b) $y = 1.5 \sin \dfrac{x}{3} + 1.0$

41. Write an equation that describes each function.

a)

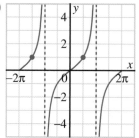

b)

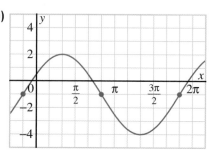

42. Given the function $y = 3\cos 2\left(x + \frac{\pi}{4}\right) - 1$, determine the period, amplitude, phase shift, domain, and range of the function.

43. The number of spots on the surface of the sun varies periodically from 0 to about 100, with a period of approximately 11 years. There was a sunspot minimum in 1997. Determine an equation that can be used to estimate the number sunspots during any year after 1997.

44. Complete the table of values, then sketch the function $y = \tan\left(x + \frac{\pi}{8}\right)$ for $0 \le x \le \pi$.

x	0	$\frac{\pi}{6}$	$\frac{\pi}{3}$	$\frac{\pi}{2}$	$\frac{2\pi}{3}$	$\frac{5\pi}{6}$	π
y							

45. Given $f(x) = 2x^2 - 3x + 5$, determine each value.

a) $f(2.4)$ **b)** $f(-3)$ **c)** $f(x + 1)$

46. The function $y = f(x)$ consists of two straight line segments. One segment joins the points $(0, 0)$ and $(1, 2)$. The second segment joins the points $(1, 2)$ and $(2, 0)$. Sketch each of the following functions on a separate grid.

a) $y = f(x)$ **b)** $y = f(x) + 2$ **c)** $y = 2f(x)$

d) $y = f(x - 2)$ **e)** $y = f(2x)$ **f)** $y = f\left(\frac{1}{2}x + 1\right) - 2$

47. Graph $y = |2x - 5|$ and $y = 2|x| - 3$ on the same grid.

48. a) Describe the transformations applied to $y = \sqrt{x}$ to produce $y = 2\sqrt{x + 3} - 1$.

    b) Graph both functions in part a on the same grid.

49. a) Determine the inverse of each function.

      i) $y = 2x - 1$ **ii)** $f(x) = x^2 + 2$

    b) Graph each function and its inverse on the same grid.

INSIGHTS INSI
INTO A INTO
RICH RICH RI
PROBLEM
INSIGHT

The July 2000 issue of *New Scientist* magazine contains an article about "atomic ghosts."

At the end of this chapter, you will investigate this phenomenon. You will use the reflection property of an ellipse.

Curriculum Expectations

By the end of this chapter, you will:

- Construct a geometric model to represent a described locus of points; determine the properties of the geometric model; and use the properties to interpret the locus.

- Explain the process used in constructing a geometric model of a described locus.

- Determine an equation to represent a described locus.

- Construct geometric models to represent the locus definitions of the conics.

- Determine equations for conics from their locus definitions, by hand for simple particular cases.

- Describe the importance, with applications, of the focus of a parabola, an ellipse, or a hyperbola.

- Illustrate the conics as intersections of planes, with cones, using concrete materials or technology.

1. New: What Is a Relation?

Remember that a function is a rule that gives a single output number for every valid input number. The definition of a relation is similar, but there does not have to be a single output number.

Take Note

A *relation* is a rule that gives one or more output numbers for every valid input number.

All these graphs represent relations.

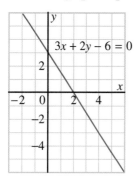

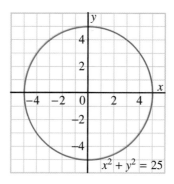

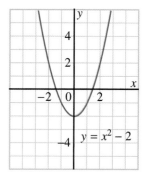

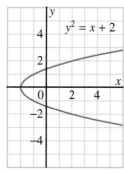

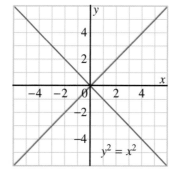

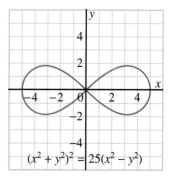

The graph of a relation does not have to satisfy the vertical line test.

Exercises

1. Explain why the graph of a relation does not have to satisfy the vertical line test.

2. **a)** Is every relation a function? Explain.

   b) Is every function a relation? Explain.

3. Use the equation on each graph on page 450 to determine its x- and y-intercepts. Check your results using the graph.

4. A relation whose equation contains quadratic terms but no terms of a higher degree is a *quadratic relation*. Only four of the relations on page 450 are quadratic relations. Which ones are they? Explain why the other two relations are not quadratic relations.

2. Review: Geometry Properties

Perpendicular Bisector of a Line Segment

The perpendicular bisector of segment AB is the line that is perpendicular to AB and divides AB into two equal parts.

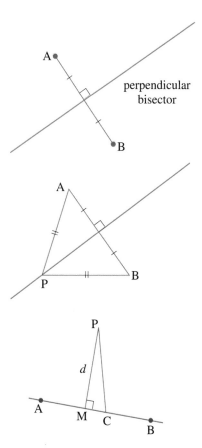

Any point P on the perpendicular bisector is equidistant from A and B. That is, PA = PB

Conversely, any point P that is equidistant from two points A and B must lie on the perpendicular bisector of AB.

The Distance from a Point to a Line

The distance from a point to a line is the shortest distance to the line.

The shortest distance is measured along the perpendicular from the point to the line.

PM is shorter than PC.
PM is the shortest distance from P to AB.

3. Review: Distance between Two Points

Remember the formula for the distance between two points $A(x_1, y_1)$ and $B(x_2, y_2)$.

Take Note

Distance Formula and Length of a Line Segment

The distance between two points $A(x_1, y_1)$ and $B(x_2, y_2)$ is also the length of segment AB.

$AB = \sqrt{(x_2 - x_1)^2 + (y_2 - y_1)^2}$.

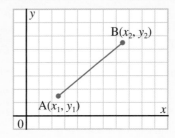

Example

Determine the distance between $A(7, -10)$ and $B(-3, 5)$.

Solution

Use the formula $AB = \sqrt{(x_2 - x_1)^2 + (y_2 - y_1)^2}$.

Substitute $x_2 = -3$, $x_1 = 7$, $y_2 = 5$, and $y_1 = -10$.

$$AB = \sqrt{(-3 - 7)^2 + (5 - (-10))^2}$$
$$= \sqrt{(-10)^2 + 15^2}$$
$$= \sqrt{325}$$
$$\doteq 18.0$$

The distance between A and B is approximately 18.0 units.

Exercises

1. Determine the distance between each pair of points.

  a) $A(1, 3)$, $B(1, 5)$ **b)** $C(3, -2)$, $D(8, -2)$

  c) $O(0, 0)$, $F(-7, 4)$ **d)** $G(-5, -8)$, $O(0, 0)$

  e) $H(-2, -3)$, $J(-5, -9)$ **f)** $K(7, 3)$, $L(4, 10)$

2. Determine the length of the line segment that joins each pair of points.

  a) $M(5, 8)$, $N(3, 1)$ **b)** $Q(-3, -1)$, $R(10, 0)$

  c) $S(-2, 6)$, $T(-10, 2)$ **d)** $U(6, -4)$, $V(4, -9)$

  e) $W(-8, -10)$, $A(-3, -1)$ **f)** $B(-5, 4)$, $C(11, -7)$

4. New: Squaring Expressions Containing Radicals

In this chapter, you will use the distance formula to write equations of relations. Since the distance formula involves a radical, you will need to square expressions that contain radicals.

Example

Determine the square of each expression.

a) $\sqrt{(x-2)^2 + y^2}$

b) $6 - \sqrt{(x-2)^2 + y^2}$

Solution

a) $\sqrt{(x-2)^2 + y^2}$

Remember that, by definition, $(\sqrt{a})^2 = a$.

Therefore, $\left(\sqrt{(x-2)^2 + y^2}\right)^2 = (x-2)^2 + y^2$

$$= x^2 - 4x + 4 + y^2$$

b) $6 - \sqrt{(x-2)^2 + y^2}$

Remember that $(a-b)^2 = a^2 - 2ab + b^2$.

The expression $6 - \sqrt{(x-2)^2 + y^2}$ has the form $6 - \sqrt{a}$.

$$(6 - \sqrt{a})^2 = 36 - 12\sqrt{a} + a$$

Therefore,

$$\left(6 - \sqrt{(x-2)^2 + y^2}\right)^2 = 36 - 12(\sqrt{(x-2)^2 + y^2}) + \left(\sqrt{(x-2)^2 + y^2}\right)^2$$

$$= 36 - 12(\sqrt{(x-2)^2 + y^2}) + (x-2)^2 + y^2$$

$$= 36 - 12(\sqrt{(x-2)^2 + y^2}) + x^2 - 4x + 4 + y^2$$

$$= x^2 + y^2 - 4x + 40 - 12(\sqrt{(x-2)^2 + y^2})$$

Exercises

1. Determine the square of each expression.

a) $\sqrt{(x+1)^2 + y^2}$

b) $\sqrt{(x+4)^2 + y^2}$

c) $\sqrt{x^2 + (y-3)^2}$

2. Determine the square of each expression.

a) $8 + \sqrt{(x+1)^2 + y^2}$

b) $5 - \sqrt{(x+4)^2 + y^2}$

c) $10 + \sqrt{x^2 + (y-3)^2}$

3. Determine the square of each expression.

a) $4 + \sqrt{(x-2)^2 + y^2}$

b) $3 - \sqrt{x^2 + (y-5)^2}$

c) $6 + \sqrt{(x-4)^2 + y^2}$

d) $1 - \sqrt{x^2 + (y+6)^2}$

e) $5 + \sqrt{x^2 + (y-8)^2}$

f) $2 - \sqrt{(x-3)^2 + y^2}$

g) $10 - \sqrt{(x-8)^2 + y^2}$

h) $7 - \sqrt{(x-6)^2 + y^2}$

i) $9 + \sqrt{x^2 + (y-9)^2}$

5. Review: Using *The Geometer's Sketchpad*

This chapter contains several investigations and exercises in which you use *The Geometer's Sketchpad* to explore geometric ideas in a dynamic way. If you have used this software, check that you are familiar with the information in the checklist below. If you have not used this software, you may want to experiment with it before you begin the computer activities. Refer to the checklist as you do this.

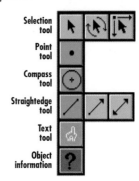

Selection tool

Point tool

Compass tool

Straightedge tool

Text tool

Object information

Skills Checklist

- **The Toolbox**
  One tool is always active. The appearance of the cursor and the things you can do with it depend on the tool you have chosen.

- **The Menus**
  The available options depend on the tool chosen and the objects selected. Some menu options show shortcuts that let you use the keyboard instead.

- **Selecting Objects**
  Use the Selection tool, then click on the object.
  Shift-click to select more than one object.

- **Naming Objects**
  Use the Text tool, then click on the object. To change the name, double-click the name, then enter the new name.

- **Dragging Objects**
  You can move objects or parts of objects by dragging them with the mouse. What happens depends on how the objects are constructed.

- **Horizontal or Vertical Lines**
  Hold down the Shift key as you use the Straightedge tool.

Making Corrections

- To delete an object, select it, then press the Delete key.

- To undo previous steps, choose Undo in the Edit menu.

- To erase everything, use the Selection tool. Choose Select All in the Display menu, then press the Delete key.

If something is not working the way you think it should, you may be using the wrong tool.

To name points automatically, choose Preferences in the Display menu. Make sure Autoshow Labels for Points is selected. Try some of the other options in Preferences.

Check the options in the menus to see what is available. For example, you can:
- hide objects
- measure objects
- change colours of objects
- do calculations
- use a coordinate grid
- undo previous steps
- get help

To make this photograph, a point source of light was mounted on a wheel. A camera recorded the light at split-second intervals as the wheel rolled along a flat surface. The path traced out by the light is an example of a locus.

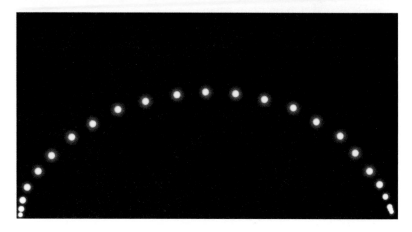

A similar example is the path of a point P as a circle rolls along a straight line.

 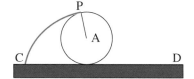 

As the circle, centre A, rolls along CD, a pencil at point P draws the curve shown. This curve is an example of a locus.

Another example of a locus is the path traced by a pencil point when compasses are used to construct a circle.

Take Note

Locus

A *locus* is the path traced by a point that moves according to a given condition.

When the locus condition is simple enough, we can find an equation to represent the path.

Example 1

Point N has coordinates (1, –2). Point P moves so the slope of NP is always $\frac{3}{4}$.

a) Determine the equation of the locus of P.

b) Identify the locus.

Solution

a) Draw a sketch on plain paper.

Plot point N and a point P so the slope of NP is $\frac{3}{4}$.

Draw segment NP.

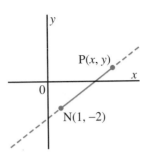

Let P(x, y) be any point on the locus.

Use the constant slope property.

Slope of NP $= \frac{3}{4}$

$$\frac{y+2}{x-1} = \frac{3}{4}$$

$$4(y + 2) = 3(x - 1)$$

$$4y + 8 = 3x - 3$$

$$3x - 4y - 11 = 0$$

The equation of the locus is $3x - 4y - 11 = 0$.

b) The equation in part b is that of a straight line. So, the locus of P is a straight line with slope $\frac{3}{4}$, passing through N(1, –2).

Discuss

What other way could we use to determine the equation of the locus?

Example 2

Point P moves so it is equidistant from R(3, 0) and S(0, 2).

a) Determine the equation of the locus of P.

b) Identify the locus.

Solution

a) Draw a sketch on plain paper.

Plot points R and S, and a point P so that PR = PS.

Draw segments PR and PS.

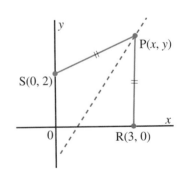

Let P(x, y) be any point on the locus.

Since P is equidistant from R and S,

PR = PS

Use the distance formula to determine the lengths of PR and PS.

$$\sqrt{(x - 3)^2 + (y - 0)^2} = \sqrt{(x - 0)^2 + (y - 2)^2}$$

Square each side.

$$(x - 3)^2 + (y - 0)^2 = (x - 0)^2 + (y - 2)^2$$

$$x^2 - 6x + 9 + y^2 = x^2 + y^2 - 4y + 4$$

Collect like terms.

$$-6x + 4y + 5 = 0$$

The equation of the locus is $6x - 4y - 5 = 0$.

Discuss

How is the locus related to line segment RS?

b) The locus is a straight line.

Here are some properties of a locus.

Take Note

Properties of a Locus

- The coordinates of every point on a locus satisfy the equation of the locus.
- Every point whose coordinates satisfy the equation of a locus is on the locus.

In each of *Examples 1* and *2*, we might have found the locus by first guessing that it is a straight line. Then we could use a geometric argument (or some other method) to determine the equation. In *Example 1*, we could use the point slope formula for the equation of a line. In *Example 2*, we could use the property of a perpendicular bisector or we could use a symmetry argument. In other situations, we may not be able to identify or describe the locus in advance. This is illustrated in *Example 3*.

Example 3

Point P moves so the line segments that join P to A(–4, 0) and B(4, 0) are perpendicular.

a) Determine the equation of the locus of P.

b) Identify the locus.

Solution

a) Draw a sketch on plain paper.
Plot points A and B, and a point P so that PA is perpendicular to PB. Draw segments PA and PB.
Let P(x, y) be any point on the locus.
Since AP and BP are perpendicular, their slopes are negative reciprocals.

The slope of AP is $\frac{y-0}{x+4}$.

The slope of BP is $\frac{y-0}{x-4}$.

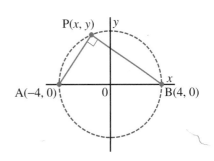

Since the slopes are negative reciprocals,

$$\frac{y}{x+4} = -\frac{x-4}{y}$$
$$-y^2 = (x+4)(x-4)$$
$$-y^2 = x^2 - 16$$
$$x^2 + y^2 = 16$$

The equation of the locus is $x^2 + y^2 = 16$.

b) The equation in part a is that of a circle. The locus is a circle with centre O(0, 0) and radius 4.

The locus in *Example 3* is the basis of the construction in the following Investigation.

Using *The Geometer's Sketchpad* to Construct a Locus

You will construct the diagram below. Study the diagram before you begin the construction. Make sure you understand the following information about it.

A and B are two fixed points.

D is a variable point on a fixed circle with centre A.

A line is drawn through A and D.

Line BP is perpendicular to this line and intersects it at P.

As D moves around the circle, the line AP rotates about A. The line BP moves so that ∠APB is always a right angle.

Point P will trace the locus.

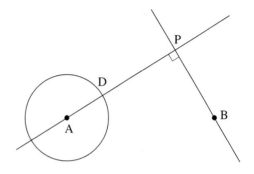

Set-Up
- From the File menu, choose New Sketch.
- Construct two points. Label them A and B.
- Use the circle tool to construct a circle with centre A.
- A point will be on the circumference of the circle. Hide this point.

You now have the fixed circle with centre A.

Before you use the computer, identify a few points on the locus by choosing some special directions for the line AD. Can you guess the locus of P?

Constructing a Point P on the Locus
- Construct a point on the circle. This is a variable point. Label it D.
- Construct the line through A and D.
- Construct the line through B that is perpendicular to this line.
- Construct the point of intersection, P, of these two lines.

P is a point on the locus.

Tracing the Locus of P
- Drag point D around the circle. Observe how the position of P changes. Check visually that ∠APB is a right angle.
- Click point P to select it. From the Display menu, choose Trace Point.
- Drag point D again. Point P leaves a trail of points as it moves.

The points lie on a circle. Hence, the locus of P is a circle.

Constructing the Locus of P

- Shift-click point P and point D. From the Construct menu, choose Locus. The computer will construct the locus of P, which is a circle.

Point D is called the *driver point* for the locus. Every locus construction that uses *The Geometer's Sketchpad* requires:

- a driver point D that moves along a path
- a point P that traces the locus

In this chapter, we will always use D for the driver point and P for the point on the locus. Moving D along its path is what causes P to trace the locus.

1. Suppose B is moved closer to A, or farther from A. Predict how the circle will change. Use the computer to check your prediction.

2. Try dragging point P. Why is the effect not the same as dragging point D?

3. In this construction, the circle with centre A is the path for the driver point.

   a) Repeat the construction using each of these paths for the driver point.
      i) a circle that contains point A, but A is not the centre
      ii) a circle that does not contain point A
      iii) a line

   b) Some paths in part a will not result in a complete circle. Suggest how you might obtain the rest of the circle in each case.

8.1 Exercises

A

1. Describe the locus that a point P must satisfy to lie on each graph.

a)

b)

c)

d)
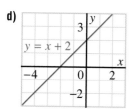

e)
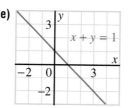

f)
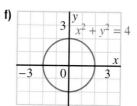

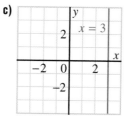

2. Describe the graph of each equation as a locus.

a) $y = 3$ b) $x = -2$ c) $y = 3x$

d) $y = 3x - 2$ e) $x^2 + y^2 = 25$ f) $x^2 + y^2 = 5$

3. a) Sketch a graph of the line $x = 5$.

b) Sketch the locus of a point P that moves according to each condition.
 i) P is always 2 units to the right of the line $x = 5$.
 ii) P is always 2 units to the left of the line $x = 5$.

c) Sketch the locus of a point P that moves so its distance from the line $x = 5$ is always 2 units.

 4. A point P moves so it is always the same distance from the lines $y = 2$ and $y = 8$.

a) Sketch the locus of P. b) Describe the locus of P.

c) Determine the equation of the locus.

5. Point A has coordinates $(0, 1)$. Point P moves so the slope of AP is always 2.

a) Identify the locus of P, then sketch its graph.

b) Determine the equation of the locus.

 6. A point Q moves so it is always 8 units from the origin $O(0, 0)$.

a) Identify the locus of Q, then sketch its graph.

b) Determine the equation of the locus.

B

7. Point B has coordinates $(-6, 3)$. Point C moves so the slope of BC is always -3.

a) Sketch the locus of C. b) Describe the locus of C.

c) Determine the equation of the locus.

 8. Knowledge/Understanding Determine the equation of the locus of P. Identify the locus, then sketch its graph.

a) The slope of the line through P and $A(2, 1)$ is equal to the slope of the line through P and $B(-1, 4)$.

b) P is always the same distance from $C(-2, 3)$ as it is from $D(8, -1)$.

 9. Thinking/Inquiry/Problem Solving Points $A(2, 0)$ and $B(-2, 0)$ are given. Point P moves so the slope of PA is the opposite of the slope of PB.

a) Determine the equation of the locus of P.

b) Graph the equation, then describe the locus.

c) Choose two points on the locus. Verify that the slopes of the segments that join each point to A and to B are opposites.

10. Points C(0, 2) and D(0, –2) are given. Point P moves so the slopes of PC and PD are opposite numbers.

   a) Determine the equation of the locus of P.

   b) In exercise 9, you should have found that the locus is two intersecting lines. In part a, the locus is one line. Explain why the loci in these two similar situations are different.

11. Application Points O(0, 0) and A(6, 0) are given. Point P moves so the slope of OP is 1 less than the slope of AP.

   a) Determine the equation of the locus of P.

   b) Identify the locus.

   c) Graph the locus on grid paper.

   d) Choose two different points on the locus. Verify the locus condition for each point.

12. Repeat exercise 11, where P moves so the slope of OP is 1 more than the slope of AP.

13. Points O(0, 0) and A(6, 0) are given. Point P moves according to each given condition. Determine the equation of the locus of P.

   a) The slope of OP is double the slope of AP.

   b) The slope of OP is one-half the slope of AP.

14. Point P moves so it is always 5 units from point B(3, 0).

   a) Identify the locus of P, then sketch its graph.

   b) Determine the equation of the locus of P.

15. Point P moves so it is always 4 units from point C(–2, 3).

   a) Identify the locus of P, then sketch its graph.

   b) Determine the equation of the locus of P.

16. Points A(8, 0) and B(2, 0) are given. Point P moves so it is always twice as far from A as it is from B.

   a) Determine the equation of the locus of P.

   b) Identify the locus, then sketch its graph.

   c) Determine the coordinates of the points where the locus intersects the x-axis. Verify that these points satisfy the locus condition.

   d) Determine the coordinates of the points where the locus intersects the y-axis. Verify that these points satisfy the locus condition.

17. Refer to exercise 16. Suppose P were to move so it is always twice as far from B as it is from A.

a) Use your results from exercise 16. Predict the locus of P, then sketch its graph.

b) Determine the equation of the locus of P.

 18. Point P moves so it is always three times as far from point B(8, 0) as it is from point O(0, 0).

a) Determine the equation of the locus of P.

b) Sketch the graph of the locus.

c) Determine the intercepts of this graph. Verify that the corresponding points are three times as far from B as they are from A.

19. Point F has coordinates (0, 3). Line d has equation $y = 1$. Point P(x, y) moves so its distance from F is always equal to its distance from d.

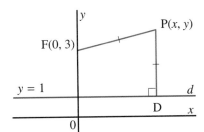

a) Determine the equation of the locus of P.

b) Identify the locus.

c) Graph the locus.

20. Point F has coordinates (3, 0). Line d has equation $x = 1$. A point P moves so its distance from F is always equal to its distance from d.

a) Determine the equation of the locus of P.

b) Identify the locus.

c) Graph the locus.

21. Communication Compare the results of exercises 19 and 20. Explain any patterns you find.

 22. Point F(0, 4) is given. Point P moves according to each given condition. Determine the equation of the locus of P.

a) P is equidistant from F and the x-axis.

b) P is twice as far from F as it is from the x-axis.

c) P is twice as far from the x-axis as it is from F.

23. Point P is the intersection of perpendicular lines drawn through point A(5, 0) and point B(−5, 0).

a) Sketch a diagram to show several different pairs of perpendicular lines and the corresponding positions of P.

b) Determine the equation of the locus of P.

c) Identify the locus, then sketch its graph.

24. A line segment is 10 units long. It has its endpoints on the *x*- and *y*-axes. Point P is the midpoint of the line segment.

a) Determine the equation of the locus of P.

b) Identify the locus, then sketch its graph.

25. Use *The Geometer's Sketchpad*. You will construct this diagram.

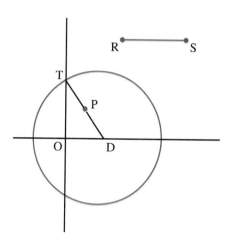

RS is a fixed line segment.

Horizontal and vertical lines intersect at O.

Point D is a variable point on the horizontal line.

The circle has centre D and radius equal to the length of RS.

The circle intersects the vertical line at T.

Point P is the midpoint of segment DT.

Point D is the driver point for the locus of P. As D moves along the horizontal line, P traces the locus.

Set-Up
- From the File menu, choose New Sketch. Construct a segment RS.
- Construct a horizontal line.
- Construct a vertical line. Label the point of intersection O.

Constructing the Point P
- Construct a variable point on the horizontal line. Label it D.
- Construct a circle with centre D and radius equal to the length of segment RS.
- Construct the points of intersection of the circle and the vertical line. Label one of these points T. Construct segment DT.
- Construct the midpoint of segment DT. Label it P.

Constructing the Locus of P
- Drag point D along the horizontal line to observe the effect on P.
- Shift-click point D (the driver point) and point P (the point on the locus). From the Construct menu, choose Locus.

a) Fully describe the locus.

b) Predict how the locus will change when segment RS is made longer or shorter. Use the computer to check your prediction.

c) Your locus appears to be incomplete. Improve your construction so the computer displays more parts of the locus.

Spotlights are used in theatres. A spotlight is shone on the stage from the back of the theatre. The light rays illuminate an elliptical region on the stage.

An ellipse also results when a cylindrical tube is cut at an angle.

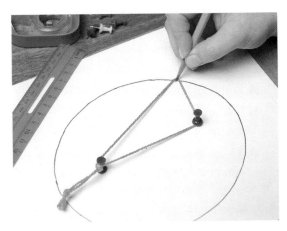

An ellipse can be drawn on paper, with the use of two thumb tacks, a loop of string, a pencil, and cardboard.

Place the paper on the cardboard. Push the thumb tacks into the cardboard. Loop the string around the tacks. Use a pencil to keep the string taut. Move the pencil to trace an ellipse.

This construction illustrates the definition of an ellipse.

Definition of an Ellipse

An ellipse is the locus of a point P that moves so the sum of its distances to two fixed points is constant.

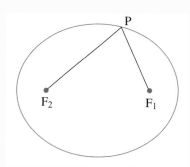

Each fixed point is a *focus*.
Each distance from a focus to P is a *focal radius*.

F_1 and F_2 are the foci.
PF_1 and PF_2 are the focal radii.

The locus definition states that the sum of the focal radii is constant.

$$PF_1 + PF_2 = \text{constant}$$

Notice that focus F_1 is drawn to the right of focus F_2. In Chapter 9, we will draw ellipses on a coordinate grid with foci on the *x*-axis, where F_1 is to the right of the origin and F_2 is to the left of the origin.

Using a Grid to Construct an Ellipse

You will need grid paper with two sets of concentric circles, as shown below.

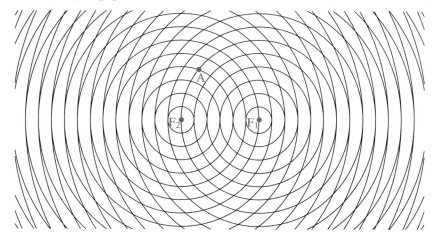

The centres of the circles are the foci. Point A is 4 units from F_2 and 6 units from F_1.
That is, $AF_1 + AF_2 = 10$

   1. Locate all the points on the grid so the sum of the distances of each point from the foci is 10 units.

2. Draw a smooth curve through the points to form an ellipse. Describe the ellipse.

3. In each case, describe how the ellipse would be different from the ellipse you drew.

   a) The sum of the focal radii is less than 10 units.

   b) The sum of the focal radii is greater than 10 units.

   c) On the circular grid paper, the centres of the circles are closer together.

4. Explain why the ellipse you constructed has:

   a) a horizontal line of symmetry

   b) a vertical line of symmetry

Another construction of an ellipse is based on this idea:

Visualize a circle with centre F_2 large enough to enclose F_1. If we could find a point P on the radius F_2D so that $PF_1 = PD$, then P would trace an ellipse as D rotates around the circle.

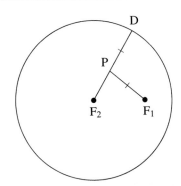

This idea is the basis of the constructions in *Investigations 2* and *3*.

Using Geometry to Construct an Ellipse

1. Start with two fixed points F_1 and F_2. These are the foci of the ellipse. Use compasses to construct a circle with centre F_2. Make the radius large enough so F_1 is inside the circle.

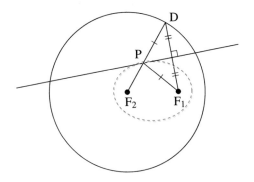

2. Mark a point D on the circle. Join D to F_1 and F_2.

   Construct the perpendicular bisector of segment F_1D; it intersects segment F_2D at P. Join P to F_1.

   P is a point on the locus.

3. Repeat exercise 2 several times, using other positions of D on the circle. Draw a smooth curve through all the points labelled P.

4. a) Explain why the locus is an ellipse.

   b) How is the perpendicular bisector related to the ellipse?
      In 8.2 Exercises, exercise 22, you will explain this relationship.

Using *The Geometer's Sketchpad* to Construct an Ellipse

You will construct a dynamic model of an ellipse using the idea described preceding *Investigation 2*. Point P is on the locus and point D is the driver point for the locus.

Set-Up

- From the File menu, choose New Sketch.
- Construct two points. Label them F1 and F2.
- Construct a point H that is farther from F2 than F1 is from F2.
- Shift-click point F2, then point H. From the Construct menu, choose Circle by Center and Point. Hide point H.
- Construct a variable point D on the circle.

Constructing a Point P on the Locus

- Construct segments F1D and F2D.
- Construct the perpendicular bisector of F1D.
- Construct the point P where the perpendicular bisector intersects F2D.

P is a point on the locus.

Constructing the Locus of P

- Drag point D around the circle. Observe how the position of P changes. Check visually that PF1 + PF2 is always equal to the length of F2D.
- Shift-click point P (the point on the locus) and point D (the driver point). From the Construct menu, choose Locus.

The computer will construct the locus of P, which is an ellipse.

1. Predict how the ellipse will change in each situation. Use the computer to check your prediction.

   a) F1 moves closer to F2, or farther from F2.

   b) The circle is larger or smaller.

2. If possible, make a printout of your construction. Otherwise, make an accurate drawing of it.

The definition of an ellipse can be used to determine the equation of an ellipse in a coordinate system.

Example

The foci of an ellipse are $F_1(3, 0)$ and $F_2(-3, 0)$. The sum of the focal radii is 10 units.

a) Determine the equation of the ellipse.

b) Graph the ellipse on grid paper.

Solution

a) Draw a sketch on plain paper.
Show points F_1 and F_2, and a point P so that
$PF_1 + PF_2 = 10$. Draw segments PF_1 and PF_2.

Let $P(x, y)$ be any point on the ellipse.
Use the fact that the sum of the focal radii is 10
to write an equation.

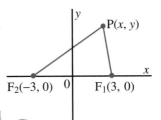

$$PF_1 + PF_2 = 10$$
$$\sqrt{(x - 3)^2 + y^2} + \sqrt{(x + 3)^2 + y^2} = 10$$

Isolate one radical.
$$\sqrt{(x - 3)^2 + y^2} = 10 - \sqrt{(x + 3)^2 + y^2}$$

Square each side.
$$\left(\sqrt{(x - 3)^2 + y^2}\right)^2 = \left(10 - \sqrt{(x + 3)^2 + y^2}\right)^2$$
$$(x - 3)^2 + y^2 = 100 - 20\sqrt{(x + 3)^2 + y^2} + (x + 3)^2 + y^2$$
$$x^2 - 6x + 9 + y^2 = 100 - 20\sqrt{(x + 3)^2 + y^2} + x^2 + 6x + 9 + y^2$$

Isolate the term containing the radical.
$$20\sqrt{(x + 3)^2 + y^2} = 100 + 12x$$

Divide each side by 4.
$$5\sqrt{(x + 3)^2 + y^2} = 25 + 3x$$

Square each side.
$$\left(5\sqrt{(x + 3)^2 + y^2}\right)^2 = (25 + 3x)^2$$
$$25(x^2 + 6x + 9 + y^2) = 625 + 150x + 9x^2$$
$$25x^2 + 150x + 225 + 25y^2 = 625 + 150x + 9x^2$$
$$16x^2 + 25y^2 = 400$$

quation of the ellipse is $16x^2 + 25y^2 = 400$.

b) To sketch the ellipse, determine the intercepts.

Substitute $x = 0$ in the equation of the ellipse.

$16(0)^2 + 25y^2 = 400$

$$y^2 = \frac{400}{25}$$

$$y = \pm\sqrt{\frac{400}{25}}$$

$$= \pm 4$$

The y-intercepts are 4 and –4.

Substitute $y = 0$.

$16x^2 + 25(0)^2 = 400$

$16x^2 = 400$

$$x^2 = \frac{400}{16}$$

$$x = \pm\sqrt{25}$$

$$= \pm 5$$

The x-intercepts are 5 and –5.

Four points on the ellipse are $(0, \pm 4)$ and $(\pm 5, 0)$.
Substitute any valid value of x, say $x = 2$.

$16(2)^2 + 25y^2 = 400$

$$y^2 = \frac{336}{25}$$

$$y \doteq \pm 3.7$$

Substituting $x = -2$ produces the same values for y.
Four more points on the ellipse are $(\pm 2, \pm 3.7)$.
Plot these points, then draw a smooth curve through them.

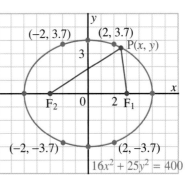

---

1. The equation of an ellipse is $x^2 + 9y^2 = 9$.

    a) Determine the intercepts of the graph of this ellipse.

    b) Determine the coordinates of 4 other points on the graph.

2. The equation of an ellipse is $9x^2 + 4y^2 = 36$.

    a) Determine the intercepts of the graph of this ellipse.

    b) Determine the coordinates of 4 other points on the graph.

3. Describe how a circle can be regarded as a special case of an ellipse.

✓ 4. **Knowledge/Understanding** The foci of an ellipse are $F_1(4,0)$ and $F_2(-4, 0)$. The sum of the focal radii is 12 units.

   a) Determine the equation of the ellipse.

   b) Sketch the ellipse.

✓ 5. The foci of an ellipse are $F_1(0,4)$ and $F_2(0, -4)$. The sum of the focal radii is 12 units.

   a) Determine the equation of the ellipse.

   b) Sketch the ellipse.

✓ 6. Look at the results from exercises 4 and 5.

   a) How are the ellipses and their equations similar?

   b) How are the ellipses and their equations different?

✓ 7. The base of $\triangle ABP$ is AB. Point P moves so the sum of the lengths of AP and BP is 8 units. Determine the equation of the locus of P in each case.

   a) The coordinates of A and B are A(1, 0) and B(−1, 0).

   b) The coordinates of A and B are A(0, 1) and B(0, −1).

   c) Compare the results of parts a and b. What do you notice?

8. The foci of an ellipse are $F_1(5, 0)$ and $F_2(-5, 0)$. Determine the equation of the ellipse for each condition.

   a) The sum of the focal radii is 12 units.

   b) The sum of the focal radii is 15 units.

   c) The sum of the focal radii is 20 units.

9. The sum of the focal radii of an ellipse is 20 units. Determine the equation of the ellipse for each condition.

   a) The foci are $F_1(4, 0)$ and $F_2(-4, 0)$.

   b) The foci are $F_1(0, 2)$ and $F_2(0, -2)$.

   c) The foci are O(0, 0) and A(3, 0).

   d) The foci are O(0, 0) and C(0, 3).

✓ 10. The sum of the focal radii of an ellipse is 8 units. Determine the equations of two different ellipses with this property.

✓ 11. Determine the equations of two different ellipses that have foci $F_1(2, 0)$ and $F_2(-2, 0)$.

12. Use the definition of an ellipse. Explain why an ellipse has two lines of symmetry.

13. Communication Point O lies on a horizontal line and is the centre of two circles. Segment CP is parallel to the horizontal line. Segment PD is perpendicular to the horizontal line. Hence, △CPD is a right triangle. As D moves around the larger circle, P traces a locus.

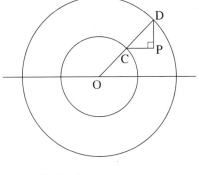

a) Draw the diagram. Show D in different positions around the circle.

b) Sketch the locus of P. Describe the locus.

c) Visualize a rectangle with two sides CP and PD and diagonal CD. Let Q be the fourth vertex of the rectangle. Is the locus of Q the same as the locus of P? If your answer is yes, explain. If your answer is no, sketch the locus of Q and explain why it is different.

14. Application A gardener wishes to make a flower bed. She ties a length of string around two pegs at A and B as shown. The diagram is not drawn to scale.

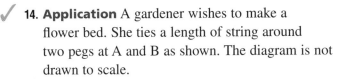

The gardener places a stick at P. She keeps the string taut and uses the stick to outline the flower bed.

a) What is the shape of the flower bed? Sketch it.

b) Suppose A and B were moved closer. How would the shape of the flower bed change?

c) What would happen to the shape of the flower bed if A and B were moved farther apart?

15. Suppose the gardener in exercise 14 places three pegs A, B, and C at the vertices of an equilateral triangle with side length 1 m. She uses a 4-m string to trace the outline of a new flower bed. The diagram is not drawn to scale.

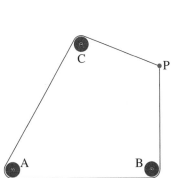

a) Predict the shape of the flower bed. Support your prediction.

b) Sketch the flower bed.

16. An ellipse has foci $F_1(4, 0)$ and $F_2(-4, 0)$. Determine the equation of the ellipse in each case.

a) One x-intercept is 5.   b) One y-intercept is 2.

17. An ellipse has foci $F_1(0, 6)$ and $F_2(0, -6)$. Determine the equation of the ellipse in each case.

a) One x-intercept is 3.   b) One y-intercept is 10.

18. **Thinking/Inquiry/Problem Solving** In the diagram, P is a point on an ellipse with foci F_1 and F_2. The line through F_1 and F_2 intersects the ellipse at points A_1 and A_2, called the *vertices*. Line segment A_1A_2 is the *major axis*. The perpendicular bisector of A_1A_2 intersects the ellipse at points B_1 and B_2. Line segment B_1B_2 is the *minor axis*. The major and minor axes intersect at the *centre* O.

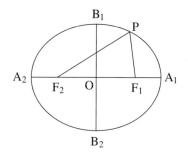

a) The property that $PF_1 + PF_2$ is constant applies to every point on the ellipse. Assume P is at A_1. Show that this constant is the length of the major axis.

b) Assume P is at B_1. Show that the distance from B_1 to either focus is equal to one-half the length of the major axis.

19. Cut out a cardboard right triangle. Draw two lines that intersect at right angles. Place the triangle as shown. The vertex of the right angle is on one line and another vertex is on the second line. Move the triangle so these vertices always stay on the lines. Mark points to illustrate the path of the third vertex. Identify the locus of the third vertex.

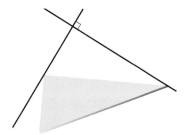

20. Use *The Geometer's Sketchpad*. You will construct this diagram. Point D is the centre of a circle with fixed radius equal to the length of segment AB. Horizontal and vertical lines are drawn through a point O inside the circle. Point C is one of the points of intersection of the horizontal line and the circle. Point P is any point on the radius DC. Point D is a driver point for the locus of P. As D moves along the vertical line, P traces the locus.

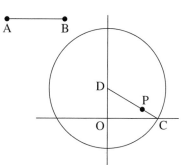

Set-Up
- From the File menu, choose New Sketch. Construct a segment AB.
- Construct two perpendicular lines that intersect at O.

Constructing the Point P
- Construct a variable point D on the vertical line.
- Construct a circle with centre D and radius equal to the length of AB.
- Construct one of the points of intersection of the circle and the horizontal line. Label it C.
- Construct segment DC. Construct a point P on segment DC.

Constructing the Locus of P
- Drag point D along the vertical line to observe the effect on P.
- Shift-click point D (the driver point) and point P (the point on the locus). From the Construct menu, choose Locus.

a) Describe the locus fully.

b) Predict how the locus will change in each situation. Use the computer to check your prediction.
   i) Point P moves closer to D.
   ii) Point P is the midpoint of DC.
   iii) Segment AB is made longer or shorter.

c) In part a, you should have found that the locus is a semi-ellipse.
   i) How could you obtain the other half of the ellipse?
   ii) Which point is the centre of the ellipse?
   iii) How are the major and minor axes of the ellipse related to the diagram on page 472?

21. Use *The Geometer's Sketchpad*. Repeat exercise 25 in 8.1 Exercises, but use lines that are not perpendicular.

C

22. Refer to the ellipse construction in *Investigation 2*. The perpendicular bisector of segment DF_1 touches the ellipse at P. This line is a *tangent* to the ellipse. Explain why the perpendicular bisector is a tangent to the ellipse.

23. An ellipse has major axis of length $2a$ units and minor axis of length $2b$ units. The foci of the ellipse are $F_1(c, 0)$ and $F_2(-c, 0)$.

a) Determine a relationship between a, b, and c.

b) Show that the equation of the ellipse is $\dfrac{x^2}{a^2} + \dfrac{y^2}{b^2} = 1$.

24. Refer to exercise 13. Let the larger circle have radius a and the smaller circle have radius b. Suppose O is the origin of a coordinate grid. Determine the equation of the locus of P, and thus verify that it is an ellipse.

25. Use *The Geometer's Sketchpad*. You will construct this diagram. Point D is a variable point on a line through the centre O of a circle. Segment DM is constructed perpendicular to the diameter. Point P is a variable point on DM.

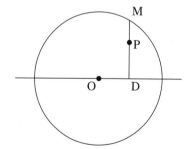

Point D is the driver point for the locus of P, which moves so the ratio DP : PM is constant.

a) Create a dynamic model of this situation, then construct the locus of P.

b) Predict what will happen to the locus when you drag point P. Check your prediction.

c) Your locus is a semi-ellipse. Find a way to add the other half of the ellipse to your construction.

d) Show that the locus is a semi-ellipse.

1. Point Q has coordinates (2, 3). Point R moves so the slope of QR is always $-\frac{1}{3}$.

   a) Determine the equation of the locus of R.

   b) Identify the locus of R.

   c) Sketch the locus of R.

2. Point E moves so it is always the same distance from the lines $x = 2$ and $x = -6$.

   a) Sketch the locus of E.

   b) Determine the equation of the locus of E.

   c) Describe the locus of E.

3. Point F moves so it is always the same distance from the lines
   $2x - 3y + 15 = 0$ and $2x - 3y - 3 = 0$.

   a) Sketch the locus of F.

   b) Determine the equation of the locus of F.

   c) Describe the locus of F.

4. Point P moves so the product of the slopes of the line segments that join P
   to Q(0, −4) and to R(0, 4) is −1.

   a) Determine the equation of the locus of P.

   b) Sketch the locus of P.

   c) Describe the locus of P.

5. Point P is the intersection of perpendicular lines drawn through point A(4, 0)
   and point B(−4, 0).

   a) Sketch a diagram to show several possible pairs of perpendicular lines
      and the corresponding positions of P.

   b) Determine the equation of the locus of P.

   c) Identify the locus, then draw its graph.

6. The equation of an ellipse is $x^2 + 16y^2 = 16$.

   a) Determine the intercepts of the graph of this ellipse.

   b) Determine the coordinates of 4 other points on the graph.

7. The foci of an ellipse are $F_1(4, 0)$ and $F_2(-4, 0)$. The sum of the focal radii
   is 10 units. Determine the equation of the ellipse.

8. The sum of the focal radii of an ellipse is 8 units. Determine the equation of
   an ellipse with this property.

9. Determine the equation of one ellipse that has foci $F_1(0, 2)$ and $F_2(0, -2)$.

8.3 The Hyperbola

A flashlight casts a shadow on the wall. The shadow has the shape of a hyperbola. The light forms a cone. The wall intersects the cone to form a hyperbolic shadow.

A hyperbola can be drawn on paper with the use of two thumb tacks, a piece of string, a pencil, and cardboard.

Place the paper on the cardboard. Push the thumb tacks into the cardboard. Make a knotted loop in the string to hold the pencil point. Pass the string around the tacks. Hold the ends of the string together. Use the pencil to keep the string taut. Place the hand that holds the string close to the nearer tack. Move the hand away from the tack to draw one branch of the hyperbola. Reverse the position of the string to draw the other branch of the hyperbola.

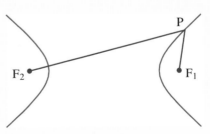

This construction illustrates the definition of a hyperbola.

Take Note

Definition of a Hyperbola

A hyperbola is the locus of a point P that moves so the difference of its distances from two fixed points is constant.

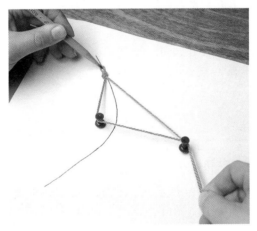

Each fixed point is a *focus*.
Each distance from a focus to P is a *focal radius*.
F_1 and F_2 are the foci.
PF_1 and PF_2 are the focal radii.

The locus definition states that the difference of the focal radii is constant.

$$|PF_1 - PF_2| = \text{constant}$$

In the diagram on page 475, since $PF_1 < PF_2$, then $PF_1 - PF_2$ is negative.

Since the definition applies to P on both branches, we use the absolute value symbol to denote the constant is positive.

Using a Grid to Construct a Hyperbola

You will need grid paper with two sets of concentric circles, as shown below.

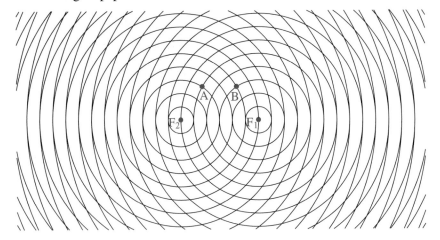

The centres of the circles are the foci.

Point A is 5 units from F_1 and 3 units from F_2; that is, $AF_1 - AF_2 = 2$
Point B is 3 units from F_1 and 5 units from F_2; that is, $|BF_1 - BF_2| = 2$

1. Locate all the points on the grid so the difference of the distances of each point from the foci is 2 units.

2. Draw smooth curves through the points to form two branches of a hyperbola. Describe the hyperbola.

3. In each case, describe how the hyperbola would be different from the hyperbola you drew.

   a) The difference of the focal radii is less than 2 units.

   b) The difference of the focal radii is greater than 2 units.

   c) On the circular grid paper, the centres of the circles are closer together.

4. Explain why the hyperbola you constructed has:

   a) a horizontal line of symmetry

   b) a vertical line of symmetry

Another construction of a hyperbola is based on an idea similar to that used for the ellipse in Section 8.2.

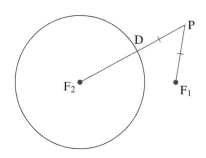

Visualize a circle with centre F_2 that is not large enough to enclose F_1. If we could find a point P on the line containing the radius F_2D so that $PF_1 = PD$, then P would trace a hyperbola as D rotates around the circle.

This idea is the basis of the constructions in *Investigations 2* and *3*.

Investigation 2

Using Geometry to Construct a Hyperbola

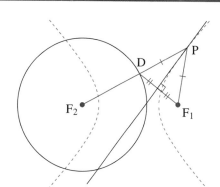

1. Start with two fixed points F_1 and F_2.
   These are the foci of the hyperbola.
   Use compasses to construct a circle with centre F_2. Make the radius small enough so F_1 is outside the circle.

2. Mark a point D on the circle.
   Join D to F_1 and F_2.
   Construct the perpendicular bisector of segment F_1D; it intersects the line through F_2 and D at P.
   Join P to F_1. P is a point on the locus.

3. Repeat exercise 2, using other positions of D on the circle. Draw smooth curves through all the points labelled P. These curves are the branches of the hyperbola.

4. a) Explain why the locus is a hyperbola.

   b) How is the perpendicular bisector related to the hyperbola?
      In 8.3 Exercises, exercise 17, you will explain this relationship.

Using *The Geometer's Sketchpad* to Construct a Hyperbola

You will construct a dynamic model of a hyperbola using the idea described preceding *Investigation 2*. Point P is on the locus and point D is the driver point for the locus.

Set-Up

- From the File menu, choose New Sketch.
- Construct two points. Label them F1 and F2.
- Construct a point H that is closer to F2 than F1 is to F2.
- Shift-click point F2, then point H. From the Construct menu, choose Circle by Center and Point. Hide point H.
- Construct a variable point D on the circle.

Constructing a Point P on the Locus

- Construct segments F1D and F2D.
- Construct the perpendicular bisector of F1D.
- Construct the line through F2 and D.
- Construct the point P where the perpendicular bisector intersects F2D.

P is a point on the locus.

Constructing the Locus of P

- Drag point D around the circle. Observe how the position of P changes. Check visually that |PF2 − PF1| is always equal to the length of F2D.
- Shift-click point P (the point on the locus) and point D (the driver point). From the Construct menu, choose Locus.

The computer will construct the locus of P, which is a hyperbola. Notice that it has two branches.

1. Predict how the hyperbola will change in each situation. Use the computer to check your prediction.

   a) F1 moves closer to F2, or farther from F2.

   b) The circle is larger or smaller.

2. If possible, make a printout of your construction. Otherwise, make an accurate drawing of it.

Note: See 8.3 Exercises, exercise 16, for an extension of this investigation.

The definition of a hyperbola can be used to determine the equation of a
hyperbola in a coordinate system.

Example

The foci of a hyperbola are $F_1(5, 0)$ and $F_2(-5, 0)$. The difference of the
focal radii is 8 units.

a) Determine the equation of the hyperbola.

b) Graph the hyperbola on grid paper.

Solution

a) Draw a sketch on plain paper. Show points
F_1 and F_2, and a point P so that $PF_1 - PF_2 = 8$.
Draw segments PF_1 and PF_2. Let $P(x, y)$ be a point
on the hyperbola, where PF_1 is longer than PF_2. Use
the fact that the difference of the focal radii is 8 to
write an equation.

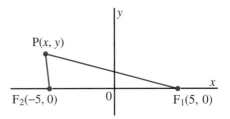

$$PF_1 - PF_2 = 8$$
$$\sqrt{(x-5)^2 + y^2} - \sqrt{(x+5)^2 + y^2} = 8$$

Isolate one radical.

$$\sqrt{(x-5)^2 + y^2} = 8 + \sqrt{(x+5)^2 + y^2}$$

Square each side.

$$\left(\sqrt{(x-5)^2 + y^2}\right)^2 = \left(8 + \sqrt{(x+5)^2 + y^2}\right)^2$$
$$(x-5)^2 + y^2 = 64 + 16\sqrt{(x+5)^2 + y^2} + (x+5)^2 + y^2$$
$$x^2 - 10x + 25 + y^2 = 64 + 16\sqrt{(x+5)^2 + y^2} + x^2 + 10x + 25 + y^2$$

Isolate the term containing the radical.

$$-20x - 64 = 16\sqrt{(x+5)^2 + y^2}$$

Divide each side by 4.

$$-5x - 16 = 4\sqrt{(x+5)^2 + y^2}$$

Square each side.

$$(-5x - 16)^2 = \left(4\sqrt{(x+5)^2 + y^2}\right)^2$$
$$25x^2 + 160x + 256 = 16(x^2 + 10x + 25 + y^2)$$
$$25x^2 + 160x + 256 = 16x^2 + 160x + 400 + 16y^2$$
$$9x^2 - 16y^2 = 144$$

The equation of the hyperbola is $9x^2 - 16y^2 = 144$.

Discuss

Suppose PF_1 is shorter
than PF_2. How would
the solution change?

b) To sketch the hyperbola, determine the intercepts.

Substitute $x = 0$ in the equation of the hyperbola.
$$9(0)^2 - 16y^2 = 144$$
$$-16y^2 = 144$$
This equation has no real roots, so there are no y-intercepts.

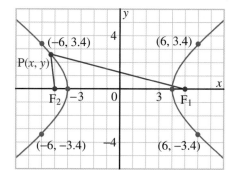

Substitute $y = 0$ in the equation.
$$9x^2 - 16(0)^2 = 144$$
$$9x^2 = 144$$
$$x^2 = 16$$
$$x = \pm 4$$
The x-intercepts are 4 and –4.
Two points on the hyperbola are (4, 0) and (–4, 0).

Substitute any valid value of x, say $x = 6$.
$$9(6)^2 - 16y^2 = 144$$
$$16y^2 = 180$$
$$y^2 = 11.25$$
$$y = \pm\sqrt{11.25}$$
$$\doteq \pm 3.4$$

Substituting $x = -6$ produces the same values for y.
Four more points on the hyperbola are (±6, ±3.4).

Plot these points, then draw two smooth curves through them.

8.3 Exercises

1. The equation of a hyperbola is $9x^2 - 4y^2 = 36$.

   a) Determine the intercepts of the graph of this hyperbola.

   b) Determine the coordinates of 4 other points on the graph.

2. The equation of a hyperbola is $16x^2 - y^2 = -16$.

   a) Determine the intercepts of the graph of this hyperbola.

   b) Determine the coordinates of 4 other points on the graph.

B

3. **Knowledge/Understanding** The foci of a hyperbola are $F_1(3, 0)$ and $F_2(-3, 0)$. The difference of the focal radii is 4 units.

  a) Determine the equation of the hyperbola.

  b) Sketch the hyperbola.

4. The foci of a hyperbola are $F_1(0, 5)$ and $F_2(0, -5)$. The difference of the focal radii is 8 units.

  a) Determine the equation of the hyperbola.

  b) Sketch the hyperbola.

5. **Communication** Look at the results from exercises 3 and 4.

  a) How are the hyperbolas and their equations similar?

  b) How are the hyperbolas and their equations different?

  c) By looking at the equation of a hyperbola, how can you tell whether it intersects the x-axis or the y-axis? Explain.

6. The base of $\triangle ABP$ is AB. Point P moves so the difference of the lengths of AP and BP is 4 units. Determine the equation of the locus of P in each case.

  a) The coordinates of A and B are A(−3, 0) and B(3, 0).

  b) The coordinates of A and B are A(0, −3) and B(0, 3).

  c) Compare the results of parts a and b. What do you notice?

7. The foci of a hyperbola are $F_1(0, 8)$ and $F_2(0, -8)$. Determine the equation of the hyperbola for each condition.

  a) The difference of the focal radii is 4 units.

  b) The difference of the focal radii is 5 units.

  c) The difference of the focal radii is 6 units.

8. The difference of the focal radii of a hyperbola is 2 units. Determine the equation of the hyperbola for each condition.

  a) The foci are $F_1(0, 3)$ and $F_2(0, -3)$.

  b) The foci are $F_1(5, 0)$ and $F_2(-5, 0)$.

  c) The foci are O(0, 0) and A(4, 0).

  d) The foci are O(0, 0) and C(0, 4).

9. The difference of the focal radii of a hyperbola is 6 units. Determine the equations of two different hyperbolas with this property.

10. Determine the equations of two different hyperbolas that have foci $F_1(3, 0)$ and $F_2(-3, 0)$.

11. **Application** Suppose the sound of a cannon is heard in the distance by two observers who are 2 km apart. One observer hears the sound 2 s later than the other observer. Sound travels at about 335 m/s.

   a) How much farther is the cannon from the second observer than the first observer?

   b) What information does your answer to part a give you about the location of the cannon relative to the two observers?

   c) What additional information would be needed to determine the exact location of the cannon? Explain.

12. Use the definition of a hyperbola and the hyperbola you drew in *Investigation 1*. Explain why the hyperbola has:

   a) a horizontal line of symmetry   **b)** a vertical line of symmetry

13. A hyperbola has foci $F_1(10, 0)$ and $F_2(-10, 0)$. One x-intercept is 6. Determine the equation of the hyperbola.

14. A hyperbola has foci $F_1(0, 5)$ and $F_2(0, -5)$. One y-intercept is 4. Determine the equation of the hyperbola.

15. **Thinking/Inquiry/Problem Solving** In the diagram, P is a point on a hyperbola with foci F_1 and F_2. The line through F_1 and F_2 intersects the hyperbola at points A_1 and A_2, called the *vertices*. Line segment A_1A_2 is the *transverse axis*. The midpoint of A_1A_2 is the *centre* O. The property that $|PF_1 - PF_2|$ is constant applies to every point on the hyperbola. Assume P is at A_1. Show that this constant is the length of the transverse axis.

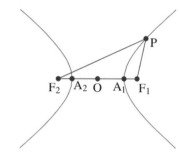

16. Use *The Geometer's Sketchpad*. In *Investigation 3*, you found that the locus of P had two branches. You will investigate what happens when P moves from one branch of the hyperbola to the other branch.

   a) Repeat the construction in *Investigation 3*.

   b) Construct segment F_1F_2 and its midpoint, O, which is the centre of the hyperbola. Your diagram should look like the one at the right.

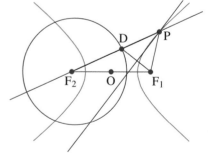

   c) The perpendicular bisector of F_1D does not pass through the centre of the hyperbola. Drag point D until it does.
   i) What special property does the perpendicular bisector of F_1D have when it passes through O?
   ii) Where is point P in this case?

d) Find a different position of D on the circle so the perpendicular bisector passes through O. Do the results you found in part c still apply?

e) Describe how the two perpendicular bisectors are related.

17. Refer to the hyperbola construction in *Investigation 2*. The perpendicular bisector of segment DF_1 touches the hyperbola at P. This line is a *tangent* to the hyperbola. Explain why the perpendicular bisector is a tangent to the hyperbola.

18. A hyperbola has transverse axis of length $2a$ units. The foci of the hyperbola are $F_1(c, 0)$ and $F_2(-c, 0)$. Show that the equation of the hyperbola is
$$\frac{x^2}{a^2} - \frac{y^2}{c^2 - a^2} = 1.$$

19. Use *The Geometer's Sketchpad*. Point A is inside a fixed circle. D is a variable point on the circle. A line perpendicular to segment AD is constructed through D.

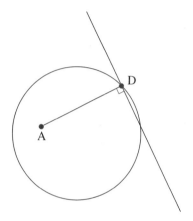

a) Create a dynamic model of this situation.

b) Slowly drag point D around the circle, and observe the effect on the line. Try this for different positions of A inside the circle.

c) Shift-click the line and the point D (the driver point). From the Construct menu, choose Locus. Drag point A to different positions inside and outside the circle, and observe the effect on the locus.

d) This example illustrates a locus of a line. How would you define the locus of a line?

20. Use *The Geometer's Sketchpad*.

a) Create a dynamic model of an ellipse and a hyperbola that have the same foci.

b) Drag the driver point for the hyperbola to observe how it intersects the ellipse as the hyperbola changes. Repeat, using the driver point for the ellipse.

c) Look at one of the points where the ellipse and the hyperbola intersect. Drag the point on the ellipse to the point of intersection. Drag the point on the hyperbola to the same point of intersection. What property do the tangents to the curves appear to have at the point of intersection?

d) An ellipse and a hyperbola with the same foci are *confocal*. State a property of a confocal ellipse and hyperbola that is suggested by your results.

8.4   The Parabola

Television pictures are transmitted worldwide. The signals from a communications satellite are reflected off the surface of a dish antenna and focused at the receiver. The dish antenna has a cross section that is a parabola.

In Chapter 4, you reviewed the parabola and its equations, $y = ax^2 + bx + c$ and $y = a(x - p)^2 + q$.

A parabola can be defined as a locus.

Take Note

Definition of a Parabola

A parabola is the locus of a point P that moves so it is always the same distance from a fixed point and a fixed line.

The fixed point is the focus, F.
The fixed line is the *directrix*, d.

From the locus definition, PF = PD

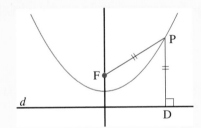

Investigation 1

Using a Grid to Construct a Parabola

You will need grid paper with concentric circles and parallel lines.

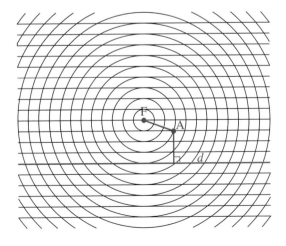

This grid paper can be used to construct a parabola with focus at the centre of the circles. Any line on the grid paper can be used as a directrix.

1. a) Mark the centre of the circles, F.

  b) Draw the line *d* that is 4 units from F.

You will construct a parabola with focus F and directrix *d*.

2. a) Mark point A that is 3 units from F and 3 units from *d*, as shown on page 484. Since A is equidistant from F and *d*, A is a point on the parabola.

  b) Mark as many other points as you can that are equidistant from F and *d*.

  c) Draw a smooth curve through the points to form the parabola.

3. Explain why the parabola you constructed has a line of symmetry.

4. The line of symmetry intersects the parabola at its vertex. How is the vertex related to the focus and the directrix?

5. In each case, describe how the parabola would be different from the parabola you drew.

  a) The directrix is closer to the focus.

  b) The directrix is farther from the focus.

Using *The Geometer's Sketchpad* to Construct a Parabola

You will construct a dynamic model of a parabola. Study the diagram below before you begin the construction. Make sure you understand the following information about it.

F is a fixed point, and *d* is a fixed line. These are the focus and directrix of the parabola, respectively. P is a point on the parabola.

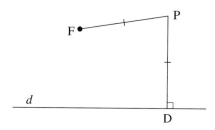

PD is perpendicular to *d*, and PF = PD. Hence, P is equidistant from F and *d*.

D is the driver point for the locus. As D moves along the directrix, PF and PD are always equal in length. The locus of P will be a parabola.

Set-Up

- From the File menu, choose New Sketch.
- Construct a point, then label it F.
- Construct a line that does not pass through F, then label it *d*.
- Construct a variable point D on the line.

Constructing a Point P on the Locus

- Construct segment DF.
- Construct the perpendicular bisector of DF.
- Construct a line through D perpendicular to the line *d*.
- Construct the point of intersection, P, of these two lines.
- Construct segment PF.

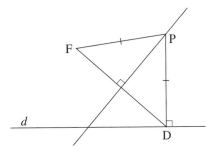

P is a point on the locus.

Constructing the Locus of P

- Drag point D along the directrix. Observe how the position of P changes. Check visually that the lengths of PF and PD are always equal.
- Shift-click point P (the point on the locus) and point D (the driver point). From the Construct menu, choose Locus.

The computer will construct the locus of P, which is a parabola.

1. **a)** Explain why the locus of P is a parabola.

   b) How is the perpendicular bisector of DF related to the parabola?

2. Predict how the parabola will change in each situation. Use the computer to check your prediction.

   a) F moves closer to the directrix.

   b) F moves farther from the directrix.

3. Explain why the parabola you constructed has a line of symmetry.

4. If possible, make a printout of your construction. Otherwise, make an accurate drawing of it.

The definition of a parabola can be used to determine the equation of a parabola in a coordinate system.

Example

A parabola has focus F(2, 0) and directrix $x = -2$.

a) Determine the equation of the parabola.

b) Graph the parabola on grid paper.

Solution

a) Draw a sketch on plain paper.
Show the focus and the directrix.
Let P(x, y) be any point on the parabola.
Draw the perpendicular from P to meet the directrix at D. The coordinates of D are (-2, y).

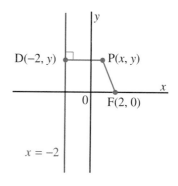

From the definition of a parabola,

$$PD = PF$$

$$\sqrt{(x + 2)^2 + (y - y)^2} = \sqrt{(x - 2)^2 + (y - 0)^2}$$

Square each side.

$$x^2 + 4x + 4 = x^2 - 4x + 4 + y^2$$

Collect like terms.

$$y^2 = 8x$$

The equation of the parabola is $y^2 = 8x$.

b) To sketch the parabola, locate the vertex and two other points on the parabola. The vertex V is halfway between the directrix and focus, so V has coordinates (0, 0).

Substitute any valid value of x in $y^2 = 8x$, say $x = 2$.

$$y^2 = 8(2)$$
$$y = \pm\sqrt{16}$$
$$= \pm 4$$

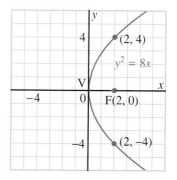

Two other points on the parabola are (2, ±4).
Plot the points, then join them with a smooth curve.

8.4 Exercises

 A

1. Determine the equation of each parabola, then sketch its graph.

   a) Focus F(2, 0); directrix $x = -2$

   b) Focus F(0, 2); directrix $y = -2$

   c) Focus F(–2, 0); directrix $x = 2$

   d) Focus F(0, –2); directrix $y = 2$

 2. **Communication** Look at the results of exercise 1.

   a) How are the parabolas and their equations similar?

   b) How are the parabolas and their equations different?

   c) Suppose you are given the coordinates of the focus and the equation of the directrix of a parabola. How can you determine which way it opens?

 B

3. **Knowledge/Understanding** A point P moves so it is always the same distance from the point B(0, 3) as it is from the line $y = -3$.

   a) Determine the equation of the locus of P.

   b) Identify the locus, then sketch its graph.

 4. A point P moves so it is always the same distance from the point A(–5, 0) as it is from the line $x = 5$.

   a) Determine the equation of the locus of P.

   b) Identify the locus, then sketch its graph.

5. A parabola has directrix $x = -3$ and vertex O(0, 0).

   a) What are the coordinates of the focus?

   b) What is the equation of the parabola?

 6. A parabola has focus F(10, 0) and vertex O(0, 0).

   a) What is the equation of the directrix?

   b) What is the equation of the parabola?

7. **Application** Determine the equation of the parabola with the given focus and directrix.

   a) Focus F(0, 4); directrix x-axis

   b) Focus F(3, 4); directrix x-axis

   c) Focus O(0, 0); directrix $y = 4$

8. Determine the equation of the parabola with the given focus and directrix.

    a) Focus F(6, 0); directrix y-axis

    b) Focus F(6, 3); directrix y-axis

    c) Focus O(0, 0); directrix $x = 6$

9. Thinking/Inquiry/Problem Solving A line segment that joins two points on a parabola is a *chord*. The chord that passes through the focus, and is perpendicular to the line of symmetry, is the *latus rectum*. How is the length of the latus rectum related to the perpendicular distance from the focus to the directrix? Explain.

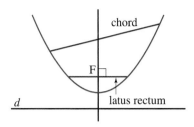

10. Point P moves so the slope of the line through P and S(2, 0) is always 2 greater than the slope of the line through P and T(−2, 0).

    a) Determine the equation of the locus of P.

    b) Identify the locus, then sketch its graph.

    c) Point M(t, 16) is on the graph. Determine the value of t.

11. Determine the equation of the parabola with each given focus and directrix.

    a) Focus F(0, p); directrix $y = -p$

    b) Focus F(p, 0); directrix $x = -p$

12. On grid paper, draw square OACB with side length 8 units.

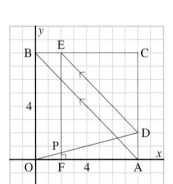

    a) Mark a point D on AC so AD = 2 units. Join OD. Draw DE parallel to diagonal AB. Draw EF perpendicular to OA. Mark point P where EF intersects OD.

    b) Repeat part a for other positions of point D on AC.

    c) Sketch the locus of P. Describe the locus.

    d) Determine the equation of the locus.

13. In the diagram, OACB is a rectangle.
D is any point on side AC.
DE is parallel to the diagonal AB.
EF is perpendicular to OA.
OD and EF intersect at P.
As D moves along AC, point P traces a locus.

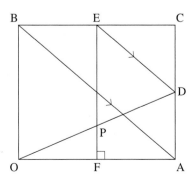

    a) Draw the diagram, with D in the approximate position shown.

b) Repeat part a at least three times, with D in different positions. Include the cases where D is very close to A and very close to C.

c) On one diagram, sketch the locus of P. Describe the locus.

d) Consider the special case where OA = 2 and OB = 1. Suppose O is the origin of a coordinate grid and A lies on the *x*-axis. Determine the equation of the locus of P, and thus verify that it is a parabola.

14. Use *The Geometer's Sketchpad.* Two perpendicular lines intersect at O. Point T is a fixed point on one line. Point D is a variable point on the other line. Point O′ is the reflection of O in segment DT. A line is constructed through D, perpendicular to DT. The line through T and O′ intersects this line at P. Point D is the driver point for the locus of P.

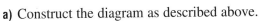

a) Construct the diagram as described above.

b) Construct the locus of P. Drag point D to observe how P traces the locus.

c) Describe the locus.

d) Consider the special case where OT = 4. Suppose O is the origin of a coordinate grid, and D lies on the *x*-axis. Suppose the *y*-coordinate of P is *a*.
  i) Determine the *x*-coordinate of P in terms of *a*.
  ii) Determine the equation of the locus, and thus verify that it is a parabola.

C

15. Determine the equation of the locus of a point P that moves according to each condition. Then graph the locus.

a) The sum of the distances from P to the origin and to the *x*-axis is 4.

b) The sum of the distances from P to the point (0, 6) and the *x*-axis is 10.

16. The line $x + y = 0$ is the directrix of a parabola. The point F(2, 2) is the focus.

a) Determine the equation of the parabola.

b) Sketch a graph of the parabola.

17. Use *The Geometer's Sketchpad.* Refer to exercise 9.

a) Construct a parabola, and its latus rectum.

b) Construct the tangents to the parabola at the endpoints of its latus rectum. What properties do these tangents have?

1. The equation of a hyperbola is $16x^2 - 9y^2 = 144$.

   a) Determine the intercepts of the graph.

   b) Determine the coordinates of 4 other points on the graph.

2. The foci of a hyperbola are $F_1(4, 0)$ and $F_2(-4, 0)$. The difference of the focal radii is 4 units. Determine the equation of the hyperbola.

3. The difference of the focal radii of a hyperbola is 8 units. Determine the equations of two different hyperbolas with this property.

4. Determine the equations of two different hyperbolas with foci $F_1(0, 6)$ and $F_2(0, -6)$.

5. A hyperbola has foci $F_1(8, 0)$ and $F_2(-8, 0)$. One x-intercept is 5. Determine the equation of the hyperbola.

6. Determine the equation of each parabola, then sketch it.

   a) Focus $F(3, 0)$; directrix $x = -3$

   b) Focus $F(0, 4)$; directrix $y = -4$

   c) Focus $O(0, 0)$; directrix $y = 3$

   d) Focus $O(0, 0)$; directrix $x = -4$

7. Point P moves so it is always the same distance from the line $y = -2$ as it is from the point $A(0, 2)$.

   a) Determine the equation of the locus of P.

   b) Identify the locus, then sketch its graph.

8. Point P moves so the slope of the segment that joins the origin $O(0, 0)$ to P is always equal to the x-coordinate of P.

   a) Determine the equation of the locus of P.

   b) Identify the locus, then sketch its graph.

8.5 Relating the Ellipse, Hyperbola, and Parabola

Everyone is familiar with an ice cream cone. Imagine cutting an empty cone at an angle. The cross section would look like an ellipse. If we cut the cone at other angles, it is possible to obtain cross sections that look like a parabola and a hyperbola. But it would not be possible to obtain both branches of the hyperbola.

In mathematics, there are different ways to define a cone. We will use the following definition because it accounts for the fact that a hyperbola has two branches.

Take Note

Definition of a Cone

A *cone* is the surface generated when a line is rotated in space about a fixed point P on the line.

To represent a cone, you could drill a small hole near the end of a pencil and insert a bent piece of wire. Visualize spinning the pencil rapidly between the palms of your hands. The wire traces a three-dimensional surface that forms a cone. Each position of the wire is a line on the cone. These lines are *generators* of the cone. The pencil forms the *axis* of the cone. All the generators intersect at a point called the *vertex*. The cone has two symmetrical parts, or *nappes*, on either side of the vertex.

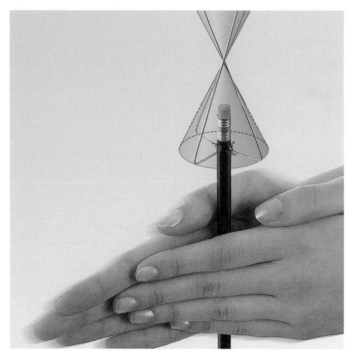
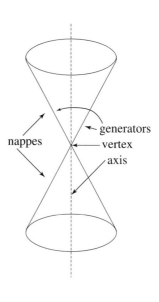

The curves that result when a plane intersects a cone are *conic sections*, or simply *conics*.

The Circle

The plane is perpendicular to the axis of the cone. The curve of intersection is a circle. Hence, a circle is a conic section.

Both the sun and the moon appear to us as circular disks of about the same size. When they are aligned correctly, they can cause a total solar eclipse.

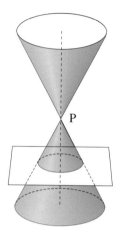

The Ellipse

The plane is not perpendicular to the axis of the cone. The curve of intersection is an ellipse.

Satellites, planets, and some asteroids travel in elliptical orbits. In 1998, astronomers found an asteroid circling the sun inside Earth's orbit. The asteroid, named 1998 DK36, has a diameter of about 40 m.

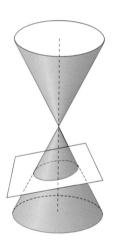

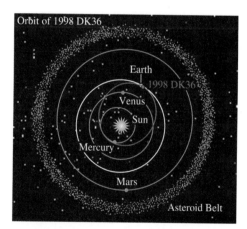

Orbit of 1998 DK36

Earth · 1998 DK36 · Venus · Sun · Mercury · Mars · Asteroid Belt

The Parabola

The plane is parallel to a generator AB on the cone. The curve of intersection is a parabola.

Parabolas have many applications in astronomy. The mirrors in some telescopes have surfaces whose cross sections are parabolas.

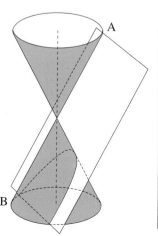

The Hyperbola

The plane intersects both nappes of the cone. The curves of intersection form a hyperbola. A hyperbola has two distinct parts, or branches.

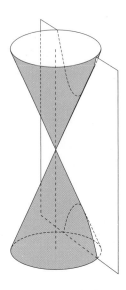

The *Voyager 2* space probe, launched in 1977, provides examples of hyperbolic paths. The arrangement of Jupiter, Saturn, Uranus, and Neptune during the 1980s allowed *Voyager 2* to pass by one planet on its way to the next. On each segment of this journey, *Voyager 2* followed a hyperbolic path. The diagram shows the hyperbolic path of *Voyager 2* as it passed by Neptune in August 1989.

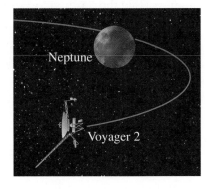

Flashlight Patterns

1. **a)** Hold a flashlight perpendicular to a wall. Identify the curve formed by the edge of the shadow.

   b) Move the flashlight farther from the wall, or closer to the wall, while you still hold it perpendicular to the wall. How does the curve change?

   c) Move the flashlight closer and closer to the wall until it touches the wall. Describe what happens to the curve.

2. **a)** Tilt the flashlight upward. Identify the curve formed.

   b) Increase the angle of elevation of the flashlight. How does the curve change?

3. **a)** Hold the flashlight vertical, close to the wall. Identify the curve formed.

   b) Decrease the angle of elevation. How does the curve change?

4. As the angle of elevation increases, the curve changes from an ellipse to a hyperbola.

   a) Try to determine the position where the curve changes from an ellipse to a hyperbola.

   b) At the position in part a, the curve is neither an ellipse nor a hyperbola. Look closely at the curve. What curve do you think this is?

   c) What is unusual about the position of the flashlight at that position?

5. a) Hold the flashlight to form an ellipse on the wall. Move the flashlight farther from, or closer to the wall, without changing its angle of elevation. How does the ellipse change?

b) Move the flashlight closer and closer to the wall until it touches the wall. Describe what happens to the ellipse.

c) Repeat parts a and b for the hyperbola.

6. Explain how a hyperbola differs from a parabola.

8.5 Exercises

1. A table lamp is near a wall. Describe the shadow formed on the wall when the lamp is turned on.

2. Suppose a plane intersects a cone. Does every plane parallel to this plane intersect the cone? Explain.

3. Refer to the diagram on page 493 that shows a plane intersecting a cone to form a circle. Assume the plane moves parallel to its original position. Describe what happens to the circle when the plane moves as described.

a) farther from the vertex of the cone

b) closer to the vertex of the cone

c) across the vertex of the cone

4. Knowledge/Understanding Repeat exercise 3, using the diagrams on pages 493 and 494 that show a plane intersecting a cone to form each conic section.

a) an ellipse   **b)** a parabola   **c)** a hyperbola

5. Communication Visualize a set of parallel planes that intersect a cone.

a) Suppose the conic section on one plane is a circle. Describe the conic sections on the other planes. Explain how they are related to the first circle.

b) Repeat part a, replacing the word circle with:
  i) ellipse   ii) parabola   iii) hyperbola

6. **Application** Visualize shining a flashlight on a basketball on the floor. When the flashlight is directly above the centre of the basketball, the shadow of the basketball forms a circle on the floor.

Assume the light is always aimed toward the centre of the ball. Describe the position of the light relative to the ball for the shadow to be each conic section.

a) an ellipse   **b)** a parabola   **c)** a hyperbola

7. When a jet airplane breaks the sound barrier, it creates a shock wave that has the shape of a cone. As the jet flies overhead, the shock wave affects points on the ground that form a curve. Describe the shape of this curve for each position of the jet.

a) flying parallel to the ground   **b)** gaining altitude

c) losing altitude   **d)** flying straight up

8. **Thinking/Inquiry/Problem Solving** List as many different ways as possible in which a plane can intersect a cone and not form a curve. Describe how each is obtained.

9. Some comets follow elliptical orbits around the sun. Other comets originate from interstellar space, follow hyperbolic orbits around the sun, then return to interstellar space. Some comets have been observed on only one journey around the sun. Explain why it could be difficult to tell if the orbits of these comets are elliptical or hyperbolic.

10. A flashlight is directed toward a wall. Suppose the angle formed at the flashlight by the rays of light is 60°. Assume the angle of elevation of the flashlight increases from 0° to 90°. For what angles of elevation does each conic section appear on the wall?

a) a circle   **b)** an ellipse

c) a hyperbola   **d)** a parabola

Finding the Ghost –
The Reflection Property of an Ellipse

The July 2000 issue of *New Scientist* magazine contains an interesting article about "atomic ghosts." A team of physicists conducted the following experiment using an empty chamber in the shape of an ellipse.

> *Using the precise motions of a scanning tunneling microscope (STM), Eigler's team placed an atom of cobalt at one focus. In the frigid temperature and ultra-high vacuum of the STM chamber, the atom stuck there like a refrigerator magnet. When the physicists probed the cobalt atom with the STM, they saw a swarm of electrons around it. Then, when they scanned the other focus, they saw an unmistakable signature. The swarm surrounding the real atom was mirrored at the empty focus, even though there was no atom there... It all seems rather surreal.*
>
> [They've seen a ghost, New Scientist 2246, July 8, 2000 p. 25.]

The scientists labelled the cloud of electrons at the empty focus an "atomic ghost."

This phenomenon could have applications for those who study or observe atoms. An atom is observed by using a "probe" such as a light ray or an X ray. Unfortunately, the probe disturbs the atom so you are no longer looking at exactly what you wanted to see. A possible solution is to study and learn from the ghost instead.

Formulating Questions

1. Where does the ghost come from?

2. Why does it appear at a focus?

The answer to these two questions is contained in a fundamental reflection property of the ellipse. Suppose you have an elliptical pool table. When you shoot a ball through a focus, the ball bounces off the wall and passes through the other focus. This happens irrespective of the angle at which you shoot the ball. As long as the ball passes through one focus, it will bounce off the wall and pass through the other focus. The ball will continue this course through the two foci for as long as it keeps moving.

Now think of the electrons at one focus as waves, as in a source of light. The rays emanate from the focus in all directions, reflect off the wall of the chamber, *and they will all pass through the other focus*. The concentration of energy at the focus forms the ghost.

We state this result formally.

> *Proposition*: A light ray emanating from one focus of an ellipse will bounce off the wall of the ellipse and pass through the other focus.

Our mathematics problem is to find a geometric proof of this proposition.

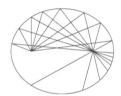

The reflection property of the ellipse is used in a number of applications. A whispering gallery is a large elliptical room where a whisper at one focus can be clearly heard at the other focus. In *lithotripsy*, a person with a kidney stone is placed in an elliptical bath so the stone is at one focus. High-intensity sound waves generated at the other focus are reflected to the stone and shatter it without damaging the surrounding tissue.

Selecting Strategies, Resources, Technology, and Tools

There are several ways to prove the proposition. Here is one approach.

From physics, we know the following properties of light.

- Light reflects from a curved surface, such as an ellipse, as if it was reflecting from a tangent to the ellipse at the point of reflection.
- The incoming and reflected rays make equal angles with the tangent at the point of reflection.

Consider an ellipse with foci F_1 and F_2 and a line l that is tangent to the ellipse at point P. We will prove the proposition in two steps.

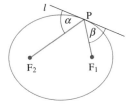

Step 1 The shortest path that contains F_1, F_2, and a point on l is the path $F_2P + PF_1$.

Step 2 PF_1 and PF_2 make equal angles with the tangent l.
That is, $\alpha = \beta$ as shown in the diagram at the right.

Interpreting Information and Forming Conclusions

Proof of Step 1

Suppose Q is any point on the line l different from P. The diagram at the right shows two possible positions of Q. Consider paths $F_2P + PF_1$ and $F_2Q + QF_1$. For the reasons given below, $F_2P + PF_1$ has the shortest total length.

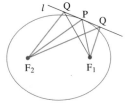

- P is on the ellipse.
- Since P is on the ellipse, $F_2P + PF_1$ is the sum of the focal radii; that is, $F_2P + PF_1 = 2a$.
- Since Q lies outside the ellipse, $F_2Q + QF_1$ is greater than the sum of the focal radii; that is, $F_2Q + QF_1 > 2a$.
- The path $F_2P + PF_1$ is shorter than all other paths $F_2Q + QF_1$.

The shortest path that contains F_1, F_2, and a point on l is the path $F_2P + PF_1$.

Proof of Step 2

We begin with a construction. Let point D be the reflection of F_1 in l. For the reasons given below, F_2PD is a straight line.

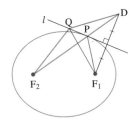

- Line l is the perpendicular bisector of F_1D, so any point on l is the same distance from F_1 as from D.
  Thus, $PF_1 = PD$ and $F_2P + PF_1 = F_2P + PD$
  Similarly, $QF_1 = QD$ and $F_2Q + QF_1 = F_2Q + QD$

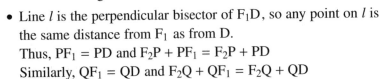

- In Step 1, we showed that $F_2P + PF_1$ is shorter than $F_2Q + QF_1$. Thus, $F_2P + PD$ is shorter than $F_2Q + QD$ for all other points Q on l.

- Since $F_2P + PD$ is the shortest possible path, F_2PD must be a straight line.

- Since F_2PD is a straight line, α and γ are opposite angles. Thus, $\gamma = \alpha$

- D is the reflection of F_1 in the tangent. By symmetry, $\gamma = \beta$

- Since α and β are both equal to γ, they must be equal to each other. That is, $\alpha = \beta$

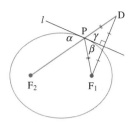

Since PF_1 and PF_2 make equal angles with tangent l, $F_2P + PF_1$ is the path of the light ray from F_2 to F_1 that reflects off l. We have proved the proposition.

The technique of using the reflection of a focus in a tangent is a powerful construction in the geometry of conic sections. It is used in the "circle" construction of the ellipse in Section 8.2, *Investigations 2* and *3*. This construction is more complex than that using the sum of the focal radii definition of an ellipse. In constructing the perpendicular bisector of F_1D, we not only obtain point P on the ellipse, but also the tangent to the ellipse at P. (In Section 8.2, exercise 22, you explained why the line is a tangent to the ellipse.) This gives us an argument for the equal angle result: that the rays F_1P and F_2P make the same angle with the tangent. The result is no different from what we have shown here except that it is done in a different order. In *Investigation 2*, we started with D and used it to construct the tangent. Here, we started with the tangent and used it to construct D.

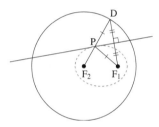

Problems

1. Kursti and Steve are discussing how to draw the tangent to an ellipse at a point P.

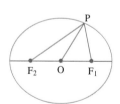

   Kursti: I'm not sure, but an ellipse is just like a circle except it's stretched out. A tangent to a circle is always at right angles to the radius. Shouldn't that be true here?

   Steve: But an ellipse doesn't have a radius.

   Kursti: That's true, but you can still draw a line from the centre of the ellipse. As P moves, the length of the line will change, but maybe it will always be perpendicular to the tangent.

   Steve: Maybe. It works if P is at the top or at the side. Let's try it.

   Investigate Kursti's suggestion using the equal angle property developed in this section. There is an interesting result to be found.

For each of problems 2 to 7, use either a pencil and paper argument, or use *The Geometer's Sketchpad* to produce a construction.

Challenge Problems

2. Consider two points F_1 and F_2 and a line l that neither contains the points nor passes between them. Show that there is a unique ellipse with foci F_1 and F_2 that is tangent to l.

3. Consider point F and two intersecting lines l_1 and l_2, neither of which passes through F.

   a) Is there a unique ellipse with a focus at F that is tangent to both l_1 and l_2? Explain.

   b) Is there is a unique parabola with focus F that is tangent to both l_1 and l_2? Explain.

4. Consider a point F, two lines l_1 and l_2 (neither of which passes through F), and a point P_1 on l_1. Is there a unique ellipse with one focus at F that is tangent to l_1 at P_1 and also tangent to l_2? Explain.

5. Consider a point F inside a triangle. Show that there is a unique ellipse with one focus at F that is tangent to all three sides of the triangle.

6. Consider a point F, a line l not passing through F, and a point P on l. Show that there is a unique parabola with focus at F that is tangent to l at P.

7. Consider three mutually intersecting lines that do not pass through a common point. Show that there is a parabola that is tangent to all three lines. Is this parabola unique? Explain.

8. Since the hyperbola is related to the ellipse, the reflection property of the hyperbola is similar to that for the ellipse. Consider a mirror shaped like one branch of a hyperbola. A light ray that emanates from the focus is reflected off the surface of the hyperbola. If the reflected ray is extended backwards, it passes through the other focus. The proof of this is similar to the proof for the ellipse. Show the proof.

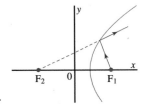

> Problems 2–7 form an interesting class of explorations. All of them deal with the number and type of conditions needed to specify an ellipse or parabola. The conditions could involve a given focus, a given tangent, or a given point of tangency. If you have too few conditions, you will get many loci of the desired kind, but if you have too many conditions, you will not get a locus at all. The objective is to find the right mix that gives a unique locus.

Mathematics Toolkit

Geometry Tools

- A locus is the path traced by a point that moves according to a given condition.
- A circle is the locus of a point that moves so it is always the same distance from a fixed point. This distance is the radius. The fixed point is the centre of the circle.
- An ellipse is the locus of a point that moves so the sum of its distances to two fixed points is constant. Each fixed point is a focus. Each distance from a focus to the fixed point is a focal radius.
- A hyperbola is the locus of a point that moves so the difference of its distances from two fixed points is constant. Each fixed point is a focus. Each distance from a focus to the fixed point is a focal radius.
- A parabola is the locus of a point that moves so it is always the same distance from a fixed point and a fixed line. The fixed point is the focus. The fixed line is the directrix.
- A cone is the surface generated when a line is rotated in space about a fixed point on the line.
- A circle, an ellipse, a hyperbola, and a parabola are conic sections, or simply conics. Each conic results from the intersection of a plane and a cone.

8.1

1. Point B has coordinates $(-1, 2)$. Point C moves so the slope of BC is always $\frac{2}{5}$.

   a) Determine the equation of the locus of C.

   b) Identify the locus, then sketch it.

2. Point D moves so it is always the same distance from the lines $y = 3$ and $y = -5$.

   a) Sketch the locus of D.

   b) Determine the equation of the locus of D.

   c) Describe the locus of D.

3. Point F moves so it is always the same distance from the lines $x = 5$ and $y = 0$.

   a) Sketch the locus of F.

   b) Determine the equation of the locus of F.

   c) Describe the locus of F.

4. Point F moves so its distance from point A(2, 3) is always equal to its distance from point B(4, –5).

a) Determine the equation of the locus of F.

b) Sketch the locus of F, then describe it.

5. Point T moves so the slope of the line segment that joins T to A(5, 2) is equal to the slope of the line segment that joins T to B(0, –2).

a) Determine the equation of the locus of T.

b) Sketch the locus of T, then describe it.

6. Point P moves so the slope of the line segment that joins P to A(0, 2) is three times the slope of the line segment that joins P to B(0, –2).

a) Determine the equation of the locus of P.

b) Sketch the locus of P, then describe it.

7. Point P moves so it is always one-half as far from point A(–5, 0) as it is from point B(5, 0).

a) Determine the equation of the locus of P.

b) Sketch the locus of P, then describe it.

8. Point P moves so the line segment that joins P to Q(0, –1) is always perpendicular to the line segment that joins P to R(0, 1).

a) Determine the equation of the locus of P.

b) Sketch the locus of P, then describe it.

8.2 9. The equation of an ellipse is $9x^2 + 4y^2 = 36$.

a) Determine the intercepts of the graph of this ellipse.

b) Determine the coordinates of 4 other points on the graph, then sketch the ellipse.

10. The foci of an ellipse are $F_1(0, 3)$ and $F_2(0, -3)$. Determine an equation of the ellipse for each condition.

a) The sum of the focal radii is 14 units.

b) The sum of the focal radii is 11 units.

c) The sum of the focal radii is 8 units.

11. The sum of the focal radii of an ellipse is 15 units. Determine an equation of the ellipse for each condition.

a) The foci are $F_1(0, 4)$ and $F_2(0, -4)$.   b) The foci are $F_1(2, 0)$ and $F_2(-2, 0)$.

c) The foci are O(0, 0) and C(4, 0).   d) The foci are O(0, 0) and D(–4, 0).

12. An ellipse has foci $F_1(6, 0)$ and $F_2(-6, 0)$. Determine the equation of the ellipse for which the sum of the focal radii is 16 units.

13. The distance between the foci of an ellipse, centre the origin, is 8 units. The sum of the focal radii is 10 units. Determine the equations of two different ellipses with this property.

14. Use *The Geometer's Sketchpad.*

RS is a fixed line segment. Horizontal and vertical lines intersect at O. Point D is a variable point on the horizontal line. The circle has centre D and radius equal to the length of RS. The circle intersects the vertical line at T. Point P is a point on the line through D and T.
Point D is the driver point for the locus of P. As D moves along the horizontal line, P traces the locus.

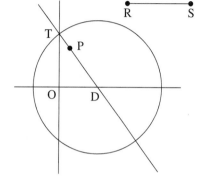

a) Create a dynamic model of this situation, then construct the locus of P.

b) Predict what will happen to the locus when you drag point P. Check your prediction.

c) What special cases occur for each position of P?
   i) on the horizontal line   **ii)** below the horizontal line
   iii) on the vertical line   **iv)** to the left of the vertical line

d) The locus is part of an ellipse with foci on either the horizontal line or the vertical line. Where is P when the ellipse changes from having its foci on the horizontal line to having its foci on the vertical line?

e) What special properties does the ellipse have when P is on the circumference of the circle, and opposite T? Explain how you determined these properties.

f) Explain how you could add the other half of the ellipse to your construction.

8.3   **15.** The foci of a hyperbola are $F_1(5, 0)$ and $F_2(-5, 0)$. Determine the equation of the hyperbola for each condition.

   a) The difference of the focal radii is 3 units.

   b) The difference of the focal radii is 5 units.

   c) The difference of the focal radii is 7 units.

16. The difference of the focal radii of a hyperbola is 4 units. Determine the equation of the hyperbola for each condition.

   a) The foci are $F_1(4, 0)$ and $F_2(-4, 0)$.

   b) The foci are $F_1(0, 3)$ and $F_2(0, -3)$.

c) The foci are O(0, 0) and E(–6, 0).

d) The foci are O(0, 0) and G(8, 0).

17. A hyperbola has foci $F_1(0, 8)$ and $F_2(0, -8)$. Determine the equation of the hyperbola for which the difference of the focal radii is 9 units.

18. The distance between the foci of a hyperbola, centre the origin, is 16 units. The difference of the focal radii is 10 units. Determine the equations of two different hyperbolas with this property.

8.4 19. Determine the equation of each parabola, then sketch it.

a) Focus F(6, 0); directrix $x = -2$

b) Focus F(0, –3); directrix $y = -5$

c) Focus F(4, –3); directrix $x = -2$

20. Point P moves so it is always the same distance from the line $y = -2$ as it is from the point A(0, 2).

a) Determine the equation of the locus of P.

b) Identify the locus, then sketch its graph.

21. Point P moves so the slope of the segment that joins the origin O(0, 0) to P is always equal to the y-coordinate of P.

a) Determine the equation of the locus of P.

b) Identify the locus, then sketch its graph.

22. Point P moves so the slope of the segment that joins the origin O(0, 0) to P is always equal to twice the x-coordinate of P.

a) Determine the equation of the locus of P.

b) Identify the locus, then sketch its graph.

8.5 23. Visualize a pair of perpendicular planes that intersect a cone.

a) Suppose the conic section on one plane is a circle. Describe the conic section on the other plane.

b) Suppose the conic section on one plane is an ellipse. Describe the conic section on the other plane.

24. As Earth rotates about the sun in an elliptical orbit, countries in the Northern Hemisphere experience winter, while countries in the Southern Hemisphere experience summer. Explain why this happens.

1. **Knowledge/Understanding** Point Q has coordinates $(-1, 2)$. Point R moves so it is always 5 units from Q.

   a) Sketch the locus of R.

   b) Describe the locus of R.

   c) Determine the equation of the locus of R.

   d) The point $S(a, 6)$ lies on the locus of R. Determine the value of a.

2. Point P moves so that $AP = 2BP$, where A has coordinates $(-2, -3)$ and B has coordinates $(4, 6)$.

   a) Describe the locus of P.

   b) Sketch the locus of P.

   c) Determine the equation of the locus of P.

3. **Communication** Describe the graph of the function $y = x^2 + 1$ as a locus.

4. Point P moves so it is always the same distance from the line $y = -1$ as it is from the point $A(0, 1)$.

   a) Determine the equation of the locus of P.

   b) Identify the locus, then sketch its graph.

5. **Application** Determine the equation of an ellipse with the same intercepts as the hyperbolas $16x^2 - 9y^2 = -144$ and $16x^2 - 49y^2 = 784$.

6. Consider the foci $F_1(3, 0)$ and $F_2(-3, 0)$.

   a) Determine the equation of the ellipse for which the sum of the focal radii is 8 units.

   b) Determine the equation of the hyperbola for which the difference of the focal radii is 4 units.

   c) Sketch these two conics on the same grid.

7. **Thinking/Inquiry/Problem Solving** Visualize two parallel planes that intersect a cone. Describe and compare the possible resulting conic sections.

8. Point F has coordinates $(-4, 0)$. Point D lies on the line $x = 2$. Point $P(x, y)$ is a variable point. Segment PD is the perpendicular distance from P to D.

   a) Determine the locus of P when $PD = 2PF$, then sketch it.

   b) Determine the locus of P when $PF = 2PD$, then sketch it.

   c) Identify each locus in parts a and b. How are the loci related?

Assessment Tasks

1. Suppose two distinct points F_1 and F_2 are d units apart. A point P moves so the sum of its distances from F_1 and F_2 is $2d$.

  a) Describe the locus of P.

  b) Draw a diagram. Mark all points and distances of particular interest on the diagram.

  c) Introduce a coordinate system on your diagram in part b. Determine an equation for the locus of P. You may choose to use a particular value for d or work with the general parameter d.

2. Suppose you are given two intersecting lines, l_1 and l_2. A point P moves so its distance from l_1 is twice its distance from l_2. Describe the locus of P. In your description, be as specific as you can: provide arguments to support your conclusions and use suitable diagrams. Look at special cases, if you wish.

3. Use *The Geometer's Sketchpad*. You will construct this diagram. A and B are two fixed points. Point P is twice as far from B as it is from A. To arrange this, the top diagram is used. Points T and U are the midpoints of RS and RD. This means that SD is twice as long as TU.

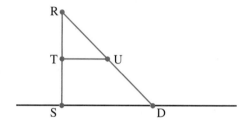

The larger circle has radius equal to the length of SD. The smaller circle has radius equal to the length of TU.

Point D is the driver point for the locus of P, which moves so it is always twice as far from B as it is from A.

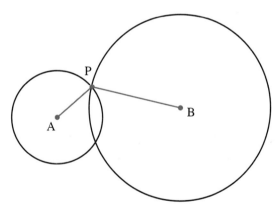

  a) Create a dynamic sketch of this situation, then construct the locus of P.

  b) Explain why SD is twice as long as TU.

  c) Show that the locus is a circle. To do this, introduce a coordinate system so the origin is the centre of the circle, then find the equation of the locus in that coordinate system.

Conics: From Algebra to Geometry (Functions and Relations)

9

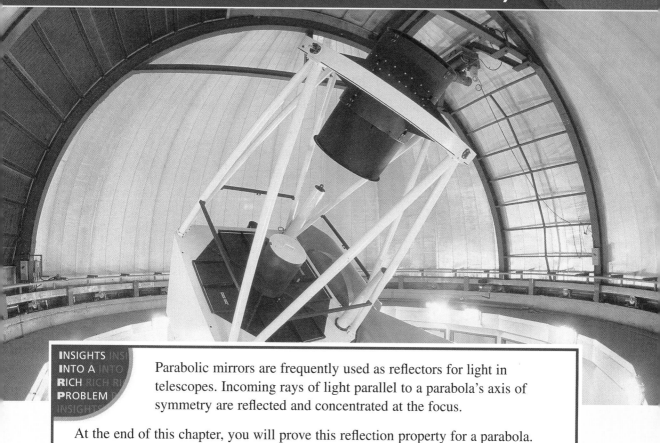

INSIGHTS INSI
INTO A INTO
RICH RICH RI
PROBLEM P
INSIGHTS

Parabolic mirrors are frequently used as reflectors for light in telescopes. Incoming rays of light parallel to a parabola's axis of symmetry are reflected and concentrated at the focus.

At the end of this chapter, you will prove this reflection property for a parabola.

Curriculum Expectations

By the end of this chapter, you will:

- Identify the standard forms for the equations of parabolas, circles, ellipses, and hyperbolas having centres at $(0, 0)$ and at (h, k).

- Identify the type of conic, given its equation in the form
  $Ax^2 + By^2 + 2Gx + 2Fy + C = 0$.

- Determine the key features of a conic whose equation is given in the form
  $Ax^2 + By^2 + 2Gx + 2Fy + C = 0$, by hand in simple cases.

- Sketch the graph of a conic whose equation is given in the form
  $Ax^2 + By^2 + 2Gx + 2Fy + C = 0$.

- Describe the importance, within applications, of the focus of a parabola, an ellipse, or a hyperbola.

- Pose and solve problems drawn from a variety of applications involving conics, and communicate the solutions with clarity and justification.

- Solve problems involving the intersections of lines and conics.

1. Review: The Quadratic Formula

Remember, from Chapter 4, that the roots of the quadratic equation $ax^2 + bx + c = 0$ are given by the quadratic formula,

$x = \dfrac{-b \pm \sqrt{b^2 - 4ac}}{2a}$, where $a \neq 0$. The nature of the roots depends on the value of the discriminant, $b^2 - 4ac$.

- If $b^2 - 4ac > 0$, there are two different real roots.
- If $b^2 - 4ac = 0$, there are two equal real roots.
- If $b^2 - 4ac < 0$, there are two complex roots.

Example 1

Solve the quadratic equation $3x^2 - 38x + 100 = 0$.

Solution

$3x^2 - 38x + 100 = 0$

Use the quadratic formula. Substitute $a = 3$, $b = -38$, $c = 100$.

$$x = \frac{38 \pm \sqrt{(-38)^2 - 4(3)(100)}}{6}$$

$$x = \frac{38 \pm \sqrt{244}}{6}$$

$$x \doteq 8.94 \qquad \text{or} \qquad x \doteq 3.73$$

Example 2

Without solving the equation $9x^2 - 24x + 16 = 0$, determine the nature of its roots.

Solution

$9x^2 - 24x + 16 = 0$

Calculate the discriminant. Substitute $a = 9$, $b = -24$, $c = 16$.

$$\begin{aligned} b^2 - 4ac &= (-24)^2 - 4(9)(16) \\ &= 576 - 576 \\ &= 0 \end{aligned}$$

Since the discriminant is 0, the equation has two equal real roots.

Example 3

For what value(s) of k does each equation have two equal real roots?

a) $4x^2 + kx + 25 = 0$

b) $2x^2 + 2kx + (k^2 - 8) = 0$

Solution

a) $4x^2 + kx + 25 = 0$

Impose the condition that there are two equal real roots.
$$b^2 - 4ac = 0$$

Substitute $a = 4$, $b = k$, $c = 25$.
$$k^2 - 4(4)(25) = 0$$

Solve for k.
$$k^2 = 400$$
$$k = \pm 20$$

When $k = 20$ or -20, the equation has two equal real roots.

b) $2x^2 + 2kx + (k^2 - 8) = 0$

Impose the condition that there are two equal real roots.
$$b^2 - 4ac = 0$$

Substitute $a = 2$, $b = 2k$, $c = (k^2 - 8)$.
$$(2k)^2 - 4(2)(k^2 - 8) = 0$$

Solve for k.
$$4k^2 - 8k^2 + 64 = 0$$
$$-4k^2 = -64$$
$$k^2 = 16$$
$$k = \pm 4$$

When $k = 4$ or -4, the equation has two equal real roots.

Exercises

1. Solve each equation.

a) $4x^2 + 4x - 3 = 0$ **b)** $3x^2 - 11x - 20 = 0$

c) $5x^2 - 2x - 1 = 0$ **d)** $2x^2 + 19x - 30 = 0$

2. Determine the nature of the roots of each equation.

a) $3x^2 - 7x + 4 = 0$ **b)** $x^2 + x + 1 = 0$

c) $4x^2 - 36x + 81 = 0$ **d)** $49x^2 + 154x + 221 = 0$

3. For what value(s) of k does each equation have two equal real roots?

a) $4x^2 - 20x + k = 0$ **b)** $x^2 + kx + (k^2 - 3) = 0$

c) $2x^2 + 2kx + (k^2 - 32) = 0$ **d)** $(1 + k^2)x^2 - 10x + 20 = 0$

2. New: Standard Equation of a Circle

A circle is defined as the locus of a point P that moves so it is always the same distance from a fixed point. We can use this definition to determine the equation of any circle with centre $C(h, k)$ and radius r.

Let $P(x, y)$ be any point on the circle. Then,

$$CP = r$$

Use the distance formula.

$$\sqrt{(x - h)^2 + (y - k)^2} = r$$

Square each side.

$$(x - h)^2 + (y - k)^2 = r^2$$

This is the *standard equation* of a circle.

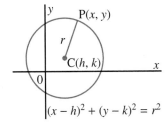

$(x - h)^2 + (y - k)^2 = r^2$

Take Note

Standard Equation of a Circle

A circle, centre $C(h, k)$, radius r, has equation $(x - h)^2 + (y - k)^2 = r^2$.

Example 1

A circle has centre $C(-2, 3)$ and radius 5 units.

a) Write the equation of the circle.

b) Graph the circle.

Solution

a) Use the standard equation $(x - h)^2 + (y - k)^2 = r^2$.
Substitute $h = -2$, $k = 3$, and $r = 5$.
The equation of the circle is $(x + 2)^2 + (y - 3)^2 = 25$.

b) Plot the centre. Mark the points that are 5 units left, right, above, and below the centre. Draw a circle through these points.

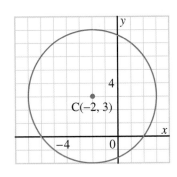

In *Example 1*, 25 can be written as the sum of two squares, $25 = 3^2 + 4^2$. More points on the circle can be marked by moving 3 units left (or right) then 4 units up (or down) from the centre, and vice versa.

In *Example 1*, we could have started with the equation $x^2 + y^2 = 25$, which represents a circle with centre O(0, 0) and radius 5. To translate the circle 2 units left and 3 units up, replace x with $x + 2$ and replace y with $y - 3$. Therefore, the equation of the circle with centre C(–2, 3) and radius 5 is $(x + 2)^2 + (y - 3)^2 = 25$.

In *Example 1*, we can expand the binomial squares on the left side of the equation.
$$(x + 2)^2 + (y - 3)^2 = 25$$
$$x^2 + 4x + 4 + y^2 - 6y + 9 = 25$$
Write all the terms on the left side, with the squared terms first.
$$x^2 + y^2 + 4x - 6y - 12 = 0$$

This equation is in *general form*. When the equation of a circle is in general form, we cannot identify the radius from the equation. To do that, we must write the equation in standard form.

Example 2

Determine the coordinates of the centre, and the radius of the circle defined by $x^2 + y^2 - 8x + 10y + 31 = 0$.

Solution

$$x^2 + y^2 - 8x + 10y + 31 = 0$$

Collect the terms containing x, and the terms containing y.
$$x^2 - 8x + y^2 + 10y + 31 = 0$$

Complete each square.
$$(x^2 - 8x + (16 - 16)) + (y^2 + 10y + (25 - 25)) + 31 = 0$$
$$(x - 4)^2 - 16 + (y + 5)^2 - 25 + 31 = 0$$
$$(x - 4)^2 + (y + 5)^2 = 10$$

The circle has centre (4, –5) and radius $\sqrt{10}$.

Exercises

1. State the radius and the coordinates of the centre of the circle defined by
   each equation.

   a) $x^2 + y^2 = 81$

   b) $x^2 + y^2 = 15$

   c) $(x + 1)^2 + (y + 1)^2 = 36$

   d) $(x - 2)^2 + (y + 3)^2 = 100$

   e) $(x - 4)^2 + (y + 5)^2 = 12$

   f) $(x - 3)^2 + (y - 6)^2 = 55$

2. Write the equation of the circle with the given centre and radius.

   a) $O(0, 0)$; 5

   b) $O(0, 0)$; 1

   c) $C(1, 2)$; 7

   d) $D(-3, 2)$; 6

   e) $E(4, -2)$; 2

   f) $F(-6, -8)$; 8

3. Write each equation in general form.

   a) $(x + 3)^2 + (y + 1)^2 = 4$

   b) $(x - 5)^2 + (y + 2)^2 = 20$

   c) $(x + 6)^2 + (y - 3)^2 = 30$

   d) $\left(x - \frac{7}{2}\right)^2 + \left(y - \frac{3}{2}\right)^2 = 25$

4. Write each equation in standard form. Graph the circle, then show the
   coordinates of its centre, and its radius.

   a) $x^2 + y^2 + 8x + 10y - 1 = 0$

   b) $x^2 + y^2 - 10x - 8y - 2 = 0$

   c) $x^2 + y^2 - 6x + 12y + 5 = 0$

   d) $x^2 + y^2 - 3x + 4y - 3 = 0$

3. Review: Solving a Linear System

A linear system is a pair of linear equations in x and y. To solve a linear system
means to determine the ordered pairs (x, y) that satisfy both equations.

One method to solve a linear system is by substitution.

Example

Solve this linear system.

$3x + 4y = 8$

$2x - y = -13$

Solution

$3x + 4y = 8$ ①

$2x - y = -13$ ②

Solve equation ② for y.

$$2x - y = -13$$
$$y = 13 + 2x$$

Substitute this expression for y in equation ①, then solve for x.

$$3x + 4(13 + 2x) = 8$$
$$3x + 52 + 8x = 8$$
$$11x = 8 - 52$$
$$11x = -44$$
$$x = -4$$

Substitute $x = -4$ in equation ① to determine y.

$$3(-4) + 4y = 8$$
$$-12 + 4y = 8$$
$$4y = 20$$
$$y = 5$$

The solution of the linear system is $(-4, 5)$.

Exercises

1. Solve each linear system.

a) $x + y = 3$
$x - y = 7$

b) $2x + y = 8$
$-2x + y = -4$

c) $x - 2y = 5$
$x + 2y = 4$

d) $3x + y = -2$
$-2x + y = -6$

2. Solve each linear system.

a) $2x + y = 11$
$3x - 2y = 6$

b) $3x + y = -9$
$2x + 3y = -13$

c) $3x + y = 14$
$4x - 3y = 23$

d) $2x - 5y = -34$
$4x + y = -2$

When we graph two different equations on the same grid, we can estimate the coordinates of the points of intersection. For example, this graph shows the circle $x^2 + y^2 = 20$ and the line $2x + y = 6$. One point of intersection appears to be $(4, -2)$, but we cannot determine the other point of intersection accurately from the graph. To determine the coordinates of this point accurately, we use algebra.

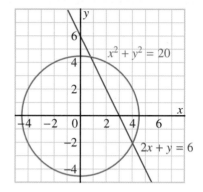

To distinguish the line and the circle, we use y_L for points on the line and y_C for points on the circle:

$$x^2 + y_C^2 = 20 \qquad ①$$
$$2x + y_L = 6 \qquad ②$$

For any value of x, y_C is the height of the circle at that x, and y_L is the height of the line. At any point where the circle and the line intersect, these heights are equal. Therefore, we want the values of x for which:

$$y_C = y_L$$

From equation ②, we determine an expression for y_L. Since we want $y_C = y_L$, we substitute this expression for y_C into equation ①. This method is used in *Example 1*.

Example 1

Determine the coordinates of the points of intersection of the circle $x^2 + y^2 = 20$ and the line $2x + y = 6$.

Solution

$$x^2 + y^2 = 20 \qquad ①$$
$$2x + y = 6 \qquad ②$$

Solve equation ② for y.

$$y = 6 - 2x \qquad ③$$

Substitute for y from ③ into ①, then solve for x.

$$x^2 + (6 - 2x)^2 = 20$$
$$x^2 + 36 - 24x + 4x^2 = 20$$
$$5x^2 - 24x + 16 = 0$$

Solve the quadratic equation by factoring.

$$(5x - 4)(x - 4) = 0$$

Either
$$5x - 4 = 0 \qquad \text{or} \qquad x - 4 = 0$$
$$5x = 4 \qquad\qquad x = 4$$
$$x = 0.8$$

There are two solutions for x. We expect this from the graph, because these solutions are the x-coordinates of the two points of intersection.

Substitute each value of x into equation ③ to calculate the corresponding values of y.

When $x = 0.8$, $y = 6 - 2(0.8)$
$$y = 4.4$$

When $x = 4$, $y = 6 - 2(4)$
$$y = -2$$

Discuss

Why did we substitute the values of x into equation ③ and not equation ①?

The points of intersection of the circle and the line are $(4, -2)$ and $(0.8, 4.4)$.

If we had used the line $2x + y = 10$ in *Example 1*, we would have obtained the equation $x^2 + (10 - 2x)^2 = 20$, which reduces to $x^2 - 8x + 16 = 0$, or $(x - 4)^2 = 0$. This equation has two equal real roots, $x = 4$, that correspond to the point of intersection $(4, 2)$ shown on the graph. The line touches the circle at only one point. The line is called a *tangent* to the circle.

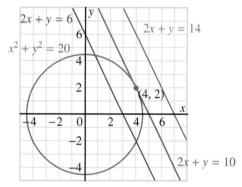

If we had used the line $2x + y = 14$ in *Example 1*, we would have obtained the equation $x^2 + (14 - 2x)^2 = 20$, which reduces to $5x^2 - 56x + 176 = 0$. The discriminant of this quadratic equation is negative, and the equation has no real roots. This indicates that the line does not intersect the circle.

The system of equations in *Example 1* is a *linear-quadratic* system. It contains a linear equation in x and y and a quadratic equation in x and y.

Take Note

Solving a Linear-Quadratic System

To solve a linear-quadratic system, follow these steps:

- Solve the linear equation for either variable.
- Substitute into the quadratic equation, then solve for the second variable.
- Substitute the result into the linear equation, then solve it.

We can use a linear-quadratic system to determine the equation of a tangent to a circle.

Example 2

a) Determine the equations of the tangents with slope 1 to the circle $x^2 + y^2 = 18$.

b) Graph the circle and the lines.

Solution

a) Sketch the circle and two lines with slope 1.

Let the equations of the tangents have the form $y = x + k$, where k is to be determined. Consider the linear-quadratic system:

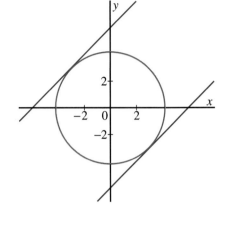

$$x^2 + y^2 = 18 \qquad ①$$
$$y = x + k \qquad ②$$

Solve the system. Substitute for y from ② into ①.

$$x^2 + (x + k)^2 = 18$$
$$x^2 + x^2 + 2kx + k^2 - 18 = 0$$
$$2x^2 + 2kx + (k^2 - 18) = 0$$

This is a quadratic equation in x, where $a = 2$, $b = 2k$, and $c = k^2 - 18$.

For the lines $y = x + k$ to be tangents, this equation must have two equal real roots. For this to be true, the discriminant of the quadratic equation must be 0.

Impose the condition that the discriminant is 0.

$$b^2 - 4ac = 0$$
$$(2k)^2 - 4(2)(k^2 - 18) = 0$$
$$4k^2 - 8(k^2 - 18) = 0$$

Divide each side by 4.

$$k^2 - 2(k^2 - 18) = 0$$
$$k^2 - 2k^2 + 36 = 0$$
$$k^2 = 36$$
$$k = \pm 6$$

The equations of the tangents are $y = x + 6$ and $y = x - 6$.

b) On grid paper, graph the circle with centre O(0, 0) and radius $\sqrt{18} \doteq 4.2$, and the lines $y = x + 6$ and $y = x - 6$.

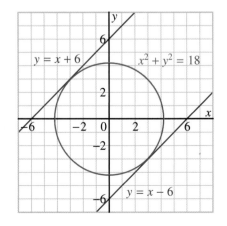

In *Example 2*, the two tangents are members of the family of lines with slope 1. The equation $y = x + b$ represents this family, where b is the y-intercept. When $b = \pm 6$, the members of the family are tangents to the circle (red lines on diagram). When $-6 < b < 6$, the members of the family intersect the circle in two different points (green lines). When $b < -6$ or $b > 6$, the members of the family do not intersect the circle (blue lines).

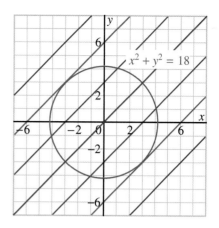

Example 3

a) Graph the circle $(x - 10)^2 + y^2 = 25$.

b) Write an equation to represent the family of lines passing through $O(0, 0)$. Draw some of these lines on the diagram to show the different ways they can intersect the circle.

c) Determine the equations of the members of the family that are tangents to the circle.

Solution

a) The circle has centre $(10, 0)$ and radius 5.

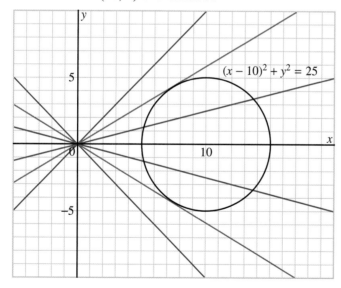

b) The equation $y = mx$ represents the family of lines passing through $O(0, 0)$, where m is the slope. The lines can intersect the circle in 2 different points (green lines on diagram), one point (red lines), or no points (blue lines).

c) Consider the linear-quadratic system:

$$(x - 10)^2 + y^2 = 25 \qquad ①$$
$$y = mx \qquad ②$$

Solve the system. Substitute for y from ② into ①.

$$(x - 10)^2 + (mx)^2 = 25$$
$$x^2 - 20x + 100 + m^2x^2 = 25$$
$$(1 + m^2)x^2 - 20x + 75 = 0$$

This is a quadratic equation in x, where $a = 1 + m^2$, $b = -20$, and $c = 75$. For the line $y = mx$ to be a tangent, this equation must have two equal real roots. For this to be true, its discriminant must be 0.

Impose the condition that the discriminant is 0.

$$b^2 - 4ac = 0$$
$$(-20)^2 - 4(1 + m^2)(75) = 0$$
$$400 - 300(1 + m^2) = 0$$

Divide each side by 100.

$$4 - 3 - 3m^2 = 0$$

Solve for m.

$$m^2 = \frac{1}{3}$$
$$m = \pm\sqrt{\frac{1}{3}}$$

The equations of the tangents are $y = \pm\sqrt{\frac{1}{3}}x$, or $y \doteq \pm0.577x$.

We could have completed *Examples 2* and *3* using the geometric property that the tangent to a circle is perpendicular to the radius. However, the geometric method only works for circles. The method used in the solutions of *Examples 2* and *3* is a general method that applies to other conics. You can use this method in the exercises of Sections 9.2, 9.3, and 9.4.

9.1 Exercises

1. Check the solution of *Example 1* by substituting the coordinates of each point of intersection into the equation of the line and also into the equation of the circle.

2. Check the solution of *Example 2* by solving the linear-quadratic system formed by the equation of each tangent with the equation of the circle.

a) $x^2 + y^2 = 18$
  $y = x + 6$

b) $x^2 + y^2 = 18$
  $y = x - 6$

3. Refer to the diagram that follows *Example 2*.

    a) Write the equation of any line that intersects the circle in two different points. Solve the equation of the line with the equation of the circle. Explain the result.

    b) Write the equation of any line that does not intersect the circle. Solve the equation of the line with the equation of the circle. Explain the result.

4. Check the solution of *Example 3* by solving the linear-quadratic system formed by the equation of each tangent with the equation of the circle.

    a) $(x - 10)^2 + y^2 = 25$
$$y = \sqrt{\frac{1}{3}}x$$

    b) $(x - 10)^2 + y^2 = 25$
$$y = -\sqrt{\frac{1}{3}}x$$

5. Repeat exercise 3, using the circle and lines in *Example 3*.

B

6. Knowledge/Understanding Determine the coordinates of the points of intersection of each line and circle.

    a) $x^2 + y^2 = 5$
       $y = -2x$

    b) $x^2 + y^2 = 5$
       $x - 2y = 0$

    c) $y = 3x$
       $x^2 + y^2 = 10$

    d) $x + y = 2$
       $x^2 + y^2 = 10$

7. Solve each linear-quadratic system. Check the solution.

    a) $x^2 + y^2 = 25$
       $2x + y = -5$

    b) $x^2 + y^2 = 13$
       $x - 2y = 1$

    c) $x^2 + y^2 = 13$
       $y = x - 5$

    d) $x^2 + y^2 = 40$
       $x = 3y$

    e) $y = 2x - 1$
       $x^2 + y^2 = 13$

    f) $x^2 + y^2 = 40$
       $y = x + 9$

8. Solve each linear-quadratic system. Check the solution.

    a) $x^2 + y^2 = 17$
       $y = 2x + 2$

    b) $x^2 + y^2 = 20$
       $2x + 3y = -2$

    c) $4x + 3y = 17$
       $x^2 + y^2 = 26$

    d) $5x + 4y - 32 = 0$
       $x^2 + y^2 = 25$

9. Solve each linear-quadratic system.

    a) $(x + 3)^2 + (y + 2)^2 = 5$
       $y = x$

    b) $x + 2y = 7$
       $(x - 4)^2 + (y + 1)^2 = 10$

    c) $x + 5y = 33$
       $(x - 5)^2 + (y - 3)^2 = 13$

    d) $(x + 1)^2 + (y - 4)^2 = 26$
       $3x + 2y = -8$

10. Thinking/Inquiry/Problem Solving

a) The sum of two numbers is 9. The sum of their squares is 65.
   i) Use a linear-quadratic system to determine the numbers algebraically.
   ii) On grid paper, draw an accurate diagram of a line and a circle to illustrate a graphical solution to the problem.
   iii) Explain why the problem has only one answer, but there are two points where the line intersects the circle.

b) The difference of two numbers is 9. The sum of their squares is 65.
   i) Determine the numbers.
   ii) On the graph from part a, draw a different line to illustrate the solution of this problem.

c) Use the graph to explain how you could have solved the problem in part b using only the answer to the problem in part a.

11. A rectangle has a perimeter of 66 cm and an area of 140 cm^2. Determine the dimensions of the rectangle.

12. A right triangle has a hypotenuse length 10 cm. The perimeter of the triangle is 22 cm. Determine the lengths of the legs of the triangle.

13. Point P is on the line defined by $3x + 5y + 45 = 0$, and P is 13 units from the origin. Determine the coordinates of P.

14. Point Q is on the line defined by $3x - 4y + 31 = 0$, and Q is 10 units from the point C(3, –2). Determine the coordinates of Q.

15. Application From a lighthouse, the range of visibility is 30 km. On a coordinate system, the lighthouse is at O(0, 0). A ship travels on a course represented by $y + 3x + 85 = 0$. Between which two points on the course can the ship be seen from the lighthouse? Write the coordinates to the nearest kilometre.

16. Communication

a) Determine the equations of the tangents with slope 2 to the circle $x^2 + y^2 = 5$.

b) Explain the method you used in part a. Use a diagram to illustrate your explanation.

c) Explain how you can be certain that your solution is correct.

d) Explain how you can use your results to write the equations of the tangents with slope –2 to the same circle.

17. Determine the equations of the tangents to the given circle, with the given slope.

a) $x^2 + y^2 = 10$; slope 3   b) $x^2 + y^2 = 25$; slope $\frac{4}{5}$

18. In *Example 3*, suppose the equation of the circle had been $(x - 5)^2 + y^2 = 25$.

   a) What differences would there be in the ways that lines through $O(0, 0)$ can intersect the circle?

   b) Solve the equation $y = mx$ with the equation of the circle. Explain how the algebra accounts for the differences you noted in part a.

   c) Repeat part b using the circle $(x - 3)^2 + y^2 = 25$.

✓ **19. a)** Graph the circle $(x - 10)^2 + (y - 5)^2 = 25$.

   b) Write an equation to represent the family of lines passing through $O(0, 0)$. Draw some of these lines on your diagram to show the different ways they can intersect the circle.

   c) Determine the equations of the members of the family that are tangents to the circle.

✓ **20.** In exercise 19, suppose the equation of the circle had been $(x - 5)^2 + (y - 5)^2 = 25$.

   a) What differences would there be in the ways that lines through $O(0, 0)$ can intersect the circle?

   b) Solve the equation $y = mx$ with the equation of the circle. Explain how the algebra accounts for the differences you noted in part a.

   c) Repeat part b using the circle $(x - 3)^2 + (y - 5)^2 = 25$.

21. For each circle, determine the equations of the tangents that pass through $O(0, 0)$.

   a) $x^2 + (y - 10)^2 = 10$ **b)** $(x - 5)^2 + (y - 5)^2 = 25$

✓ **22.** Show that the line $3x + 4y = 15$ is a tangent to the circle $x^2 + y^2 = 9$.

23. Show that each line is a tangent to the given circle.

   a) $x^2 + y^2 = 25$ **b)** $x^2 + y^2 = 10$ **c)** $x^2 + y^2 = 20$
   $3x + 4y = 25$ $3x + y = 10$ $2x - 4y = 20$

C

24. In exercise 23, notice the patterns in the pairs of equations. In each pair, the constant terms are the same. The coefficients of x and y in the equation of the line satisfy the equation of the circle. This means they are the coordinates of a point on the circle. For example, in part a, $3^2 + 4^2 = 25$, so $(3, 4)$ is a point on the circle.

   a) Suppose (x_1, y_1) represents a point on the circle $x^2 + y^2 = r^2$. Show that the equation of the tangent to the circle at this point is $x_1 x + y_1 y = r^2$.

   b) Explain how the result of part a can be used to complete exercise 23.

25. Determine the equations of the two lines through the point $P(3, 4)$ that are tangent to the circle $x^2 + y^2 = 9$. Write to explain how you determined the equations.

Remember that an ellipse is defined as the locus of a point P that moves so the sum of its distances from two fixed points is constant.

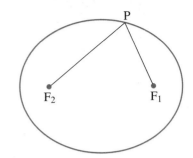

The two fixed points are the foci F_1 and F_2.
$PF_1 + PF_2$ is constant.

Additional definitions

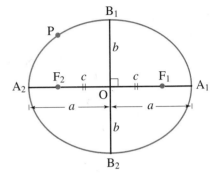

- The line joining the foci intersects the ellipse at the *vertices* A_1 and A_2.

- The perpendicular bisector of line segment A_1A_2 intersects the ellipse at B_1 and B_2.

- Line segment A_1A_2 is the *major axis*.
  Its length is represented by $2a$.

- Line segment B_1B_2 is the *minor axis*.
  Its length is represented by $2b$.

- The major and minor axes intersect at the *centre*.

Properties of an ellipse

The following properties are consequences of the definitions.

- The major and minor axes are axes of symmetry of the ellipse.

- The major axis is longer than the minor axis. Hence, $a > b$

- When P is at one vertex, say A_1, then
  $$PF_1 + PF_2 = A_1F_1 + A_1F_2$$
  $$= A_1A_2$$
  $$= 2a$$
  The sum of the focal radii equals the length of the major axis.
  This is called the *focal radii property*.

- When P is at B_1, then $B_1F_1 + B_1F_2 = 2a$.
  Since $B_1F_1 = B_1F_2$,
  then $B_1F_1 = B_1F_2$
  $$= a$$
  The distance from B_1 or B_2 to either focus equals the length of the semi-major axis.

- The distance from the centre to either focus is represented by c, and $c < a$.

- The right triangle OF_1B_1 has sides a, b, and c, which satisfy $a^2 = b^2 + c^2$.
  This is called the *Pythagorean property*.

Focal Radii Property

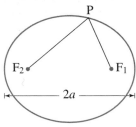

$$PF_1 + PF_2 = 2a$$

Pythagorean Property

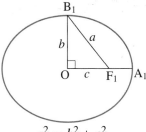

$$a^2 = b^2 + c^2$$

We use the definition of an ellipse to derive the equation of an ellipse with centre $O(0, 0)$ and foci on the x-axis.

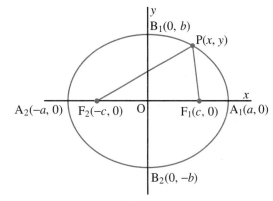

Let the coordinates of the foci be $F_1(c, 0)$ and $F_2(-c, 0)$. Let $P(x, y)$ be any point on the ellipse.

Then, according to the focal radii property, the sum of the focal radii is $2a$.

$$PF_1 + PF_2 = 2a$$
$$\sqrt{(x - c)^2 + y^2} + \sqrt{(x + c)^2 + y^2} = 2a$$

Isolate one radical, then square each side.

$$\sqrt{(x - c)^2 + y^2} = 2a - \sqrt{(x + c)^2 + y^2}$$
$$\left(\sqrt{(x - c)^2 + y^2}\right)^2 = \left(2a - \sqrt{(x + c)^2 + y^2}\right)^2$$
$$(x - c)^2 + y^2 = 4a^2 - 4a\sqrt{(x + c)^2 + y^2} + (x + c)^2 + y^2$$
$$x^2 - 2cx + c^2 + y^2 = 4a^2 - 4a\sqrt{(x + c)^2 + y^2} + x^2 + 2cx + c^2 + y^2$$

Isolate the term containing the radical.

$$4a\sqrt{(x + c)^2 + y^2} = 4a^2 + 4cx$$

Divide each side by 4.

$$a\sqrt{(x + c)^2 + y^2} = a^2 + cx$$

Square each side again.

$$a^2(x^2 + 2cx + c^2 + y^2) = a^4 + 2a^2cx + c^2x^2$$
$$a^2x^2 + 2a^2cx + a^2c^2 + a^2y^2 = a^4 + 2a^2cx + c^2x^2$$

Collect like terms.

$$a^2x^2 - c^2x^2 + a^2y^2 = a^4 - a^2c^2$$

This equation may be written as:

$$(a^2 - c^2)x^2 + a^2y^2 = a^2(a^2 - c^2)$$

By the Pythagorean property, $a^2 - c^2 = b^2$

Hence, the equation becomes $b^2x^2 + a^2y^2 = a^2b^2$.
Divide each side by a^2b^2.

$$\frac{x^2}{a^2} + \frac{y^2}{b^2} = 1 \qquad (a > b)$$

This is the *standard equation* of an ellipse with centre $O(0, 0)$ and foci on the x-axis.

When the equation of an ellipse is given in this form, the values of a and b can be determined from the equation. To determine the coordinates of the foci, the value of c is required. This can be obtained from the Pythagorean property, $a^2 = b^2 + c^2$. Since we usually need this property to determine c, we write the property in the form $c^2 = a^2 - b^2$.

When we reflect the graph of the ellipse with foci on the x-axis in the line $y = x$, we get the graph of the ellipse with foci on the y-axis.

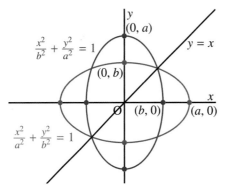

Interchange x and y in the equation $\frac{x^2}{a^2} + \frac{y^2}{b^2} = 1$ to get $\frac{y^2}{a^2} + \frac{x^2}{b^2} = 1$.

This equation is written as $\frac{x^2}{b^2} + \frac{y^2}{a^2} = 1$.

This is the standard equation of an ellipse with foci on the y-axis.

Take Note

Standard Equations of an Ellipse, Centre (0, 0)

Foci on the x-axis

$$\frac{x^2}{a^2} + \frac{y^2}{b^2} = 1 \qquad (a > b)$$

↑

Largest denominator occurs under x^2.

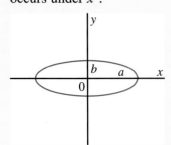

Foci on the y-axis

$$\frac{x^2}{b^2} + \frac{y^2}{a^2} = 1 \qquad (a > b)$$

↑

Largest denominator occurs under y^2.

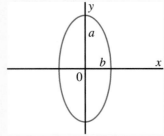

Length of major axis: $2a$
Length of minor axis: $2b$

Vertices: $(a, 0), (-a, 0)$
Foci: $(c, 0), (-c, 0)$ $c^2 = a^2 - b^2$

Vertices: $(0, a), (0, -a)$
Foci: $(0, c), (0, -c)$

When the equation of an ellipse is given in standard form, the values of a and b can be determined from the equation. We can use these values to plot the endpoints of the major and minor axes, then graph the ellipse.

Example 1

Consider the ellipse $\dfrac{x^2}{36} + \dfrac{y^2}{16} = 1$.

a) Graph the ellipse. Show the coordinates of the vertices and the endpoints of the minor axis.

b) Determine the coordinates of the foci. Show the foci on the graph.

Solution

a) $\dfrac{x^2}{36} + \dfrac{y^2}{16} = 1$

Since the larger denominator occurs under x^2, the foci are on the x-axis.
For this equation, $a^2 = 36$ and $b^2 = 16$, so $a = 6$ and $b = 4$
The coordinates of the vertices are $(\pm 6, 0)$.
The endpoints of the minor axis are $(0, \pm 4)$.
Plot these points, then sketch the ellipse.

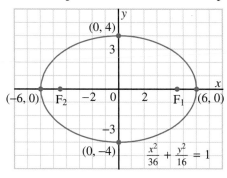

For a more accurate graph, we could substitute values of x to determine the coordinates of other points on the ellipse.

b) Use $c^2 = a^2 - b^2$.
$$c^2 = 36 - 16$$
$$c^2 = 20$$
$$c = \sqrt{20}$$

The coordinates of the foci are $(\pm\sqrt{20}, 0)$, or approximately $F_1(4.5, 0)$ and $F_2(-4.5, 0)$.

Discuss

When we solve $c^2 = 20$, why do we not write $c = \pm\sqrt{20}$?

In *Example 1*, suppose the given equation had been $\frac{x^2}{16} + \frac{y^2}{36} = 1$. Since the larger denominator is under y^2, the foci are on the y-axis. The values of a and b are the same as before. The coordinates of the foci are $(0, \pm\sqrt{20})$, or about $(0, \pm 4.5)$.

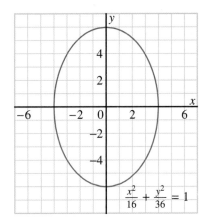

In *Example 1*, suppose the given equation had been $\frac{(x-2)^2}{36} + \frac{(y+3)^2}{16} = 1$. Compare this equation with the original equation. x is replaced with $x - 2$ and y is replaced with $y + 3$. The ellipse in *Example 1* is translated 2 units right and 3 units down.

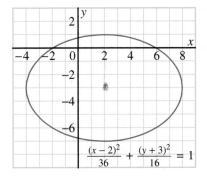

Example 2

Consider the ellipse $\frac{(x+1)^2}{9} + \frac{(y-2)^2}{25} = 1$.

a) Graph the ellipse. Show the coordinates of the centre, the vertices, and the endpoints of the minor axis.

b) Determine the coordinates of the foci. Show the foci on the graph.

Solution

a) $\frac{(x+1)^2}{9} + \frac{(y-2)^2}{25} = 1$

Since the larger denominator occurs under y^2, the major axis is vertical.
For this equation, $a^2 = 25$ and $b^2 = 9$, so $a = 5$ and $b = 3$
The coordinates of the centre are $(-1, 2)$. Plot this point on a grid.

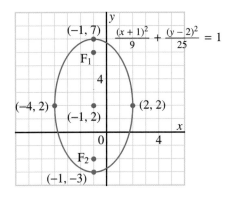

The vertices are 5 units above and below the centre: $(-1, 7)$ and $(-1, -3)$.
Plot these points.
The endpoints of the minor axis are 3 units left and right of the centre: $(-4, 2)$ and $(2, 2)$. Plot these points.
Sketch the ellipse.

b) Use $c^2 = a^2 - b^2$.

$c^2 = 25 - 9$

$c^2 = 16$

$c = 4$

The foci are 4 units above and below the centre. Their coordinates are $F_1(-1, 6)$ and $F_2(-1, -2)$.

In *Example 2*, suppose the given equation had been $\dfrac{(x + 1)^2}{25} + \dfrac{(y - 2)^2}{9} = 1$.

Since the larger denominator is under x^2, the major axis is horizontal. The values of a and b are the same as before. The foci are 4 units left and right of the centre, $C(-1, 2)$. Their coordinates are $F_2(-5, 2)$ and $F_1(3, 2)$.

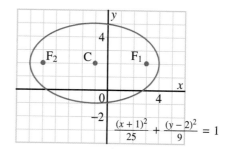

Standard Equations of an Ellipse, Centre (h, k)

Major axis is horizontal.

$$\frac{(x - h)^2}{a^2} + \frac{(y - k)^2}{b^2} = 1 \quad (a > b)$$

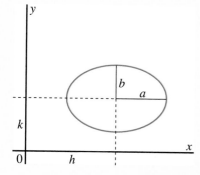

Major axis is vertical.

$$\frac{(x - h)^2}{b^2} + \frac{(y - k)^2}{a^2} = 1 \quad (a > b)$$

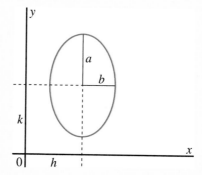

Length of major axis: $2a$

Length of minor axis: $2b$

$$c^2 = a^2 - b^2$$

A

1. For each ellipse:

  i) State the coordinates of the centre.

  ii) State whether the foci are on the x-axis or the y-axis.

  iii) Determine the values of a and b.

a) $\dfrac{x^2}{9} + \dfrac{y^2}{4} = 1$ **b)** $\dfrac{x^2}{16} + \dfrac{y^2}{25} = 1$ **c)** $\dfrac{x^2}{36} + \dfrac{y^2}{1} = 1$

d) $\dfrac{x^2}{49} + \dfrac{y^2}{36} = 1$ **e)** $\dfrac{x^2}{100} + \dfrac{y^2}{4} = 1$ **f)** $\dfrac{x^2}{81} + \dfrac{y^2}{100} = 1$

 2. For each ellipse:

  i) State the coordinates of the centre.

  ii) State whether the major axis is horizontal or vertical.

  iii) Determine the values of a and b.

a) $\dfrac{(x-1)^2}{16} + \dfrac{(y-2)^2}{4} = 1$ **b)** $\dfrac{(x+2)^2}{49} + \dfrac{(y-3)^2}{81} = 1$

c) $\dfrac{(x+3)^2}{9} + \dfrac{(y+4)^2}{25} = 1$ **d)** $\dfrac{x^2}{36} + \dfrac{(y-1)^2}{9} = 1$

e) $\dfrac{(x-5)^2}{100} + \dfrac{y^2}{144} = 1$ **f)** $\dfrac{(x+1)^2}{121} + \dfrac{(y+10)^2}{64} = 1$

3. Write an equation to represent each graph.

a)

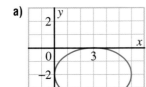

b)

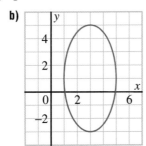

B

4. Knowledge/Understanding

  For each ellipse:

  i) Graph the ellipse. Show the coordinates of the centre, the vertices, and the endpoints of the minor axis.

  ii) Determine the coordinates of the foci.

a) $\dfrac{x^2}{25} + \dfrac{y^2}{49} = 1$ **b)** $\dfrac{x^2}{100} + \dfrac{y^2}{36} = 1$

c) $\dfrac{(x-3)^2}{16} + \dfrac{(y+4)^2}{25} = 1$ **d)** $\dfrac{(x-2)^2}{4} + \dfrac{(y-1)^2}{9} = 1$

5. For each ellipse:

    i) Graph the ellipse. Show the coordinates of the centre, the vertices, and the endpoints of the minor axis.

    ii) Determine the coordinates of the foci.

a) $\dfrac{x^2}{64} + \dfrac{y^2}{9} = 1$ **b)** $\dfrac{x^2}{81} + \dfrac{y^2}{16} = 1$

c) $\dfrac{(x+4)^2}{36} + \dfrac{(y-2)^2}{4} = 1$ **d)** $\dfrac{(x+1)^2}{100} + \dfrac{(y+3)^2}{64} = 1$

 6. For each ellipse:

    i) Write the standard equation.

    ii) Graph the ellipse. Show the coordinates of the centre, the vertices, and the endpoints of the minor axis.

    iii) Determine the coordinates of the foci.

a) $x^2 + 9y^2 = 9$ **b)** $x^2 + 9y^2 = 36$ **c)** $4x^2 + 9y^2 = 36$

d) $4x^2 + y^2 = 16$ **e)** $2x^2 + 3y^2 = 6$ **f)** $2x^2 + 3y^2 = 12$

7. An ellipse has centre O(0, 0) and foci on the x-axis. Determine the equation of each ellipse.

a) $a = 6$, $b = 2$ **b)** $a = 5$, $c = 4$

c) The x-intercepts are ± 12 and the y-intercepts are ± 8.

d) The major axis has length 6 and the minor axis has length 2.

e) One vertex is A(4, 0) and one y-intercept is 3.

 8. An ellipse has centre O(0, 0) and foci on the y-axis. Write the equation of each ellipse.

a) $a = 7$, $b = 4$ **b)** $a = 10$, $c = 6$

c) The y-intercepts are ± 10 and the x-intercepts are ± 5.

d) The major axis has length 15 and the minor axis has length 11.

e) One vertex is A(0, 9) and one x-intercept is 4.

9. An ellipse has centre C(2, 4) and major axis on the x-axis. Determine the equation of each ellipse.

a) $a = 5$, $b = 3$ **b)** $a = 8$, $c = 5$

c) The minor axis has length 6 and the sum of the focal radii is 10.

10. An ellipse has centre C(−1, 5) and major axis on the y-axis. Determine the equation of each ellipse.

a) $a = 8$, $b = 5$ **b)** $a = 8$, $c = 5$

c) The major axis has length 12 and the minor axis has length 6.

11. There are two different ellipses that satisfy the following conditions. Determine their equations.

The centre is C(4, 5). The major axis has length 10. The minor axis has length 8.

12. There are infinitely many ellipses that satisfy the following conditions. The centre is C(4, 0). One vertex is A(0, 0).

a) Determine the equations of two of these ellipses.

b) Let $2b$ represent the length of the minor axis of the ellipses. Write a single equation to represent the family of ellipses that satisfy this condition.

13. a) Write the equations of two ellipses that satisfy the following condition. The endpoints of the minor axis are $B_1(0, 5)$ and $B_2(0, 1)$.

b) Write a single equation to represent the family of ellipses that satisfy this condition.

14. Thinking/Inquiry/Problem Solving

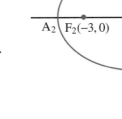

An ellipse has foci $F_1(3, 0)$ and $F_2(-3, 0)$. Determine, if possible, the equation of the ellipse so that:

a) quadrilateral $F_1B_1F_2B_2$ is a square.

b) quadrilateral $A_1B_1A_2B_2$ is a square.

If either of these is not possible, explain why.

15. An ellipse has foci $F_1(3, 0)$ and $F_2(-3, 0)$. Determine, if possible, the equation of the ellipse so that:

a) $\triangle F_1B_1B_2$ is equilateral.   **b)** $\triangle A_1B_1B_2$ is equilateral.

c) $\triangle F_1B_1F_2$ is equilateral.   **d)** $\triangle A_1B_1A_2$ is equilateral.

If any of these is not possible, explain why.

16. Visualize all possible ellipses with foci $F_1(3, 0)$ and $F_2(-3, 0)$.

a) What angles are possible for $\angle F_1B_1F_2$?

b) What angles are possible for $\angle A_1B_1A_2$?

17. A square is inscribed in the ellipse $\dfrac{x^2}{16} + \dfrac{y^2}{9} = 1$. The sides of the square are parallel to the axes. Determine the area of the square.

18. An ellipse has centre C(-2, 3) and one vertex A(-12, 3). The ellipse passes through the point R(4, 7). Determine the equation of the ellipse.

19. **Application**

  a) Graph the equation $x^2 + y^2 = 1$. On the same grid, sketch the graph after each transformation.

  i) Expand horizontally by a factor of 2.

  ii) Expand vertically by a factor of 3.

  iii) Expand horizontally by a factor of 2 and expand vertically by a factor of 3.

  b) For each transformation, describe the image graph and how it relates to the circle.

20. **Communication** Use the results of exercise 19. Explain how transformations could be used to graph the ellipse $\dfrac{x^2}{25} + \dfrac{y^2}{16} = 1$, beginning with the graph of a unit circle, centre O(0, 0).

21. Use the results of exercise 19. Explain how transformations could be used to graph the ellipse $\dfrac{(x-1)^2}{36} + \dfrac{(y+2)^2}{4} = 1$, beginning with the graph of a unit circle, centre O(0, 0).

22. Determine the coordinates of the points of intersection of each line and ellipse.

  a) $9x^2 + y^2 = 9$
    $y = -x + 3$

  b) $x^2 + 16y^2 = 16$
    $x - 4y = 4$

  c) $2x + 3y = 6$
    $25x^2 + 9y^2 = 225$

  d) $16x^2 + 25y^2 = 400$
    $4x + 5y = -20$

23. The diagram shows the ellipses $\dfrac{(x-5)^2}{16} + \dfrac{y^2}{9} = 1$ and $\dfrac{(x-5)^2}{9} + \dfrac{y^2}{16} = 1$, and the lines $y = \pm x$.

  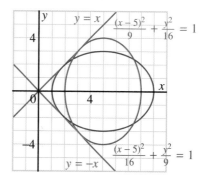

  a) Show that the two lines are tangents to both ellipses.

  b) The ellipses and tangents appear to form a pattern. Describe the pattern.

  c) Use the pattern to write the equations of two other ellipses with centre (5, 0) that have the lines $y = \pm x$ as tangents.

24. Use the results of exercise 23. Write the equations of two ellipses with centre (10, 0) that have the lines $y = \pm x$ as tangents.

25. Consider the ellipse $25x^2 + 64y^2 = 1600$ and a line that form a linear-quadratic system. Determine the equation of a line for each situation.

  a) The system has one solution.

  b) The system has two solutions.

  c) The system has no solutions.

1. Write each equation in general form.

a) $(x + 2)^2 + (y + 4)^2 = 9$ **b)** $(x + 3)^2 + (y - 1)^2 = 4$

c) $(x - 5)^2 + (y - 6)^2 = 1$ **d)** $(x - 1)^2 + (y - 3)^2 = 49$

2. Graph the circle represented by each equation.

a) $x^2 + y^2 - 6x + 4y - 51 = 0$ **b)** $x^2 + y^2 + 2x - 2y - 34 = 0$

c) $x^2 + y^2 - 7x - 9y - 4 = 0$ **d)** $x^2 + y^2 + 12x + 14y + 60 = 0$

3. Determine the equation of a circle with A(7, 3) and B(–1, –3) as the endpoints of a diameter.

4. A circle has centre C(–2, –1) and radius 4 units.

a) Write the equation of the circle.

b) Determine the intercepts of the circle.

c) Graph the circle.

5. Solve this linear-quadratic system.

$x + 2y = 3$
$x^2 + y^2 = 26$

6. Determine the equations of the tangents to the circle $x^2 + y^2 = 12$, with slope 2.

7. Determine the coordinates of the points of intersection of the circle $x^2 + y^2 - x - 3y = 0$ and the line $y = x - 1$.

8. Sketch each ellipse. Identify the coordinates of its foci.

a) $\dfrac{x^2}{49} + \dfrac{y^2}{36} = 1$ **b)** $\dfrac{(x + 2)^2}{9} + \dfrac{(y - 4)^2}{16} = 1$

9. An ellipse has centre O(0, 0) and its major axis on the y-axis. Determine the equation of each ellipse.

a) $a = 6, b = 3$

b) The major axis has length 10 and the minor axis has length 8.

c) One vertex is A(0, 11) and one x-intercept is 2.

10. The centre of an ellipse is C(2, 3). The major axis has length 8. The minor axis has length 6. Determine the equations of two possible ellipses.

11. Determine the equations of the tangents to the given ellipse with the given slope.

a) $16x^2 + y^2 = 16$; slope 3   **b)** $\dfrac{x^2}{9} + \dfrac{y^2}{4} = 1$; slope $\dfrac{1}{2}$

Remember that a hyperbola is defined as the locus of a point P that moves so the difference of its distances from two fixed points is constant.

The two fixed points are the foci F_1 and F_2.
$|PF_1 - PF_2|$ is constant.

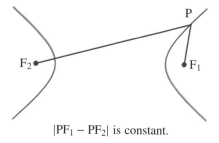

$|PF_1 - PF_2|$ is constant.

Additional definitions

- The line joining the foci intersects the hyperbola at the *vertices* A_1 and A_2.
- Line segment A_1A_2 is called the *transverse axis*.
  Its length is represented by $2a$.
- The midpoint of segment A_1A_2 is the *centre*.

Properties of a hyperbola

The following properties are consequences of the definitions.

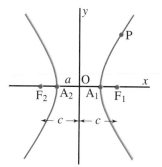

- The line containing the transverse axis is an axis of symmetry of the hyperbola.
- The perpendicular bisector of the transverse axis is an axis of symmetry.
- The distance from the centre to either focus is represented by c, and $c > a$.
- When P is at one vertex, say A_1, then
$$|PF_1 - PF_2| = |A_1F_1 - A_1F_2|$$
$$= |A_2F_2 - A_1F_2|$$
$$= A_1A_2$$
$$= 2a$$
The difference of the focal radii equals the length of the transverse axis. This is called the focal radii property.

We can use the definition of a hyperbola to derive the equation of a hyperbola with centre $O(0, 0)$ and foci on the x-axis.

Let the coordinates of the foci be $F_1(c, 0)$ and $F_2(-c, 0)$.
Let $P(x, y)$ be any point on the hyperbola.

Then, according to the focal radii property, the difference of the focal radii is $2a$.

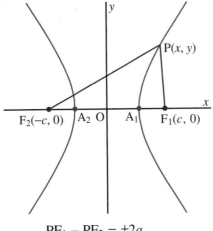

$$PF_1 - PF_2 = \pm 2a$$
$$\sqrt{(x-c)^2 + y^2} - \sqrt{(x+c)^2 + y^2} = \pm 2a$$

Isolate one radical, then square each side.

$$\sqrt{(x-c)^2 + y^2} = \pm 2a + \sqrt{(x+c)^2 + y^2}$$
$$\left(\sqrt{(x-c)^2 + y^2}\right)^2 = \left(\pm 2a + \sqrt{(x+c)^2 + y^2}\right)^2$$
$$(x-c)^2 + y^2 = 4a^2 \pm 4a\sqrt{(x+c)^2 + y^2} + (x+c)^2 + y^2$$
$$x^2 - 2cx + c^2 + y^2 = 4a^2 \pm 4a\sqrt{(x+c)^2 + y^2} + x^2 + 2cx + c^2 + y^2$$

Isolate the term containing the radical.

$$-4a^2 - 4cx = \pm 4a\sqrt{(x+c)^2 + y^2}$$

Divide each side by 4.

$$-a^2 - cx = \pm a\sqrt{(x+c)^2 + y^2}$$

Square each side again.

$$a^4 + 2a^2cx + c^2x^2 = a^2(x^2 + 2cx + c^2 + y^2)$$
$$a^4 + 2a^2cx + c^2x^2 = a^2x^2 + 2a^2cx + a^2c^2 + a^2y^2$$

Collect like terms.

$$c^2x^2 - a^2x^2 - a^2y^2 = a^2c^2 - a^4$$

This equation may be written as $(c^2 - a^2)x^2 - a^2y^2 = a^2(c^2 - a^2)$.
To simplify this equation, we *define* $b^2 = c^2 - a^2$.

Hence, the equation becomes $b^2x^2 - a^2y^2 = a^2b^2$.

Divide each side by a^2b^2.

$$\frac{x^2}{a^2} - \frac{y^2}{b^2} = 1$$

This is the *standard equation* of a hyperbola with centre O(0, 0) and foci on the *x*-axis. Both *a* and *b* can be any positive numbers.

When the equation of a hyperbola is given in standard form, the values of a and b can be determined from the equation. To determine the coordinates of the foci, the value of c is required. This can be obtained from the definition, $b^2 = c^2 - a^2$. Since we usually need this equation to determine c, we write the equation in the form $c^2 = a^2 + b^2$.

Consider the equation $\dfrac{x^2}{36} - \dfrac{y^2}{16} = 1$.

For this equation, $a^2 = 36$ and $b^2 = 16$, so $a = 6$ and $b = 4$

To determine the x-intercepts, substitute $y = 0$ to obtain $\dfrac{x^2}{36} = 1$, or $x = \pm 6$. These intercepts correspond to the vertices $A_1(6, 0)$ and $A_2(-6, 0)$.

There are no y-intercepts. If we substitute $x = 0$, we get $-\dfrac{y^2}{16} = 1$, which has no real solution.

However, for the equation, $b = 4$

Although they are not on the hyperbola, we plot the points $B_1(0, 4)$ and $B_2(0, -4)$ on the y-axis.

The points A_1, A_2, B_1, and B_2 are the midpoints of the sides of a rectangle. We draw this rectangle and the lines containing its diagonals. These lines are asymptotes to the hyperbola (see exercise 27). We use the vertices and the asymptotes as guides to graph the hyperbola.

From the diagram, the slopes of the asymptotes are $\pm\dfrac{4}{6}$.

Since the asymptotes pass through the origin, their equations are $y = \dfrac{4}{6}x$ and $y = -\dfrac{4}{6}x$; that is, in general, $y = \pm\dfrac{b}{a}x$.

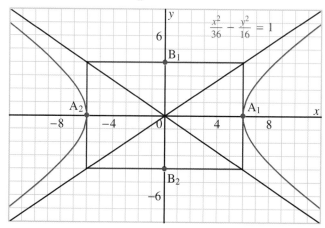

Line segment B_1B_2 is the *conjugate axis*.

For the hyperbola $\dfrac{x^2}{a^2} - \dfrac{y^2}{b^2} = 1$, the endpoints of the conjugate axis are $B_1(0, b)$ and $B_2(0, -b)$.

When we reflect the graph of the hyperbola $\dfrac{x^2}{a^2} - \dfrac{y^2}{b^2} = 1$ with foci on the x-axis

in the line $y = x$, we get the graph of the hyperbola with foci on the y-axis.

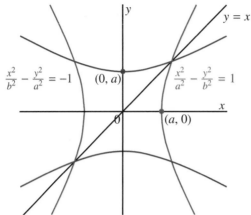

Interchange x and y in the equation $\dfrac{x^2}{a^2} - \dfrac{y^2}{b^2} = 1$ to get $\dfrac{y^2}{a^2} - \dfrac{x^2}{b^2} = 1$.

This equation is usually written as $\dfrac{x^2}{b^2} - \dfrac{y^2}{a^2} = -1$. This is the standard equation

of a hyperbola with foci on the y-axis.

Take Note

Standard Equations of a Hyperbola, Centre O(0, 0)

Foci on the x-axis

$$\frac{x^2}{a^2} - \frac{y^2}{b^2} = 1$$

$\uparrow$ $\uparrow$ same sign as x^2 term

a^2 occurs under x^2.

Foci on the y-axis

$$\frac{x^2}{b^2} - \frac{y^2}{a^2} = -1$$

$\uparrow$ $\uparrow$ same sign as y^2 term

a^2 occurs under y^2.

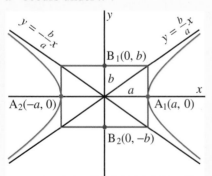

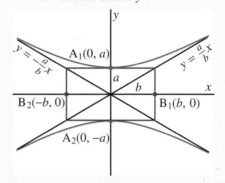

Length of transverse axis: $2a$

Length of conjugate axis: $2b$

Vertices: $(a, 0)$ and $(-a, 0)$

Foci: $(c, 0)$ and $(-c, 0)$ $c^2 = a^2 + b^2$

Asymptotes: $y = \pm \dfrac{b}{a}x$

Vertices: $(0, a)$ and $(0, -a)$

Foci: $(0, c)$ and $(0, -c)$

Asymptotes: $y = \pm \dfrac{a}{b}x$

Example 1

Consider the hyperbola $\frac{x^2}{49} - \frac{y^2}{9} = -1$.

a) Graph the hyperbola. Show the asymptotes and the coordinates of the vertices and the endpoints of the conjugate axis.

b) Determine the coordinates of the foci. Show the foci on the graph.

Solution

a) $\frac{x^2}{49} - \frac{y^2}{9} = -1$

Since the right side is negative, the foci are on the y-axis.
For this equation, $a^2 = 9$ and $b^2 = 49$, so $a = 3$ and $b = 7$
The coordinates of the vertices are $(0, \pm 3)$.
The endpoints of the conjugate axis are $(\pm 7, 0)$.

Graph these points, then draw vertical and horizontal segments to form a rectangle.

Graph the lines containing the diagonals of the rectangle, which are the asymptotes of the hyperbola.

Use the vertices and the asymptotes as guides to graph the hyperbola.

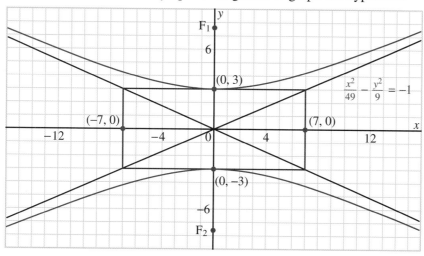

b) The coordinates of the foci are $(\pm c, 0)$.

$c^2 = a^2 + b^2$
$\quad = 9 + 49$
$\quad = 58$
$c = \sqrt{58}$
$\quad \doteq 7.6$

The coordinates of the foci are $(0, \pm\sqrt{58})$, or, approximately $F_1(0, 7.6)$ and $F_2(0, -7.6)$.

In *Example 1*, suppose the given equation had been $\frac{x^2}{49} - \frac{y^2}{9} = 1$. Since the right side is positive, the foci are on the *x*-axis. The values of *a* and *b* are the same as before. The coordinates of the foci are $(\pm\sqrt{58}, 0)$. This hyperbola has the same asymptotes as the hyperbola $\frac{x^2}{49} - \frac{y^2}{9} = -1$.

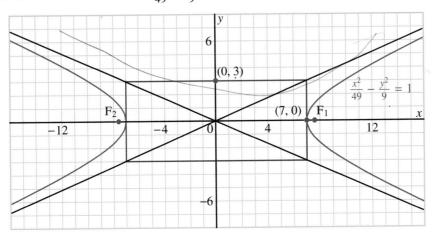

Example 2

Consider the hyperbola $\frac{(x+2)^2}{4} - \frac{(y-1)^2}{16} = 1$.

a) Graph the hyperbola. Show the asymptotes and the coordinates of the centre, the vertices, and the endpoints of the conjugate axis.

b) Determine the coordinates of the foci.

Solution

a) $\frac{(x+2)^2}{4} - \frac{(y-1)^2}{16} = 1$

Since the right side is positive, the transverse axis is horizontal.
For this equation, $a^2 = 4$ and $b^2 = 16$, so $a = 2$ and $b = 4$

The coordinates of the centre are $(-2, 1)$.
The vertices are 2 units left and right of the centre: $(-4, 1)$ and $(0, 1)$
The endpoints of the conjugate axis are 4 units above and below the centre: $(-2, 5)$ and $(-2, -3)$

Graph these points, then draw vertical and horizontal segments to form a rectangle. Graph the lines containing the diagonals of the rectangle, which are the asymptotes of the hyperbola. Use the vertices and the asymptotes as guides to graph the hyperbola.

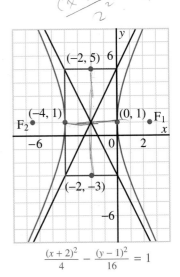

b) Use $c^2 = a^2 + b^2$.

$$c^2 = 4 + 16$$
$$= 20$$
$$c = \sqrt{20}$$
$$\doteq 4.5$$

The foci are $\sqrt{20}$ units right and left of the centre: $(-2 \pm \sqrt{20}, 1)$, or, approximately $F_1(2.5, 1)$ and $F_2(-6.5, 1)$.

Take Note

Standard Equations of a Hyperbola, Centre (h, k)

Transverse axis is horizontal.

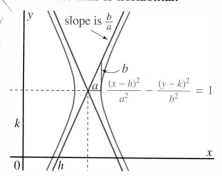

Asymptotes have slopes $\pm\dfrac{b}{a}$.

Transverse axis is vertical.

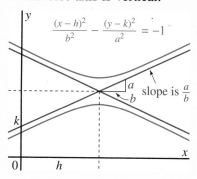

Asymptotes have slopes $\pm\dfrac{a}{b}$.

9.3   Exercises

A

1. For each hyperbola:

   i) State the coordinates of the centre.

   ii) State whether the foci are on the x-axis or the y-axis.

   iii) Determine the values of a and b.

   iv) Determine the slopes of its asymptotes.

   a) $\dfrac{x^2}{4} - \dfrac{y^2}{9} = 1$ **b)** $\dfrac{x^2}{9} - \dfrac{y^2}{16} = -1$ **c)** $\dfrac{x^2}{64} - \dfrac{y^2}{25} = 1$

   d) $\dfrac{x^2}{36} - \dfrac{y^2}{64} = -1$ **e)** $\dfrac{x^2}{16} - \dfrac{y^2}{100} = -1$ **f)** $\dfrac{x^2}{4} - \dfrac{y^2}{81} = 1$

2. The equation $x^2 + y^2 = 1$ represents a circle with centre $O(0, 0)$ and radius 1. Describe what each equation represents.

   a) $x^2 - y^2 = 1$ **b)** $x^2 - y^2 = -1$

3. For each hyperbola:

    i) State the coordinates of the centre.

    ii) State whether the transverse axis is horizontal or vertical.

    iii) Determine the values of a and b.

    iv) Determine the slopes of its asymptotes.

a) $\dfrac{(x-5)^2}{9} - \dfrac{(y+3)^2}{25} = 1$ **b)** $\dfrac{(x+1)^2}{16} - \dfrac{(y+4)^2}{36} = -1$

c) $\dfrac{(x-3)^2}{4} - \dfrac{(y-2)^2}{16} = -1$ **d)** $\dfrac{(x-4)^2}{64} - \dfrac{(y+4)^2}{25} = 1$

e) $\dfrac{(x+2)^2}{1} - \dfrac{(y-1)^2}{9} = 1$ **f)** $\dfrac{(x+7)^2}{49} - \dfrac{(y+5)^2}{4} = -1$

4. Write an equation to represent each graph.

a)
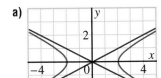

b)
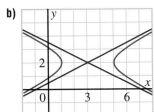

c)
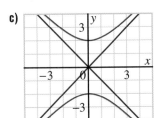

d)
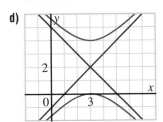

B

5. Knowledge/Understanding

For each hyperbola:

    i) Graph the hyperbola. Show the asymptotes and the coordinates of the centre, the vertices, and the endpoints of the conjugate axis.

    ii) Determine the coordinates of the foci.

a) $\dfrac{x^2}{9} - \dfrac{y^2}{4} = -1$ **b)** $\dfrac{x^2}{49} - \dfrac{y^2}{16} = 1$

c) $\dfrac{(x+3)^2}{49} - \dfrac{(y-2)^2}{9} = -1$ **d)** $\dfrac{(x-2)^2}{36} - \dfrac{(y-3)^2}{1} = 1$

6. For each hyperbola:

    i) Graph the hyperbola. Show the asymptotes and the coordinates of the centre, the vertices, and the endpoints of the conjugate axis.

    ii) Determine the coordinates of the foci.

a) $\dfrac{x^2}{16} - \dfrac{y^2}{49} = -1$ **b)** $\dfrac{x^2}{4} - \dfrac{y^2}{36} = 1$

c) $\dfrac{(x+2)^2}{9} - \dfrac{(y-3)^2}{4} = 1$ **d)** $\dfrac{(x-4)^2}{16} - \dfrac{(y-5)^2}{64} = -1$

7. For each hyperbola:

    i) Write the standard equation.

    ii) Graph the hyperbola. Show the asymptotes and the coordinates of the centre, the vertices, and the endpoints of the conjugate axis.

    iii) Determine the coordinates of the foci.

a) $x^2 - 4y^2 = 4$ **b)** $x^2 - 4y^2 = 36$ **c)** $9x^2 - 4y^2 = 36$

d) $9x^2 - y^2 = 81$ **e)** $5x^2 - 2y^2 = 10$ **f)** $5x^2 - 2y^2 = 20$

8. A hyperbola has centre O(0, 0) and transverse axis horizontal. Determine the equation of each hyperbola.

    a) $a = 5$ and $b = 4$ **b)** $a = 9$ and $b = 12$

    c) $a = 6$ and $c = 10$ **d)** $b = 8$ and $c = 12$

    e) The transverse axis has length 8 and the conjugate axis has length 12.

    f) One vertex is A(3, 0) and one focus is F(5, 0).

    g) One x-intercept is 8 and one asymptote is $y = -2x$.

9. A hyperbola has centre O(0, 0) and transverse axis vertical. Determine the equation of each hyperbola.

    a) $a = 6$ and $b = 8$ **b)** $a = 10$ and $b = 5$

    c) $a = 8$ and $c = 14$ **d)** $b = 10$ and $c = 15$

    e) One vertex is A(0, –4) and one focus is F(0, –6).

    f) The conjugate axis has length 15 and one focus is F(0, 8).

    g) One y-intercept is 6 and one asymptote is $y = \frac{2}{3}x$.

10. A hyperbola has centre O(0, 0) and one vertex A($\sqrt{6}$, 0). The hyperbola passes through B(9, 5).

    a) Determine the equation of the hyperbola.

    b) Sketch the hyperbola.

11. Write the equations of the circle and the two hyperbolas shown on the graph at the right.

12. On the same grid:

    a) Graph the circle $x^2 + y^2 = 9$.

    b) Graph the hyperbola $x^2 - y^2 = 9$.

    c) Graph the hyperbola $x^2 - y^2 = -9$.

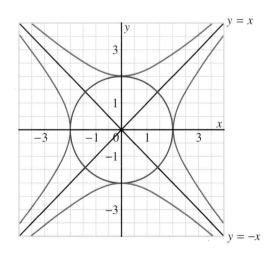

13. Each hyperbola in exercises 11 and 12 is an example of a *rectangular hyperbola*. A rectangular hyperbola has its transverse axis and conjugate axis equal in length.

   a) Write the equation of a rectangular hyperbola with vertices $A_1(a, 0)$ and $A_2(-a, 0)$.

   b) Determine the coordinates of the foci and the equations of the asymptotes.

   c) What special property do the asymptotes have?

   d) Sketch the hyperbola.

14. A rectangular hyperbola has centre $O(0, 0)$ and vertices on the y-axis. The hyperbola passes through $B(2, 8)$. Determine the equation of the hyperbola.

15. Communication Four hyperbolas that have similar equations are given below. Graph the first hyperbola. Then describe how the other three hyperbolas are related to the first hyperbola. Use graphs to illustrate your descriptions.

$$\frac{x^2}{25} - \frac{y^2}{4} = 1 \qquad \frac{x^2}{4} - \frac{y^2}{25} = 1 \qquad \frac{x^2}{25} - \frac{y^2}{4} = -1 \qquad \frac{x^2}{4} - \frac{y^2}{25} = -1$$

16. Application Two hyperbolas are *conjugate hyperbolas* when the transverse axis of one is the conjugate axis of the other.

   a) Write the equations of two conjugate hyperbolas.

   b) Sketch the hyperbolas on the same grid.

   c) Suppose you know the equation of one hyperbola. How can you find the equation of its conjugate hyperbola?

   d) Is it possible to define conjugate ellipses in a similar way? Explain.

17. A hyperbola has centre $C(-3, -5)$ and transverse axis vertical. Determine the equation of each hyperbola.

   a) $a = 6, b = 10$ **b)** $a = 12, b = 8$

   c) $a = 5, c = 20$ **d)** $b = 3, c = 10$

   e) One vertex is $A(-3, -2)$ and the conjugate axis has length 8.

18. a) Write the equations of two hyperbolas that satisfy the following condition. The endpoints of the transverse axis are $A_1(7, 0)$ and $A_2(-1, 0)$.

   b) Write a single equation to represent the family of hyperbolas that satisfy this condition.

19. A hyperbola has foci $F_1(3, 0)$ and $F_2(-3, 0)$. Determine, if possible, the equation of the hyperbola so that:

a) quadrilateral $F_1B_1F_2B_2$ is a square.

b) quadrilateral $A_1B_1A_2B_2$ is a square.

If either of these is not possible, explain why.

20. A hyperbola has foci $F_1(3, 0)$ and $F_2(-3, 0)$. Determine, if possible, the equation of the hyperbola so that:

a) $\triangle F_1B_1B_2$ is equilateral.

b) $\triangle A_1B_1B_2$ is equilateral.

c) $\triangle F_1B_1F_2$ is equilateral.

d) $\triangle A_1B_1A_2$ is equilateral.

If any of these is not possible, explain why.

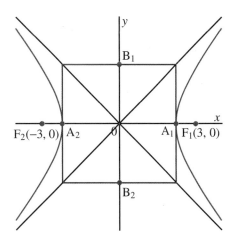

21. A rectangular hyperbola has centre $C(3, 4)$ and transverse axis horizontal. The hyperbola passes through the point $B(7, 6)$. Determine the equation of the hyperbola.

22. Thinking/Inquiry/Problem Solving

a) A square is inscribed in the hyperbola $\dfrac{x^2}{9} - \dfrac{y^2}{25} = 1$. The sides of the square are parallel to the axes. Determine the area of the square.

b) Is it always possible to inscribe a square in the hyperbola defined by $\dfrac{x^2}{a^2} - \dfrac{y^2}{b^2} = 1$? Explain.

23. Determine the coordinates of the points of intersection of each line and hyperbola.

a) $x + 2y = 0$
$x^2 - y^2 = 4$

b) $y = -3x + 3$
$9x^2 - 16y^2 = -144$

c) $x + 4y = 3$
$4x^2 - 9y^2 = 36$

24. Draw a graph of the rectangular hyperbola $x^2 - y^2 = 9$.

a) Determine, if possible, the coordinates of the points of intersection of each line and the hyperbola.

i) $y = \dfrac{1}{2}x$

ii) $y = x$

iii) $y = 2x$

b) Determine the equations of the tangents with slope 2 to the hyperbola.

c) What slopes are possible for tangents to the hyperbola? Explain.

25. What slopes are possible for tangents to the hyperbola $\dfrac{x^2}{a^2} - \dfrac{y^2}{b^2} = 1$? Explain.

C

26. A square, centre the origin, has horizontal and vertical sides 4 units long. The midpoints of the two vertical sides are the foci of a hyperbola. The hyperbola passes through the vertices of the square. Determine the equation of the hyperbola.

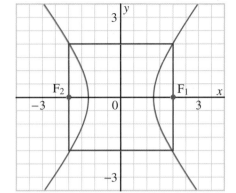

27. Consider the hyperbola $\dfrac{x^2}{36} - \dfrac{y^2}{16} = 1$.

   a) Solve the equation for y.

   b) What happens to the values of y when $|x|$ becomes very large?

   c) Explain why the equations of the asymptotes are $y = \dfrac{2}{3}x$ and $y = -\dfrac{2}{3}x$.

28. From Chapter 7, remember the graph of $y = \dfrac{2}{x}$. We write this equation in the form $xy = 2$. In this exercise, you will show that the graph is a rectangular hyperbola. You will do this by showing that there are points F_1 and F_2 so that $|PF_1 - PF_2|$ is constant for all positions of P on the curve.

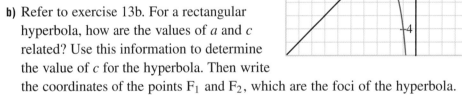

   a) Point A_1 is the point where the line $y = x$ intersects the graph of $xy = 2$. Calculate the length of OA_1. This is the value of a for the hyperbola.

   b) Refer to exercise 13b. For a rectangular hyperbola, how are the values of a and c related? Use this information to determine the value of c for the hyperbola. Then write the coordinates of the points F_1 and F_2, which are the foci of the hyperbola.

   c) Let P be a point that moves so the difference of its distances from F_1 and F_2 is constant. What is the value of the constant in this case? Use this constant to show that the equation of the locus of P is $xy = 2$.

29. Consider the points $O(0, 0)$ and $A(6, 0)$. A point P moves so the slope of OP is twice the slope of AP.

   a) Determine the equation of the locus of P.

   b) Identify the locus, then sketch its graph.

   c) Determine the coordinates of two different points on the locus. Verify that these points satisfy the locus condition.

30. Repeat exercise 29, when the slope of AP is twice the slope of OP.

Remember that a parabola is defined as the locus of a point P that moves so it is always the same distance from a fixed point and a fixed line.

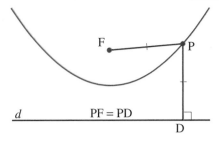

Additional definitions

- The fixed point is the focus, F.
- The fixed line is the directrix, *d*.
- The line through the focus and perpendicular to the directrix intersects the parabola at the vertex, V.
- The chord LR through F and parallel to the directrix is the *latus rectum*.

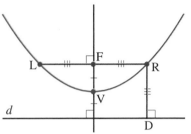

Properties of a parabola

The following properties are consequences of the definitions.

- The line through F and V is the axis of symmetry of the parabola.
- The vertex V is halfway between F and *d*.
- When P is at R, then RF = RD.
  Hence, FR = RD = 2FV
  The distance from F to R is twice the distance from F to V.
  This is the *latus rectum property*.
  We will use this property to graph parabolas.

We can use the definition of a parabola to derive the equation of a parabola with vertex O(0, 0) and focus on the *x*-axis.

The focus is F(*p*, 0) and the directrix is the line $x = -p$.
Let P(*x*, *y*) be any point on the parabola.
Then, D is the point (−*p*, *y*).

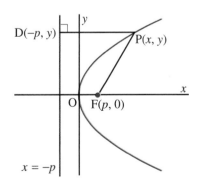

$$PF = PD$$
$$\sqrt{(x-p)^2 + y^2} = \sqrt{(x+p)^2}$$

Square each side.
$$(x-p)^2 + y^2 = (x+p)^2$$
$$x^2 - 2px + p^2 + y^2 = x^2 + 2px + p^2$$
$$y^2 = 4px$$

This is the *standard equation* of a parabola with vertex O(0, 0) and focus F(*p*, 0) on the *x*-axis.

When we reflect the graph of the parabola with focus on the x-axis in the line $y = x$, we get the graph of a parabola with focus on the y-axis. Interchange x and y in the equation $y^2 = 4px$ to get $x^2 = 4py$. This is the standard equation of a parabola with vertex O(0, 0) and focus on the y-axis.

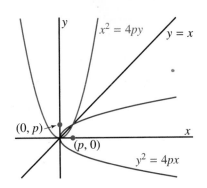

Take Note

Standard Equations of a Parabola, Vertex (0, 0)

Focus on the *x*-axis

$y^2 = 4px$

↑

    x is not squared.

When $p > 0$, the parabola opens right.

When $p < 0$, the parabola opens left.

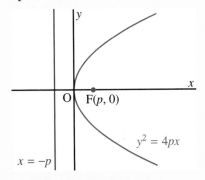

Coordinates of focus: $(p, 0)$

Equation of directrix: $x = -p$

Focus on the *y*-axis

$x^2 = 4py$

↑

    y is not squared.

When $p > 0$, the parabola opens up.

When $p < 0$, the parabola opens down.

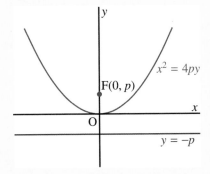

Coordinates of focus: $(0, p)$

Equation of directrix: $y = -p$

When the equation of a parabola is given in standard form, the value of p can be determined from the equation. We can use this value to determine the coordinates of the focus. When we know the coordinates of the focus and the vertex, we can graph other points on the parabola using the following rule.

The 2-3-4 Rule for Graphing a Parabola

A parabola is completely determined by its vertex and focus.

1. Plot the vertex V and the focus F. Let the distance FV be p.

2. From F, move $2p$ units perpendicular to the axis to each of points L and R.

3. From F, move $3p$ units farther along the axis to G, then $4p$ units perpendicular to the axis to each of points S and T.

4. Draw the parabola through S, L, V, R, and T.

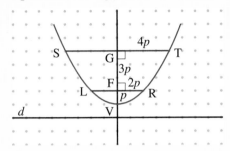

Segments FR, FG, and GT are 2, 3, and 4 times as long as segment VF.

In the 2-3-4 Rule, the latus rectum property tells us that L and R are on the parabola. To explain why S and T are on the parabola, see exercise 5.

Example 1

A parabola has the equation $y^2 = -6x$.

a) Determine the coordinates of the focus and the equation of the directrix.

b) Graph the parabola.

Solution

a) $y^2 = -6x$

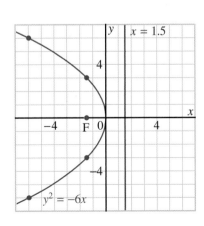

Since x is not squared, the focus is on the x-axis. Compare the given equation, $y^2 = -6x$, with the standard equation, $y^2 = 4px$.

$4p = -6$

$p = -1.5$

Since $p < 0$, the parabola opens to the left. The coordinates of the focus are $(-1.5, 0)$. The equation of the directrix is $x = 1.5$.

b) Plot the vertex $(0, 0)$.

Use the 2-3-4 Rule. The focus is 1.5 units from the vertex.

From F, move 2×1.5 units = 3 units up and down to $(-1.5, 3)$ and $(-1.5, -3)$. Plot these points.

From F, move 3×1.5 units = 4.5 units left and 4×1.5 units = 6 units up and down to $(-6, 6)$ and $(-6, -6)$. Plot these points.

Draw a parabola through the four plotted points and the origin.

In *Example 1*, if the equation had been $y^2 = 6x$, the parabola would have opened right.

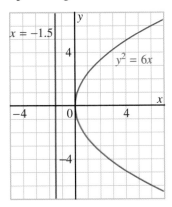

If the equation had been $x^2 = 6y$, the parabola would have opened up.

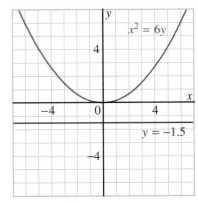

If the equation had been $x^2 = -6y$, the parabola would have opened down.

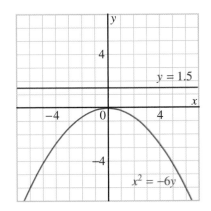

Example 2

Graph the parabola $(x + 2)^2 = 8(y - 1)$. Show the coordinates of the vertex, the focus, and the equations of the directrix and the axis of symmetry.

Solution

$(x + 2)^2 = 8(y - 1)$

Since $(y - 1)$ is not squared, the axis of symmetry is vertical.

$$4p = 8$$
$$p = 2$$

Since $p > 0$, the parabola opens up.

The coordinates of the vertex are $(-2, 1)$.

Since $p = 2$, the focus is 2 units above the vertex.

Its coordinates are $F(-2, 3)$.

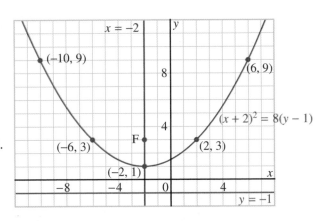

Use the 2-3-4 Rule. The focus is 2 units above the vertex. From the focus, move 2×2 units = 4 units left and right to $(-6, 3)$ and $(2, 3)$. Plot these points.

From the focus, move 3×2 units = 6 units up, then 4×2 units = 8 units left and right to $(-10, 9)$ and $(6, 9)$. Plot these points.

Draw a parabola through the four plotted points and the vertex. The directrix is 2 units below the vertex. Its equation is $y = -1$. The equation of the axis of symmetry is $x = -2$.

Take Note

Standard Equations of a Parabola, Vertex (h, k)

Axis of symmetry is horizontal.

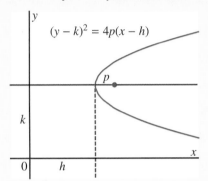

$(y - k)^2 = 4p(x - h)$

Axis of symmetry is vertical.

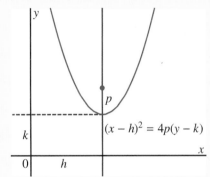

$(x - h)^2 = 4p(y - k)$

Coordinates of focus: $(h + p, k)$
Equation of directrix: $x = h - p$
Equation of axis of symmetry: $y = k$
Opening: right when $p > 0$,
        left when $p < 0$

Coordinates of focus: $(h, k + p)$
Equation of directrix: $y = k - p$
Equation of axis of symmetry: $x = h$
Opening: up when $p > 0$,
        down when $p < 0$

9.4   Exercises

1. State the coordinates of the focus and the equation of the directrix of the parabola defined by each equation.

a) $y^2 = 4x$

b) $y^2 = 12x$

c) $y^2 = -20x$

d) $x^2 = 8y$

e) $x^2 = -2y$

f) $x^2 = 3y$

g) $y^2 = -9x$

h) $x^2 = -5y$

2. State the coordinates of the vertex, the equation of the axis of symmetry, and the direction of opening of the parabola defined by each equation.

a) $(y - 2)^2 = 4(x - 3)$

b) $(y + 1)^2 = -8(x - 2)$

c) $(x + 1)^2 = 4(y + 5)$

d) $(x - 4)^2 = -12(y - 1)$

e) $(y - 3)^2 = 8x$

f) $x^2 = 16(y - 2)$

B

3. For each parabola:

> **i)** Determine the coordinates of the focus and the equation of the directrix.
>
> **ii)** Graph the parabola.

a) $y^2 = 8x$ **b)** $y^2 = -3x$ **c)** $x^2 = 4y$ **d)** $x^2 = -10y$

4. Knowledge/Understanding Sketch the parabola defined by each equation. Show the coordinates of the vertex and the focus, and the equations of the axis of symmetry and the directrix.

a) $(y + 2)^2 = 4(x - 1)$

b) $(y - 3)^2 = -2(x + 4)$

c) $(x - 3)^2 = 2(y + 2)$

d) $x^2 = -3(y - 1)$

e) $y^2 = -8(x - 2)$

f) $x^2 = 4(y + 1)$

5. Communication Refer to the 2-3-4 Rule on page 547.

a) Explain why a parabola is completely determined by its vertex and focus.

b) Explain why TF = TE.

c) Explain why T is on the parabola with vertex V and focus F.

d) Explain why S is on the parabola.

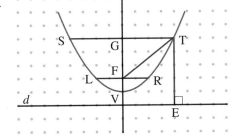

6. Write the equation of the parabola that satisfies each description.

a) directrix $y = 2$, focus $O(0, 0)$

b) vertex $O(0, 0)$, focus $F(0, 4)$

c) vertex $V(2, 2)$, focus $F(2, 0)$

d) vertex $V(0, 4)$, directrix $y = 0$

7. A parabola has vertex $O(0, 0)$ and focus on a coordinate axis. Write the equation of the parabola in each case.

a) The focus is: **i)** $F(4, 0)$ **ii)** $F(-6, 0)$ **iii)** $F(0, 3)$

b) The directrix is the line defined by $y = 8$.

8. Determine the equation of the parabola defined by the given conditions.

a) The vertex is $V(1, 2)$ and the focus is $F(3, 2)$.

b) The vertex is $V(-1, 3)$ and the equation of the directrix is $x = 2$.

c) The focus is $F(2, 0)$ and the equation of the directrix is $y = -6$.

9. A square, centre the origin, has horizontal and vertical sides 2 units long. Consider the side RS of the square. One parabola has focus R and vertex S. Another parabola has focus S and vertex R.

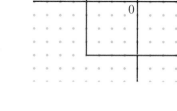

a) Sketch the square and the two parabolas.

b) Determine the equations of the parabolas.

c) Determine the x- and y-intercepts of the graphs of the parabolas.

d) Draw a large, accurate graph of the square and the two parabolas.

e) Write the equations of two other parabolas whose foci and vertices are the endpoints of one of the other sides of the square. Show these parabolas on your graph.

10. Use the definition of a parabola to derive the standard equation of a parabola, with vertex $O(0, 0)$, and focus $F(0, p)$ on the y-axis.

11. Application In your previous work with parabolas, equations had the form $y = ax^2$. At that time, you were told that the equation represents a parabola. In Chapter 8, a parabola was defined as the locus of a point that moves so it is equidistant from a fixed point and a fixed line. How can you be certain that the graph of the equation $y = ax^2$ satisfies this definition?

12. There are infinitely many parabolas with a vertical axis of symmetry and focus at the origin.

a) Write the equations of two of these parabolas.

b) Write a single equation to represent the family of parabolas with a vertical axis of symmetry and focus at the origin.

13. A parabola with focus $F(0, 1)$ and vertex $O(0, 0)$ is given. Chord AB is perpendicular to the axis of the parabola. Determine the coordinates of A and B so that:

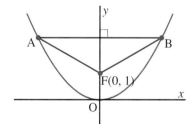

a) $\triangle AFB$ is a right triangle.

b) $\triangle AFB$ is an equilateral triangle.

c) $\triangle AOB$ is a right triangle.

d) $\triangle AOB$ is an equilateral triangle.

14. **Thinking/Inquiry/Problem Solving** Sketch the graph of $y^2 = 4x$. Sketch the directrix. Label each point: the focus F; a general point P(x, y) on the parabola; and D, the point where the perpendicular from P meets the directrix. Determine the coordinates of P in each case.

a) Triangle PFD is a right triangle. b) Triangle PFD is equilateral.

15. Point P moves so it is always 2 units farther from the point A(4, 0) than it is from the line $x = -4$.

a) Determine the equation of the locus of P.

b) Explain how you can tell that the locus is a parabola. Identify the coordinates of its vertex and its focus, and the equation of its directrix.

c) Draw a large, accurate graph of the parabola. Show the focus and the directrix on the graph.

d) Since the graph is a parabola, it is the locus of point P that moves so it is equidistant from its focus and directrix. Explain why it is possible for P to satisfy this locus condition and the locus condition at the beginning of the exercise.

16. a) Determine the coordinates of the points of intersection of the lines in each list with the parabola $y = x^2$.

   i) $y = x + 2$ ii) $y = -2x - 1$
      $y = 2x + 3$ $y = -3x - 2$
      $y = 3x + 4$ $y = -4x - 3$

b) Graph the parabola and the six lines in part a on the same grid. Write the next line in each list, then determine the coordinates of its points of intersection with the parabola $y = x^2$.

c) Extend each list upward. Determine the coordinates of the points of intersection of each line with the parabola $y = x^2$. What do you notice about the two lists?

17. a) Draw a large, accurate graph of the parabola $y = x^2$ on grid paper.

b) Determine the equations of the tangents to the parabola with each slope.
   i) 1   ii) 2   iii) 3   iv) 4

c) Draw the tangents on the graph.

d) Use the graph. Write the equations of the tangents to the parabola with each slope.
   i) –1   ii) –2   iii) –3   iv) –4

18. Determine the coordinates of the points of intersection of each line and parabola.

a) $y = x^2$ b) $y = x^2$ c) $y = x^2 - 4$ d) $y^2 = x - 2$
   $y = x$ $x - y = -2$ $y = -x + 6$ $y = x - 4$

C

19. Determine whether the 2-3-4 Rule can be extended to plot more points on a parabola. If it can, explain how you can be sure that it can. If it cannot, give an example to show why not.

20. What condition(s) must be satisfied by p, h, and k, for each equation to represent a parabola whose focus is at the origin?

a) $(y - k)^2 = 4p(x - h)$ **b)** $(x - h)^2 = 4p(y - k)$

21. This diagram shows a parabola, an ellipse, and a hyperbola that share a common focus at the point F(6, 0). The line d with equation $x = 12$ is the directrix of the parabola.

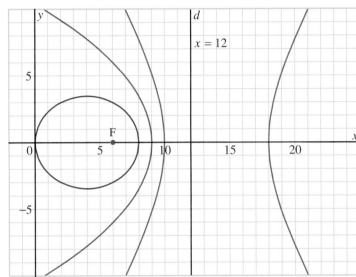

Parabola
$y^2 = -12(x - 9)$

Ellipse
$\dfrac{(x - 4)^2}{16} + \dfrac{y^2}{12} = 1$

Hyperbola
$\dfrac{(x - 14)^2}{16} - \dfrac{y^2}{48} = 1$

a) Verify that the equations listed beside the graph are correct.

b) A *conic* can be defined as the locus of a point P that moves so the ratio of its distance to a fixed point F to its distance to a fixed line d is constant. For example, in the diagram above, this ratio is as follows, where N is on the line $x = 12$:

$$\frac{PF}{PN} = \frac{\text{distance from P to (6, 0)}}{\text{distance from P to the line } x = 12}$$

i) Choose three different points on the parabola. Verify that $\dfrac{PF}{PN} = 1$.

ii) Choose three different points on the ellipse. Verify that $\dfrac{PF}{PN}$ is constant. What is the value of the constant for this ellipse?

iii) Repeat part ii for the hyperbola.

c) Visualize other ellipses on this diagram that have one focus at F. How would the value of $\dfrac{PF}{PN}$ change for these ellipses?

d) Repeat part c for hyperbolas.

1. Sketch each hyperbola. Identify the coordinates of its foci.

   a) $\dfrac{x^2}{16} - \dfrac{y^2}{9} = 1$

   b) $\dfrac{x^2}{25} - \dfrac{y^2}{4} = -1$

2. A hyperbola has centre O(0, 0) and a horizontal transverse axis. Determine the equation of each hyperbola.

   a) $a = 5, b = 12$

   b) The hyperbola passes through P(2, 3) and one focus is F(2, 0).

   c) One vertex is A(3, 0) and one focus is F(5, 0).

3. Sketch each hyperbola. Label each sketch with the equations of the asymptotes.

   a) $\dfrac{(x - 1)^2}{9} - \dfrac{(y + 2)^2}{4} = 1$

   b) $\dfrac{(x + 3)^2}{9} - \dfrac{(y - 1)^2}{16} = -1$

4. A hyperbola has centre C(1, −2) and a horizontal conjugate axis. Determine the equation of each hyperbola.

   a) $a = 4, c = 10$

   b) One vertex is A(1, 1) and the conjugate axis has length 5.

   c) The transverse axis has length 2 and the conjugate axis has length 8.

5. Sketch the parabola defined by each equation. Show the coordinates of the focus and the equation of the directrix.

   a) $y^2 = 10x$

   b) $x^2 = -5y$

6. Determine the equation of each parabola.

   a) The focus is F(2, 3) and the directrix is $y = -1$.

   b) The vertex is O(0, 0), the axis of symmetry is the y-axis, and the parabola passes through P(−1, 8).

7. Determine the equation of each parabola.

   a) The focus is F(2, 4) and the directrix is $x = 6$.

   b) The vertex is V(8, 3), the axis of symmetry is horizontal, and the parabola passes through A(−10, 0).

8. Determine the coordinates of the point of intersection of each line and conic.

   a) $x + y = 9$
   $xy = 14$

   b) $y = -x^2 + 3$
   $x + y = 1$

9.5 Applications of Quadratic Relations

The signals from a communications satellite reflect off the surface of a dish antenna and are concentrated at the receiver.

A dish antenna works because it has a cross section that is a parabola. When incoming signals are parallel to the axis of symmetry, the signals reflect off the parabola and pass through the focus. The receiver is placed at the focus.

Conversely, in a parabolic headlight reflector, the bulb is placed at the focus, so the light rays reflect off the surface and are emitted as parallel rays.

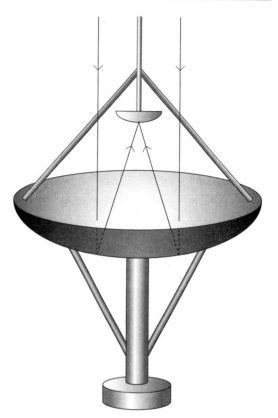

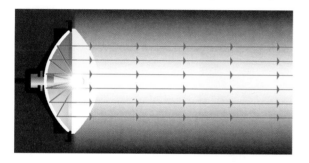

We can use the equation of a parabola to solve problems that involve parabolic reflectors.

Example 1

The parabolic dish antenna above is 60 cm wide and 7 cm deep. Calculate the distance from the centre of the dish to the receiver.

Solution

Sketch a cross section of the parabola, with its vertex at the origin.

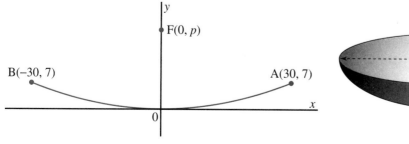

The equation of the parabola has the form $x^2 = 4py$.

The receiver is placed at the focus $F(0, p)$.

Since the dish is 60 cm wide and 7 cm deep, points A(30, 7) and B(–30, 7) lie on the parabola.

Substitute $x = 30$ and $y = 7$ in $x^2 = 4py$.

$$30^2 = 4p(7)$$
$$28p = 900$$
$$p = \frac{900}{28}$$
$$\doteq 32.14$$

The coordinates of the focus are approximately F(0, 32).

The receiver is 32 cm from the centre of the dish.

The planets move in elliptical orbits around the sun. The centre of the sun is at one focus of each ellipse.

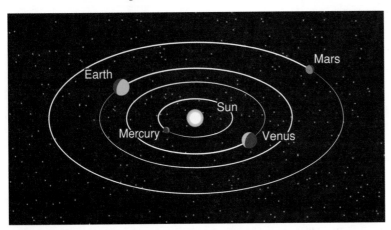

Many satellites travel in elliptical orbits with the centre of Earth at one focus (see *Example 2*).

We can use this property of elliptical orbits to solve problems that involve the motion of planets or satellites.

Example 2

The path of a satellite around Earth is an ellipse, with the centre of Earth at one focus.

A satellite has a minimum altitude of 1000 km and a maximum altitude of 3500 km. The radius of Earth is approximately 6400 km. Determine an equation for the path of the satellite.

Solution

Sketch a cross section with the centre of the ellipse at the origin of coordinate axes, and the centre of Earth at the right focus, F. The vertices of the ellipse are A_1 and A_2.

The equation of the ellipse has the form
$$\frac{x^2}{a^2} + \frac{y^2}{b^2} = 1.$$

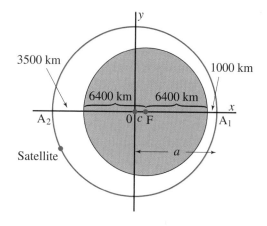

The distance between the vertices is:
$$2a = 3500 + 6400 + 6400 + 1000$$
$$= 17\ 300$$
$$a = 8650$$

The distance from F to A_1 is 7400 km; so
$$c = a - 7400$$
$$= 8650 - 7400$$
$$= 1250$$

But $c^2 = a^2 - b^2$; so $b^2 = a^2 - c^2$

Substitute $a = 8650$ and $c = 1250$.
$$b^2 = 8650^2 - 1250^2$$
$$= 73\ 260\ 000$$
$$b \doteq 8559$$

An equation for the path of the satellite is:
$$\frac{x^2}{8650^2} + \frac{y^2}{8559^2} = 1$$

9.5) Exercises

B

 1. A bridge over a river is supported by a parabolic arch. The arch is 200 m wide at water level. The maximum height of the arch is 80 m.

a) Write an equation to represent the arch.

b) What is the height of the arch measured from a point on the water 40 m from the centre of the arch?

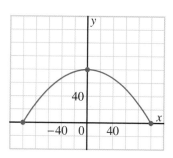

2. Before the use of the Global Positioning System (GPS), the LORAN (LOng RAnge Navigation) system was used to determine the position of a ship. The LORAN system is based on the definition of a hyperbola. Equipment on a ship determines the difference of the distances to two transmitters on shore by measuring the time difference for simultaneous signals to reach the ship from the transmitters. Suppose the transmitters are 300 km apart and are at the foci of a hyperbola. The ship is 200 km farther from one transmitter than the other. The foci are $F_1(150, 0)$ and $F_2(-150, 0)$. The position of the ship is $S(x, y)$. Determine the equation of the hyperbola on which the ship is located.

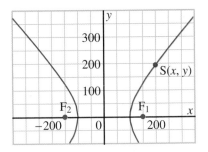

3. An ornamental pool has the shape of an ellipse. The major axis is 15 m long and the minor axis is 9 m long.

a) Write an equation for the ellipse.

b) Calculate the width of the pool at a point on the major axis that is 5 m from the centre.

4. The cables of a suspension bridge hang in a curve that approximates a parabola. The road passes through the vertex. The supporting towers are 550 m apart and 50 m high.

a) Determine an equation of the parabola.

b) Determine the height of the cables at a point 25 m from the vertex.

5. Knowledge/Understanding The roof of an ice rink is supported by parabolic arches. Each arch is 20 m high and spans 80 m.

a) Determine an equation of the parabolic arch.

b) Calculate the height of the arch at a point 15 m from the centre of the base of the arch.

6. The Colosseum in Rome has the shape of an ellipse 188 m long and 156 m wide. The formula for the area of an ellipse with semi-major axis a units and semi-minor b units is $A = \pi ab$.

a) Calculate the area of the Colosseum.

b) How is the area of an ellipse related to the area of a circle?

c) Pose a problem about the Colosseum. Solve the problem you posed.

7. The arch of a bridge has the shape of one branch of a rectangular hyperbola. The arch is 100 m wide at its base. The highest point on the arch is 27 m above its base.

a) Determine an equation of the hyperbola.

b) Calculate the height of the arch at a point 20 m from the centre of its base.

8. A parabolic dish antenna is 80 cm wide and 9 cm deep. The receiver is placed at the focus of the parabola. Calculate the distance from the centre of the dish to the receiver.

9. Pluto's orbit around the sun is elliptical, with the centre of the sun at one focus. The diameter of the sun is approximately 1 392 000 km. The closest distance between Pluto and the sun is 4.48 billion kilometres, and the farthest distance is 7.36 billion kilometres.

a) Determine an equation of the orbit.

b) Derive a formula that could be used to determine similar equations for other planets.

10. Application A stone is thrown horizontally from a bridge over a river. The path of the stone is a parabola. When the stone is thrown, it is 30 m above the river. The stone hits the water at a horizontal distance of 45 m from where it was thrown. Pose a problem about this situation. Solve the problem you posed.

11. Communication In the 1800s, a large deep parabolic reflector, called a sounding board, was placed behind the podium in a meeting room. The purpose was to direct the sound of the person speaking toward the audience. Explain why the sounding board did not work as intended.

12. A road bridge is supported by a hyperbolic arch. The arch is 250 m wide at its base. The maximum height of the arch is 60 m. Pose a problem about this situation. Solve the problem you posed.

13. A plane, flying at a constant altitude of 10 000 m, is observed from an airport's control tower. Show that the equation that relates the horizontal distance, x, and the direct distance, d, from the tower to the plane is that of a hyperbola.

14. A stream of water from a hose fastened on the ground follows a parabolic curve. The stream of water reaches a maximum height of 20 m at a horizontal distance of 32 m from the nozzle of the hose. Determine an equation for the stream of water, then sketch its graph.

15. Thinking/Inquiry/Problem Solving A tunnel is built through a mountain. The tunnel is 20 m wide. The road is 15 m wide and each sidewalk is 2.5 m wide. The cross section of the tunnel is half an ellipse. For trucks to drive through the tunnel, it must be at least 4 m high at all points above the road. The smallest possible tunnel is used. Calculate the height of the tunnel at the centre of the road.

C

16. The orbit of a satellite is an ellipse with the centre of Earth at one focus. One satellite has an orbit with major axis 15 540 km and minor axis 15 490 km. The centre of the orbit is 600 km from the centre of Earth. The radius of Earth is 6370 km. Calculate the height of the satellite at each point.

a) its lowest point (the *perigee*)   **b)** its highest point (the *apogee*)

9.6 The General Equation of a Conic

When the equation of a conic is written in standard form, the numbers in the equation indicate certain properties of the graph.

For example, in Section 9.2, *Example 2*, we graphed the ellipse $\dfrac{(x+1)^2}{9} + \dfrac{(y-2)^2}{25} = 1$.

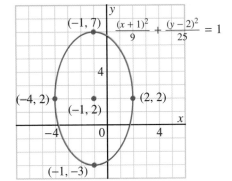

From the equation, we can identify the coordinates of the centre of the ellipse, and the lengths of its major and minor axes.

We can expand the left side of the equation and write it in a different form.

$$\frac{(x+1)^2}{9} + \frac{(y-2)^2}{25} = 1$$

Multiply by the common denominator 225.

$$25(x+1)^2 + 9(y-2)^2 = 225$$
$$25(x^2 + 2x + 1) + 9(y^2 - 4y + 4) = 225$$
$$25x^2 + 50x + 25 + 9y^2 - 36y + 36 - 225 = 0$$
$$25x^2 + 9y^2 + 50x - 36y - 164 = 0$$

This equation is in *general* form.

When an equation is in general form, we cannot identify the properties of the graph from the equation. To determine the properties, we must first write the equation in standard form.

Example 1

Consider the conic defined by $4x^2 - 9y^2 + 32x + 18y + 91 = 0$.

a) Write the equation in standard form.

b) Describe, then sketch, the graph of the conic.

c) Determine the coordinates of the foci.

Solution

a) $4x^2 - 9y^2 + 32x + 18y + 91 = 0$

Collect the terms that contain x, and the terms that contain y.
$$4x^2 + 32x - 9y^2 + 18y + 91 = 0$$

Complete each square.

$$4(x^2 + 8x) - 9(y^2 - 2y) + 91 = 0$$
$$4(x^2 + 8x + 16 - 16) - 9(y^2 - 2y + 1 - 1) + 91 = 0$$
$$4(x + 4)^2 - 64 - 9(y - 1)^2 + 9 + 91 = 0$$
$$4(x + 4)^2 - 9(y - 1)^2 = -36$$

Divide each side by 36.

$$\frac{(x + 4)^2}{9} - \frac{(y - 1)^2}{4} = -1$$

b) The equation represents a hyperbola.

The coordinates of the centre: $(-4, 1)$
The length of the transverse axis: $2a = 4$
The length of the conjugate axis: $2b = 6$
The transverse axis is vertical.

Coordinates of the vertices:
$(-4, 1 + 2)$, or $(-4, 3)$
$(-4, 1 - 2)$, or $(-4, -1)$

c) For a hyperbola:
$$c^2 = a^2 + b^2$$
$$= 4 + 9$$
$$= 13$$
$$c = \sqrt{13}$$

The coordinates of the foci: $(-4, 1 + \sqrt{13})$ and $(-4, 1 - \sqrt{13})$;
or approximately $(-4, 4.6)$ and $(-4, -2.6)$

In *Example 1*, we could have predicted that the given equation represents a hyperbola because the quadratic terms are separated by a $-$ sign.

An equation that represents a parabola contains only one squared term; hence, only one square can be completed.

Example 2

Consider the conic defined by $x^2 + 10x + 4y + 13 = 0$.

a) Write the equation in standard form.

b) Describe, then sketch, the graph of the conic.

Solution

a) $x^2 + 10x + 4y + 13 = 0$

Complete the square for the x terms.

$x^2 + 10x + 25 - 25 + 4y + 13 = 0$

$(x + 5)^2 + 4y - 12 = 0$

$(x + 5)^2 = -4y + 12$

$(x + 5)^2 = -4(y - 3)$

b) The equation represents a parabola.
It has the form $(x - h)^2 = 4p(y - k)$.
The coordinates of the vertex are $(-5, 3)$.
The parabola opens down.
The equation of the axis of symmetry is $x = -5$.
Use the 2-3-4 Rule to sketch the parabola.

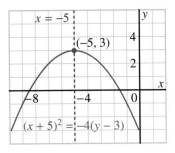

The equations in *Examples 1* and *2* are particular cases of the general equation $Ax^2 + By^2 + 2Gx + 2Fy + C = 0$. Remember, from Section 8.5, that when a plane intersects a cone the result is usually a circle, an ellipse, a hyperbola, or a parabola. However, special cases including a single point, a line, or two intersecting lines can occur. The same is true for this general equation. It usually represents a circle, an ellipse, a hyperbola, or a parabola, but it can also represent a single point, two intersecting lines, or nothing at all (see exercise 14).

9.6 Exercises

A

1. State which equations represent each conic.

    i) a circle   **ii)** an ellipse   **iii)** a hyperbola   **iv)** a parabola

    a) $x^2 - 6y - 3 = 0$ **b)** $4x^2 - 4y^2 - 9 = 0$ **c)** $x^2 + 4y^2 - 8 = 0$

    d) $3x^2 + 3y^2 - 5 = 0$ **e)** $x = 6y^2$ **f)** $2x^2 - 3y^2 + 6 = 0$

 2. Each equation represents a conic. State which equation represents each conic.

    i) a circle   **ii)** an ellipse   **iii)** a hyperbola   **iv)** a parabola

    a) $9x^2 + 4y^2 - 54x + 16y + 61 = 0$ **b)** $2x^2 - 3y^2 - 8x - 6y + 11 = 0$

    c) $y^2 - 4x + 6y - 23 = 0$ **d)** $x^2 + y^2 + 4x + 5y = 0$

3. Determine which equations represent circles. For each circle, determine the radius and the coordinates of its centre.

a) $x^2 + y^2 - 10x + 4y + 20 = 0$

b) $x^2 + y^2 - 6x - 2y - 15 = 0$

c) $x^2 + y^2 + 6x - 2y + 12 = 0$

d) $x^2 + y^2 + x + y - 4 = 0$

e) $2x^2 + 2y^2 - 4x + 3y - 5 = 0$

f) $3x^2 + 3y^2 + 5x - 9y + 40 = 0$

B

4. Sketch the circle represented by each equation.

a) $x^2 + y^2 - 6x + 5 = 0$

b) $x^2 + y^2 + 2y - 8 = 0$

c) $x^2 + y^2 - 2x - 6y = 0$

d) $x^2 + y^2 + 6x - 4y + 9 = 0$

e) $x^2 + y^2 - 6x + 10y + 25 = 0$

f) $x^2 + y^2 + 8x + 8y + 16 = 0$

5. Convert each equation to standard form.

a) $x^2 - 2x - 3y - 8 = 0$

b) $x^2 + 6x + 5y - 1 = 0$

c) $y^2 - 4x + 4y + 24 = 0$

d) $y^2 + 3x - 2y + 7 = 0$

6. Write the standard form of the equation for each ellipse.

a) $9x^2 + 64y^2 - 36x - 128y - 476 = 0$

b) $4x^2 + y^2 + 24x - 6y + 41 = 0$

c) $9x^2 + 4y^2 - 18x - 24y + 9 = 0$

d) $4x^2 + 25y^2 + 16x - 100y + 16 = 0$

7. Identify each equation as representing a circle, a parabola, or an ellipse.

a) $x^2 + 2y^2 + 12x + 4y + 8 = 0$

b) $3x^2 + 18x + 3y + 5 = 0$

c) $8x^2 + 8y^2 - 32x - 32y = 0$

d) $-2x^2 - 5y^2 + 10 = 0$

e) $5y^2 + 2x + 30y + 9 = 0$

f) $3x^2 + 3y^2 + 6x + 9y + 7 = 0$

8. For each hyperbola whose equation is given below:

   i) Write the standard equation.

   ii) Determine the lengths of the transverse and conjugate axes, the coordinates of the vertices and foci, and the equations of the asymptotes.

a) $4x^2 - 8x - 9y^2 = -40$

b) $x^2 - 4x - 4y^2 = -20$

c) $16x^2 + 32x - 25y^2 - 50y = -391$

d) $4x^2 - y^2 - 6y = -91$

e) $x^2 - 2y^2 = -50$

f) $3(x + 2)^2 - 4(y + 1)^2 = -24$

9. **Knowledge/Understanding** Each equation defines a conic. Write the equation in standard form. Sketch the conic.

a) $2x^2 + y^2 + 12x - 2y + 15 = 0$

b) $4x^2 + 9y^2 - 8x + 36y + 4 = 0$

c) $x^2 - 9y^2 - 4x + 18y - 14 = 0$

d) $x^2 - 4y^2 - 2x - 3 = 0$

e) $y^2 - 4x + 8y + 3 = 0$

f) $x^2 + 2x + 3y + 4 = 0$

10. Communication Describe the graph of each equation.

a) $x^2 + y^2 - 8x + 6y + 9 = 0$

b) $x^2 + 4y^2 - 2x + 16y + 13 = 0$

c) $3x^2 + 4y^2 + 18x - 16y + 31 = 0$

d) $3x^2 - 2y^2 - 36x + 96 = 0$

e) $y^2 - 8x - 8y = 0$

f) $6x^2 + 24x - y + 19 = 0$

11.
i) Classify each equation as representing a circle, a parabola, an ellipse, or a hyperbola.

ii) Write each equation in standard form.

iii) Identify the vertices and foci where appropriate.

iv) Sketch the curve.

a) $16x^2 - 9y^2 - 64x + 72y - 224 = 0$ b) $x^2 + y^2 - 10x - 10y + 25 = 0$

c) $4y^2 - x - 24y + 40 = 0$

d) $4x^2 + 9y^2 + 24x - 90y + 225 = 0$

e) $9x^2 + 4y^2 + 54x - 40y + 145 = 0$ f) $x^2 + y^2 + 4x - 2y - 5 = 0$

g) $4x^2 - 9y^2 - 8x - 54y - 77 = 0$ h) $x^2 - 4y^2 + 8x + 20 = 0$

i) $8x^2 + 32x - y + 35 = 0$ j) $3x^2 + 3y^2 - 18x - 24y - 33 = 0$

12. Application The diagram shows three overlapping squares.

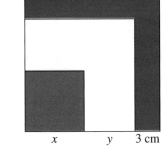

a) The green region has the same area as the blue region. What is the equation that relates x and y?

b) Graph the equation that relates x and y.

13. Consider the equation $Ax^2 + By^2 + 2Gx + 2Fy + C = 0$. What conditions must be satisfied by the coefficients for this equation to represent each conic section?

a) a circle with centre O(0, 0)

b) a rectangular hyperbola with centre O(0, 0) and vertices on the x-axis

c) a rectangular hyperbola with centre O(0, 0) and vertices on the y-axis

d) a parabola with vertex O(0, 0) and a horizontal axis of symmetry

e) an ellipse with centre O(0, 0) and vertices on the y-axis

14. Thinking/Inquiry/Problem Solving

a) Describe the graph of each equation, if it exists.

i) $3x^2 + 2y^2 - 6x + 16y + 35 = 0$

ii) $2x^2 + y^2 - 12x - 2y + 20 = 0$

iii) $x^2 - y^2 + 4x + 6y - 5 = 0$

b) Write the simplest equation you can that represents the same picture as each equation in part a.

1. A building's entrance is a parabolic arch 2.8 m high at the centre and 3.7 m wide at the base. Determine an equation that represents the arch.

2. A design on a coordinate grid consists of a series of triangles. Each triangle has the line segment that joins $A(0, -2)$ and $B(0, 2)$ as its base. The perimeter of each triangle is 12 units. Determine the equation of the curve on which the third vertex lies.

3. A pool is elliptical. The major axis is 10 m long and the minor axis is 6 m long.
   a) Write an equation for the ellipse.
   b) Calculate the width of the pool at a point on the minor axis that is 1 m from the centre.
   c) Pose a problem about the pool. Solve the problem.

4. Write the standard form for each ellipse.
   a) $16x^2 + 49y^2 - 32x + 98y - 719 = 0$
   b) $36x^2 + 25y^2 + 144x - 150y - 531 = 0$

5. Write the standard form for each hyperbola.
   a) $64x^2 - 4y^2 - 256x - 32y - 64 = 0$
   b) $16x^2 - 9y^2 + 96x + 36y + 252 = 0$

6. Write the standard form for each parabola.
   a) $x^2 + 4x + 4y = 0$
   b) $y^2 - 2y - 4x - 19 = 0$

7. i) Identify each conic.
    ii) Write each equation in standard form.
    iii) Identify the vertices and foci where appropriate.
    iv) Sketch each curve.
    a) $x^2 + 4y^2 - 6x + 1 = 0$ b) $2x^2 - y^2 - 4x - 4y = 0$
    c) $x^2 + 8x - 8y + 16 = 0$ d) $2x^2 + 2y^2 - 3y - 1 = 0$

The Reflection Property of a Parabola

In Section 9.5, you learned the following reflection property of a parabola: all incoming light rays parallel to the axis of symmetry reflect to the focus.

This has practical applications. A parabolic mirror has a cross section that has the shape of a parabola. Parabolic mirrors are used in telescopes to focus the light from distant stars. When a parabolic mirror is pointed at the sun, the parallel rays upon reflection are concentrated at the focus; a dry stick placed there will burst into flames. This is the origin of the word "focus" in the study of conics; in Latin, focus translates to hearth or fireplace.

We will verify that incoming rays parallel to the axis of symmetry of a parabola reflect to the focus. We will use algebra. We start with the equation of the parabola and a ray of light parallel to its axis of symmetry. We then determine the path of the reflected ray, and verify that it passes through the focus.

Formulating Questions

Consider the parabola $y^2 = 16x$. Its focus is F(4, 0) and its axis of symmetry is the x-axis. Suppose a horizontal ray at height 4 units strikes the parabola at the point C(1, 4).

Does the reflected ray pass through the focus F(4, 0)?

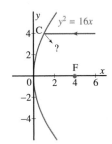

Selecting Strategies, Resources, Technology, and Tools

From physics, we know the following properties of light.

• In general, light travels in straight lines.

• Light reflects from a curved surface, such as a parabola, as if it was reflecting from a line that is tangent to the parabola at the point of reflection.

• The angle of incidence and the angle of reflection are equal. By symmetry, the incoming and reflected rays make equal angles with the tangent at the point of reflection.

Thus, the ray will reflect off the parabola at the point (1, 4) as if it was reflecting off the tangent at (1, 4). So, that's our first job — to determine the equation of the tangent at (1, 4). We can then construct the reflected ray and check whether it passes through the focus.

In *Insights into a Rich Problem* in Chapter 4, we found a tangent to a parabola by moving a line with a given slope parallel to itself until the line intersected the parabola at a single point. However, in that problem, we knew the slope of the tangent and did not know the point of tangency. Here, the reverse is true. We know the point of tangency, but do not know the slope of the tangent. So, we represent the slope as an unknown parameter m.

Representing the Tangent in Mathematical Form

Let m be the slope of the tangent at C(1, 4). Members of the family of lines with slope m that pass through the point C(1, 4) have equation

$$y - 4 = m(x - 1)$$

To determine the coordinates of the points of intersection of the line and the parabola, we solve this system of equations.

$$y - 4 = mx - m \qquad \text{①}$$
$$y^2 = 16x \qquad \text{②}$$

The algebra will be simpler if we solve equation ② for x, then substitute into equation ①. From equation ②, $x = \dfrac{y^2}{16}$

$$y - 4 = m\left(\frac{y^2}{16}\right) - m$$
$$16y - 64 = my^2 - 16m$$
$$my^2 - 16y + 64 - 16m = 0$$

This is a quadratic equation in y where $a = m$, $b = -16$, and $c = 64 - 16m$.

The solutions are $y = \dfrac{16 \pm \sqrt{256 - 4m(64 - 16m)}}{2m}$.

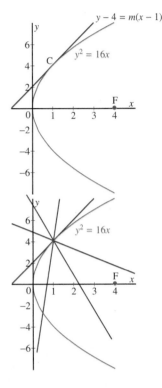

Interpreting Information and Forming Conclusions

There is a single point of intersection when the discriminant is zero; that is, when $b^2 - 4ac = 0$.

$$256 - 4m(64 - 16m) = 0$$
$$256 - 256m + 64m^2 = 0$$
$$m^2 - 4m + 4 = 0$$
$$(m - 2)^2 = 0$$
$$m = 2$$

From equation ①, the equation of the tangent is $y - 4 = 2x - 2$, or $y = 2x + 2$.

Reflecting on the Reasonableness of Results

From the diagram above, there is a unique line that is tangent to the parabola at (1, 4). The other lines intersect the parabola at one or more points. This is confirmed by the algebra. The equation simplifies to a perfect square; and any perfect square equation has a single solution!

To draw the reflected ray, we ignore the parabola and use the tangent instead. Point A is on the incoming ray, $y = 4$. Point B is on the tangent, $y = 2x + 2$. Point D is at the x-intercept of the tangent. Point D has coordinates $(-1, 0)$. The problem now reduces to this:

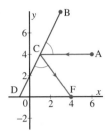

A horizontal light ray at $y = 4$ reflects off the line $y = 2x + 2$ at $x = 1$. Does the reflected ray pass through F(4, 0)?

One way to do this is to draw the line from C(1, 4) to F(4, 0) and show that it is the reflected ray. If the line CF makes the same angle with the tangent as the incoming ray, then CF is the reflected ray. So, we need to show that $\angle ACB = \angle FCD$.

First, we show that $\triangle FCD$ is isosceles with FC = FD. We do this by calculating the distances FC and FD.

$$\begin{aligned} FC &= \sqrt{(4-1)^2 + (0-4)^2} & FD &= 4 - (-1) \\ &= \sqrt{9 + 16} & &= 5 \\ &= \sqrt{25} \\ &= 5 \end{aligned}$$

So, FC = FD and $\triangle FCD$ is isosceles.

Now, all that is required is to show that $\angle ACB = \angle FCD$.

- Since CA and DF are parallel, $\angle ACB = \angle FDC$ (corresponding angles are equal).
- Since FC = FD, $\angle FCD = \angle FDC$ (property of an isosceles triangle)
- Both $\angle ACB$ and $\angle FCD$ are equal to $\angle FDC$. Therefore, they are equal to each other; that is, $\angle ACB = \angle FCD$.

Hence, the reflected ray passes through the focus F(4, 0).

Problems

1. Verify that the parabola, $y^2 = 16x$, has focus F(4, 0). What is the equation of the directrix?

2. Repeat the process of the solution to show that a horizontal ray of light striking the parabola $y^2 = 16x$ at each given point also reflects to the focus F(4, 0).

   a) (4, 8)

   b) $(\frac{1}{4}, 2)$

3. Consider the parabola $x^2 = 4y$. Suppose an incoming vertical ray of light strikes the parabola at $x = 4$. Show that the reflected ray passes through the focus of the parabola.

4. The method used to determine the equation of the tangent, given the coordinates of the point of tangency, can be applied to any conic. For each conic whose equation is given, determine an equation for the tangent at the given point, with the given slope.

a) $x^2 + y^2 = 25$; $(4, 3)$; $m = -\dfrac{4}{3}$

b) $x^2 + 4y^2 = 20$; $(2, 2)$; $m = -\dfrac{1}{4}$

c) $4x^2 - y^2 = 75$; $(5, 5)$; $m = 4$

Challenge Problems

5. Repeat the process of the solution using the same parabola, $y^2 = 16x$, but a general point.

a) Consider the general point $(a^2, 4a)$ on the parabola. Determine the slope of the tangent at that point.

b) Consider the general slope m of a tangent to the parabola. Determine the coordinates of the point on the parabola at which the tangent has slope m.

c) Explain how each of parts a and b verifies the reflection property.

6. In Chapter 8, you learned about the ellipse and its reflection property. All rays emitted from one focus are reflected off the ellipse to concentrate at the other focus. The ellipse $\dfrac{x^2}{16} + \dfrac{y^2}{12} = 1$ has foci at $(\pm 2, 0)$. Suppose a ray emitted from $(-2, 0)$ strikes the ellipse at point $P(2, 3)$. The tangent to the ellipse at P has slope $-\dfrac{1}{2}$. Verify that the reflected ray passes through the focus $(2, 0)$.

7. Use the ellipse in problem 6. In that problem, you found the equation of the tangent at the point $P(2, 3)$. Suppose a horizontal ray strikes the ellipse at that point. Where does the reflected ray intersect the x-axis?

Review Exercises

Algebra Tools

Standard equations of conics

- A circle, centre C(h, k), radius r
  $(x - h)^2 + (y - k)^2 = r^2$

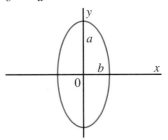

$(x - h)^2 + (y - k)^2 = r^2$

- An ellipse, centre O(0, 0), major axis length $2a$, minor axis length $2b$; where $a > b$

Major axis horizontal

$$\frac{x^2}{a^2} + \frac{y^2}{b^2} = 1$$

Major axis vertical

$$\frac{x^2}{b^2} + \frac{y^2}{a^2} = 1$$

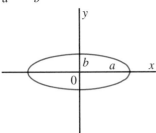

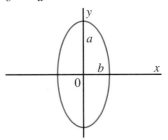

Vertices: $(a, 0)$, $(-a, 0)$

Foci: $(c, 0)$, $(-c, 0)$ $c^2 = a^2 - b^2$

Vertices: $(0, a)$, $(0, -a)$

Foci: $(0, c)$, $(0, -c)$

- When the centre of an ellipse has coordinates (h, k), the equations are
  $$\frac{(x - h)^2}{a^2} + \frac{(y - k)^2}{b^2} = 1 \text{ and } \frac{(x - h)^2}{b^2} + \frac{(y - k)^2}{a^2} = 1, \text{ respectively. There are}$$
  corresponding changes in the coordinates of the vertices and the foci.

- A hyperbola, centre O(0, 0), transverse axis length $2a$, conjugate axis length $2b$

Transverse axis horizontal

$$\frac{x^2}{a^2} - \frac{y^2}{b^2} = 1$$

Transverse axis vertical

$$\frac{x^2}{b^2} - \frac{y^2}{a^2} = -1$$

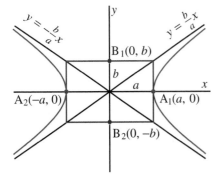

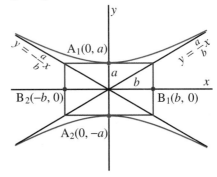

Vertices: $(a, 0)$, $(-a, 0)$

Foci: $(c, 0)$, $(-c, 0)$ $\qquad c^2 = a^2 + b^2$

Asymptotes: $y = \pm\dfrac{b}{a}x$

Vertices: $(0, a)$, $(0, -a)$

Foci: $(0, c)$, $(0, -c)$

Asymptotes: $y = \pm\dfrac{a}{b}x$

- When the centre of a hyperbola has coordinates (h, k), the equations are $\dfrac{(x - h)^2}{a^2} - \dfrac{(y - k)^2}{b^2} = 1$ and $\dfrac{(x - h)^2}{b^2} - \dfrac{(y - k)^2}{a^2} = -1$, respectively. There are corresponding changes in the coordinates of the vertices and the foci; and in the equations of the asymptotes.

- A parabola, vertex O(0, 0)

Axis of symmetry horizontal

$y^2 = 4px$

Axis of symmetry vertical

$x^2 = 4py$

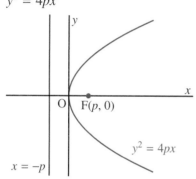

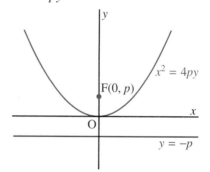

Focus: $(p, 0)$

Directrix: $x = -p$

Focus: $(0, p)$

Directrix: $y = -p$

- When the vertex of a parabola has coordinates (h, k), the equations are $(y - k)^2 = 4p(x - h)$ and $(x - h)^2 = 4p(y - k)$, respectively. There are corresponding changes in the coordinates of the focus, and in the equation of the directrix.

A parabola may be graphed using the 2-3-4 Rule (see page 547).

The general equation of a conic is $Ax^2 + By^2 + 2Gx + 2Fy + C = 0$.

NS **1.** A circle has centre C(2, 1) and radius 3 units.

   a) Write the equation of the circle.

   b) Graph the circle.

2. Write each equation in general form.

   a) $(x - 2)^2 + (y + 3)^2 = 9$

   b) $(x + 4)^2 + (y + 1)^2 = 49$

3. Write each equation in standard form. Graph the circle. Show the coordinates of the centre, and the radius.

   a) $x^2 + y^2 + 6x - 4y - 3 = 0$

   b) $x^2 + y^2 - 2x - 10y - 10 = 0$

9.1   4. Solve each linear-quadratic system. Check the solution.

   a) $x^2 + y^2 = 35$
   $y = 2x + 4$

   b) $x^2 + y^2 = 18$
   $2x + 3y = 1$

   c) $x + y = 1$
   $x^2 + y^2 = 1$

5. The difference of two numbers is 17. The sum of their squares is 689. Determine the numbers.

6. Determine the equations of the tangents with slope 1 to the circle $x^2 + y^2 = 6$.

7. a) Graph the circle $(x + 5)^2 + (y + 10)^2 = 25$.

   b) Write an equation to represent the family of lines passing through $O(0, 0)$. Draw some of these lines on the graph, to show the different ways the lines can intersect the circle.

   c) Determine the equations of the members of the family that are tangents to the circle.

9.2   8. Sketch each ellipse. Identify the coordinates of its foci, and the lengths of the major and minor axes.

   a) $\dfrac{x^2}{16} + \dfrac{y^2}{36} = 1$

   b) $\dfrac{x^2}{9} + \dfrac{y^2}{49} = 1$

   c) $\dfrac{(x - 1)^2}{9} + \dfrac{(y + 2)^2}{4} = 1$

   d) $\dfrac{(x + 3)^2}{81} + \dfrac{(y - 2)^2}{64} = 1$

9. An ellipse has centre $O(0, 0)$ and major axis on the x-axis. Determine the equation of each ellipse.

   a) $b = 3$, $c = 4$

   b) The major axis has length 12, and the minor axis has length 9.

   c) The x-intercepts are ± 3, and the y-intercepts are ± 2.

10. A point P moves so the sum of its distances from $A(4, 1)$ and $B(4, 5)$ is 12. Determine the equation of the locus of P.

11. Determine the coordinates of the points of intersection of the line and the ellipse.
    $6y - x = 6$
    $x^2 + 3y^2 = 36$

12. Determine the equation of each ellipse.

    a) Centre $D(-1, -5)$, major axis vertical with length 10, minor axis length 6

    b) Centre $E(1, 4)$, major axis horizontal, one focus $F(5, 4)$, minor axis length 4

13. Sketch each ellipse. Label each sketch with the coordinates of the foci, the centre, the vertices, and the endpoints of the minor axis.

a) $\dfrac{(x+3)^2}{9} + \dfrac{(y-4)^2}{16} = 1$

b) $\dfrac{(x-2)^2}{49} + \dfrac{(y+6)^2}{25} = 1$

9.3 14. A hyperbola has centre O(0, 0) and one vertex A(–2, 0). The hyperbola passes through P(3, 2.5).

a) Determine the equation of the hyperbola.

b) Sketch the hyperbola.

15. A hyperbola has centre O(0, 0). It passes through A(1, 2) and B(2, $2\sqrt{2}$).

a) Determine the equation of the hyperbola.

b) Determine the equations of the asymptotes of the hyperbola.

16. A rectangular hyperbola has equation $xy = 4$.

a) Sketch the hyperbola.

b) Determine the equations of the asymptotes.

c) Determine the equations of the transverse and conjugate axes.

17. Sketch each hyperbola. Label each sketch with the coordinates of the foci and the equations of the asymptotes.

a) $\dfrac{(x-1)^2}{4} - \dfrac{(y-2)^2}{9} = 1$

b) $\dfrac{(y-4)^2}{16} - \dfrac{(x+2)^2}{4} = 1$

18. Determine the equation of the hyperbola with asymptotes $y = \pm\dfrac{2}{3}x$ and one vertex A(3, 0).

19. Determine the coordinates of the points of intersection of each line and hyperbola.

a) $x + y = 2$
   $2x^2 - y^2 = 1$

b) $2x - y = 4$
   $x^2 - y^2 = 4$

9.4 20. Write an equation for the parabola that satisfies each description.

a) Vertex V(3, 3); focus F(3, 0)

b) Vertex V(0, 2); directrix $x = 1$

c) Focus F(0, –3); directrix $y = 3$

d) Vertex V(4, –3); axis parallel to the y-axis; parabola passes through (8, 5)

21. Sketch the parabola defined by each equation. Label each sketch with the coordinates of the vertex and focus, and the equations of the axis of symmetry and directrix.

a) $x^2 = -10y$

b) $y^2 = 16x$

c) $(y-3)^2 = -2(x+1)$

d) $(x+4)^2 = -3(y+2)$

22. Determine the coordinates of the points of intersection of the line and the parabola.
$$y^2 = x + 2$$
$$y = -x + 4$$

9.5 23. Many famous buildings (for example, the Taj Mahal) have elliptical ceilings. An ellipse has the property that a light ray or sound wave from a source at one focus will be reflected through the other focus. Suppose a building has a ceiling whose cross section can be described by the equation $25x^2 + 256y^2 = 6400$. All measurements are in metres. How far apart must two people be to be able to whisper to each other using this focal property?

24. The arch of a viaduct has the shape of a rectangular hyperbola. The arch is 100 m wide at its base. The maximum height of the arch is 40 m.

a) How high is the arch at a point 10 m from the centre of its base?

b) Pose a problem about the arch. Solve the problem you posed.

25. A ray of light that is directed toward one focus of a hyperbolic mirror is reflected through the other focus. Determine an equation for the hyperbolic mirror. The dimensions are shown in the diagram below.

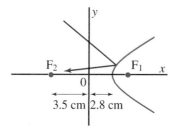

9.6 26. Each equation defines a conic. Write the equation in standard form. Sketch the conic.

a) $x^2 + 4y^2 - 8x - 5 = 0$ b) $2x^2 + 2y^2 - 3x - 1 = 0$

c) $y^2 - 2x - 2y - 9 = 0$ d) $5x^2 - 4y^2 + 20x + 8y - 4 = 0$

27.   i) Identify the curve represented by each equation.
      ii) Write each equation in standard form.
      iii) Identify the vertices and foci where appropriate.
      iv) Sketch each curve.

a) $2x^2 - y^2 + 12x + 14 = 0$ b) $2x^2 = 3 - 2y^2$

c) $3x^2 - 6x = 3 - y^2$ d) $4x^2 - 16x - 12y - 23 = 0$

1. Determine the equation of a circle that passes through A(1, –4) and whose centre is C(–5, –1).

2. Determine the coordinates of the points of intersection of each line and conic.

   a) $x^2 + y^2 = 2$
   $x - 2y + 3 = 0$

   b) $x^2 - y^2 = 25$
   $x + y = 3$

3. **Knowledge/Understanding** Determine the equation of an ellipse that satisfies each set of conditions.

   a) The length of the minor axis is 8; the foci are $(0, \pm 3)$.

   b) The foci are $(\pm 3, 0)$; $a = 4$.

   c) The foci are A(2, 1) and B(2, 3); the length of the major axis is 6.

4. **Communication** A certain computer part costs c dollars. A number, n, of these computer parts can be bought for \$1000. If one computer part costs \$5 less, then 10 extra parts can be bought for \$1000. Here are the equations that represent this situation:

   $$cn = 1000$$
   $$(c - 5)(n + 10) = 1000$$

   a) Explain how each equation was derived.

   b) What is the cost of 1 computer part?

   c) Explain how you completed part b.

5. A hyperbola has vertices A(1, 0) and B(–1, 0). The equations of its asymptotes are $y = \pm 2x$. Determine the equation of the hyperbola.

6. Sketch the hyperbola $\dfrac{(x + 1)^2}{25} - \dfrac{(y - 2)^2}{16} = 1$. Label the sketch with the coordinates of the foci and the vertices, and the equations of the asymptotes.

7. A lamp has a parabolic reflector. The bulb of the lamp is at the focus of the parabola, as shown. The reflector is 10 cm deep.

   a) Determine an equation of the parabola.

   b) Determine the width of the reflector at its widest point.

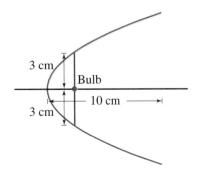

3 cm

Bulb

10 cm

3 cm

8. A graphic designer draws a series of triangles on a grid. Each triangle has its base from (–3, 0) to (3, 0), and a perimeter of 14 units. Determine the equation of the curve on which the third vertex of each triangle is located.

9. **Application** The radiator grill on a car has the shape of an ellipse, 16 cm high and 60 cm wide. Determine the width of the radiator grill 10 cm from the top.

10.   i) Classify each equation as a circle, an ellipse, a parabola, or a hyperbola.
    ii) Write each equation in standard form.
    iii) Identify the coordinates of the vertices and foci where appropriate.
    iv) Sketch each curve.

    a) $4x^2 + 9y^2 + 24x = 0$ b) $x^2 + 2x - 4y - 3 = 0$
    c) $2x^2 + 9y^2 + 8x - 72y + 134 = 0$ d) $2y^2 - 4y = 9x - 2$

11. **Thinking/Inquiry/Problem Solving** The equation of a conic is $x^2 + ky^2 = 1$. Identify and describe the conic in each case. Use examples in your description.

    a) $k < 0$ b) $k = 1$ c) $0 < k < 1$ d) $k > 1$

Assessment Tasks

1. Describe the type of curve represented by the equation $x^2 + ky^2 = a^2$ in each case.

    a) $k = 1$ b) $k < 0$ c) $0 < k < 1$ d) $k > 1$

2. Determine the locus of a point that moves so its distance from the line $x = -3$ is two times its distance from the point A(3, 0). Sketch the curve. Identify and describe any special points.

3. A sealed-beam car headlight is backed by a parabolic mirror whose cross-section can be represented by the equation $x^2 = 4py$. The bulb at the focus of this parabola produces a parallel beam of light. Determine the shortest distance from the bulb to the mirror.

4. Consider the ellipse $\frac{x^2}{25} + \frac{y^2}{16} = 1$. One foci is the focus of a parabola. One vertex is the vertex of this parabola.

    a) How many different parabolas are possible?

    b) Determine the equations of the parabolas.

    c) Illustrate your results on a graph that shows the ellipse and the parabolas.

    d) Determine the coordinates of the points of intersection of the parabolas.

5. Create a problem similar to exercise 4, about a hyperbola and a parabola, then solve it.

Answers

Chapter 1 Sequences and Series

Necessary Skills

1 Review: Percent

Exercises, page 3

1. a) 0.2 **b)** 0.04 **c)** 0.15 **d)** 0.75
e) 1.1 **f)** 0.0875 **g)** 0.015 **h)** 0.0325
i) 0.005 **j)** 0.001

2. a) 25% **b)** 47.2% **c)** 8%
d) 0.3% **e)** 137%

3. a) $94.65 **b)** $9840 **c)** $224.31 **d)** $984

4. a) 56% **b)** 46% **c)** 180% **d)** 218%

5. a) $339.15 **b)** $390.02

6. $1433.50

2 New: Exponent Laws for Integer Exponents

Exercises, page 5

1. a) 8 **b)** $\frac{1}{3}$ **c)** $\frac{1}{25}$ **d)** 4
e) $\frac{16}{81}$ **f)** 2 **g)** 1 **h)** 1
i) 100 **j)** 8

2. a) 16 **b)** $\frac{1}{16}$ **c)** 16 **d)** -16
e) $\frac{1}{16}$ **f)** $-\frac{1}{16}$ **g)** $\frac{1}{16}$ **h)** 16
i) $\frac{1}{16}$ **j)** $-\frac{1}{16}$

3. a) 8 **b)** $\frac{1}{128}$ **c)** $\frac{1}{8}$ **d)** 128
e) $\frac{1}{128}$ **f)** $\frac{3125}{4}$ **g)** 12 500 **h)** $\frac{1}{8}$
i) $\frac{1}{1024}$ **j)** 1024 **k)** $\frac{1}{1024}$ **l)** 1024

4. a) 10^{19} **b)** 6^{15} **c)** 3^{-4}

5. a) $2^{20} = 1\ 048\ 576$ **b)** $\left(\frac{1}{2}\right)^3 = 0.125$
c) $\frac{3^{16}}{2^4} = 2\ 690\ 420.1$

6. Answers may vary; $3^5 \div 3^2 = 3^{5-2} = 3^3; (2^2)^3 = 2^{2 \times 3} = 2^6$

3 New: Numerical Roots

Exercises, page 7

1. a) 7 **b)** 3 **c)** 3 **d)** -2
e) 10 **f)** -4 **g)** 9 **h)** 10

2. a) 2.49 **b)** 2.61 **c)** 2.78
d) -2.42 **e)** 1.11

3. a) 3.46 m by 3.46 m **b)** 2.45 m

4. a) 44.72 cm **b)** 447.21 cm

5. 73.42 cm by 73.42 cm by 73.42 cm

4 New: Patterns and Sequences

Exercises, page 7

1. a) 20 Add 5 to the number to find the next number.
b) 80 Double the number to find the next number.
c) 45 Add 9 to the number to find the next number.
d) 0.1 Divide the number by 10 to find the next number.
e) 6.25 Divide the number by 4 to find the next number.
f) 21 The difference between consecutive numbers increases by 1 each time.

2. a) 7 Add 1 to each number.
b) 1 The pattern 1, 2, 3 is repeated.
c) 7 Each sequential odd number is followed by a 2.
d) 21 Add the previous two numbers to find the next number.
e) 48 Add all the previous numbers to find the next number.

3. a) 23 The difference between consecutive numbers increases by 1 each time.
b) 34 Add the previous two numbers to find the next number.
c) 80 Add all previous numbers to find the next number.
d) 11 A number is added to each number following the pattern 1, 2, 1, 2, ...
e) 11 Add 3 to a number in an odd position to find the next number; all numbers in even positions are 3.
f) 65 The differences between consecutive numbers form a series of powers of 2.

4. a) 9, 11 Add 2 to each number.
b) 160, 320 Double each number.
c) 60, 75 Add 15 to each number.
d) 60, 50 Subtract 10 from each number.
e) 81, 243 Multiply each number by 3.
f) 2, -2 Multiply each number by -1.
g) 10 000, $-100\ 000$ Multiply each number by -10.
h) $-12, -17$ Subtract 5 from each number.
i) $\frac{7}{8}, \frac{9}{10}$ Add 2 to the numerator and denominator of each term.
j) $\frac{1}{9}, \frac{1}{27}$ Multiply each number by $\frac{1}{3}$.
k) 17, 21 Add 4 to each number.
l) 25, 36 Squares of consecutive numbers

5. a) a, c, d, h, k **b)** b, e, f, g, j **c)** i, l

6. Answers may vary.
2, 4, 8, 16, 32, ...; multiply by 2.
2, 4, 8, 32, 256, ...; multiply the two preceding numbers to get the next number.

1.1 Exercises, page 12

1. a) Yes; 4   **b)** Yes; –2   **c)** No   **d)** No
   e) Yes; 7   **f)** No   **g)** No   **h)** Yes; –2
   i) Yes; 1   **j)** No

2. a) 3; 21, 24, 27   **b)** –4; 13, 9, 5
   c) 10; 57, 67, 77   **d)** –10; 1, –9, –19
   e) 3; 1, 4, 7   **f)** 0.5; 3.3, 3.8, 4.3
   g) –5; –18, –23, –28   **h)** 50; 350, 400, 450
   i) –11; 33, 22, 11   **j)** 0.64; 3.15, 3.79, 4.43

3. $26

4. a) No; there is no common difference.
   b) Yes; the common difference is 128.
   c) No; there is no common difference.

5. a)   **i)** 36   **ii)** –3   **iii)** 122
     iv) –19   **v)** 60   **vi)** 44

6. a) 17, 20, 23, 26, 29
   b) Row1

7. a) Each row is an arithmetic sequence with a common
     difference of 1.
   b) Each column is an arithmetic sequence with a common
     difference of 7.
   c) Every diagonal is an arithmetic sequence with a common
     difference of 8.

8. a) 2012, 2024, 2036   **b)** Pig
   c) **i)** 2022, 2034, 2046   **ii)** 2017, 2029, 2041
     iii) 2020, 2032, 2044

9. a) 39 million years ago and 13 million years ago
   b) 13 million years from now

10. All terms would be multiples of the first term.

11. a) This year; 112 000 ounces
     Next year; 134 000 ounces

   b)

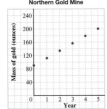

Total Output of a Northern Gold Mine

   c) The line would be steeper.

12. a) 1924, 1928, 1932, 1936, 1940, 1944
   b) The 1940 and 1944 Olympics were cancelled due to
     World War II.
   c) 16
   d) Answers may vary. The Olympic committee wanted to
     alternate the summer and winter game years.

13. a) Yes, the common differences must be 0. For example,
     2, 2, 2, … .
   b) No, there would be no common difference between the
     terms. For example, 2, 3, 5, 3, 2.

14. a)   **i)** 2, 7, 12, 17, 22   **ii)** 37, 33, 29, 25, 21
     iii) 5, 13, 21, 29, 37   **iv)** 50, 45, 40, 35, 30
     v) –18, –8, 2, 12, 22, 32   **vi)** 43, 51.5, 60, 68.5, 77

15. 8, $15\frac{1}{3}$, $22\frac{2}{3}$, 30

16. 10, 21.25, 32.5, 43.75, 55

17. a) 11, 14, 17, 20, 23   **b)** 25, 30, 35, 40, 45
   c) 12, 10, 8, 6, 4

1.2 Exercises, page 22

1. a) Yes; 2   **b)** No   **c)** Yes; $-\frac{1}{2}$ **d)** Yes; $-\frac{1}{3}$
   e) No   **f)** Yes; 0.1   **g)** No   **h)** Yes; 10
   i) Yes; 10^{-2} **j)** Yes; 1.08

2. a) 10; 2000, 20 000, 200 000
   b) $\frac{1}{2}$; 6, 3, $\frac{3}{2}$ **c)** –2; –40, 80, –160
   d) 3; 81, 243, 729   **e)** $-\frac{1}{2}$; $-\frac{1}{2}$, $\frac{1}{4}$, $-\frac{1}{8}$
   f) –1; –1, 1, –1   **g)** 2; 16, 32, 64
   h) 3, –27, –81, –243   **i)** $\frac{1}{3}$; $\frac{1}{54}$, $\frac{1}{162}$, $\frac{1}{486}$
   j) $\frac{3}{2}$; $\frac{8}{3}$, 4, 6

3. a) Geometric; there is a common ratio of 100.
   b) Neither; there is no common difference or ratio.
   c) Arithmetic; there is a common difference of 4.
   d) Neither; there is no common difference or ratio.
   e) Arithmetic; there is a common difference of –7.
   f) Geometric; there is a common ratio of 0.1.
   g) Geometric; there is a common ratio of –1.
   h) Both; there is a common ratio of 1, and a common
     difference of 0.
   i) Neither; there is no common difference or ratio.
   j) Neither; there is no common difference or ratio.

4. a) 400   **b)** 1600   **c)** 6400

5. a) No; there is no common ratio.
   b) Yes; the common ratio is 2.
   c) No; there is no common ratio.

6. a) 0.9 m, 0.81 m, 0.729 m
   b) There is a common ratio of 0.9.
   c) 0.35 m

7. a)   **i)** 96   **ii)** –96   **iii)** 0.02
     iv) 20 480   **v)** $\frac{4}{25}$ **vi)** $-\frac{2}{81}$

8. a) Yes; 2, 2, 2, …   **b)** Yes; 2, –2, 2, –2, …
   c) Yes; 2, 2, 2, …

9. a) $600.29

   b)

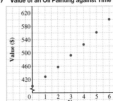

Value of an Oil Painting against Time

   c) More than $400: curve shifts up; less than $400: curve
     shifts down.
   d) More than 7%: curve gets steeper more quickly; less than
     7%: curve gets steeper less quickly.

10. $591.84

11. $1593.85

12. a) $9380.40

b)

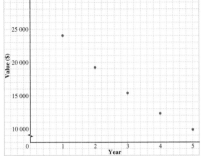

Value of a Vehicle against Time

c) More than $30 000: curve shifts up; less than $30 000: curve shifts down.

d) More than 20% decrease: curve decreases faster; less than 20% decrease: curve decreases more slowly.

13. $225.00, $202.50, $182.25, $164.03, $147.62

14. $1248.06

15. a)

Step	Number of pieces	Length of one piece (cm)	Width of one piece (cm)	Area of one piece (cm²)
Start	1	30	20	600
1	4	15	10	150
2	16	7.5	5	37.5
3	64	3.75	2.5	9.375
4	256	1.875	1.25	2.344

b) Column 2: there is a common ratio of 4

Columns 3 and 4: there is a common ratio of $\frac{1}{2}$

Column 5: there is a common ratio of $\frac{1}{4}$

16. The other terms are powers of the first term.

17. a) 2, 4, 8, 16, 32, 64, 128, 256

b)

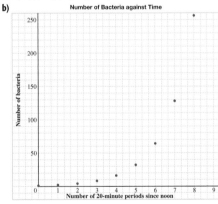

Number of Bacteria against Time

No; you cannot have a fraction of a bacterium.

18. Answers may vary.

a) Rates of growth for individual bacteria can vary.

b) No; the bacteria will run out of space and resources.

20. a) 4, 8, 16, 32, 64 **b)** 108, 36, 12, 4, $\frac{4}{3}$

c) 1, –3, 9, –27, 81

d) 1, 4, 16, 64, 256 or 1, –4, 16, –64, 256

e) 320, 160, 80, 40, 20, 10 or –320, 160, –80, 40, –20, 10

f) 10, 50, 250, 1250, 6250 or 10, –50, 250, –1250, 6250

21. 2, 6, 18, 54

22. 4, 20, 100, 500, 2500

24. a) 4, 4.29, 4.59, 4.92, 5.28

b) The sequence is geometric; the common ratio is $2^{0.1}$.

25. Yes, it is possible for a sequence to be geometric and arithmetic, for example 2, 2, 2.

26. a) 1, 3, 9, 27, 81 **b)** $\frac{9}{5}, \frac{6}{5}, \frac{4}{5}, \frac{8}{15}$, or 9, –6, 4, $\frac{-8}{3}$

1.3 Exercises, page 29

1. a) 7, 12, 17, 22 **b)** 16, 14, 12, 10

c) 2, 4, 8, 16 **d)** 6, 18, 54, 162

e) 2, 5, 10, 17 **f)** 2, 6, 12, 20

2. Arithmetic sequences: a, b
Geometric sequences: c, d
Neither: e, f

3. a) 27 **b)** 10 **c)** –4

d) 99 **e)** $\frac{1}{10}$ **f)** 90

4. a) $-2 + 6n$ **b)** 58 **c)** 118

5. a) $14 - 3n$ **b)** –10 **c)** –61

6. a) $3(2)^{n-1}$ **b)** 192 **c)** 6144

7. a) $3(-2)^{n-1}$ **b)** 192 **c)** –6144

9. a) $t_n = 2 + 3n$ **b)** $t_n = 7 - 2n$

c) $t_n = -6 + 2n$ **d)** $t_n = -3 + 6n$

10. a) $t_n = -1 + 3n$; 59 **b)** $t_n = 8 + 2n$; 108

c) $t_n = 23 - 3n$; –217 **d)** $t_n = 47 - 2n$; –153

11. a) $t_n = 2^{n-1}$ **b)** $t_n = (-2)^{n-1}$

c) $t_n = 8\left(\frac{1}{2}\right)^{n-1}$ **d)** $t_n = 8\left(-\frac{1}{2}\right)^{n-1}$

12. a) $t_n = 2(3)^{n-1}$; 486 **b)** $t_n = 3(5)^{n-1}$; 1 171 875

c) $t_n = 10\left(\frac{1}{2}\right)^{n-1}$; 0.078 125 **d)** $t_n = 4(-3)^{n-1}$; –78 732

13. a) Sequence 1: 2, 3, 4, 5
Sequence 2: 3, 5, 7, 9
Sequence 3: 4, 7, 10, 13
Sequence 4: 5, 9, 13, 17

b) The first terms form an arithmetic sequence with a common difference of 1.

c) The second terms form an arithmetic sequence with a common difference of 2.

d) The third terms form an arithmetic sequence with a common difference of 3.

e) The fourth terms form an arithmetic sequence with a common difference of 4.

14. a) Row 9 **b)** 11 rows

15. 15th term

16. a) 32 **b)** 59 **c)** 38

d) 33 **e)** 21 **f)** 101

17. 27

18. a) 32 **b)** 1024

c) 1 048 576 **d)** 1.1×10^{12}

19. Answers may vary. Mortality rates were higher in previous generations.

20. a) $17\,500.00, $12\,250.00, $8575.00, $6002.50, $4201.75

b)

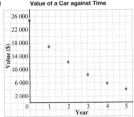

Value of a Car against Time

c) $t_n = 25\,000(0.7)^n$

22. a) $t_n = \dfrac{n}{n+1}$ **b)** $t_n = \dfrac{2n-1}{n}$ **c)** $t_n = \dfrac{4n-2}{2n-1}$

23. a) $t_n = n^2 + n$ **b)** $t_n = (2n-1)(3n-1)$
c) $t_n = n(2^n)$ **d)** $t_n = (4n-2)(2n+1)$

24. b) 8100, 7290, 6561, 5905
5129, 4616, 4155, 3739
c) $_n\$x(0.9)^n$, where n is the number of weeks

25. a) $176\,319.37   **b)** $259\,071.00
c) $120\,000(1.08)^n$

26. a) 2, 4, 6, 8, 10, 24
b) For the first 5 terms, $t_n = 2n$. When $n > 5$, the second term is not zero so the pattern changes.

27. -10

Self-Check 1.1–1.3 (Functions), page 33

1. $1102.50

2. a) -8 **b)** 2560

3. a) 0, 3, 8   **b)** 15, 22.5, 33.75

4. a) 2a   **b)** 2b, 3b   **c)** 3a

5. a) $t_n = 2 + 3n$ **b)** $t_n = 7 - 2n$

6. a) $t_n = 2^{n-1}$ **b)** $t_n = 8\left(-\dfrac{1}{2}\right)^{n-1}$

7. a) $t_n = 2(5)^{n-1}$ **b)** $t_n = \dfrac{2n-1}{3n-1}$

8. a) $t_n = (2n-1)(3n-2)$ **b)** $t_n = \dfrac{(2n-1)(2n+1)}{2n(2n+2)}$

1.4 Exercises, page 35

1. a) 1, 3, 5, 7, 9   **b)** 2, 5, 8, 11, 14
c) 5, 10, 15, 20, 25   **d)** $-4, -2, 0, 2, 4$
e) 8, 3, $-2, -7, -12$ **f)** 10, 110, 210, 310, 410

2. a) 1, 2, 4, 8, 16   **b)** 2, 4, 8, 16, 32
c) 3, 6, 12, 24, 48   **d)** 3, -6, 12, -24, 48
e) 1, 10, 100, 1000, 10 000   **f)** 16, 8, 4, 2, 1

3. a) The second part of the formula tells you how to generate other terms of the sequence.
b) The first part of the formula gives the starting point of the sequence.

4. a) i) 1, 2, 3, 4, 5   **ii)** 1, 2, 3, 4, 5
1, 3, 5, 7, 9   2, 4, 6, 8, 10
1, 4, 7, 10, 13   3, 6, 9, 12, 15
1, 5, 9, 13, 17   4, 8, 12, 16, 20

5. a) i) 1, 1, 1, 1, 1   **ii)** 1, -1, 1, -1, 1
1, 2, 4, 8, 16   1, -2, 4, -8, 16
1, 3, 9, 27, 81   1, -3, 9, -27, 81
1, 4, 16, 64, 256   1, -4, 16, -64, 256

6. a) 100, 107, 114, 121, 128
b) -9, 1, 11, 21, 31
c) 1, 0.5, 0.25, 0.125, 0.0625
d) 1, -0.5, 0.25, -0.125, 0.0625
e) 2, 0, 2, 0, 2
f) 6, 18, 72, 360, 2160

7. a) Geometric; common ratio is -1.
b) Neither; there is no common difference or common ratio.
c) Neither; there is no common difference or common ratio.
d) Neither; there is no common difference or common ratio.

8. a) 993

9. a) 3 906 250

10. a) 1, 3, 6, 10, 15   **b)** 1, 5, 11, 19, 29
c) 1, 3, 7, 15, 31   **d)** 1, 4, 10, 22, 46

11. a) 1, 2, 3, 5, 8   **b)** 1, 3, 4, 7, 11
c) 1, 2, 4, 8, 16   **d)** 1, 2, 5, 11, 26

12. a) i) $t_1 = 4$, $t_n = t_{n-1} + 7, n > 1$
ii) $t_1 = 32$, $t_n = t_{n-1} - 6, n > 1$
iii) $t_1 = 1$, $t_n = -10t_{n-1}, n > 1$
iv) $t_1 = 32$, $t_n = \dfrac{1}{2}t_{n-1}, n > 1$

b) i) The first term is $t_1 = 4$; after the first term, each term is 7 more than the previous one, so $t_n = t_{n-1} + 7$.

13. a) $t_1 = a$, $t_n = t_{n-1} + d$ **b)** $t_1 = a$, $t_n = rt_{n-1}$

14. a) $m = 1$, b is any real number
b) $b = 0$, $m \neq 0$ **c)** $m \neq 1$, $b \neq 0$

15. a) 1, 1, 2, 3, 5, 8, ...
b) $t_1 = 1$, $t_2 = 1$, $t_n = t_{n-2} + t_{n-1}, n > 2$

16. a) 1, 1, 4, 9
b) $t_1 = 1$, $t_2 = 1$, $t_n = (\sqrt{t_{n-1}} + \sqrt{t_{n-2}})^2, n > 2$

17. Yes; for example, 2, 4, 8, 16, 32
$t_1 = 2$, $t_n = 2t_{n-1}, n > 1$
$t_1 = 2$, $t_n = t_{n-1} + 2^{n-1}, n > 1$

Self-Check 1.1–1.4 (Functions and Relations), page 38

1. $5624.32

2. a) 8   **b)** 512

3. a) 2, 5, 10   **b)** 11.2, 15.68, 21.952

4. a) 2a   **b)** 2b, 3b   **c)** 3a

5. a) $t_n = 4 + 3n$ **b)** $t_n = 10 - 3n$

6. a) $t_n = 2(4)^{n-1}$ **b)** $t_n = 99\left(-\dfrac{1}{3}\right)^{n-1}$

7. a) $t_n = 3(4)^{n-1}$ **b)** $t_n = \dfrac{4n-3}{2n}$

8. a) $t_n = 2n(3n)$ **b)** $t_n = \dfrac{(3n-2)(3n+1)}{(n+1)(n+2)}$

9. a) 7, 8, 7, 2, -11
b) 2.5, 6.25, 97.66, 2 328 306.4, 7.35×10^{25}

10. a) $t_1 = 32$, $t_n = t_{n-1} - 6, n > 1$
b) $t_1 = p$, $t_n = t_{n-1}(q^2), n > 1$

1.5 Exercises, page 42

1. a) 1   **b)** 2   **c)** 3   **d)** 4   **e)** 5
f) 1   **g)** 8   **h)** 27   **i)** 64   **j)** 125

2. a) 1   **b)** 2   **c)** 3   **d)** 4   **e)** 5
f) 1   **g)** 4   **h)** 9   **i)** 16   **j)** 25

3. a) −1   **b)** −2   **c)** −3   **d)** −4   **e)** −5
f) 1   **g)** 4   **h)** 9   **i)** 16   **j)** 25

4. a) i) 2   **ii)** 4   **iii)** −2   **iv)** −4
   v) −2   **vi)** 4   **vii)** 2   **viii)** −4

5. a) 2   **b)** 4   **c)** 8   **d)** 16   **e)** 32
f) 1   **g)** $\frac{1}{2}$ **h)** $\frac{1}{4}$ **i)** $\frac{1}{8}$ **j)** $\frac{1}{16}$

6. a) 3   **b)** 9   **c)** 27   **d)** 81   **e)** 243
f) 1   **g)** $\frac{1}{3}$ **h)** $\frac{1}{9}$ **i)** $\frac{1}{27}$ **j)** $\frac{1}{81}$

7. a) 2.175   **b)** 28.635   **c)** 83.593
d) 55.330   **e)** 19.973   **f)** 0.459
g) 0.035   **h)** 0.012   **i)** 0.018
j) 0.050

8. a) 0.616 kg   **b)** 0.859 g

9. a) 1.05 kg

10. a) 0.244 m^2 **b)** 3.05 m^2

11. a) $40^{\frac{3}{4}} = (\sqrt[4]{40})^3$ **b)** 15.91

12. a) i) 8   **ii)** 4   **iii)** 343   **iv)** 128
   v) 100 000   **vi)** $\frac{1}{5}$ **vii)** $\frac{1}{27}$ **viii)** $\frac{1}{81}$
   ix) $\frac{1}{3}$ **x)** $\frac{1}{100}$

13. a) 7.622   **b)** 4.050   **c)** 332.554   **d)** 279.508
e) 97 518.719   **f)** 0.204   **g)** 0.032   **h)** 0.012
i) 0.334   **j)** 0.010

15. a) 5 cm, 125 cm^3 **b)** $A^{\frac{1}{2}}$ cm, $A^{\frac{3}{2}}$ cm^3
c) $A^{\frac{1}{2}}, A, A^{\frac{3}{2}}$; geometric; common ratio $A^{\frac{1}{2}}$

16. a) 9.28 cm, 86.18 cm^2 **b)** $V^{\frac{1}{3}}$ cm, $V^{\frac{2}{3}}$ cm^3
c) $V^{\frac{1}{3}}, V^{\frac{2}{3}}, V$; geometric; common ratio $V^{\frac{1}{3}}$

17. a) −2   **b)** −216   **c)** 16   **d)** 8000
e) 400   **f)** $\frac{4}{3}$ **g)** $\frac{125}{343}$ **h)** $\frac{1}{4}$
i) $-\frac{9}{4}$ **j)** $\frac{8}{27}$

18. a) Elephant: 3.45 kg
    Cat: 0.0345 kg
    Shrew: 0.000 345 kg
b) The body masses form a geometric sequence with
   common ratio 1000. The brain masses form a geometric
   sequence with common ratio $1000^{\frac{2}{3}}$.

20. a) Elephant: 27 beats/min, 6 breaths/min
    Cat: 152 beats/min, 34 breaths/min
    Shrew: 852 beats/min, 189 breaths/min
b) Frequencies increase as masses decrease.

21. a) $900^{0.7} = 900^{\frac{7}{10}}$ **b)** 116.94
     $= \sqrt[10]{900^7}$

22. a) Approximately 11.84 $m^{0.25}$
b) Elephant: approximately 106 years
    Cat: approximately 19 years
    Shrew: approximately 3 years

23. a) 16   **b)** 0.755

24. $\sqrt[10]{2.3^{37}} \doteq 21.7968$

1.6 Exercises, page 50

1. a) $x^{\frac{3}{4}}$ **b)** $x^{\frac{7}{6}}$ **c)** $x^{\frac{1}{8}}$ **d)** $x^{\frac{1}{6}}$
e) $x^{\frac{1}{4}}$ **f)** $x^{\frac{5}{12}}$ **g)** $x^{-\frac{1}{4}}$ **h)** $x^{-\frac{5}{12}}$

2. a) $36^{-\frac{3}{2}} = \frac{1}{216}$ **b)** $25^{\frac{1}{2}} = 5$
c) $64^{-\frac{1}{2}} = \frac{1}{8}$ **d)** $16^{\frac{3}{4}} = 8$
e) $9^{\frac{3}{2}} = 27$ **f)** $(-8)^{\frac{2}{3}} = 4$
g) $9^{\frac{5}{2}} = 243$ **h)** $(-8)^{\frac{4}{3}} = 16$

3. a) 128   **b)** 256   **c)** 32   **d)** 16
e) $\frac{1}{32}$ **f)** $\frac{1}{16}$ **g)** $\frac{1}{128}$ **h)** $\frac{1}{256}$

4. a) 32   **b)** 8   **c)** 4   **d)** $\frac{1}{4}$
e) 8   **f)** 32   **g)** $\frac{1}{8}$ **h)** $\frac{1}{32}$

5. a) $a^{\frac{3}{2}}$ **b)** $b^{\frac{4}{3}}$ **c)** $s^{\frac{3}{4}}$ **d)** k^2
e) $y^{\frac{2}{3}}$ **f)** $c^{\frac{3}{5}}$ **g)** $p^{\frac{1}{4}}$ **h)** $n^{\frac{1}{6}}$

6. a) $3^{\frac{5}{2}}$ **b)** $3^{\frac{7}{2}}$ **c)** $3^{\frac{9}{2}}$ **d)** $3^{\frac{11}{2}}$

7. a) $7^{\frac{3}{4}}$ **b)** $7^{\frac{1}{4}}$ **c)** $7^{-\frac{1}{4}}$ **d)** $7^{-\frac{3}{4}}$

8. a) $5^{1.4} = 9.52$ **b)** $3^{3.90} = 72.57$
c) $2^{5.54} = 46.53$ **d)** $7^{0.06} = 3.21$

9. a) 1   **b)** 4   **c)** 7   **d)** −1
e) 0   **f)** 1   **g)** $\frac{3}{2}$ **h)** $-\frac{1}{2}$

10. a) i) −9   **ii)** −6   **iii)** −3   **iv)** 0
   v) 3   **vi)** 6   **vii)** 9   **viii)** 12

11. −4

12. a) $x = 3, 0$ **b)** $x = 2, 1$ **c)** $x = 2$ **d)** $x = 2$
e) $x = 4, 1$ **f)** $x = 0$ **g)** $x = 1$ **h)** $x = 2, 0$
i) $x = 1$

13. a) 0.277 $m^{-0.23}$ **b)** 0.0482 $e^{0.132}$

14. 1.13 $m^{-0.128}$%

15.

Year	Population
1985	200
1986	221
1987	245
1988	271
1989	301
1990	333
1991	368
1992	408
1993	452
1994	500

16.

Year	Population
1977	300
1980	378
1983	476
1986	600
1989	755
1992	952
1995	1199
1998	1510
2001	1902

17. a) i) 2.8075   **ii)** 0.3563

18. a) 19.95   **b)** 199.5   **c)** 1995   **d)** 19 950
e) 0.1995   **f)** 0.019 95   **g)** 0.001 995   **h)** 0.000 199 5

Self-Check 1.5, 1.6, page 53

1. a) 1 **b)** 16 **c)** 32 **d)** −625
e) 1 **f)** $\frac{1}{2}$ **g)** $\frac{1}{9}$ **h)** $-\frac{1}{125}$

2. a) 2.609 **b)** 15.385 **c)** 828.956
d) 0.003 **e)** 7.622 **f)** −0.547

3. a) $x^{\frac{31}{20}}$ **b)** $x^{\frac{7}{6}}$ **c)** $x^{\frac{1}{5}}$ **d)** $x^{\frac{1}{12}}$

4. a) 256 **b)** 64

5. a) $5^{2.1} = 29.365$ **b)** $7.2^{2.59} = 166.146$

6. a) 6 **b)** 0

1.7 Exercises, page 56

1. a) 30 **b)** 40 **c)** −30 **d)** −40

2. a) 153 **b)** 385 **c)** 244 **d)** 441

3. a) 375 **b)** −98 **c)** 35 000 **d)** −357

4. a) 11.04 **b)** 55.56 **c)** −109.2 **d)** −168

5. a) 400 **b)** 590 **c)** 970 **d)** 115

6. a) 210 **b)** 320 **c)** −290 **d)** 180
e) 519 **f)** 37.5

7. a) 55 **b)** 5050
c) 500 500 **d)** 50 005 000

8. a) i) 416 **ii)** −598 **iii)** 3604 **iv)** −110

9. a) 1380 **b)** −637 **c)** 646 **d)** 246.5
e) −383.5 **f)** −137.6

10. Job A

11. Job B pays more over the summer.

12. $\frac{n^2 + n}{2}$

13. a) 63 **b)** 690

14. 272

15. a) 44 **b)** 15 **c)** 345

17. a) $9000 **b)** $18 000

18. a) $1520 **b)** $29 885 **c)** Year 5 **d)** $209 195

19. −59, 38

20. 90

21. 5, 7, 9, 11

22. a) Doctors prescribe the correct pharmaceuticals, but you cannot read the prescription.
b) Each word has one more letter than the word before.
c) 210

24. a) 125 **b)** 15

25. 16, 18, 20, 22, 24, 26, 28, 30, 32, 34; or
7, 11, 15, 19, 23, 27, 31, 35, 39, 43

26. 3, 4, 5, 6, 7, 8, …, 17; or
7, 8, 9, 10, …, 18; or
28, 29, 30, 31, 32; or
36, 37, 38, 39; or
49, 50, 51

1.8 Exercises, page 61

1. a) 62 **b)** 22 **c)** −22
d) 363 **e)** 183 **f)** −183

2. a) 63 **b)** 1092 **c)** 682
d) 77.5 **e)** −21 **f)** 27.5

3. a) 1562 **b)** 484 **c)** 93
d) 46.5 **e)** 605 **f)** 55

4. a) 0.1111 **b)** 254.1 **c)** −363
d) 133.2 **e)** 0.9375 **f)** 6.6968

5. a) 78 732 **b)** 118 096

6. a) −1365 **b)** 24 570 **c)** 16 777 215
d) 4920.741 **e)** 191.953 **f)** 63.984

7. a) 5115 **b)** −1705 **c)** 1.5
d) 0.75 **e)** 9.99 **f)** 3.33

8. a) Prize 1 **b)** $1 048 575

9. a) 11 **b)** 6141

10. a) 254 **b)** 3906.24 **c)** 4372 **d)** 2047.75

11. a) 62 **b)** 2046
c) 2 097 150 **d)** 2.2×10^{12}

12. a) 7 **b)** 128 **c)** 254 **d)** $2^n - 2$ **e)** 9

14. a) 15 **b)** 31 **c)** 63
d) Number of players: 2^n; number of games: $2^n - 1$

15. 127.996

16. c)

17. 9841

Self-Check 1.7, 1.8, page 65

1. a) 133; arithmetic **b)** 1050; arithmetic
c) 2032; geometric **d)** 3.283 68; geometric

2. a) 167.5 **b)** 32.5 **c)** 29 524
d) −14 762 **e)** 1.998 **f)** 0.666

3. 49.5; 515

4. 131 072; 174 762.5

5. a) 138 601 **b)** 69 432

6. 2, 11, 20, 29, 38, 47, 56; or
11, 17, 23, 29, 35, 41, 47; or
26, 27, 28, 29, 30, 31, 32; or
20, 23, 26, 29, 32, 35, 38; or
17, 21, 25, 29, 33, 37, 41; or
14, 19, 24, 29, 34, 39, 44; or
8, 15, 22, 29, 36, 43, 50; or
5, 13, 21, 29, 37, 45, 53

7. 6141

8. $67 108 863

Insights Into a Rich Problem— The Bouncing Ball, page 68

1. 8.747 m, 6.75 s

2. Neither D_n nor T_n is geometric as there is no common ratio.

4. a) $h_n = 0.8^n$

b)

Height of Ball against Bounce Number

5. a) The time when the ball reaches maximum height; yes
b) Maximum height; yes

6. a) The time between bounces; no
b) The change in height between bounces; no

7. Yes

8. a) No   **b)** Yes

9. a) The distance the ball falls in one bounce; they are opposites.
b) $h = -4.9t^2 + 1, 0 \le t \le 452$
c) $h = -4.9(t - 0.856)^2 + 0.8, 0.452 \le t \le 1.26$
d) $t = 0.452$ and $h = 0$

11.

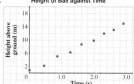

Height of Ball against Time

Chapter 1 Review Exercises, page 71

1. a) i) 34   **ii)** −67   **iii)** 123   **iv)** −49

2. a) −1, 7, 15, 23, 31   **b)** 58, 47, 36, 25, 14
c) 5, 14, 23, 32, 41   **d)** 50, 43, 36, 29, 22
e) −17, −8, 1, 10, 19, 28   **f)** 41, 55, 69, 83, 97

3. a) $t_n = 8n - 1$ **b)** 79   **c)** 159

4. a) 23, 42, 61, 80, 99, 118, 137, 156
b) −7.56, −4.6, −1.64, 1.32, 4.28, 7.24, 10.2, 13.16

5. a) Neither; no common ratio or common difference
b) Neither; no common ratio or common difference
c) Arithmetic; common difference is 3
d) Neither; no common ratio or common difference
e) Neither; no common ratio or common difference
f) Geometric; common ratio is 0.1
g) Both; common ratio is 1, common difference is 0
h) Geometric; common ratio is −1
i) Neither; no common ratio or common difference
j) Neither; no common ratio or common difference

6. a) i) 256   **ii)** $\frac{1}{8}$ **iii)** 19 683   **iv)** 1458

7. a) $\frac{8}{3}$, 8, 24, 72, 216   **b)** 192, 48, 12, 3, $\frac{3}{4}$
c) 1, −4, 16, −64, 256
d) 1, 5, 25, 125, 625 or 1, −5, 25, −125, 625
e) 168 070, 24 010, 3430, 490, 70, 10 or
−168 070, 24 010, −3430, 490, −70, 10
f) 6, 36, 216, 1296, 7776 or 6, −36, 216, −1296, 7776

8. a) $t_n = 3(2)^{n-1}$ **b)** 48   **c)** 3072

9. a) −8, 20, −50, 125, −312.5
b) 2.7, 8.37, 25.947, 80.4357, 249.350 67

10. a) Arithmetic; −3, −8, −13, −18
b) Arithmetic; 16, 19, 22, 25
c) Neither; 3, 6, 11, 20
d) Geometric; 15, 45, 135, 405
e) Neither; 5, 11, 21, 35
f) Neither; 3, 8, 15, 24

11. a) $t_n = 4n - 2$; 78   **b)** $t_n = 80 + 20n$; 1080
c) $t_n = 36 - 3n$; −204   **d)** $t_n = 45.5 - 0.5n$; −4.5

12. a) $t_n = 2(3)^{n-1}$; 1458   **b)** $t_n = 3(0.5)^{n-1}$; 0.093 75
c) $t_n = 10(-0.5)^{n-1}$; −0.078 125
d) $t_n = -4(3)^{n-1}$; −78 732

13. a) $t_n = \dfrac{2^{n-1}}{n+2}$ **b)** $t_n = \dfrac{2n-1}{2n}$
c) $t_n = n(2)^{6-n}$ **d)** $t_n = (4n-2)(n+2)$

14. a) 1 **b)** −2 **c)** 3 **d)** −4 **e)** 5
f) 1 **g)** 4 **h)** 9 **i)** 16 **j)** 25
k) 3 **l)** 27 **m)** $\frac{1}{27}$ **n)** 81 **o)** −243
p) 4 **q)** 16 **r)** 256 **s)** 1024 **t)** $\frac{1}{256}$

15. a) 8.739   **b)** 3.505   **c)** 419.066
d) 29 897.688   **e)** 31 543 779   **f)** 0.209
g) 0.001   **h)** 0.063   **i)** 0.273
j) 0.046   **k)** 3.106   **l)** 0.056
m) 0.016   **n)** 15.709   **o)** 2.278×10^{13}

16. a) −5 **b)** 216 **c)** 36 **d)** 8000 **e)** 900
f) $\frac{4}{3}$ **g)** $\frac{5}{7}$ **h)** $\frac{1}{4}$ **i)** $\frac{9}{4}$ **j)** $\frac{8}{27}$

17. a) −192 **b)** 36 **c)** 8 **d)** $\frac{25}{4}$
e) $\frac{1}{2}$ **f)** 4 **g)** $-\frac{1}{192}$ **h)** $\frac{1}{16}$
i) 27 **j)** 2048 **k)** $\frac{1}{4}$ **l)** $\frac{1}{32}$

18. a) 24 300   **b)** 53 144 100   **c)** 1.046×10^{12}

19. a) $6^{1.4} = 12.286$ **b)** $8^{3.9} = 3326.986$
c) $5^{8.04} = 416\ 599.59$ **d)** $7^{6.9} = 677\ 916.92$

20. a) 1 **b)** 10 **c)** −7 **d)** 1

21. a) 610 **b)** −360 **c)** 1170 **d)** 153

22. −1, 1, 3, 5

23. a) 147 620 **b)** 1705 **c)** 13.986 **d)** 3.34

24. a) $1720   **b)** $1992.56

25. a) 555 **b)** 795 **c)** 16 383 **d)** 357

26. a) 6 **b)** 2187 **c)** 3280 **d)** 9

27. 20, 80, 320; or −20, 80, −320

28. a) 1, 4, 7, 10, 13   **b)** 2, −1, −4, −7, −10
c) 5, 11, 23, 47, 95
d) −4, −11.8, −35.2, −105.4, −316

29. a) 100, 107, 114, 121, 128
   b) −4, −9, −14, −19, −24
   c) 1, 0.5, 0.25, 0.125, 0.0625
   d) 1, 3, −0.8, 2.5, −1.81

30. a) Arithmetic; common difference of 7
   b) Neither; no common ratio or common difference
   c) Neither; no common ratio or common difference
   d) Neither; no common ratio or common difference

Chapter 1 Self-Test, page 75

1. a) Arithmetic; common difference of 4
   b) Geometric; common ratio of 2
   c) Neither; no common ratio or difference
   d) Neither; no common ratio or difference

2. a) 83   **b)** −17

3. a) 156 250   **b)** 262 144

4. 117.5

5. 137 781

6. a) −27   **b)** 144
   c) $\frac{9}{2}$ **d)** 2
   e) 3   **f)** 512
   g) $\frac{1}{4}$ **h)** 9

7. a) 1740   **b)** 562

8. a) 2 441 406   **b)** −6.66

9. a) 12.172   **b)** 0.244
   c) 0.008   **d)** 0.044
   e) 37.674   **f)** 11 391 573.800

10. 34.5, 42, 49.5, 57, 64.5, 72, 79.5, 87

11. −50, 100, −200, 400, −800

12. 787 552

13. $t_{33} = 432$; $S_{33} = 7920$

14. $t_9 = 0.1875$; $S_9 = 95.8125$

15. a) $-\frac{1}{4}$ **b)** −7

16. 31

17. a) 1, 3, 5, 7, 9, 11
   b) 2.4, 4.32, 7.776, 13.9968, 25.194 24, 45.349 632

Assessment Tasks, page 76

1. a) Geometric; common ratio of 101
   b) $101^{\frac{5}{2}} \div 101^{\frac{3}{2}} = 101$, $101^{\frac{3}{2}} \div 101^{\frac{1}{2}} = 101$

2. a) No

3. a) Answers may vary; $2 \times 3 + 4 \times 9 + 6 \times 27 + 8 \times 81$
   b) 4072

Chapter 2 Rational Expressions

Necessary Skills

1 Review: Operations with Fractions

Exercises, page 78

1. a) $\frac{12}{5}$ **b)** $\frac{15}{2}$ **c)** $\frac{3}{4}$

2. a) $\frac{1}{12}$ **b)** $-\frac{8}{5}$ **c)** $-\frac{4}{21}$
   d) $-\frac{4}{15}$ **e)** $\frac{5}{9}$ **f)** $\frac{11}{4}$

3. a) $\frac{1}{10}$ **b)** 2   **c)** $\frac{8}{5}$
   d) $\frac{4}{3}$ **e)** −1   **f)** $\frac{7}{9}$

4. a) $\frac{3}{5}$ **b)** $\frac{1}{6}$ **c)** $\frac{31}{24}$
   d) $\frac{71}{60}$ **e)** $\frac{15}{22}$ **f)** $\frac{13}{60}$

2 Review: Operations with Monomials

Exercises, page 80

1. a) $9x + 4$ **b)** $-4a - 1$
   c) $2x^2 - 6xy + 8y^2$ **d)** $3a^2 - 2a$

2. a) $6a^2$ **b)** $-6a^3$ **c)** $6a^5$

3. a) $18xy$ **b)** $32p^2q$ **c)** $-45r^2s^5$

4. a) $4x^3$ **b)** $-9m^6$ **c)** $4d^2$

5. Answers may vary.
   a) $(9a^4)(4b^2)$, $(4a^3)(9ab^2)$, $(6a^2b)(6a^2b)$
   b) $(5x)(-3yz)$, $(-5xy)(3z)$, $(-15xy)(2)$
   c) $(-2m^2)(2m^2)$, $(-4m)(m^3)$, $(-2m^3)(2m)$

6. Answers may vary.
   a) $\frac{72a^5b^3}{2ab}$, $\frac{36a^6b^4}{a^2b^2}$, $\frac{72a^6b^2}{a^2}$
   b) $\frac{-30x^2y^2z^2}{2xyz}$, $\frac{-15x^2yz}{x}$, $\frac{-45xy^2z^2}{3yz}$
   c) $\frac{-8m^4n}{2n}$, $\frac{-16m^6}{4m^2}$, $\frac{-12m^4n^4}{3n^4}$

7. a) $54x^{11}$ **b)** $-12a^{10}b$ **c)** $45s^{10}t^5$

8. a) $\frac{9r^4s^2}{2}$ **b)** $\frac{3x^4y}{2}$ **c)** $14a^2b^3$

3 Review: Factoring Polynomials

Exercises, page 83

1. a) $x(x + 2)$ **b)** $3(x - 2)(x + 2)$
   c) $(x - 3)(x + 3)$ **d)** $(2m + 5)(2m - 5)$
   e) $2(k - 6)(k + 6)$ **f)** $5(x + 2)(x - 2)$
   g) $9(2x + 3)(2x - 3)$ **h)** $2(5x - y)(5x + y)$
   i) $(a^2 + b^2)(a - b)(a + b)$

2. a) $(x + 4)(x + 3)$ **b)** $(x + 4)(x - 3)$
   c) $(x - 4)(x + 3)$ **d)** $(x - 4)(x - 3)$
   e) $(m - 6)(m - 5)$ **f)** $(a + 6)(a - 3)$
   g) $(a + 3)(a + 1)$ **h)** $(y - 7)(y + 1)$
   i) $3(a + 2)(a - 1)$ **j)** $2(m^2 - 11m - 30)$
   k) $2(x + 9)(x - 8)$ **l)** $13(x - 1)^2$
   m) $2(x - 5)(x - 2)$ **n)** $3m(m - 3)(m + 2)$

3. Answers may vary.
  a) $(3x - 5)^2$
  $$16x^2 - 16x + 4 = (4x - 2)^2$$
  $$x^2 - 6x + 9 = (x - 3)^2$$
  $$4x^2 - 4x + 1 = (2x - 1)^2$$
  b) $(3x + 5)(3x - 5)$
  $$4x^2 - 9 = (2x + 3)(2x - 3)$$
  $$x^2 - 4 = (x + 2)(x - 2)$$
  $$25x^2 - 16 = (5x + 4)(5x - 4)$$
  c) Cannot be factored
  $$4x^2 + 9$$
  $$x^2 + 4$$
  $$5x^2 + 16$$

4. a) $(2x - 3)^2$ **b)** $(2m + 3)(m + 5)$
  c) $(3a + 2b)(a - 5b)$ **d)** $(2p + 1)(p - 3)$
  e) $(2m - 3)^2$ **f)** $(5x - 1)^2$

5. a) $7(x - 2y)(x + 2y)$ **b)** $5(n - 9)(n + 1)$
  c) $(4a + 3b)(a + b)$ **d)** $(2x - 1)(x - 1)$
  e) $-2(2x - 3)^2$ **f)** $3y(x^2 - 3y^2)$

6. If we take a common factor of -1 from $a - b$, the result is $-(b - a)$.

7. a) 1 **b)** 8, -5 **c)** $\frac{4}{3}, -\frac{4}{3}$
  d) $-\frac{1}{2}$, 2 **e)** $\frac{3}{2}$ **f)** 3, $-\frac{2}{3}$

2.1 Exercises, page 86

1. a) $5x - 1$ **b)** $12a - 5$ **c)** $2b - 1$
  d) $-5y + 5$ **e)** $3a - 2b$ **f)** $4m - 3n$

2. a) $x + 9$ **b)** $2a + 1$ **c)** $6b - 11$
  d) $3y - 1$ **e)** $-11a - 18b$ **f)** $-2m + 7n$

3. a) $13m^2 - 3m$ **b)** $4a^3 + 4a^2 + 3a$
  c) $7x^2 + 10x - 5y$ **d)** $5x^2 - xy + y^2$
  e) $-5m^2 - 9m + 16$ **f)** $12a^3 - 10a^2 + 9a$
  g) $-3x^2 - 22x + 19y$ **h)** $x^2 + 9xy + 9y^2$

4. a) $20m - 8$ **b)** $12p - 18q$
  c) $-12mn - 6n + 3$ **d)** $10x + 15y + 20$
  e) $-7p + 56pq^2$ **f)** $3mn^2 - 33mn + 3n^3 - 12$

5. a) $24m - 21n$ **b)** $3x^2 - 13x - 10$
  c) $4x^2 + 44xy + 121y^2$ **d)** $-44m^2 + 92mn - 8n^2$
  e) $12x^2 - 4x - 5$ **f)** $9x^2 - 42xy + 49y^2$

6. a) $10x^2 - 20$ **b)** $12a - 20$
  c) $-21k^2 + 24k$ **d)** $4b^2 - 10b + 18$
  e) $72m^2 - 63m + 45$ **f)** $44p^2 - 55p + 66$
  g) $84x^2 - 36x$ **h)** $-20a^2 + 32a$
  i) $14p^2 - 21pq$ **j)** $-40n^2 + 90n^3$
  k) $24m^4n - 30m^3$ **l)** $-14x^3 - 21x^2y$

7. a) $x^2 + 7x + 12$ **b)** $2a^2 - 8$
  c) $-3b^2 - 3b + 6$ **d)** $t^2 - 10t + 9$
  e) $2x^2 + x - 15$ **f)** $-k^2 + 2k + 24$
  g) $4y^2 + 23y - 35$ **h)** $k^2 - 11k + 24$
  i) $m^2 + m - 30$

8. a) i) $k^2 + 4k + 4$ **ii)** $9m^2 + 18m + 9$
  iii) $a^2 - 12a + 36$ **iv)** $4b^2 + 28b + 49$
  v) $y^2 - 2y + 1$ **vi)** $z^2 + 12z + 36$
  vii) $16x^2 - 64x + 64$ **viii)** $a^2 - 6ab + 9b^2$
  ix) $16m^2 + 24mn + 9n^2$

b) $(a + b)^2 = a^2 + 2ab + b^2$

9. $12a + 10$

10. Answers may vary.
  a) $(4a + 6) + (4a + 4)$ **b)** $(-4b + 5) + (-2b + 10)$
  c) $(-3m - 7n) + (-m - 4n)$ **d)** $(10 - 7x) + (6 - 10x)$

11. Answers may vary.
  a) $(12a + 12) - (4a + 2)$ **b)** $(-5b - 2) - (b - 17)$
  c) $(6m + n) - (10m + 12n)$ **d)** $(15 - 2x) - (-1 + 15x)$

12. $9x^2 + x - 2$

13. b) $893; 4x^2 + 43x + 63$
  c) Each has four individual multiplications.

14. a) $x^2 + 5x + 6$ **b)** $x^2 + 5x + 4$
  $x^2 - x - 6$ $x^2 - 3x - 4$
  $x^2 + x - 6$ $x^2 + 3x - 4$
  $x^2 - 5x + 6$ $x^2 - 5x + 4$
  c) $x^2 + 9x + 18$
  $x^2 + 3x - 18$
  $x^2 - 3x - 18$
  $x^2 - 9x + 18$

15. a) $-5x^2 - 3y^2 - 3$ **b)** $13m^2 - 3n^2$
  c) $9a^3 + 2a^2 - 19$ **d)** $-7x^2 - 12x + 6$
  e) $-2x^2 + 2x^2y + 4xy^2 - 3y$ **f)** $-2p^3q^2 + p^2q^2 - 4p + 3q$
  g) $5xy + x^2y - 8xy^2$ **h)** $a^2b^2 - 2b^2 - a^2b$

16. Answers may vary; $-6x^2 + 5x + 4; -3x^2 - 6x - 2$

18. a) $2x + 18$ **b)** $-107a - 448$
  c) $6y - 35$ **d)** $21m - 28$
  e) $-10p^2 - 63p$ **f)** $-23x - 16y$
  g) $5x - 15$ **h)** $3x - 57$
  i) $16a + 88b - 84c$ **j)** $20m - 27n + 36$

19. a) $4x^2 + 17xy + 18y^2$ **b)** $9a^2 - 30ab + 25b^2$
  c) $30x^2 + 19xy - 4y^2$ **d)** $14x^2 - 57xy - 27y^2$
  e) $24m^2 - 22mn + 3n^2$ **f)** $72x^2 + 77xy + 20y^2$

20. a) $17x^3 - 20x^2y$ **b)** $-23a^4 - 53a^3b$
  c) $-4p^3 + 40p^2q$ **d)** $-17a^4 + 44a^3b - 57a^3$
  e) $-32m^3n^2 - 8m^3n^3 + 12m^2n^3$
  f) $12x^2 - y^2 - 43xy + 30y$
  g) $6b^4 - 15b^3c - 14bc + 7c^2 + 4bc^2$
  h) $6x^3 - 12xy^2 - 5xy - 63x^2y - 14y^3$

21. a) $6x^3 - 13x^2 - 38x + 35$
  b) $6n^4 + 18n^3 + 13n^2 + 45n - 70$
  c) $3a^3 - 20a^2 + 39a - 28$
  d) $26p^3 + 29p^2 - 13p + 3$
  e) $6m^3 + 17m^2 - 31m + 63$
  f) $200y^3 + 20y^2z - 10y^2 + yz + 13z$

22. a) $x^3 + 3x^2 + 3x + 1$ **b)** $x^3 + 3x^2y + 3xy^2 + y^3$
  c) $8x^3 + 12x^2y + 6xy^2 + y^3$ **d)** $8x^3 + 36x^2 + 54x + 27$
  e) $27x^3 - 54x^2y + 36xy^2 - 8y^3$

23. a) $7x - 11$ **b)** $-2x^2 - 21x - 4$
  c) $6a^2 + 3a - 29$ **d)** $13a^2 + 9a + 3$

24. a) $6x^3 + 2x^2 - 128x - 160$
  b) $3b^3 - b^2 - 172b + 224$
  c) $18x^3 + 3x^2 - 88x - 80$
  d) $50a^3 - 235a^2 + 228a - 63$
  e) $75m^3 - 10m^2 - 28m + 8$
  f) $8k^3 + 12k^2 - 18k - 27$

25. a) i) $x^2 + 4x + 3$;
$x^2 + 5x + 6$;
$x^2 + 6x + 9$
ii) $x^2 - 1$;
$x^2 + x - 2$;
$x^2 + 2x - 3$
iii) $x^2 - 25$;
$x^2 + x - 20$;
$x^2 + 2x - 15$

c) i) $(x + 3)(x + 4) = x^2 + 7x + 12$;
$(x + 3)(x + 5) = x^2 + 8x + 15$;
$(x + 3)(x + 6) = x^2 + 9x + 18$
ii) $(x + 4)(x - 1) = x^2 + 3x - 4$;
$(x + 5)(x - 1) = x^2 + 4x - 5$;
$(x + 6)(x - 1) = x^2 + 5x - 6$
iii) $(x + 5)(x - 2) = x^2 + 3x - 10$;
$(x + 5)(x - 1) = x^2 + 4x - 5$;
$(x + 5)(x - 0) = x^2 + 5x$

d) i) $(x + 3)(x + 0) = x^2 + 3x$;
$(x + 3)(x - 1) = x^2 + 2x - 3$;
$(x + 3)(x - 2) = x^2 + x - 6$
ii) $(x + 0)(x - 1) = x^2 - x$;
$(x - 1)(x - 1) = x^2 - 2x + 1$;
$(x - 2)(x - 1) = x^2 - 3x + 2$
iii) $(x + 5)(x - 6) = x^2 - x - 30$;
$(x + 5)(x - 7) = x^2 - 2x - 35$;
$(x + 5)(x - 8) = x^2 - 3x - 40$

26. $A = -4x^2 + 200$

27. a) $0 < x < 5$
b) No; as x increases, the surface area decreases.

28.

Side length of square cut out (cm)	Total surface area (cm²)
1	196
2	184
3	164
4	136

29. b) Approximately 3.54 cm

30. a) $x^2 + 2x + 1$;
$x^3 + 2x^2 + 2x + 1$;
$x^4 + 2x^3 + 2x^2 + 2x + 1$;
$(x + 1)(x^4 + x^3 + x^2 + x + 1) =$
$x^5 + 2x^4 + 2x^3 + 2x^2 + 2x + 1$;
$(x + 1)(x^5 + x^4 + x^3 + x^2 + x + 1) =$
$x^6 + 2x^5 + 2x^4 + 2x^3 + 2x^2 + 2x + 1$;
$(x + 1)(x^6 + x^5 + x^4 + x^3 + x^2 + x + 1) =$
$x^7 + 2x^6 + 2x^5 + 2x^4 + 2x^3 + 2x^2 + 2x + 1$

b) $x^2 - 1$;
$x^3 + 1$;
$x^4 - 1$;
$(x + 1)(x^4 - x^3 + x^2 - x + 1) = x^5 + 1$;
$(x + 1)(x^5 - x^4 + x^3 - x^2 + x - 1) = x^6 - 1$;
$(x + 1)(x^6 - x^5 + x^4 - x^3 + x^2 - x + 1) = x^7 + 1$

31. a) $x^2 + 2x + 1$; $x^3 + 3x^2 + 3x + 1$;
$x^4 + 4x^3 + 6x^2 + 4x + 1$;
$(x + 1)^5 = x^5 + 5x^4 + 10x^3 + 10x^2 + 5x + 1$;
$(x + 1)^6 = x^6 + 6x^5 + 15x^4 + 20x^3 + 15x^2 + 6x + 1$;
$(x + 1)^7 = x^7 + 7x^6 + 21x^5 + 35x^4 + 35x^3 + 21x^2 + 7x + 1$
b) $x^2 - 2x + 1$; $x^3 - 3x^2 + 3x - 1$;
$x^4 - 4x^3 + 6x^2 - 4x + 1$;

$(x - 1)^5 = x^5 - 5x^4 + 10x^3 - 10x^2 + 5x - 1$;
$(x - 1)^6 = x^6 - 6x^5 + 15x^4 - 20x^3 + 15x^2 - 6x + 1$;
$(x - 1)^7 = x^7 - 7x^6 + 21x^5 - 35x^4 + 35x^3 - 21x^2 + 7x - 1$
c) $x^2 - 1$; $x^4 - 2x^2 + 1$; $x^6 - 3x^4 + 3x^2 - 1$;
$(x + 1)^4(x - 1)^4 = x^8 - 4x^6 + 6x^4 - 4x^2 + 1$;
$(x + 1)^5(x - 1)^5 = x^{10} - 5x^8 + 10x^6 - 10x^4 + 5x^2 - 1$;
$(x + 1)^6(x - 1)^6 =$
$x^{12} - 6x^{10} + 15x^8 - 20x^6 + 15x^4 - 6x^2 + 1$

2.2 Exercises, page 93

1. a) $-\frac{7}{4}$
b) $\frac{1}{3}$
c) $\frac{2}{3}$
d) $\frac{5}{2}$
e) $\frac{1}{5}$
f) $\frac{2}{3}$
g) -6
h) Undefined
i) $-\frac{1}{8}$

2. a) 2
b) $-\frac{3}{4}$
c) 0
d) 37
e) 13
f) $-\frac{14}{5}$
g) $-\frac{3}{7}$
h) Undefined
i) $-\frac{14}{3}$

3. a) $-\frac{1}{2}$
b) 3
c) $\frac{5}{3}$
d) -3
e) 0
f) Undefined
g) 6
h) $\frac{1}{5}$
i) $\frac{1}{3}$

4. The denominator is equal to zero.

5. A rational number is a fraction of two integers; a rational expression is a fraction that contains at least one variable.

6. a) -2
b) 3
c) $\frac{5}{2}$
d) -2
e) 0
f) 0
g) $-\frac{3}{2}$
h) $\frac{5}{4}$
i) $\frac{1}{3}$

7. The expressions in parts g and h cannot be evaluated because the denominator cannot be 0.

8. a) 0
b) Undefined
c) Numerators can be 0, but denominators cannot.

9. a) 0
b) -1
c) 0
d) None
e) $\frac{7}{2}$
f) 1
g) 3 or -3
h) None
i) None

10. b) $\frac{2x + 1}{5}$, $\frac{x^2 - 9}{x^2 + 1}$ and $\frac{x^2 + 16}{x^2 + 3}$; there are no values of x that make the denominator zero.

11. a) i) 0.48
ii) 10
iii) 0.29
iv) -0.92
v) -0.5
vi) -3.49
b) i) $x \neq 3y, y \neq \frac{x}{3}$
ii) $y \neq -2x, x \neq -\frac{y}{2}$
iii) $x \neq \frac{7}{2}y, y \neq \frac{2}{7}x$
iv) $x \neq 7y, y \neq \frac{x}{7}$
v) $x \neq \frac{4}{3}y, y \neq \frac{3}{4}x$
vi) $y \neq \sqrt{3x}, x \neq \frac{y^2}{3}$

12. a) $y = 1$
b) $x = 6$
c)

x	y
2	1
6	3
0	0
4	2
8	4

d)

e) The equation is the denominator equated to zero.

13. a) 40 mm
b) 120 mm
c) 60.55 mm

2.3 Exercises, page 99

1. a) $5x$ **b)** $-\dfrac{4x}{y}$ **c)** $\dfrac{a}{18}$ **d)** $\dfrac{b}{2c}$

   e) $\dfrac{2m}{3n^2}$ **f)** $\dfrac{9x^3}{y^3}$ **g)** $-\dfrac{x}{2z}$ **h)** $-2b$

2. a) $\dfrac{x+1}{x}$ **b)** $\dfrac{2a}{a-1}$ **c)** $\dfrac{1+3x}{2}$ **d)** $\dfrac{-2}{m+2}$

   e) $\dfrac{b-2}{2b}$ **f)** $\dfrac{3n}{1+n}$ **g)** $\dfrac{2x-1}{3}$ **h)** $\dfrac{-5m}{3+4m}$

3. a) $\dfrac{3}{5}, x \ne -2$ **b)** $\dfrac{1}{3}, x \ne 5$ **c)** $2x+3, x \ne 0$

   d) $\dfrac{x}{3}, x \ne 5$ **e)** $4x, x \ne 3$ **f)** $-\dfrac{2}{3}, a \ne -\dfrac{5}{2}$

   g) $\dfrac{-3m+2}{2m+2}, m \ne 0; m \ne -1$

   h) $-\dfrac{3}{n}, n \ne 0; n \ne \dfrac{4}{3}$

4. a) 1 **b)** 1 **c)** 1

   d) -1 **e)** $\dfrac{x+1}{x-1}$ **f)** $\dfrac{x+1}{1-x}$

5. a) $\dfrac{2}{a+2}$ **b)** $\dfrac{x-3}{x}$ **c)** $\dfrac{3}{m-3}$

   d) $\dfrac{-n}{n-2}$ **e)** $\dfrac{-2}{b+2}$ **f)** $-x-2$

   g) $\dfrac{-5}{x+3}$ **h)** $x-3$ **i)** $\dfrac{1}{x+4}$

6. a) 4 **b)** $x \ne -3$ and $x \ne 1; \dfrac{2x}{x-1}$

   c) 4 **d)** Same

7. a) $x+1; x \ne 1$

   c) Same line, except one has a gap at $x = 1$.

   d) The first screen represents $y = \dfrac{x^2-1}{x-1}$ and the second screen represents $y = x + 1$.

   e) No; we must include the restriction $x \ne 1$.

8. a) $-\dfrac{5}{3}$ **b)** -1 **c)** $-\dfrac{2}{3}$

   d) $-\dfrac{3}{2}$ **e)** $\dfrac{-5y}{2}$ **f)** $-\dfrac{3}{2}$

9. a) $\dfrac{a+7}{a-4}$ **b)** $\dfrac{1}{x+6}$ **c)** $m-5$

   d) $\dfrac{r-3}{r+3}$ **e)** $\dfrac{1}{x-4}$ **f)** $\dfrac{x-3}{x^2+9}$

10. a) $\dfrac{m^2-7m+10}{m-2}$

   b) $\dfrac{a^2+5a-14}{a^2-6a+8}$

11. a) $-\dfrac{2}{3}$ **b)** $\dfrac{-1}{x+3}$ **c)** $-\dfrac{3}{2}$

   d) $\dfrac{x}{x-1}$ **e)** $\dfrac{3(x-2)}{x+12}$ **f)** $\dfrac{x-3}{x+4}$

   g) $\dfrac{-3(4+a)}{4(a+7)}$ **h)** $\dfrac{2(x-5)}{3x}$ **i)** $\dfrac{2(a+6)}{3(a+5)}$

12. a) $\dfrac{x-2}{x+1}$ **b)** $\dfrac{a+2}{a+1}$ **c)** $\dfrac{m-2}{m+2}$

   d) $\dfrac{d+1}{d-1}$ **e)** $\dfrac{3n+1}{2n-1}$ **f)** $\dfrac{3x-2}{x-1}$

   g) $\dfrac{b+3}{b+1}$ **h)** $\dfrac{2a+1}{2a-1}$ **i)** $\dfrac{(2y-1)(y+1)}{2y^2+4y+3}$

13. a) $\dfrac{x}{x-1}$ **b)** $\dfrac{5(x-2)}{x+12}$ **c)** $\dfrac{(a+4)}{-2(a-7)}$

   d) $\dfrac{x-5}{2x}$ **e)** $\dfrac{17-x}{x-3}$ **f)** $\dfrac{3(b+5)}{2(b+6)}$

   g) $\dfrac{5(g+1)}{5g+1}$ **h)** $\dfrac{h-2}{h+1}$ **i)** $\dfrac{3x-1}{3x+2}$

14. Chantelle

Self-Check 2.1–2.3, page 102

1. a) x^2+x-4 **b)** $6m^2+2m-3$

   c) $-15n^2-8n-3$ **d)** $-2b^2+14b+19$

2. a) $14x^2+x$ **b)** $18y^2+9y-20$

3. a) $25x^2+20x+4$ **b)** $36m^2-84mn+49n^2$

4. a) $-3x^2-16x-14$ **b)** $125y^3-150y^2+60y-8$

5. a) $x = 0$ and $y = 0$

   b) The expression is defined for all values of x.

   c) $x = 2$ and $x = -2$

6. a) -6 **b)** 2 **c)** $-\dfrac{1}{2}$

7. a) $\dfrac{x}{4y^3}$ **b)** $\dfrac{4(a+3)}{5}$ **c)** $\dfrac{3a-4b^2}{b^2(2a+b)}$

8. a) $x \ne -1$ and $x \ne -2; \dfrac{x-3}{x+1}$

   b) $x \ne -6$ and $x \ne 4; \dfrac{x+4}{x+6}$

   c) $x \ne 1$ and $x \ne 4$x; $\dfrac{(x+2)(x-2)}{(x-1)(x-4)}$

9. a) $\dfrac{4a-5}{2a-5}$ **b)** $\dfrac{2x+1}{3x-1}$ **c)** $\dfrac{a^2(3+4a)}{2b^3}$

10. a) $a \ne -1$ and $a \ne 1; \dfrac{a+1}{a-1}$

   b) $b \ne -1; \dfrac{b-1}{b+1}$

   c) $c \ne -1$ and $c \ne 1; \dfrac{c-1}{c+1}$

2.4 Exercises, page 105

1. a) $\dfrac{6a}{7}$ **b)** $\dfrac{x}{3}$ **c)** $\dfrac{-m^2}{10}$ **d)** $\dfrac{3b}{14}$

   e) $\dfrac{-8}{5}$ **f)** $\dfrac{r}{6}$ **g)** $25x^2$ **h)** $\dfrac{a}{2b}$

2. a) $\dfrac{3b}{2}$ **b)** $\dfrac{a}{2}$ **c)** -15

   d) $6ab$ **e)** $\dfrac{-20}{t^2}$ **f)** $\dfrac{2r^3}{21}$

   g) $\dfrac{2m}{7n}$ **h)** $\dfrac{2x}{3}$ **i)** $\dfrac{2}{3a}$

3. a) $\dfrac{8y}{5}$ **b)** $\dfrac{3}{4x^2}$ **c)** $\dfrac{45ab}{2}$

   d) $\dfrac{3m^5}{40}$ **e)** 1 **f)** $\dfrac{ac}{12b}$

4. a) i) $\dfrac{3}{2mn}$ **ii)** $9xy$ **iii)** $\dfrac{-16x^2}{3}$

   iv) $\dfrac{-1}{2b^2}$ **v)** $\dfrac{m}{10n}$ **vi)** $\dfrac{ac}{12b}$

   vii) $\dfrac{5a}{16}$ **viii)** $4xy$ **ix)** $\dfrac{3p}{4u^2}$

5. a) 1 **b)** $\dfrac{15a^2b^3}{4}$ **c)** $\dfrac{m}{2}$

   d) $\dfrac{8z}{9x}$ **e)** $\dfrac{2c}{ab^2}$ **f)** $\dfrac{4m^4}{3}$

6. Answers may vary.

   a) $\dfrac{6m}{9x^2} \times \dfrac{9x}{6m}$ **b)** $\dfrac{2x}{3} \times \dfrac{3}{2y}$ **c)** $\dfrac{6m}{8} \times \dfrac{4}{-2n}$

   d) $\dfrac{7a}{5} \times \dfrac{5}{14}$ **e)** $\dfrac{8a}{5b} \times \dfrac{15b^2}{8a}$ **f)** $\dfrac{12ab}{3a^2b^3} \times \dfrac{-b}{4c}$

7. Answers may vary.

   a) $\dfrac{2x}{3} \div \dfrac{2x^2}{3}$ **b)** $\dfrac{5x^2}{y^3} \div \dfrac{5x}{y^2}$ **c)** $\dfrac{-3}{n} \div \dfrac{12mn}{6m^2n}$

   d) $\dfrac{5a^2}{6} \div \dfrac{5a}{3}$ **e)** $\dfrac{12ab}{7} \div \dfrac{4a}{7}$ **f)** $\dfrac{-4}{8a^2b^2c} \div \dfrac{4}{8ab}$

8. a) i) $10, x \ne -1$ and $x \ne 0$ **ii)** $\dfrac{1}{9}, x \ne 0$ and $x \ne 3$

   iii) $3(x-2), x \ne -1$ **iv)** $12s, s \ne 0$ and $s \ne 4$

   v) $-4(t-3), t \ne 2$

   vi) $\dfrac{2(x+1)}{-3x}, x \ne -1, x \ne 0$ and $x \ne 3$

9. a) $\dfrac{2}{3}$ **b)** $\dfrac{3a}{5b^2}$ **c)** $\dfrac{4y}{5(y+3)}$

d) $\dfrac{3(3a+4)}{ab}$ **e)** $\dfrac{5m}{n}$ **f)** $3(x+3y)$

g) $\dfrac{4x(x+1)}{27}$ **h)** $\dfrac{25b^3}{8a^4(a+b)}$ **i)** $\dfrac{9(n-m)}{2mn}$

10. a) n^2 **b)** $\dfrac{2(x+1)}{5(x-1)}$ **c)** $\dfrac{a+2}{a}$

d) $\dfrac{b-2}{b+4}$ **e)** $\dfrac{c+2}{c-1}$ **f)** $\dfrac{x-2}{x+1}$

11. a) $\dfrac{2(x+2)}{3(x+1)}$ **b)** $\dfrac{3(e^2-2)}{4e(e-2)}$ **c)** $\dfrac{a+3}{a-3}$

d) $\dfrac{n-2}{n-1}$ **e)** $\dfrac{(m-2)(m+2)}{(m+1)^2}$ **f)** $\dfrac{c+3}{c-3}$

12. a) $\dfrac{-(x+3)}{x-5}$ **b)** $-(a+5)(a+2)$ **c)** 1

d) $\dfrac{a-2}{a-1}$ **e)** $\dfrac{(x-3)^2}{(x+3)^2}$ **f)** $\dfrac{m+1}{m+7}$

13. Answers may vary.

a) $\dfrac{x}{x^2+2x+1} \times \dfrac{x^2-1}{x^2-x}$

b) $\dfrac{x^2-4x+4}{x^2+4x+4} \times \dfrac{x^2+2x}{x^2-2x}$

c) $\dfrac{a^2+2a}{a^2+2ab+b^2} \times \dfrac{a^2+ab+2a+2b}{a^2+4a+4}$

d) $\dfrac{(x+y)^3}{x^3} \times \dfrac{x^2(x-y)}{x^2-y^2}$

14. Answers may vary.

a) $\dfrac{3x+6}{3x^2+3x} \div \dfrac{2x+4}{2x}$

b) $\dfrac{x^2-4x+4}{x^2+4x+4} \div \dfrac{x^2-3x+2}{x^2+x-2}$

c) $\dfrac{a^2+ab}{a^2-b^2} \div \dfrac{a^2+2ab+b^2}{a^2-b^2}$

d) $\dfrac{x^2+2xy+y^2}{x^2-xy} \div \dfrac{x+y}{x^2-y^2}$

15. a) $\dfrac{-2(x+3y)}{3}$ **b)** $\dfrac{-3(a+b)}{2}$ **c)** $\dfrac{-n}{3m(2m+3)}$

d) $\dfrac{-6m}{n(2n+m)}$ **e)** $\dfrac{-2(3a+4)}{a}$ **f)** $\dfrac{-y}{4}$

16. a) 1 **b)** -1

c) $2a+5b$ **d)** $-(2a+5b)$

2.5 Exercises, page 109

1. a) $\dfrac{8y}{36xy}$ **b)** $\dfrac{15x^2}{36xy}$ **c)** $\dfrac{-18x^2y}{36xy}$

d) $\dfrac{66x^2y^2}{36xy}$ **e)** $\dfrac{-14y}{36xy}$ **f)** $\dfrac{-52xy}{36xy}$

g) $\dfrac{252}{36xy}$ **h)** $\dfrac{-33y^2}{36xy}$ **i)** $\dfrac{-30x^2y}{36xy}$

j) $\dfrac{-44xz}{36xy}$

2. a) $\dfrac{5m}{10}, \dfrac{2m}{10}$ **b)** $\dfrac{x^2}{3x}, \dfrac{9}{3x}$ **c)** $\dfrac{4}{3p}, \dfrac{-3}{3p}$

d) $\dfrac{15}{18x}, \dfrac{4x}{18x}$ **e)** $\dfrac{8xz}{12yz}, \dfrac{3xy}{12yz}$ **f)** $\dfrac{x^2+3x}{2x^2}, \dfrac{2x-10}{2x^2}$

3. a) $\dfrac{7}{x}, x \neq -0$ **b)** $\dfrac{4}{x}, x \neq 0$ **c)** $\dfrac{6+5x}{7x}, x \neq 0$

d) $\dfrac{1}{m^2}, m \neq 0$ **e)** $\dfrac{a}{b}, b \neq 0$ **f)** $\dfrac{4x}{3y}, y \neq 0$

g) $\dfrac{3x}{2y^2}, y \neq 0$ **h)** $\dfrac{26a^2+11b^2}{17ab}, a \neq 0$ and $b \neq 0$

4. a) $\dfrac{3}{x}$ **b)** $\dfrac{2}{5x}$ **c)** $\dfrac{3+5x}{2x^2}$

d) $\dfrac{7-6m}{2m^3}$ **e)** $\dfrac{x}{2y}$ **f)** $\dfrac{25a^2}{7b^3}$

g) $\dfrac{4m}{3n}$ **h)** $\dfrac{-12}{11x^2}$

5. a) $\dfrac{19a}{6}$ **b)** $\dfrac{27}{10m}, m \neq 0$

c) $\dfrac{15x^2+14}{6x}, x \neq 0$ **d)** $\dfrac{14+15a^2}{35a}, a \neq 0$

e) $\dfrac{17}{12a}, a \neq 0$ **f)** $\dfrac{5x+4}{6x^2}, x \neq 0$

g) $\dfrac{9x^2+4y^2}{6xy}, x \neq 0$ and $y \neq 0$ **h)** $\dfrac{7a^2b+6c}{3ac}, a \neq 0$ and $c \neq 0$

i) $\dfrac{3y+5x}{4xy}, x \neq 0$ and $y \neq 0$

6. a) $\dfrac{-2x}{15}$ **b)** $\dfrac{-1}{12a}$ **c)** $\dfrac{20-3a}{12a}$

d) $\dfrac{-2}{15x}$ **e)** $\dfrac{3b-7a^2}{4ab}$ **f)** $\dfrac{24ab-35}{56b^2}$

g) $\dfrac{7a^2b-20}{5a}$ **h)** $\dfrac{22b-15a^2}{33ab}$ **i)** $\dfrac{9x-7}{6y}$

7. a) $\dfrac{10xy-28x}{35y}$ **b)** $\dfrac{-8-15a}{20a^2}$ **c)** $\dfrac{3a+20b}{12ab}$

d) $\dfrac{25y^2-6}{15xy}$ **e)** $\dfrac{3a^2-b^2}{4ab^2}$ **f)** $\dfrac{24ab-21a}{56b^2}$

g) $\dfrac{-8ab-10b}{5a}$ **h)** $\dfrac{22b-35a^2}{77ab}$ **i)** $\dfrac{15x^2-1}{6xy}$

8. a) $\dfrac{17a}{5}$ **b)** $\dfrac{-7m}{12}$ **c)** $\dfrac{19}{20a}$

d) $\dfrac{17}{20y}$ **e)** $\dfrac{10n-18m+45}{15mn}$ **f)** $\dfrac{23y-9x}{3xy}$

g) $\dfrac{21x-8}{20xy}$ **h)** $\dfrac{6b-6a+6}{5ab}$ **i)** $\dfrac{385y-99x-42}{231xy}$

9. a) $\dfrac{2a+5}{2}$ **b)** $\dfrac{-1}{2}$ **c)** $\dfrac{6x-2}{x}$

d) $\dfrac{-2x+8}{x}$ **e)** $\dfrac{3m-5n}{mn}$ **f)** $\dfrac{m-n}{mn}$

g) $\dfrac{5y+8}{6}$ **h)** $\dfrac{-5d-13}{6}$ **i)** $\dfrac{1}{4}$

j) $\dfrac{10-17b}{12}$ **k)** $\dfrac{n-8}{10}$ **l)** $\dfrac{7-19x}{12}$

10. a) i) $\dfrac{69-10m}{15}$ **ii)** $\dfrac{17-5m}{3}$

iii) $\dfrac{12a+8b-1}{4a}$ **iv)** $\dfrac{7-19y}{4y}$

v) $\dfrac{4mn+m+6}{2mn}$ **vi)** $\dfrac{3xy-5y-3x}{xy}$

vii) $\dfrac{8pr-15q^2-80qr^2}{20qr}$ **viii)** $\dfrac{3b+4a-10ab}{5ab}$

ix) $\dfrac{25y-45xy-9}{15xy}$

11. Answers may vary.

a) $\dfrac{1}{a} + \dfrac{1}{a}$ **b)** $\dfrac{a}{4b} + \dfrac{a}{2b}$ **c)** $\dfrac{1-a^2}{9ab} + \dfrac{a}{9b}$

d) $\dfrac{x}{4y^2} + \dfrac{2x}{4y^2}$ **e)** $\dfrac{-1}{4x} + \dfrac{2}{y}$

12. Answers may vary.

a) $\dfrac{3}{a} - \dfrac{1}{a}$ **b)** $\dfrac{a}{b} - \dfrac{a}{4b}$ **c)** $\dfrac{1}{ab} - \dfrac{8}{9ab}$

d) $\dfrac{x}{y^2} - \dfrac{x}{4y^2}$ **e)** $\dfrac{2}{y} - \dfrac{1}{4x}$

13. a) $\dfrac{12a-13}{10}$ **b)** $\dfrac{-8x+5}{6}$

c) $\dfrac{6xy+5x-2}{3y^2}, y \neq 0$ **d)** $\dfrac{m^3+4m^2+15}{5m^2}, m \neq 0$

e) $\dfrac{6a^2-5a-14}{7a}, a \neq 0$ **f)** $\dfrac{-10x-3}{6x^2}, x \neq 0$

14. b) 8.86 cm

15. Answers may vary.

a) $4 - \dfrac{a}{3}$ **b)** $\dfrac{1}{5} - \dfrac{1}{2x}$

c) $\dfrac{x}{y} + 1$ **d)** $\dfrac{7x^2+1}{x} + 1$

16. a) $\dfrac{1+4x}{1-4x}$ **b)** $\dfrac{4x-1}{4x+1}$

c) $\dfrac{4x-1}{4x+1}$ **d)** $\dfrac{2+6x}{4-3x}$

2.6 Exercises, page 114

1. a) $\dfrac{6+x}{x-1}$ **b)** $\dfrac{a-3}{a+3}$ **c)** 1

d) $\dfrac{2k+9}{3k-2}$ **e)** $\dfrac{4a-6}{a^2+3}$ **f)** $\dfrac{x+8}{x+5}$

g) $\dfrac{9-k}{3k-1}$ **h)** $\dfrac{5m+10}{m^2+4}$ **i)** $\dfrac{a+100}{a-9}$

2. a) $\dfrac{5x-1}{x(x-1)}$ **b)** $\dfrac{5(2a+3)}{a(a+5)}$ **c)** $\dfrac{20-3y}{y(y-4)}$

d) $\dfrac{2(2a+7)}{a(a+2)}$ **e)** $\dfrac{x^2+2x-6}{2(x+2)}$ **f)** $\dfrac{2(11-3a)}{5(a+3)}$

g) $\dfrac{2(m-3)}{m(m-1)}$ **h)** $\dfrac{(x-6)(x+2)}{(x-4)(x+1)}$ **i)** $\dfrac{-a^2-8a+5}{5(a+8)}$

3. a) $\dfrac{2(3a-8)}{a-3}$ **b)** $\dfrac{20+7a}{a+2}$ **c)** $\dfrac{3y+1}{y+2}$

d) $\dfrac{-10m-1}{2m+1}$ **e)** $\dfrac{-x^2-x+8}{x-1}$ **f)** $\dfrac{-a^2+a+11}{a+3}$

g) $\dfrac{3m+4}{m+1}$ **h)** $\dfrac{-2x^2+3x+37}{x-5}$ **i)** $\dfrac{8a^2-12a-3}{2a-3}$

4. a) $\dfrac{2x}{(x+3)(x-3)}$ **b)** $\dfrac{-6}{(x+3)(x-3)}$ **c)** $\dfrac{2(3a-4)}{(a-3)(a+2)}$

d) $\dfrac{x-10}{(2x+1)(x-1)}$ **e)** $\dfrac{x(7x+39)}{(x+2)(x+7)}$ **f)** $\dfrac{a(-2a+31)}{(a-5)(a+2)}$

g) $\dfrac{7x-8}{(x+1)(2x-1)}$ **h)** $\dfrac{x(9x-53)}{(x-2)(x-7)}$ **i)** $\dfrac{m(m-1)}{(m+3)(m+2)}$

5. a) $\dfrac{x^2+6x-23}{(x-3)(x-2)}$ **b)** $\dfrac{a^2-8a-26}{(a+2)(a-4)}$ **c)** $\dfrac{2m^2+5m+5}{(m+3)(m-1)}$

d) $\dfrac{-5x-7}{(x-1)(x-5)}$ **e)** $\dfrac{41a-29}{10(a-1)(a+1)}$ **f)** $\dfrac{11x-49}{6(x+1)(x-3)}$

g) $\dfrac{-3x^2-10x+10}{(2x+1)(x-1)}$ **h)** $\dfrac{7w^2+14w-5}{4(w-1)(w+1)}$ **i)** $\dfrac{-2(4a^2+a-35)}{15(a+4)(a-1)}$

6. a) $\dfrac{x^2+8x-28}{(x-3)(x-2)}$ **b)** $\dfrac{a(a-13)}{(a+2)(a-4)}$ **c)** $\dfrac{5m+7}{(m+3)(m-1)}$

d) $\dfrac{5x-7}{(x+1)(x+5)}$ **e)** $\dfrac{7a^2+22a-41}{12(a+1)(a-1)}$ **f)** $\dfrac{-a^2-20a+41}{2(a-9)(a+1)}$

g) $\dfrac{-x^2-11x-7}{(x+1)(x-2)}$ **h)** $\dfrac{m(17m+8)}{4(m-2)(m+1)}$ **i)** $\dfrac{x(5x-27)}{6(x+1)(x-3)}$

7. Answers may vary.

a) $\dfrac{1}{x+1}+\dfrac{1}{x+1}$ **b)** $\dfrac{x}{x-6}+\dfrac{2}{x-6}$ **c)** $\dfrac{b}{a+b}+\dfrac{b}{a+b}$

8. Answers may vary.

a) $\dfrac{x}{x+1}-\dfrac{x-2}{x+1}$ **b)** $\dfrac{x+4}{x-6}-\dfrac{2}{x-6}$ **c)** $\dfrac{5b}{a+b}-\dfrac{3b}{a+b}$

9. a) $\dfrac{2x+1}{x(x+1)}, \dfrac{2x+3}{(x+1)(x+2)}, \dfrac{2x+5}{(x+2)(x+3)}$

$\dfrac{1}{x+3}+\dfrac{1}{x+4}=\dfrac{2x+7}{(x+3)(x+4)}$

$\dfrac{1}{x+4}+\dfrac{1}{x+5}=\dfrac{2x+9}{(x+4)(x+5)}$

b) $\dfrac{3x+4}{(x+1)(x+2)}, \dfrac{5x+12}{(x+2)(x+3)}, \dfrac{7x+24}{(x+3)(x+4)}$

$\dfrac{4}{x+4}+\dfrac{5}{x+5}=\dfrac{9x+40}{(x+4)(x+5)}$

$\dfrac{5}{x+5}+\dfrac{6}{x+6}=\dfrac{11x+60}{(x+5)(x+6)}$

c) $\dfrac{2}{(x-1)(x+1)}, \dfrac{2}{(x-2)(x+2)}, \dfrac{2}{(x-3)(x+3)}$

$\dfrac{1}{x(x-4)}+\dfrac{1}{x(x+4)}=\dfrac{2}{(x-4)(x+4)}$

$\dfrac{1}{x(x-5)}+\dfrac{1}{x(x+5)}=\dfrac{2}{(x-5)(x+5)}$

10. Answers may vary.

a) $\dfrac{1}{x}+\dfrac{1}{x-1}$

$\dfrac{1}{x-1}+\dfrac{1}{x-2}$

$\dfrac{1}{x-2}+\dfrac{1}{x-3}$

b) $\dfrac{-1}{x-1}+\dfrac{-2}{x-2}$

$\dfrac{-2}{x-2}+\dfrac{-3}{x-3}$

$\dfrac{-3}{x-3}+\dfrac{-4}{x-4}$

c) $\dfrac{1}{x(x-1)}+\dfrac{1}{x(x+1)}$

$\dfrac{2}{2x(x-2)}+\dfrac{2}{2x(x+2)}$

$\dfrac{3}{3x(x-3)}+\dfrac{3}{3x(x+3)}$

11. a) $\dfrac{29}{6(x-1)}$ **b)** $\dfrac{-1}{12(x-4)}$ **c)** $\dfrac{18}{5(x-2)}$

d) $\dfrac{19}{6(x-3)}$ **e)** $\dfrac{7x+10}{2x(y-1)}$ **f)** $\dfrac{2(9-b)}{3b(ab-1)}$

g) $\dfrac{4(x+10)}{(3x-4)(3x+4)}$ **h)** $\dfrac{2(x^2-4x+6)}{(x+2)(x-2)}$ **i)** $\dfrac{2(x^2+3x-12)}{(x-3)(x+3)}$

12. a) $\dfrac{7a-2}{(a-2)(a+2)}$ **b)** $\dfrac{-7x-38}{(5-x)(5+x)}$ **c)** $\dfrac{-2(2m+5)}{(m-3)(m+3)}$

d) $\dfrac{4x+23}{(5-x)(5+x)}$ **e)** $\dfrac{2x+13}{(x-4)(x+4)}$ **f)** $\dfrac{-18a+17}{(3a-2)(3a+2)}$

13. a) i) $60°$ **ii)** $90°$

iii) $108°$ **iv)** $120°$

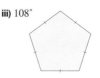 

v) $135°$

b) $\dfrac{180(n-2)}{n}$, where n is the number of sides and $n>2$

c) $144°$

14. a) $\dfrac{7x+4}{(x-1)(x+1)}$ **b)** $\dfrac{-x^2-6x+3}{(x-2)(x+2)}$

c) $\dfrac{m(m+15)}{(m+4)(m+3)}$ **d)** $\dfrac{-4n^2+2n-5}{(2n+1)(2n+3)}$

e) $\dfrac{-10c-29}{(c+7)(c-2)}$ **f)** $\dfrac{8m^2+3m-10}{(2m-1)(2m-3)}$

g) $\dfrac{3(2n^2+n-2)}{(2n-1)(2n-5)}$ **h)** $\dfrac{-a^2-22a-13}{(2a+3)(a-6)}$

15. a) $\dfrac{a(9a-8)}{(a-4)(a-2)(a+3)}$ **b)** $\dfrac{3x}{(x-4)(x-1)}$

c) $\dfrac{b(5b-2)}{(b+4)(b+2)(b-2)}$ **d)** $\dfrac{-2m(m-15)}{(m-3)(m-2)(m+3)}$

e) $\dfrac{6n(n+3)}{(n-5)(n-2)(n+4)}$ **f)** $\dfrac{-a(a+10)}{(a+8)(a+1)(a+7)}$

g) $\dfrac{2x(4x+11)}{(x-5)(x+3)(x+2)}$ **h)** $\dfrac{x(x-8)}{(x+4)(x-3)(x+1)}$

16. a) $\dfrac{2(x^2-x-3)}{(x-5)(x+2)(x-4)}$ **b)** $\dfrac{-3(3a-5)}{(a+5)(a+3)(a-5)}$

c) $\dfrac{(3x-14)(x-1)}{(x-5)(x-4)(x-3)}$ **d)** $\dfrac{-2(2x^2-x-14)}{(6-x)(6+x)(2-x)}$

e) $\dfrac{2}{(a-4)(a-1)}$ **f)** $\dfrac{-2(a^2+22a-9)}{(a+7)(a+3)(a-5)}$

g) $\dfrac{5b^2+16b-30}{(b-5)(b+3)(b+6)}$ **h)** $\dfrac{-2(x^2-x-15)}{(x+6)(x-3)(x+4)}$

17. a) $\dfrac{14x-3}{(2x-3)(x+1)(2x+3)}$ **b)** $\dfrac{-11x-8}{(3x+2)(x+1)(2x+1)}$

c) $\dfrac{a(3a+7)}{(2a+3)(a+2)(a+3)}$ **d)** $\dfrac{2n(4-7n)}{(2n+1)(n-3)(n-7)}$

e) $\dfrac{m(3m+7)}{(m+3)(m+1)(m+2)}$ **f)** $\dfrac{c(4c+13)}{(3c+1)(c+4)(2c+3)}$

18. a) $\dfrac{x^2 + 10x - 4}{(2x+1)(x+3)(x-2)}$

b) $\dfrac{-19a - 14}{2(a+1)(a+1)(2a+1)}$

c) $\dfrac{2}{c-5}$

d) $\dfrac{-2}{m+2}$

e) $\dfrac{11x^2 + 19x + 10}{(3x+2)(2x+1)(x+2)}$

f) $\dfrac{-(n+6)(n+3)}{(3n+1)(n+2)(2n-5)}$

19. a) $2x$

b) $-5y$

c) $\dfrac{5x-6y}{6}$

d) $\dfrac{2a}{(a-3b)(a+3b)}$

20. Answers may vary.

a) $\dfrac{2}{x-4} - \dfrac{4}{(x^2-4x)}$

b) $\dfrac{1}{x+y} + \dfrac{1}{x-y}$

c) $\dfrac{2}{x+3} + \dfrac{1}{x+4}$

21. a) $\dfrac{1}{x-1} + \dfrac{1}{x} = \dfrac{2x-1}{x(x-1)}$

$\dfrac{1}{x-2} + \dfrac{1}{x-1} = \dfrac{2x-3}{(x-2)(x-1)}$

$\dfrac{1}{x-3} + \dfrac{1}{x-2} = \dfrac{2x-5}{(x-3)(x-2)}$

b) $\dfrac{0}{x} + \dfrac{1}{x+1} = \dfrac{1}{x+1}$

$\dfrac{-1}{x-1} + \dfrac{0}{x} = \dfrac{-1}{x-1}$

$\dfrac{-2}{x-2} + \dfrac{-1}{x-1} = \dfrac{-3x+4}{(x-2)(x-1)}$

c) $\dfrac{1}{x(x)} + \dfrac{1}{x(x)} = \dfrac{2}{x^2}$

$\dfrac{1}{x(x+1)} + \dfrac{1}{x(x-1)} = \dfrac{2}{(x-1)(x+1)}$

$\dfrac{1}{x(x+2)} + \dfrac{1}{x(x-2)} = \dfrac{2}{(x-2)(x+2)}$

Self-Check 2.4–2.6, page 117

1. a) $\dfrac{5y^2}{8x^3}$ **b)** $\dfrac{8a^3}{3b^2c}$ **c)** $\dfrac{7z}{18x}$

d) $\dfrac{6c}{5b^3}$ **e)** $4s$ **f)** $-\dfrac{2}{3}$

2. a) $\dfrac{3(x-5)}{8x^3}$ **b)** $\dfrac{3a}{2(4-a)}$ **c)** 1 **d)** $\dfrac{x+2}{x-1}$

3. a) $\dfrac{2}{5}$ **b)** $\dfrac{3(x-4)}{2(3x-1)}$ **c)** $\dfrac{a-2}{5a^2}$ **d)** $\dfrac{4(2x-3)}{x-1}$

4. a) $\dfrac{13}{6a}$ **b)** $\dfrac{7m+15}{m(m+3)}$ **c)** $\dfrac{13a}{5}$

d) $\dfrac{191}{60y}$ **e)** $\dfrac{40-93x}{60xy}$ **f)** $\dfrac{75y-54x-35}{45xy}$

5. a) $\dfrac{a^2+8a-13}{(a+1)(a-3)}$, $a \neq -1$ and $a \neq 3$

b) $\dfrac{-17x-11}{(3x+1)(x-1)}$, $x \neq 1$ and $x \neq -\dfrac{1}{3}$

c) $\dfrac{-2x^2-x-3}{(2x-1)(2x+1)}$, $x \neq \dfrac{1}{2}$ and $x \neq -\dfrac{1}{2}$

d) $\dfrac{11m^2+17m-4}{4(m-1)(m+1)}$, $m \neq 1$ and $m \neq -1$

e) $\dfrac{-y^2-26y-13}{2(y+7)(y-3)}$, $y \neq 3$ and $y \neq -7$

f) $\dfrac{3x+4}{(x+2)(x-2)(x+1)}$, $x \neq 2$, $x \neq -2$, and $x \neq -1$

Insights Into a Rich Problem— How Much Time Does Extra Speed Save?, page 120

1. 50 min

2. a) 27.3 min **b)** No

3. a) 75 min **b)** No

4. a) 2 min **b)** $3\dfrac{1}{3}$ min

5. $\dfrac{1}{5}$

6. a) No

b) Approximately 95.2% of the original amount

c) $\dfrac{1}{1+r}$

7. a) No **b)** $\dfrac{1}{3}$ **c)** $\dfrac{r}{1-r}$

8. B also increases by 20%.

9. b) As r approaches 1, s approaches $\dfrac{1}{2}$.

10. a) 36%

b) The height is decreased by a fraction $\dfrac{p^2 + 2p}{(1+p)^2}$.

c) The radius is decreased by a fraction $1 - \sqrt{\dfrac{1}{1+q}}$.

11. A wins the race. B loses the race by a fraction of $\left(\dfrac{s^2}{1-s^2}\right)$ of A's time.

Chapter 2 Review Exercises, page 122

1. a) $2x^3 + 5x^2 + 4x + 3$ **b)** $2x^4 + x^3 + 2x^2 - 4x - 4$

c) $7x^2 - x - 5$ **d)** $3x^2y - 2xy - 2y^2$

2. a) $x^2 - 3x - 2$ **b)** $2y^3 + y^2 + 9y - 7$

c) $x^2 + 3xy + 4y^2$ **d)** $3a^2b^2 + 8a^3b - 4ab^3$

3. a) $-9x^2 + 20xy$ **b)** $3m^2 - 8mn + 7n^2$

c) $-4x^2 + 11xy$ **d)** $3a^2 - 12ab$

e) $-5x^2y - 20xy^2$ **f)** $-12m^2n + 5mn^2$

4. a) $23x^2 - 69x$ **b)** $-14c + 12d - 57c$

c) $8m^2 - 17mn + 13m$ **d)** $8x^3 + 16x^2y - 26x^2$

5. a) $2x^2 + 2x - 12$ **b)** $5x^2 + 22x + 8$

c) $4m^2 - 12m + 9$ **d)** $16a^2 + 8a + 1$

e) $4x^3 - 24x^2 + 27x + 20$ **f)** $24y^3 + 41y^2 - 9y - 28$

6. a) 1 **b)** 1 **c)** 7

d) $-\dfrac{5}{7}$ **e)** $\dfrac{1}{6}$ **f)** $\dfrac{5}{7}$

7. a) $x \neq 5$ **b)** $x \neq -1$

c) $x \neq \dfrac{3}{2}$ **d)** $x \neq -5$ and $x \neq 5$

e) $x \neq -4$ and $x \neq 3$ **f)** $x \neq -2$ and $x \neq -5$

8. a) $\dfrac{10ab}{3}$ **b)** $2m + 1$ **c)** $\dfrac{2(5x-1)}{5}$

d) $\dfrac{-2(3a-b)}{3a}$ **e)** $\dfrac{2}{x-3}$ **f)** $\dfrac{-3m^2}{2n(3m+1)}$

9. a) -4, $y \neq \dfrac{1}{2}$ **b)** $\dfrac{x+3}{7x}$, $x \neq 0$ and $x \neq 3$

c) $\dfrac{x+3}{x+4}$, $x \neq 4$ and $x \neq -4$ **d)** $\dfrac{-3(a+2)}{a-3}$, $a \neq 2$ and $a \neq 3$

e) $\dfrac{m-3}{m-1}$, $m \neq 1$ and $m \neq 4$ **f)** $\dfrac{-x}{x+2}$, $x \neq 6$ and $x \neq -2$

10. a) $2a^2$ **b)** $-2n$ **c)** $\dfrac{21}{5xy^3}$

d) $\dfrac{4x^3}{9}$ **e)** $\dfrac{14}{5b}$ **f)** $48a^2b^2$

11. a) $\dfrac{9}{a^2}$ **b)** $\dfrac{-9}{y}$ **c)** $\dfrac{9m}{a}$

d) $\dfrac{-7}{16a^5}$ **e)** $\dfrac{1}{12x^2}$ **f)** $8b^2$

12. a) $\dfrac{1}{3x}$ **b)** $\dfrac{a-3}{2a(a+3)}$ **c)** $\dfrac{1}{2}$

d) $2a(a+1)$ **e)** $\dfrac{1}{4x}$ **f)** $\dfrac{-(m+2)^2}{(m-3)^2}$

13. a) $\dfrac{a^2}{(a-3)^2}$ **b)** $\dfrac{2}{2x+1}$ **c)** -1

d) $2x$ **e)** $\dfrac{a+6}{4ab}$ **f)** $\dfrac{a^2}{(a+b)^2}$

14. a) $\dfrac{5}{2a}$ b) $\dfrac{23}{4x}$ c) $\dfrac{m+4}{3m}$
d) $\dfrac{17x}{24}$ e) $\dfrac{5}{6a}$ f) $\dfrac{38b-3}{14b^2}$

15. a) $\dfrac{3x-2}{x}$ b) $\dfrac{5x+1}{6}$ c) $\dfrac{24a^2+a-10}{20a}$
d) $\dfrac{13x+7}{12x}$ e) $\dfrac{7a^2-5a-8}{4a}$ f) $\dfrac{28m^2-4m-3}{18m^2}$

16. a) $\dfrac{9a-10}{a(a-2)}$ b) $\dfrac{7m+10}{m(m+5)}$ c) $\dfrac{2(2-x)}{x(x-1)}$
d) $\dfrac{3m-5}{m-2}$ e) $\dfrac{-5a-11}{a+3}$ f) $\dfrac{6y+4}{y+1}$

17. a) $\dfrac{19}{6(2x-1)}$ b) $\dfrac{2(9-a)}{3a(b-1)}$ c) $\dfrac{20-7n}{5n(mn-1)}$
d) $\dfrac{5x+13}{(x-3)(x+3)}$ e) $\dfrac{-6a+17}{(2a-5)(2a+5)}$ f) $\dfrac{6x+11}{(x-2)(x+2)}$

18. a) $\dfrac{5-2x}{(x-3)(x-1)}$ b) $\dfrac{3x+49}{(x+7)(x-4)}$
c) $\dfrac{6x^2+11x+8}{(2x+3)(x+4)(2x-3)}$ d) $\dfrac{6x-1}{(3x+2)(3x-1)}$

Chapter 2 Self-Test, page 125

1. a) $5m-2n+3n^2$ b) $-a^2+17ab^2$
c) $5x^2-13xy-6y^2$ d) a^3+8

2. a) $x \neq 0$ and $y \neq 0$ b) $x \neq 0$ and $x \neq 2$
c) $x \neq 1$ and $x \neq 7$
d) The expression is defined for all values of y.

3. a) $-\dfrac{5}{18}$ b) $\dfrac{1}{15}$ c) $-\dfrac{9}{2}$ d) 1

4. a) $\dfrac{3b}{4a}$ b) $3x-2$
c) $\dfrac{x-6}{x-3}$ d) $\dfrac{-3(x+2)}{x+1}$

5. Answers may vary.
a) $\dfrac{9ab}{12a^2} = \dfrac{3ab}{6a^2} + \dfrac{3b}{12a}$ b) $\dfrac{9ab}{12a^2} = \dfrac{21b}{12a} + \dfrac{ab}{a^2}$

6. a) $\dfrac{3}{2}$ b) $\dfrac{7t(t-3)}{12(t-1)(14-t)}$
c) $\dfrac{4(x+4)}{15x}$

7. a) $a-3; a \neq -1, a \neq \dfrac{1}{2}, a \neq 1$
b) $-2(x+1); x \neq -\dfrac{3}{4}, x \neq \dfrac{3}{4}, x \neq 3$
c) $\dfrac{-3x-14}{(x+4)(x-3)(x+3)}, x \neq -4, x \neq -3, x \neq 3$
d) $\dfrac{-5a-9}{a(a-1)(a+3)}, a \neq 0, a \neq 1, a \neq -3$

8. Answers may vary.
a) $\dfrac{6}{x^2} \times \dfrac{x}{2}$ b) $\dfrac{10}{b} \times \dfrac{b^2}{12}$
c) $\dfrac{4}{m} \times \dfrac{1}{2m+2}$

9. Answers may vary.
a) $\dfrac{2+x}{x} + \dfrac{3-3x}{3x}$ b) $\dfrac{b}{2} + \dfrac{b}{3}$
c) $\dfrac{2-m}{m} + \dfrac{m-1}{m+1}$

10. a) $z = \dfrac{xy}{y+x}$ b) 5.45 ohms

Assessment Tasks, page 126

1. a)

Width (m)	Length (m)	Area (m²)
1	14	14
2	13	26
3	12	36
4	11	44
5	10	50
6	9	54
7	8	56
8	7	56
9	6	54
10	5	50
11	4	44
12	3	36
13	2	26
14	1	14

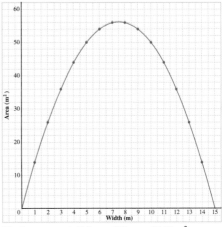

Area of Rectangle whose Perimeter is 30 m

Maximum area is 7.5 m × 7.5 m = 56.25 m²

2. a) i) $\dfrac{3}{10}$ ii) $\dfrac{1}{6}$ iii) $\dfrac{3}{28}$

Chapter 3 Financial Mathematics

Necessary Skills
1 New: Simple Interest
Exercises, page 130

1. a) $3.33 b) $13.67 c) $1941.18
d) 5% e) 9 months f) $51.11

2. $36.94

3. 88 days

4. 7.40%

5. $5.37

6. $467.92

7. a)

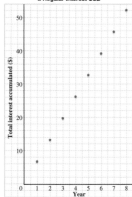

Interest Accumulated on a Regular Interest CSB

b) Linear growth

c) The yearly accumulated interest is an arithmetic sequence with $a = 6.50$ and $d = 6.50$.

2 Review: Solving Equations

Exercises, page 131

1. a) $\frac{8}{7}$ **b)** $\frac{24}{7}$ **c)** $-\frac{14}{3}$

d) 20   **e)** $\frac{d-a}{4}$ **f)** $\frac{h+2}{g}$

g) $\pm\sqrt{5}$ **h)** $\pm\sqrt{2}$ **i)** $\pm\sqrt{\frac{b}{A}}$

3 Review: Geometric Series

Exercises, page 134

1. a) 3.3333   **b)** 3.45×10^{10}
c) 1020   **d)** 6.2500

4 Review: Using a Calculator to Evaluate Expressions

Exercises, page 134

1. a) 1.3   **b)** 1.5   **c)** 0.7

2. a) 584.21   **b)** 4630.74   **c)** 77 632.00

3. a) 1149.47   **b)** 12 043.93

3.1 Exercises, page 138

1. a) $562.43   **b)** $1124.86
c) $629.86   **d)** $632.66

2. a) $796.92   **b)** $1648.83
c) $1322.52   **d)** $1552.42

3. a) $841.97   **b)** $1683.95
c) $712.99   **d)** $708.92

4. a) $644.61   **b)** $924.08
c) $1629.00   **d)** $3862.47

5. a) $2676.47   **b)** $1770.14   **c)** $1790.87

6. Part a; when you double the principle the amount is doubled.

7. a) $6393.77   **b)** $2093.01   **c)** $2044.01

8. Part a; the divisor $(1.0575)^8$ does not change, so if the numerator doubles, the present value also doubles.

9. a) i) $1550   **ii)** $2300   **iii)** $3500
    iv) $5250   **v)** $8000
b) Estimates may vary.
    i) 9.9 years   **ii)** 16.5 years   **iii)** 26 years
c) The amount grows exponentially.
d) i) The graph would start at the same point but rise more rapidly.
    ii) The graph would start at a higher point and rise more rapidly.
e) No

10. a) i) $2800   **ii)** $1600   **iii)** $900
    iv) $500   **v)** $300   **vi)** $280
b) Estimates may vary.
    i) 21.5 years   **ii)** 16.5 years   **iii)** 9 years
c) The rate of decrease of the present values gets smaller as the number of years increases.
d) i) The graph would start at the same point, but would rise more rapidly.
    ii) The graph would start at a higher point and fall more slowly; that is, the graph would be stretched by a factor that is determined by the increase in the mortgage.

12. a) i) $1129.87   **ii)** $1407.10
    iii) $1579.70   **iv)** $1857.59
b) i) $1086.81   **ii)** $1181.15
    iii) $1516.21   **iv)** $1866.99

13. a) $581.87   **b)** 10.31%   **c)** 11.91 years

14. a) $1286.47   **b)** $1459.14   **c)** $1655.00

15. a) $380.47   **b)** $760.95   **c)** $1521.89

16. a) i) $1047.50   **ii)** $2782.56   **iii)** $5913.04
    iv) $12 744.29   **v)** $137 008.67

17. a) $2904.93   **b)** $2409.93
    c) $9928.40   **d)** $4905.55

18. $2726.97

19. a) $7107.90   **b)** $6838.43   **c)** $6581.62
    d) $6336.75   **e)** $6103.16

20. a) $1000 today if I could invest it at a rate of 15% or more
b) $1000 today
c) $1000 today
d) part a: 14.9%; part b: 14.9%

21. Yes

23. $1 586 874.32

24. $33 947.76

25. a) 14 years   **b)** 12 years   **c)** 10 years
    d) 9 years   **e)** 8 years

26. a) 18.92%   **b)** 9.05%   **c)** 5.95%
    d) 4.43%   **e)** 3.53%

27. 10.31%

29. a) i) 7.2 years   **ii)** 4.9 years
    b) i) 12.1%   **ii)** 7.1%

30. $396.88

31. $3701.07

32. $1020.06

33. a) $4900.88   **b)** 5.50%

3.2 Exercises, page 146

1. a) $132.39   **b)** $273.71
c) $275.95   **d)** $221.85

2. a) $468.38   **b)** $274.14   **c)** $745.55

3. a) $835.26   **b)** $1317.81
c) $2264.31   **d)** $3896.33

4. a) $3069.57   **b)** $4370.67   **c)** $7430.63

5. a) $645.08   **b)** $445.35
c) $860.64   **d)** $2398.66

6. a) $317.62   **b)** $661.26   **c)** $877.63
d) $7839.65   **e)** $489.85   **f)** $1142.50

7. a) $45.51   **b)** $45.94

8. a) $290.37   **b)** $289.92

9. a) $875.02   **b)** $873.94

10. 7.72%

11. $1061.42

12. a)

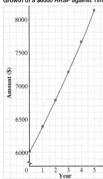

Growth of a $6000 RRSP against Time

b) Exponential growth
c) 15 years
d) Estimates may vary. $9100.00

13. $2030.14

14. a) $0.90   **b)** $0.46   **c)** $0.31

15. Plan A: $569.78; Plan B: $570.35

17. a) Plan B   **b)** $5.57

18. $546.90

19. 5.84%

20. a) $1380.42   **b)** 9.5 years   **c)** $5064.82

21. a) 7.64%   **b)** 7.71%   **c)** 7.76%

22. 25 years

23. 24 years 2 months

24. The investment schedule in part b

25. a) 10.07 years   **b)** 13.38 years   **c)** 8.2 years

26. a) $Y_1 = \$816.48$, $Y_2 = \$816.61$, $Y_3 = \$816.63$
b) Each is just over $4.00 more.

Self-Check 3.1, 3.2, page 150

1. a) $958.62   **b)** 10.22%   **c)** 14.3 years

2. a) $1162.84   **b)** $3379.47

3. a) $651.60   **b)** $986.15

4. a) $5418.33   **b)** $2095.60

5. a) $877.63   **b)** $4069.13

6. $1640.14

7. $2826.45

8. 5.48%

9. $1354.95

10. $866.51

11. 20.25 years

3.3 Exercises, page 154

1. a) $4607.11   **b)** $9214.23
c) $5318.31   **d)** $10 912.27

2. a) $680.19   **b)** $1094.14
c) $2789.01   **d)** $1111.53

3. a) $386.49   **b)** $238.51
c) $342.93   **d)** $175.38

4. a) $523.61   **b)** $351.16
c) $229.57   **d)** $45.54

5. a) $3173.90   **b)** $1679.22   **c)** $3400.56

6. Part a

7. a) $441.20   **b)** $194.17   **c)** $95.43

8. Part a

9. Estimates may vary.
a) i) $7000   **ii)** $16 000   **iii)** $30 000
iv) $55 000   **v)** $90 000   **vi)** $150 000
b) i) 38 years   **ii)** 52 years   **iii)** 60 years
c) As the years increase, the amount grows exponentially.
d) i) The growth would occur more rapidly, so the graph would rise more rapidly.
ii) The graph would rise more rapidly and the starting point is higher.

10. a) i) $9616.52   **ii)** $784.26
iii) $10 020.10   **iv)** $3436.73
b) i) $1034.26   **ii)** $2164.79
iii) $6227.88   **iv)** $10 548.82

11. a) $787.67   **b)** 8.35 years

12. $20 892.74

13. $1146.39

14. $3488.50

15. a) Annuity C
b) A: $27 908.01; B: $32 775.87; C: $46 204.09

16. a) $4096.98   **b)** $7270.47   **c)** $11 551.02

17. $111.46

18. $194.94

19. a) $191.83   **b)** $171.42

20. $1299.85

21. $105 174.33

22. $10 078.44

24. **a)** Martha: $40 000.00; Randy: $100 000.00
    b) Martha
    c) No

25. Dave's plan

26. **a)** $2459.85 **b)** 4.86% **c)** 40 years

27. 13.1 years

28. 8.14%

29. **a)** $13 971.64 **b)** $A = \dfrac{R[(1 + i)^{n+1} - (1 + i)]}{i}$

3.4 Exercises, page 162

1. **a)** $3366.37 **b)** $6732.74
   c) $2873.32 **d)** $5826.15

2. **a)** $2030.28 **b)** $4491.56
   c) $13 365.34 **d)** $6851.31

3. **a)** $564.13 **b)** $566.73
   c) $285.99 **d)** $335.87

4. **a)** $2820.12 **b)** $1104.75
   c) $1094.41 **d)** $280.70

5. **a)** $3823.66 **b)** $1748.44 **c)** $3536.47

6. Part a

7. **a)** $435.56 **b)** $227.49 **c)** $113.62

8. Part a

9. Estimates may vary.
   a) i) $5500 **ii)** $8400 **iii)** $10 200
   iv) $11 300 **v)** $11 900 **vi)** $12 200
   b) i) 9 years **ii)** 16 years **iii)** 28.5 years
   c) The amount grows more slowly as time passes.
   d) i) The graph rise more slowly.
   ii) The graph rises faster.

12. **a) i)** $11 590.98 **ii)** $944.28
    iii) $11 062.96 **iv)** $3640.73
    b) i) $1308.80 **ii)** $2483.01
    iii) $5329.54 **iv)** $7087.26

13. $60 372.00

14. $5772.79

15. **a)** Annuity A
    b) A: $20 690.22; B: $18 014.69; C: $13 958.08

16. $13 777.03

18. $142.48

20. 7.93%

21. **a)** $7801.69 **b)** $P = \dfrac{R(1 + i)[1 - (1 + i)^{-n}]}{i}$

Self-Check 3.3, 3.4, page 166

1. **a)** $10 062.31 **b)** $11 491.32
2. **a)** $3188.49 **b)** $7494.34
3. $3621.58
4. $471.39
5. **a)** $2974.13 **b)** $7138.96

6. **a)** $14 445.19 **b)** $18 103.95

7. $2608.99

8. $373.51

9. $3488.50

10. $1526.11

3.5 Exercises, page 170

1. **a)** 0.493 862 2% **b)** 0.534 474 01% **c)** 0.575 033 95%
   d) 0.635 646 16% **e)** 0.682 417 84%

2. **a)** $888.60 **b)** $656.60 **c)** $686.89

3. **a)** $116 944.37; $55 411.94; $88 808.75
   b) $113 686.97; $50 556.37; $87 507.83
   c) $109 891.91; $45 417.60; $86 100.76
   d) $106 512.44; $39 979.09; $84 578.87

4. **a)** $758.54 **b)** $173 074.40

5. **a)** $858.56 **b)** $106 054.40

6. **a)** $779.23 **b)** $133 769

7. **a)** $811.61 **b)** $143 483

8. Estimates may vary.
   a) i) $2000 **ii)** $1200 **iii)** $975
   iv) $850 **v)** $800 **vi)** $750
   b) As the amortization period increases, the monthly
   payments decrease.
   c) i) The graph would start higher and fall more slowly.
   ii) The graph would start higher and fall more slowly.

9. Estimates may vary.
   a) i) $20 000 **ii)** $44 000 **iii)** $75 500
   iv) $104 000 **v)** $140 000 **vi)** $170 000

10. **a) i)** $2044.59 **ii)** $1232.02 **iii)** $976.16
    iv) $888.56 **v)** $795.36 **vi)** $758.54
    b) i) $763.21 **ii)** $779.23
    iii) $811.61 **iv)** $827.98

11. **a)** 20.5 years **b)** $29 508

12. **a)** $934.15 **b)** $155 245 **c)** $119 372.99

13. **a)** $1491.85 **b)** $183 044 **c)** $163 290.96

14. **a)** $1090.92 **b)** $1180.77 **c)** $1346.95

15. **a) i)** $549.97 **ii)** $607.21 **iii)** $630.83

16. **a)** $525.31 **b)** $773.92 **c)** $1211.21

18. **a)** $801 311.27 **b)** $99 999.56

19. **a)** $658.40 **b)** $711.22

20. **a) i)** $65 358.69 **ii)** $76 174.65 **iii)** $83 935.52

21. **a)** $8306.12 **b)** $40 360.52 **c)** $418.18 **d)** $8820.87

3.6 Exercises, page 176

1. 28 payments

2. 13.6%

3. $14 504.09

4. $1060.17

5. $10 790.33

6. $6190.43

7. a) 6.70%   **b)** Yes

8. 14 years

9. a)

Investment period (years)	Accumulated amount ($)
1	1233.56
5	6977.00
10	16 387.93
15	29 081.87
20	46 204.09
25	69 299.40
30	100 451.50
35	142 471.03
40	199 149.07

b)

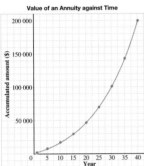

Value of an Annuity against Time

c)

Investment period (years)	Amount invested ($)
1	1200
5	6000
10	12 000
15	18 000
20	24 000
25	30 000
30	36 000
35	42 000
40	48 000

d)

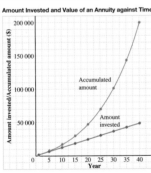

Amount Invested and Value of an Annuity against Time

e) Investing early allows more time for your money to grow.

3.7 Exercises, page 180

3. Interest paid is very high compared to the principal paid because the balance is high.

4. Interest paid is very low compared to the principal paid because the balance is low.

5. The interest payments decrease because the balance decreases. So, the principal payments increase because the monthly payment does not change.

6. Estimates may vary.
  a) $1237.71   **b)** $8306.61

7. Estimates may vary.
  a) $9125.85   **b)** $418.47

8. a) $238 611.66   **b)** $138 611.66

10. On each line of the spreadsheet, the balance has been rounded to 2 decimal places; this introduces slight errors in amounts.

11. a) The *Interest* payment decreases while the *Principal* payment increases.
  b) This is the time at which one half a monthly payment goes toward the principal and one half goes toward the interest.

12. a) i) $92 500   **ii)** $81 500   **iii)** $64 500   **iv)** $38 900
  b) 18 years

13. a) $138 611.66   **b)** $99 996.34
  c) There is still $3.66 outstanding.

14. 16 years 9 months

15. a)

Interest rate	6%	7%	8%	9%	10%
Monthly payment	$639.81	$700.42	$763.21	$827.98	$894.49

  b) 6% to 7% = $60.61; 7% to 8% = $62.79; 8% to 9% = $64.77; 9% to 10% = $66.51; No

16. a)

Interest rate	Total interest paid ($)
6%	91 940.85
7%	110 122.72
8%	128 966.11
9%	148 391.14
10%	168 343.30

  b) 6% to 7% = $18 181.92; 7% to 8% = $18 843.39; 8% to 9% = $19 425.03; 9% to 10% = $19 952.16; No

17. a) $1614.94   **b)** $1601.19; $13.75
  c) $384 507.67

18. a) $858.56
  b) i) $106 053.82   **ii)** $32 557.84

19. a) $976.16
  b) i) $75 708.04   **ii)** $62 903.61

20. b) i) $123 204.76   **ii)** $15 406.90
  iii) 22 years 8 months

21. b) i) $111 325.45   **ii)** $272 286.21
  iii) 20 years 10 months

22. b) i) $132 441.79   **ii)** $6169.87
  iii) 24 years 3 months

23. b) i) $111 549.31   **ii)** $27 062.35
  iii) 22 years 5 months

24. a) $103 520.06   **b)** $35 091.60
  c) 19 years 9 months

Self-Check 3.5–3.7, page 186

1. a) 0.493 862 2%   **b)** 0.635 646 15%   **c)** 0.682 417 84%

2. a) $888.60   **b)** $656.59

3. $938.94

4. a) $693.80   **b)** $118 140

5. a) $1102.04   **b)** $185 612   **c)** $138 655.69

6. a) $1038.19   **b)** $1120.08

7. a) $737.85   **b)** $796.75

8. a) The interest is very high and the principal low.
   b) The interest is very low and the principal is high.

9. a) Regular payment increases; total interest decreases.
   b) Total interest decreases.
   c) Regular payment is unchanged; total interest decreases.
   d) Total interest decreases.

Insights Into a Rich Problem— Where Did the $314 Come From?, page 189

1. a) $4708.69

2. a) $95.02

4. It matures in less than 1 month.

6. The price would increase.

7. Yes; $103.22

8. 40 semi-annual payments

9. $7800; this is the maximum value of the bond.

Chapter 3 Review Exercises, page 192

1. a) $1074.19   **b)** 3.25%   **c)** 11.8 years

2. a) $1926.71   **b)** $4760.75   **c)** $3081.98

3. a) $651.60   **b)** $986.15   **c)** $2507.63

4. $4446.14

5. a) $20 506.43   **b)** $1891.19   **c)** $1523.39   **d)** $5321.05

6. a) $463.94   **b)** $9439.98   **c)** $8139.64   **d)** $4226.31

7. $1870.10

8. 10.44%

9. $2755.79

10. $563.41

11. 25.2 years

12. a) $10 062.31   **b)** $11 491.32   **c)** $10 826.17

13. a) $25 662.70   **b)** $12 857.42   **c)** $8488.04

14. $7178.74

15. a) $9266.08   **b)** $4708.40   **c)** $4964.02

16. a) $2875.53   **b)** $11 479.08   **c)** $32 294.59

17. $675.11

18. $2451.55

19. $332.92

20. $10 025.91

21. $868.62

22. a) 0.655 819 69%   **b)** 0.816 484 61%
   c) 0.975 879 42%   **d)** 0.461 313 57%
   e) 0.562 853 24%   **f)** 0.715 415 15%

23. a) $1015.40   **b)** $657.79   **c)** $917.80

24. $953.86

25. a) $735.37   **b)** $123 611

26. a) $1021.02   **b)** $173 306   **c)** $127 278.58

27. a) $1132.74   **b)** $1223.39

28. a) $935.73   **b)** $1047.66

Chapter 3 Self-Test, page 195

1. a) $1914.88   **b)** 2.74%   **c)** 11.05 years

2. 6%: $290 335.90; 8%: $573 770.16;
   10%: $1 163 908.53; 12%: $2 400 018.25

3. a) $1317.19   **b)** $416.39

4. $14 049.37

5. $20 465.57

6. a) $891.01   **b)** $1512.69

7. $1772.35

8. $5221.87

9. 10.04%

10. Nearly 30 years

11. $4197.35

12. $455.63

13. $802.04

14. $1025.56

15. a) $749.27   **b)** $125 781   **c)** $94 636.80

Assessment Tasks, page 196

1. a) $63.98
   b) Leave the money in the bank account; it amounts
   to $24 644.86.

2. a) $11 098.19
   b) First aunt: $5582.38; second aunt: $3502.46;
   third aunt: $2329.33

Chapter 4 Quadratic Functions and Complex Numbers

Necessary Skills
1 Review: The Quadratic Function $y = ax^2 + bx + c$
Exercises, page 200

1. a) $y = (x + 2)^2 - 3$ **b)** $y = (x + 3)^2 - 1$

   c) $y = (x - 4)^2 - 21$ **d)** $y = \left(x - \frac{3}{2}\right)^2 - \frac{1}{4}$

   e) $y = \left(x - \frac{5}{2}\right)^2 - \frac{45}{4}$ **f)** $y = \left(x + \frac{7}{2}\right)^2 - \frac{9}{4}$

2. a) $y = -(x - 3)^2 + 17$ **b)** $y = -(x + 5)^2 + 26$

   c) $y = -(x + 2)^2 + 1$ **d)** $y = -\left(x + \frac{3}{2}\right)^2 - \frac{19}{2}$

   e) $y = -\left(x + \frac{5}{2}\right)^2 + \frac{41}{4}$ **f)** $y = -\left(x - \frac{1}{2}\right)^2 - \frac{31}{4}$

3. a) $y = (x+1)^2 + 6$

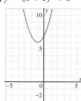

b) $y = -(x+1)^2 - 5$

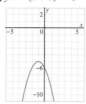

c) $y = (x+3)^2 - 10$

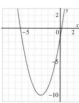

d) $y = -\left(x + \dfrac{3}{2}\right)^2 - \dfrac{23}{4}$

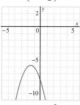

e) $y = -\left(x - \dfrac{5}{2}\right)^2 + \dfrac{17}{4}$

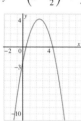

f) $y = \left(x - \dfrac{1}{2}\right)^2 - \dfrac{21}{4}$

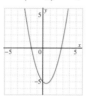

2 Review: Number Systems

Exercises, page 201

1. Answers may vary.
   a) 0, 2, 4
   b) $\dfrac{1}{2}$, −5, 0.6363...
   c) 0, sin 60°, $\dfrac{3}{4}$
   d) −3, 0, 7
   e) $\sqrt{5}$, 2.314 765..., π
   f) 5, 7, 286

2. a) Natural, whole, integer, rational, real
   b) Rational, real
   c) Rational, real
   d) Irrational, real
   e) Natural, whole, integer, rational, real
   f) Whole, integer, rational, real
   g) Integer, rational, real
   h) Natural, whole, integer, rational, real
   i) Irrational, real
   j) Irrational, real

3.

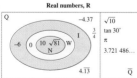

3 Review: Intercepts and Zeros

Exercises, page 203

1. a) $x = 4$, $y = 8$

b) $x = 4$, $y = 3$

c) $x = -9$, $y = 4$

d) $x = -5$ and $x = 1$, $y = -5$

e) $x = 3$ and $x = 6$, $y = -18$

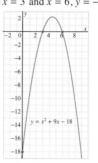

f) $x = -4$, $y = 16$

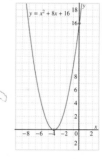

2. a) $y = -7$ **b)** $y = -5$ **c)** $y = 2$
   d) $y = 5$ **e)** $y = 81$ **f)** $y = 16$

3. a) $x = 2.7$ **b)** $x = 0.375$
   c) $x = -4$ and $x = -3$ **d)** $x = 0.75$
   e) $x = -1.6$ and $x = 3.5$ **f)** There are no x-intercepts.

4 New: Multiplying and Dividing Radicals

Exercises, page 205

1. a) $\sqrt{10}$ **b)** $\sqrt{42}$ **c)** $\sqrt{7}$ **d)** $\sqrt{5}$
2. a) $2\sqrt{2}$ **b)** $2\sqrt{3}$ **c)** $3\sqrt{3}$ **d)** $\sqrt{35}$
   e) $2\sqrt{10}$ **f)** $5\sqrt{2}$ **g)** $2\sqrt{15}$ **h)** $3\sqrt{7}$
   i) $6\sqrt{2}$ **j)** $5\sqrt{3}$ **k)** $4\sqrt{5}$ **l)** $10\sqrt{2}$

3. Answers may vary.
   a) $\sqrt{98}$ **b)** $\sqrt{21}$

4.1 Exercises, page 210

1. a) −3; minimum **b)** 5; minimum
   c) 2; maximum **d)** −1; minimum
   e) 0; maximum **f)** 16; maximum

2. a) i) −4; minimum **ii)** −2
   b) i) −2; maximum **ii)** −3
   c) i) 3; maximum **ii)** −1
   d) i) −10; maximum **ii)** 1
   e) i) 6; minimum **ii)** 0
   f) i) 0; maximum **ii)** −4

3. a) $y = (x - 3)^2 - 1$ **b)** $y = (x + 5)^2 - 16$
c) $y = (x + 2)^2 - 11$ **d)** $y = (x - 1)^2$
e) $y = \left(x + \dfrac{5}{2}\right)^2 - \dfrac{37}{4}$ **f)** $y = \left(x + \dfrac{1}{2}\right)^2 - \dfrac{9}{4}$

4. a) $y = 2\left(x + \dfrac{3}{2}\right)^2 - \dfrac{23}{2}$ **b)** $y = 3(x + 1)^2 - 11$
c) $y = -3\left(x + \dfrac{3}{2}\right)^2 + \dfrac{59}{4}$ **d)** $y = -2(x - 2)^2 + 12$
e) $y = 4\left(x + \dfrac{1}{2}\right)^2 + 1$ **f)** $y = -4(x + 1)^2 + 5$

5. a) $y = 2\left(x + \dfrac{5}{4}\right)^2 - \dfrac{33}{8}$ **b)** $y = 3\left(x - \dfrac{2}{3}\right)^2 + \dfrac{14}{3}$
c) $y = -2\left(x + \dfrac{3}{4}\right)^2 - \dfrac{39}{8}$ **d)** $y = -3\left(x - \dfrac{5}{6}\right)^2 - \dfrac{23}{12}$
e) $y = 4\left(x + \dfrac{3}{4}\right)^2 - \dfrac{21}{4}$ **f)** $y = -4\left(x + \dfrac{5}{4}\right)^2 + \dfrac{29}{4}$

6. a) $y = 2(x - 3)^2 - 3$; minimum is -3
b) $y = 3(x - 1)^2 + 5$; minimum is 5
c) $y = 2\left(x - \dfrac{5}{2}\right)^2 + \dfrac{15}{2}$; minimum is $\dfrac{15}{2}$
d) $y = -(x + 3)^2 + 14$; maximum is 14
e) $y = -5(x - 4)^2 + 77$; maximum is 77
f) $y = -4(x + 3)^2 + 42$; maximum is 42

7. a) $y = \dfrac{1}{2}(x + 3)^2 - \dfrac{5}{2}$ **b)** $y = \dfrac{1}{3}(x - 3)^2 - 2$
c) $y = -\dfrac{1}{4}(x - 2)^2 - 2$ **d)** $y = -\dfrac{1}{2}(x - 6)^2 + 16$
e) $y = -\dfrac{1}{3}(x + 6)^2 + 18$ **f)** $y = \dfrac{1}{10}(x + 10)^2 - 6$

8. a) $y = (x - 1)^2 - 4$ **b)** $y = -(x - 3)^2 + 17$

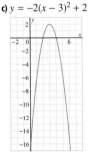
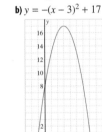

c) $y = -2(x - 3)^2 + 2$ **d)** $y = 3(x - 4)^2 - 12$

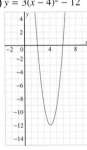
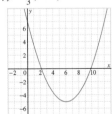

e) $y = -\dfrac{1}{2}(x - 2)^2 - 1$ **f)** $y = \dfrac{1}{3}(x - 6)^2 - 5$

9. a) Minimum is -5; 4
b) Maximum is -5; 1
c) Maximum is 14; -4
d) Minimum is -13; 2
e) Minimum is $-\dfrac{249}{4}$; 25
f) Maximum is 59; $\dfrac{27}{2}$

10. Answers may vary.
a) $y = 3(x - 4)^2 + 6$ **b)** $y = 2(x - 5)^2 - 3$
c) $y = -3(x + 2)^2 + 10$ **d)** $y = 3x^2 + 7$
e) $y = -x^2 - 3$

11. Yes; answers may vary.
a) $y = 12(x - 4)^2 + 6$ **b)** $y = 6(x - 5)^2 - 3$
c) $y = -7(x + 2)^2 + 10$ **d)** $y = 3(x - 5)^2 + 7$
e) $y = -(x + 7)^2 - 3$

13. a) 12 m   **b)** 1 s   **c)** 7 m

14. Least value: 1.875 V at 2.25 min; greatest value: 17 V at 5 min

4.2 Exercises, page 218

1. a) iii; -3 **b)** ii; 2, 5   **c)** vi; no real roots
d) i; -2, 1   **e)** iv; no real roots   **f)** v; -1.5

2. a) 3, 4   **b)** 1, 8   **c)** -2
d) -3, 8   **e)** -6, 6   **f)** -12, 12

3. a) -5, 5   **b)** $-\sqrt{6}$, $\sqrt{6}$
c) $-2\sqrt{3}$, $2\sqrt{3}$ **d)** $-\dfrac{\sqrt{2}}{3}$, $\dfrac{\sqrt{2}}{3}$
e) -3, 5   **f)** $-\sqrt{3} - 2$, $\sqrt{3} - 2$

4. a) -6, 4   **b)** 1, 5
c) 0.7639, 5.2361   **d)** -3.4142, -0.5858
e) $-\dfrac{5}{3}$, $-\dfrac{1}{3}$ **f)** -4.1794, 0.1794

5. a) -3, -2 **b)** 2, 7
c) -8.4244, 1.4244   **d)** No real roots
e) 0.8915, 5.6085   **f)** -2.1514, -0.3486

6. a) i) 1, 5   **ii)** 2   **iii)** No real roots
b)

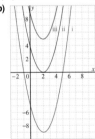

7. a) 0.89, 5.61   **b)** 0.72, 2.78
c) -1.14, 1.47   **d)** -0.11, 4.61
e) No real roots   **f)** No real roots

8. a) 3, 11   **b)** -9, 2
c) $-\dfrac{1}{3}$; $\dfrac{3}{2}$ **d)** -3, $\dfrac{1}{2}$
e) 0, 4   **f)** 0, $\dfrac{1}{2}$

9. a) i) -4.4365, -0.5635 **ii)** -3.5, -1.5
iii) -2.5
b) Answers may vary; $4x^2 + 20x + 26 = 0$

10. a) −3, 5 **b)** −8, −4

c) $-\frac{4}{3}$, −1 **d)** $-\frac{1}{2}$, 5

e) $-\frac{1}{2}$, $\frac{3}{2}$ **f)** 1, $\frac{5}{4}$

11. a) −1.4342, −0.2324 **b)** −2.8860, 1.3860

c) No real roots **d)** No real roots

e) $-\frac{3}{2}$ **f)** 3

12. a) a and b **b)** e and f

c) c and d

13. a) −1.35, 0.15 **b)** −0.16, 3.16

c) −1.90, 1.23 **d)** −1.15, 0.65

e) 0.18, 1.82 **f)** 0.18, 2.82

14. a) −0.5, 1.5 **b)** −0.2071, 1.2071

c) 0.5 **d)** No real roots

15. a) 47.42 m **b)** 3.06 s

c) 6.17 s **d)** 1.5 m

16. a) i) 3 **ii)** −5

iii) $\frac{3}{2}$ **iv)** $-\frac{5}{2}$

b) When $b^2 - 4ac = 0$

c) i) No **ii)** Yes

iii) No **iv)** Yes

17. a) i) No real roots **ii)** No real roots

iii) No real roots **iv)** No real roots

b) When $b^2 - 4ac < 0$

c) i) Yes **ii)** Yes

iii) No **iv)** No

18. a) $b > 4$ or $b < -4$ **b)** $b = 4$ or $b = -4$

c) $-4 < b < 4$

Self-Check 4.1, 4.2, page 221

1. a) $y = \left(x - \frac{5}{2}\right)^2 + \frac{11}{4}$ **b)** $y = 2(x + 1)^2 + 5$

c) $y = -2\left(x + \frac{3}{2}\right)^2 + \frac{11}{2}$ **d)** $y = 2\left(x - \frac{3}{4}\right)^2 - \frac{25}{8}$

e) $y = \frac{1}{2}(x + 2)^2 - 7$ **f)** $y = -\frac{1}{3}\left(x + \frac{3}{2}\right)^2 + \frac{19}{4}$

2. a) $y = (x - 5)^2 - 14$ **b)** $y = 2(x + 3)^2 - 27$

c) $y = -(x - 2)^2 + 5$ **d)** $y = -2\left(x + \frac{7}{4}\right)^2 + \frac{97}{8}$

e) $y = \frac{1}{10}(x - 10)^2 - 7$ **f)** $y = -\frac{1}{4}(x + 10)^2 + 24$

3. a) Minimum is −14; 5 **b)** Minimum is −27; −3

c) Maximum is 5; 2 **d)** Maximum is $\frac{97}{8}$; $-\frac{7}{4}$

e) Minimum is −7; 10 **f)** Maximum is 24; −10

4. Answers may vary; $y = -2(x + 3)^2 + 6$

5. a) −4, −3 **b)** $\frac{3}{2}$

c) $\frac{1}{2}$, $\frac{5}{2}$ **d)** −4, $-\frac{1}{3}$

e) $-\frac{2}{3}$, $\frac{5}{2}$ **f)** $-\frac{3}{2}$, 5

6. a) −9, 1 **b)** No real roots

c) −1, 3, 5 **d)** 0.0941, 2.6559

e) −0.5486, 1.2153 **f)** No real roots

7. a) No real roots **b)** No real roots

c) No real roots **d)** No real roots

e) −1.8968, 1.2301 **f)** −1.5826, 7.5826

8. a) −8.1623, −1.8377 **b)** −7.2361, −2.7639

c) −5 **d)** No real roots

4.3 Exercises, page 226

1. a) $2i$ **b)** $5i$ **c)** $7i$ **d)** $\sqrt{2}i$

e) $\sqrt{5}i$ **f)** $2\sqrt{2}i$ **g)** $3\sqrt{2}i$ **h)** $6\sqrt{2}i$

2. a) −9 **b)** −25 **c)** −6 **d)** −12

e) −1 **f)** $-i$ **g)** 1 **h)** i

3. a) Rational, real, complex

b) Irrational, real, complex

c) Integer, rational, real, complex

d) Complex

e) Complex

f) Whole, integer, rational, real, complex

g) Irrational, real, complex

h) Complex

i) Rational, real, complex

j) Rational, real, complex

k) Irrational, real, complex

l) Complex

4. a, c, f

5. a) $\pm5i$ **b)** $\pm2\sqrt{3}i$ **c)** $\pm3i$

d) $\pm4i$ **e)** $\pm2\sqrt{5}i$ **f)** $\pm\frac{3}{2}i$

6. a) ±4 **b)** $\pm4i$ **c)** $\pm\sqrt{6}$ **d)** $\pm\sqrt{6}i$

e) $\pm\frac{5}{2}$ **f)** $\pm\frac{5}{2}i$ **g)** ±2 **h)** $\pm2i$

i) $\pm\frac{\sqrt{11}}{2}$ **j)** $\pm\frac{\sqrt{11}}{2}i$

7. a) $1 \pm i$ **b)** $-2 \pm i$ **c)** $-1 \pm \sqrt{2}i$

d) $\frac{-1 \pm \sqrt{7}i}{2}$ **e)** $\frac{5 \pm \sqrt{3}i}{2}$ **f)** $1 \pm \frac{\sqrt{2}}{2}$

8. b) $\pm6i$

9. a) $1 + 2i$ **b)** $-2 \pm \sqrt{11}$ **c)** $\frac{2 \pm \sqrt{2}i}{3}$

d) $\frac{1 \pm \sqrt{5}i}{3}$ **e)** $\frac{2 \pm \sqrt{10}i}{7}$ **f)** $\frac{1 \pm \sqrt{7}i}{2}$

10. a) −4, 3 **b)** $\frac{1}{2}$, 5 **c)** $\frac{-5 \pm \sqrt{33}}{4}$

d) $\frac{-1 \pm i}{2}$ **e)** 3 **f)** $-1 \pm \sqrt{3}i$

11. a) $-\sqrt{6}$

b) For $\sqrt{a} \times \sqrt{b} = \sqrt{a \times b}$, a and b cannot be negative.

12. a), b)

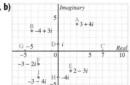

c) Answers may vary; the opposite of A is $-3 - 4i$ (point J on the grid).

13.

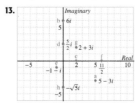

14. a) $-1, -i, 1, i, -1$

c)

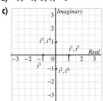

d) $i^{12} = 1, i^{21} = i, i^{30} = -1; i^{59} = -i$

15. a) $-2i, i$ **b)** $\dfrac{\pm\sqrt{7} - i}{2}$

4.4 Exercises, page 233

1. a) $9 - 3i$ **b)** $2 - 3i$ **c)** $11 + 2i$
d) $-2 + 6i$ **e)** 10 **f)** $7i$

2. a) $2 + 11i$ **b)** $6 - 22i$ **c)** $8 + 14i$
d) -3 **e)** $-9 + 3i$ **f)** $8 - 8i$

3. a) 5 **b)** 25 **c)** $-5 + 10i$
d) $22 + 14i$ **e)** $2i$ **f)** $33 - 56i$

4. a) The results are real numbers.

6. a) $-2i$ **b)** $-5i$ **c)** $-\dfrac{7}{4}i$ **d)** $-\dfrac{2}{3}i$
e) $\dfrac{1}{6}i$ **f)** $\dfrac{1}{3}i$ **g)** $3i$ **h)** $3i$

7. a) $2 - \dfrac{3}{2}i$ **b)** $-2 - \dfrac{3}{2}i$ **c)** $\dfrac{3}{2} - 2i$ **d)** $-\dfrac{3}{2} - 2i$
e) $-\dfrac{1}{4} + \dfrac{5}{4}i$ **f)** $-\dfrac{2}{3} - 2i$ **g)** $-\dfrac{7}{4} + \dfrac{1}{2}i$ **h)** $-\dfrac{1}{2} + \dfrac{5}{3}i$

8. a) $1, i, -1, -i, 1, i, -1, -i$
b) i) 1 **ii)** i **iii)** -1 **iv)** $-i$

9. a) 5 **b)** 10 **c)** 25 **d)** 29
e) $\dfrac{5}{4}$ **f)** $\dfrac{5}{16}$ **g)** 3 **h)** 1
The results are real numbers.

10. Yes; answers may vary; $(4 + 0i)(6 + 0i) = 24$

11. a) 4 **b)** 6 **c)** -8 **d)** -10
e) 1 **f)** $\dfrac{1}{2}$ **g)** $2\sqrt{2}$ **h)** 1
The results are real numbers.

12. Yes; answers may vary; $(6 + 0i) + (4 + 0i) = 10$

13. a) $10 + 6i$ **b)** $8 - 10i$ **c)** $31 - 29i$
d) $43 - 18i$ **e)** $-3 + 36i$ **f)** $8 - 25i$
g) $60 + 144i$ **h)** $-2 - 2i$

14. a) $17 - 32i$ **b)** $-6 + 23i$ **c)** $8 - 4i$
d) $14 - 15i$ **e)** $-2 + 4\sqrt{6}i$ **f)** $7 - 6\sqrt{2}i$
g) $-2 + 2i$ **h)** $-60 - 63i$

15. a) $\dfrac{3}{2} + \dfrac{1}{2}i$ **b)** $\dfrac{8}{5} - \dfrac{1}{5}i$ **c)** i **d)** $\dfrac{7}{5} - \dfrac{6}{5}i$
e) $\dfrac{2}{5} - \dfrac{6}{5}i$ **f)** $\dfrac{11}{13} - \dfrac{16}{13}i$ **g)** $6 + 4i$ **h)** $2 - 4i$
i) $\dfrac{75}{29} + \dfrac{30}{29}i$ **j)** $-\dfrac{3}{29} - \dfrac{7}{29}i$ **k)** $-\dfrac{3}{4} + \dfrac{1}{4}i$ **l)** $\dfrac{1}{5} - \dfrac{8}{5}i$

16. a) $\dfrac{a - bi}{a^2 + b^2}$
b) i) $-\dfrac{1}{2}i$ **ii)** $\dfrac{1}{5} - \dfrac{2}{5}i$ **iii)** $\dfrac{1}{5} + \dfrac{2}{5}i$ **iv)** $\dfrac{4}{25} + \dfrac{3}{25}i$
c) i and $-i$

17. a) Answers may vary;
$2 + 3i; \dfrac{2}{13} - \dfrac{3}{13}i$ $2 - 3i; \dfrac{2}{13} + \dfrac{3}{13}i$

18. Yes; answers may vary; $\dfrac{2 + 4i}{3 + 6i} = \dfrac{2}{3}$

19. a) $5 + 2i, -2 + 5i, -5 - 2i, 2 - 5i, 5 + 2i$
b) $1 + 6i, -6 + i, -1 - 6i, 6 - i, 1 + 6i$
c) $4 - i, 1 + 4i, -4 + i, -1 - 4i, 4 - i$

20. a) Answers may vary; $5 + 2i, -2 + 5i,$
$-5 - 2i, 2 - 5i, 5 + 2i$

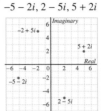

b) A rotation of 90° counterclockwise about the origin
c) A rotation of 180° about the origin

21. $a = 21; b = -20$

22. a) $-1, 1, i, -i$ **b)** $\dfrac{1}{\sqrt{2}} + \dfrac{1}{\sqrt{2}}i, -\dfrac{1}{\sqrt{2}} - \dfrac{1}{\sqrt{2}}i$

23. $a = \dfrac{1}{5}, b = \dfrac{8}{5}$

24. $\dfrac{z_1}{z_2} = \dfrac{(a_1a_2 + b_1b_2) + (a_2b_1 - a_1b_2)i}{a_2^2 + b_2^2}$

Self-Check 4.3, 4.4, page 236

1. a) $9i$ **b)** $\sqrt{82}i$ **c)** $10i$ **d)** $\sqrt{10}i$
e) -16 **f)** -16 **g)** -5 **h)** -5

2. a) $-1 \pm \sqrt{2}i$ **b)** $\dfrac{1}{6} \pm \dfrac{\sqrt{23}}{6}i$ **c)** $-\dfrac{1}{4} \pm \dfrac{\sqrt{3}}{4}i$
d) $\dfrac{7}{4} \pm \dfrac{\sqrt{7}}{4}i$ **e)** $2 \pm \sqrt{6}i$ **f)** $-20, 5$

3. a) $-1 \pm i$ **b)** $\dfrac{3}{2} \pm \dfrac{\sqrt{15}}{2}i$ **c)** $-\dfrac{3}{2} \pm \dfrac{3}{2}i$
d) $-\dfrac{1}{6} \pm \dfrac{\sqrt{59}}{6}i$ **e)** $\dfrac{3}{20} \pm \dfrac{\sqrt{31}}{20}i$ **f)** $\dfrac{5}{4} \pm \dfrac{\sqrt{7}}{4}i$

4. a) $15 + 14i$ **b)** $7 - 7i$ **c)** $1 - 9i$ **d)** $-14 + 8i$

5. a) $3 - 4i$ **b)** $3 + 4i$ **c)** $-4 - 10i$ **d)** $-6 + i$

6. a) $15 + 18i$ **b)** $26 - 13i$ **c)** $35 - 12i$ **d)** $52 + 39i$

7. a) -12 **b)** -8 **c)** $-5i$
d) $6 + 9i$ **e)** $\dfrac{1}{2} - \dfrac{11}{2}i$ **f)** $\dfrac{23}{25} - \dfrac{14}{25}i$

8. a) $-\dfrac{1}{3}i$ **b)** $\dfrac{2}{13} - \dfrac{3}{13}i$ **c)** $\dfrac{3}{25} + \dfrac{4}{25}i$

Insights Into a Rich Problem— Parabolas and Lines, page 239

1.

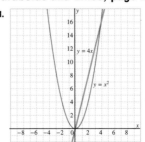

a) One of the lines is a tangent. Each line above the tangent intersects the parabola twice; each line below the tangent does not intersect the parabola.

b) The family of lines is $y = 4x + b$.

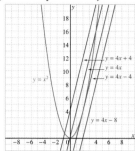

When $b > -4$, there are 2 solutions.
When $b = -4$, there is 1 solution.
When $b < -4$, there are no solutions.

2. a)

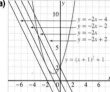

b) $y = -2x + b$
c) When $b > -2$, there are 2 solutions.
When $b = -2$, there is 1 solution.
When $b < -2$, there are no solutions.

3. a) When $b > 4$ or $b < -4$, there are 2 solutions.
When $b = \pm 4$, there is 1 solution.
When $-4 < b < 4$, there are no solutions.

4.

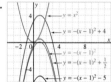

a) When $k > \frac{1}{2}$, there are 2 solutions.

When $k = \frac{1}{2}$, there is 1 solution.

When $k < \frac{1}{2}$, there are no solutions.

c) $k = \frac{1}{2}$

5. a) Each line intersects the parabola at 1 or 2 points.
c) $y = 6x$

6. a) All the parabolas pass through the origin and have a maximum value.
b) Each parabola intersects the line $y = 2x$ at least once.
d) $y = x(2 - x)$; $y = \frac{1}{3}x(6 - x)$

7.

a) When $-2 < b < 2$, there are 2 solutions.
When $b = \pm 2$, there is 1 solution.
When $b < -2$ or $b > 2$, there are no solutions.

8.

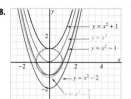

c) When $k < -\frac{5}{4}$ or $k > 1$, there are no solutions.
When $k = 1$, there is 1 solution.
When $-1 < k < 1$ or $k = -\frac{5}{4}$, there are 2 solutions.
When $k = -1$, there are 3 solutions.
When $-\frac{5}{4} < k < -1$, there are 4 solutions.

9. When $a < -\sqrt{2}$ or $a > \sqrt{2}$, there are no solutions.
When $a = -\sqrt{2}$ or $a = \sqrt{2}$, there are 2 solutions.
When $a = \pm 1$, there are 3 solutions.
When $1 < a < \sqrt{2}$, $-1 < a < 1$, or $-\sqrt{2} < a < -1$,
there are 4 solutions.
There will never be 1 or 5 solutions.

Chapter 4 Review Exercises, page 241

1. a) i) $y = \frac{1}{2}(x + 4)^2 - 13$ **ii)** $(-4, -13)$
   iii) $x = -4$ **iv)** -9.0990, 1.0990
v)

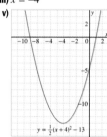

$$y = \frac{1}{2}(x + 4)^2 - 13$$

b) i) $y = -\frac{1}{3}(x + 12)^2 + 60$ **ii)** $(-12, 60)$
   iii) $x = -12$ **iv)** -25.4164, 1.4164
v)

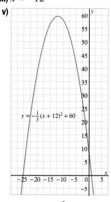

$$y = -\frac{1}{3}(x + 12)^2 + 60$$

c) i) $y = 2(x + 1)^2 - 8$ **ii)** $(-1, -8)$
   iii) $x = -1$ **iv)** -3, 1

v)

d) i) $y = 3(x - 2)^2 - 3$ ii) $(2, -3)$
  iii) $x = 2$ iv) $1, 3$

v)

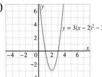

e) i) $y = -(x - 3)^2 + 4$ ii) $(3, 4)$
  iii) $x = 3$ iv) $1, 5$

v)

f) i) $y = -2(x + 1)^2 + 8$ ii) $(-1, 8)$
  iii) $x = -1$ iv) $-3, 1$

v)

2. a) Minimum is 0; -7
  b) Maximum is 4; 3
  c) Maximum is $-\frac{3}{4}, \frac{1}{2}$

3. a) 35 m   **b)** 2 s   **c)** 4.65 s

4. a) 3, 5   **b)** 3, 10   **c)** $\frac{3}{2}, 5$
  d) $-\frac{1}{3}, 2$ **e)** $-5, -1$ **f)** $3 \pm i$

5. a) $4i$ **b)** $6i$ **c)** $4\sqrt{3}i$ **d)** $2\sqrt{3}i$ **e)** -25
  f) -49 **g)** -3 **h)** -5 **i)** 1 **j)** $-i$

6. a) $-10, -4$ **b)** $2, 6$
  c) $-1.7958, 7.7958$ **d)** $-3.4495, 1.4495$
  e) $1 \pm 2i$ **f)** $-6 \pm 3i$

7. a) $9 - 2i$ **b)** $7 - 10i$ **c)** $-18 + 12i$
  d) $8 + 28i$ **e)** $26 - 7i$ **f)** $31 - i$
  g) $-21 + 20i$ **h)** $-40 - 42i$ **i)** 53

8. a) $-3i$ **b)** $-2i$ **c)** $-\frac{2}{3} - \frac{5}{3}i$
  d) $\frac{3}{2} - 3i$ **e)** $4 - 2i$ **f)** $\frac{10}{13} + \frac{15}{13}i$
  g) i **h)** $\frac{4}{29} - \frac{19i}{29}$

9. a) $-i$ **b)** $\frac{i}{2}$
  c) $\frac{2}{5} - \frac{i}{5}$ **d)** $\frac{4}{25} + \frac{3i}{25}$

Chapter 4 Self-Test, page 243

1. a) $y = 2(x - 2)^2 + 10$ **b)** $y = 3\left(x + \frac{11}{6}\right)^2 - \frac{73}{12}$
  c) $y = -2\left(x - \frac{5}{2}\right)^2 + \frac{1}{2}$ **d)** $y = \frac{1}{2}(x - 3)^2 - \frac{23}{2}$

2. a) i) 10 ii) Minimum   iii) 2
  b) i) $-\frac{73}{12}$ ii) Minimum   iii) $-\frac{11}{6}$
  c) i) $\frac{1}{2}$ ii) Maximum   iii) $\frac{5}{2}$
  d) i) $-\frac{23}{2}$ ii) Minimum   iii) 3

3. a) 80 m   **b)** 3 s   **c)** 7 s

4. The x-intercepts of each graph are the roots of the
  corresponding equation.
  a) $-1, 3$ **b)** 2 **c)** No real roots

5. a) $\pm\frac{4}{3}$ **b)** $\pm\sqrt{5}$ **c)** $\pm\sqrt{7}i$
  d) $-4, 5$ **e)** $-\frac{1}{2}, 3$ **f)** $-\frac{5}{3}$

6. a) $\pm12i$ **b)** $-0.4495, 4.4495$
  c) $-1 \pm 3i$ **d)** $-1 \pm i$
  e) $\frac{3}{4} \pm \frac{\sqrt{31}}{4}i$ **f)** $-\frac{1}{2} \pm \frac{\sqrt{7}}{2}$

7. a) $5i$ **b)** $2\sqrt{3}i$ **c)** -36 **d)** $8i$

8. Sum $= -\frac{b}{a}$; product $= \frac{c}{a}$

9. a) $7 - 8i$ **b)** $12 + 10i$
  c) 85 **d)** $7 - 24i$

10. a) -7 **b)** $-\frac{3}{2} + \frac{5}{2}i$
  c) $\frac{1}{2} - \frac{5}{2}i$ **d)** $\frac{3}{5} - \frac{4}{5}i$

11. a) $-\frac{i}{5}$ **b)** $\frac{4}{25} + \frac{3}{25}i$

Assessment Tasks, page 244

1. a)

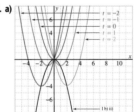

b) i) $(t, -r^2)$ ii) $y = -x^2$

2. a) Yes; 7.24 cm or 2.76 cm
  b) No   **c)** 50 cm^2; 5 cm

Chapter 5 Trigonometric Functions
Necessary Skills
1 Review: Trigonometric Ratios in Right Triangles
Exercises, page 247

1. a) $38°$ **b)** $51°$ **c)** $39°$

2. a) 2.0 cm   **b)** 3.2 cm   **c)** 1.4 cm

3. a) 3.4 cm   **b)** 3.7 cm   **c)** 1.9 cm

4. a) $\angle D = 29°$, EF $\doteq 5.9$ cm, DF $\doteq 12.1$ cm
  b) $\angle J = 53°$, HJ $\doteq 4.6$ cm, GJ $\doteq 7.6$ cm
  c) $\angle M = 61°$, KM $\doteq 2.8$ cm, LM $\doteq 5.0$ cm

d) QP ≐ 5.1 cm, ∠Q ≐ 57°, ∠P ≐ 33°
e) TV ≐ 5.2 cm, ∠V ≐ 32°, ∠S ≐ 58°

5. a) b ≐ 5.3 cm, ∠A ≐ 26°, ∠C ≐ 64°
b) a ≐ 7.6 cm, ∠A ≐ 34°, ∠C ≐ 56°
c) c ≐ 6.6 cm, ∠A ≐ 38°, ∠C ≐ 52°
d) ∠C = 47°, b ≐ 3.4 cm, c ≐ 2.5 cm
e) ∠C = 58°, a ≐ 3.5 cm, b ≐ 6.6 cm
f) ∠C = 19°, a ≐ 8.8 cm, c ≐ 3.0 cm

2 Review: The Sine Law in Acute Triangles
Exercises, page 249

1. a) 52° **b)** 56° **c)** 58°

2. a) 10.6 cm **b)** 5.8 cm **c)** 3.9 cm

3. a) 6.6 cm **b)** 12.1 cm **c)** 5.5 cm

4. a) 5.7 cm **b)** 10.1 cm **c)** 5.2 cm

5. a) ∠D = 73°, d ≐ 11.4 cm, f ≐ 5.0 cm
b) ∠J ≐ 82°, g ≐ 5.9 cm, h ≐ 2.8 cm
c) ∠P ≐ 43°, ∠M ≐ 53°, m ≐ 9.9 cm

6. a) ∠Q ≐ 76°, p ≐ 7.6 cm, r ≐ 13.2 cm
b) ∠S ≐ 47°, ∠U ≐ 51°, u ≐ 10.1 cm
c) ∠W = 51°, w ≐ 16.9 cm, x ≐ 21.8 cm

3 Review: The Cosine Law in Acute Triangles
Exercises, page 252

1. a) 5.8 cm **b)** 4.9 cm **c)** 6.5 cm

2. a) 68°, 46° **b)** 30°, 73° **c)** 64°, 33°

3. a) 86° **b)** 41° **c)** 59°

4. a) 50°, 45° **b)** 84°, 55° **c)** 50°, 71°

5. a) d ≐ 3.9 cm, ∠C ≐ 84°, ∠E ≐ 47°
b) ∠F ≐ 55°, ∠G ≐ 46°, ∠H ≐ 79°
c) k ≐ 12.6 cm, ∠J ≐ 39°, ∠L ≐ 55°

6. a) ∠B ≐ 96°, ∠C ≐ 66°, ∠D ≐ 18°
b) f ≐ 13.0 cm, ∠E ≐ 65°, ∠G ≐ 44°
c) ∠H ≐ 56°, ∠J ≐ 60°, ∠K ≐ 64°

7. Yes

5.1 Exercises, page 257

1. a) 0, 1 **b)** 0.1736, 0.9848
c) 0.3256, 0.9455 **d)** 0.4540, 0.8910
e) 0.5736, 0.8192 **f)** 0.7193, 0.6947
g) 0.8910, 0.4540 **h)** 0.9744, 0.2250
i) 0.9877, 0.1564 **j)** 1, 0

2. a) 0.8660, −0.5000 **b)** 0.2588, −0.9659
c) 0.8572, −0.5150 **d)** 0.9945, −0.1045
e) 0.3746, −0.9272 **f)** 0.6018, −0.7986
g) 0.9816, −0.1908 **h)** 0, −1
i) 0.7431, −0.6691 **j)** 0.0698, −0.9976

3. a) i) Positive **ii)** Positive

iii) Positive **iv)** Negative

v) Negative **vi)** Positive

b) For 90° < θ ≤ 180°, the cosine ratio is negative.

4. a) 0.940, −0.342 **b)** 0.996, −0.087

c) 0.669, −0.743 **d)** 0.956, 0.292

e) 0.616, −0.788 **f)** 0.574, 0.819

g) 0.139, −0.990 **h)** 0.809, 0.588

i) 0.777, −0.629 **j)** 0.485, −0.875

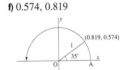

5. a) 45°, 135° **b)** 120° **c)** 68°, 112°
d) 135° **e)** 60°, 120° **f)** 180°
g) 49°, 131° **h)** 41° **i)** 139°

6. Each equation that contains the sine ratio has 2 solutions.

7. a) 65°, 115° **b)** 55° **c)** 137°
d) 25°, 155° **e)** 35°, 145° **f)** 112°
g) 30°, 150° **h)** 60° **i)** 120°
j) 42°, 138° **k)** 14°, 166° **l)** 146°

10. a) i) 0.5, 0.8660 **ii)** 0.7071, 0.7071
iii) 0.8660, 0.5
b) sin 30° = cos 60°; sin 60° = cos 30°; sin 45° = cos 45°

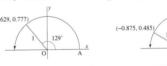

11. a) 0.714 **b)** 0.954

12. a) −0.980 **b)** 0.8

13. a) 0.968, −0.968   **b)** 0.760

14. a) i) 1, 0   **ii)** 0, 1   **iii)** −1, 0

15. a) i) 0, 1   **ii)** 0.3420, 0.9397
    iii) 0.6428, 0.7660   **iv)** 0.8660, 0.5
    v) 0.9848, 0.1736   **vi)** 0.9848, −0.1736
    vii) 0.8660, −0.5   **viii)** 0.6248, −0.7660
    ix) 0.3420, −0.9397   **x)** 0, −1
  b) 0°, 180°; 20°, 160°; 40°, 140°; 60°, 120°; 80°, 100°
    Each pair has a sum of 180°.
  c) The numerical values are the same, but the signs are
    opposite.

16. a) $\sin \theta = \cos(90° − \theta)$ and $\cos \theta = \sin(90° − \theta)$

b)

	θ	$180° − \theta$	$90° − \theta$
sine	$\sin \theta$	$\sin \theta$	$\cos \theta$
cosine	$\cos \theta$	$−\cos \theta$	$\sin \theta$

5.2 Exercises, page 263

1. a) 5.2 cm   **b)** 7.4 cm   **c)** 8.9 cm

2. a) 5.7 cm   **b)** 5.1 cm   **c)** 7.9 cm

3. a) 83°   **b)** 23°   **c)** 106°

4. a) 65°   **b)** 33°   **c)** 124°

5. a) $f \doteq 24.0$ cm, $\angle D \doteq 48°$, $\angle E \doteq 25°$
  b) $\angle G \doteq 30°$, $g \doteq 12.4$ cm, $h \doteq 19.0$ cm
  c) $\angle J \doteq 110°$, $\angle K \doteq 43°$, $\angle L \doteq 27°$
  d) $\angle M \doteq 40°$, $\angle N \doteq 104°$, $n \doteq 19.8$ cm

6. a) $\angle A \doteq 39°$ and AC $\doteq 4.7$ cm or
    $\angle A \doteq 141°$ and AC $\doteq 1.0$ cm
  b) $\angle A \doteq 53°$ and AC $\doteq 116$ cm or
    $\angle A \doteq 127°$ and AC $\doteq 1.2$ cm

7. a) AC gets longer.   **b)** AC gets shorter.

8. a) $\angle A \doteq 25°$, $\angle B \doteq 137°$, $\angle C \doteq 18°$
  b) $\angle D = 94°$, $e \doteq 13.1$ cm, $d \doteq 21.2$ cm
  c) $g \doteq 4.7$ cm, $\angle J \doteq 35°$, $\angle H \doteq 84°$
  d) $m \doteq 8.4$ cm, $\angle K \doteq 88°$, $\angle N \doteq 50°$
  e) $\angle Q \doteq 52°$, $\angle R \doteq 56°$, $r \doteq 24.8$ cm
  f) $\angle U \doteq 47°$, $\angle T \doteq 111°$, $t \doteq 8.7$ cm

9. $q \doteq 15.6$ cm, $\angle P \doteq 30°$, $\angle R \doteq 28°$

10. $\angle C \doteq 21°$, $\angle A \doteq 18°$, $a \doteq 3.8$ cm

11. 5.02 km

12. DB $\doteq 4.7$ cm, AC $\doteq 3.4$ cm

13. 48°, 58°, 74°

14. a) 118°, 62°   **b)** 9.4 cm

15. a) 13.7 cm   **b)** 21°

16. 126.6°, 50.6°, 61.7°

17. 20.5 cm

18. a) 18.8 cm   **b)** 74.4°

19. 1.6 km

20. 6.6 cm

21. 112.6°

22. a) 14.5°   **b)** 14.4°   **c)** 77.5 cm

23. 43.7 m

24. 2.3 km

25. 2.7 cm or 6.0 cm

Self-Check 5.1, 5.2, page 267

1. a) 0.9945, 0.1045   **b)** 0.1530, −0.9882
  c) 0.9925, −0.1219   **d)** 0.7157, −0.6984

3. a) 7.7 cm   **b)** 104°

4. Since $x_1 > x_2$, then $\cos 20° > \cos 50°$

5. It is not possible to construct a triangle with these
measurements.

6. a) $b \doteq 14.7$ cm, $\angle A \doteq 47°$, $\angle C \doteq 40°$
  b) $\angle P \doteq 34°$, $\angle Q \doteq 127°$, $q \doteq 16.3$ mm
  c) $\angle Z \doteq 13°$, $\angle Y \doteq 31°$, $\angle X \doteq 136°$

7. $\angle A \doteq 49°$, $\angle C \doteq 101°$, $c \doteq 7.8$ cm or
  $\angle A \doteq 131°$, $\angle C \doteq 19°$, $c \doteq 2.6$ cm

8. $\angle C \doteq 21°$, $\angle A \doteq 20°$, $a \doteq 3.9$ cm

9. 5.9 cm, 50.1 cm

10. 9.9 km

11. 9.2 units, 12.4 units

12. 14.8 cm

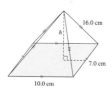

5.3 Exercises, page 270

1. a) 270°   **b)** 540°   **c)** −180°

2. a)

b)

c)

d)

e)

f)

g)

h)

3. Answers may vary.
a) 430°, −290°   **b)** 250°, −470°   **c)** 205°, −515°
d) 580°, −140°   **e)** 450°, −270°   **f)** 315°, −405°
g) 480°, −240°   **h)** 90°, −630°

4. Answers may vary.
a) 400°, −320°   **b)** 140°, −580°   **c)** 590°, −130°

5. Answers may vary.
a) 540°, −180°   **b)** 450°, −270°
c) 300°, −420°   **d)** 720°, 0°

7. a) 1.2   **b)** Quadrant I
c)

8. a) 1.05; Quadrant I   **b)** 1.3; Quadrant III

c) 2.1; Quadrant I

d) 2.5; on the axis between Quadrants II and III

9. a)   **b)**

c)   **d)**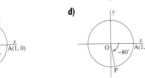

10. a) (−45 + 360n)°   **b)** (150 + 360n)°
c) (240 + 360n)°   **d)** (−30 + 360n)°
e) (180 + 360n)°   **f)** (−45 + 360n)°
g) (450 + 360n)°   **h)** (−80 + 360n)°

11. 233.1°

12. 146.3°

5.4 Exercises, page 278

1. a) 0.8, 0.6, 1.33   **b)** 0.8, −0.6, −1.33
c) −0.6, −0.8, 0.75   **d)** −0.6, 0.8, −0.75

2. a) 0.891   **b)** 0.454   **c)** 1.963   **d)** 0.485
e) −0.875   **f)** −0.554   **g)** −0.731   **h)** −0.682
i) 1.072   **j)** −0.848   **k)** 0.530   **l)** −1.600

3. a) i) 0   **ii)** 1   **iii)** 0   **iv)** 1
v) 0   **vi)** Undefined **vii)** 0   **viii)** −1
ix) 0   **x)** −1   **xi)** 0   **xii)** Undefined
xiii) 0   **xiv)** 1   **xv)** 0

4. a) 1.111   **b)** 0.839   **c)** 0.326   **d)** 0.391
e) −0.625   **f)** −0.988   **g)** 0.139   **h)** −0.974
i) 2.475   **j)** −0.052   **k)** −0.404   **l)** 0.777

5. Answers may vary for part ii.
a) i) 0.731   **ii)** 133°, 407°
b) i) 0.559   **ii)** −56°, 416°
c) i) 0.649   **ii)** 213°, 393°
d) i) 0.951   **ii)** 72°, 468°
e) i) −0.951   **ii)** 198°, 522°
f) i) −0.488   **ii)** 334°, 514°
g) i) −0.156   **ii)** 351°, 549°
h) i) −0.857   **ii)** 149°, 571°
i) i) 3.487   **ii)** 74°, 434°
j) i) −0.574   **ii)** 215°, 685°
k) i) 0.407   **ii)** 66°, 654°
l) i) −5.145   **ii)** 101°, 461°

6. a) Negative   **b)** Negative   **c)** Positive
d) Negative   **e)** Positive   **f)** Positive

8. a) 67°   **b)** 17°   **c)** 46°
d) 37°   **e)** 78°   **f)** 39°

9. a) 155°   **b)** 161°   **c)** 125°
d) 129°   **e)** 117°   **f)** 131°

10. a) 215°   **b)** 246°   **c)** 215°
d) 213°   **e)** 258°   **f)** 207°

11. a) 320°   **b)** 318°   **c)** 349°
d) 282°   **e)** 316°   **f)** 290°

12. a) 65°, 295°   **b)** 17°, 163°   **c)** 54°, 234°
d) 55°, 125°   **e)** 43°, 317°   **f)** 68°, 248°

13. a) 208°, 332°   **b)** 137°, 317°   **c)** 156°, 204°
d) 238°, 302°   **e)** 107°, 253   **f)** 100°, 280°

14. a) i) (0.866, 0.5), (−0.5, 0.866), (−0.866, −0.5), (0.5, −0.866)
ii) 30°, 120°, 210°, 300°
iii) 0.866, 0.5; −0.5, 0.866; −0.866, −0.5; 0.5, −0.866
b) i) (0.342, 0.94), (−0.94, 0.342), (−0.342, −0.94),
(0.94, −0.342)
ii) 70°, 160°, 250°, 340°
iii) 0.342, 0.94; −0.94, 0.342; −0.342, −0.94; 0.94, −0.342

15. a) −0.866; 0.5   **b)** 0.866; −0.5
    c) 0.5; 0.866   **d)** −0.5; −0.866

16. a) −0.342, 0.94   **b)** 0.342, −0.94
    c) 0.94, 0.342   **d)** −0.94, −0.342

17. a) 0.949   **b)** 0.316   **c)** 3.000

18. a) 0.857   **b)** 0.514   **c)** 1.667

19. a) $-\dfrac{5}{13}$ **b)** $\dfrac{12}{13}$ **c)** $-\dfrac{5}{12}$

20. a) Answers may vary.

    b) Answers may vary. 5   **c)** 0.8
    d) Answers may vary. (3, 4)

21. a) Answers may vary.

    b) Answers may vary. 5   **c)** 0.8
    d) Answers may vary. (−3, 4)

22. Answers may vary. (−2, −1)

23. Answers may vary. (5, −12)

25. a) $\left(-\dfrac{3}{\sqrt{58}}, -\dfrac{7}{\sqrt{58}}\right)$
    b) Corresponding ratios are equal.

5.5 Exercises, page 285

1. a) i)

ii)

iii)

iv)

v)

vi)

vii)

viii)

b) i) 45°   **ii)** 30°   **iii)** 45°   **iv)** 60°
   v) 30°   **vi)** 60°   **vii)** 45°   **viii)** 60°

2. a) $\dfrac{1}{\sqrt{2}}$ **b)** $\dfrac{1}{\sqrt{2}}$ **c)** $-\dfrac{1}{\sqrt{2}}$ **d)** $-\dfrac{1}{\sqrt{2}}$
  e) $\dfrac{1}{2}$ **f)** $\dfrac{1}{2}$ **g)** $-\dfrac{1}{2}$ **h)** $-\dfrac{1}{2}$
  i) $\dfrac{\sqrt{3}}{2}$ **j)** $\dfrac{\sqrt{3}}{2}$ **k)** $-\dfrac{\sqrt{3}}{2}$ **l)** $-\dfrac{\sqrt{3}}{2}$

3. a) 1   **b)** −1   **c)** 1   **d)** −1
  e) $\dfrac{1}{\sqrt{3}}$ **f)** $-\dfrac{1}{\sqrt{3}}$ **g)** $\dfrac{1}{\sqrt{3}}$ **h)** $-\dfrac{1}{\sqrt{3}}$
  i) $\sqrt{3}$ **j)** $-\sqrt{3}$ **k)** $\sqrt{3}$ **l)** $-\sqrt{3}$

4. a) $\dfrac{1}{\sqrt{2}}$ **b)** $-\dfrac{1}{\sqrt{2}}$ **c)** $-\dfrac{1}{\sqrt{2}}$ **d)** $\dfrac{1}{\sqrt{2}}$
  e) $\dfrac{\sqrt{3}}{2}$ **f)** $-\dfrac{\sqrt{3}}{2}$ **g)** $-\dfrac{\sqrt{3}}{2}$ **h)** $\dfrac{\sqrt{3}}{2}$
  i) $\dfrac{1}{2}$ **j)** $-\dfrac{1}{2}$ **k)** $-\dfrac{1}{2}$ **l)** $\dfrac{1}{2}$

5. The results are exact when geometric relationships are used.

6. b) i) Yes   **ii)** Yes

7. a) There is a pattern.
   b) The pattern for cosines is the reverse of the pattern for sines.

8. a) i) (0.866, 0.5), (−0.866, 0.5), (0, −1)
    ii) 30°, 150°, 270°
    iii) $\dfrac{\sqrt{3}}{2}, \dfrac{1}{2}, \dfrac{1}{\sqrt{3}}; -\dfrac{\sqrt{3}}{2}, \dfrac{1}{2}, -\dfrac{1}{\sqrt{3}}; 0, -1$, undefined
   b) i) (0.707, 0.707), (−0.707, 0.707), (−0.707, −0.707), (0.707, −0.707)
    ii) 45°, 135°, 225°, 315°
    iii) $\dfrac{1}{\sqrt{2}}, \dfrac{1}{\sqrt{2}}, 1; -\dfrac{1}{\sqrt{2}}, \dfrac{1}{\sqrt{2}}, -1; -\dfrac{1}{\sqrt{2}}, -\dfrac{1}{\sqrt{2}}, 1; \dfrac{1}{\sqrt{2}}, -\dfrac{1}{\sqrt{2}}, -1$
   c) i) (0.5, 0.866), (−0.5, 0.866), (−1, 0), (−0.5, −0.866), (0.5, −0.866), (1, 0)
    ii) 60°, 120°, 180°, 240°, 300°, 360°
    iii) $\dfrac{1}{2}, \dfrac{\sqrt{3}}{2}, \sqrt{3}, -\dfrac{1}{2}, \dfrac{\sqrt{3}}{2}, -\sqrt{3}; -1, 0, 0; -\dfrac{1}{2}, -\dfrac{\sqrt{3}}{2}, \sqrt{3}; \dfrac{1}{2}, -\dfrac{\sqrt{3}}{2}, -\sqrt{3}; 1, 0, 0$
   d) i) (0.924, 0.383), (0.383, 0.924), (−0.383, 0.924), (−0.924, 0.383), (−0.924, −0.383), (−0.383, −0.924), (0.383, −0.924), (0.924, −0.383)
    ii) 22.5°, 67.5°, 112.5°, 157.5°, 202.5°, 247.5°, 292.5°, 337.5°
    iii) 0.924, 0.383, 0.414; 0.383, 0.924, 2.414; −0.383, 0.924, −2.414; −0.924, 0.383, −0.414; −0.924, −0.383, 0.414; −0.383, −0.924, 2.414; 0.383, −0.924, −2.414; 0.924, −0.383, −0.414

9. a) $\dfrac{1+\sqrt{3}}{2}$ **b)** $\dfrac{5\sqrt{3}}{6}$
  c) $\dfrac{\sqrt{3}-1}{2}$ **d)** $\dfrac{2-\sqrt{3}}{2}$
  e) $\dfrac{2\sqrt{3}-\sqrt{2}}{2}$ **f)** $\dfrac{\sqrt{3}}{6}$

10. a) 0.9659   **b)** 0.9239   **c)** 0.8090

Self-Check 5.3–5.5, page 287

1. a)

b)

c)

d)

e)

f)

2. Answers may vary.
a) $-90°, 630°$ **b)** $-285°, 435°$
c) $-210°, 510°$ **d)** $-480°, 240°$

3. Answers may vary for part ii.
a) i) 0.407   **ii)** $156°, 384°, 516°$
b) i) 0.309   **ii)** $288°, 432°, 648°$
c) i) 0.781   **ii)** $218°, 398°, 578°$
d) i) 0.682   **ii)** $43°, 403°, 497°$
e) i) -0.122 **ii)** $263°, 457°, 623°$
f) i) -0.675 **ii)** $326°, 506°, 686°$
g) i) -0.766 **ii)** $310°, 590°, 670°$
h) i) -0.070 **ii)** $94°, 454°, 626°$
i) i) 0.325   **ii)** $18°, 378°, 558°$
j) i) -0.829 **ii)** $236°, 596°, 664°$
k) i) 0.391   **ii)** $67°, 427°, 653°$
l) i) -0.839 **ii)** $140°, 500°, 680°$

4. a) Negative **b)** Negative **c)** Positive
d) Negative **e)** Negative **f)** Negative

5. a) $125°$ **b)** $148°$ **c)** $139°$

6. a) $63°, 297°$ **b)** $194°, 346°$ **c)** $59°, 239°$

7. a) $-\dfrac{\sqrt{3}}{2}$ **b)** $-\dfrac{\sqrt{3}}{2}$ **c)** $-\dfrac{1}{\sqrt{2}}$
d) $-\dfrac{1}{\sqrt{3}}$ **e)** $-\sqrt{3}$ **f)** $\dfrac{1}{2}$

5.6 Exercises, page 292

1. a) $\dfrac{\pi}{6}$ **b)** $\dfrac{\pi}{3}$ **c)** $\dfrac{\pi}{2}$ **d)** $\dfrac{2\pi}{3}$
e) $\dfrac{5\pi}{6}$ **f)** π **g)** $\dfrac{7\pi}{6}$ **h)** $\dfrac{4\pi}{3}$
i) $\dfrac{3\pi}{2}$ **j)** $\dfrac{5\pi}{3}$ **k)** $\dfrac{11\pi}{6}$ **l)** 2π

2. a) $\dfrac{\pi}{4}$ **b)** $\dfrac{3\pi}{4}$ **c)** $\dfrac{5\pi}{4}$ **d)** $\dfrac{7\pi}{4}$

3. a) $30°$ **b)** $60°$ **c)** $90°$ **d)** $120°$
e) $150°$ **f)** $180°$ **g)** $45°$ **h)** $90°$
i) $135°$ **j)** $180°$ **k)** $225°$ **l)** $270°$

4. a) 2π radians **b)** π radians **c)** $\dfrac{\pi}{2}$ radians

5. a)

b)

c)

d)

e)

f)

g)

h)

$\dfrac{13\pi}{6}, \dfrac{25\pi}{6}$ $\dfrac{9\pi}{4}, \dfrac{17\pi}{4}$

$\dfrac{7\pi}{3}, \dfrac{13\pi}{3}$ $\dfrac{5\pi}{2}, \dfrac{9\pi}{2}$

$\dfrac{8\pi}{3}, \dfrac{14\pi}{3}$ $\dfrac{17\pi}{6}, \dfrac{29\pi}{6}$

$\dfrac{10\pi}{3}, \dfrac{16\pi}{3}$ $\dfrac{11\pi}{3}, \dfrac{17\pi}{3}$

6. a) $\dfrac{11\pi}{4}, \dfrac{19\pi}{4}$ **b)** $\dfrac{13\pi}{4}, \dfrac{21\pi}{4}$
c) $\dfrac{15\pi}{4}, \dfrac{23\pi}{4}$ **d)** $\dfrac{23\pi}{6}, \dfrac{35\pi}{6}$
e) $\dfrac{19\pi}{6}, \dfrac{31\pi}{6}$ **f)** $\dfrac{7\pi}{2}, \dfrac{11\pi}{2}$
g) $3\pi, 5\pi$ **h)** $4\pi, 6\pi$

7. a) 1.83 radians **b)** 3.84 radians **c)** 1.00 radians
d) 2.29 radians **e)** 1.43 radians **f)** 0.79 radians
g) 1.12 radians **h)** 0.40 radians **i)** 2.44 radians
j) 1.05 radians **k)** 1 radian **l)** 0.5 radians

8. a) $171.9°$ **b)** $229.2°$ **c)** $120.3°$ **d)** $91.7°$
e) $28.6°$ **f)** $68.8°$ **g)** $378.2°$ **h)** $360°$

9. a) $90°$ **b)** $330°$ **c)** $120°$ **d)** $210°$
e) $300°$ **f)** $270°$ **g)** $315°$ **h)** $405°$

10. a) Multiply by $\dfrac{\pi}{180°}$ to convert degrees to radians.

b) Multiply by $\dfrac{180°}{\pi}$ to convert radians to degrees.

11. a)

b)

c)

d)

e)

f)

g)

h)

12. a) 10 cm **b)** 12.8 cm **c)** 6.8 cm
d) 24.8 cm **e)** 18 cm **f)** 3.6 cm

13. a) 34.0 cm **b)** 18.3 cm **c)** 26.2 cm **d)** 40.6 cm
e) 55.0 cm **f)** 23.6 cm **g)** 86.4 cm **h)** 78.5 cm

14. a) i) r **ii)** $\frac{\pi}{3}r$ **b)** $\frac{\pi}{3}$

15. a) 0.5 radians, 28.6° **b)** 1.17 radians, 66.8°
c) 2.08 radians, 119.4° **d)** 2.73 radians, 156.6°

16. 5.5 cm

17. 8.9 cm

18. a) 0.009 59 radians **ii)** 3686 km

19. a) 18.52 radians/second **b)** $\frac{500x}{9d}$

20. 5009.3 km

21. a) $A = \frac{r^2\theta}{2}$ **b)** $A = \frac{\theta}{360}\pi r^2$

5.7 Exercises, page 300

1. a) 0.964 **b)** 0.622 **c)** 0.684 **d)** −0.602
e) 0.946 **f)** −0.942 **g)** −0.897 **h)** 1.424
i) −0.916 **j)** −0.926 **k)** −0.660 **l)** 0.554

2. a) 0, 1, 0 **b)** 1, 0, undefined **c)** 0, −1, 0
d) −1, 0, undefined **e)** 0, 1, 0

3. a) $\frac{\sqrt{3}}{2}$ **b)** 1 **c)** $\frac{1}{2}$ **d)** $\sqrt{3}$
e) $\frac{1}{2}$ **f)** $\frac{1}{\sqrt{2}}$ **g)** $\frac{1}{\sqrt{2}}$ **h)** $\frac{1}{\sqrt{3}}$
i) $\frac{\sqrt{3}}{2}$ **j)** −1 **k)** 0 **l)** 1

4. Answers may vary for part ii.
a) i) 0.746 **ii)** 0.842, 8.583
b) i) 0.493 **ii)** 6.742, 9.883
c) i) 0.087 **ii)** 1.483, 11.083
d) i) −0.129 **ii)** 4.583, 7.983
e) i) −0.374 **ii)** −2.758, 12.183
f) i) 1.260 **ii)** 4.042, 7.183

5. a) 0.79, 2.35 **b)** 1.25, 4.39 **c)** 1.22, 5.06
d) 1.04, 4.19 **e)** 0.45, 5.83 **f)** 0.23, 2.91

6. a) 2.08, 5.22 **b)** 2.24, 4.04 **c)** 3.71, 5.71
d) 2.37, 5.51 **e)** 3.29, 6.13 **f)** 1.91, 4.38

7. a) $-\frac{\sqrt{3}}{2}$ **b)** $-\frac{1}{2}$ **c)** $\sqrt{3}$ **d)** $-\frac{1}{2}$
e) $-\frac{1}{2}$ **f)** $-\frac{1}{\sqrt{3}}$ **g)** $-\frac{1}{\sqrt{3}}$ **h)** $\frac{1}{\sqrt{2}}$
i) $-\frac{1}{2}$

8. a) $-\frac{1}{\sqrt{2}}$ **b)** $\frac{\sqrt{3}}{2}$ **c)** $-\sqrt{3}$ **d)** $-\frac{\sqrt{3}}{2}$
e) $\frac{1}{2}$ **f)** $\frac{1}{\sqrt{3}}$ **g)** $\frac{\sqrt{3}}{2}$ **h)** $-\frac{1}{\sqrt{2}}$
i) $-\frac{\sqrt{3}}{2}$ **j)** $\frac{1}{\sqrt{2}}$ **k)** −1 **l)** −1

9. a) $-\frac{1}{\sqrt{2}}, -\frac{1}{\sqrt{2}}, 1$ **b)** $\frac{1}{2}, -\frac{\sqrt{3}}{2}, -\frac{1}{\sqrt{3}}$
c) $-\frac{\sqrt{3}}{2}, \frac{1}{2}, -\sqrt{3}$

10. a) 0.52, 2.62 **b)** 4.19, 5.24 **c)** 0.79, 3.93
d) 2.09, 5.24 **e)** 3.93, 5.50 **f)** 3.14

11. a) 2.9 m **b)** 8.2 m²

12. a) i) $-0.5 \le \theta \le 0.5$ **ii)** $-0.24 \le \theta \le 0.24$
iii) $-0.114 \le \theta \le 0.114$

5.8 Exercises, page 305

1. a) 0, π, 2π **b)** $\frac{\pi}{2}, \frac{3\pi}{2}$ **c)** 0, π, 2π
d) $\frac{\pi}{2}$ **e)** 0, 2π **f)** $\frac{\pi}{4}, \frac{5\pi}{4}$

2. a) $\frac{\pi}{6}, \frac{11\pi}{6}$ **b)** $\frac{\pi}{6}, \frac{5\pi}{6}$ **c)** $\frac{\pi}{3}, \frac{4\pi}{3}$
d) $\frac{\pi}{4}, \frac{3\pi}{4}$ **e)** $\frac{\pi}{4}, \frac{7\pi}{4}$ **f)** $\frac{\pi}{6}, \frac{7\pi}{6}$

3. a) $\frac{2\pi}{3}, \frac{4\pi}{3}$ **b)** $\frac{5\pi}{4}, \frac{7\pi}{4}$ **c)** $\frac{5\pi}{6}, \frac{11\pi}{6}$
d) $\frac{4\pi}{3}, \frac{5\pi}{3}$ **e)** $\frac{3\pi}{2}$ **f)** $\frac{2\pi}{3}, \frac{5\pi}{3}$
g) $\frac{3\pi}{4}, \frac{7\pi}{4}$ **h)** π **i)** $\frac{5\pi}{6}, \frac{7\pi}{6}$

4. a) 1.32, 4.97 **b)** 0.85, 2.29 **c)** 1.25, 4.39
d) 0.64, 2.50 **e)** 1.37, 4.91 **f)** 0.59, 3.73
g) 1.33, 4.47 **h)** 0.72, 5.56 **i)** 0.25, 2.89

5. a) 1.89, 5.03 **b)** 2.3, 3.98 **c)** 3.48, 5.95
d) 2.50, 3.79 **e)** 2.50, 5.64 **f)** 3.55, 5.87
g) 3.99, 5.44 **h)** 2.25, 5.39 **i)** 1.82, 4.46

6. a) 1.11, 4.25
b) Both sin θ and cos θ must be between −1 and 1.

7. a) $\frac{\pi}{2}, \frac{7\pi}{6}, \frac{11\pi}{6}$ **b)** $\frac{3\pi}{4}, \frac{2\pi}{3}, \frac{5\pi}{4}, \frac{4\pi}{3}$ **c)** $\frac{\pi}{4}, \frac{2\pi}{3}, \frac{5\pi}{4}, \frac{5\pi}{3}$
d) $0, \frac{\pi}{6}, \frac{11\pi}{6}, 2\pi$ **e)** $\frac{\pi}{3}, \frac{2\pi}{3}, \frac{5\pi}{4}, \frac{7\pi}{4}$ **f)** $\frac{3\pi}{4}, \frac{\pi}{6}, \frac{7\pi}{6}, \frac{7\pi}{4}$

8. a) $\cos x(\cos x + 2)$ **b)** $(\sin x + 2)(\sin x + 3)$
c) $(2\sin x - 3)(\sin x + 2)$ **d)** $(3\cos x + 1)(\cos x - 1)$
e) $(2\cos x - 1)(\cos x - 3)$ **f)** $(3\sin x - 1)(2\sin x + 1)$

9. a) $\frac{\pi}{2}, \frac{3\pi}{2}$ **b)** No solution
c) No solution **d)** 0, 2π, 1.91, 4.37
e) $\frac{\pi}{3}, \frac{5\pi}{3}$ **f)** 0.34, 2.80, $\frac{7\pi}{6}, \frac{11\pi}{6}$

10. a) $0, \frac{\pi}{2}, \pi, 2\pi$ **b)** $\frac{\pi}{2}, \pi, \frac{3\pi}{2}$
c) $\frac{\pi}{6}, \frac{5\pi}{6}, \frac{3\pi}{2}$ **d)** $\frac{\pi}{2}, \frac{7\pi}{6}, \frac{11\pi}{6}$
e) π **f)** $\frac{\pi}{2}$
g) $\frac{2\pi}{3}, \pi, \frac{4\pi}{3}$ **h)** $0, \frac{\pi}{3}, \frac{5\pi}{3}, 2\pi$
i) $\frac{3\pi}{2}$ **j)** No solution
k) $\frac{\pi}{3}, \frac{5\pi}{3}$ **l)** $\frac{\pi}{6}, \frac{5\pi}{6}, \frac{7\pi}{6}, \frac{11\pi}{6}$

11. a) $0, \frac{\pi}{4}, \pi, \frac{5\pi}{4}, 2\pi$ **b)** $0, \frac{3\pi}{4}, \pi, \frac{7\pi}{4}, 2\pi$
c) $\frac{\pi}{4}, \frac{3\pi}{4}, \frac{5\pi}{4}, \frac{7\pi}{4}$ **d)** $\frac{\pi}{4}, \frac{\pi}{3}, \frac{5\pi}{4}, \frac{4\pi}{3}$
e) 0.46, 3.61, $\frac{\pi}{4}, \frac{5\pi}{4}$ **f)** 0.99, 2.43, 4.14, 5.57

12. Answers may vary.

a) $\sin^2 \theta + 2 \sin \theta = 0$ **b)** $\sin^2 \theta - \sin \theta + \frac{1}{4} = 0$

c) $\sin \theta - 1 = 0$ **d)** $\cos^2 \theta - \cos \theta + \frac{1}{4} = 0$

e) $\tan^2 \theta - 2 \tan \theta + 1 = 0$ **f)** $\tan^2 \theta + 2 \tan \theta + 1 = 0$

13. Answers may vary.

a) $2 \sin^2 \theta - 3 \sin \theta + 1 = 0$

b) $\tan^2 \theta - (\sqrt{3} + 1) \tan \theta + \sqrt{3} = 0$

c) $\tan^2 \theta - 1 = 0$

14. a) $0, \pi, 2\pi$ **b)** $\frac{\pi}{2}, \frac{3\pi}{2}$ **c)** $0, \pi, 2\pi$

d) $\frac{\pi}{2}, \frac{3\pi}{2}$ **e)** $\frac{\pi}{6}, \frac{5\pi}{6}, \frac{3\pi}{2}$ **f)** $\frac{\pi}{3}, \frac{5\pi}{3}$

15. a) $0.73, 2.41, \frac{7\pi}{6}, \frac{11\pi}{6}$ **b)** $1.91, 4.37, \frac{\pi}{3}, \frac{5\pi}{3}$

c) $0, \pi, \frac{7\pi}{6}, \frac{11\pi}{6}, 2\pi$ **d)** $1.23, 1.74, 4.54, 5.05$

e) $0.62, 2.53, 3.76, 5.67, \frac{\pi}{2}, \frac{3\pi}{2}$

f) $0, \frac{\pi}{4}, \frac{3\pi}{4}, \pi, \frac{5\pi}{4}, \frac{7\pi}{4}, 2\pi$

Self-Check 5.6–5.9, page 310

1. a) $\frac{\pi}{12}$ radians   **b)** $\frac{7\pi}{12}$ radians

c) $\frac{2\pi}{9}$ radians   **d)** $\frac{31\pi}{18}$ radians

2. a) $120°$ **b)** $22.5°$ **c)** $315°$ **d)** $330°$

3. a) 7.2 cm   **b)** 11.7 cm   **c)** 10.2 cm   **d)** 16.8 cm

4. a) $\frac{\sqrt{3}}{2}$ **b)** $-\frac{1}{2}$ **c)** $-\sqrt{3}$

d) $\frac{1}{\sqrt{2}}$ **e)** $-\frac{1}{2}$ **f)** Undefined

5. All angles between π and $\frac{3\pi}{2}$ are in Quadrant III.

6. a) $1.07, 4.21$ **b)** $0.51, 2.63$ **c)** $1.49, 4.79$

d) $3.39, 6.03$ **e)** $2.25, 4.03$ **f)** $1.97, 5.11$

7. a) $1.16, 5.12$ **b)** $\frac{\pi}{4}, \frac{5\pi}{4}$ **c)** $4.07, 5.36$

d) $0, \frac{5\pi}{6}, \frac{7\pi}{6}, 2\pi$ **e)** $0, \frac{\pi}{4}, \frac{3\pi}{4}, \pi, 2\pi$ **f)** $\frac{\pi}{4}, \frac{2\pi}{3}, \frac{5\pi}{4}, \frac{5\pi}{3}$

8. a) $\frac{\pi}{6}, \frac{5\pi}{6}, \frac{3\pi}{2}$ **b)** $\frac{\pi}{3}, \frac{2\pi}{3}, \frac{4\pi}{3}, \frac{5\pi}{3}$ **c)** $\frac{\pi}{2}$

d) $\frac{\pi}{6}, \frac{7\pi}{6}$ **e)** $0, 2\pi$ **f)** $3.77, 5.66$

10. No

Insights Into a Rich Problem— The 2-3-4 Triangle, page 313

1. a) $41.41°, 55.77°, 82.82°$

b) (largest angle) $= 2 \times$ (smallest angle)

2. a) $44.42°, 57.12°, 78.46°; 46.57°, 57.91°, 75.52°$

b) For the 6-7-8: $2 \times$ (largest angle) $= 2 \times$ (smallest angle) $+$ (middle angle)

5. a) $a + ar + ar^2 = 180°, a + ar = 90°, ar^2 = 90°$;
$a = 34.3769°, r = 1.618034$;
$a = 34.4°, ar = 55.6°, ar^2 = 90°$

b) Same triangle.

6. a) $(r^2)^2 = r^2 + 1; r = 1.272\,019\,6; 38.2°, 51.8°$

b) Similar triangle.

7. a) $BC = \frac{2}{\sqrt{3}+1}, AC = \frac{\sqrt{6}}{\sqrt{3}+1}$

b) $\frac{\sqrt{3}+1}{2\sqrt{2}}, \frac{\sqrt{2-\sqrt{3}}}{2}, \frac{\sqrt{6}+\sqrt{2}}{2\sqrt{2-\sqrt{3}}}$

c) $\frac{\sqrt{2-\sqrt{3}}}{2}, \frac{\sqrt{3}+1}{2\sqrt{2}}, \frac{2\sqrt{2-\sqrt{3}}}{\sqrt{6}+\sqrt{2}}$

8. b) $\frac{\sqrt{5}-1}{2} < r < \frac{\sqrt{5}+1}{2}$

Chapter 5 Review Exercises, page 316

1. a) Negative   **b)** Positive

c) Negative

2. a) $61.5°$ **b)** $167.2°$ **c)** $33.2°, 146.8°$

d) $58.3°$ **e)** $20.4°, 159.6°$ **f)** $123.9°$

3. a) 0.4067 **b)** -0.2403

4. $54.7°$

5. 10.6 cm

6. a) $\angle B = 26°; AC \doteq 29.5$ cm; $AB \doteq 45.1$ cm

b) $\angle R \doteq 29.6°; \angle Q \doteq 49.9°; PR \doteq 32.8$ cm

c) $YZ \doteq 31$ mm; $\angle Z = 33°; \angle Y = 114°$

7. $107.8°; 13.0$ cm

8. Coterminal angles may vary.

a) $530°$ **b)** $653°$

c) $330°$ **d)** $40°$

e) $90°$ **f)** $240°$

g) $350°$ **h)** $560°$

9. a) 25°, 155° **b)** 108°, 252° **c)** 74°, 254°

10. a) −0.966 **b)** 0.258 **c)** −3.750

11. a) $\dfrac{4}{5}$ **b)** $-\dfrac{3}{5}$ **c)** $-\dfrac{4}{3}$

12. a) $-\dfrac{1}{\sqrt{2}}$ **b)** 1 **c)** $-\dfrac{1}{2}$ **d)** $\dfrac{1}{\sqrt{3}}$

13. a) 1 **b)** 2 **c)** $\dfrac{1-\sqrt{3}}{2}$

15. a) $\dfrac{\pi}{6}$ **b)** $\dfrac{5\pi}{4}$ **c)** $\dfrac{7\pi}{4}$ **d)** $\dfrac{7\pi}{6}$

16. a) 114.6° **b)** 34.4° **c)** 309.4° **d)** 25.7°

17. 1.1:1

18. Answers may vary for part ii.

a) i) $\dfrac{\sqrt{3}}{2}$ **ii)** $\dfrac{\pi}{3}, \dfrac{7\pi}{3}$

b) i) $\dfrac{1}{\sqrt{2}}$ **ii)** $\dfrac{\pi}{4}, \dfrac{9\pi}{4}$

c) i) $-\dfrac{1}{\sqrt{3}}$ **ii)** $\dfrac{11\pi}{6}, \dfrac{17\pi}{6}$

19. a) 0.61, 5.67 **b)** 0.96, 4.10 **c)** 0.44, 2.70
d) 3.68, 5.75 **e)** 1.78, 4.50 **f)** 1.94, 5.08

20. a) 1.13, 5.16 **b)** 0.20, 2.94 **c)** $\dfrac{2\pi}{3}, \dfrac{5\pi}{3}$

21. a) $\dfrac{\pi}{3}, \dfrac{5\pi}{3}$, 2.19, 4.10 **b)** $\dfrac{\pi}{4}, \dfrac{2\pi}{3}, \dfrac{5\pi}{4}, \dfrac{5\pi}{3}$
c) $\dfrac{\pi}{3}, \dfrac{2\pi}{3}, \dfrac{5\pi}{4}, \dfrac{7\pi}{4}$ **d)** $\dfrac{5\pi}{6}, \dfrac{7\pi}{6}$, 2.36, 5.50

22. a) $0, \dfrac{\pi}{6}, \dfrac{5\pi}{6}, \pi, 2\pi$ **b)** $\dfrac{2\pi}{3}, \dfrac{4\pi}{3}$
c) $0, \pi, 2\pi, 0.32, 3.46$ **d)** $0.25, 2.89, \dfrac{\pi}{6}, \dfrac{5\pi}{6}$

23. a) $\dfrac{\pi}{2}, \dfrac{7\pi}{6}, \dfrac{11\pi}{6}$ **b)** $\pi, \dfrac{2\pi}{3}, \dfrac{5\pi}{3}$
c) 0.79, 2.36 **d)** $1.91, 4.37, \dfrac{\pi}{3}, \dfrac{5\pi}{3}$

Chapter 5 Self-Test, page 319

1. 0.6507, −0.8570

2. a) $\angle C = 39.9°$; AC ≐ 3.47 cm; AB ≐ 4.22 cm
b) $\angle X$ ≐ 131.4°; $\angle Z$ ≐ 18.6°; XY ≐ 25.52 cm; or
$\angle X$ ≐ 48.6°; $\angle Z$ ≐ 101.4°; XY ≐ 78.42 cm

3. a) −51°, 669° **b)** −212°, 508°

c) −414°, 306°

4. a) 5.39 radians **b)** 2.58 radians **c)** −0.94 radians

5. a)

b) $\sin\theta = -\dfrac{5}{\sqrt{29}}$, $\cos\theta = -\dfrac{2}{\sqrt{29}}$, $\tan\theta = \dfrac{5}{2}$
c) 248°

6. a) 0.236, 3.377 **b)** No solution
c) $0, \dfrac{\pi}{6}, \dfrac{5\pi}{6}, \pi, \dfrac{7\pi}{6}, \dfrac{11\pi}{6}, 2\pi$ **d)** $\dfrac{7\pi}{6}, \dfrac{11\pi}{6}$

7. 0.045 km

8. Approximately 2897 mm

10. a) $\dfrac{\pi}{2}, \dfrac{7\pi}{6}, \dfrac{11\pi}{6}$ **b)** $0, 2\pi$
c) $\dfrac{\pi}{2}$ **d)** 0.97, 1.85, 4.11, 5.00

12. a) 180°/s **b)** π radians/s

Assessment Tasks, page 320

1. a) 5.70 or 1.23 **b)** 5.70 or 1.23

2. Always true

3. 4.47 units

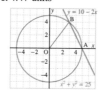

Chapter 6 Graphing Trigonometric Functions
Necessary Skills
1 Review: Transformations of Quadratic Functions
Exercises, page 323

1. a)

b)

c) $y = -(x+4)^2 + 1$

d) $y = -(x-6)^2 + 4$

e)

  $y = 0.5(x-3)^2 - 5$

f) $y = -0.5(x-3)^2 - 5$

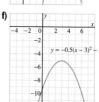

2. a) Vertical stretch by a factor of 3
b) Reflection in the x-axis
c) Reflection in the x-axis; vertical compression by a factor of 0.5
d) Translate 1 unit left and 2 units down.
e) Vertical stretch by a factor of 2; translate 3 units right and 4 units up.
f) Reflection in the x-axis; vertical stretch by a factor of 2; translate 3 units right and 4 units up.

2 New: The Domain and Range of a Function
Exercises, page 324

1. **a)** All real numbers; all real numbers
   b) All real numbers between –2 and 3, inclusive; all real numbers between 0 and 3, inclusive
   c) All real numbers between –2 and 7, inclusive; all real numbers between –1 and 5, inclusive

2. **a)** All real numbers; all real numbers

   b) All real numbers; all real numbers

   c) All real numbers; all real numbers greater than or equal to 2

   d) All real numbers; all non-negative real numbers

   e) All real numbers; all real numbers greater than or equal to 1

   f) All real numbers; all real numbers less than or equal to 1

3. **a)** All real numbers; all non-negative real numbers
   b) All real numbers; all real numbers greater than or equal to –4
   c) All real numbers; all real numbers greater than or equal to –3
   d) All real numbers; all real numbers greater than or equal to 6
   e) All real numbers; all real numbers less than or equal to 6
   f) All real numbers; all real numbers less than or equal to 4

4. **a)** $l = 10 - w$
   b) All real numbers between 0 and 10; all real numbers between 0 and 10

5. **a)** $y = 90 - x$; all real numbers between 0 and 90; all real numbers between 0 and 90
   b) $y = 180 - 2x$; all real numbers between 0 and 90; all real numbers between 0 and 180

3 New: Independent and Dependent Variables
Exercises, page 325

1. **a)** x; y **b)** n; A **c)** i; P
   d) r; V **e)** l; P **f)** x; y

2. **a)** x; y **b)** x; y **c)** n; T_n
   d) n; R
   e) i; A
   f) a; T
   g) t; h

4 New: Absolute Value
Exercises, page 328

1. **a)** 9   **b)** 4.2   **c)** 100   **d)** 15   **e)** 3.14

2. **a)** [number line from –6 to 6]   **b)** [number line from –6 to 6]
   c) [number line from –6 to 6]   **d)** [number line from –6 to 6]

3. **a)** [number line from –6 to 6]   **b)** [number line from –6 to 6]
   c) [number line from –6 to 6]   **d)** [number line from –6 to 6]

6.1 Exercises, page 331

1. **a)** 10 cm   **b)** 2 s
   c) 0.3 s, 0.7 s, 1.3 s, 1.7 s, 2.3 s, 2.7 s, 3.3 s, 3.7 s, 4.3 s, 4.7 s, 5.3 s, 5.7 s
   d) 1.2 s

2. **a)** **i)** 10 h   **ii)** 14.5 h   **iii)** 10.5 h
   b) **i)** February 10, November 11
   ii) April 5, September 7
   iii) May 20, July 19

3. **a)** The peaks would be higher and valleys would be lower.
   b) They would have the same period.
   c) The peaks would be lower and valleys would be higher.

4. A horizontal line with vertical intercept 12 h

5. **a)** 12 h   **b)** 2 m
   c) The difference between the maximum and minimum heights would be smaller.

6. **a)** $\frac{1}{256}$ s
   b) Period $= \frac{1}{\text{frequency}}$
   c) Approximately 2.71 m

7. Estimates may vary.
   a) Periodic; 8 units   **b)** Periodic; 6 units
   c) Periodic; 6 units   **d)** Not periodic
   e) Not periodic   **f)** Periodic; 6 units

6.2 Exercises, page 336

1. a)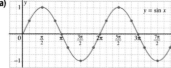

b)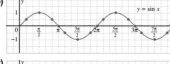

c)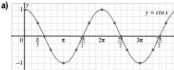

2. a)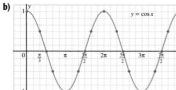

b)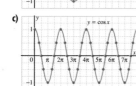

c)

4. a) 0.479; 0.878

b) 0.842; 0.540

c) 0.909; −0.416

d) 0.335; −0.942

e) −0.916; −0.401

f) −0.544; −0.839

g) −0.479; 0.878

h) 0.530; −0.848

5. a) The value of y approaches 0.
b) Yes; $y = 0$
c) $y = 1, y = -1, y = 0$
d) $x = \pi, y = -1; x = \dfrac{\pi}{2}, y = 0;$
   $x = \dfrac{3\pi}{2}, y = 0; x = 2\pi, y = 1$
e) $x = 0.785\ 398\ 16, y = 0.707\ 106\ 78$

7. a) $1; \ldots, -\dfrac{3\pi}{2}, \dfrac{\pi}{2}, \dfrac{5\pi}{2}, \dfrac{9\pi}{2}, \ldots$
b) $-1; \ldots, -\dfrac{\pi}{2}, \dfrac{3\pi}{2}, \dfrac{7\pi}{2}, \ldots$
c) All real numbers; all real numbers between −1 and 1, inclusive
d) $\ldots, -\pi, 0, \pi, 2\pi, \ldots$
e) 0   **f)** 2π

8. a) $1; \ldots, -2\pi, 0, 2\pi, 4\pi, \ldots$
b) $-1; \ldots, -\pi, \pi, 3\pi, \ldots$
c) All real numbers; all real numbers between −1 and 1, inclusive
d) $\ldots, -\dfrac{\pi}{2}, \dfrac{\pi}{2}, \dfrac{3\pi}{2}, \ldots$
e) 1   **f)** 2π

9. Between 0 and 2π: $\sin x > \cos x$ when $\dfrac{\pi}{4} < x < \dfrac{5\pi}{4}$; $\sin x = \cos x$ when $x = \dfrac{\pi}{4}$; $\sin x < \cos x$ when $0 < x < \dfrac{\pi}{4}$ and $\dfrac{5\pi}{4} < x < 2\pi$. Beyond 2π, this pattern repeats.

10. Answers may vary.
(−4.078, 0.805), (−5.347, 0.805), (2.206, 0.805)

11. Answers may vary.
(−5.347, 0.593), (−0.936, 0.593), (5.347, 0.593)

15. a) A straight line along the x-axis
b)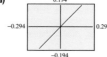

16. a) $y = 0.877$
b) Answers may vary. −5.214, −4.210, 2.073

17. a) $y = 0.481$
b) Answers may vary. −5.214, −1.609, 5.214

18. a) The horizontal scale would change to $-360 \le x \le 360$.
b) Yes

19. a) $(0.805)^2 + (0.593)^2 = 1$ **b)** True for all points

20. a)

b) They are the same.
c) For x close to 0, $\sin x \doteq x$

21. a) $(0, 0)$ **b)** $(0.739, 0.739)$

c) $(0.785 + 6.283n, 0.707)$, $(3.927 + 6.283n, -0.707)$:
where n is an integer

23. a) $\dfrac{2\pi}{3}$ **b)** 2.636; 1.445

c) i)

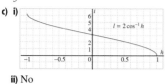

ii) No

6.3 Exercises, page 347

1. a) 1; 3; 0   **b)** 1; 0; $-\dfrac{\pi}{2}$ **c)** 2; –3; 0

2. a) $\dfrac{1}{2}$; –3; 0   **b)** 2; –2; $-\dfrac{\pi}{3}$

4. a) The graph is reflected in the x-axis and shifted up 2 units.

b) The graph shifts right $\dfrac{3\pi}{4}$ units and up 3 units.

c) The graph is stretched vertically by a factor of 2, shifted
left $\dfrac{\pi}{3}$ units, and up 1 unit.

d) The graph is compressed vertically by a factor of $\dfrac{1}{2}$,
shifted left $\dfrac{\pi}{4}$ units, and down 4 units.

7. a) Yes   **b)** No

8. (0.6, –2.175); (0.6, –1.175); (0.6, –0.175); (0.6, 1.825);
(0.6, 2.825); (0.6, 3.825)

9. (0.6, –2.475); (0.6, –1.65); (0.6, –0.825); (0.6, 0);
(0.6, 1.65); (0.6, 2.475)

10. a) $y = 0.564\ 642\ 47$
b) (0.6, –2.435); (0.6, –1.435); (0.6, –0.435); (0.6, 1.565);
(0.6, 2.565); (0.6, 3.565)

11. a) $y = 0.564\ 642\ 47$
b) (0.6, –1.695); (0.6, –1.13); (0.6, –0.565); (0.6, 0);
(0.6, 1.13); (0.6, 1.695)

12. No

13. Answers may vary. A graph can be translated horizontally
by one full period.

14. (–1.2, 0.697); (–0.2, 0.697); (1.8, 0.697); (2.8, 0.697)

15. a)

 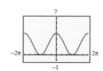

b)

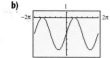 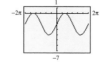

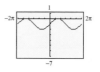

16. Answers may vary.

a) $\dfrac{\pi}{3}, -\dfrac{5\pi}{3}; y = \sin\left(x - \dfrac{\pi}{3}\right), y = \sin\left(x + \dfrac{5\pi}{3}\right)$

b) $\dfrac{5\pi}{6}, -\dfrac{7\pi}{6}; y = \cos\left(x - \dfrac{5\pi}{6}\right), y = \cos\left(x + \dfrac{7\pi}{6}\right)$

17. Equations and phase shifts may vary.

a) i) $y = \cos x + \dfrac{1}{2}$ **ii)** 1

iii) 0   **iv)** $\dfrac{3}{2}$; ..., 0, 2π, 4π, ...

v) $-\dfrac{1}{2}$; ..., π, 3π, ...   **vi)** $\dfrac{1}{2}$

vii) All real numbers; all real numbers between
$-\dfrac{1}{2}$ and $\dfrac{3}{2}$, inclusive

b) i) $y = 2 \sin x - 1$ **ii)** 2

iii) 0   **iv)** 1; ..., $\dfrac{\pi}{2}, \dfrac{5\pi}{2}, \dfrac{9\pi}{2}$, ...

v) –3; ..., $\dfrac{3\pi}{2}, \dfrac{7\pi}{2}$, ...   **vi)** –1

vii) All real numbers; all real numbers between
–3 and 1, inclusive

c) i) $y = \cos x - 2$ **ii)** 1

iii) 0   **iv)** –1; ..., 0, 2π, ...

v) –3; ..., $-\pi$, π **vi)** –2

vii) All real numbers; all real numbers between
–3 and –1, inclusive

d) i) $y = \dfrac{1}{2} \sin x + \dfrac{3}{2}$ **ii)** $\dfrac{1}{2}$

iii) 0   **iv)** 2; ..., $\dfrac{\pi}{2}, \dfrac{5\pi}{2}$, ...

v) 1; ..., $\dfrac{3\pi}{2}, \dfrac{7\pi}{2}$, ...   **vi)** $\dfrac{3}{2}$

vii) All real numbers; all real numbers between
1 and 2, inclusive

18. a) All real numbers; all real numbers between –5 and 5,
inclusive; 0; 5; 5, –5

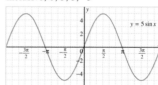

b) All real numbers; all real numbers between –3 and 3,
inclusive; 0; 3; 3, –3

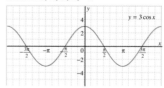

c) All real numbers; all real numbers between 3.75 and
4.25, inclusive; 0; 0.25; 4.25, 3.75

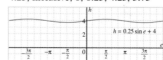

d) All real numbers; all real numbers between –5 and –1, inclusive; 0; 2; –1, –5

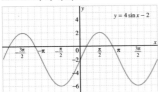

e) All real numbers; all real numbers between –6 and 2, inclusive; 0; 4; 2, –6

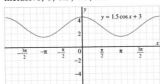

f) All real numbers; all real numbers between 1.5 and 4.5, inclusive; 0; 1.5; 4.5, 1.5

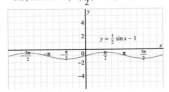

g) All real numbers; all real numbers between –1.5 and –0.5, inclusive; 0; $\frac{1}{2}$; –0.5, –1.5

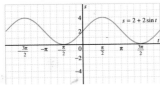

h) All real numbers; all real numbers between 0 and 4, inclusive; 0; 2; 4, 0

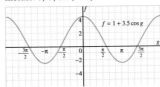

i) All real numbers; all real numbers between –2.5 and 4.5, inclusive; 0; 3.5; 4.5, –2.5

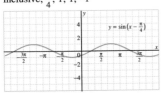

19. a) All real numbers; all real numbers between –1 and 1, inclusive; $\frac{\pi}{4}$; 1; 1, –1

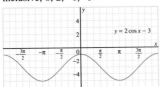

b) All real numbers; all real numbers between –1 and 1, inclusive; $\frac{4\pi}{3}$; 1; 1, –1

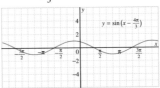

c) All real numbers; all real numbers between –2 and 2, inclusive; $-\frac{5\pi}{6}$; 2; 2, –2

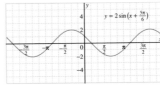

d) All real numbers; all real numbers between 0 and 6, inclusive; $\frac{\pi}{6}$; 3; 6, 0

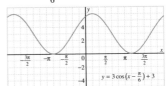

e) All real numbers; all real numbers between –4 and 0, inclusive; $-\frac{5\pi}{3}$; 2; 0, –4

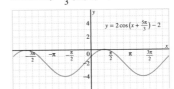

f) All real numbers; all real numbers between –3 and 7, inclusive; $\frac{7\pi}{6}$; 5; 7, –3

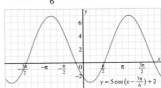

21. Maximum value = $a + c$; minimum value = $-a + c$

22. Maximum value = $a + c$; minimum value = $-a + c$

23. a) $a = \dfrac{M - m}{2}$ **b)** $c = \dfrac{M + m}{2}$
 c) $m \le R \le M$

24. a)

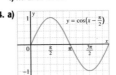

$y = \cos\left(x - \dfrac{\pi}{2}\right) = \sin x$

b) $\dfrac{\pi}{2} + 2\pi, \dfrac{\pi}{2} + 4\pi, \dfrac{\pi}{2} + 6\pi$, and so on

25. a)

$$y = \sin\left(x - \frac{\pi}{2}\right) = -\cos x \text{ or } y = \cos(x - \pi)$$

b) $-\frac{\pi}{2} + 2\pi, -\frac{\pi}{2} + 4\pi, -\frac{\pi}{2} + 6\pi,$ and so on

26. $y = 2\sin\left(x + \frac{\pi}{2}\right) = 2\cos x$

27. $y = \sin x + 1$ or $y = \sin x - 1$; 2

Self-Check 6.1–6.3, page 351

1. Estimates may vary.
  a) i) 5:10 P.M. **ii)** 9:00 P.M. **iii)** 5:50 P.M.
  b) i) April 15, August 21
   ii) March 15, September 28
   iii) February 20, October 20

2. a) 2 years **b)** 6500; 9500

3. (−5.498, −0.707); (−2.357, −0.707); (3.927, −0.707)

4. a) 1; −5; 0 **b)** 1, $\frac{\pi}{6}$, 0 **c)** 2, 0, 0

5. All real numbers; all real numbers between −1 and 3, inclusive; $\frac{\pi}{3}$; 2; 3; −1

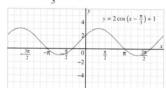

6.4 Exercises, page 357

1. a) $y = \sin x$ **b)** $y = \sin 2x$
  c) $y = \sin 4x$ **d)** $y = \sin 3x$

2. a) $y = \sin 2x$; π **b)** $y = \sin 3x$; $\frac{2\pi}{3}$
  c) $y = \sin \frac{1}{2}x$; 4π **d)** $y = \sin 6x$; $\frac{\pi}{3}$

3. Yes

4. a) 1; 2; 0; 0 **b)** 1; $\frac{1}{5}$; 0; 0

  c) 4; 3; 0; 0 **d)** 3; $\frac{1}{2}$; 0; $\frac{\pi}{3}$

5. a) The graph is compressed horizontally by a factor of $\frac{1}{2}$.
  b) The graph is expanded horizontally by a factor of 2.
  c) The graph is expanded vertically by a factor of 2, compressed horizontally by a factor of $\frac{1}{2}$, and translated down 2 units.
  d) The graph is expanded vertically by a factor of 3, expanded horizontally by a factor of 2, translated up 4 units, and translated $\frac{\pi}{6}$ units right.

6. a) i)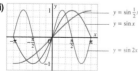

ii)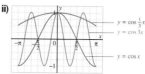

b) As b changes, the period changes by a factor of $\frac{1}{b}$.

c) As b changes, the period changes by a factor of $\frac{1}{b}$.

7. a)   **b)**

2; π 3; 4π

c)   **d)**

$\frac{1}{2}$; $\frac{2\pi}{3}$ 4; 4π

e)   **f)**

5; π $\frac{1}{3}$; $\frac{2\pi}{3}$

9. a) i) 2 **ii)** 2π
  iii) Answers may vary; $-\frac{\pi}{4}$ **iv)** 5; $\frac{\pi}{4}$, $\frac{9\pi}{4}$
  v) 1; $\frac{5\pi}{4}$ **vi)** 3
  vii) All real numbers; all real numbers between 1 and 5, inclusive
  b) i) 3 **ii)** π
  iii) Answers may vary; $\frac{\pi}{2}$ **iv)** 6; $\frac{3\pi}{4}$, $\frac{7\pi}{4}$, $\frac{11\pi}{4}$
  v) 0; $\frac{\pi}{4}$, $\frac{5\pi}{4}$, $\frac{9\pi}{4}$ **vi)** 3
  vii) All real numbers; all real numbers between 0 and 6, inclusive
  c) i) 5 **ii)** 2π
  iii) Answers may vary; $-\frac{\pi}{3}$ **iv)** 20; $\frac{\pi}{6}$, $\frac{13\pi}{6}$
  v) 10; $\frac{7\pi}{6}$, $\frac{19\pi}{6}$ **vi)** 15
  vii) All real numbers; all real numbers between 10 and 20, inclusive

10. Answers may vary.
  a) $y = 2\sin\left(x + \frac{\pi}{4}\right) + 3$ **b)** $y = 3\sin 2\left(x - \frac{\pi}{2}\right) + 3$
  c) $y = 5\sin\left(x + \frac{\pi}{3}\right) + 15$

11. a) $\frac{\pi}{3}$; π; 4; 2

  b) The domain of the graph drawn may vary.

  c) All real numbers; all real numbers between 2 and 6, inclusive

12. The domain of the graphs drawn may vary.

a) $\frac{\pi}{4}$; π; 3; 3; all real numbers; all real numbers between 0 and 6, inclusive

$y = 3\sin 2\left(x - \frac{\pi}{4}\right) + 3$

b) π; $\frac{2\pi}{3}$; 0; 5; all real numbers; all real numbers between −5 and 5, inclusive

$y = 5\cos 3(x - \pi)$

c) $\frac{\pi}{2}$; $\frac{2\pi}{3}$; 0; 2; all real numbers; all real numbers between −2 and 2, inclusive

$y = 2\sin 3\left(x - \frac{\pi}{2}\right)$

d) $-\frac{2\pi}{3}$; 2π; 0; 2.5; all real numbers; all real numbers between −2.5 and 2.5, inclusive

$y = 2.5\cos\left(x - \frac{2\pi}{3}\right)$

e) $-\frac{\pi}{4}$; $\frac{2\pi}{4}$; 0; 0.5; all real numbers; all real numbers between −0.5 and 0.5, inclusive

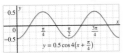
$y = 0.5\cos 4\left(x + \frac{\pi}{4}\right)$

f) $\frac{\pi}{2}$; $\frac{2\pi}{3}$; 4; 4; all real numbers; all real numbers between 0 and 8, inclusive

$y = 4\sin 3\left(x - \frac{\pi}{2}\right) + 4$

g) $-\frac{\pi}{6}$; π; −6; 3; all real numbers; all real numbers between −9 and −3, inclusive

$y = -3\cos 2\left(x + \frac{\pi}{6}\right) - 6$

h) $\frac{\pi}{6}$; $\frac{2\pi}{3}$; 2; 4; all real numbers; all real numbers between −2 and 6, inclusive

$y = 4\sin 3\left(x - \frac{\pi}{6}\right) + 2$

13. a) $-\frac{\pi}{6}$; π; 0; 2

b)

$y = 2\sin\left(2x + \frac{\pi}{3}\right)$

c) All real numbers; all real numbers between −2 and 2, inclusive.

14. a) $\frac{\pi}{4}$; π; 0; 5; all real numbers; all real numbers between −5 and 5, inclusive

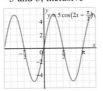
$y = 5\cos\left(2x - \frac{\pi}{2}\right)$

b) $-\frac{\pi}{4}$; π; 0; 3; all real numbers; all real numbers between −3 and 3, inclusive

$y = 3\cos\left(2x + \frac{\pi}{2}\right)$

c) $\frac{\pi}{2}$; π; 0; 2; all real numbers; all real numbers between −2 and 2, inclusive

$y = 2\sin(2x - \pi)$

d) $-\frac{\pi}{6}$; $\frac{2\pi}{3}$; 0; 2; all real numbers; all real numbers between −2 and 2, inclusive

$y = 2\sin\left(3x + \frac{\pi}{2}\right)$

15. Answers may vary.

a) $y = \cos 2\left(x - \frac{\pi}{4}\right)$ **b)** $y = \cos 3\left(x - \frac{\pi}{6}\right)$

c) $y = \cos\frac{1}{2}(x - \pi)$ **d)** $y = \cos 6\left(x - \frac{\pi}{12}\right)$

16. a) $y = \sin x$, $y = \sin 1.1x$, $y = \sin 1.2x$, ..., $y = \sin 1.9x$

b) $y = \cos x$, $y = \cos 1.1x$, $y = \cos 1.2x$, ..., $y = \cos 1.9x$

17. a) The graph expands vertically when $|a| > 1$ and compresses vertically when $0 < |a| < 1$.

b) The period increases when $0 < |b| < 1$ and decreases when $|b| > 1$.

c) The graph shifts horizontally $-d$ units.

d) The graph shifts vertically c units.

18. a) 1

$y = \cos 2\pi x$

b) i) 2

$y = \cos \frac{2\pi}{2} x$

ii) 3

$y = \cos \frac{2\pi}{3} x$

c) The graph has period p.

19. a) 1

$y = \sin 2\pi x$

b) i) 2

$y = \sin \frac{2\pi}{2} x$

ii) 3

$y = \sin \frac{2\pi}{3} x$

c) The graph has period p.

20. Answers may vary. $(0.6, 0.362); (2.4, 0.362)$

21. a)

b) Answers may vary. $(1.6, 0.717); (0.4, 0.717)$

22. a)

$y = \cos^2 x$

b) The graph repeats; π

c) Maximum is 1 at $-\pi, 0, \pi$; minimum is 0 at $-\frac{\pi}{2}, \frac{\pi}{2}$.

d) Answers may vary. $y = 0.5 \cos 2x + 0.5$

e) Answers may vary. $y = 0.5 \sin 2\left(x - \frac{\pi}{4}\right) + 0.5$

23. a) i and iii

d) Answers may vary.

i) $y = 2 \sin 2\left(x - \frac{\pi}{2}\right)$ **ii)** $y = 2 \cos 2x$

iii) $y = 2 \cos 2\left(x + \frac{\pi}{4}\right)$ **iv)** $y = 2 \sin 2(x - \pi)$

24. a) $a + c; \frac{\pi}{2b} + d + \frac{2n\pi}{b}$ where n is an integer

b) $c - a; d + \frac{3\pi}{2b} + \frac{2n\pi}{b}$, where n is an integer

25. a) $a + c; d + \frac{2n\pi}{b}$, where n is an integer

b) $c - a; d + \frac{\pi}{b} + \frac{2n\pi}{b}$, where n is an integer

6.5 Exercises, page 366

1. a) 2; 5; 3; 4 **b)** 6; 3; 1; 10
c) 12; 6; 1; 12 **d)** 15; 100; 30; 75

2. a) 10; $y = \cos \frac{2\pi}{10} x$ **b)** 2; $y = \cos \frac{2\pi}{2} x$
c) 0.025; $y = \cos \frac{2\pi}{0.025} x$ **d)** 0.25; $y = \cos \frac{2\pi}{0.25} x$

3. Answers for phase shift may vary.
a) i) 6 **ii)** 4 **iii)** 4
iv) 14; 0, 4, 8, 12 **v)** 2; −2, 2, 6, 10
vi) All real numbers between −2 and 14 **vii)** 8
b) i) 10 **ii)** 40 **iii)** 30
iv) 30; 0, 40, 80, 120 **v)** 10; −20, 20, 60, 100
vi) All real numbers between 10 and 30 **vii)** 20

4. Equations may vary.
a) $y = 6 \cos \frac{2\pi}{4} x + 8$ **b)** $y = 10 \cos \frac{2\pi}{40} x + 20$

5. Equations may vary.
a) $y = 3 \cos \frac{2\pi}{7} x + 2$ **b)** $y = 0.005 \cos \frac{2\pi}{0.001} x$
c) $y = 0.2 \cos \frac{2\pi}{0.1} x + 0.10$ **d)** $y = -2 \cos \frac{2\pi}{5} x + 3$

7. a) The graph shifts up; $h = 25 \cos \frac{2\pi}{1.6} (t - 0.8) + 60$

b) The amplitude is smaller; $h = 20 \cos \frac{2\pi}{1.6} (t - 0.8) + 50$

c) The graph is expanded horizontally;
$h = 25 \cos \frac{2\pi}{2} (t - 1) + 50$

8. a) 40; 12 **b)** $y = 40 \sin \frac{2\pi}{12} x$
c) The amplitude and the period would both be greater.

9. a) Only 2 periods are shown on this graph.

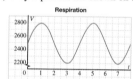
Respiration

b) 4 s; 300; 0; 2500 **c)** $V = 300 \sin \frac{2\pi}{4} t + 2500$
d) i) The period would decrease.
ii) The amplitude would be greater.

10. a) i)

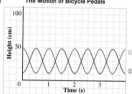
The Motion of Bicycle Pedals

ii) ① $h = 18 \cos 2\pi t + 30$
② $h = -18 \cos 2\pi t + 30$

b) i)

The Motion of Bicycle Pedals

ii) ③ $h = -18 \sin (2\pi t) + 100$
④ $h = 18 \sin (2\pi t) + 100$

11. a) Change 2π, 0.8 radians, and 1.6 radians to degrees.

12. a) 7:47 P.M. **b)** Answers may vary. October 5

13. a) 360 days; 3.1; 172; 12.2

  b) $y = 3.1 \cos \frac{2\pi}{365}(n - 172) + 12.2$

  c) 12.7 h **d)** Answers may vary. April 26

14. a) $y = 3.8 \cos \frac{2\pi}{365}(n - 172) + 11.9$

  b)

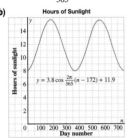

Hours of Sunlight

$y = 3.8 \cos \frac{2\pi}{365}(n - 172) + 11.9$

  c) 9.5 h **d)** Answers may vary. April 25

15. a) Answers may vary. 5.3 m

16. a) A: $h = 10 \sin \frac{2\pi}{0.15}t + 12$;

  B: $h = 10 \sin \frac{2\pi}{0.15}(t - 0.05) + 12$;

  C: $h = 10 \sin \frac{2\pi}{0.15}(t - 0.1) + 12$

  b) 6.67 cycles per second

6.6 Exercises, page 375

2. a)

$y = \tan x$

  b)

$y = \tan x$

  c)

$y = \tan x$

3. a)

  b)

$Q(1, 0.9474)$

3.9

$A(1, 0)$

P

  c)

O -1.25 $A(1, 0)$

P

  d)

P

O

-4.0 $A(1, 0)$

$Q(1, -1.1578)$

$Q(1, -3.0096)$

e)

2π

O

$A(1, 0)$
P
Q

f)

P

$\frac{3\pi}{4}$

O $A(1, 0)$

$Q(1, -1)$

g)

$Q(1, 1)$

$\frac{5\pi}{4}$

O $A(1, 0)$

P

h)

O $\frac{\pi}{2}$ $A(1, 0)$

P

4. Answers may vary. $(-2.206, 1.357)$, $(4.078, 1.357)$, $(-5.347, 1.357)$

5. $1.357 \doteq \frac{0.805}{0.593} \doteq \frac{\sin x}{\cos x}$

7. b) All real numbers except $\pm\frac{\pi}{2}, \pm\frac{3\pi}{2}, \pm\frac{5\pi}{2}, \dots$; all real numbers

  c) $\dots, -\pi, 0, \pi, 2\pi, \dots$ **d)** 0 **e)** π

9. $\tan x$

10. a) $h = 100 \tan x$

  b)

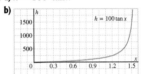

$h = 100 \tan x$

11. a) The value of y increases rapidly.

  b) Yes

Y1=tan(X)

-4.7 4.7

X=1.5707963 Y=

  c) $x = \frac{\pi}{4}, y = 1$; $x = \frac{3\pi}{4}, y = -1$; $x = -\frac{\pi}{2}$, y is undefined.

12. a)

Y1=tan(X)

-2π 2π

X=1.069 Y=1.825

  b) Answers may vary. $-2.073, 4.211$

13. a)

$y = 2 \cos x$

$y = \sin x$

  b)

2.5

0 2π

-2.5

  c) $(1.1071, 0.8944)$, $(4.2487, -0.8944)$

14. a)

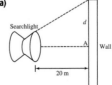

Searchlight d

A Wall

20 m

  b) $d = 20 \tan \frac{2\pi}{10}t$

c)

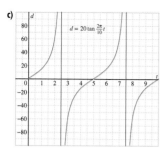

$d = 20 \tan \frac{2\pi}{10}t$

15. a) It appears to be a horizontal line.
b) Yes; only the horizontal scale changes.
c) For values of x close to 0, $\sin x \doteq \tan x$

Self-Check 6.4–6.6, page 378

1. a) $\frac{\pi}{4}$; π; 5; 4

b)

$y = 4\sin\left(x - \frac{\pi}{4}\right) + 5$

c) All real numbers; all real numbers between 1 and 9, inclusive

2. a) $\frac{\pi}{2}$; π

$y = \sin(2x - \pi)$

b) $\frac{\pi}{3}$, $\frac{2\pi}{3}$

$y = 2\cos(3x - \pi) + 1$

c) $\frac{\pi}{3}$, $\frac{2\pi}{3}$

$y = 2\cos(3x - \pi) + 4$

d) $-\frac{\pi}{4}$; $\frac{\pi}{2}$

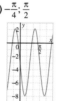

$y = 5\sin(4x + \pi) - 3$

3. Answers may vary. $(-2.6, 0.809)$, $(0.6, 0.809)$, $(4.6, 0.809)$, $(5.4, 0.809)$

4. a) 0.017; 160   **b)** 160 V
c) $V = 160 \sin \frac{2\pi}{0.017}t$

5. $-\frac{5\pi}{6}$, $\frac{7\pi}{6}$, $\frac{13\pi}{6}$

Insights Into a Rich Problem—
The Equation of a Damped Spring, page 382

1. a) $y = 40(0.997\ 692)^t \sin \frac{2\pi}{0.67}t$
b) $y = -40(0.997\ 692)^t \cos \frac{2\pi}{0.67}t$

2. a) $y = 50(0.9)^t \sin \frac{2\pi}{4}t$

b)

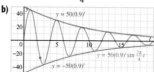

c) -27.168 cm

3. a) $y = (t - 10)^2 \sin \frac{2\pi}{2}t$
b) 1.29, 1.67

4. a)

b) For $0 \le t \le 5$, $x = \frac{1}{5}t\cos\frac{\pi}{20}t$, $y = \frac{1}{5}t\sin\frac{\pi}{20}t$
For $5 \le t \le 10$, $x = 2\cos\frac{\pi}{20}t - \frac{1}{5}t\cos\frac{\pi}{20}t$,
$y = 2\sin\frac{\pi}{20}t - \frac{1}{5}t\sin\frac{\pi}{20}t$
For $10 \le t \le 15$, $x = \frac{1}{5}t\cos\frac{\pi}{20}t - 2\cos\frac{\pi}{20}t$,
$y = \frac{1}{5}t\sin\frac{\pi}{20}t - 2\sin\frac{\pi}{20}t$
For $15 \le t \le 20$, $x = 4\cos\frac{\pi}{20}t - \frac{1}{5}t\cos\frac{\pi}{20}t$,
$y = 4\sin\frac{\pi}{20}t - \frac{1}{5}t\sin\frac{\pi}{20}t$; and so on

Chapter 6 Review Exercises, page 384

1. a) 1   **b)** 0   **c)** π

2. No

3. 11 years

4. a)

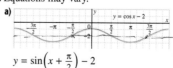

$y = \cos x$

b) 1; -1; all real numbers; all real numbers between -1 and 1, inclusive; $\pm\frac{3\pi}{2}$, $\pm\frac{\pi}{2}$, ...; 1; 2π

5. a)

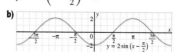

$y = \sin x$ $y = \cos x$

b) They are congruent.
c) 2π
d) $\left(\frac{\pi}{4}, \frac{1}{\sqrt{2}}\right)$, $\left(\frac{5\pi}{4}, -\frac{1}{\sqrt{2}}\right)$

6. 11

7. Equations may vary.
a)

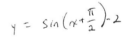

$y = \cos x - 2$

$y = \sin\left(x + \frac{\pi}{2}\right) - 2$

$y = \sin\left(x + \frac{\pi}{2}\right) - 2$

b)

$y = 2\sin\left(x - \frac{\pi}{2}\right)$

$y = -2\cos x$

c)

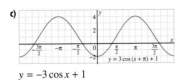

$y = -3\cos x + 1$

8. a) iii   **b)** i   **c)** iv   **d)** ii

9. Equations may vary.

a) $y = \cos\left(x - \dfrac{2\pi}{3}\right)$ **b)** $y = \cos\left(x - \dfrac{\pi}{6}\right)$

c) $y = \cos\left(x - \dfrac{\pi}{4}\right)$ **d)** $y = \cos(x - \pi)$

10. a) iii   **b)** ii   **c)** i

11. a) All real numbers; all real numbers between −2.5 and 2.5, inclusive; 0; 2.5; 2.5; −2.5

b) All real numbers; all real numbers between −5.5 and 1.5, inclusive; 0; 3.5; 1.5; −5.5

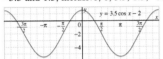

c) All real numbers; all real numbers between −1.5 and 4.5, inclusive; 0; 3; 4.5; −1.5

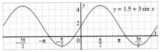

d) All real numbers; all real numbers between −1 and 1, inclusive; $-\dfrac{\pi}{4}$; 1; 1; −1

e) All real numbers; all real numbers between −3 and 3, inclusive; $\dfrac{5\pi}{6}$; 3; 3; −3

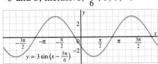

f) All real numbers; all real numbers between −5 and 3, inclusive; $\dfrac{\pi}{6}$; 4; 3; −5

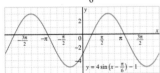

12. a) 1; π; $-\dfrac{\pi}{4}$ **b)** 2; $\dfrac{2\pi}{3}$; $-\dfrac{\pi}{6}$

13. a) 3; π

b) 2; 6π

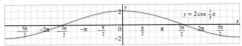

c) $\dfrac{1}{2}$; $\dfrac{2\pi}{3}$

14. a) $-\dfrac{\pi}{2}$; π; −1; 3

b)

c) All real numbers; all real numbers between −4 and 2, inclusive

15. a) $\dfrac{\pi}{4}$; $\dfrac{2\pi}{3}$; 2; 2; all real numbers; all real numbers between 0 and 4, inclusive

b) $-\dfrac{\pi}{3}$; 2π; 0; 0.5; all real numbers; all real numbers between −0.5 and 0.5, inclusive

c) $-\dfrac{3\pi}{4}$; π; −1; 3; all real numbers; all real numbers between −4 and 2, inclusive

d) $\dfrac{7\pi}{6}$; $\dfrac{2\pi}{3}$; 1; 4; all real numbers; all real numbers between −3 and 5, inclusive

16. a) It expands vertically when $|a| > 1$ and compresses vertically when $0 < |a| < 1$.

b) The period increases when $0 < |b| < 1$ and decreases when $|b| > 1$.

c) The graph shifts horizontally −d units.

d) The graph shifts vertically c units.

17. a) $y = 3.565\cos\dfrac{2\pi}{365}(n - 172) + 12.015$

b) i) 11.91 h   **ii)** 14.39 h
iii) 12.03 h

18. $h = 4.5\cos\dfrac{\pi}{13.6}(t - 6) + 13.5$

19. Estimates and answers may vary.
   a) 0.0038   **b)** 263.16   **c)** $y = \sin \dfrac{2\pi}{0.0038}x$

20. $\tan x = \dfrac{\sin x}{\cos x}$; when $\cos x = 0$, $\tan x$ is undefined.

21.

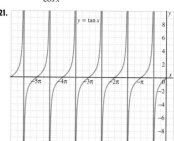

Chapter 6 Self-Test, page 389

1. -3.534

2. $P\left(\dfrac{\pi}{6}, \dfrac{1}{2}\right)$; $Q\left(\dfrac{3\pi}{4}, \dfrac{1}{\sqrt{2}}\right)$; $R\left(\dfrac{5\pi}{3}, -\dfrac{\sqrt{3}}{2}\right)$

3. $\left(0.452, \dfrac{\pi}{4}\right)$, $\left(1.119, \dfrac{\pi}{4}\right)$, $\left(3.593, \dfrac{\pi}{4}\right)$, $\left(4.261, \dfrac{\pi}{4}\right)$

4. a) $-\dfrac{\pi}{2}$, π, -1, 1

b)

$$y = \cos 2\left(x + \tfrac{\pi}{2}\right) - 1$$

c) All real numbers; all real numbers between -2 and 0, inclusive

5. a) $h = 20 \sin \dfrac{2\pi}{40}(t - 10) + 21$

b) 35.1 m   **c)** 20 m

6. a)

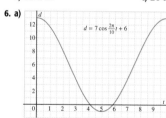

$$d = 7\cos \tfrac{2\pi}{10}t + 6$$

b) $d = 7\cos \dfrac{2\pi}{10}t + 6$ **c)** 8.2 m

7. a) i) 1.57 m   **ii)** -0.95 m   **iii)** 18.51 m
   b) -1 m

8.

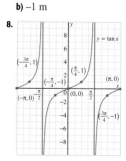

9. $4b + 1$ if b is a non-zero positive integer

1. a) 0.314 s   **b)** $y = 0.3\cos 20t + 0.3$
   c)

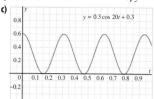

2. a) 24 s   **b)** 13.7 m

Chapter 7 Transformations of Functions
Necessary Skills
1 New: The Vertical Line Test
Exercises, page 393

1. No; for most values of x, there are two values of y.

2. a) No   **b)** Yes   **c)** No   **d)** Yes
   e) Yes   **f)** No   **g)** Yes

3. a) Yes   **b)** Yes   **c)** No
   d) Yes   **e)** No   **f)** Yes

2 New: Solving Linear Inequalities
Exercises, page 395

1. a) $x \le 4$ **b)** $x < -2$ **c)** $x > 2$
   d) $n \ge \dfrac{3}{4}$ **e)** $x < \dfrac{5}{4}$ **f)** $c \le -13$

2. a) $x \le 2$ **b)** $x > -3$

c) $x \le -4$ **d)** $k < -3$

e) $x \ge -4$ **f)** $n < -12$

7.1 Exercises, page 399

2. a) 9 m   **b)** Approximately 4.3 s

3. a) i) 15.6 h   **ii)** 8.8 h   **iii)** 12.2 h
   c) The amplitude would be smaller.

4. a)

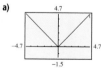

c)

d)

5. a), b)

x	-4	-2	0	2	4
$y = |x|$	4	2	0	2	4

See exercise 4d for graph.

6. a) All real numbers; $y \geq 0$

  b) For $x < 0$, $y = |x|$ is a reflection of $y = x$ in the x-axis, for $x \geq 0$, $y = |x|$ is equal to $y = x$.

  c) i) Yes, $x = 0$ **ii)** Minimum is $y = 0$.

  iii) No

7. a)

  c) There is no real solution.

8. a)

9.

10. a)

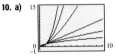

7.2 Exercises, page 404

1. a) 7   **b)** 19   **c)** 0   **d)** –1   **e)** –5

2. a) 110   **b)** 20   **c)** 6   **d)** –0.09   **e)** 0

3. a) 319   **b)** 279   **c)** 84   **d)** 0   **e)** –1

4. a) 2; 2.5; 0.5   **b)** 4; 6.25; 0.25

  c) 1.414; 1.581; 0.7071   **d)** 0.5; 0.4; 2

  e) 0.909; 0.598; 0.479   **f)** –0.416; –0.801; 0.878

5. a) 11; 9.5; 10.5   **b)** –3; 2.25; –1.75

  c) –10; –2.5; –7.5   **d)** 0; –3.75; –1.75

  e) –1; 2; –2   **f)** 0.25; 2; 0.5

6. a) i) 20π **ii)** 10π **iii)** 5π **iv)** 2π

  b) $A(r) = \pi r^2$

  c) i) 100π **ii)** 25π **iii)** 6.25π **iv)** π

7. a) $f(x - 2)$ is a function.

8. a) $0; \dfrac{1}{\sqrt{2}}; 1$ **b)** $1; \dfrac{1}{\sqrt{2}}; 0$

  c) $0; 1; 0$ **d)** $\dfrac{1}{\sqrt{2}}; 0; -\dfrac{1}{\sqrt{2}}$

  e) $1; \dfrac{1}{\sqrt{2}}; 0$ **f)** $1; 1; 1$

9. a) 2; 4; 2   **b)** –1.5; 3; 1   **c)** 2; –1; 2

10. a) –2, 3   **b)** 1.5   **c)** –2, 3

11. a) All real numbers; all real numbers

b) All real numbers; $y \geq -4$

c) All real numbers; $y \geq 0$

d) All real numbers except 0; $y \neq 0$

e) All real numbers; $-1 \leq y \leq 1$

f) $x \geq 0$, $y \geq 0$

12. a) All real numbers; all real numbers

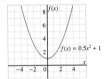

b) All real numbers; $y \geq 1$ **c)** All real numbers; $y \geq 1$

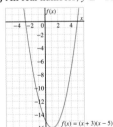

d) All real numbers; $y \geq -16$ **e)** $-3 \leq x \leq 3$; $0 \leq y \leq 3$

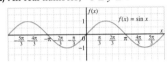

f) $x \geq 0$; $y \geq 0$

13. a) $2r + 5$ **b)** $4x + 5$
c) $-2x + 5$ **d)** $2x + 1$
e) $2x^2 + 5$ **f)** $\dfrac{2}{x} + 5$

14. a) $x^2 - x - 1$ **b)** $x^2 + x - 1$
c) $x^2 + 3x + 1$ **d)** $4x^2 - 6x + 1$
e) $9x^2 - 9x + 1$ **f)** $x^2 + 3x + 1$

15. a) $\dfrac{n^2 + 1}{n}$ **b)** $\dfrac{4x^2 + 1}{2x}$
c) $\dfrac{x^2 - 4x + 5}{x - 2}$ **d)** $\dfrac{x^2 - 2x + 2}{1 - x}$
e) $\dfrac{x^4 + 1}{x^2}$ **f)** $\dfrac{1}{x} + x$

16. a) $6x - 1$ **b)** $6x - 3$
c) $4x - 3$

17. Answers may vary.
a) $f(x) = x + 3$ **b)** $g(x) = 9 - x$

18. Answers may vary.
a) $f(x) = 1 + x^2$ **b)** $g(x) = 3x - 1$

19. Answers may vary; $f(x) = x + 4$, $g(x) = 6 - x$

20. a) 0 **b)** 3 **c)** -1

21. a) **b)**

c) There is only 1 output number (t_n or $t(n)$) for each input number (n).
d) Yes

22. a) i) $\dfrac{2}{3}$ **ii)** $\dfrac{1}{3}$ **iii)** 1
iv) $\dfrac{3}{4}$ **v)** $\dfrac{1}{4}$ **vi)** 1
b) 1 **c)** All values except 0 and -1

23. a) $m = \dfrac{2}{5}, b = -3$ **b)** $b = 2, m = 3$
c) $b = -3, m = 0$

24. a) i) 3; 4.5; -2.7
ii)

b) i) 5; 5; 5
ii)

25. a) i) Answers may vary. $f(x) = |x|$; $f(x) = -x^2$

ii) The graph has axis of symmetry $x = 0$.

b) i) Answers may vary. $f(x) = x$; $f(x) = \dfrac{1}{x}$

ii) The graph is symmetrical about the origin.

Self-Check NS, 7.1, 7.2, page 408

1. a) $a \geq 9$ **b)** $c \leq 2$
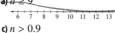 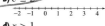
c) $n > 0.9$ **d)** $x > 1$
e) $m > 4$ **f)** $x \leq 3.75$

2. a)

b) The graph is a straight line because it represents a linear function.
c) All real numbers; all real numbers

3. a)

b) The graph is a parabola because it represents a quadratic function.
c) All real numbers; $y \geq 5$

4. a)

b) The graph is a semicircle because it represents part of a circle, centre the origin, for which y is non-negative.
c) $-4 \leq x \leq 4$; $0 \leq y \leq 4$

5. a)

c) All real numbers; $y \geq 4$

6. a) 4 **b)** -2 **c)** 1
d) Approximately 5.24 **e)** Approximately -3.24

7. a) -5 **b)** -4.5 **c)** -4.5 **d)** 1 **e)** 1

8. Decimal answers are approximate.
a) -1 **b)** -0.0625 **c)** -2.0625
d) 2.9443 **e)** -14.9443

9. a) 0 **b)** 30 **c)** 0 **d)** 6 **e)** 1386

10. a) $-3x + 10$ **b)** $x^2 - 8x + 20$ **c)** $\sin(x - 3)$

    d) $\cos(x - 3)$ **e)** $\dfrac{1}{x - 3}$ **f)** $\sqrt{x - 3}$

11. a) Graphs may vary.

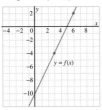

    b) No

7.3 Exercises, page 413

1. a) $y = \sqrt{x - 5} + 2$ **b)** $y = |x - 5| + 2$

    c) $y = \cos(x - 5) + 2$ **d)** $y = x - 3$

    e) $y = \sin(x - 5) + 2$ **f)** $y = f(x - 5) + 2$

2. a) $y = \dfrac{1}{2}\sqrt{3x}$ **b)** $y = \dfrac{1}{2}\sin 3x$

    c) $y = \dfrac{9x^2}{2}$ **d)** $y = \dfrac{3x}{2}$

    e) $y = \dfrac{1}{2}|3x|$ **f)** $y = \dfrac{1}{2}f(3x)$

4. a) Translated 3 units right or translated 3 units down.

    b) Translated 3 units right.

    c) Translated 3 units right.

    d) Compressed horizontally by a factor of $\dfrac{1}{3}$.

    e) Compressed horizontally by a factor of $\dfrac{1}{3}$ or expanded vertically by a factor of 9.

    f) Compressed horizontally by a factor of $\dfrac{1}{3}$.

5. a) Translated 4 units right.

    b) Translated 1 unit up.

    c) Compressed horizontally by a factor of $\dfrac{1}{3}$.

    d) Compressed vertically by a factor of $\dfrac{1}{2}$.

    e) Expanded horizontally by a factor of 2.

    f) Expanded vertically by a factor of 2.

    g) Compressed horizontally by a factor of $\dfrac{1}{2}$, then reflected in the y-axis.

    h) Compressed vertically by a factor of $\dfrac{1}{2}$, then reflected in the x-axis.

    i) Translated 3 units left.

    j) Translated 2 units down.

6. a) $y = f(x - 2)$ **b)** $y = f(x) - 5$ **c)** $y = f(3x)$

    d) $y = f\left(\dfrac{1}{2^x}\right)$ **e)** $y = 4f(x)$ **f)** $y = \dfrac{1}{2}f(x)$

    g) $y = f(-2x)$ **h)** $y = -5f(x)$

7. a)

    $g(x) = \cos\left(x - \dfrac{\pi}{3}\right)$; all real numbers; $-1 \le y < 1$

    b)

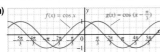

    $g(x) = 2\cos\left(x - \dfrac{\pi}{3}\right)$; all real numbers; $-2 \le y \le 2$

    c)

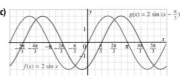

    $g(x) = 2\sin\left(x - \dfrac{\pi}{3}\right)$; all real numbers; $-2 \le y \le 2$

8. a)

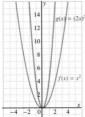

Horizontally compressed by a factor of $\dfrac{1}{2}$, all real numbers; $y \ge 0$

    b)

Horizontally compressed by a factor of $\dfrac{1}{2}$, all real numbers; $-1 \le y < 1$

    c)

Horizontally compressed by a factor of $\dfrac{1}{2}$, all real numbers; all real numbers.

9. a) i) Vertically expanded by a factor of 2 and translated 3 units up.

    ii) Vertically expanded by a factor of 2 and translated 3 units up.

    iii) Vertically expanded by a factor of 2 and translated 3 units up.

    b) Answers may vary.

    i) $y = -x$ **ii)** $y = x^3$ **iii)** $y = \dfrac{1}{x}$

      $y = -2x + 3$ $y = 2x^3 + 3$ $y = \dfrac{2}{x} + 3$

10. a)

    b)

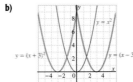

c)

11. a), c)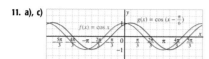

b) The graph of $f(x) = \cos x$ is translated $\frac{\pi}{6}$ units right.

d) All real numbers; $-1 \leq y \leq 1$

12. a) Horizontally compressed by a factor of $\frac{1}{2}$.

b) Vertically compressed by a factor of $\frac{1}{2}$.

c) Horizontally compressed by a factor of $\frac{1}{2}$ and reflected in the y-axis.

d) Vertically compressed by a factor of $\frac{1}{2}$ and reflected in the x-axis.

e) Translated 3 units right.

f) Translated 3 units up.

g) Horizontally expanded by a factor of 2.

h) Vertically expanded by a factor of 3.

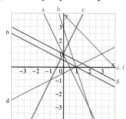

13. a), b)

c) The graph of $f(x)$ is translated 3 units right.

14. a), b)

c) The graph of $f(x)$ is translated $\frac{\pi}{4}$ units left.

15. Each graph of $f(x)$ is compressed horizontally by a factor of $\frac{1}{2}$.

a)    **b)**

c)

16. a) Translated 1 unit right.

b) Translated 4 units down.

c) Translated 9 units left and 2 units down.

d) Reflected in the x-axis.

e) Vertically expanded by a factor of 4.

f) Horizontally compressed by a factor of $\frac{1}{4}$.

g) Horizontally compressed by a factor of $\frac{1}{5}$ and reflected in the y-axis.

h) Vertically expanded by a factor of 3 and horizontally compressed by a factor of $\frac{1}{2}$.

17. a), b), d)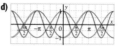

18. a)

b) i) $y = \sqrt{4x}$ **ii)** $y = 2\sqrt{x}$

d) Answers may vary. $y = \frac{1}{x}$

19. a), b)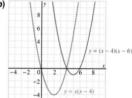

c) i) $y = (x - 6)(x - 4)$ **ii)** $y = (x - 5)^2 - 1$

d) i) x-intercepts   **ii)** Coordinates of the vertex

20. a), c)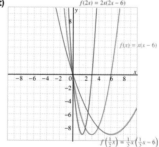

b) $y = 2x(2x - 6); \ y = \frac{1}{2}x\left(\frac{1}{2}x - 6\right)$

24. a) $y = \sqrt{x + 4}, y = \sqrt{x + 3}, y = \sqrt{x + 2}, y = \sqrt{x + 1},$
$y = \sqrt{x}, y = \sqrt{x - 1}, y = \sqrt{x - 2}, y = \sqrt{x - 3},$
$y = \sqrt{x - 4}, y = \sqrt{-x + 4}, y = \sqrt{-x + 3}, y = \sqrt{-x + 2},$
$y = \sqrt{-x + 1}, y = \sqrt{-x}, y = \sqrt{-x - 1}, y = \sqrt{-x - 2},$
$y = \sqrt{-x - 3}, y = \sqrt{-x - 4}$

b) $y = \sqrt{x} + 1, y = \sqrt{x} - 1, y = \sqrt{x} + 0.5, y = \sqrt{x} - 0.5,$
$y = \sqrt{x}, y = -\sqrt{-x} + 1, y = -\sqrt{-x} - 1, y = -\sqrt{-x} + 0.5,$
$y = -\sqrt{-x} - 0.5, y = -\sqrt{-x}$

25. a)

b) $L \geq 0; T \geq 0$

26. a)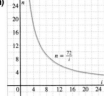

b) $i > 0; n > 0$

c) The graph of $y = \dfrac{1}{x}$ has been expanded vertically by a factor of 72.

28. Answers may vary. $y = \sin x; y = x$

29. a)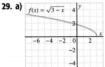

b) Reflected $y = \sqrt{x}$ in the y-axis then translated it 3 units right.

c) The graph is reflected in the y-axis then horizontally translated k units.

30. a) Answers may vary. $f(x) = \dfrac{2}{3}x$

b) An infinite number; any straight line with slope $\dfrac{2}{3}$

31. a), b)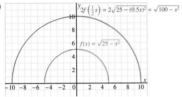

7.4 Exercises, page 419

1. a) $y = 2x + 3$
b) $y = 2x^2 + 3$
c) $y = 2\sin x + 3$
d) $y = 2\cos x + 3$
e) $y = 2f(x) + 3$

2. a) $y = 2(x + 3)$
b) $y = [2(x + 3)]^2$
c) $y = \sin 2(x + 3)$
d) $y = \cos 2(x + 3)$
e) $y = f[2(x + 3)]$

3. a)–c) The graph of $f(x)$ is translated 4 units left and 1 unit down.

d)–f) The graph of $f(x)$ is horizontally compressed by a factor of $\dfrac{1}{3}$ and vertically expanded by a factor of 2.

4. a) Horizontally compressed by a factor of $\dfrac{1}{3}$ then translated 2 units right.

b) Translated 2 units right then horizontally compressed by a factor of $\dfrac{1}{3}$.

c) Reflected in the y-axis then translated 4 units left.

d) Translated 4 units right then reflected in the y-axis.

5. a) $y = f(x - 3) + 7$
b) $y = f(x + 4) - 2$
c) $y = \dfrac{1}{3}f(2x)$
d) $y = \dfrac{1}{2}f\left(\dfrac{1}{3}x\right)$

6. a)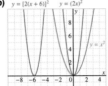

b)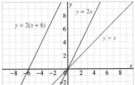

c)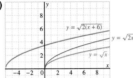

7. a)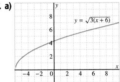
b)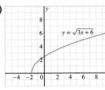

c)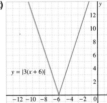
d)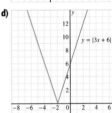

e)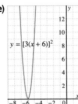
f)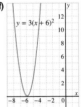

8. $y = 2\sqrt{x} + 6$

9. $y = \sqrt{2x + 3}$

10. a) The graph of $y = \sqrt{x}$ is horizontally compressed by a factor of $\dfrac{1}{4}$ then translated 2 units left.

11. a) The graph of $y = |x|$ is translated 5 units right, vertically expanded by a factor of 3, then translated 1 unit up.

12. a)

b) The graph of $y = x^2$ is horizontally expanded by a factor of 2 then translated 4 units right.

c) All real numbers; $y \geq 0$

13. a)

The graph of $y = \sqrt{x}$ is horizontally compressed by a factor of $\frac{1}{2}$ then translated 2.5 units right.

$x \geq 0;\ y \geq 0$
$x \geq 2.5;\ y \geq 0$

b)

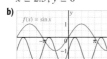

The graph of $f(x)$ is horizontally compressed by a factor of $\frac{1}{2}$ then translated 1 unit down.
All real numbers; $-1 \leq y \leq 1$
All real numbers; $-2 \leq y \leq 0$

14. a) The graph of $f(x)$ is vertically expanded by a factor of 2, then translated $\frac{\pi}{3}$ units right and 1 unit up.

b) All real numbers; $-1 \leq y \leq 3$

15. a) $-2;\ 7$ **b)** $-\frac{1}{2};\ \frac{7}{2}$ **c)** $-\frac{2}{3};\ 3$ **d)** $-\frac{1}{6};\ \frac{23}{6}$

17. a) $(0.827, 3.346)$ **b)** $y = 4.89t^2$

20. a) $V = L(d - 4)^2$

b) $V = 12(d-4)^2;\ V = 16(d-4)^2;\ V = 20(d-4)^2$

c)

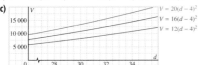

21. a)

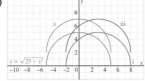

b) i) $y = \sqrt{25 - (x-3)^2}$

ii) $y = \sqrt{25 - x^2} + 2$

iii) $y = \sqrt{25 - (x-3)^2} + 2$

c) $-5 \leq x \leq 5;\ 0 \leq y \leq 5$

i) $-2 \leq x \leq 8;\ 0 \leq y \leq 5$

ii) $-5 \leq x \leq 5;\ 2 \leq y \leq 7$

iii) $-2 \leq x \leq 8;\ 2 \leq y \leq 7$

22. a)

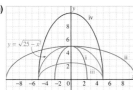

b) i) $y = \sqrt{25 - (2x)^2}$ **ii)** $y = \sqrt{25 - \left(\frac{1}{2}x\right)^2}$

ii) $y = \frac{1}{2}\sqrt{25 - x^2}$ **iv)** $y = 2\sqrt{25 - x^2}$

c) $-5 \leq x \leq 5;\ 0 \leq y \leq 5$

i) $-2.5 \leq x \leq 2.5;\ 0 \leq y \leq 5$

ii) $-10 \leq x \leq 10;\ 0 \leq y \leq 5$

iii) $-5 \leq x \leq 5.;\ 0 \leq y \leq 2.5$

iv) $-5 \leq x \leq 5;\ 0 \leq y \leq 10$

23. b) $y = 3f(x) + 12$

7.5 Exercises, page 430

1. a) $r = \frac{d}{2}$ **b)** $d = \frac{C}{\pi}$ **c)** $r = \sqrt{\frac{A}{\pi}}$

d) $r = \sqrt{\frac{A}{4\pi}}$ **e)** $r = \sqrt[3]{\frac{3V}{4\pi}}$

3. a) $f^{-1}(x) = x - 4$ **b)** $f^{-1}(x) = \frac{x+1}{2}$

c) $f^{-1}(x) = \frac{x}{3}$ **d)** $f^{-1}(x) = 1 - x$

e) $f^{-1}(x) = 2x - 10$ **f)** $f^{-1}(x) = \frac{3x-3}{2}$

4. a) $y = \pm\sqrt{x}$ **b)** $y = \pm\sqrt{x+2}$ **c)** $y = \pm\sqrt{3-x}$

d) $y = \pm\sqrt{\frac{x-2}{3}}$ **e)** $y = \pm\sqrt{2x+2}$ **f)** $y = \pm\sqrt{\frac{5-x}{2}}$

5. a) No   **b)** No

7. a) i) $f^{-1}(x) = x;\ f^{-1}(x) = x - 1;\ f^{-1}(x) = x - 2;$
$f^{-1}(x) = x - 3$

ii) $f^{-1}(x) = -x;\ f^{-1}(x) = 1 - x;\ f^{-1}(x) = 2 - x;$
$f^{-1}(x) = 3 - x$

iii) $f^{-1}(x) = x;\ f^{-1}(x) = \frac{x}{2};\ f^{-1}(x) = \frac{x}{3};\ f^{-1}(x) = \frac{x}{4}$

iv) $f^{-1}(x) = x - 1;\ f^{-1}(x) = \frac{x}{2} - 1;\ f^{-1}(x) = \frac{x}{3} - 1;$
$f^{-1}(x) = \frac{x}{4} - 1$

8. a) i) $y = 1 \pm \sqrt{x};\ y = 2 \pm \sqrt{x};\ y = 3 \pm \sqrt{x};\ y = 4 \pm \sqrt{x}$

ii) $f^{-1}(x) = \frac{1}{x};\ f^{-1}(x) = \frac{1}{2x};\ f^{-1}(x) = \frac{1}{3x};\ f^{-1}(x) = \frac{1}{4x}$

iii) $f^{-1}(x) = \frac{1}{x};\ f^{-1}(x) = \frac{1}{x} - 1;\ f^{-1}(x) = \frac{1}{x} - 2;$
$f^{-1}(x) = \frac{1}{x} - 3$

iv) $f^{-1}(x) = \frac{1}{x};\ f^{-1}(x) = \frac{1}{x-1};\ f^{-1}(x) = \frac{1}{x-2};$
$f^{-1}(x) = \frac{1}{x-3}$

9. a) Yes   **b)** No   **c)** No
d) Yes   **e)** Yes   **f)** Yes

10. a) $y = \frac{-6 - 2x}{5}$ **b)** $y = 2 \pm \sqrt{2 - x}$

11. a) Yes   **b)** No

12. a) $n = \frac{C - 8000}{4}$ **b)** $t = \frac{\sqrt{9 - h}}{0.7}$

c) $h = \frac{d^2}{12\,769}$ **d)** $C = \frac{F - 30}{2}$

e) $C = \frac{5}{9}(F - 32)$ **f)** $d = \left(\frac{T}{0.2}\right)^{\frac{2}{3}}$

13. a) $y = \pm\sqrt{x}$

b)

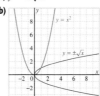

c) No; it does not pass the vertical line test.

$f^{-1}(x) = x^2, x \geq 0$

c) Yes

15. a) $f^{-1}(x) = x + 4$ **b)** $f^{-1}(x) = \dfrac{-x}{3}$

c) $f^{-1}(x) = 2x - 14$ **d)** $g^{-1}(x) = \dfrac{x-1}{x}$

e) $g^{-1}(x) = \dfrac{1-x}{x}$ **f)** $h^{-1}(x) = \dfrac{3}{x}$

16. a) $y = \dfrac{x-3}{2}$; all real numbers; all real numbers; function

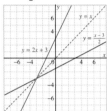

b) $y = 10 - x$; all real numbers; all real numbers; function

c) $y = \pm\sqrt{x+4}$; $x \geq -4$; all real numbers; not a function

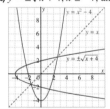

d) $y = 1 \pm \sqrt{x}$; $x \geq 0$; all real numbers; not a function

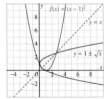

e) $f^{-1}(x) = \dfrac{6}{x}$; all real numbers except 0; all real numbers except 0; function

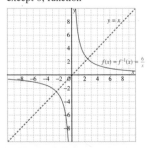

f) $g^{-1}(x) = x^2 + 2$, $x \geq 0$; $x \geq 0$; $y \geq 2$; function

17. a) $f^{-1}(x) = \dfrac{x+7}{4}$ **b)** $f^{-1}(x) = 5 - x$ **c)** $f^{-1}(x) = \dfrac{8-x}{3}$

d) $f^{-1}(x) = \dfrac{2}{x}$ **e)** $f^{-1}(x) = \dfrac{1-3x}{x}$ **f)** $f^{-1}(x) = x^2 - 1$

18. a) Answers may vary; $f(x) = \dfrac{2}{x}$

b) An infinite number

19. Restrictions may vary.

a) $x \geq 0$ **b)** $x \geq 0$

c) $x \geq 1$ **d)** $x \geq -2$

e) $x \geq 1$

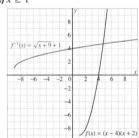

f) $x \geq 2$

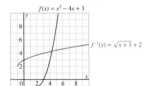

20. a)

x	−1	−0.5	0	0.5	1
y	−1.571	−0.524	0	0.524	1.571

b)

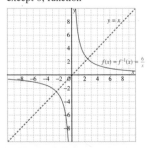

d) $-1 \leq x \leq 1$; all real numbers

21. a), b)

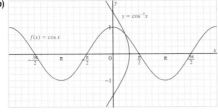

$y = \cos^{-1} x$; no

23. Answers may vary. $f(x) = x - 4$, $f(f^{-1}(x)) = f^{-1}(f(x)) = x$

24. b) Yes

25. b) (b, a)

Self-Check 7.3–7.5, page 434

1. a), b)

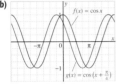

c) $g(x) = \cos\left(x + \dfrac{\pi}{4}\right)$

d) All real numbers; $-1 \le y \le 1$

2. a), b)

c) Horizontally expanded by a factor of 2.

d) $x \ge 0$; $y \ge 0$
 $x \ge 0$; $y \ge 0$

3. a) Translated 3 units left.
 b) Translated 2 units up.
 c) Horizontally compressed by a factor of $\dfrac{1}{2}$.
 d) Vertically compressed by a factor of $\dfrac{1}{4}$.
 e) Horizontally expanded by a factor of 3.
 f) Vertically expanded by a factor of 5.
 g) Horizontally compressed by a factor of $\dfrac{1}{3}$ then reflected in the y-axis.
 h) Vertically compressed by a factor of $\dfrac{1}{3}$ then reflected in the x-axis.

4. a), b)

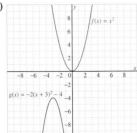

c) The graph of $f(x)$ is compressed horizontally by a factor of $\dfrac{1}{2}$, reflected in the x-axis, then translated 3 units left and 4 units down.

d) All real numbers; $y \ge 0$
 All real numbers; $y \le -4$

5. a) Horizontally compressed by a factor of $\dfrac{1}{2}$ then translated 1 unit left.
 b) Translated 1 unit left then horizontally compressed by a factor of $\dfrac{1}{2}$.
 c) Horizontally compressed by a factor of $\dfrac{1}{2}$, reflected in the y-axis, then translated 1 unit right.
 d) Translated 1 unit right, horizontally compressed by a factor of $\dfrac{1}{2}$, then reflected in the y-axis.

6. a) $y = \dfrac{7 - x}{2}$; function

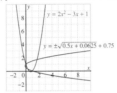

b) $y = \pm\sqrt{0.5x + 0.0625} + 0.75$; not a function

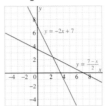

c) $y = \dfrac{1}{4}(x - 4)^2 + 1$, $x \ge 4$; function

7. a) All real numbers; all real numbers
 All real numbers; $y \ge -\dfrac{1}{8}$
 $x \ge 1$; $y \ge 4$
 b) All real numbers; all real numbers
 $x \ge -\dfrac{1}{8}$; all real numbers
 $x \ge 4$; $y \ge 1$

Insights Into a Rich Problem— Inverting a Quartic Function, page 437

1. $f(x)$: $x \ge 0$; $y \ge 1$ $\qquad$ $g(x)$: $0 \le x \le 1$; $0 \le y \le 1$
 $k(x)$: $x \ge 0$; $y \le -1$ $\qquad$ $h(x)$: $0 \le x \le 1$; $-1 \le y \le 0$

3.

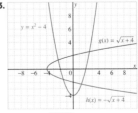

a) $y = \pm\sqrt{x + 4}$
c) $x \ge -4$; $x \ge -4$

4.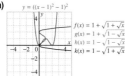

a) $y = \pm\sqrt{x+1} + 1$

c) $x \geq -1; x \geq -1$

5. a)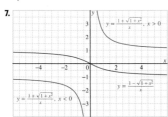

$y = \pm\sqrt{\dfrac{1}{x} + 4}$

c) For each piece, the domain is $x \leq -0.25$ or $x > 0$.

6. a)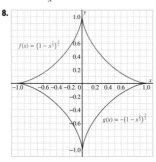

b) $y = ((x-1)^2 - 1)^2$

c) $y = 1 \pm \sqrt{1 \pm \sqrt{x}}$;

$f(x) = 1 + \sqrt{1 + \sqrt{x}}$; $g(x) = 1 + \sqrt{1 - \sqrt{x}}$;

$h(x) = 1 - \sqrt{1 - \sqrt{x}}$; $k(x) = 1 - \sqrt{1 + \sqrt{x}}$

d) Yes

7.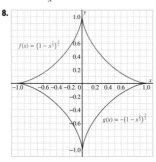

$y = \dfrac{1 \pm \sqrt{1 + x^2}}{x}$

8.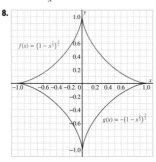

b) $y = \pm\left(1 - x^{\frac{2}{3}}\right)^{\frac{3}{2}}$

d) $-1 \leq x \leq 1; f(x) = \left(1 - x^{\frac{2}{3}}\right)^{\frac{3}{2}}; -1 \leq x \leq 1;$

$g(x) = -\left(1 - x^{\frac{2}{3}}\right)^{\frac{3}{2}}$

Chapter 7 Review Exercises, page 440

1. a) $x > -\dfrac{5}{2}$ **b)** $a \geq 9$

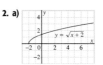

c) $n < 2$ **d)** $x \leq 4$

e) $a > -\dfrac{1}{5}$ **f)** $x > \dfrac{1}{2}$

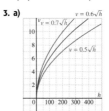

2. a)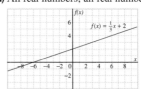

b) $x \geq -2; y \geq 0$

c) i) No   **ii)** Minimum at $(-2, 0)$ **iii)** No

3. a)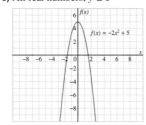

b) i) $0 \leq h \leq 500; 0 \leq y \leq 11.2$

ii) $0 \leq h \leq 350; 0 \leq y \leq 11.2$

iii) $0 \leq h \leq 200; 0 \leq y \leq 9.9$

4. a) -7 **b)** -6 **c)** -12 **d)** -6 **e)** -9

5. a) $8; 0; 4.196$ **b)** $-7; 1.889; -1$

c) $2; 1.155; 1.653$ **d)** $0.250; 0.750; 0.366$

e) $-0.990; 0.945; -0.161$ **f)** $0.141; 0.327; 0.987$

6. a) All real numbers; all real numbers

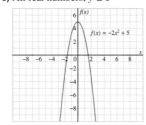

b) All real numbers; $y \leq 5$

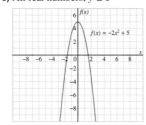

c) All real numbers; $y \geq -4$

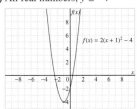

$f(x) = 2(x + 1)^2 - 4$

d) $x \geq 1$; $y \geq 0$

$f(x) = \sqrt{x - 1}$

e) All real numbers except 1; all real numbers except 0

$f(x) = \dfrac{1}{x - 1}$

f) All real numbers; $-2 \leq y \leq 0$

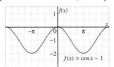

$f(x) = \cos x - 1$

7. a) $3a^2 - a - 1$　　**b)** $12a^2 + 2a - 1$
c) $3a^2 + 5a + 1$　　**d)** $3a^4 - a^2 - 1$
e) $3a - \sqrt{a} - 1$

8.

$f(x) = \sqrt{x}$

a) $x \geq 0$; $y \geq 0$
b) The graph of $f(x)$ is the inverse of the graph of $g(x) = x^2$, $x \geq 0$.

9.

$f(x) = \dfrac{1}{x}$

a) All real numbers except 0; all real numbers except 0
b) The graph of $g(x)$ is a line of symmetry for the graph of $f(x)$.

10. a)

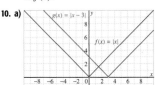

$g(x) = |x - 3|$　$f(x) = |x|$

b) The graph of $f(x)$ is translated 3 units right.
c) All real numbers; $y \geq 0$

11. a) The graph of $y = x^2$ is vertically expanded by a factor of 500 then translated 1 unit left.
b) $i \geq 0$; $A \geq 500$

12. The graph of $y = \sqrt{x}$ is expanded vertically by a factor of 113.

13. a) The graph of temperature in degrees Celsius is expanded vertically by a factor of 1.8 then translated 32 units up.

b)

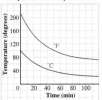

Temperature of a Cup of Coffee

14.

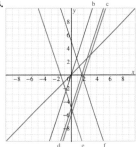

b) The graph of $y = x$ is vertically expanded by a factor of 3.
c) The graph of $y = x$ is vertically expanded by a factor of 3 then translated 2 units right.
d) The graph of $y = x$ is vertically expanded by a factor of 3, then translated 2 units right and 1 unit up.
e) The graph of $y = x$ is vertically expanded by a factor of 3, then translated 2 units right and 1 unit up, and reflected in the y-axis.
f) The graph of $y = x$ is vertically expanded by a factor of 3, then translated 2 units right and 1 unit up, and reflected in the x-axis.

15.

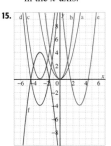

b) The graph of $y = x^2$ is vertically expanded by a factor of 2.
c) The graph of $y = x^2$ is vertically expanded by a factor of 2, then translated 3 units left.
d) The graph of $y = x^2$ is vertically expanded by a factor of 2, then translated 3 units left and 4 units down.

e) The graph of $y = x^2$ is vertically expanded by a factor of 2, then translated 3 units left and 4 units down, and reflected in the *y*-axis.

f) The graph of $y = x^2$ is vertically expanded by a factor of 2, then translated 3 units left and 4 units down, and reflected in the *x*-axis.

16.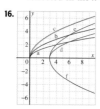

b) The graph of $f(x)$ is horizontally compressed by a factor of $\frac{1}{2}$.

c) The graph of $f(x)$ is vertically expanded by a factor of 2.

d) The graph of $f(x)$ is horizontally compressed by a factor of $\frac{1}{2}$, then translated 3 units right.

e) The graph of $f(x)$ is vertically expanded by a factor of 2, then translated 3 units right.

f) The graph of $f(x)$ is vertically expanded by a factor of 2, then translated 3 units right, and reflected in the *x*-axis.

17.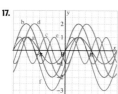

b) The graph of $f(x)$ is vertically expanded by a factor of 2.

c) The graph of $f(x)$ is horizontally compressed by a factor of $\frac{1}{2}$.

d) The graph of $f(x)$ is vertically expanded by a factor of 2, then translated 1 unit right.

e) The graph of $f(x)$ is horizontally compressed by a factor of $\frac{1}{2}$, then translated 1 unit right.

f) The graph of $f(x)$ is vertically expanded by a factor of 2, then translated 1 unit down.

18. a), b) $g(x) = \frac{1}{2}\cos\left(x + \frac{\pi}{6}\right) + 2$

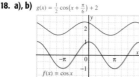

c) The graph of $f(x)$ is vertically compressed by a factor of $\frac{1}{2}$, then translated $\frac{\pi}{6}$ units left and 2 units up.

d) $f(x)$: All real numbers; $-1 \le y \le 1$
$g(x)$: All real numbers; $1.5 \le y \le 2.5$

19. a) $y = \dfrac{x - 5}{2}$ 　　　　　**b)** $y = \pm\sqrt{x - 4} + 1$

c) $y = \pm\sqrt{\dfrac{3x + 19}{9}} - \dfrac{2}{3}$ 　　**d)** $f^{-1}(x) = (x + 3)^2 - 2, x \le 0$

e) $g^{-1}(x) = \dfrac{2 - x}{x}$ 　　　**f)** $g^{-1}(x) = \dfrac{2}{x - 1}$

20. a) $y = \pm\sqrt{x - 2} + 3$

b)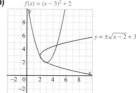

c) No; it does not pass the vertical line test.

21. a) i) $f^{-1}(x) = 2x + 2$

ii)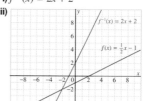

iii) All real numbers; all real numbers
iv) All real numbers; all real numbers
v) Yes

b) i) $y = -2 \pm \sqrt{\dfrac{x - 2}{2}}$

ii)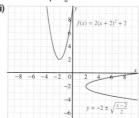

iii) All real numbers; $y \ge 2$
iv) $x \ge 2$; all real numbers
v) No
vi) $x \ge -2$ or $x \le -2$

c) i) $f^{-1}(x) = \frac{1}{4}(x + 2)^2 - 2, x \ge -2$

ii)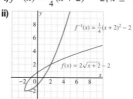

iii) $x \ge -2$; $y \ge -2$
iv) $x \ge -2$; $y \ge -2$
v) Yes

Chapter 7 Self-Test, page 443

1. Answers may vary.
a) $f(x) = x - 7$ 　　　　　**b)** $g(x) = \sqrt{x} + 1$
c) $h(x) = \frac{7}{3}x - 2$

2. a), b)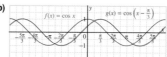

c) The graph of $f(x)$ is translated $\frac{\pi}{3}$ units right.

d) $f(x)$: all real numbers; $-1 \leq y \leq 1$
$g(x)$: all real numbers; $-1 \leq y \leq 1$

3. a) No

4. a)

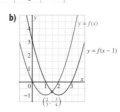

b) $g(x) = \frac{1}{2}\sqrt{\frac{x}{2}}$

c) $f(x)$: $x \geq 0$; $y \geq 0$; $g(x)$: $x \geq 0$; $y \geq 0$

6. a) $y = \pm\sqrt{\frac{5-x}{2}}$

b)

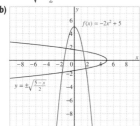

c) All real numbers; $y \leq 5$
$x \leq 5$; all real numbers

d) No   **e)** $x \geq 0$ or $x \leq 0$

7. a) 100 L   **b)** Tank never empties.
c) 64 L; 36 L
d) $t = 8 \pm \sqrt{V - 36}$; $36 \leq V \leq 100$; $t \geq 0$

Assessment Tasks, page 444

1. a)

x	$f(x)$	$f(x+1)$	$f(2x)$	$f(3x-2)$	$3f(x)-2$	$f^{-1}(x)$
1	1	3	3	1	1	1
2	3	5	7	7	7	9
3	5	7	8	6	13	2
4	7	9	4	0	19	8
5	9	8	0		25	3
6	8	6			22	7
7	6	4			16	4
8	4	2			10	6
9	2	0			4	5
10	0				-2	

2. a)

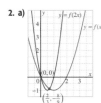

b)

Cumulative Review Chapters 1–7

Exercises, page 445

2. a) 8   **b)** $\frac{1}{25}$ **c)** 256

3. 34.2, 41, 47.8, 54.6, 61.4

4. 4, 6, 9, 13.5, 20.25

5. a) 26   **b)** $\frac{13}{7}$

6. a) 504   **b)** -6560

7. $s[3q + 4(s - 1)p]$

8. ± 80

9. a) $3p^3 + 7p^2 - 8p - 20$ **b)** $97x^2 - 38x - 3$

10. a) $\frac{y+3}{y-2}$, $y \neq 2, 8$ **b)** $\frac{9x^2 - 29x + 2}{6x(x-1)}$, $x \neq 0, 1$

11. a) $\frac{1}{9x - 7y}$ **b)** $\frac{(5x + 8y)(x + 5y)}{(5x - 8y)}$

12. a) $\frac{x}{(x+2)(x+3)}$ **b)** $\frac{7x+1}{(4x+3)(3x-2)}$

14. a) \$2303.23   **b)** \$2336.87   **c)** \$2366.51

15. 23

16. \$9493.44

17. \$1098.85

18. \$1024.18

19. a) \$709.21   **b)** \$85 210.40   **c)** \$79 129.25

20. a) $y = 2(x-3)^2 - 15$ **b)** $y = -\frac{1}{3}(x-12)^2 + 50$

21. a) Minimum; -15 **b)** Maximum; 50

22. a) $\frac{5 \pm \sqrt{17}}{2}$ **b)** $\frac{-3 \pm \sqrt{15}}{3}$

23. a) $-1.306, 0.306$ **b)** $0.451; 2.215$

24. a) $-i$ **b)** $5\sqrt{2}i$ **c)** $3\sqrt{6}i$

25. a) $1 \pm 2i$ **b)** $\frac{-1 \pm \sqrt{2}i}{3}$

26. a) 7.5625 cm^2 **b)** 1.25

27. a) $-17 + 67i$ **b)** $44 - 28i$

28. a) $\frac{1}{10} + \frac{11}{30}i$ **b)** $60 - 32i$

29. $146 - 48i$

30. AC = 41.0 cm, $\angle$BAC = 37°, $\angle$ACB = 30°

31. $-0.928; -0.371; 2.500$

32. $\frac{-(\sqrt{2} + \sqrt{3})}{2}$

33. Approximately 0.314 m/s

34. 1.344

36. a) 56.3°   **b)** 63.4°

38.

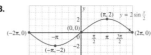

39. a)

b)

40. a) Amplitude: 2.5; period: π

b) Amplitude: 1.5; period: 6π

41. a) $y = \tan\left(\dfrac{x}{2}\right)$ **b)** $y = 3\sin\left(x + \dfrac{\pi}{6}\right) - 1$

42. π; 3; $-\dfrac{\pi}{4}$; all real numbers; $-4 \le y \le 2$

43. $n = -50\cos\dfrac{2\pi}{11}(t - 1997) + 50$

44.

x	0	$\frac{\pi}{6}$	$\frac{\pi}{3}$	$\frac{\pi}{2}$	$\frac{2\pi}{3}$	$\frac{5\pi}{6}$	π
y	0.41	1.30	7.60	−2.41	−0.77	−0.13	0.41

45. a) 9.32 **b)** 32 **c)** $2x^2 + x + 4$

46. a)

   b)

c)

   d)

e)

   f)

47.
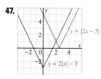

48. a) The graph of $y = \sqrt{x}$ is vertically expanded by a factor of 2, then translated 3 units left and 1 unit down.

b)
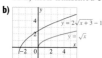

49. a) i) $y = \dfrac{x+1}{2}$ **ii)** $y = \pm\sqrt{x-2}$

b) i)

   ii)
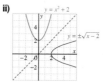

Chapter 8 Loci: From Geometry to Algebra (Functions and Relations)

Necessary Skills
1 New: What Is a Relation?
Exercises, page 451

1. In a relation, one value of x can produce more than one value of y.

2. a) No   **b)** Yes

3. a) 2; 3 **b)** -5, 5; 5, -5 **c)** $\pm\sqrt{2}$; -2
   d) -2; $\pm\sqrt{2}$ **e)** 0; 0 **f)** ± 5, 0; 0

4. $x^2 + y^2 = 25$, $y = x^2 - 2$, $y^2 = x + 2$, $y^2 = x^2$

3 Review: Distance between Two Points
Exercises, page 452

1. a) 2 **b)** 5 **c)** 8.1
   d) 9.4 **e)** 6.7 **f)** 7.6

2. a) 7.3 **b)** 13.0 **c)** 8.9
   d) 5.4 **e)** 10.3 **f)** 19.4

4 New: Squaring Expressions Containing Radicals
Exercises, page 453

1. a) $x^2 + 2x + 1 + y^2$ **b)** $x^2 + 8x + 16 + y^2$
   c) $x^2 + y^2 - 6y + 9$

2. a) $x^2 + y^2 + 2x + 65 + 16\sqrt{(x+1)^2 + y^2}$
   b) $x^2 + y^2 + 8x + 41 - 10\sqrt{(x+4)^2 + y^2}$
   c) $x^2 + y^2 - 6y + 109 + 20\sqrt{x + (y-3)^2}$

3. a) $x^2 + y^2 - 4x + 20 + 8\sqrt{(x-2)^2 + y^2}$
   b) $x^2 + y^2 - 10y + 34 - 6\sqrt{x^2 + (y-5)^2}$
   c) $x^2 + y^2 - 8x + 52 + 12\sqrt{(x-4)^2 + y^2}$
   d) $x^2 + y^2 + 12y + 37 - 2\sqrt{x^2 + (y+6)^2}$
   e) $x^2 + y^2 - 16y + 89 + 10\sqrt{x^2 + (y-8)^2}$
   f) $x^2 + y^2 - 6x + 13 - 4\sqrt{(x-3)^2 + y^2}$
   g) $x^2 + y^2 - 16x + 164 - 20\sqrt{(x-8)^2 + y^2}$
   h) $x^2 + y^2 - 12x + 85 - 14\sqrt{(x-6)^2 + y^2}$
   i) $x^2 + y^2 - 18y + 162 + 18\sqrt{x^2 + (y-9)^2}$

8.1 Exercises, page 459

1. Answers may vary.
   a) P is always 2 units below the x-axis.
   b) P is always 2 units away from the x-axis.
   c) P is always 3 units to the right of the y-axis.
   d) Point N has coordinates $(0, 2)$, P moves so the slope of NP is always 1.
   e) Point R has coordinates $(1, 0)$, P moves so the slope of RP is always -1.
   f) P moves so it is always 2 units from the origin.

2. Answers may vary.
   a) P is always 3 units above the x-axis.
   b) P is always 2 units left of the y-axis.
   c) Point O has coordinates $(0, 0)$, P moves so the slope of OP is always 3.

d) Point A has coordinates (2, 4), P moves so the slope of AP is always 3.

e) P moves so it is always 5 units from the origin.

f) P moves so it is always $\sqrt{5}$ units from the origin.

3. a), b)

c)

4. a)

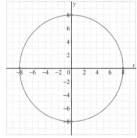

b) A horizontal line through (0, 5)

c) $y - 5 = 0$

5. a) A straight line with slope 2, through (0, 1)

b) $y - 2x - 1 = 0$

6. a) A circle with radius 8 and centre (0, 0)

b) $x^2 + y^2 = 64$

7. a)

b) A straight line with slope −3, through (−6, 3)

c) $y + 3x + 15 = 0$

8. a) $x + y - 3 = 0$; a straight line with slope −1, through (0, 3)

b) $5x - 2y - 13 = 0$; a straight line with slope $\frac{5}{2}$, through (2, −1.5)

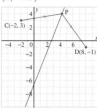

9. a) $x = 0$ and $y = 0$

b)

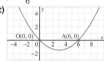

The locus is the x- and y-axes.

10. a) $y = 0$, excluding the origin

11. a) $y = \frac{1}{6}x^2 - x$ **b)** It is a parabola.

c)

12. a) $y = -\frac{1}{6}x^2 + x$ **b)** It is a parabola.

c)

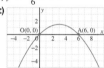

13. a) $x + 6 = 0$ and $y = 0$ **b)** $x - 12 = 0$ and $y = 0$

14. a) A circle with centre (3, 0) and radius 5

b) $(x - 3)^2 + y^2 = 25$

15. a) A circle with centre (−2, 3) and radius 4

b) $(x + 2)^2 + (y - 3)^2 = 16$

16. a) $x^2 + y^2 = 16$

b) A circle with centre (0, 0) and radius 4

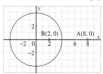

c) (4, 0), (−4, 0)   **d)** (0, 4), (0, −4)

17. a) A circle with centre (10, 0) and radius 4

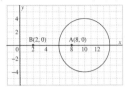

b) $x^2 - 20x + 84 + y^2 = 0$

18. a) $x^2 + 2x - 8 + y^2 = 0$

b)

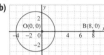

c) x-intercepts: -4, 2; y-intercepts: $\pm 2\sqrt{2}$

19. a) $y = \dfrac{1}{4}x^2 + 2$

b) A parabola with a minimum at (0, 2)

c)

20. a) $x = \dfrac{1}{4}y^2 + 2$

b) A parabola that opens to the right with vertex at (2, 0)

c)

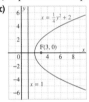

22. a) $y = \dfrac{1}{8}x^2 + 2$ **b)** $3y^2 + 8y - 16 - x^2 = 0$

c) $4x^2 + 3y^2 - 32y + 64 = 0$

23. a)

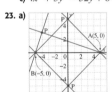

b) $x^2 + y^2 = 25$

c) A circle with centre (0, 0) and radius 5

24. a) $x^2 + y^2 = 25$

b) A circle with centre (0, 0) and radius 5

25. a) A portion of a circle with centre O and radius DP

b) As RS gets longer or shorter, the radius of the circle gets larger or smaller, respectively.

8.2 Exercises, page 469

1. a) x-intercepts: ± 3; y-intercepts: ± 1

b) Answers may vary. $(-2, 0.7)$, $(-2, -0.7)$, $(2, 0.7)$, $(2, -0.7)$

2. a) x-intercepts: ± 2; y-intercepts: ± 3

b) Answers may vary. $(-1, 2.6)$, $(-1, -2.6)$, $(1, 2.6)$, $(1, -2.6)$

3. A circle is an ellipse in which F_1 and F_2 coincide.

4. a) $5x^2 + 9y^2 = 180$

b)

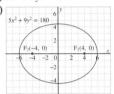

5. a) $9x^2 + 5y^2 = 180$

b)

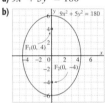

7. a) $15x^2 + 16y^2 = 240$ **b)** $16x^2 + 15y^2 = 240$

8. a) $11x^2 + 36y^2 = 396$ **b)** $20x^2 + 36y^2 = 1125$

c) $3x^2 + 4y^2 = 300$

9. a) $21x^2 + 25y^2 = 2100$ **b)** $25x^2 + 24y^2 = 2400$

c) $1564x^2 - 4692x - 152\ 881 + 1600y^2 = 0$

d) $1600x^2 + 1564y^2 - 4692y - 152\ 881 = 0$

10. Answers may vary. $15x^2 + 16y^2 = 240$, $16x^2 + 15y^2 = 240$

11. Answers may vary. $36x^2 + 100y^2 = 225$, $5x^2 + 9y^2 = 45$

13. a)

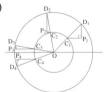

b) An ellipse

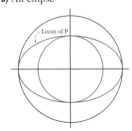

c) No

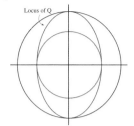

Locus of Q

14. a) An ellipse

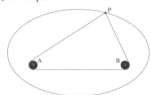

b) The ellipse would be more circular.
c) The ellipse would be stretched horizontally.

15. a) Parts of three congruent semi-ellipses with the vertices of triangle ABC as the foci.
b)

16. a) $9x^2 + 25y^2 = 225$ **b)** $x^2 + 5y^2 = 20$

17. a) $5x^2 + y^2 = 45$ **b)** $25y^2 + 16x^2 = 1600$

19. The locus is one-quarter of an ellipse.

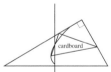

20. a) The locus is a semi-ellipse.
b) **i)** The semi-ellipse increases in length and gets closer to the vertical axis.
  i) The semi-ellipse becomes a semicircle.
  iii) The semi-ellipse expands and contracts as AB expands and contracts.
c) **i)** By repeating the construction of a locus on a segment between D and the other point of intersection
  ii) Point O

21. a) The locus is part of an ellipse.
b) The semi-ellipse gets larger and smaller as the line RS increases and decreases in length.
c) Repeat the construction of a locus using point D and the other point of intersection of the circle and the line.

23. a) $b^2 = a^2 - c^2$

24. $\dfrac{x^2}{a^2} + \dfrac{y^2}{b^2} = 1$

25. b) The semi-ellipse is expanded horizontally as P moves closer to the line and becomes more circular as P moves away from the line.
c) Repeat the construction of P on DM on the other side of the horizontal line.

Self-Check 8.1, 8.2, page 474

1. a) $x + 3y - 11 = 0$
b) A straight line with slope $-\dfrac{1}{3}$, through $(2, 3)$
c)

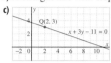

2. a)

b) $x = -2$
c) A vertical line through $x = -2$

3. a)

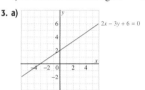

b) $2x - 3y + 6 = 0$
c) A straight line with slope $\dfrac{2}{3}$, passing through $(0, 2)$

4. a) $x^2 + y^2 = 16$
b)

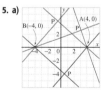

c) A circle with centre $(0, 0)$ and radius 4

5. a)

b) $x^2 + y^2 = 16$
c) A circle with centre $(0, 0)$ and radius 4

6. a) x-intercepts: ± 4; y-intercepts: ± 1
b) Answers may vary. $(-2, 0.9)$, $(-2, -0.9)$, $(2, 0.9)$, $(2, -0.9)$

7. $9x^2 + 25y^2 = 225$

8. Answers may vary. $9x^2 + 16y^2 = 144$

9. Answers may vary. $25x^2 + 21y^2 = 525$

8.3 Exercises, page 480

1. a) x-intercepts: ± 2; no y-intercepts
   b) Answers may vary. $(-3, 3.4)$, $(-3, -3.4)$, $(3, 3.4)$, $(3, -3.4)$

2. a) No x-intercepts; y-intercepts: ± 4
   b) Answers may vary. $(1.1, -6)$, $(-1.1, -6)$, $(1.1, 6)$, $(-1.1, 6)$

3. a) $5x^2 - 4y^2 = 20$
   b)

4. a) $16x^2 - 9y^2 = -144$
   b)

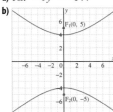

6. a) $5x^2 - 4y^2 = 20$ **b)** $4x^2 - 5y^2 = -20$
   c) Each hyperbola is a reflection of the other in $y = x$.

7. a) $x^2 - 15y^2 = -60$
   b) $100x^2 - 924y^2 = -5775$
   c) $9x^2 - 55y^2 = -495$

8. a) $x^2 - 8y^2 = -8$
   b) $24x^2 - y^2 = 24$
   c) $3x^2 - y^2 - 12x + 9 = 0$
   d) $x^2 - 3y^2 + 12y - 9 = 0$

9. Answers may vary. $16x^2 - 9y^2 = 144$, $9x^2 - 16y^2 = -144$

10. Answers may vary. $12x^2 - 4y^2 = 27$, $5x^2 - 4y^2 = 20$

11. a) 670 m

13. $16x^2 - 9y^2 = 576$

14. $9y^2 - 16x^2 = 144$

16. c) i) The perpendicular bisector is an asymptote to the hyperbola.
   ii) Point P is jumping between the branches of the hyperbola.
   d) Yes
   e) The slopes of the perpendicular bisectors are opposite numbers.

20. c) The tangents appear to be perpendicular.
   d) The tangents at a point of intersection of a confocal ellipse and hyperbola are perpendicular.

8.4 Exercises, page 488

1. a) $y^2 = 8x$

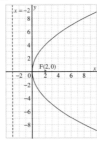

   b) $x^2 = 8y$

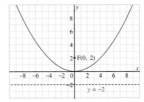

   c) $y^2 = -8x$

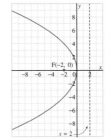

   d) $x^2 = -8y$

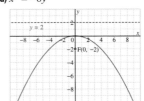

3. a) $x^2 = 12y$
   b)

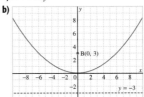

A parabola, with vertex $(0, 0)$, that opens up

4. a) $y^2 = -20x$

b)

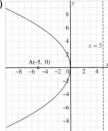

A parabola, with vertex $(0, 0)$, that opens left

5. a) $(3, 0)$ **b)** $y^2 = 12x$

6. a) $x = -10$ **b)** $y^2 = 40x$

7. a) $y = \frac{1}{8}x^2 + 2$ **b)** $8y = x^2 - 6x + 25$
   c) $y = -\frac{1}{8}x^2 + 2$

8. a) $y^2 = 12x - 36$ **b)** $y^2 - 6y - 12x + 45 = 0$
   c) $y^2 = 36 - 12x$

9. The length of the latus rectum is twice the perpendicular distance from the focus to the directrix.

10. a) $x^2 = 2y + 4$
   b) A parabola, with vertex $(0, -2)$, that opens up

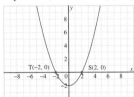

   c) $t = \pm 6$

11. a) $x^2 = 4py$ **b)** $y^2 = 4px$

12. b), c)

   A parabola, with vertex $(0, 0)$, that opens up
   d) $x^2 = 8y$

13. b), c) A parabola, with vertex $(0, 0)$, that opens up

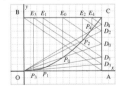

   d) $x^2 = 18y$

14. c) A parabola, with vertex $(0, 0)$, that opens up
   d) i) $4\sqrt{a}$ **ii)** $x^2 = 16y$

15. a) $y = \frac{-(x^2 - 16)}{8}$ **b)** $y = \frac{64 - x^2}{8}$

16. a) $x^2 + y^2 - 2xy - 8x - 8y + 16 = 0$

b)

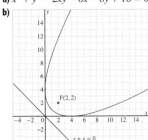

17. b) The tangents are perpendicular lines that pass through the point of intersection of the directrix and the axis of symmetry.

Self-Check 8.3, 8.4, page 491

1. a) x-intercepts: ± 3; no y-intercepts
   b) Answers may vary. $(-4, 3.5)$, $(-4, -3.5)$, $(4, 3.5)$, $(4, -3.5)$

2. $3x^2 - y^2 = 12$

3. Answers may vary. $5x^2 - 4y^2 = 80$; $4x^2 - 5y^2 = -80$

4. Answers may vary. $4x^2 - 5y^2 = -80$; $x^2 - 8y^2 = -32$

5. $39x^2 - 25y^2 = 975$

6. a) $y^2 = 12x$

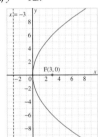

b) $x^2 = 16y$

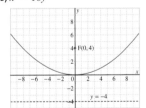

c) $x^2 = 9 - 6y$

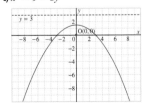

d) $y^2 = 8x + 16$

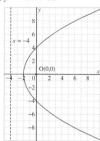

7. a) $x^2 = 8y$
  b) A parabola, with vertex (0, 0), that opens up

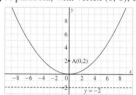

8. a) $y = x^2$
  b) A parabola, with vertex (0, 0), that opens up

8.5 Exercises, page 495

1. It is a hyperbola.

2. Yes

3. a) The circle gets bigger.
  b) The circle gets smaller.
  c) The circle becomes a point.

4. a) The ellipse gets bigger; gets smaller; becomes a point.
  b) The parabola gets wider; gets smaller; becomes a point.
  c) The two branches of the hyperbola get farther apart; the two branches get closer; the hyperbola becomes a pair of intersecting lines.

5. a) Circles
  b) i) Ellipses   **ii)** Parabolas
  iii) Hyperbolas

6. a) Move the flashlight so it makes an angle less than 45° with the vertical.
  b) Move the flashlight so it makes an angle of 45° with the vertical.
  c) Move the flashlight so it makes an angle of 90° with the vertical.

7. a) One branch of a hyperbola
  b) Parabola or ellipse   **c)** Parabola or ellipse
  d) Circle

10. θ is the angle of elevation.
  a) $\theta = 0°$ **b)** $0° < \theta < 60°$
  c) $60° < \theta < 90°$ **d)** $\theta = 60°$

Chapter 8 Review Exercises, page 501

1. a) $2x - 5y + 12 = 0$
  b) A straight line with slope $\frac{2}{5}$, through (−6, 0)

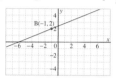

2. a)

  b) $y = -1$
  c) A horizontal line through $y = -1$

3. a)

  b) $y = \pm(x - 5)$
  c) A pair of perpendicular lines through (5, 0)

4. a) $x - 4y - 7 = 0$
  b)

  A straight line with slope $\frac{1}{4}$, through (7, 0)

5. a) $4x - 5y - 10 = 0$
  b)

  A straight line with slope $\frac{4}{5}$, through (0, −2)

6. a) $y = -4$
  b)

  A horizontal line through (0, −4), excluding the point (0, −4)

7. a) $3x^2 + 3y^2 + 50x + 75 = 0$

b)

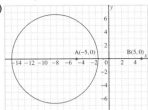

A circle with radius $\frac{20}{3}$, centre on the negative x-axis

8. a) $x^2 + y^2 = 1$

b)

A circle with radius 1 and centre $(0, 0)$

9. a) x-intercepts: ± 2; y-intercepts: ± 3

b) Coordinates may vary. $(1, 2.6)$, $(-1, 2.6)$, $(-1, -2.6)$, $(1, -2.6)$

10. a) $49x^2 + 40y^2 = 1960$

b) $484x^2 + 340y^2 = 10\ 285$

c) $16x^2 + 7y^2 = 112$

11. a) $900x^2 + 644y^2 = 36\ 225$

b) $836x^2 + 900y^2 = 47\ 025$

c) $836x^2 + 900y^2 - 3344x - 43\ 681 = 0$

d) $836x^2 + 900y^2 + 3344x - 43\ 681 = 0$

12. $7x^2 + 16y^2 = 448$

13. Answers may vary. $9x^2 + 25y^2 = 225$, $25x^2 + 9y^2 = 225$

14. c) i) The locus is a horizontal line.

ii) The foci are on the horizontal line and the ellipse is below the line.

iii) The locus is a vertical line.

iv) The ellipse gets larger.

d) At the midpoint between T and D

e) The major axis has length two times the diameter of the circle. Check by measuring.

f) Repeating the construction with the other point of intersection of the vertical line and the circle.

15. a) $364x^2 - 36y^2 = 819$ **b)** $12x^2 - 4y^2 = 75$

c) $204x^2 - 196y^2 = 2499$

16. a) $4x^2 - y^2 = 12$ **b)** $5x^2 - 4y^2 = 20$

c) $5x^2 - 4y^2 + 30x + 25 = 0$

d) $3x^2 - y^2 - 24x + 36 = 0$

17. $324x^2 - 700y^2 = -14\ 175$

18. $39x^2 - 25y^2 = 975$, $25x^2 - 39y^2 = -975$

19. a) $y^2 = 16x - 32$

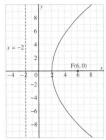

b) $x^2 = 4y + 16$

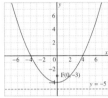

c) $y^2 + 6y - 12x + 21 = 0$

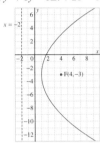

20. a) $x^2 = 8y$

b) A parabola, with vertex $(0, 0)$, that opens up

21. a) $x = 1$ and $y = 0$

b) A horizontal line and a vertical line through $(1, 0)$

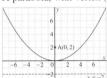

22. a) $y = 2x^2$

b) A parabola, with vertex $(0, 0)$, that opens up

23. a) Hyperbola **b)** Parabola

24. Earth's axis is tilted so there are times during the year when the Southern Hemisphere is closer to the sun (summer) while the Northern Hemisphere is farther from the sun (winter).

Chapter 8 Self-Test, page 505

1. a)

b) A circle with radius 5 and centre $(-1, 2)$
c) $x^2 + 2x + y^2 - 4y - 20 = 0$ **d)** $-4, 2$

2. a) A circle
b)

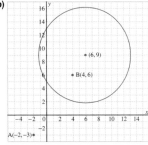

c) $x^2 + y^2 - 12x - 18y + 65 = 0$

4. a) $x^2 = 4y$
b) A parabola, with vertex $(0, 0)$, that opens up

5. $16x^2 + 49y^2 = 784$

6. a) $7x^2 + 16y^2 = 112$
b) $5x^2 - 4y^2 = 20$
c)

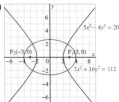

8. a), b)

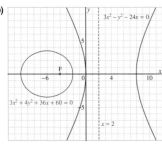

c) The locus in part a is an ellipse. The locus in part b is a hyperbola. Both of them have $(-4, 0)$ as one focus.

1. a) An ellipse
b), c)

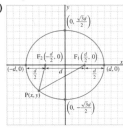

$3x^2 + 4y^2 = 3d^2$

Chapter 9 Conics: From Algebra to Geometry (Functions and Relations)

Necessary Skills
1 Review: The Quadratic Formula
Exercises, page 509

1. a) $\frac{1}{2}, -\frac{3}{2}$ **b)** $5, -\frac{4}{3}$
c) $0.69, -0.29$ **d)** $1.38, -10.88$

2. a) Two different real roots
b) No real roots   **c)** Two equal roots
d) No real roots

3. a) 25 **b)** ± 2 **c)** ± 8 **d)** $\pm\frac{1}{2}$

2 New: Standard Equation of a Circle
Exercises, page 512

1. a) $9, (0, 0)$ **b)** $\sqrt{15}, (0, 0)$ **c)** $6, (-1, -1)$
d) $10, (2, -3)$ **e)** $\sqrt{12}, (4, -5)$ **f)** $\sqrt{55}, (3, 6)$

2. a) $x^2 + y^2 = 25$ **b)** $x^2 + y^2 = 1$
c) $(x - 1)^2 + (y - 2)^2 = 49$ **d)** $(x + 3)^2 + (y - 2)^2 = 36$
e) $(x - 4)^2 + (y + 2)^2 = 4$ **f)** $(x + 6)^2 + (y + 8)^2 = 64$

3. a) $x^2 + y^2 + 6x + 2y + 6 = 0$
b) $x^2 + y^2 - 10x + 4y + 9 = 0$
c) $x^2 + y^2 + 12x - 6y + 15 = 0$
d) $x^2 + y^2 - 7x - 3y - \frac{21}{50} = 0$

4. a) $(x + 4)^2 + (y + 5)^2 = 42$ **b)** $(x - 5)^2 + (y - 4)^2 = 43$

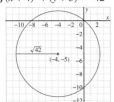

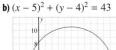
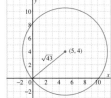

c) $(x - 3)^2 + (y + 6)^2 = 40$ **d)** $\left(x - \dfrac{3}{2}\right)^2 + (y + 2)^2 = \dfrac{37}{4}$

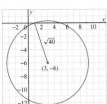

3 Review: Solving a Linear System
Exercises, page 513

1. a) $(5, -2)$ **b)** $(3, 2)$ **c)** $\left(\dfrac{9}{2}, -\dfrac{1}{4}\right)$ **d)** $\left(\dfrac{4}{5}, -\dfrac{22}{5}\right)$

2. a) $(4, 3)$ **b)** $(-2, -3)$ **c)** $(5, -1)$ **d)** $(-2, 6)$

9.1 Exercises, page 518

2. a) $(-3, 3)$ **b)** $(3, -3)$

4. a) Approximately $(7.5, 4.33)$
b) Approximately $(7.5, -4.33)$

6. a) $(1, -2), (-1, 2)$ **b)** $(2, 1), (-2, -1)$
c) $(1, 3), (-1, -3)$ **d)** $(-1, 3), (3, -1)$

7. a) $(0, -5), (-4, 3)$ **b)** $(-3, -2), \left(\dfrac{17}{5}, \dfrac{6}{5}\right)$
c) $(3, -2), (2, -3)$ **d)** $(6, 2), (-6, -2)$
e) $(2, 3) \left(-\dfrac{6}{5}, -\dfrac{17}{5}\right)$ **f)** No solution

8. a) $(1, 4), \left(-\dfrac{13}{5}, -\dfrac{16}{5}\right)$ **b)** $(-4, 2), \left(\dfrac{44}{13}, -\dfrac{38}{13}\right)$
c) $\left(\dfrac{11}{25}, \dfrac{127}{25}\right), (5, -1)$ **d)** $(4, 3), \left(\dfrac{156}{41}, \dfrac{133}{41}\right)$

9. a) $(-4, -4), (-1, -1)$ **b)** $(7, 0), (3, 2)$
c) $(3, 6), (5, 8)$ **d)** $(-6, 5), (-2, -1)$

10. a) i) $1, 8$
ii)

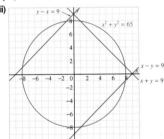

b) i) $1, -8; -1, 8$ **ii)** See part a) ii).

11. 28 cm by 5 cm

12. 2.26 cm, 9.74 cm

13. $(5, -12), \left(-\dfrac{220}{17}, -\dfrac{21}{17}\right)$

14. $(-5, 4), \left(-\dfrac{13}{25}, \dfrac{184}{25}\right)$

15. $(-21, -21), (-30, 4)$

16. a) $y = 2x + 5, y = 2x - 5$
b)

c) Solve the linear-quadratic system.

17. a) $y = 3x + 10, y = 3x - 10$
b) $y = \dfrac{4}{5}x + \sqrt{41}, y = \dfrac{4}{5}x - \sqrt{41}$

18. b) $(0, 0); \left(\dfrac{10}{1 + m^2}, \dfrac{10m}{1 + m^2}\right)$

c) $\left(\dfrac{3 + \sqrt{25 + 16m^2}}{1 + m^2}, \dfrac{3m + m\sqrt{25 + 16m^2}}{1 + m^2}\right);$
$\left(\dfrac{3 - \sqrt{25 + 16m^2}}{1 + m^2}, \dfrac{3m - m\sqrt{25 + 16m^2}}{1 + m^2}\right)$

19. a)

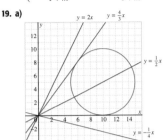

b) $y = mx$ **c)** $y = 0, y = \dfrac{4}{3}x$

20. b) $\left(\dfrac{5 + 5m + \sqrt{50m}}{1 + m^2}, \dfrac{5m + 5m^2 + m\sqrt{50m}}{1 + m^2}\right);$
$\left(\dfrac{5 + 5m - \sqrt{50m}}{1 + m^2}, \dfrac{5m + 5m^2 - m\sqrt{50m}}{1 + m^2}\right)$

c) $\left(\dfrac{3 + 5m + \sqrt{16m^2 + 30m}}{1 + m^2}, \dfrac{3m + 5m^2 + m\sqrt{16m^2 + 30m}}{1 + m^2}\right);$
$\left(\dfrac{3 + 5m - \sqrt{16m^2 + 30m}}{1 + m^2}, \dfrac{3m + 5m^2 - m\sqrt{16m^2 + 30m}}{1 + m^2}\right)$

21. a) $y = 3x, y = -3x$ **b)** $x = 0, y = 0$

25. $x = 3, -21x + 72y = 225$

9.2 Exercises, page 528

1. a) i) $(0, 0)$ **ii)** x-axis   **iii)** 3; 2
b) i) $(0, 0)$ **ii)** y-axis   **iii)** 5; 4
c) i) $(0, 0)$ **ii)** x-axis   **iii)** 6; 1
d) i) $(0, 0)$ **ii)** x-axis   **iii)** 7; 6
e) i) $(0, 0)$ **ii)** x-axis   **iii)** 10; 2
f) i) $(0, 0)$ **ii)** y-axis   **iii)** 10; 9

2. a) i) $(1, 2)$ **ii)** Horizontal   **iii)** 4; 2
b) i) $(-2, 3)$ **ii)** Vertical   **iii)** 9; 7
c) i) $(-3, -4)$ **ii)** Vertical   **iii)** 5; 3
d) i) $(0, 1)$ **ii)** Horizontal   **iii)** 6; 3
e) i) $(5, 0)$ **ii)** Vertical   **iii)** 12; 10
f) i) $(-1, -10)$ **ii)** Horizontal   **iii)** 11; 8

3. a) $\dfrac{(x - 3)^2}{9} + \dfrac{(y + 2)^2}{4} = 1$ **b)** $\dfrac{(x - 3)^2}{4} + \dfrac{(y - 1)^2}{16} = 1$

4. a) i)

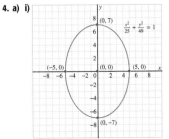

ii) $(0, 4.9), (0, -4.9)$

b) i)

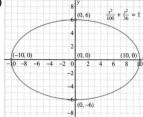

$$\frac{x^2}{100} + \frac{y^2}{36} = 1$$

ii) $(8, 0)$, $(-8, 0)$

c) i)

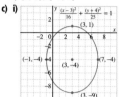

$$\frac{(x-3)^2}{16} + \frac{(y+4)^2}{25} = 1$$

ii) $(3, -1)$, $(3, -7)$

d) i)

$$\frac{(x-2)^2}{4} + \frac{(y-1)^2}{9} = 1$$

ii) $(2, 3.2)$, $(2, -1.2)$

5. a) i)

ii) $(7.4, 0)$, $(-7.4, 0)$

b) i)

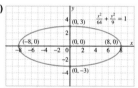

ii) $(8.1, 0)$, $(-8.1, 0)$

c) i)

ii) $(1.7, 2)$, $(-9.7, 2)$

d) i)

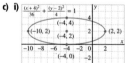

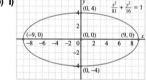

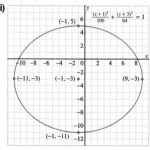

ii) $(5, -3)$, $(-7, -3)$

6. a) i) $\dfrac{x^2}{9} + y^2 = 1$

ii)

iii) $(2.8, 0)$, $(-2.8, 0)$

b) i) $\dfrac{x^2}{36} + \dfrac{y^2}{4} = 1$

ii)

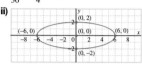

iii) $(5.7, 0)$, $(-5.7, 0)$

c) i) $\dfrac{x^2}{9} + \dfrac{y^2}{4} = 1$

ii)

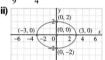

iii) $(2.2, 0)$, $(-2.2, 0)$

d) i) $\dfrac{x^2}{4} + \dfrac{y^2}{16} = 1$

ii)

iii) $(0, 3.5)$, $(0, -3.5)$

e) i) $\dfrac{x^2}{3} + \dfrac{y^2}{2} = 1$

ii)

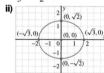

iii) $(1, 0)$, $(-1, 0)$

f) i) $\dfrac{x^2}{6} + \dfrac{y^2}{4} = 1$

ii)

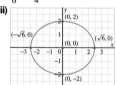

iii) $(1.4, 0)$, $(-1.4, 0)$

7. a) $\dfrac{x^2}{36} + \dfrac{y^2}{4} = 1$　　**b)** $\dfrac{x^2}{25} + \dfrac{y^2}{9} = 1$　　**c)** $\dfrac{x^2}{144} + \dfrac{y^2}{64} = 1$

d) $\dfrac{x^2}{9} + \dfrac{y^2}{1} = 1$　　**e)** $\dfrac{x^2}{16} + \dfrac{y^2}{9} = 1$

8. a) $\dfrac{x^2}{16} + \dfrac{y^2}{49} = 1$　　**b)** $\dfrac{x^2}{64} + \dfrac{y^2}{100} = 1$　　**c)** $\dfrac{x^2}{25} + \dfrac{y^2}{100} = 1$

d) $\dfrac{4x^2}{121} + \dfrac{4y^2}{225} = 1$　　**e)** $\dfrac{x^2}{16} + \dfrac{y^2}{81} = 1$

9. a) $\dfrac{(x-2)^2}{25} + \dfrac{(y-4)^2}{9} = 1$　　**b)** $\dfrac{(x-2)^2}{64} + \dfrac{(y-4)^2}{39} = 1$

c) $\dfrac{(x-2)^2}{25} + \dfrac{(y-4)^2}{9} = 1$

10. a) $\dfrac{(x+1)^2}{25} + \dfrac{(y-5)^2}{64} = 1$　　**b)** $\dfrac{(x+1)^2}{39} + \dfrac{(y-5)^2}{64} = 1$

c) $\dfrac{(x+1)^2}{9} + \dfrac{(y-5)^2}{36} = 1$

11. $\dfrac{(x-4)^2}{25} + \dfrac{(y-5)^2}{16} = 1$; $\dfrac{(x-4)^2}{16} + \dfrac{(y-5)^2}{25} = 1$

12. a) Answers may vary. $\dfrac{(x-4)^2}{16} + \dfrac{y^2}{4} = 1$; $\dfrac{(x-4)^2}{16} + \dfrac{y^2}{25} = 1$

b) $\dfrac{(x-4)^2}{16} + \dfrac{y^2}{b^2} = 1$; $b^2 < 16$

13. a) $\dfrac{x^2}{9} + \dfrac{(y-3)^2}{4} = 1$; $\dfrac{x^2}{16} + \dfrac{(y-3)^2}{4} = 1$

b) $\dfrac{x^2}{a^2} + \dfrac{(y-3)^2}{4} = 1$; $a^2 > 4$

14. a) $\dfrac{x^2}{18} + \dfrac{y^2}{9} = 1$ **b)** Not possible

15. a) $\dfrac{x^2}{12} + \dfrac{y^2}{3} = 1$ **b)** $\dfrac{2x^2}{27} + \dfrac{2y^2}{9} = 1$

c) $\dfrac{x^2}{36} + \dfrac{y^2}{27} = 1$ **d)** Not possible

16. a) $90° < \angle B_1 < 180°$ **b)** $90° < \angle B_1 < 180°$

17. Approximately 23.04 units^2

18. $\dfrac{(x+2)^2}{100} + \dfrac{(y-3)^2}{25} = 1$

19. a)

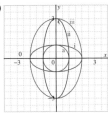

20. Expand horizontally by a factor of 5 and expand vertically by a factor of 4.

21. Expand horizontally by a factor of 6, expand vertically by a factor of 2, and translate 1 unit right and 2 units down.

22. a) $(0, 3)$, $\left(\dfrac{3}{5}, \dfrac{12}{5}\right)$ **b)** $(4, 0)$, $(0, -1)$

c) $(3, 0)$, $\left(-\dfrac{63}{29}, \dfrac{100}{29}\right)$ **d)** $(0, -4)$, $(-5, 0)$

23. c) Answers may vary. $\dfrac{(x-5)^2}{21} + \dfrac{y^2}{4} = 1$; $\dfrac{(x-5)^2}{4} + \dfrac{y^2}{21} = 1$

24. Answers may vary. $\dfrac{(x-10)^2}{36} + \dfrac{y^2}{64} = 1$; $\dfrac{(x-10)^2}{36} + \dfrac{y^2}{64} = 1$

25. Answers may vary.

a) $x = 8$ **b)** $y = x$ **c)** $y = 6$

Self-Check NS, 9.1, 9.2, page 532

1. a) $x^2 + y^2 + 4x + 8y + 11 = 0$
b) $x^2 + y^2 + 6x - 2y + 6 = 0$
c) $x^2 + y^2 - 10x - 12y + 60 = 0$
d) $x^2 + y^2 - 2x - 6y - 39 = 0$

2. a)

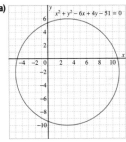

b)

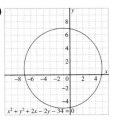

c)

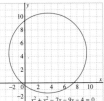

d)

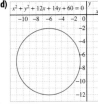

3. $(x - 3)^2 + y^2 = 25$

4. a) $(x + 2)^2 + (y + 1)^2 = 16$

b) x-intercepts: 1.87, -5.87; y-intercepts: 2.46, -4.46

c)

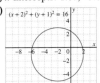

5. $(5, -1)$, $\left(-\dfrac{19}{5}, \dfrac{17}{5}\right)$

6. $y = 2x + 7.75$, $y = 2x - 7.75$

7. $(2, 1)$, $(1, 0)$

8. a) $(3.6, 0)$, $(-3.6, 0)$

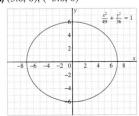

b) $(-2, 6.6)$, $(-2, 1.4)$

9. a) $\dfrac{x^2}{9} + \dfrac{y^2}{36} = 1$ **b)** $\dfrac{x^2}{16} + \dfrac{y^2}{25} = 1$

c) $\dfrac{x^2}{4} + \dfrac{y^2}{121} = 1$

10. Answers may vary. $\dfrac{(x-2)^2}{9} + \dfrac{(y-3)^2}{16} = 1$,

$\dfrac{(x-2)^2}{16} + \dfrac{(y-3)^2}{9} = 1$

11. a) $y = 3x + 5$, $y = 3x - 5$ **b)** $y = \dfrac{1}{2}x + \dfrac{3}{2}$, $y = \dfrac{1}{2}x - \dfrac{5}{2}$

1. a) i) $(0, 0)$ **ii)** x-axis **iii)** 2; 3 **iv)** $\pm\frac{3}{2}$

b) i) $(0, 0)$ **ii)** y-axis **iii)** 4; 3 **iv)** $\pm\frac{4}{3}$

c) i) $(0, 0)$ **ii)** x-axis **iii)** 8; 5 **iv)** $\pm\frac{5}{8}$

d) i) $(0, 0)$ **ii)** y-axis **iii)** 8; 6 **iv)** $\pm\frac{4}{3}$

e) i) $(0, 0)$ **ii)** y-axis **iii)** 10; 4 **iv)** $\pm\frac{5}{2}$

f) i) $(0, 0)$ **ii)** x-axis **iii)** 2; 9 **iv)** $\pm\frac{9}{2}$

2. a) A hyperbola, centre $(0, 0)$, foci on the x-axis, lengths of transverse axis and conjugate axis = 2

b) A hyperbola, centre $(0, 0)$, foci on the y-axis, lengths of transverse axis and conjugate axis = 2

3. a) i) $(5, -3)$ **ii)** Horizontal **iii)** 3; 5 **iv)** $\pm\frac{5}{3}$

b) i) $(-1, -4)$ **ii)** Vertical **iii)** 6; 4 **iv)** $\pm\frac{3}{2}$

c) i) $(3, 2)$ **ii)** Vertical **iii)** 4; 2 **iv)** ± 2

d) i) $(4, -4)$ **ii)** Horizontal **iii)** 8, 5 **iv)** $\pm\frac{5}{8}$

e) i) $(-2, 1)$ **ii)** Horizontal **iii)** 1; 3 **iv)** ± 3

f) i) $(-7, -5)$ **ii)** Vertical **iii)** 2; 7 **iv)** $\pm\frac{2}{7}$

4. a) $\dfrac{x^2}{4} - y^2 = 1$ **b)** $\dfrac{(x-3)^2}{4} - (y-2)^2 = 1$

c) $\dfrac{x^2}{4} - \dfrac{y^2}{4} = -1$ **d)** $\dfrac{(x-3)^2}{4} - \dfrac{(y-2)^2}{4} = -1$

5. a) i)

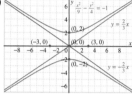

ii) $(0, 3.6)$, $(0, -3.6)$

b) i)

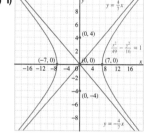

ii) $(8.1, 0)$, $(-8.1, 0)$

c) i)

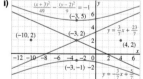

ii) $(-3, 9.6)$, $(-3, -5.6)$

d) i)

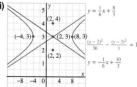

ii) $(8.1, 3)$, $(-4.1, 3)$

6. a) i)

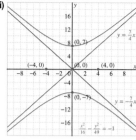

ii) $(0, 8.1)$, $(0, -8.1)$

b) i)

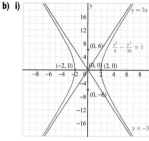

ii) $(6.3, 0)$, $(-6.3, 0)$

c) i)

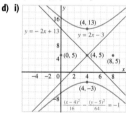

ii) $(1.6, 3)$, $(-5.6, 3)$

d) i)

ii) $(4, 13.9)$, $(4, -3.9)$

7. a) i) $\dfrac{x^2}{4} - y^2 = 1$

ii)

iii) $(2.2, 0)$, $(-2.2, 0)$

b) i) $\dfrac{x^2}{36} - \dfrac{y^2}{9} = 1$

ii)

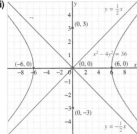

iii) $(6.7, 0), (-6.7, 0)$

c) i) $\dfrac{x^2}{4} - \dfrac{y^2}{9} = 1$

ii)

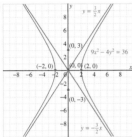

iii) $(3.6, 0), (-3.6, 0)$

d) i) $\dfrac{x^2}{9} - \dfrac{y^2}{81} = 1$

ii)

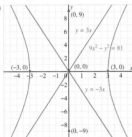

iii) $(9.5, 0), (-9.5, 0)$

e) i) $\dfrac{x^2}{2} - \dfrac{y^2}{5} = 1$

ii)

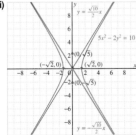

iii) $(2.6, 0), (-2.6, 0)$

f) i) $\dfrac{x^2}{4} - \dfrac{y^2}{10} = 1$

ii)

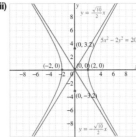

iii) $(3.7, 0), (-3.7, 0)$

8. a) $\dfrac{x^2}{25} - \dfrac{y^2}{16} = 1$ **b)** $\dfrac{x^2}{81} - \dfrac{y^2}{144} = 1$ **c)** $\dfrac{x^2}{36} - \dfrac{y^2}{64} = 1$

d) $\dfrac{x^2}{80} - \dfrac{y^2}{64} = 1$ **e)** $\dfrac{x^2}{16} - \dfrac{y^2}{36} = 1$ **f)** $\dfrac{x^2}{9} - \dfrac{y^2}{16} = 1$

g) $\dfrac{x^2}{64} - \dfrac{y^2}{256} = 1$

9. a) $\dfrac{x^2}{64} - \dfrac{y^2}{36} = -1$ **b)** $\dfrac{x^2}{25} - \dfrac{y^2}{100} = -1$

c) $\dfrac{x^2}{132} - \dfrac{y^2}{64} = -1$ **d)** $\dfrac{x^2}{100} - \dfrac{y^2}{125} = -1$

e) $\dfrac{x^2}{20} - \dfrac{y^2}{16} = -1$ **f)** $\dfrac{4x^2}{225} - \dfrac{4y^2}{31} = -1$

g) $\dfrac{x^2}{81} - \dfrac{y^2}{36} = -1$

10. a) $\dfrac{x^2}{6} - \dfrac{y^2}{2} = 1$

b)

11. $x^2 + y^2 = 4;\ \dfrac{x^2}{4} - \dfrac{y^2}{4} = 1;\ \dfrac{x^2}{4} - \dfrac{y^2}{4} = -1$

12.

13. a) $\dfrac{x^2}{a^2} - \dfrac{y^2}{a^2} = 1$

b) $(\sqrt{2}a, 0), (-\sqrt{2}a, 0);\ y = \pm x$

c) The slopes of the asymptotes are always ± 1.

d)

14. $\dfrac{x^2}{60} - \dfrac{y^2}{60} = -1$

15.

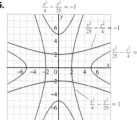

$$\frac{x^2}{4} - \frac{y^2}{25} = -1$$

(graph labels: $\frac{x^2}{25} - \frac{y^2}{4} = -1$, $\frac{x^2}{25} - \frac{y^2}{4} = 1$, $\frac{x^2}{4} - \frac{y^2}{25} = 1$)

16. a) Answers may vary; $\frac{x^2}{16} - \frac{y^2}{9} = 1$, $\frac{x^2}{9} - \frac{y^2}{16} = 1$

b)

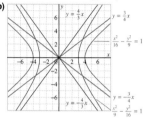

(graph labels: $y = \frac{4}{3}x$, $y = \frac{3}{4}x$, $\frac{x^2}{16} - \frac{y^2}{9} = 1$, $y = -\frac{3}{4}x$, $y = -\frac{4}{3}x$, $\frac{x^2}{9} - \frac{y^2}{16} = 1$)

c) Interchange the denominators.
d) Answers may vary.

17. a) $\frac{(x+3)^2}{100} - \frac{(y+5)^2}{36} = -1$ **b)** $\frac{(x+3)^2}{64} - \frac{(y+5)^2}{144} = -1$
c) $\frac{(x+3)^2}{375} - \frac{(y+5)^2}{25} = -1$ **d)** $\frac{(x+3)^2}{9} - \frac{(y+5)^2}{91} = -1$
e) $\frac{(x+3)^2}{16} - \frac{(y+5)^2}{9} = -1$

18. a) Answers may vary. $\frac{(x-3)^2}{16} - \frac{y^2}{16} = 1$, $\frac{(x-3)^2}{16} - \frac{y^2}{9} = 1$
b) $\frac{(x-3)^2}{16} - \frac{y^2}{b^2} = 1$

19. a) Not possible **b)** $\frac{2x^2}{9} - \frac{2y^2}{9} = 1$

20. a) $\frac{x^2}{6} - \frac{y^2}{3} = 1$ **b)** $\frac{4x^2}{27} - \frac{4y^2}{9} = 1$
c) Not possible **d)** $\frac{4x^2}{9} - \frac{4y^2}{27} = 1$

21. $\frac{(x-3)^2}{12} - \frac{(y-4)^2}{12} = 1$

22. a) 36 units^2
b) Yes; the square will have side length $2a$.

23. a) $(-2.3, 1.2), (2.3, -1.2)$
b) $(0, 3), \left(\frac{32}{15}, -\frac{17}{5}\right)$ **c)** $(3, 0), \left(-\frac{219}{55}, \frac{96}{55}\right)$

24.

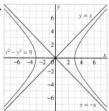

(graph labels: $y = x$, $x^2 - y^2 = 9$, $y = -x$)

a) i) $(3.46, 1.73), (-3.46, -1.73)$
ii) No solution   **iii)** No solution
b) $y = 2x + \sqrt{\frac{27}{7}}$, $y = 2x - \sqrt{\frac{27}{7}}$
c) $m > 1$ or $m < -1$

25. $m > \frac{b}{a}$ or $m < -\frac{b}{a}$

26. $\frac{x^2}{1.53} - \frac{y^2}{2.47} = 1$

27. a) $y = \frac{\pm\sqrt{4x^2 - 144}}{3}$
b) The value of y approaches $\frac{2}{3}|x|$.

28. a) 2   **b)** $c = \sqrt{2}a$; $(2, 2), (-2, -2)$

29. a) $x = -6$ and $y = 0$
b) Horizontal and vertical lines through $(-6, 0)$.

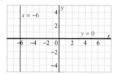

30. a) $x = 12$ and $y = 0$
b) Horizontal and vertical lines through $(12, 0)$

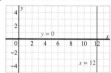

9.4 Exercises, page 549

1. a) $(1, 0), x = -1$ **b)** $(3, 0), x = -3$
c) $(-5, 0), x = 5$ **d)** $(0, 2), y = -2$
e) $(0, -0.5), y = 0.5$ **f)** $(0, 0.75), y = -0.75$
g) $(-2.25, 0), x = 2.25$ **h)** $(0, -1.25), y = 1.25$

2. a) $(3, 2), y = 2$, right **b)** $(2, -1), y = -1$, left
c) $(-1, -5), x = -1$, up **d)** $(4, 1), x = 4$, down
e) $(0, 3), y = 3$, right **f)** $(0, 2), x = 0$, up

3. a) i) $(2, 0), x = -2$
ii)

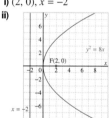

(graph labels: $y^2 = 8x$, $F(2, 0)$, $x = -2$)

b) i) $(-0.75, 0), x = 0.75$
ii)

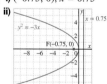

(graph labels: $x = 0.75$, $y^2 = -3x$, $F(-0.75, 0)$)

c) i) $(0, 1), y = -1$
ii)

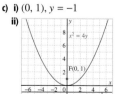

(graph labels: $x^2 = 4y$, $F(0, 1)$, $y = -1$)

d) i) $(0, -2.5)$, $y = 2.5$

ii)

4. a)

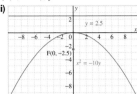

b)

c)

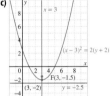

d)

e)

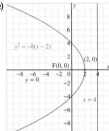

f)

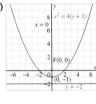

6. a) $x^2 = 4(y - 1)$ **b)** $x^2 = 16y$
c) $(x - 2)^2 = -8(y - 2)$ **d)** $x^2 = 16(y - 4)$

7. a) i) $y^2 = 16x$ **ii)** $y^2 = -24x$ **iii)** $x^2 = 12y$
b) $x^2 = -32y$

8. a) $(y - 2)^2 = 8(x - 1)$ **b)** $(y - 3)^2 = -12(x + 1)$
c) $(x - 2)^2 = 12(y + 3)$

9. b) $(x - 1)^2 = 8(y + 1)$, $(x - 1)^2 = -8(y - 1)$
c) $(0, -0.875)$, $(-1.828, 0)$, $(3.828, 0)$; $(0, 0.875)$

d)

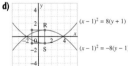

e) Equations may vary.

10. $x^2 = 4py$

12. a) Answers may vary. $x^2 + 8(y + 2)$, $x^2 = 12(y + 3)$
b) $x^2 = 4p(y + p)$

13. a) $(4.83, 5.83)$, $(-4.83, 5.83)$ or $(-0.83, 0.17)$, $(0.83, 0.17)$
b) $(7.46, 13.93)$, $(-7.46, 13.93)$ or $(-0.54, 0.07)$, $(0.54, 0.07)$
c) $(4, 4)$, $(-4, 4)$ **d)** $(6.93, 12)$, $(-6.93, 12)$

14.

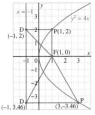

a) $(1, 2)$, $(1, -2)$ **b)** $(3, 3.46)$, $(3, -3.46)$
15. a) $y^2 = 20(x + 1)$ **b)** $(-1, 0)$; $(4, 0)$; $x = -6$
c)

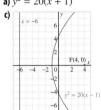

16. a) i) $(2, 4)$, $(-1, 1)$; $(3, 9)$, $(-1, 1)$; $(4, 16)$, $(-1, 1)$
    ii) $(-1, 1)$; $(-2, 4)$, $(-1, 1)$; $(-3, 9)$, $(-1, 1)$
b)

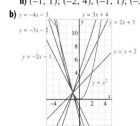

  i) $y = 4x + 5$; $(-1, 1)$, $(5, 25)$
  ii) $y = -5x - 4$; $(-4, 16)$, $(-1, 1)$
c) i) $y = 0x + 1$; $(-1, 1)$, $(1, -1)$
  ii) $y = -x - 0$; $(-1, 1)$, $(0, 0)$

17. b) i) $y = x - \dfrac{1}{4}$ **ii)** $y = 2x - 1$
   iii) $y = 3x - \dfrac{9}{4}$ **iv)** $y = 4x - 4$
c)

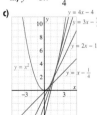

d) i) $y = -x - \dfrac{1}{4}$ **ii)** $y = -2x - 1$
   iii) $y = -3x - \dfrac{9}{4}$ **iv)** $y = -4x - 4$

18. a) $(0, 0)$, $(1, 1)$ **b)** $(2, 4)$, $(-1, 1)$
c) $(2.7, 3.3)$, $(-3.7, 9.7)$ **d)** $(6, 2)$, $(3, -1)$

19. The 2-3-4 Rule can be extended.

20. a) $k = 0$, $h = -p$ **b)** $h = 0$, $k = -p$

21. b) ii) $\dfrac{1}{2}$ **iii)** 2
c) The values for $\dfrac{\text{PF}}{\text{PN}}$ would change, but $0 < \dfrac{\text{PF}}{\text{PN}} < 1$.
d) The values for $\dfrac{\text{PF}}{\text{PN}}$ would change, but $\dfrac{\text{PF}}{\text{PN}} > 1$.

Self-Check 9.3, 9.4, page 554

1. a)

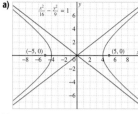

b)

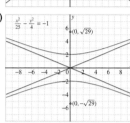

2. a) $\dfrac{x^2}{25} - \dfrac{y^2}{144} = 1$ **b)** $x^2 - \dfrac{y^2}{3} = 1$ **c)** $\dfrac{x^2}{9} - \dfrac{y^2}{16} = 1$

3. a)

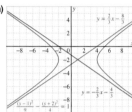

b)

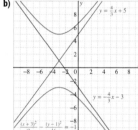

4. a) $\dfrac{(x-1)^2}{84} - \dfrac{(y+2)^2}{16} = -1$ **b)** $\dfrac{4(x-1)^2}{25} - \dfrac{(y+2)^2}{9} = -1$

c) $\dfrac{(x-1)^2}{16} - (y+2)^2 = -1$

5. a)

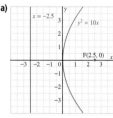

b)

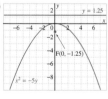

6. a) $(y-1)^2 = 8(x-2)$ **b)** $x^2 = \dfrac{1}{8}y$

7. a) $(y-4)^2 = -8(x-4)$ **b)** $(y-3)^2 = -\dfrac{1}{2}(x-8)$

8. a) $(2, 7), (7, 2)$ **b)** $(2, -1), (-1, 2)$

9.5 Exercises, page 557

1. a) $x^2 = -125(y - 80)$ **b)** $y = 67.2$ m

2. $\dfrac{x^2}{10\ 000} - \dfrac{y^2}{12\ 500} = 1$

3. a) Equation may vary. $\dfrac{4x^2}{225} + \dfrac{4y^2}{81} = 1$ **b)** 3.4 m

4. a) Equation may vary. $x^2 = 1512.50y$ **b)** 0.41 m

5. a) Equation may vary. $x^2 = -80y$ **b)** 17.19 m

6. a) 23 034.2 m^2

b) The area of a circle is the area of an ellipse for which $a = b = r$.

7. a) Equation may vary. $\dfrac{(54x)^2}{1771^2} - \dfrac{(54y)^2}{1771^2} = -1$

b) 21.4 m

8. 44.4 cm

9. a) $\dfrac{x^2}{3.5 \times 10^{19}} + \dfrac{y^2}{3.3 \times 10^{19}} = 1$

b) $\dfrac{4x^2}{(d_1 + d_2 + 1\ 392\ 000)^2} - \dfrac{y^2}{(d_1d_2 + 696\ 000(d_1 + d_2 + 696\ 000))^2} = 1,$

where d_1 is the shortest distance and d_2 is the longest distance

11. The speaker would have to face the reflector for the sound to be directed toward the audience; therefore, her back would be toward the audience.

13. $x^2 - d^2 = -10\ 000^2$

14. Equation may vary. $x^2 = -\dfrac{256}{5}y$

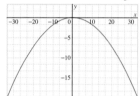

15. 6.05 m

16. a) 800 km **b)** 2000 km

9.6 Exercises, page 562

1. a) Parabola **b)** Hyperbola **c)** Ellipse
d) Circle **e)** Parabola **f)** Hyperbola

2. a) Ellipse **b)** Hyperbola
c) Parabola **d)** Circle

3. a) 3; $(5, -2)$ **b)** 5; $(3, 1)$ **c)** Not a circle

d) $\dfrac{3}{\sqrt{2}}$; $\left(-\dfrac{1}{2}, -\dfrac{1}{2}\right)$ **e)** $\dfrac{\sqrt{65}}{4}$; $\left(1, -\dfrac{3}{4}\right)$

f) Not a circle

4. a)

b)

c)

$x^2 + y^2 - 2x - 6y = 0$

d)

$x^2 + y^2 + 6x - 4y + 9 = 0$

e)

$x^2 + y^2 - 6x + 10y + 25 = 0$

f)

$x^2 + y^2 + 8x + 8y + 16 = 0$

5. a) $(x - 1)^2 = 3(y + 3)$ **b)** $(x + 3)^2 = -5(y - 2)$
c) $(y + 2)^2 = 4(x - 5)$ **d)** $(y - 1)^2 = -3(x + 2)$

6. a) $\dfrac{(x - 2)^2}{64} + \dfrac{(y - 1)^2}{9} = 1$ **b)** $(x + 3)^2 + \dfrac{(y - 3)^2}{4} = 1$
c) $\dfrac{(x - 1)^2}{4} + \dfrac{(y - 3)^2}{9} = 1$ **d)** $\dfrac{(x + 2)^2}{25} + \dfrac{(y - 2)^2}{4} = 1$

7. a) Ellipse   **b)** Parabola   **c)** Circle
d) Ellipse   **e)** Parabola   **f)** Circle

8. a) i) $\dfrac{(x - 1)^2}{9} - \dfrac{y^2}{4} = -1$
ii) 4; 6; (1, 2), (1, –2); (1, 3.6), (1, –3.6); $y = \dfrac{2}{3}x - \dfrac{2}{3}$, $y = -\dfrac{2}{3}x + \dfrac{2}{3}$

b) i) $\dfrac{(x - 2)^2}{16} - \dfrac{y^2}{4} = -1$
ii) 4; 8; (2, 2), (2, –2); (2, 4.5), (2, –4.5); $y = \dfrac{1}{2}x - 1$, $y = -\dfrac{1}{2}x + 1$

c) i) $\dfrac{(x + 1)^2}{25} - \dfrac{(y + 1)^2}{16} = -1$
ii) 8; 10; (–1, 3), (–1, –5); (–1, 5.4), (–1, –7.4); $y = \dfrac{4}{5}x - \dfrac{1}{5}$, $y = -\dfrac{4}{5}x - \dfrac{9}{5}$

d) i) $\dfrac{x^2}{25} - \dfrac{(y + 3)^2}{100} = -1$
ii) 20; 10; (0, 7), (0, –13); (0, 8.2), (0, –14.2); $y = 2x - 3$, $y = -2x - 3$

e) i) $\dfrac{x^2}{50} - \dfrac{y^2}{25} = -1$
ii) 10; $10\sqrt{2}$; (0, 5), (0, –5); (0, 8.7), (0, –8.7); $y = \pm\dfrac{1}{\sqrt{2}}x$

f) i) $\dfrac{(x + 2)^2}{8} - \dfrac{(y + 1)^2}{6} = -1$
ii) $2\sqrt{6}$; $4\sqrt{2}$; (–2, 1.4), (–2, –3.4); (–2, 2.7), (–2, –4.7); $y = \dfrac{\sqrt{3}}{2}x - 1 + \sqrt{3}$, $y = -\dfrac{\sqrt{3}}{2}x - 1 - \sqrt{3}$

9. a) $\dfrac{(x + 3)^2}{2} + \dfrac{(y - 1)^2}{4} = 1$ **b)** $\dfrac{(x - 1)^2}{9} + \dfrac{(y + 2)^2}{4} = 1$

c) $\dfrac{(x - 2)^2}{9} - (y - 1)^2 = 1$

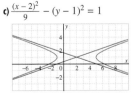

d) $\dfrac{(x - 1)^2}{4} - y^2 = 1$

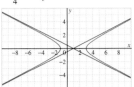

e) $(y + 4)^2 = 4\left(x + \dfrac{13}{4}\right)$ **f)** $(x + 1)^2 = -3(y + 1)$

10. a) A circle with centre (4, –3) and radius 4
b) An ellipse with centre (1, –2), major axis 4, and minor axis 2
c) An ellipse with centre (–3, 2), major axis 4, and minor axis $2\sqrt{3}$
d) A hyperbola with centre (6, 0), vertices at (4, 0) and (8, 0), and asymptotes with slope $\pm\dfrac{\sqrt{6}}{2}$
e) A parabola that opens right with vertex (4, –2), focus (6, –2), and directrix $x = 2$
f) A parabola that opens up with vertex at (–2, –5), focus $\left(-2, -\dfrac{119}{24}\right)$, and directrix $y = -\dfrac{121}{24}$

11. a) i) Hyperbola   **ii)** $\dfrac{(x - 2)^2}{9} - \dfrac{(y - 4)^2}{16} = 1$
iii) (5, 4), (–1, 4); (7, 4), (–3, 4)
iv)

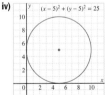

b) i) Circle   **ii)** $(x - 5)^2 + (y - 5)^2 = 25$
iv)

$(x - 5)^2 + (y - 5)^2 = 25$

c) i) Parabola   **ii)** $(y - 3)^2 = \dfrac{1}{4}(x - 4)$
iii) (4, 3), $\left(\dfrac{65}{16}, 3\right)$
iv)

$(y - 3)^2 = \dfrac{1}{4}(x - 4)$

d) i) Ellipse   **ii)** $\dfrac{(x + 3)^2}{9} + \dfrac{(y - 5)^2}{4} = 1$
iii) (0, 5), (–6, 5); (–0.8, 5), (–5.2, 5)

iv)

e) i) Ellipse   **ii)** $\dfrac{(x+3)^2}{4} + \dfrac{(y-5)^2}{9} = 1$

iii) (–3, 8), (–3, 2); (–3, 7.2), (–3, 2.8)

iv)

f) i) Circle   **ii)** $(x+2)^2 + (y-1)^2 = 10$

iv)

g) i) A pair of intersecting lines

ii) $\dfrac{y+3}{x-1} = \pm\dfrac{2}{3}$ **iii)** (1, –3)

iv)

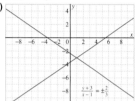

h) i) Hyperbola   **ii)** $\dfrac{(x+4)^2}{4} - y^2 = -1$

iii) (–4, 1), (–4, –1), (–4, 2.2), (–4, –2.2)

iv)

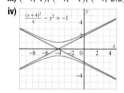

i) i) Parabola   **ii)** $(x+2)^2 = \dfrac{1}{8}(y-3)$

iii) (–2, 3); (–2, 3.03)

iv)

j) i) Circle   **ii)** $(x-3)^2 + (y-4)^2 = 36$

iii) (–3, 4), (9, 4), (3, 10), (3, –2); (3, 4)

iv)

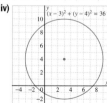

12. a) $(x-3)^2 = 6(y+3)$

b)

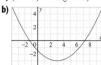

13. a) $G = 0$, $F = 0$, $A = B$; if $C > 0$, then $A < 0$ and $B < 0$; if $C < 0$, then $A > 0$ and $B > 0$

b) $G = 0$, $F = 0$, $A = -B$; if $A > 0$, then $C < 0$; if $A < 0$, then $C > 0$

c) $G = 0$, $F = 0$, $A = -B$; if $A > 0$, then $C > 0$; if $A < 0$, then $C < 0$

d) $A = 0$, $F = 0$, $C = 0$

e) $G = 0$, $F = 0$; if $A > B$, then $A > 0$, $B > 0$, $C < 0$; if $A < B$, then $A < 0$, $B < 0$, $C > 0$

14. a) i) The point (1, –4)   **ii)** Does not exist.

iii) Two lines; one with slope 1 and y-intercept 5, the other with slope –1 and y-intercept 1.

b) iii) $y = x + 5$; $y = -x + 1$

Self-Check 9.5, 9.6, page 565

1. Equation may vary. $x^2 = -0.55y$

2. $\dfrac{x^2}{16} + \dfrac{y^2}{12} = 1$

3. Equation may vary.

a) $\dfrac{x^2}{25} + \dfrac{y^2}{9} = 1$ **b)** 5.88 m

4. a) $\dfrac{(x-1)^2}{49} + \dfrac{(y+1)^2}{16} = 1$ **b)** $\dfrac{(x+2)^2}{25} + \dfrac{(y+3)^2}{36} = 1$

5. a) $\dfrac{(x-2)^2}{4} - \dfrac{(y+4)^2}{64} = 1$ **b)** $\dfrac{(x+3)^2}{9} - \dfrac{(y-2)^2}{16} = -1$

6. a) $(x+2)^2 = -4(y-1)$ **b)** $(y-1)^2 = 4(x+5)$

7. a) i) Ellipse   **ii)** $\dfrac{(x-3)^2}{8} + \dfrac{y^2}{2} = 1$

iii) (5.8, 0), (0.2, 0); (5.4, 0), (0.6, 0)

iv)

b) i) Hyperbola   **ii)** $(x-1)^2 - \dfrac{(y+2)^2}{2} = -1$

iii) (1, –0.6), (1, –3.4); (1, –0.3), (1, –3.7)

iv)

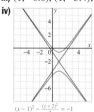

c) i) Parabola   **ii)** $(x+4)^2 = 8y$

iii) (–4, 0); (–4, 2)

iv)

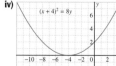

d) i) Circle   **ii)** $x^2 + \left(y - \dfrac{3}{4}\right)^2 = \dfrac{17}{16}$

iv)

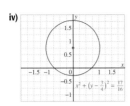

Insights Into a Rich Problem—
The Reflection Property of a Parabola, page 568

1. $x = -4$

4. a) $y = -\frac{4}{3}x + \frac{25}{3}$ **b)** $y = -\frac{1}{4}x + \frac{5}{2}$ **c)** $y = 4x - 15$

5. a) $\frac{2}{a}$ **b)** $\left(\frac{4}{m^2}, \frac{8}{m}\right)$

7. $(4.25, 0)$

Chapter 9 Review Exercises, page 571

1. a) $(x - 2)^2 + (y - 1)^2 = 9$

b)

2. a) $x^2 + y^2 - 4x + 6y + 4 = 0$
b) $x^2 + y^2 + 8x + 2y - 32 = 0$

3. a) $(x + 3)^2 + (y - 2)^2 = 16$

b) $(x - 1)^2 + (y - 5)^2 = 36$

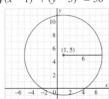

4. a) $(0.9, 5.8)$, $(-4.1, -4.2)$ **b)** $(-3.4, 2.6)$, $(3.7, -2.1)$
  c) $(0, 1)$, $(1, 0)$

5. 25, 8 or −25, −8

6. $y = x \pm 3.5$

7. a), b) $y = mx$

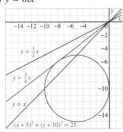

c) $y = \frac{3}{4}x$ and $x = 0$

8. a) $(0, \pm\sqrt{20})$; 12; 8

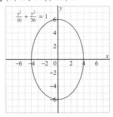

b) $(0, \pm\sqrt{40})$; 14; 6

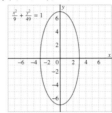

c) $(1 \pm \sqrt{5}, -2)$; 6; 4

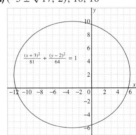

d) $(-3 \pm \sqrt{17}, 2)$; 18; 16

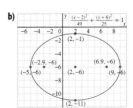

9. a) $\frac{x^2}{25} + \frac{y^2}{9} = 1$ **b)** $\frac{x^2}{36} + \frac{4y^2}{81} = 1$
  c) $\frac{x^2}{9} + \frac{y^2}{4} = 1$

10. $\frac{(x - 4)^2}{32} + \frac{(y - 3)^2}{36} = 1$

11. $(-6, 0)$, $(5.1, 1.8)$

12. a) $\frac{(x + 1)^2}{9} + \frac{(y + 5)^2}{25} = 1$
  b) $\frac{(x - 1)^2}{20} + \frac{(y - 4)^2}{4} = 1$

13. a)

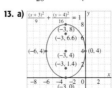

b)

14. a) $\dfrac{x^2}{4} - \dfrac{y^2}{5} = 1$

b)

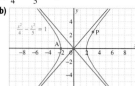

15. a) $\dfrac{x^2}{2} - \dfrac{3y^2}{8} = -1$

b) $y = \pm 2x$

16. a)

b) $x = 0,\ y = 0$

c) $y = x;\ y = -x$

17. a)

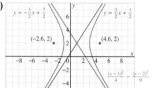

b)

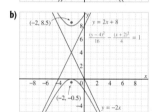

18. $\dfrac{x^2}{9} - \dfrac{y^2}{4} = 1$

19. a) $(-5, 7),\ (1, 1)$ **b)** $\left(\dfrac{10}{3}, \dfrac{8}{3}\right),\ (2, 0)$

20. a) $(y - 3)^2 = 12(x - 3)$ **b)** $(y - 2)^2 = -4x$

c) $(x - 4)^2 = 2(y + 3)$ **d)** $(x - 4)^2 = \dfrac{1}{4}x$

21. a)

b)

c)

d)

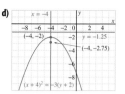

22. $(7, -3),\ (2, 2)$

23. 30.4 m

24. a) 36.2 m

25. $\dfrac{100x^2}{784} - \dfrac{100y^2}{441} = 1$

26. a) $\dfrac{(x - 4)^2}{21} + \dfrac{y^2}{5.25} = 1$ **b)** $\left(x - \dfrac{3}{4}\right)^2 + y^2 = \dfrac{17}{16}$

c) $(y - 1)^2 = 2(x + 5)$ **d)** $\dfrac{(x + 2)^2}{4} - \dfrac{(y - 1)^2}{5} = 1$

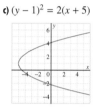   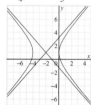

27. a) i) Hyperbola

ii) $\dfrac{(x + 3)^2}{2} - \dfrac{y^2}{4} = 1$

iii) $(-4.4, 0)\ (-1.6, 0);$
$(-0.6, 0),\ (-5.4, 0)$

iv)

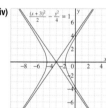

b) i) Circle

ii) $x^2 + y^2 = \dfrac{3}{2}$

iv)

c) i) Ellipse

ii) $\dfrac{(x - 1)^2}{2} + \dfrac{y^2}{6} = 1$

iii) $(1, 2.5),\ (1, -2.5);$
$(1, 2),\ (1, -2)$

iv)

d) i) Parabola

ii) $(x - 2)^2 = 3\left(y + \dfrac{13}{4}\right)$

iii) $\left(2, -\dfrac{13}{4}\right);\ \left(2, -\dfrac{5}{2}\right)$

iv)

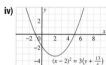

Chapter 9 Self-Test, page 575

1. $(x + 5)^2 + (y + 1)^2 = 45$

2. a) $\left(-\frac{1}{5}, \frac{7}{5}\right)$, $(-1, 1)$ **b)** $\left(\frac{17}{3}, -\frac{8}{3}\right)$

3. a) $\frac{x^2}{16} + \frac{y^2}{25} = 1$ **b)** $\frac{x^2}{16} + \frac{y^2}{7} = 1$

  c) $\frac{(x-2)^2}{8} + \frac{(y-2)^2}{9} = 1$

4. b) \$25

5. $x^2 - \frac{y^2}{4} = 1$

6.

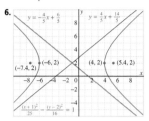

7. a) Equation may vary. $y^2 = 6x$
  b) 15.5 cm

8. $\frac{x^2}{16} + \frac{y^2}{7} = 1$

9. 58.1 cm

10. a) i) Ellipse
   ii) $\frac{(x+3)^2}{9} + \frac{y^2}{4} = 1$
   iii) $(-6, 0)$, $(0, 0)$;
     $(-3 - \sqrt{5}, 0)$,
     $(-3 + \sqrt{5}, 0)$
  iv)

  b) i) Parabola
   ii) $(x + 1)^2 = 4(y - 1)$
   iii) $(-1, 1)$; $(-1, 2)$
  iv)

  c) i) Ellipse
   ii) $\frac{(x+2)^2}{9} + \frac{(y-4)^2}{2} = 1$
   iii) $(1, 4)$, $(-5, 4)$;
     $(-2 + \sqrt{7}, 4)$,
     $(-2 - \sqrt{7}, 4)$
  iv)

  d) i) Parabola
   ii) $(y - 1)^2 = \frac{9}{2}x$
   iii) $(0, 1)$; $\left(\frac{9}{8}, 1\right)$
  iv)

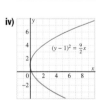

11. a) Hyperbola **b)** Circle **c)** Ellipse **d)** Ellipse

Assessment Tasks, page 576

1. a) Circle **b)** Hyperbola **c)** Ellipse **d)** Ellipse

2.

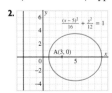

3. p

4. a) 4
  b) $y^2 = 8(x + 5)$, $y^2 = 32(x + 5)$, $y^2 = -8(x - 5)$,
    $y^2 = -32(x - 5)$
  c)

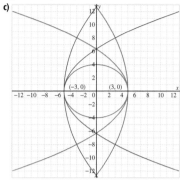

  d) $(\pm3, \pm8)$, $(0, \pm\sqrt{40})$, $(0, \pm\sqrt{160})$, $(\pm5, 0)$

Glossary

absolute value: the distance between any real number and 0 on a number line; for example, $|-3| = 3$, $|3| = 3$

acute angle: an angle measuring less than 90°

acute triangle: a triangle with three acute angles

algebraic expression: a mathematical expression containing a variable: for example, $6x - 4$ is an algebraic expression

altitude: the perpendicular distance from the base of a figure to the opposite side or vertex

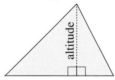

amortization: the repayment of the principal and interest of a loan by equal payments over a fixed period of time

amount: the value of the principal plus interest

amplitude of a function: the distance from the central axis to the minimum or maximum value of a periodic function

angle bisector: the line that divides an angle into two equal angles

angular velocity: the angle per unit time through which an object rotates about the centre of a circle

annuity: a series of regular, equal payments paid into, or out of, an account

approximation: a number close to the exact value; the symbol $\doteq$ means "is approximately equal to"

area: the number of square units needed to cover a region

arithmetic sequence: a sequence of numbers in which each term after the first term is calculated by adding the same number to the preceding term; for example, in the sequence 1, 4, 7, 10, …, each number is calculated by adding 3 to the previous number

arithmetic series: the indicated sum of the terms of an arithmetic sequence

asymptote: a line that a curve approaches, but never reaches

average: a single number that represents a set of numbers; see *mean*, *median*, and *mode*

axis of symmetry: a line that divides a figure into two congruent parts

balance: the result when money is added to or subtracted from an original amount

bar notation: the use of a horizontal bar over a decimal digit to indicate that it repeats; for example, $1.\overline{3}$ means 1.333 333 …

base: the side of a polygon or the face of a solid from which the height is measured; the factor repeated in a power

binomial: a polynomial with two terms; for example, $3x - 8$

bisector: a line that divides a line segment into two equal parts

The dotted line is a bisector of AB.

branches: the two distinct parts of a hyperbola

chord: a line segment whose endpoints lie on a conic

circle: the curve that results when a plane intersects a cone, parallel to the base of the cone; or the locus of a point P that moves so it is the same distance from a fixed point (the centre of the circle)

circumference: the distance around a circle, and sometimes the circle itself

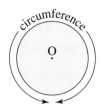

coefficient: the numerical factor of a term; for example, in the terms $3x$ and $3x^2$, the coefficient is 3

collinear points: points that lie on the same line

commission: a fee or payment given to a sales-person, usually a specified percent of the person's sales

common denominator: a number that is a multiple of each of the given denominators; for example, 12 is a common denominator for the fractions $\frac{1}{3}, \frac{5}{4}, \frac{7}{12}$

common difference: the number obtained by subtracting any term from the next term in an arithmetic sequence

common factor: a monomial that is a factor of each of the given monomials; for example, $3x$ is a common factor of $15x$, $9x^2$, and $21xy$

common ratio: the ratio formed by dividing any term after the first one in a geometric sequence by the preceding term

complete the square: add or subtract constants to rewrite a quadratic expression $ax^2 + bx + c$ as $a(x - p)^2 + q$

complex number: any number of the form $a + bi$, where a and b are real numbers and $i^2 = -1$

compound interest: see *interest*; if the interest due is added to the principal and thereafter earns interest, the interest earned is compound interest

compression of a function: a transformation that results in the graph of a function being compressed horizontally or vertically

compounding period: the time interval for which interest is calculated

cone: the surface generated when a line is rotated in space about a fixed point P on the line

congruent: figures that have the same size and shape

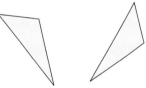

conjugate complex numbers: two numbers of the form $a + bi$ and $a - bi$, where a and b are real numbers and $i^2 = -1$

consecutive numbers: integers that come one after the other without any integers missing; for example, 34, 35, 36 are consecutive numbers, so are $-2, -1, 0$, and 1

constant function: $f(x) = c$, where c is a constant

constant term: a number

coordinate axes: the x- and y-axes on a grid that represents a plane

coordinate plane: a two-dimensional surface on which a coordinate system has been set up

coordinates: the numbers in an ordered pair that locate a point in the plane

corresponding angles in similar triangles: two angles, one in each triangle, that are equal

cosine of θ: the first coordinate of point P, where P is on the unit circle, centre $(0, 0)$, and θ is the measure of the angle in standard position

cube root: a number which, when raised to the power 3, results in a given number; for example, 4 is the cube root of 64, and –4 is the cube root of –64

cylinder: a solid with two parallel, congruent, circular bases

data: facts or information

database: an organized collection of facts or information, often stored on a computer

degree of a term: the sum of the exponents of the variables in that term
  The degree of $3x^2y^3$ is 5.
  The degree of $2ab^2$ is 3.
  The degree of $-4x$ is 1.
  The degree of a constant, such as 7, is 0.

degree of a polynomial: the degree of its highest-degree term
  The degree of $x^3 + 2xy + y^2$ is 3.
  The degree of $3x - 2y + 5$ is 1.

denominator: the term below the line in a fraction

diagonal: a line segment that joins two vertices of a polygon, but is not a side

diameter: the distance across a circle, measured through the centre; a line segment through the centre of the circle with its endpoints on the circle

difference of squares: a polynomial that can be expressed in the form $x^2 - y^2$; the product of two monomials that are the sum and difference of the same quantities, $(x + y)(x - y)$

directrix of a parabola: the fixed line such that the distance from any point P on the parabola to the fixed line is equal to the distance from P to the focus F

discriminant: the discriminant of the quadratic equation $ax^2 + bx + c = 0$ is $b^2 - 4ac$

distributive law: the property stating that a product can be written as a sum or difference of two or more products; for example, for all real numbers a, b, and c: $a(b + c) = ab + ac$ and $a(b - c) = ab - ac$

domain of a function: the set of x-values (or valid input numbers) represented by the graph or the equation of a function

doubling time: the term used in exponential growth problems; the time it takes the quantity of an item to double

effective rate: the annual interest rate that produces the same amount of interest per year as the given rate compounded several times per year

ellipse: the closed curve that results when a plane intersects a cone, or the locus of a point P that moves so the sum of its distances from two fixed points (the foci) is constant

equation: a mathematical statement that two expressions are equal

equidistant: the same distance

equilateral triangle: a triangle with three equal sides

equivalent rates: rates of interest with different compounding periods that have the same effect on a given amount of money over the same time

evaluate: to substitute a value for each variable in an expression and simplify the result

even number: an integer that has 2 as a factor; for example, 2, 4, –6

even function: a function with the property $f(-x) = f(x)$

expanding: multiplying a polynomial by a polynomial

expansion of a function: a transformation that results in the graph of a function being expanded horizontally or vertically

exponent: a number, shown in a smaller size and raised, that tells how many times the number before it is used as a factor; for example, 2 is the exponent in 6^2

exponential growth: a situation where an original amount is repeatedly multiplied by a constant; see *geometric sequence*

expression: a mathematical phrase made up of numbers and/or variables connected by operations

extrapolate: to estimate a value beyond known values

factor: to factor means to write as a product; to factor a given integer means to write it as a product of integers, the integers in the product are the factors of the given integer; to factor a polynomial with integer coefficients means to write it as a product of polynomials with integer coefficients

fifth root: a number which, when raised to the power 5, results in a given number; for example, 3 is the fifth root of 243 since $3^5 = 243$, and -3 is the fifth root of -243 since $(-3)^5 = -243$

foci of an ellipse: the two points F_1 and F_2 on the major axis of an ellipse such that $PF_1 + PF_2$ is constant for all points P on the ellipse

focus (plural, foci): the point in a parabolic dish antenna where the receiver is located; parallel signals are reflected off the surface and concentrated at this point

foci of a hyperbola: the two points F_1 and F_2 on the transverse axis of a hyperbola such that $|PF_1 - PF_2|$ is constant for all points P on the hyperbola

focus of a parabola: the point F on the axis of symmetry of a parabola such that the distance of any point P on the parabola from F is equal to the distance of P from the directrix

formula: a rule that is expressed as an equation

45-45-90 triangle: a triangle with angles 45°, 45°, and 90°

fourth root: a number which, when raised to the power 4, results in a given number; for example, -2 and 2 are the fourth roots of 16

fraction: an indicated quotient of two quantities

function: a rule that gives a single output number for every valid input number

future value: see *amount*

general term of an arithmetic sequence (or series): used to determine any term by substitution; that is, t_n is the nth term in the sequence, and $t_n = a + (n - 1)d$, where a is the first term, n the number of terms, and d the common difference

general term of a geometric sequence (or series): used to determine any term by substitution; that is, t_n is the nth term in the sequence, and $t_n = ar^{n-1}$, where a is the first term, n is the number of terms, and r is the common ratio

geometric growth: see *exponential growth*

geometric sequence: a sequence of numbers in which each term after the first term is calculated by multiplying the preceding term by the same number; for example, in the sequence 1, 3, 9, 27, 81, ..., each number is calculated by multiplying the preceding number by 3

geometric series: the indicated sum of the terms of a geometric sequence

greatest common factor: the greatest factor that two or more terms have in common; for example, $4x^2$ is the greatest common factor of $4x^3 + 16x^2 - 64x^4$

guaranteed investment certificate (GIC): see *term deposit*; an account with a guaranteed rate of interest for a specified term where the deposit cannot be withdrawn before the end of the term

horizontal intercept: the horizontal coordinate of the point where the graph of a function or a relation intersects the horizontal axis

hyperbola: the curve that results when a plane intersects both nappes of the cone; or the locus of a point P that moves so the difference of its distances from two fixed points (the foci) is constant

hypotenuse: the side that is opposite the right angle in a right triangle

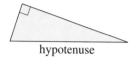
hypotenuse

hypothesis: something that seems likely to be true

identity: an equation that is satisfied for all values of the variable for which both sides of the equation are defined

image: the figure or graph that results from a transformation

inequality: a statement that one quantity is greater than (or less than) another quantity

initial arm: the horizontal ray of an angle in standard position

integers: the set of numbers… −3, −2, −1, 0, +1, +2, +3, …

interest: money that is paid for the use of money, usually according to a predetermined percent

interpolate: to estimate a value between two known values

interval: a regular distance or space between numbers

inverse of a function: a relation whose rule is obtained from that of a function by interchanging x and y

irrational number: a number that cannot be written in the form $\frac{m}{n}$, where m and n are integers ($n \neq 0$)

isosceles triangle: a triangle with at least two equal sides

lattice point: on a coordinate grid, a point at the intersection of two grid lines

latus rectum: the chord in a parabola that passes through the focus and is perpendicular to the line of symmetry

leading coefficient: the coefficient of the highest power of a polynomial expression

like radicals: radicals that have the same radical part; for example, $\sqrt{5}$, $3\sqrt{5}$, and $-7\sqrt{5}$

like terms: terms that have the same variables; for example, $4x$ and $-3x$ are like terms

line of best fit: a line that passes as close as possible to a set of plotted points

line segment: the part of a line between two points on the line

line symmetry: a figure that maps onto itself when it is reflected in a line is said to have line symmetry; for example, line l is the line of symmetry for figure ABCD

linear equation: an equation in which the degree of the highest-degree term is 1; for example, $x = 6$, $y = 2x - 3$, and $4x + 2y - 5 = 0$

linear inequality: an inequality in which the degree of the highest term is 1; for example, $2x - 3 > 5 - 4x$

linear function: a function whose defining equation can be written in the form $y = mx + b$, where m and b are constants

linear growth: a situation where a constant is repeatedly added to an original amount; see *arithmetic sequence*

linear system: two or more linear equations in the same variables

locus: the path traced by a point that moves according to a given condition

maturity value: see *amount*; the value of the principal plus interest at the end of the term

mean: the sum of a set of numbers divided by the number of numbers in the set

median: the middle number when data are arranged in numerical order

median of a triangle: a line from one vertex to the midpoint of the opposite side

midpoint: the point that divides a line segment into two equal parts

mixed radical: an expression of the form $a\sqrt{x}$; for example, $2\sqrt{5}$ is a mixed radical

mode: the number that occurs most often in a set of numbers

monomial: a polynomial with one term; for example, 14 and $5x^2$ are monomials

mortgage: a long-term loan on real estate that gives the person or firm providing the money a claim on the property if the loan is not repaid

multiple: the product of a given number and a natural number; for example, some multiples of 8 are 8, 16, 24, …

multiplicative inverses: a number and its reciprocal; the product of multiplicative inverses is 1; for example, $3 \times \frac{1}{3} = 1$

napped of a cone: the 2 symmetrical parts of a cone on either side of the vertex

natural numbers: the set of numbers 1, 2, 3, 4, 5, …

negative number: a number less than 0

negative reciprocals: two numbers whose product is −1; for example, $\frac{3}{4}$ is the negative reciprocal of $-\frac{4}{3}$, and vice versa

non-linear relation: a relation that cannot be represented by a straight-line graph

numerator: the term above the line in a fraction

obtuse angle: an angle greater than 90° and less than 180°

obtuse triangle: a triangle with one angle greater than 90°

odd function: a function with the property $f(-x) = -f(x)$

odd number: an integer that does not have 2 as a factor; for example, 1, 3, −7

operation: a mathematical process or action such as addition, subtraction, multiplication, or division

opposite angles: the equal angles that are formed by two intersecting lines

opposites: two numbers whose sum is zero; each number is the opposite of the other

optimization: making a system or object as efficient as possible

order of operations: the rules that are followed when simplifying or evaluating an expression

ordered pair: a pair of numbers, written as (x, y), that represents a point on a coordinate grid

ordinary annuity: an annuity where a payment is made at the end of each payment period; see *annuity*

parabola: the name given to the shape of the graph of a quadratic function

parallel lines: lines in the same plane that do not intersect

percent: the number of parts per 100; the numerator of a fraction with denominator 100

perfect square: a number that is the square of a whole number; a polynomial that is the square of another polynomial

perimeter: the distance around a closed figure

period: the length of one cycle, measured along the horizontal axis

period of a loan: the time it takes to pay back the loan

periodic function: a function that repeats in a regular way, or, a function that has a number p such that $f(x + p) = f(x)$ for all values of x in the domain

perpendicular: intersecting at right angles

perpendicular bisector: the line that is perpendicular to a line segment and divides it in two equal parts

   The dotted line is the perpendicular bisector of AB.

pi (π): the ratio of the circumference of a circle to its diameter; $\pi \doteq 3.1416$

point of intersection: a point that lies on two or more figures

point slope form: the equation of a line in the form $y = m(x - p) + q$, where (p, q) are the coordinates of a point on the line and m is its slope

point symmetry: a figure that maps onto itself after a rotation of $180°$ about a point is said to have point symmetry

polygon: a closed figure that consists of line segments; for example, triangles and quadrilaterals

polynomial: a mathematical expression with one or more terms, in which the exponents are whole numbers and the coefficients are numbers

polynomial function: a function where $f(x)$ is a polynomial expression

positive number: a number greater than 0

power: an expression of the form a^n, where a is the base and n is the exponent; it represents a product of equal factors; for example, $4 \times 4 \times 4$ can be expressed as 4^3

power function: a function that has the form $f(x) = x^a$, where a is a constant

present value: the principal required to obtain a specific amount in the future

principal: money invested or loaned

prime number: a natural number with exactly two factors, itself and 1; for example, 2, 5, 11

product: the quantity resulting from the multiplication of two or more quantities

Pythagorean Theorem: for any right triangle, the area of the square on the hypotenuse is equal to the sum of the areas of the squares on the other two sides

quadrant: one of the four regions into which coordinate axes divide a plane

quadratic equation: an equation of the form $ax^2 + bx + c = 0$, where $a \neq 0$; for example, $x^2 + 5x + 6 = 0$ is a quadratic equation

quadratic function: a function with defining equation $y = ax^2 + bx + c$, where a, b, and c are constants, and $a \neq 0$

quotient: the quantity resulting from the division of one quantity by another

radian: a unit for measuring angles; 1 radian is about $57.295\,78°$

radical: the root of a number; for example, $\sqrt{400}$, $\sqrt[3]{8}$, $\sqrt[4]{72}$, $\sqrt[5]{24}$

radical equation: an equation where the variable occurs under a radical sign

radical sign: the symbol $\sqrt{}$ that denotes the positive square root of a number

radius (plural, radii): the distance from the centre of a circle to any point on the circumference, or a line segment joining the centre of a circle to any point on the circumference

range: the difference between the highest and lowest values (the *extremes*) in a set of data

range of a function: the set of *y*-values (or output numbers) represented by the graph or the equation of a function

rate: a certain quantity or amount of one thing considered in relation to a unit of another thing

ratio: the quotient of two numbers or quantities

rational expression: a fraction where both numerator and denominator are polynomials

rational number: a number that can be written in the form $\frac{m}{n}$, where *m* and *n* are integers ($n \neq 0$)

rationalize the denominator: write the denominator as a rational number, to replace the irrational number; for example, $\frac{6}{\sqrt{2}}$ is written $\frac{6\sqrt{2}}{2}$, or $3\sqrt{2}$

ray: a figure formed by a point P on a line and all the points on the line on one side of P

real numbers: the set of rational numbers and the set of irrational numbers; that is, all numbers that can be expressed as decimals

reciprocals: two numbers whose product is 1; for example, $\frac{3}{4}$ and $\frac{4}{3}$ are reciprocals, 2 and $\frac{1}{2}$ are reciprocals

rectangular hyperbola: a hyperbola that has perpendicular asymptotes

recursion formula: a rule by which each term of a sequence is generated from the preceding term or terms

reference angle: the acute angle between the terminal arm and the *x*-axis

reflection of a function: a transformation that results in the graph of a function being reflected in a horizontal or vertical line

reflex angle: an angle between 180° and 360°

registered retirement savings plan (RRSP): a savings plan, for people who earn income, where money invested and interest earned are not taxed until money is withdrawn

regular polygon: a polygon that has all sides equal and all angles equal

relation: a rule that produces one or more output numbers for every valid input number

right angle: a 90° angle

right circular cone: a cone in which a line segment from the centre of the circular base to the vertex is perpendicular to the base; see *cone*

right triangle: a triangle that has one right angle

rise: the vertical distance between two points

root of an equation: a value of the variable that satisfies the equation

rotational symmetry: a figure that maps onto itself in less than one full turn is said to have rotational symmetry; for example, a square has rotational symmetry about its centre O

run: the horizontal distance between two points

scale: the ratio of the distance between two points on a map, model, or diagram to the distance between the actual locations; the numbers on the axes of a graph

scalene triangle: a triangle with no two sides equal

scatter plot: a graph of data that is a set of points

scientific notation: a way of expressing a number as the product of a number greater than −10 and less than −1 or greater than 1 and less than 10, and a power of 10; for example, 4700 is written as 4.7×10^3

semi-annual: every six months

semicircle: half a circle

significant digits: the meaningful digits of a number representing a measurement

similar figures: figures with the same shape, but not necessarily the same size

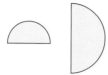

simple harmonic motion: a periodic up-and-down motion commonly created by the motion of a weight on a spring

simple interest: see *interest*; interest calculated according to the formula $I = Prt$

sine of θ: the second coordinate of P, where P is on the unit circle, centre $(0, 0)$ and θ is the measure of the angle in standard position

sinusoidal functions: functions of curves that look like waves

sinusoids: curves that look like waves

slope: describes the steepness of a line or line segment; the ratio of the rise of a line or line segment to its run

slope y-intercept form: the equation of a line in the form $y = mx + b$, where m is the slope and b is the y-intercept

spreadsheet: a computer-generated arrangement of data in rows and columns, where a change in one entry results in appropriate calculated changes in the other entries

square of a number: the product of a number multiplied by itself; for example, 25 is the square of 5

square root: a number which, when multiplied by itself, results in a given number; for example, 5 and -5 are the square roots of 25

standard position: an angle is in standard position when the initial arm starts at $(0, 0)$ and lies on the positive x-axis; the terminal arm is rotated about $(0, 0)$

statistics: the branch of mathematics that deals with the collection, organization, and interpretation of data

straight angle: an angle measuring $180°$

sum of an arithmetic series: the formula for the sum of the first n terms is $S_n = \left(\frac{a + t_n}{2}\right) \times n$, where a is the first term, t_n is the nth term, and n is the number of terms; or $S_n = \frac{n}{2}[2a + (n - 1)d]$, where d is the common difference

sum of a geometric series: the formula for the sum of the first n terms is $S_n = \frac{a(r^n - 1)}{r - 1}$, $r \neq 1$, where a is the first term, r is the common ratio, and n is the number of terms

symmetrical: possessing symmetry; see *line symmetry*, *point symmetry*, and *rotational symmetry*

tangent of θ: the y-coordinate of Q, where P is on the unit circle and AQ is perpendicular to OA

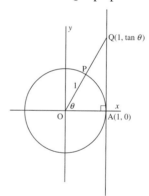

term: of a fraction is the numerator or the denominator of the fraction; when an expression is written as the sum of several quantities, each quantity is a term of the expression

term deposit: an account whose rate of interest is guaranteed for a specified term where withdrawal before the end of the term may result in loss of interest

terminal arm: the final ray when defining an angle

30-60-90 triangle: a triangle with angles $30°$, $60°$, and $90°$

three-dimensional: having length, width, and depth or height

trajectory: the curved path of an object moving through space

transformation of a function: the change in a function that results in changes to its equation and its graph; see *compression*, *expansion*, *reflection*, and *translation*

translation of a function: a transformation that results in the graph of a function being moved horizontally or vertically

trigonometric equation: an equation involving one or more trigonometric functions of a variable

trigonometric identity: an identity involving one or more trigonometric functions of a variable

trinomial: a polynomial with three terms; for example, $3x^2 + 6x + 9$

two-dimensional: having length and width, but no thickness, height, or depth

unlike radicals: radicals that have different radical parts; for example, $\sqrt{5}$ and $\sqrt{11}$

unlike terms: terms that have different variables, or the same variable but different exponents; for example, $3x$, $-4y$ and $3x^2$, $-3x$

variable: a letter or symbol representing a quantity that can vary

vertex (plural, vertices): the corner of a figure or a solid

vertex of a cone: the point where all the generators intersect

vertex of a parabola: the point where the axis of symmetry of a parabola intersects the parabola

vertical intercept: the vertical coordinate of the point where the graph of a function or a relation intersects the vertical axis

vertical line test: if no two points on a graph can be joined by a vertical line, then the graph represents a function

vertices of a hyperbola: the endpoints of the transverse axis

vertices of an ellipse: the endpoints of the major axis

volume: the amount of space occupied by an object

whole numbers: the set of numbers 0, 1, 2, 3,…

x-axis: the horizontal number line on a coordinate grid

x-intercept: the x-coordinate of the point where the graph of a function or a relation intersects the x-axis

y-axis: the vertical number line on a coordinate grid

y-intercept: the y-coordinate of the point where the graph of a function or a relation intersects the y-axis

zero of a function: the horizontal coordinate of the point where the graph of a function intersects the horizontal axis drawn through the origin

Index

Even function, 407

Expanding, 84

Exponent
  integer, 3–5
  rational, 39–42

Exponent laws
  integer exponents, 3, 4
  rational exponents, 47–50

Exponential decay, 381

Exponential equations
  solving, 48, 51, 53, 73

Exponential function, 381

Exponential growth, 16–21
  related to compound interest,
    135, 137

F

Factoring polynomials, 81, 82,
  96–99, 105, 113

Family
  of lines, 238–240, 517, 518
  of parabolas, 239, 240

Fibonacci, Leonardo, 35

Fibonacci sequence, 34

Fifth root, 6

Focal length of a lens, 95

Focal radius/radii
  for a hyperbola, 475, 501
  for an ellipse, 465, 501
  property for a hyperbola, 533
  property for an ellipse, 522

Focus, 465, 475, 484

4-5-6 triangle, 245, 313

45-45-90 triangle, 282, 283

Fourth root, 6

Frequency of sound, 332

Functions, 392, 450
  absolute value, 399
  constant, 407
  definition of, 392, 429
  dependent variable, 325
  domain of, 323, 324, 375, 383,
    396, 397
  equation test for, 393, 439
  even, 407
  identity, 407

independent variable, 325
inverse of, 424–429
notation, 401, 402
odd, 407
periodic, 329–331, 333–336,
  340–347, 352–357,
  362–366, 372–375, 381
quadratic, 197–199, 206–210,
  215, 216, 241
quartic, 435, 436
range of, 323, 324, 375, 383,
  396, 397
square root, 403
transforming, 322, 409–412,
  418, 419, 439
vertical line test for, 392, 439
zeros of, 203, 215

Future value/amount, FV, *see*
  TI-83 graphing calculator

G

General equation
  of a circle, 511
  of a conic, 560–562, 571
  of a hyperbola, 560
  of a parabola, 561
  of an ellipse, 560

General quadratic equation, 212
  roots of, 215, 241

General term of a geometric
  sequence, 28

General term of a sequence,
  26–29

General term of an arithmetic
  sequence, 26

Geometer's Sketchpad, The, 454
  constructing a hyperbola, 478,
    481, 482
  constructing a locus, 458, 459,
    463, 503, 506
  constructing a parabola, 485,
    486, 490
  constructing an ellipse, 467,
    472, 473

Geometric sequence, 8, 20, 21,
  27–29, 70
  related to compound interest,
    135, 137

Geometric series
  sum of, 60, 61, 66, 70, 132,
    144, 151, 159, 160

Goods and Services Tax (GST),
  3

Graphing calculator, 209
  amounts under compound
    interest, 149
  calculating in radians, 288
  quadratic function, 209, 210,
    215
  semicircle function, 398
  sinusoidal functions, 337–341,
    348, 349, 352, 361, 364,
    365
  tangent function, 376, 377
  TVM Solver, 174–176

Graphing trigonometric
  functions
  $y = a \cos x$, 340, 342
  $y = a \sin x$, 340, 342
  $y = \cos bx$, 352–354
  $y = \cos x$, 334, 335
  $y = \cos x + c$, 341, 343
  $y = \cos (x - d)$, 341, 344, 345
  $y = \sin bx$, 352–354
  $y = \sin x$, 333, 334
  $y = \sin x + c$, 341, 343
  $y = \sin (x - d)$, 341, 344, 345
  $y = \tan x$, 373–375

Graphmatica, 332, 360

Greatest common factor, 81, 96,
  97

Guaranteed Investment
  Certificate (GIC), 141, 147,
  148, 150, 192

H

Harmonic mean, 126

Horizontal compression, 354,
  384, 409–411, 439

Horizontal expansion, 354, 384,
  409–411, 418, 439

Horizontal translation, 344, 385,
  409, 411, 418, 439

Hyperbola(s), 475–480, 501,
  533–539
  as a conic section, 494

for present value of a bond, 188

for present value of an annuity, 159, 160, 161

for present value of monthly mortgage payments, 169

for principal (present value) with annual compounding, 136, 137

for regular deposit of an annuity, 153

Time saved by extra speed, 118–120

Transforming graphs of functions; 409, 439; *see also* Trigonometric functions
horizontal compression, 409, 410, 411, 439
horizontal expansion, 409, 410, 411, 418, 439
horizontal translation, 409, 411, 418, 439
quadratic functions, 322, 409, 410
reflection in horizontal axis, 410, 439
reflection in vertical axis, 410, 439
trigonometric functions, 340–347, 352–357, 411–412
vertical compression, 409, 410, 411, 439
vertical expansion, 409, 410, 411, 418, 439
vertical translation, 409, 411, 418, 439

Transverse axis, *see* Hyperbola

Trigonometric equations
solving linear, 254–257, 276–278, 296–298, 302
solving quadratic, 303, 304

Trigonometric functions
of angles in degrees in standard position, 272–278
of angles in radians in standard position, 296–299
of special angles in degrees, 282–285, 316

of special angles in radians, 299, 316

transformations of, 340–347, 352–357, 383, 384, 409, 411, 412

Trigonometric identities, 307–309

Trigonometric ratios
in a right triangle, 246

Trinomial, 80

TVM (Time Value of Money) Solver, 174–176

2-3-4 triangle, 245, 311, 312

Unit circle, 268, 272, 333

Variables
restrictions on, 96
using in applications, 424
using conventionally, 425

Vertex/vertices
of a cone, 492
of a hyperbola, 482, 533, 536
of a parabola, 198, 199, 206–210, 241, 322, 545, 549
of an ellipse, 472, 522

Vertical compression, 342, 383, 409–411, 439

Vertical displacement, 342–344, 363, 384

Vertical expansion, 342, 383, 410, 411, 418, 439

Vertical line test, 392, 393, 439

Vertical translation, 343, 384, 409, 411, 418, 439

Weight on a spring, 342, 343, 345, 353, 362, 363

Whole numbers, 200

x-axis, 201
x-coordinate, 201

x-intercept, 201, 202, 241, 375, 383

y-axis, 201
y-coordinate, 201
y-intercept, 201, 202, 375, 383
Yield rate of a bond, 188, 189

Z

Zero exponent law, 3, 4
Zeros of a function, 203
Zeros of a quadratic function, 203, 215, 216

PHOTO CREDITS AND ACKNOWLEDGMENTS

The publisher wishes to thank the following sources for photographs, illustrations, articles, and other materials used in this book. Care has been taken to determine and locate ownership of copyright material used in the text. We will gladly receive information enabling us to rectify any errors or omissions in credits.

PHOTOS

Cover Orion Press/STONE; **Inside Front Page** Orion Press/STONE; **Back Cover** (top) Orion Press/STONE, (bottom) Randy Wells/STONE; **p xi.** Orion Press/STONE; **p 1.** (top centre), Dianne Norman/Allsport; **p 14.** (bottom right), Artbase Inc.; **p 16.** Dave Starrett; **p 32.** (top left), Gary Braasch/Stone; **p 42.** (top left), © John MacPherson/The Stock Market/First Light Associated Photographers; **p 42.** (top right), Zefa-Reinhard/Masterfile; **p 52.** (centre right), Henry Ausloos/Animals Animals; **p 58.** (centre right), Shooting Star; **p 77.** (top centre), © Bill Brooks/Masterfile; **p 90.** (top right), George Kavanagh/Stone; **p 95.** (centre right), Artbase Inc.; **p 118.** (top right), Dean Siracusa/Masterfile; **p 127.** (top centre), Dave Starrett; **p 127.** (top centre), Artbase Inc.; **p 142.** (bottom right), courtesy of Canada Post Corporation; **p 167.** (top right), Masterfile; **p 177.** (top right), Tom Mcarthy/Index Stock Imagery; **p 197.** (top centre), Spectrum Stock; **p 208.** (bottom right), Artbase Inc.; **p 245.** (top left), Science Photo Library/Photo Researchers Inc; **p 245.** Dave Starrett; **p 253.** Dave Starrett; **p 282.** Dave Starrett; **p 321.** (top centre), © R. Kord/First Light; **p 329.** (top right), © Phil Degginger/Stone; **p 352.** Dave Starrett; **p 368.** (centre right), First Light; **p 391.** (top centre), Dave Starrett; **p 396.** (top right), Dave Starrett; **p 449.** (top centre), Dr. Mitsuo Ohtsuki/Science Photo Library/Photo Researchers; **p 464.** (top left), © Robert Daly/Stone; **p 464.** (top left), Robert Daly/STONE; **p 464.** (middle right), Dave Starrett; **p 464.** (bottom left), Dave Starrett; **p 464.** (bottom right), Dave Starrett; **p 475.** (top right), Dave Starrett; **p 475.** (middle left), Dave Starrett; **p 475.** (middle right), Dave Starrett; **p 484.** (top left), © John Gillmoure/The Stock Market/First Light Associated Photographers; **p 492.** (bottom left), Dave Starrett; **p 493.** (top right), Pat O'Hara/Tony Stone Images; **p 493.** (bottom right), William James Warren/First Light; **p 495.** (middle right), Dave Starrett; **p 507.** (top centre), Spectrum Stock

ILLUSTRATIONS

Mike Herman: **p 376.** (bottom right), **p 496.** (middle centre)
Dave McKay: **p 265.** (bottom right), **p 362.** (top right), **p 369.** (top centre), **p 379.** (middle right), **p 426.** (middle centre), **p 494.** (top right), **p 555.** (middle left), **p 556.** (middle centre)
Jun Park: **p 496.** (top right)
from original reference courtesy of David J. Tholen: **p 493.** (middle right)